MANAGEMENT

MANAGEMENT
Sixth Edition

JUSTIN G. LONGENECKER
Baylor University

CHARLES D. PRINGLE
Sam Houston State University

Charles E. Merrill Publishing Company
A Bell & Howell Company
Columbus Toronto London Sydney

Cover photo by Michel Tcherevkoff

Published by
Charles E. Merrill Publishing Company
A Bell & Howell Company
Columbus, Ohio 43216

This book was set in Melior.
Production Coordination: Constantina Geldis
Text Designer: Cynthia Brunk
Cover Designer: Tony Faiola

Library of Congress Catalog Card Number: 83-61931
International Standard Book Number: 0-675-20099-7
Printed in the United States of America
1 2 3 4 5 6 7 8 9 10—88 87 86 85 84

Title page photo courtesy Tom Brunk; Part One photo courtesy Redwood
Empire Association; Part Two photo courtesy Steven G. Smith; Part Three
photo courtesy New Orleans Chamber of Commerce; Part Four photo courtesy
Dallas Chamber of Commerce; Part Five photo courtesy New Orleans Chamber
of Commerce; Part Six photo courtesy Dallas Chamber of Commerce.

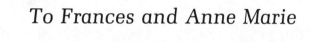
To Frances and Anne Marie

PREFACE

We believe that you will find the sixth edition of *Management* to be comprehensive, contemporary, balanced, and realistic. Towards these goals a number of changes have been made in this edition.

To make the text more comprehensive, we have expanded coverage of several topics to form the following new chapters:

Chapter 2, "Historical Trends in Management Thought and Practice," traces the evolution and development of our knowledge about management from the early classical school to contemporary contingency theory.

Chapter 15, "Human Resource Management," gives an overview of human resources, including planning, recruiting, selection, compensation, orientation, socialization, performance appraisal, and management development.

Chapter 17, "Organization Change and Development," examines the forces that lead to change, the process of planned change, and the role of organization development.

Chapter 23, "Operations Management," examines management of the subsystem that is responsible for transforming inputs into outputs.

New and added coverage includes these significant areas:

organizational environments
Japanese management practices
modern management information systems
organizational culture
job design
stress management
financial control

To maintain the contemporary nature of the text, we have thoroughly updated every chapter to reflect current theory and practice. In addition to the four new chapters, eleven others contain between 25 and 50 percent new text.

Not only does this book provide a balanced overview of management through coverage of the basic management functions, but it also helps integrate the valuable insights provided by open systems theory, contingency theory, organization theory, organizational behavior, and management science. We believe that each of these areas has much to offer and that reliance on any one approach to the exclusion of the others results in a too narrow perspective of managers and their work.

Because the institutions in which you will work are real organizations, we have been careful to make the text realistic. Hence, you will find the book liberally illustrated with examples of real people in actual organizational situations. For example, the number of boxed examples illustrating management practices in real organizations has been increased by 38 percent over the previous edition. Throughout the text, you will find evidence of our belief that management theory and practice are inextricably intertwined.

Other major improvements in this edition include

- a 59 percent increase in visual aids to heighten interest and increase understanding.
- more cases that involve you in concrete situations confronting managers at different levels in varied organizations.

Each chapter begins with a statement of learning objectives and an outline to provide an overview of the chapter's content and purpose. A summary is provided at the end of each chapter along with questions to test understanding of the chapter's major concepts. Each chapter concludes with a supplementary reading list for those wishing to pursue the subject matter further. A glossary of key terms at the end of the text succinctly defines central words and phrases.

We are deeply indebted to many individuals for their assistance and support in this project. We particularly wish to thank our manuscript reviewers, identified below. These colleagues were particularly able and deserve considerable credit for their helpful and extensive suggestions.

Allen C. Bluedorn, University of Missouri at Columbia
Melvin Blumberg, Fairleigh Dickinson University
Charles W. Cole, University of Oregon
Steven E. Markham, Virginia Polytechic Institute and State University
Timothy A. Matherly, The Florida State University
Gerald Perselay, Winthrop College
Mike Shaner, St. Louis University
John Zeiger, Bryant College

In addition, Dean Richard C. Scott of the Hankamer School of Business, Baylor University, has been most supportive of our work and we thank him. The aid and understanding of Dean Rosemary Pledger and Program Director William A. Staples of the School of Business and Public Administration, University of Houston at Clear Lake City, were most appreciated. We are also grateful to Mr. and Mrs. Harry J. Chavanne. And a special word of thanks goes to several colleagues for permission to use their cases.

Finally, but certainly not least, the support, patience, and understanding of our wives, Frances and Anne Marie, were not only helpful but essential in making this book a reality.

Justin G. Longenecker
Charles D. Pringle

CONTENTS

PART ONE INTRODUCTION TO MANAGEMENT

1

THE TASK OF MANAGEMENT IN PERSPECTIVE

This chapter will enable you to

- *Define management and identify the unique features of managerial activities.*
- *Indicate the need for management in cooperative endeavors and explain the concept of the professional manager.*
- *Become familiar with the manager's job, including managerial behavior patterns, the skills required for effective management, differences in managerial work, and the manager's multiple roles.*
- *Identify and discuss the basic managerial functions.*
- *Discuss the significant challenges facing management today.*

"If a company has nothing going for it except one thing—good management—it will make the grade. If it has everything *except* good management, it will flop."[1]

Consider the following examples:

Lee Iacocca, upon becoming chairman of Chrysler Corporation during its financial crisis, admits before the Senate Banking Committee that more than half of his company's problems result from "terrible management" in the past.

Tom Landry becomes coach of a newly formed National Football League team comprised of rookies and the cast-offs of more established teams. Under his management, the Dallas Cowboys quickly become a perennial contender for the NFL championship.

Several teachers in an elementary school request transfers to other schools in the city, citing as their reason a lack of support from their principal (the school's manager) when they deal with sensitive student or parental problems.

A dying inner city church is taken over by an enthusiastic new pastor who, through the development and management of church programs, fresh approaches to service, and inspirational leadership, revives the church and quadruples its membership.

Organizations of all types—hospitals, schools, government offices, and churches, as well as business firms—require good management to accomplish their objectives. Not only can the quality of management increase the effectiveness of a single organization, but society as a whole benefits when its constituent organizations function as they should.

The topic of this book is *management*. In it you will learn what managers do, and you will become familiar with various theories, techniques, and tools designed to increase managerial effectiveness. This knowledge is useful for anyone who works in, deals with, or belongs to a formal organization. An understanding of organizational functioning is based, to a considerable extent, upon knowledge of *managerial roles* and *processes*.

If you are interested in a managerial career, this book is a starting point. As you may have already guessed, the demand for managerial talent far exceeds the supply of good managers. This book, in itself, will not make you a "good manager," but it will acquaint you with the underlying theory and the actual practice of management. As such, it will provide you with a basic start toward developing a successful career that will involve both managing and being managed.

THE FIELD OF MANAGEMENT

Definition of Management

Management is the process of acquiring and combining human, financial, and physical resources to attain the organization's primary goal of producing a product or service desired by some segment of society. This process is essential to the functioning of all organizations—profit and nonprofit; essential resources must be acquired and combined in some way to produce an output. A hospital administrator, for instance, must staff a hospital with physicians, nurses, and technicians; provide modern equipment for diagnosis, treatment, and recovery; and raise funds from patients, private donors, and the government. These resources must then be combined to produce healed patients. The same general process, illustrated in Figure 1–1, applies to the production of an automobile, an

FIGURE 1–1   The managerial process

audit of accounting records, the issuance of a government regulation, or the education of a student.

The manager provides the dynamic force or direction necessary to acquire and combine static resources into a functioning, productive organization. He or she is the individual in charge and is expected to get results and to see that things happen as they should.

Types of Managers

The manager may carry any one of many different titles. At the top, a manager is identified by such titles as chairman of the board, president, or chief executive officer (CEO). At somewhat lower levels, a manager is called vice-president (an infinite variety), divisional manager, or regional manager. At the lowest managerial levels, such titles as department manager, assistant department manager, supervisor, and office manager appear. In each instance, the title is expected to give some indication of the function and level of the manager.

There is some similarity in the activities of all types of managers. Thus, the duties of an assistant department manager have something in common with those of the president of the organization. Figure 1–2 indicates some of the activities that are performed at the top, middle, and supervisory levels of management. This statement of activities reveals

Top Management:
Develops and reviews comprehensive, long-range plans.
Evaluates overall performance of major departments.
Evaluates leading management personnel preparatory to key executive selection.
Confers with subordinate managers on subjects or problems of general scope.

Middle Management:
Makes plans of intermediate range based on top management's long-range plans.
Analyzes managerial performance to determine capability and readiness for promotion.
Establishes departmental policies.
Reviews daily and weekly reports on production or sales.
Counsels-subordinate managers on production, personnel, or other problems.

Supervisory Management:
Makes detailed, short-range operating plans based on middle management's intermediate-range plans.
Reviews performance of "operatives" and minor supervisors.
Supervises day-to-day operations.
Makes specific task assignments to personnel.
Maintains close contact with operative employees.

FIGURE 1–2 Management activities at three different levels

some of the similarities and differences in focus and outlook at these levels. Each level, for instance, has the responsibility for planning and evaluating performance, but the types of plans and the focus of the performance evaluation differ significantly from level to level.

The Distinctive Skill of Management

We have come to recognize that management and the abilities of the manager are separate and distinct from the activities and abilities required of operating personnel. At one time, it was customary to promote the most proficient worker when filling a management vacancy. Although this procedure had much to recommend it, it ignored the fact that ability to direct the work of others is substantially different from that of doing one's own work.

As an example, consider the case of a professor who accepted an offer to become the head of a large department at another university. The offer was based primarily upon the professor's impressive research and publication record. Once the professor took over his new administrative position, however, it quickly became apparent to the members of the department that expertise in research did not necessarily qualify one to manage a department. While unanswered department correspondence piled up, scheduling deadlines passed unnoticed, and meetings of department heads went unattended, the professor stayed ensconced in his office at home turning out more articles!

The distinctive nature of managerial ability was further revealed by the discovery that managerial skills are somewhat transferable from one field of endeavor to another. George Schultz, for instance, has served as Dean of the Graduate School of Business at the University of Chicago, as Secretary of the Treasury in the Nixon administration, as President of the Bechtel Group—a worldwide construction company—and as Secretary of State in the Reagan administration. Those positions and their settings differed greatly, but all required managerial skill.

There are, however, practical limits to the transferability of managerial skills. John Kotter points out that the successful general managers he has studied have spent years in a single organization, acquiring knowledge about the company and its industry. During those years, the executive developed an extensive network of relationships with key people, both inside and outside the firm. Those interpersonal relationships and detailed knowledge of the organization are rarely transferable to other firms.[2] Robert L. Katz suggests that the transferability of managerial skills is possible only in large organizations where the manager has extensive staff assistance and highly competent technical operators throughout the organization.[3] A new manager in such a setting could rely on other individuals for the daily operations of the organization while he or she concentrated on planning and goal setting.

Need for Management

The need for some type of management arises as soon as cooperative endeavor is required to accomplish an objective. Of course, one might visualize a very simple operation—hunting or fishing by two or three individuals, for example—in which there is little apparent management. Very soon, however, any project or undertaking that involves the contribution of more than one person necessitates someone's taking the lead. If the operation is quite small and the tasks relatively unspecialized—such as those in a hair styling shop—the amount of managerial leader-

THE CHIEF EXECUTIVE OFFICER

Researchers periodically survey top-level managers in U.S. corporations to construct a profile of the "typical" chief executive. The following reflect some of the findings of recent surveys:

Almost all of the chief executives surveyed had completed college, and over 40 percent had earned graduate degrees.

Almost one-fifth of the CEOs had financial backgrounds, between 15 and 17 percent had risen through the ranks of general management, and about 12 percent each had either marketing/sales or legal backgrounds. The training of the manager varied by industry, however. All of the chief executives in household products firms had marketing/sales backgrounds, for example, while 60 percent of the top managers of electric utility companies had come up through the legal department.

The age of the top executives ranged from thirty-seven to eighty-two. Most had spent at least one-half to two-thirds of their work life with the same firm. Only 11 percent of the companies had hired their chief executive officers from outside the firm.

The highest paid executive in the country in 1982 was Frederick W. Smith, chairman of Federal Express, who received over $51.5 million in total compensation ($414,000 in salary and $51.1 million from a long-term income plan).

SOURCES: James E. Piercy and J. Benjamin Forbes, "Industry Differences in Chief Executive Officers," *MSU Business Topics* 29 (Winter 1981): 17–29; David L. Kurtz and Louis E. Boone, "A Profile of Business Leadership," *Business Horizons* 24 (September/October 1981): 28–32; and "How America's Top Moneymakers Fared in the Recession," *Business Week*, 9 May 1983, p. 84.

ship required is minimal. In most establishments with as few as a half dozen employees, however, the need for careful organization and direction of individual contributions is quite evident.

In a large institution involving a great amount of work specialization, the task of organization and management becomes gargantuan. The General Motors Corporation, for example, must blend the contributions of some 800,000 different employees in producing and selling the corporation's products and achieving profits for its stockholders. These employees perform thousands of different tasks, each making some contribution to the organization and its objective. It is the task of managers to provide the leadership necessary to secure the individual efforts of organization members and to direct the order and nature of this work.

Emergence of the Professional Manager

At one time, our economy was controlled by small-scale enterprises such as general stores, craft shops, and blacksmiths. The operations of these small concerns were primarily local, and ownership was generally combined with management of the business. An entrepreneur would launch a new enterprise and operate it during his lifetime—passing it on to his children or selling it to some other *owner-manager.*

Development of national markets and the economics of mass production led to growth in the size of industrial concerns. Capital requirements often exceeded the resources of the individual entrepreneur and his immediate family. Public sale of stock became necessary to finance such business ventures. Some of these corporations have grown to the point that they now have hundreds of thousands of stockholders and invested capital amounting to billions of dollars. With such diffusion of ownership, the concept of the owner-manager became obsolete.

As a result of these developments, a new type of manager, the *professional manager,* appeared. Professional management is based not on ownership, but on qualifications derived from knowledge and experience in engineering, production, financial administration, or sales. It is an ability to understand and deal with complex problems in these areas and to make intelligent decisions concerning such problems that qualifies an individual to lead the corporation. This significant transition from the owner-manager to the professional manager has been described as a "managerial revolution."[4]

Managers today constitute an essential class, distinct from labor and separate from ownership. At all levels, managers are generally responsible for allocating resources under their authority, supervising their subordinates, and, in turn, reporting to their own superiors. The emergence of management may be, according to Peter F. Drucker, the "pivotal event of our time." "Rarely, if ever," as Drucker sees it, "has a new basic institution, a new leading group, a new central function, emerged as fast as has management since the turn of the century."[5]

THE MANAGER'S JOB: AN OVERVIEW

What a manager does is the focus of this section.* We will examine the manager's job from a number of different perspectives: managerial behavior patterns, the skills required for effective management, differences in managerial work, the multiple roles of the manager, and the functions of the manager. These are simply alternative ways of viewing managerial work. Taken together, they give us a more complete view of the manager's job than would a single perspective.

Managerial Behavior Patterns

Observation of managers in action reveals that most managers are extremely busy. One survey of top executives revealed that they worked an average of 57.5 hours a week, while another survey indicated that such executives devoted most of their energies to their companies and to outside activities closely related to business.[6] Vacations tended to be infrequent and of short duration. These executives often spent lunch periods on business; sometimes they ate sandwiches at their desks and sometimes they had business lunches with customers, public officials, or staff members.

The fact that a manager works hard and spends long hours on the job tells us little about the patterning of managerial activities. We might surmise that an efficient manager would take one project at a time, complete it, and move on to the next project. Studies of managers in action, however, have shown that the systematic, orderly executive seldom exists in the real world.[7] Rather, the manager's activities are characterized by "brevity, variety, and fragmentation."[8] One study of managers in Great Britain revealed that they could not explicitly state what they wanted to achieve in their jobs, perhaps because of "the episodic and fragmented patterns of their days. . . ."[9]

The characteristic of brevity is particularly pronounced at lower levels of the organization. In separate studies, Guest and Ponder found extreme brevity in activities at the foreman level, with an average duration of forty-eight seconds in the former study and about two minutes in the latter.[10] A study of 1,476 lower-level managers in New York City government indicated that they spent one to three hours each, per week, on fourteen different tasks, and less than one hour each, weekly, on forty-three other tasks.[11]

---

*The practice of management is both a *science* and an *art*. In recent decades, management has become a branch of knowledge concerned with establishing and systematizing facts, principles, and methods through experiments and hypotheses. To the extent this has been accomplished—and you will see some evidence of this accomplishment throughout the text—management is scientific. Few scholars would claim, however, that management is a science. Our knowledge of planning, organizing, leading, controlling, and so on, remains incomplete. To the extent our knowledge is deficient, management continues to be an art, dependent upon personal aptitudes, skills, applications, and intuition.

THE EXECUTIVE'S VARIED ACTIVITIES

In Henry Mintzberg's study of chief executives, he found that they averaged thirty-six written and sixteen verbal contacts each day.

> A subordinate calls to report a fire in one of the facilities; then the mail, much of it insignificant, is processed; a subordinate interrupts to tell of an impending crisis with a public group; a retiring employee is ushered in to receive a plaque; later there is a discussion of bidding on a multi-million-dollar contract; after that, the manager complains that office space in one department is being wasted. Throughout each working day the manager encounters this great variety of activity. Most surprising, the significant activity is interspersed with the trivial in no particular pattern. Hence the manager must be prepared to shift moods quickly and frequently.

SOURCE: Henry Mintzberg, *The Nature of Managerial Work*, p. 31. Copyright © 1973 by Henry Mintzberg. Reprinted by permission of Harper & Row, Publishers, Inc.

Managerial Skills

Robert L. Katz suggests that managerial positions require three types of basic skills: *technical, human, and conceptual*.[12] Although managerial positions differ in the technical skill required, most necessitate some technical ability. A laboratory supervisor, for example, needs to understand the nature of laboratory tests conducted under his or her supervision. A controller requires a knowledge of accounting. Even at top levels, knowledge of the industry is required, particularly in smaller companies where extensive staff assistance is unavailable.

Competence in interpersonal relations is an important asset to the administrator because a manager accomplishes work through the efforts of others. A manager must blend the efforts of subordinate managers who frequently differ in backgrounds, areas of specialization, and viewpoints. The ability to integrate diverse interests and simultaneously preserve the loyalty and enthusiasm of team members contributes directly to organizational effectiveness.

Conceptual skills are essential if the manager is to be able to discern problems, devise solutions, analyze data, and exercise judgment. These tasks are often difficult and intellectually demanding because organizational problems do not always lend themselves to easy solutions. In strategic planning, financial administration, designing control systems, and other areas, the issues may call for the very best thinking of which the manager is capable.

The need for these skills varies from position to position within the

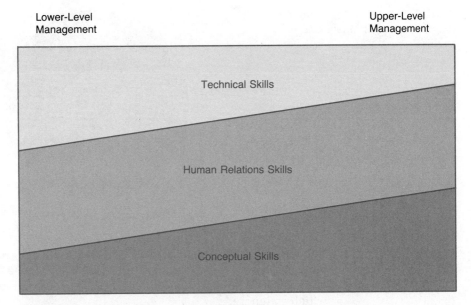

Lower-Level
Management

Upper-Level
Management

Technical Skills

Human Relations Skills

Conceptual Skills

FIGURE 1–3   Skills required at different managerial levels

organization, as illustrated in Figure 1–3. At lower levels, managers direct routine work and can perform successfully with minimum conceptual ability as long as they have the appropriate technical knowledge and human relations skills. As more complex activities are planned and directed at higher levels, the demand for conceptual skills increases, and the need for technical skills becomes less important, although some technical knowledge is required. The focus of the manager's human relations skills changes as he or she is promoted upward. At lower levels, the manager requires leadership ability within his or her own unit. But, at higher levels, skills in intergroup relationships—being able to resolve interdepartmental conflict and promote cooperation—become increasingly important.

Differences in Managerial Work

Athough all managerial jobs have certain elements in common, even managerial jobs at the same hierarchical level can differ considerably. Rosemary Stewart, a British researcher, suggests that managerial jobs vary along three lines, shown below and in Figure 1–4:[13]

1. The *behavioral demands* made upon the manager by his or her subordinates, peers, superiors, external contacts, and so on—these are the things that the manager *must* do.
2. The internal and external *constraints* that limit the manager's behavior—these include monetary and personnel constraints, provisions in the union contract, the organization's technology, and so on.

FIGURE 1–4 A model for understanding managerial jobs and behavior

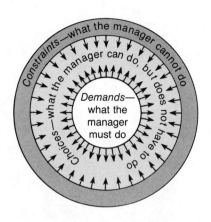

3. The *choices* that a manager has in doing a job differently from another manager—these include the freedom to choose which aspects of the job to emphasize, which to delegate to subordinates, and which to ignore.

These three variables provide a means of identifying the nature and difficulty of various managerial jobs. If we can develop systematic ways of distinguishing among managerial jobs, our efforts to select and prepare people for management will be vastly improved.[14]

Roles of the Manager

Another way to understand the nature of complex managerial work is to identify the manager's multiple *roles*. This use of activity categories helps us to see the tremendous variety that characterizes the manager's job. Although identification of specific roles is somewhat arbitrary, one of the better known categorizations is shown below.[15] These ten roles, grouped into three general categories, are also shown diagrammatically in Figure 1–5.

Interpersonal Roles

1. *Figurehead*
As symbolic head of an organization, the manager must perform duties of a legal or ceremonial nature. Examples of such activities are welcoming official visitors and signing letters to retiring employees.

2. *Leader*
In performing this widely recognized role, the manager guides and motivates subordinates.

3. *Liaison*
This role is concerned primarily with horizontal relationships. The manager establishes a web of external relationships, getting to know his or her peers and building a relationship of mutual assistance.

FIGURE 1–5 Roles of the manager

SOURCE: These roles are described by Henry Mintzberg in *The Nature of Managerial Work* (New York: Harper & Row, Publishers, 1973), Chapter 4.

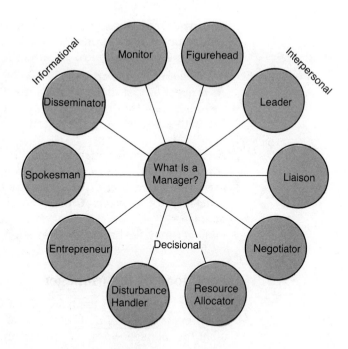

Informational Roles

1. *Monitor*
The manager receives information and analyses related to both operations and external events. Keeping up with trends and learning about new ideas also fall within this area.

2. *Disseminator*
This role entails the transmission of information received from outside to members of the organization. The manager who calls a staff meeting following a business trip is playing the disseminator role.

3. *Spokesman*
The manager speaks on behalf of the organization and transmits information out to the organizational environment. An example is the manager's speech to the trade association or press.

Decisional Roles

1. *Entrepreneur*
In initiating change, the manager performs an entrepreneurial role. A decision to launch a computer feasibility study, for example, would illustrate this role.

2. *Disturbance Handler*
Unexpected problems or disturbances—loss of an important customer or feud between two subordinates, for example—require the manager to play a disturbance-handler role.

3. *Resource Allocator*
In the resource-allocator role, a manager determines the distribution of

organizational resources such as money, time, and equipment. A manager's approval of a budget or establishment of a personal time schedule involves the allocation of resources.

4. *Negotiator*

As a negotiator, a manager bargains with customers or other outsiders or insiders. Representing the organization in labor negotiations or bargaining with a key employee illustrates the negotiator role.

A number of different roles may be evident in a given situation. The study of lower-level managers in New York City government referred to earlier revealed that those managers engaged in eight of these ten roles. (The roles of spokesman and figurehead were reserved for higher-level managers.)[16] In view of the varied relationships that are involved, the manager may find that the roles sometimes conflict.

Functions of the Manager

Another approach to analysis of management activity identifies certain basic *management functions*. In attempting to classify, in this manner, what the manager does, we are seeking some fundamental categories that permit a logical grouping of managerial activities according to their purpose and nature. A number of basic functions are widely recognized, even though there is some variation in labeling them.

In this book, the following functions will provide the framework for our analysis of management activities:

1. Planning and decision making
2. Organizing for effective performance
3. Leading and motivating
4. Controlling performance

Each of these functions is discussed briefly below and also serves as the basis for a major part of the book. In practice, these functions are intertwined in the day-to-day performance of a manager.[17]

Planning. Managerial planning involves thought and decision concerning a proposed course of action. The plan may be concerned with not only a decision to take action but also such aspects as "who," "when," and "how."

The first step in the planning process is setting organizational objectives or goals. These objectives provide direction for the organization and also serve as a basis for teamwork among organizational components and individuals. Attaining the objectives requires strategic planning; that is, devising a basic approach or strategy to reach the organization's objectives. The strategy for the organization is typically broken down and supplemented with policies—guidelines for administrative action—

and specific operating plans for particular organizational units. Middle- and lower-level managers, guided by top management's strategy, formulate more specific goals and plans for their particular divisions or departments. This interlocking set of policies and plans serves as a program of action for managers at all organizational levels.

Decision Making. Although decision making is involved in planning, motivating, and the other managerial functions, this activity is considered so important that it is emphasized here as a separate function. Basically, decision making is a conscious choice from among two or more alternative courses of action. Ideally, the manager makes this choice by identifying the problem or opportunity being faced, searching for possible alternative solutions, evaluating the alternatives, and choosing and implementing one or more of the alternatives.

Because the future is uncertain, the manager uses various types of tools to reduce the risk and subjectivity of decision making. Management information systems, for instance, are designed to provide data on internal operations and the external environment. In some situations, data analysis is aided by quantitative techniques using mathematical models.

Organizing for Effective Performance. Implementing plans requires an organization. Viewed broadly, organizing includes providing for physical facilities, capital, and personnel.* Building an organization also concerns determining relationships among functions, jobs, and personnel. Each of these is a part of the creation of the organizational machine that is designed to accomplish some objective.

The organization function might be visualized as breaking down an overall objective into the specific functions and assignments necessary for the accomplishment of that objective. This involves creating jobs and specifying job content and then grouping jobs and activities into departments and divisions. The organizing function is concerned with the relationships among these units and the jobs within the units and, more broadly, with the fit between the organization's overall structure and its external environment.

Leading and Motivating. The organizational machine must be activated in order to carry out management plans. The functions of leading and motivating set the organization in motion.

A major responsibility of managers at all organizational levels is to direct and inspire the work of others. High-performing employees can make the difference between a marginal organization and a highly effective one. Through leadership, a manager secures the cooperation of others in accomplishing an objective. And, in motivating, the manager en-

---

*The design and provision of physical facilities are basically technical or engineering functions and for this reason are excluded from detailed consideration in a study of general management. Much the same reasoning applies to the provision of capital, which is a part of the specialized field of financial management.

courages subordinates to strive persistently for high job performance. These functions require the manager to understand individual and group behavior and to communicate clearly.

Controlling Performance.   Controlling performance means monitoring the organization to insure the achievement of objectives and the completion of plans. Perhaps the most obvious feature of controlling is the comparison of organizational or individual performance with pre-established standards, or expected results. If deviations from standards are revealed, it is the manager's responsibility to take corrective action. He or she must get performance back up to the time schedule, get quality up to par, or make other adjustments necessary to meet the expectations previously established. Corrective action takes many forms, such as improving work processes, motivating subordinates, correcting communication breakdowns, revising decision-making procedures, or modifying the organization's structure.

A Synthesis.   The approaches we have taken to viewing managerial work are not unrelated. For instance, consider the function of *managerial planning*. Planning requires the use of *conceptual skills* and, later, *human relations skills* in communicating those plans to others. The final plans will reflect the *constraints* under which the manager must operate and the *behavioral demands* made upon him or her by peers, superiors, and subordinates. While planning, the manager may well play such *roles* as *liaison* in discussing the plans with managers of other units which may be affected; *monitor* in collecting and interpreting information from the environment and other parts of the organization; *entrepreneur* in initiating change for the organization; and *resource allocator* in determining the allocation of financial and human resources necessary for carrying out the plan. Hence, we have viewed the manager's job from alternative, but highly related, perspectives.

THE CHALLENGE OF MANAGEMENT

Increasing Complexity of Management

The opportunities and problems that management faces have grown in complexity during recent decades. A number of factors have contributed to this increase in the challenge to management. Consider the following, for instance.

Organizational Size and Geographic Scope.   As organizations become larger and more international in scope, the task of managing them also grows in difficulty. It is easier to provide leadership and coordinate the activities of a few hundred employees in a local area than to manage thousands of individuals spread across several geographic regions, cultures, and legal entities.

Specialization of Labor and Complexity of Work. Consider the design and assembly of a product such as an airplane. The design and specifications may require thousands of labor hours and tons of paper. Thousands of different parts become part of the finished plane. Some of these are manufactured within the company, while others are purchased. Managers must integrate and schedule the work of purchasing clerks, inventory and supply clerks, draftspersons, engineers of various types, welders, sheet metal workers, instrument mechanics, electricians, supervisors, personnel clerks, top management personnel, and hundreds of other types of employees.

Changed Status of Employees. A few decades ago, there was no question as to who was boss. The right of the manager—who was frequently the owner—to hire and fire was both recognized and exercised. But members of present-day organizations are far more independent than their predecessors. They have more education, broader interests in outside affairs, stronger desires for individual identity and recognition, and less patience for seemingly meaningless work. They are often represented by unions and, as citizens, carry greater political power. This transformation calls for greater finesse on the part of contemporary managers.

Government Regulation. In recent years, many new regulatory bodies, such as OSHA (Occupational Safety and Health Administration), EEOC (Equal Employment Opportunity Commission), EPA (Environmental Protection Agency), and CPSC (Consumer Product Safety Commission), have joined with such older agencies as the FTC (Federal Trade Commission) and FDA (Food and Drug Administration) to regulate almost all major—and many minor—aspects of organizational policy and behavior. As a result, today's managers must be acutely aware of the legal environment in which planning and decision making take place.

Accelerating Change. In addition to the changes discussed above, managers must cope with rapid inflation, energy shortages, changing social trends, and growing consumerism, as well as with scientific and technological innovation. The acceleration in the rate of innovation has altered the requirements for managerial success. A manager today can ill afford to emphasize tradition, accept the status quo, or rely upon "experience (Figure 1–6)."

Management and Productivity

A major challenge to management in the 1980s is the need to increase the productivity of American business. Productivity is a measure of economic output per person. It is important because economic and, to a large extent, social progress depend upon an upward trend in productivity. In the twenty years following World War II, output per worker in the United States increased by 3.2 percent annually. But, beginning in 1965,

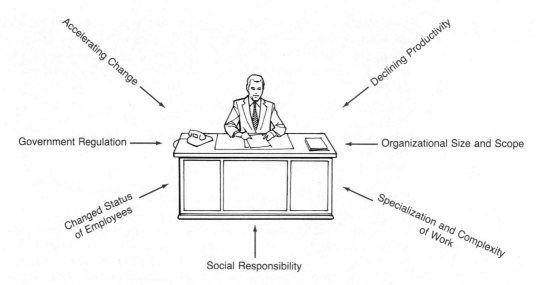

FIGURE 1–6   Some of the challenges facing today's professional manager

this figure declined to an average annual increase of only 1.9 percent. By 1976, our annual productivity increase was down to 0.5 percent, and since 1979, the average annual output per worker has actually fallen.[18]

A number of factors external to organizations affect productivity. For instance, a tax system that discourages the savings that are needed for new investment, government regulations that drain resources from productive endeavors, and the declining work ethic are often cited as culprits. A number of observers, however, feel that American managers are ultimately responsible for the productivity problem. Economist Lester C. Thurow, for example, believes that the problem lies in two areas: (1) managers have failed to generate an environment in which labor can play an active role in increasing their firm's productivity, and (2) managers emphasize short-run returns on investment at the expense of long-range research and development.[19]

In truth, our productivity problem has multiple causes—both internal and external to organizations. Although managers cannot be expected to solve all of these problems, they do have the ability to improve productivity through many types of decisions. Managers must provide appropriate motivational appeals to organization members and design jobs to encourage enthusiastic and effective performance. Capital and labor must be combined in the right proportions. In serving a changing environment, managers must introduce new product and service innovations and apply new technologies to production processes. The quality of these and many other decisions depends on the quality of management insight and the wisdom of management choices. In the final analysis, productivity may be regarded "as a measure of management's efficiency, or lack of efficiency, in employing all the necessary resources—natural, human, and financial."[20]

THE CHALLENGE OF MANAGEMENT

Top Management's Challenge

In a study of forty-seven top-level executives, George Steiner concluded that future CEOs (chief executive officers) will require qualities that differ from those of current CEOs. Some of these differences include the following:

1. The future CEO must be charismatic and articulate enough to influence public opinion. In fact, CEOs must, of necessity, become public figures and "plunge into the seas of controversy." They must be politically active and understand how government works.
2. Future top executives must be more concerned with external than internal organizational duties.
3. The CEO must have a global perspective.
4. The CEO must be a generalist with a knowledge of history, literature, the arts, and current events.

Supervisory Management's Challenge

Studies over the past thirty years have indicated that first-level supervisors serve in a unique position. Although members of management, they often have little authority or decision-making power, and although they are not part of the work force, they are dependent upon its acceptance. Current studies show that these problems continue to exist today. In addition, supervisors face other challenges:

1. Many supervisors feel overwhelmed by the amount of paperwork and record keeping they are required to handle.
2. Although confident of their problem-solving abilities and human relations skills, supervisors are less sure of themselves in such areas as counseling, using statistics and computers, enforcing OSHA regulations, and developing ideas for improving productivity.
3. The supervisor increasingly must be able to communicate effectively with workers who often "view their jobs as necessary evils to provide the resources for fulfilling their lives in leisure time, which they are pressing harder and harder to increase."

SOURCE: Based on George A. Steiner, "The New Class of Chief Executive Officer," *Long Range Planning* 14 (August 1981): 12–14; Lester R. Bittel and Jackson E. Ramsey, "The Limited, Traditional World of Supervisors," *Harvard Business Review* 60 (July–August 1982): 26–28; and W. Earl Sasser, Jr. and Frank S. Leonard, "Let First-Level Supervisors Do Their Job," *Harvard Business Review* 58 (March–April 1980): 114–16. Quote is from Sasser and Leonard, p. 114.

Management Power and Responsibility

In the last 100 years, management has come to possess immense power. The corporation occupies a position of key importance in contemporary society. To a great extent, our national welfare depends upon its effective performance. Social improvements and military strength can be achieved only by the contribution of industrial concerns. Economic growth, as noted above, is realized through the progress of America's business corporations. These corporations are, in turn, dependent upon the quality of their management.

With power comes responsibility. As a result of their powerful position, managers can no longer be self-centered or capricious in their actions. Society expects a capable, responsible performance and is inclined to tolerate little less. The nineteenth-century corporate leader has often been villainized (with some justification, of course). Today business leadership has a greater degree of public acceptance despite the lack of sympathy for those who ignore accepted standards of business behavior. In fact, the lessening public tolerance of improper behavior reflects some measure of acceptance of business management as an institution. People realize that business leaders have great influence and expect them to act responsibly.

This chapter has presented an overview of the field of management and the manager's job. Chapter 2 adds perspective to this view as it traces the evolution of management thought from its early days to contemporary times.

SUMMARY

Management is the process of acquiring and combining human, financial, and physical resources to attain the organization's primary goal of producing a product or service desired by some segment of society. This process is essential to all organizations, profit and nonprofit alike. The need for management arises in any sizable cooperative endeavor, and this need today is fulfilled most often by *professional managers*, having qualifications based on knowledge and experience in dealing with complex organizational problems.

Examination of the managerial job reveals that most managers are extremely busy and engage in activities characterized by brevity, variety, and fragmentation; effective management requires *technical, human,* and *conceptual* skills; managerial jobs differ along a number of dimensions involving behavioral *demands, constraints,* and *choices*; and managers play a variety of *roles* in their work.

A useful approach to analysis of management activity identifies certain basic management *functions*. Regardless of the type of organization or the level of the manager, most managers must engage in certain activities. Although the nature of the function varies among settings and levels, managers must *plan and make decisions, organize* for effective performance, *lead and motivate* subordinates, and *control* performance.

Increasing organizational size, extensive specialization of labor, the growing independence of employees, government regulations, decreasing productivity, and the need to exercise power responsibly are some of the important challenges facing the modern manager. The accelerating rate of environmental change likewise complicates the managerial process.

DISCUSSION QUESTIONS

1. How is the process of management similar in both profit and nonprofit organizations? How is it different?

2. Are the management skills of an individual universal; that is, are they transferable from setting to setting without any significant loss of effectiveness?

3. What factors have encouraged the professionalization of management?

4. Why do managers seem to have such fragmented work schedules? Does it reflect a lack of planning?

5. What is the relative importance of *technical* skills, *human relations* skills, and *conceptual* skills at the top-management level versus the first-line supervisory level?

6. How does identification of the manager's *multiple roles* help one understand the complexity of the management process?

7. What is the relationship between *managerial functions* and *managerial roles*?

8. What relationships exist between the functions of *planning and decision making* and *organizing for effective performance*? Between *planning and decision making* and *controlling performance*?

9. What are some of the factors contributing to the increased complexity of management today?

10. What is meant by the phrase "*productivity* is a measure of management's efficiency"?

NOTES

1. "Management," *Forbes*, 15 September 1967, p. 51.

2. John P. Kotter, "General Managers Are Not Generalists," *Organizational Dynamics* 10 (Spring 1982): 16–17.

3. Robert L. Katz, "Skills of an Effective Administrator," *Harvard Business Review* 52 (September–October 1974): 101.

4. James Burnham, *The Managerial Revolution* (New York: The John Day Co.,

1941). For an intriguing look at the problems one company is facing in making the transition from a family-run business to a professionally managed firm, see "The Outsiders' Touch That's Shaking Up Mennen," *Business Week*, 1 February 1982, pp. 58–59.

5. Peter F. Drucker, *Management: Tasks, Responsibilities, Practices* (New York: Harper & Row, Publishers, 1974), p. 10.

6. "The Organization Man, Cont'd," *Newsweek*, 27 October 1980, p. 96.

7. Examples of studies of managerial behavior are the following: Robert Dubin, "Business Behavior *Behaviorally* Viewed," in *Social Science Approaches to Business Behavior*, ed. George B. Strother (Homewood, Ill.: Richard D. Irwin, 1962), pp. 11–15; Rosemary Stewart, *Managers and Their Jobs* (London: Macmillan, 1968); and Henry Mintzberg, *The Nature of Managerial Work* (New York: Harper & Row, Publishers, 1973). The Mintzberg study is particularly useful because it reports extensive observations over time of managers at work and also provides excellent summaries of related research.

8. Mintzberg, *Managerial Work*, p. 31. (See note 7 above.)

9. Rosemary Stewart, "Managerial Agendas—Reactive or Proactive?" *Organizational Dynamics* 8 (Autumn 1979): 45.

10. These studies are summarized in Mintzberg, *Managerial Work*, p. 34.

11. Peter Allan, "Managers at Work: A Large-Scale Study of the Managerial Job in New York City Government," *Academy of Management Journal* 24 (September 1981): 613–19.

12. Katz, "Skills of an Effective Administrator," pp. 90–112.

13. Rosemary Stewart, "A Model for Understanding Managerial Jobs and Behaviors," *Academy of Management Review* 7 (January 1982): 9–11; and Rosemary Stewart, "To Understand the Manager's Job: Consider Demands, Constraints, Choices," *Organizational Dynamics* 4 (Spring 1976): 27.

14. Peter D. Couch, "Learning to be a Middle Manager," *Business Horizons* 22 (February 1979): 35.

15. Abridged and adapted from Chapter 4 in *The Nature of Managerial Work* by Henry Mintzberg. Copyright © 1973 by Henry Mintzberg. Reprinted by permission of Harper & Row, Publishers, Inc. For a set of roles partially contrasting to those described by Mintzberg, see Edmond H. Curcuru and James H. Healey, "The Multiple Roles of the Manager," *Business Horizons* 15 (August 1972): 15–24.; and Ichak Adizes, "Mismanagement Styles," *California Management Review* 19 (Winter 1976): 5–20.

16. Allan, "Managers at Work," pp. 613–19.

17. Myron D. Fottler, "Is Management Really Generic?" *Academy of Management Review* 6 (January 1981): 1–12, suggests that management functions may differ in emphasis and form across organizational types due to different external, internal, and motivational influences.

18. Gerald Egger, "A Cure for 3 P.M. Syndrome Could Produce Major Changes," *The Houston Post*, 10 August 1980.

19. Lester C. Thurow, "Where Management Fails," *Newsweek*, 7 December 1981, p. 78.

20. Richard C. Gerstenberg, quoted in "Management Itself Holds the Key," *Business Week*, 9 September 1972, p. 142.

SUPPLEMENTARY READING

Allan, Peter. "Managers at Work: A Large-Scale Study of the Managerial Job in New York City Government." *Academy of Management Journal* 24 (September 1981): 613–19.

Bittel, Lester R., and **Ramsey, Jackson E.** "The Limited, Traditional World of Supervisors." *Harvard Business Review* 60 (July–August 1982): 26–36.

Couch, Peter D. "Learning to be a Middle Manager." *Business Horizons* 22 (February 1979): 33–41.

Drucker, Peter F. *People and Performance: The Best of Peter Drucker on Management.* New York: Harper's College Press, 1977.

Finn, David. "Public Invisibility of Corporate Leaders." *Harvard Business Review* 58 (November–December 1980): 102–10.

Fottler, Myron D. "Is Management Really Generic?" *Academy of Management Review* 6 (January 1981): 1–12.

Kelly, James N. "Management Transitions for Newly Appointed CEOs." *Sloan Management Review* 22 (Fall 1980): 37–45.

Keys, Bernard, and **Bell, Robert.** "Four Faces of the Fully Functioning Middle Manager." *California Management Review* 24 (Summer 1982): 59–67.

Koprowski, Eugene J. "Exploring the Meaning of 'Good' Management." *Academy of Management Review* 6 (July 1981): 459–67.

Kotter, John P. "General Managers Are Not Generalists." *Organizational Dynamics* 10 (Spring 1982): 5–19.

_____. "What Effective General Managers Really Do." *Harvard Business Review* 60 (November–December 1982): 156–67.

Levinson, Harry. "Criteria for Choosing Chief Executives." *Harvard Business Review* 58 (July–August 1980): 113–20.

Mintzberg, Henry. "The Manager's Job: Folklore and Fact." *Harvard Business Review* 53 (July–August 1975): 49–61.

Peters, Thomas J. "Putting Excellence into Management." *Business Week,* 21 July 1980, pp. 196–205.

Sasser, W. Earl, Jr., and **Leonard, Frank S.** "Let First-Level Supervisors Do Their Job." *Harvard Business Review* 58 (March–April 1980): 113–21.

Steiner, George A. "The New Class of Chief Executive Officer." *Long Range Planning* 14 (August 1981): 10–20.

Stewart, Rosemary. "Managerial Agendas—Reactive or Proactive?" *Organizational Dynamics* 8 (Autumn 1979): 34–47.

_____. "A Model for Understanding Managerial Jobs and Behaviors." *Academy of Management Review* 7 (January 1982): 7–13.

Swinyard, Alfred W., and **Bond, Floyd A.** "Who Gets Promoted?" *Harvard Business Review* 58 (September–October 1980): 6–18.

2

HISTORICAL TRENDS IN MANAGEMENT THOUGHT AND PRACTICE

This chapter will enable you to

- *Describe the early classical school of management thought and its objectives.*
- *Understand how later management researchers and theorists expanded the classical concept of management to include human behavior in organizations.*
- *View and understand organizations as open systems with interrelated subsystems.*
- *Explain the modern contingency approach to management and its current state of development.*

An understanding of current management thought and practice requires an historical perspective. The management process is as old as history itself. The construction of the Great Pyramids, for instance, was a project of such complexity that it could not possibly have been completed without superb managerial planning and supervision. Yet, even though management has been practiced for centuries, a systematic analysis of the field and the development of a theory of management did not begin until about 1900.

Even a detailed description of management thought since the turn of the twentieth century would fill a very large book.[1] Hence, this chapter will examine only some of the major highlights in the evolution of management in the twentieth century. Our discussion will follow the diagram shown in Figure 2–1, beginning with the classical school of management thought.

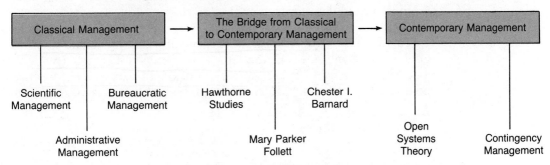

FIGURE 2–1 Major trends in the development of management thought

THE CLASSICAL SCHOOL
OF MANAGEMENT THOUGHT

Classical (meaning "of historical importance") *management thought* was a compilation of three separate, but related, fields of endeavor—(1) *scientific management*, (2) *administrative management*, and (3) *bureaucratic management*.[2] Each field is closely associated with the work of a particular person, and our discussion will focus on the contributions of these three individuals.

Scientific Management

Any description of classical management thought must begin with Frederick W. Taylor (1856–1915), the "father of *scientific management*." As Drucker has stated: "Taylor was the first man in history who actually studied work seriously. This is his historical importance."[3]

Job design, at the beginning of this century, can best be described as "casual." Workers performed tasks according to tradition and subjective judgment, and managers gave little systematic thought to techniques for improving worker efficiency. Scientific management grew out of Taylor's questioning these traditional ways of managing work as he progressed from a machinist to shop superintendent in the Midvale Steel Company in the 1880s. For the next thirty years, as a consultant, and later as a manager with Bethlehem Steel Company, Taylor refined his approach to work analysis and wrote about his ideas.[4]

The basic goal of scientific management was to increase employee productivity through a systematic, "scientific" analysis of the employee's work. This research and experimentation with the task would culminate in "one best way" to perform the job. Workers who were appropriate for the task would then be selected, given detailed instructions in the new method, and required to perform exactly in the manner prescribed.

Workers who followed the prescribed methods earned wages which were significantly higher than they had received before. Taylor felt that economic incentives served as the major motivator of industrial workers. Employees would be willing to follow the "one best way," Taylor reasoned, if high wages were tied to high production. Management, in turn, would be pleased because, even with the higher wages, labor costs per unit would be lower than before, because of increased worker productivity.

Taylor, then, saw scientific management as the systematic—or scientific—investigation of all the facts and elements connected with the work being managed. It was the very opposite of management by tradition and rule of thumb.* Much of his work—such as job analysis, careful

---

*The scientific management movement in the U.S.S.R. and the role of Walter N. Polakov as a consultant to the Soviet planners are presented in Daniel A. Wren, "Scientific Management in the U.S.S.R., with Particular Reference to the Contribution of Walter N. Polakov," *Academy of Management Review* 5 (January 1980): 1–11.

selection of workers, and employee training—serves as the foundation for modern personnel management. His scientific approach to problem solving also can be found in more modern forms today, as we will see in the discussion of the managerial decision-making process in Chapters 8 and 9.

Many criticisms were made of the work of Taylor and the scientific management movement.[5] Some people objected to the dehumanization potential of scientific management. The work of an employee was analyzed as one might analyze the operation of a machine, and the goal was maximization of efficiency of this human "machine." Although Taylor exhibited a sense of fairness toward employees and a desire to see them share the benefits of higher productivity, the potential for misuse of scientific management was exploited by other managers.

In fact, the scientific management movement fell into such disrepute that Congress undertook an investigation of it. In 1912, Taylor appeared before an investigating committee of the House of Representatives and gave a careful exposition of scientific management as he understood and practiced it. He vigorously defended the basic concepts of scientific management against the attacks of those who felt that these concepts had served to exploit and take advantage of labor. In spite of these criticisms of Taylor's work, it does stand as a pioneer, revolutionary approach to management that makes its creator one of the outstanding figures in management history.*

② Administrative Management

While Taylor focused on the planning of work and management techniques for the supervisor, across the Atlantic a French business executive analyzed management from a top-level perspective. Henri Fayol's (1841–1925) analysis was based on his lengthy experience as the managing director of a large coal mining business and resulted in the publication of *General and Industrial Management* in 1916.[6] This work made two significant contributions to management thought: (1) the delineation of the *functions*—or duties—of a manager; and (2) the establishment of a set of *principles*—or guidelines—which managers might apply as they performed their functions.

Fayol felt that management consisted of five essential functions: *planning, organizing, commanding, coordinating,* and *controlling,* shown in diagrammatic form in Figure 2–2. Planning was the act of forecasting the future—up to ten years in advance—and then preparing to deal with the forecasted events. The organization, according to Fayol, should have an overall general plan from which department managers could derive plans for their own areas of responsibility. Once planning was accomplished, the manager should organize by acquiring the nec-

---

*Taylor was, of course, only one of many contributors to the development of a scientific approach to management. Other pioneers included Henry L. Gantt, Frank and Lillian Gilbreth, Harrington Emerson, Wallace Clark, and Henry R. Towne, to name but a few.

SCHMIDT AND THE PIG IRON EXPERIMENT

Taylor and his associates studied a group of 75 men at Bethlehem Steel Company who loaded pig iron (each pig weighed about 92 pounds) onto railroad cars. Based on "scientific" calculations of the distance the men had to walk to the railroad car, how fast they walked, how often they should rest, and so on, Taylor determined that, instead of the 12½ tons per day each man was loading, 47½ tons was actually a "proper day's work."

In order to demonstrate the accuracy of his calculations, Taylor selected a physically fit worker to act as an experimental subject. This worker has become known to management history as "Schmidt."

The task before us, then, narrowed itself down to getting Schmidt to handle 47 tons of pig iron per day and making him glad to do it. This was done as follows. Schmidt was called out from among the gang of pig-iron handlers and talked to somewhat in this way:

"Schmidt, are you a high-priced man?"

"Vell, I don't know vat you mean."

"Oh yes, you do. What I want to know is whether you are a high-priced man or not."

"Vell, I don't know vat you mean."

"Oh, come now, you answer my questions. What I want to find out is whether you are a high-priced man or one of these cheap fellows here. What I want to find out is whether you want to earn $1.85 a day or whether you are satisfied with $1.15, just the same as all those cheap fellows are getting."

"Did I vant $1.85 a day? Vas dot a high-priced man? Vell, yes, I vas a high-priced man."

"Oh, you're aggravating me. Of course you want $1.85 a day—every one wants it! You know perfectly well that that has very little to do with your being a high-priced man. For goodness sake answer my questions, and don't waste any more of my time. Now come over here. You see that pile of pig iron?"

"Yes."

"You see that car?"

"Yes."

"Well, if you are a high-priced man, you will load that pig iron on that car to-morrow for $1.85. Now do wake up and answer my question. Tell me whether you are a high-priced man or not."

"Vell—did I got $1.85 for loading dot pig iron on dot car tomorrow?"

"Yes, of course you do, and you get $1.85 for loading a pile like that every day right through the year. That is what a high-priced man does, and you know it just as well as I do."

"Vell, dot's all right. I could load dot pig iron on the car tomorrow for $1.85, and I get it every day, don't I?"

"Certainly you do—certainly you do."

"Vell, den, I vas a high-priced man."

"Now, hold on, hold on. You know just as well as I do that a high-priced man has to do exactly as he's told from morning till night. You have seen this man here before, haven't you?"

"No, I never saw him."

"Well, if you are a high-priced man, you will do exactly as this man tells you to-morrow, from morning till night. When he tells you to pick up a pig and walk, you pick it up and you walk, and when he tells you to sit down and rest, you sit down. You do that right straight through the day. And what's more, no back talk. Now a high-priced man does just what he's told to do, and no back talk. Do you understand that? When this man tells you to walk, you walk; when he tells you to sit down, you sit down, and you don't talk back at him. Now you come on to work here to-morrow morning and I'll know before night whether you are really a high-priced man or not. . . ."

Schmidt started to work, and all day long, and at regular intervals, was told by the man who stood over him with a watch, "Now pick up a pig and walk. Now sit down and rest. Now walk—now rest," etc. He worked when he was told to work, and rested when he was told to rest, and at half-past five in the afternoon had his 47½ tons loaded on the car. And he practically never failed to work at this pace and do the task that was set him during the three years that the writer was at Bethlehem. And throughout this time he averaged a little more than $1.85 per day, whereas before he had never received over $1.15 per day, which was the ruling rate of wages at that time in Bethlehem. That is, he received 60 per cent higher wages than were paid to other men who were not working on task work. One man after another was picked out and trained to handle pig iron at the rate of 47½ tons per day until all of the pig iron was handled at this rate, and the men were receiving 60 per cent more wages than other workmen around them.

SOURCE: Frederick Winslow Taylor, *The Principles of Scientific Management* (New York: W. W. Norton & Co., 1911), pp. 44–47.

essary material and human resources and structuring the human resources into jobs, departments, and so on to enable them to carry out the organization's plans.

Planning and organizing were basic preparations for the operating functions. Commanding consisted of setting the human resources in motion toward the organization's objectives; coordinating involved harmo-

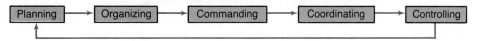

FIGURE 2–2 Fayol's five functions of management

nizing and uniting all activities; and controlling served to make certain that all operations were proceeding according to plan.

As the manager engaged in these functions, a number of principles were useful in guiding his behavior. Fayol formulated fourteen such principles, some of which are shown in Figure 2–3. Because management deals with people in a wide variety of circumstances, these principles had to be flexible and adaptable to varying situations, and the process of applying them would be more of an art than a science.

Much of Fayol's work seems relatively self-evident and obvious to readers today, and changing conditions and ideas have made other parts of his work obsolete. But some of Fayol's writings have had significant impact on modern management thought. Even today, for example, the functions of planning, organizing, and controlling are major areas of research and teaching in collegiate schools of business and public administration. As another example, the principle of equity has become so important to organizations that much of it has been formalized into law in the United States. Certainly, Fayol's place in history as the first management theoretician remains secure.

Bureaucratic Management

At the same time that Fayol and Taylor were independently developing their ideas, a German intellectual, Max Weber (1864–1920), was analyzing how managers should structure organizations. Weber was concerned with constructing a model of organization structure that would be rational and highly efficient for the operation of large organizations. The resulting model he termed *bureaucracy*.

Weber believed that large organizations in business, government, religion, and the military required a new type of management that was

> *Division of Work*—specialization of labor, in managerial and nonmanagerial jobs, increases organizational productivity.
> *Authority and Responsibility*—authority is the right of a manager to give orders and require conformity to those orders. Responsibility goes with and must match authority.
> *Unity of Command*—each employee should receive orders from only one superior.
> *Subordination of Individual Interest to General Interest*—the interests of one employee or a group of employees must be subordinated to the overall interests of the organization.
> *Scalar Chain*—the scalar chain is the line of authority, from superior to subordinate, running from the top to the bottom of the organization. This chain should be the channel used for communication and decision making.
> *Equity*—all employees should be treated with fairness, kindness, and justice.

FIGURE 2–3   Selected principles of management from Fayol

SOURCE: Henri Fayol, *General and Industrial Management*, trans. Constance Storrs (London: Pitman Publishing, 1949), pp. 19–42 (the explanations of the principles have been paraphrased).

unlike that of the old family-based organization. The basic elements of this new system of management are shown in Figure 2–4.

Today, of course, the word *bureaucracy* conjures up visions of red tape, excruciating slowness of operations, and inefficiency. This connotation, however, is quite unlike the meaning Weber intended. He felt that a bureaucracy, managed by competent individuals hired solely on the basis of their qualifications, was "capable of attaining the highest degree of efficiency."[7] The primary reason for the superiority of this management system lay in the organization's technical knowledge, regardless of whether the organization existed in a capitalistic or socialistic economy.[8]

Weber's ideas, of course, are reflected in large contemporary organizations. Indeed, managing an organization consisting of thousands of employees could not be accomplished without a rational organizational system. Although the extremes to which bureaucracy has often led have been decried, and bureaucratic principles have often proved inefficient in rapidly changing situations, Weber certainly deserves to be remembered as the "founder of organization theory."

A Synthesis of Classical Thought

Although these three theorists worked independently without knowledge of each others' contributions and wrote from different perspectives and cultures, they shared the same goal. Their basic intent was to make organizations operate more efficiently and productively. Whether the organization is a small business or a mammoth corporation, rational, scientific procedures should be applied to its operations.

---

1. A specific division of labor among organizational members exists. Each member's authority and responsibility are clearly defined.
2. A well-defined chain of command is present. All positions are organized into a hierarchy. Each lower position is under the control and supervision of a higher one. There is a right of appeal and an established grievance procedure from lower to higher positions.
3. Members of the organization are selected on the basis of adequate technical training which can be demonstrated through educational qualifications or examination.
4. Promotion is based on seniority or achievement, or both, and is dependent on the judgment of superiors.
5. All administrative acts, decisions, and rules are recorded in writing even when oral discussion is traditional.
6. The managers of the organization should not be the owners.
7. All organizational members are subject to strict and systematic discipline and control in the conduct of their duties.

FIGURE 2–4 Elements of a bureaucracy

SOURCE: Max Weber, *The Theory of Social and Economic Organization,* trans. and ed. A. M. Henderson and Talcott Parsons (New York: The Free Press, 1947): 329–34 (the elements have been paraphrased).

The work of these theorists, and the work of others we have been unable to mention, reflected certain assumptions about human beings. Among these assumptions were the following:[9]

1. Human beings act rationally.
2. Individuals need clear job limits to avoid confusion. They cannot work out the relationships among their jobs without detailed guidance from their superiors.
3. Management involves primarily the formal, official activities of individuals and should be administered without regard to their personal problems or characteristics.
4. People do not like to work and, hence, need to be closely supervised.

In the next section, we shall see how management thinkers began to move away from these assumptions.

THE BRIDGE FROM CLASSICAL TO CONTEMPORARY MANAGEMENT

The number of events, theorists, and writings which could be included in this section is very large. At the risk of excluding a number of important ideas, we have elected to focus on three areas which illustrate well the movement of management thought away from the classical assumptions.

The Hawthorne Studies

The Hawthorne Studies refer to a series of experiments conducted in the Western Electric Company's Hawthorne plant in Chicago and Cicero, Illinois, beginning in 1924.[10] The studies, carried out initially by researchers from the National Academy of Sciences, were designed to discover the relationship between the level of illumination in the workplace and the production level of employees. The underlying assumption that at some level of lighting workers would be most productive had obvious roots in scientific management.

In one phase of the experiments, workers were divided into two groups—a test group and a control group. Lighting affecting the test group was increased from twenty-four to forty-six to seventy foot-candles, while control group lighting was held constant. It was assumed that output of the test group would show some increase in contrast to that of the control group. Results were surprising, however, because production of both groups increased in roughly the same proportion!

In another experiment, lighting of a test group was reduced from ten to three foot-candles, while lighting of the control group was held constant. Rather than declining, however, test group output increased—as did that of the control group! At a later stage, illumination was reduced until it reached the level of moonlight (.06 of a foot-candle), but not until then did output drop appreciably.

Certainly, "rational" behavior was not being observed. The employees involved were aware that their performance was being recorded, and the researchers assumed that they were reacting to being observed and to the attention they were receiving. The results were so confusing that the researchers were prepared to abandon the project until a group of faculty members from Harvard University agreed to act as consultants to the study. The leaders of this new research team, Elton Mayo (1880–1949) and Fritz J. Roethlisberger (1898–1974), were to leave an enduring mark on the field of management thought.

Through interviews, observation, and experimentation (such as the study shown in the accompanying box), the researchers began to conclude that the human element in production was more significant than had been realized. Workers' personal problems affected their work performance. Additionally, workers brought to their jobs various social needs which led them to form informal groups, characterized by elaborate sets of norms.

The researchers began to view the organization as a social system, which brought together the formal organization with its hierarchy and rules and the informal organization based on human interactions and sentiments. Although the technical aspects of efficiency and productivity were important, they should be balanced by a concern for human beings and their needs. As Wren has so aptly put it:

> In short, the outcome of the Hawthorne research was a call for a new mix of managerial skills. These skills were ones which were crucial to handling human situations: first, diagnostic skills in understanding human behavior and second, interpersonal skills in counseling, motivating, leading, and communicating with workers. Technical skills alone were not enough to cope with the behavior discovered at the Hawthorne Works.[11]

The Hawthorne Studies have been widely criticized on a number of grounds; among them, inappropriate research methodology, misinterpretation of results, biased samples of workers, and overemphasis on social factors while underemphasizing the actual work being performed and the employees' economic incentives.[12] Yet, despite these faults, this series of studies modified the rational/technical assumptions of the classical school by emphasizing the importance of the human element in management.

Mary Parker Follett's Work

The emphasis on human behavior in the workplace received further impetus from the writings of Mary Parker Follett (1868–1933), an American political philosopher. Throughout her work is an emphasis on the group as the primary building block of organizations. It was only through relationships with others in groups, she believed, that an individual could find his or her true identity and be fully creative.[13]

BANK WIRING
OBSERVATION ROOM STUDY

A later phase of the Hawthorne Studies focused upon a group of fourteen workmen engaged in wiring certain types of telephone equipment. They were paid on an incentive basis so that the more they produced, the more they earned. Contrary to "rational" economic need predictions, however, most of the workers produced significantly below their capacity even though they did not appear to be fatigued and seemed to have some free time during the work day.

Further investigation revealed that the workers had established their own informal production standard—or norm—for a "fair day's work." Reasons for the norm were voiced by two of the workers as follows:

> No one can turn out the [standard that management has set] consistently. Well, occasionally some of them do. Now since the layoff started there's been a few fellows down there who have been turning out around 7,300 a day. . . . I think it is foolishness to do it because I don't think it will do them any good, and it is likely to do the rest of us a lot of harm. . . . If they start turning out around 7,300 a day over a period of weeks and if three of them do it, then they can lay one of the men off, because three men working at that speed can do as much as four men working at the present rate.
>
> You know, the supervisors came around and told us that . . . if we would turn out more work we would make more money, but we can't see it that way. Probably what would happen is that our [standard] would be raised, and then we would just be turning out more work for the same money. I can't see that.

This informal standard was enforced through "binging"—the administration of a fist to the offending "rate buster's" arm—ridicule, sarcasm, and other techniques. Rather than being motivated by management's incentive system, the workers seemed more concerned with being accepted by their fellow workers. The activities which determined the production of the group were not formal, but informal—devised by the employees themselves.

SOURCE: Quotes are from F. J. Roethlisberger and William J. Dickson, *Management and the Worker* (Cambridge: Harvard University Press, 1939), pp. 417–18.

In a larger sense, an organization was a group. Members of the organization, whether managers or workers, were members of the same group and, hence, shared common interests. The attainment of the common interests of the organization's members became a "collective responsibility," and as the members worked together, the group attained an *integrative unity* or "oneness."[14]

It was not the responsibility of the manager to give orders but rather to define and articulate the group's common purpose. Rather than work *for* the manager, the workers worked *with* him or her, and all alike took their orders from the *situation* they faced.[15] "Our job is not how to get people to obey orders, but how to devise methods by which we can best *discover* the order integral to a particular situation."[16] Responding to the situation were individuals who, on the basis of their knowledge and expertise and in recognition of their common interest, would control their tasks to meet the overall objective.[17]

SOLVING CONFLICT THROUGH INTEGRATION

Compromise is the accepted, the approved, way of ending controversy. Yet no one really wants to compromise, because that means a giving up of something. Is there then any other method of ending conflict? There is a way beginning now to be recognized at least, and even occasionally followed: when two desires are *integrated*, that means that a solution has been found in which both desires have found a place, that neither side has had to sacrifice anything. Let us take some very simple illustration. In the Harvard Library one day, in one of the smaller rooms, someone wanted the window open; I wanted it shut. We opened the window in the next room, where no one was sitting. This was not a compromise because there was no curtailing of desire; we both got what we really wanted. For I did not want a closed room, I simply did not want the north wind to blow directly on me; likewise the other occupant did not want that particular window open, he merely wanted more air in the room.

SOURCE: Mary Parker Follett, "Constructive Conflict," in *Dynamic Administration: The Collected Papers of Mary Parker Follett,* ed. Henry C. Metcalf and L. Urwick (New York: Harper & Row, Publishers, 1940), p. 32.

These ideas, although more theoretical than pragmatic, reflected Follett's optimistic view of individuals. In work organizations, people would demonstrate integrity and responsibility as they cooperatively sought to attain their common goals. The concepts that each individual was an integral part of the organization, that shared goals were desirable, and that each member could effectively participate in organizational decision making underlie the work of more modern writers such as Douglas McGregor, Rensis Likert, and Chris Argyris. These concepts, too, are reflected in the present field of organization development, discussed in Chapter 17.

Chester I. Barnard's Work

Perhaps no practicing executive has contributed more to the study of management than did Chester I. Barnard (1886–1961), president of New Jersey Bell Telephone Company. His book, *The Functions of the Executive*, developed his perspective on management and organization.

Barnard believed that a manager had three essential functions.[18] The first was to provide a system of organizational communication. By this, Barnard meant that the manager was responsible for defining the organization's structure; staffing it with loyal, responsible, able managers; and maintaining, informally, a general condition of compatibility among executive personnel. The second function involved recruiting and hiring personnel to staff the nonmanagerial ranks within the organization. Finally, the executive was to formulate and define the purpose and objectives of the organization.

The basic challenge the manager faced, Barnard felt, was how to induce individuals to cooperate in attaining the organization's objectives. To accomplish this, the manager must offer positive incentives to the organization's members or reduce negative burdens (such as lowering the work required).[19] If suitable incentives were unavailable, the only alternative was to change the worker's attitudes so that the available incentives would be effective.

Barnard recognized that potential incentives included the following: (1) money and material things; (2) opportunities for distinction, prestige, personal power, or attainment of a dominating position; (3) desirable working conditions; (4) satisfaction of personal ideals; (5) an attractive social situation; (6) familiar working conditions, practices, and attitudes; (7) opportunity for the feeling of participation in the course of events; and (8) the opportunity for communication, comradeship, and mutual support. Which of these to use and in what manner was the question. He emphasized that "the difficulties of securing the means of offering incentives, of avoiding conflict of incentives, and of making effective persuasive efforts, are inherently great; and . . . the determination of the precise combinations of incentives and of persuasion that will be both effective and feasible is a matter of great delicacy."[20] Management's goal

IMPORTANCE OF EFFORT

To try and fail is at least to learn; to fail to try is to suffer the inestimable loss of what might have been.

SOURCE: Chester I. Barnard, *The Functions of the Executive* (Cambridge, Mass.: Harvard University Press, 1938), p. v.

was to synthesize the organization's need for efficiency with the satisfaction of the employees' needs.

Perhaps Barnard's major contribution, however, came in his conceptualization of an organization as a *"system of consciously coordinated activities or forces of two or more persons."*[21] Within this system, composed of the coordinated efforts and activities of human beings, each part was related to every other part in a significant way. If the system had many parts, they might well be grouped into subsidiary or partial systems. The system, as a whole, differed in quantity and quality from the sum of its parts.

The organizational system itself, Barnard indicated, included more than its employees. Suppliers furnishing supplies, customers making purchases, or investors contributing capital were also included in the organizational system. In fact, an organization could not be understood without reference to those groups and individuals who, although not employees, interacted with the organization and influenced it through their behavior.

Overall, Barnard's work focused on the manager's role as a professional, moral leader who was able to elicit the cooperative efforts of individuals to enhance the effectiveness of their organization and their own well-being. He was the first management theorist to examine the organization as a system, using concepts from the field of biology. The power of the systems view was not immediately evident to other management theorists, however, and did not achieve general recognition until the 1960s, as we shall see in the following section.

CONTEMPORARY MANAGEMENT

The remainder of this book is devoted to contemporary management thought and practice. In this section we will lay a foundation for what is to follow by examining two current perspectives from which management is viewed.

Open Systems Theory

In contemporary management theory, an organization is visualized as a *system*—an entity comprised of parts or subsystems. Within this system, managers serve as the decision-making or regulating subsystem.

The Systems Concept. A *system* is a set of components that are related in the accomplishment of some purpose. Examples of systems abound. A physical organism, for instance, is composed of circulatory, muscular, skeletal, and nervous subsystems—all of which function together to sustain life. An automobile consists of pistons, spark plugs, axles, wheels, and so on, which work in unison to propel the car.

In the study of management, our principal concern is *organizational systems;* that is, systems composed of human beings, money, materials, equipment, and so on, which are related in the accomplishment of some goal or goals. Such systems differ significantly from biological or physical systems. The systems described in the paragraph above have identifiable structures, even when they are not functioning. An organizational system, however, has no structure apart from its functioning.[22] The basic structure of an organizational system is the "patterned activities" of individuals.[23] A building without people, even though it contains machinery and equipment and has a logo painted on its side, is not an organizational system any more than is a desert ghost town.

Organizational systems are essentially social systems comprised of human beings who interact with one another in patterned activities. "The cement that holds social systems together is essentially psychological rather than biological. Social systems are anchored in the attitudes, perceptions, beliefs, motivations, habits, and expectations of human beings."[24]

Elements of Organizational Systems.   Organizational systems share certain elements. These include *input, process, output,* and *feedback,* as indicated in Figure 2–5. The inputs in a manufacturing firm, for instance, consist of raw materials, technical knowledge, labor, equipment, and financing, all of which are combined under managerial direction into a process that results in a finished output or product. Consumer acceptance of the product results in a financial return (feedback) to the firm which reactivates the cycle. Low sales, on the other hand, indicate that a change in the input or process is necessary to produce a more acceptable output. Through cycles such as these, organizations maintain their existence. And many organizations outlive by decades and even centuries those human beings who founded them.

Organizational systems, then, are open to their environment. They import inputs, export outputs, and interpret the feedback they receive from the environment. What happens in the environment affects them, and as the environment changes, management must monitor the changes and adapt the organization to the new situation. For instance, as enrollments of full-time freshmen in colleges have declined, many schools have responded by offering evening classes to older, part-time students, by emphasizing continuing education, and by establishing degree programs "on-site" at major companies.

Although all organizations are open to their environment, the degree of openness varies. Some systems are designed to be relatively closed— a maximum security prison, for example—while others are deliberately quite open—a state legislature, for instance. Some managers believe that increasing the openness of their systems can be beneficial. Companies

FIGURE 2–5   Elements of an organizational system

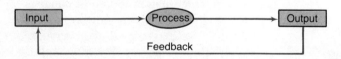

such as IBM and Sperry Corporation, for instance, have established panels of outsiders to evaluate technological trends and assess the potential of new opportunities. Such advisory boards help keep management informed of new developments in the environment and are able to advise without feeling constrained by corporate policy.[25]

FEEDBACK IGNORED

In its early days, Ford Motor Company almost went out of business because Henry Ford, Sr., refused to acknowledge that the Model T was outdated. In the 1970s, Henry Ford II made a similar mistake. During an era of increasing gasoline prices and decreasing car sizes, Ford stuck firmly by his large, fuel-inefficient cars despite warnings from his top managers. By the time the damage was evident, Ford Motor Company found itself two years behind General Motors in downsizing its cars, and two years, and eighteen months, respectively, behind Chrysler and General Motors in introducing front-wheel drive automobiles.

At the same time, Ford Motor Company found itself with an image problem that could have been reduced had it acted faster. Years after Ford became aware of its Pinto's fire-prone gasoline tank, the company was still resisting any change in its design. Although one conservative estimate indicated that the design was responsible for five hundred to nine hundred burn deaths of individuals who otherwise would not have been seriously injured, Ford refused to redesign the tank for eight years. Although Ford eventually dropped the Pinto from its line, it continues to feel the effect of its intransigence.

SOURCES: Based on "Driving to Rebuild Ford for the Future," *Business Week,* 4 August 1980, p. 70; and Elizabeth Gatewood and Archie B. Carroll, "The Anatomy of Corporate Social Response: The Rely, Firestone 500, and Pinto Cases," *Business Horizons* 24 (September/October 1981): 14–15.

Components of Organizational Systems. Organizational systems consist of a number of interrelated *subsystems*. Major subsystems of a university, for example, are the school of business, school of engineering, the athletic program, the bookstore, and so on. Corporate subsystems include the marketing division, production division, personnel department, and others. Each of these subsystems has a purpose which, if attained, aids the larger system in reaching its overall goals. Each subsystem, in attaining its purpose, must mesh its activities with the activities of the other subsystems. Within a system, there is no provision for an autonomous subsystem.

INTERRELATED SUBSYSTEMS

Chinese soldiers stationed in the Xisha Islands in the South China Sea unwittingly upset their island's natural system by their desire to eat eggs for breakfast. To satisfy their appetites, the soldiers had chickens brought in from the mainland. The chickens, however, began to wander into the bush where they were attacked by rats, some weighing over two pounds. To protect the chickens, cats were imported to kill the rats. The rats were soon gone, so the cats turned to the rare seabirds on the islands. Dogs had to be flown in to control the cats. Once the cat problem was solved, the dogs began to spend their time fighting and barking. The soldiers were still trying to remedy that problem when this report appeared in the *China Daily*.

SOURCE: Based on "Fowl Play on Isles Led to Menu Mania," *The Houston Post*, 18 April 1982.

Although we commonly equate organizational subsystems with departments or divisions, it is also possible to view subsystems in a considerably broader context, as shown in Figure 2–6. In this conceptualization, organizations are viewed as goal-directed entities consisting of people. To achieve organizational goals, people must perform tasks, using technical knowledge and equipment, and they must work together in structured relationships. However, human beings are not mere robots—they will, and indeed must, enter into social relationships, both formal (job-related) and informal (non-job-related). The task of the managerial subsystem is to coordinate all of these subsystems and plan future activities.

Management, then, constitutes the decision-making or regulating subsystem of the organizational system. Managers are thus not only parts, but they are special—planning, directing, and controlling—parts

Goal subsystem:	People with a purpose.
Technical subsystem:	People using knowledge, techniques, equipment and facilities.
Structural subsystem:	People working together on integrated activities.
Psychosocial subsystem:	People in social relationships.
Managerial subsystem:	People coordinating the other subsystems by planning and controlling the overall endeavor.

FIGURE 2–6   Major organizational subsystems
SOURCE: Adapted from Fremont E. Kast and James E. Rosenzweig, "Evolution of Organization and Management Theory," in *Contingency Views of Organization and Management*, Part 1, ed. Kast and Rosenzweig (Chicago: Science Research Associates, 1973), p. 13.

of the total organizational system. Consequently, the managerial role should be seen in its relationship to the total organization.

The thread that binds together the seemingly disparate activities of managers is revealed by this view of the managerial task. Individual managers do not work in isolation, and one function or activity is not performed without reference to another. The planning of Manager *A* must be harmonized with that of Manager *B* if organizational goals are to be achieved.

Value of the Open Systems Approach.   There are two overriding lessons for the manager contained in open systems theory. The first is that no organization exists in a vacuum. The environment constrains what the manager can do, but it also offers opportunities and potentialities. Managers must be aware of and understand environmental events and trends because the organization's well-being and even survival depend upon appropriate adaptation to change.

The second lesson of the systems approach is its stress on the interrelatedness of the parts of an organization. A manager is often tempted to see organizational problems and activities in isolation. In an extreme case, a manager may concentrate upon the efficient functioning of his or her own department and give only secondary attention to its relationships with other parts of the organization. Any neglect of important relationships results in some degree of inefficiency.

Contingency Management

Today's manager, although perhaps well-schooled in the need to monitor the environment and in understanding how different subsystems within his or her organization must mesh for overall effectiveness, also requires more specific guidance. Early managers were guided by such principles as Taylor's view that workers could be motivated primarily by economic reward and Fayol's belief that each worker should have only one boss. The behavioral sciences, too, postulated certain managerial principles. Among them, at various times, were such statements as "the most effective leaders are those who are equally interested in their subordinates' job satisfaction and in task accomplishment," and "human beings are motivated more by recognition, responsibility, and achievement than by pay, working conditions, or status."

The difficulty with these principles is simply that they are not universal; they work in some situations but not in others. The crucial point, of course, is to determine the circumstances under which certain managerial action will yield a particular set of results. The knowledge we have compiled in this area has become known as the field of *contingency management*.

To date, the development of contingency principles is still relatively limited.[26] Contingency concepts have their strongest empirical support in such areas as organization design and leadership. Other areas, such as decision making, have only recently become the focus of formal contingency-based research.

Although not yet well-developed, the contingency concept is intuitively appealing. Even Little League baseball coaches know that shouting at one player for missing a fly ball will motivate him or her to practice harder while shouting at another player for the same error will cause that individual to psychologically withdraw from the team and begin to miss practice. Not all techniques work with different individuals in the same setting, nor do all work with the same individual in different settings. Contingency management is realistic in recognizing that management is more complex than earlier theorists believed it to be.

Our Approach to Management

Elements of each of the schools of thought just reviewed influence our approach to contemporary management. For instance, Chapter 9 is devoted to the mathematical management-science approach to decision making, an outgrowth of Taylor's scientific management. Weber's ideas on organization structure will reappear in Chapter 10, and Follett's emphasis on the self-actualization of human beings will be incorporated into chapters on human resource management (Chapter 15) and organization development (Chapter 17). And, of course, contingency concepts will be discussed throughout the book where appropriate. Finally, the basic open systems approach serves as the foundation for much of our analysis. This will quickly become evident in the following chapter which examines the environment of organizations.

SUMMARY

Although the management process is as old as history itself, a systematic analysis of the field and the development of a theory of management did not begin until this century. In the early 1900s, theorists and practitioners of the *classical school* analyzed how to make organizations operate more efficiently and productively. An American manager and engineer, Frederick W. Taylor, developed the field of *scientific management,* which systematically analyzed a worker's task to discover the "one best way" to perform it. Henri Fayol, a French business executive, identified the basic *functions* performed by managers and established a set of *principles* to guide them. The question of the most efficient way to structure a large organization was addressed by Max Weber, a German sociologist, who developed the concept of *bureaucracy.*

A broader view of management, which indicated the importance and complexity of human behavior in organizations, was ushered in by the Hawthorne Studies. The emphasis on the human element in management received further impetus from the writings of Mary Parker Follett, an American political philosopher. An American business executive, Chester I. Barnard, enlarged upon these bases and developed a view of the organization as a *system,* composed of the coordinated efforts and activities of individuals.

Contemporary theorists have expanded upon this perspective to develop *open systems theory.* Organizations are viewed as systems made up of human beings, money, materials, equipment, and so on, which are related in the accomplishment of some goal or goals. Organizational systems are, of necessity, open to their environment, importing inputs, exporting outputs, and interpreting the feedback received from the environment. Within the organizational system exist a number of interrelated subsystems. Each has a purpose which, if attained, aids the larger system in reaching its overall goals. Each subsystem must mesh its activities with those of the other subsystems.

The current state of the managerial art is reflected in *contingency management.* Rather than relying on universal principles of management, this approach focuses on the situational factors that affect the managerial process. The crucial point is to determine the circumstances under which certain managerial actions will yield a particular set of results. Although not yet well developed, contingency management is realistic in recognizing the complexities of modern organizations.

DISCUSSION QUESTIONS

1. What was the major contribution of Frederick W. Taylor to management thought?

2. Henri Fayol's *general* theory of management was based on his own *specific* experience as a manager. What might an advocate of the contingency approach say about Fayol's method of theory building?

3. How did Max Weber's concept of *bureaucracy* differ from its common meaning today?

4. Explain why it can be said that the three classical theorists discussed in the chapter shared the same goal.

5. How did the conclusions of the Hawthorne Studies modify some of the assumptions held by early management theorists?

6. Explain Mary Parker Follett's view of the individual.

7. According to Chester I. Barnard, what was the basic challenge the manager faced? How was the manager to meet this challenge?

8. Explain the *open systems* concept. What are the benefits to the manager of viewing the organization in this way?

9. Identify the major *subsystems* of your college or university.

10. What is the purpose of the *managerial subsystem* in an organization?

11. The *contingency* approach to management stresses the existence of significant variables in given situations. What are some variables that might affect proper management practice?

NOTES

1. One of the best—and most readable—sources on management history is Daniel A. Wren, *The Evolution of Management Thought,* 2d ed. (New York: John Wiley & Sons, 1979).

2. This categorization is based on Fremont E. Kast and James E. Rosenzweig, *Contingency Views of Organization and Management* (Chicago: Science Research Associates, 1973), pp. 2–6.

3. Peter F. Drucker, "The Coming Rediscovery of Scientific Management," *The Conference Board Record* 13 (June 1976): 26.

4. For a collection of Taylor's writings, see Frederick Winslow Taylor, *Scientific Management* (New York: Harper & Row, Publishers, 1947).

5. For an excellent contemporary criticism of Taylor and his work, see Edwin A. Locke, "The Ideas of Frederick W. Taylor: An Evaluation," *Academy of Management Review* 7 (January 1982): 14–24.

6. Henri Fayol, *General and Industrial Management,* trans. Constance Storrs (London: Pitman Publishing, 1949).

7. Max Weber, *The Theory of Social and Economic Organization,* trans. and ed. A. M. Henderson and Talcott Parsons (New York: Oxford University Press, 1947), p. 337.

8. Ibid., pp. 337–38.

9. These assumptions are adapted from a more complete list of assumptions identified by Joseph L. Massie, "Management Theory," in *Handbook of Organizations,* ed. James G. March (Chicago: Rand McNally & Co., 1965), p. 405.

10. Descriptions of the Western Electric experiments, including both the illumination and other phases, may be found in F. J. Roethlisberger and William J. Dickson, *Management and the Worker* (Cambridge: Harvard University Press, 1946); F. J. Roethlisberger, *Management and Morale* (Cambridge: Harvard University Press, 1941), Chapter 2; and Stuart Chase, *Men at Work* (New York: Harcourt Brace Jovanovich, 1945), Chapter 2.

11. Wren, *Evolution of Management Thought,* p. 313.

12. For a representative criticism, see Alex Carey, "The Hawthorne Studies: A Radical Criticism," *American Sociological Review* 32 (June 1967): 403–16; for a response to the criticism, see Jon M. Shepard, "On Alex Carey's Radical Criticism of the Hawthorne Studies," *Academy of Management Journal* 14 (March 1971): 23–32; for a recent criticism, see Berkeley Rice, "The Hawthorne Effect: Persistence of a Flawed Theory," *Psychology Today* 16 (February 1982): 70–74.

13. Mary Parker Follett, *The New State: Group Organization the Solution of Popular Government* (London: Longmans, Green and Co., 1918), and *Creative Experience* (London: Longmans, Green and Co., 1924).

14. Mary Parker Follett, "Business as an Integrative Unity," in *Dynamic Administration: The Collected Papers of Mary Parker Follett,* ed. Henry C. Metcalf and L. Urwick (New York: Harper & Row, Publishers, 1940), pp. 71–94.

15. Mary Parker Follett, "The Giving of Orders," in *Dynamic Administration: The Collected Papers of Mary Parker Follett,* ed. Henry Metcalf and L. Urwick (New York: Harper & Row, Publishers, 1940), pp. 50–70.

16. Ibid., p. 59.

17. Wren, *Evolution of Management Thought,* p. 332.

18. Chester I. Barnard, *The Functions of the Executive* (Cambridge, Mass.: Harvard University Press, 1938), pp. 217–34.

19. Ibid., pp. 140–60.

20. Ibid., p. 158.

21. Ibid., p. 73. See pp. 65–81 for the entire discussion of the organization as a system.

22. Daniel Katz and Robert L. Kahn, *The Social Psychology of Organizations,* 2d ed. (New York: John Wiley & Sons, 1978), p. 36.

23. Ibid., p. 20.

24. Ibid., p. 37.

25. "An Advisory Council to Back up the Board," *Business Week,* 12 November 1979, p. 131.

26. Justin G. Longenecker and Charles D. Pringle, "The Illusion of Contingency Theory as a General Theory," *Academy of Management Review* 3 (July 1978): 679–83.

SUPPLEMENTARY READING

Barnard, Chester I. *The Functions of the Executive.* Cambridge, Mass.: Harvard University Press, 1938.

Chang, Y. N. "Early Chinese Management Thought." *California Management Review* 19 (Winter 1976): 71–76.

Follett, Mary Parker. *Dynamic Administration: The Collected Papers of Mary Parker Follett.* Edited by Henry C. Metcalf and L. Urwick. New York: Harper & Row, Publishers, 1940.

Fry, Louis W. "The Maligned F. W. Taylor: A Reply to His Many Critics." *Academy of Management Review* 1 (July 1976): 124–29.

Katz, Daniel, and **Kahn, Robert L.** *The Social Psychology of Organizations,* 2d ed., Chapter 2. New York: John Wiley & Sons, 1978.

Koontz, Harold. "The Management Theory Jungle Revisited." *Academy of Management Review* 5 (April 1980): 175–87.

Locke, Edwin A. "The Ideas of Frederick W. Taylor: An Evaluation." *Academy of Management Review* 7 (January 1982): 14–24.

Longenecker, Justin G. "Systems: Semantics and Significance." *Advanced Management Journal* 35 (April 1970): 63–67.

Massie, Joseph L. "Management Theory." In *Handbook of Organizations,* Chapter 9, edited by James G. March. Chicago: Rand McNally & Co., 1965.

Roethlisberger, F. J., and **Dickson, William J.** *Management and the Worker.* Cambridge, Mass.: Harvard University Press, 1939.

Ross, Joel E., and **Murdick, Robert G.** "What Are the Principles of 'Principles of Management'?" *Academy of Management Review* 2 (January 1977): 143–46.

Smith, George David, and **Steadman, Laurence E.** "Present Value of Corporate History." *Harvard Business Review* 59 (November–December 1981): 164–73.

Smith, H. R., and **Carroll, Archie B.** "Is There Anything 'New' in Management? A 'Rip Van Winkle' Perspective." *Academy of Management Review* 3 (July 1978): 670–74.

Von Bertalanffy, Ludwig. "The History and Status of General Systems Theory." *Academy of Management Journal* 15 (December 1972): 407–26.

Weber, Max. "Bureaucracy." In *From Max Weber: Essays in Sociology,* Chapter 8, translated and edited by H. H. Gerth and C. Wright Mills. New York: Oxford University Press, 1946.

_____. *The Theory of Social and Economic Organization.* Translated and edited by A. M. Henderson and Talcott Parsons. New York: Oxford University Press, 1947.

Wren, Daniel A. "Scientific Management in the U.S.S.R., with Particular Reference to the Contribution of Walter N. Polakov." *Academy of Management Review* 5 (January 1980): 1–11.

_____. *The Evolution of Management Thought.* 2d ed. New York: John Wiley & Sons, 1979.

3

MANAGEMENT
IN A CHANGING
ENVIRONMENT

This chapter will enable you to

- *Show the importance of the interface between organizations and their environments.*
- *Understand the significance of an organization's general and specific environments.*
- *Identify key features of organizational environments, such as economic, technological, social, and governmental.*
- *Recognize the nature and importance of boundary-spanning management, including the process of environmental scanning.*

Hospitals, business firms, churches, government offices, indeed all types of human organizations, are *open systems*. This means that they *interact* with their respective environments and are subject to *constraints* imposed by those environments. Many managerial practices evolve as adaptive responses to environmental changes. During the last twenty-five years, for example, managers have responded to the technological development of computers by incorporating them into managerial planning and control systems. By other actions, managers attempt to modify and control the external environment—lobbying for desired legislation, for example.

The first section of this chapter discusses the *relationship of organizations, as open systems, to their environment.* Attention then shifts to the *nature of our contemporary environment*—particularly to changes occurring in economic conditions, technology, social institutions, and government relationships.

In the final section of the chapter, we examine the *management problems and responsibilities related to the boundary area.* If organizations are to achieve success, their managers must adequately monitor and control this interface between organization and environment.

THE ORGANIZATION AND ITS ENVIRONMENT

The Environmental Interface

As explained in the preceding chapter, an open system interacts with its environment—any condition or component that is not part of the organization itself. Figure 3–1 shows some of the components of this complex environment and the varied types of interactions that are involved.

Observation of Figure 3–1 leads to the conclusion that interactions with some environmental components (customers, for instance) have more immediate significance to an organization than do interactions with others (trade associations, for example). Furthermore, a component, such as a labor union, may be extremely important to an organization that is undergoing a strike and yet largely irrelevant to another organization, such as a small, family-owned pharmacy. A number of theorists have helped us understand the differing impact of environmental components on varying organizations by distinguishing between *general* and *specific* environments.[1]

The General Environment

The general environment is comprised of components, such as the federal government, and conditions, such as inflation, which are of common concern to all organizations. These general components and conditions are potentially relevant to any organization, although most organizations are not in touch with these elements on a daily basis.[2]

Because the impact of the general environment on a particular organization may be, at first, only indirect, managers often fail to detect important changes in this environment. In the early 1970s, for example, Timex Corporation accounted for 50 percent of all watches sold in the United States. Complacent in their success, Timex's management failed

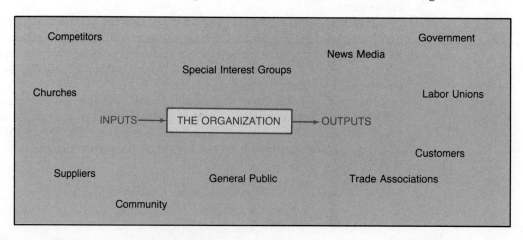

FIGURE 3–1   The organization's environment

to recognize the potential impact of developments in the semiconductor industry. Transfer of these electronic advances to the watch industry eventually occurred, permitting low-cost but highly accurate digital watches to be manufactured. Even as this effect became obvious, Timex dismissed the digital watch as a gimmick that would have no effect on their mechanical watch business. Analysts now predict that digital watches will account for almost two-thirds of all watches sold in the world by 1990. Timex, meanwhile, has seen its sales stagnate, its profits drop, and its market share erode. The corporate owners fired the chief executive officer in 1980 and set about to rejuvenate the organization's operations, making them more responsive to the environment.[3]

The Specific Environment

In contrast to the general environment, an organization's specific environment is comprised of elements that directly affect that organization's operations. Although all organizations share a common general environment, each organization has a unique specific environment (Figure 3–2).

The department store's products, prices, decor, location, and type of employees reflect various elements of the store's specific environment. Of course, certain elements of the specific environment are more important at times than are others. Construction of a discount store across the street, for instance, will require certain immediate responses from the department store's management. Managers of a store in financial difficulty will be concerned primarily about creditors and cutting costs.

Events that occur in the general environment may eventually affect one or more elements of the specific environment. Then the store itself will be affected. For instance, the generalized move of Americans to the suburbs a few decades ago ultimately translated into the migration of a specific store's actual customers and its competitors to shopping areas away from the central business district. Stores, such as Sears, Roebuck

FIGURE 3–2 Specific environment of a department store

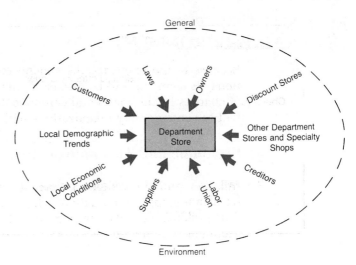

and Company, which detected and acted upon the general environmental trend in its infancy beat other stores to the competitive punch by closing their downtown locations and building new stores in suburban areas. One of these competitors was Montgomery Ward & Company, which failed to discern the trend until its customer traffic and growth began to decline precipitously.

Failure to Monitor the Environment

With the large number of elements in an organization's environment and the complex interactions among these elements, it is not surprising that managers often fail to "read" the environment correctly. Yet, there are other reasons besides complexity for management's failure to discern significant changes in the environment.

Complacency, based on past success, can lull a manager to sleep. The Great Atlantic & Pacific Tea Company, long the dominant force in the U.S. grocery business, failed to monitor the demographic and social changes that significantly altered that industry's profile. A&P's management, infamous for their smugness, eventually found themselves with too many small, uneconomical inner-city stores stocked with their own brands while consumers demanded national brands.[4]

Perhaps a more common reason for the failure to monitor environmental trends is management's preoccupation with internal operating problems. Minimizing internal frictions, achieving economy of performance, and coordinating activities of subsystems are tasks which absorb a manager's time and energy. Operational problems are constantly demanding solutions and providing pressure. It is no wonder that a manager tends to concentrate on the functioning of the system and to overlook the seriousness of boundary problems. Hence, open systems are often operated as if they were closed.

ELEMENTS OF THE
GENERAL ENVIRONMENT

Because of the relevance the general environment has for all organizations, its elements will be discussed more fully in this section. A number of changes in environmental components and conditions that are important to contemporary organizations will be noted (Figure 3–3).

Economic and Technological Factors

Inflation and Recession. In recent years, the economy has suffered from an unhappy combination of high inflation and high unemployment. This problem, described by some as "stagflation," has continued to baffle economic and political leaders.

THE COST
OF COMPLACENCY

The *New York Daily News,* which once boasted a daily circulation of 2.4 million readers, found itself in dire financial straits as it entered the 1980s. Having built its circulation by selling snappy headlines and articles to the blue-collar legions of New York City, the *News'* management continued to offer its readers the same formula decade after decade. Unfortunately, the environment changed while the *News* did not.

As the city lost population to the suburbs, management continued to market the *News* through the corner newstand even though other newspapers offered home delivery. New competition arose, such as *Newsday,* which better reflected the nation's changing social patterns. As the *News'* circulation declined, its costs increased, resulting in a profit squeeze.

Recognizing the problems too late, management in 1980 attempted to market an afternoon paper aimed at both their traditional blue-collar audience and managerial/professional readers. The mixture resulted only in blurring the paper's image, and the problems involved in printing the closing stock market prices and distributing the paper during evening rush hour were never overcome. The evening edition folded after one year, selling only 70,000 copies a day when it was removed from the stands. *The News* itself, losing money at a record pace, was put up for sale in 1982.

SOURCE: Based on "The Daily News on the Brink," *Newsweek,* 25 January 1982, pp. 85–88.

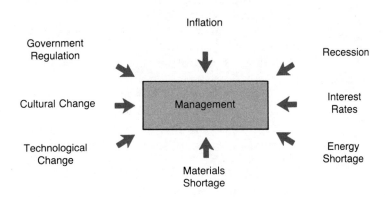

FIGURE 3–3   Environmental pressures on management

Economists have viewed stagflation the way a physicist would view an object suspended in midair in violation of the laws of gravity—as a scientific obscenity. And being unable to understand stagflation, they have, of course, encountered difficulties in trying to find ways to deal with it.[5]

Moderate inflation has been tolerated. In fact, the general consensus holds that a little inflation is necessary to avoid the pitfall of recession. Thus, federal fiscal and monetary policy tends to be at least mildly inflationary.

Recent inflation, however, has been characterized by several unusually destructive features. As noted, it has occurred simultaneously with high unemployment. The effects have been worldwide, with many countries experiencing double-digit inflation. Because of these, and perhaps other, aspects of inflation, the problem has been exceedingly difficult to diagnose and cure. Various prescriptions—for example, price control—have been advanced and tried to some extent without spectacular success. Political considerations have often limited the adoption of better remedies.

Recessions also continue to occur in spite of these inflationary forces. As the economy moved into a recession in the 1980s, some industries faced conditions similar to those of the Great Depression of the 1930s. The forest products industry, for example, experienced its worst slump in three decades with lumber and plywood orders 25 to 30 percent below normal levels. Many companies closed mills and laid off employees in unprecedented numbers. The economic and political difficulties involved in "fine tuning" the economy have obviously made avoidance of recessions impossible.

Economic Growth and Interest Rates. The more attractive scenario for the future, of course, is not recession but economic growth. Prospects for economic growth are unclear, however. Some observers feel that the world is headed for a prolonged period of economic stagnation. On the other hand, the remainder of the 1980s may see a resumption of growth and increasing productivity.

One of the major obstacles to growth in the 1980s has been high interest rates, even in the face of severe recession and unemployment. High interest rates stifle economic growth in two ways:

1. Business firms are less able to borrow money to build new plants and replace aging facilities.
2. Consumers are less likely to borrow money to finance purchases of such items as houses and automobiles.

Both conditions affect the economy in the present—through declining sales and profits and the closing of plants—and in the future—through obsolete plants and equipment that make our economy less productive and less competitive internationally.

Energy and Materials Shortages.   Throughout most of its history, the United States enjoyed an abundance of natural resources. The problem of energy shortages became abundantly clear, however, with the Arab oil embargo of 1973, the Iranian revolution of 1979, and the skyrocketing oil prices which followed.

High energy prices contribute to inflation by raising the cost of heating homes and driving automobiles and also by increasing production costs. An indirect effect also occurs because high energy prices tend to depress demand for capital goods and thereby slow the growth of productivity.

The 1970s also brought the United States face to face with a materials shortage, a shortage in metals and other basic commodities such as cotton, lumber, and plastics. Although the nation did not reach a crisis point to the same extent as experienced with energy, warnings of metals and materials shortages were abundant.

Technological Changes.   The present age is an exciting one from the standpoint of increasing scientific knowledge. Discoveries in "pure" science have extended people's knowledge of the world in which they live, and applications of this knowledge have provided the means for a more comfortable (as well as a more dangerous) life. Even within the lifetime of those living now, the airplane has been invented, nuclear energy has been discovered, and space flight has been introduced.

TECHNOLOGY'S EFFECT ON ONE INDUSTRY

Experts predict a sharp slowdown this decade in growth in the U.S. paper industry. Already technological change—in the form of copiers—has reduced demand for carbon paper and mimeograph paper. Now, other changes are evident:

1. Optical discs which can be used for storing information are beginning to replace paper stored in file cabinets.
2. Personal computers are enabling individuals to send and receive paperless messages.
3. Video systems that permit consumers to view and purchase products in their homes will reduce the need for classified ads, telephone directories, and catalogs.

SOURCE: Based on "Paper Chases the Electronic Age," *Business Week*, 5 April 1982, pp. 112–15.

The same discoveries that make it an exciting world also make it a bewildering world; scientific advances provide both threats and opportunities. Technological change contributes to and is a part of the other environmental features discussed in this chapter. Technological change makes it difficult for managers to relax and maintain the status quo. And the tempo of development is such that the organization, its methods, and its personnel may be obsolete before management appreciates the significance of the change.

Few technological developments have had a greater impact on organizational life and people in general than the computer. In less than three decades, it has revolutionized many administrative practices. Furthermore, some feel that its potential is far greater than that realized to date. The traditional approach to the solution of managerial problems relied heavily upon the judgment of the manager. However, managers often lacked professional training or time to use the scientific method. Instead, they were inclined to fall back on intuition and hunch in solving problems. Great strides now are being made in using electronic computers and related quantitative methods to increase rationality and logic in the problem-solving process.

Social Values and Governmental Relationships

Social and Cultural Change.   Our nation and world are experiencing constant change in basic institutions and values. In recent years, for example, we have observed substantial changes in life style, attitudes toward work and leisure, the role of women, organization of family life, level of public confidence in social institutions, and attitudes toward authority. All types of organizations are affected by such changes.

One area of particular concern to leaders in both the public and private sector is the changing attitudes toward social institutions—government, education, business, medicine, and others. The public has become more cynical, more insistent that its institutions should operate in the best interests of society as a whole.

As one of the major institutions of society, the modern corporation has been subjected to particular scrutiny. According to the concept of *social responsibility,* business firms are increasingly expected to promote the public welfare as well as to provide profits for shareholders. There is a growing insistence that business should provide equal employment opportunities, meaningful work for employees, support for education and the arts, solutions for urban problems, safety for consumers, and cleanliness for the environment.

Government Regulation of Business.   Although the government regulatory process has grown throughout the nation's history, the rate of growth in recent years has been striking. The costs of regulation include not only higher taxes but also higher prices to customers, which contribute to inflation, lessen our competitiveness in foreign markets, and lower dividends to stockholders. At issue, of course, is whether the costs of regulation are justified by the benefits society receives from regulation.

COSTS OF
GOVERNMENT REGULATION

A study commissioned by the Business Roundtable (an independent association of business executives who analyze specific public issues that affect the economy) and conducted by Arthur Andersen and Company investigated the impact of six federal agencies on forty-eight major firms in twenty industries in one year. The six agencies—EPA(Environmental Protection Agency), EEOC (Equal Employment Opportunity Commission), OSHA (Occupational Safety and Health Administration, DOE (Department of Energy), FTC (Federal Trade Commission), and ERISA (Employee Retirement Income Security Agency)—had the following impact in 1977:

> Direct costs imposed by these agencies that the companies would otherwise not have incurred amounted to $2.6 billion. This total was equivalent to an increase in the corporate tax rate for these firms from 48 to 55 percent. The amount equalled 16 percent of the net income of these companies, or 43 percent of their annual research and development expenditures.

The study did not calculate the costs imposed by dozens of other federal regulatory agencies, nor did it include such indirect costs of compliance as productivity losses, misallocation of resources, and added inflation.

SOURCE: Michael E. Simon, "Government Regulation: Adding Up the Cost," *Journal of Contemporary Business* 9 (2nd Quarter, 1980): 5–16.

Not only the growth, but also the pattern of regulation is changing. Until the 1960s, regulatory agencies exercised surveillance over prices and licensing in such fields as transportation, utilities, communications, and oil and gas production. The Federal Communications Commission, Civil Aeronautics Board, Interstate Commerce Commission, Federal Reserve Board, and Federal Maritime Commission are examples of such regulatory agencies.

The new wave of government regulation has featured such agencies as the Environmental Protection Agency, Consumer Product Safety Commission, and the Occupational Safety and Health Administration. Whereas the old style of regulation focused primarily on specific industries, the new regulations have cut across industry lines and focused on the quality of life, dealing with such issues as environmental protection, customer safety, and equality of employment opportunity.[6]

The newer pattern of regulation differs in its impact on business firms. Agencies such as OSHA issue voluminous rule books spelling out safety and health standards. Regulators, because of their focus, are also less directly concerned with industry problems and industry obligations for public service.

Government has become an increasingly active participant in the decision-making process of industry.

> First, government regulation is widely believed to be playing some role now in almost all major corporate decisions in this economy—particularly, a major role in hiring decisions, in the establishment of work conditions, in prices, in quantities and qualities of goods and services provided. . . . All of industry now undertakes pollution and safety-related investments, checks price increases, monitors output quality, with a federal agency in mind.[7]

BOUNDARY-SPANNING MANAGEMENT

So far in this chapter, we have examined the openness of organizational systems—that is, the way they interact with the world around them—and the changing nature of the environment. Because organizations are open and because environments change, managers must concern themselves with organizational boundaries, the interface between organizations and their environment. This section analyzes the process by which managers monitor environmental change and adapt their organizations to maintain survival and growth.

Nature of Environmental Scanning

Environmental scanning is the gathering of information about relevant parts of an organizational environment. Which aspects of an environment are most significant depend upon the type of organization. A high-technology growth company, for example, may find its greatest threats and opportunities in the area of technological change.

In a study of twelve large business corporations, Fahey and King found that these corporations were most concerned with the following environmental systems:[8]

1. Regulatory
2. Economic
3. Financial
4. Technological
5. Marketing/Industrial

Their environmental concerns were not uniform, however. Two public utilities involved in the study specified financial and capital considerations as their most significant environmental factors, followed by regulatory and energy concerns. The emphasis of utilities on capital and regulation seems entirely logical in view of their huge capital outlays and their dependence on government rate setting and environmental controls. The nature of the firm, thus, affects the focus of its environmental concerns. We should note, however, that the emphasis on environmental scanning is relatively new and that managers may not fully appreciate the relative importance of all environmental systems.

In fact, one study of eighty-six firms suggests that scanning activities too often are devoted to understanding present conditions at the expense of understanding future trends.

> Executives may ignore trends that appear to be irrelevant to their firms. There is significant danger associated with this behavior. History teaches that most new developments which threaten existing business practices and technologies do not come from traditional industries.[9]

Effectiveness and Environmental Scanning

Appropriate environmental scanning apparently contributes to organizational success. Open systems cannot function properly without regard for external conditions. Environmental scanning enables management to avoid surprise, to identify and capitalize on opportunities, and helps ensure the long-run viability of the firm.[10]

A study by three Purdue University scholars examined the corporate "turnaround" strategies of sixty-eight major corporations which had experienced four years of uninterrupted decline followed by four years of recovery.[11] The researchers found that an inadequate response to environmental change contributed to the downhill slide of the corporations involved in this study.

> The evidence suggests that it takes unfavorable changes in the environment coupled with either (1) inefficient operations under an existing corporate strategy, or (2) a strategy no longer suited to its competition, markets, or the economy, to cause a sustained decline in earnings.[12]

The researchers concluded, moreover, that decline was not inevitable even though the environment changed adversely.

> The cases examined here all suggest that the environmental changes would not have made the downturn impact they did unless management's inaction had not left the corporate body in a weakened state.[13]

Another study compared the environmental concerns expressed by managers of more successful firms in the food-processing industry with the concerns of less successful firms in the same industry.[14] Annual reports of these firms were analyzed to discover the amount of space devoted to discussion of coming changes in their environment, product/market portfolio, and "where they are going." Presumably, managers would express their orientation and environmental concerns in such projections. The study found significant differences between stated concerns of the least successful (or "fourth-quartile") firms and most successful (or "first-quartile") firms.

> While it is difficult to adequately convey the quantitative sense of this differentiating characteristic, there were virtually no real discussions of such important issues in the fourth-quartile annual reports.
>   The first-quartile companies were replete with them.[15]

According to these studies, therefore, effectiveness of corporate management is correlated with awareness of environmental issues. Successful managers, therefore, must find ways to monitor their environments and to adapt to environmental change.

Procedures for Environmental Scanning

As might be expected, environmental scanning efforts differ tremendously in nature and degree of sophistication. Every manager interacts with the external environment to some extent and thereby learns about events, relationships, and changes in that environment. Such interaction occurs informally as an incidental part of management. At the other extreme, environmental factors may be studied on a continuing basis by a specialized staff agency. Variations in environmental scanning processes, therefore, may be described as in Figure 3–4.

	Less Sophisticated Approaches	More Sophisticated Approaches
Continuity:	Spasmodic, ad hoc studies	Continuous review
Rigor:	Haphazard inquiries	Systematic, structured analyses
Scope:	Fragmented observations of specific events or issues	Comprehensive examination of broad range of factors
Posture:	Reactive response to specific problems	Proactive investigation of relevant areas

FIGURE 3–4   Environmental-scanning processes

No doubt the major scanning processes of most organizations are closely related to the organization's functional areas. Legal departments monitor changes in the legal environment, while engineering departments observe changes in technology. The various functional staffs, of course, may go beyond incidental observation to purposeful study of environmental trends.

Some organizational units have major responsibilities for environmental research. Examples of such units are the following:

1. Market research agencies
2. Public relations departments
3. Economic analysis and forecasting offices
4. Research and development organizations
5. Corporate planning offices
6. Task forces appointed to conduct broad-based studies
7. Corporate officers designated to study environmental forces impinging on the corporation

In a few cases, corporations have assigned general responsibility for environmental scanning to a corporate planning department or other control staff office. Such offices are responsible for coordinating the total corporate effort to monitor the changes and activities in the outside world.

Dynamic vs. Stable Environments

The rate of environmental change is not a constant for all organizations and industries. To illustrate, environments do not change at the same pace for computer manufacturers, city libraries, hospitals, real estate brokers, and major airlines. Some are clearly more volatile than others. Environments may be described, therefore, as ranging from relatively stable to relatively dynamic even though all are changing.

The requirement for environmental information increases as environments become more dynamic and less static.[16] As Figure 3–5 indicates, an uninformed manager may succeed in very stable situations. Two observations are important, however. First, the total environment, including the specific environment of most organizations, has been shifting in the direction of "less-stable" and "more-dynamic" and no doubt will continue to do so. Thus, the allowable margin for closed-system thinking is constantly narrowing. Second, the probability of success improves with the depth of environmental scanning. This holds true for any environment, although such information is most urgent in the highly dynamic environment.

A survey of 295 industrial corporations in the United States and Canada indicated that chief executive officers in complex, dynamic en-

VIDEO GAMES AND
BOUNDARY SPANNING

Milton Bradley Company, a successful toy and game manufacturer for over 120 years, failed to read its environment accurately in the early 1980s and is now scanning for opportunities to correct the mistake.

In the late 1970s, Milton Bradley developed a television-connected game, but failed to market it because management felt that video games were a fad. Instead, they concentrated on hand-held electronic games. The choice was a major error—video games later captured more than 25 percent of all toy/game sales while hand-held electronic games gathered dust on store shelves.

By 1982, Milton Bradley found itself scanning the environment for a niche other than console video games or game cartridges—areas that were already too competitive. Some possibilities were video game cartridges that respond to spoken words and talk to the players, education software for home video systems, or games that create sensations such as speed or vibration. In any case, Milton Bradley's scanning revealed that competitors were also attempting to develop games in those areas.

In mid-1982, Milton Bradley purchased General Consumer Electronics Corporation, a small company with a niche. It was the only company at that time to use black and white television monitors with color overlays for the screen in its video games. This made the games less expensive than those requiring color television, but the games were (theoretically at least) as attractive. To catch up with its environment, therefore, Milton Bradley was forced to purchase a company that was in tune with environmental change.

SOURCES: Based on "Milton Bradley: Playing Catch-up in the Video-game Market," *Business Week,* 24 May, 1982, pp. 110–14; and "Milton Bradley Agrees to Buy Video Game Firm," *The Dallas Morning News,* 18 July 1982.

vironments experienced the greatest difficulty in analyzing their environment, detecting trends, and deciding upon effective responses. The least difficulty was encountered by those chief executive officers who were faced with simple, stable environments.[17]

Development of a system yielding a large amount of environmental information should improve the quality of decision making and avoid some of the glaring errors of managers who confine their attention to internal operations. It should improve decisions in all types of organizations, although channels for gathering information necessarily differ.

Environmental Conditions Environmental Sensing Posture	Relatively Stable	Moderate Change and Innovation	Highly Dynamic
Internally Oriented	DANGER	EXTREME DANGER	PROBABLE FAILURE
Management Awareness of Environment		DANGER	EXTREME DANGER
Aggressive Search for Information and Continued Adaptation			DANGER

FIGURE 3–5   Environmental dangers and environmental scanning

Adaptive Management

Environmental scanning is a necessary first step, but it must be followed by appropriate decision making and action. Gathering information is not an end in itself but a means toward effective managing—responding to and/or challenging conditions in the environment. When managers observe skyrocketing fuel costs, for example, they do more than file this information. They develop energy-conservation programs.

We can see some desirable characteristics of environmentally sensitive management and organizations. Some of these features are as follows:[18]

1. Rapid reaction to external change. Trends must be detected early.
2. Prompt decision making. Because of extended deliberation, organizations sometimes become victims of "paralysis through analysis." Effective boundary management requires prompt decisions in order to keep pace with rapid external change.
3. Reversible decisions. Decisions should not be "cast in concrete." "Escape clauses" and contingency plans are desirable.
4. Flexibility in operation. Extreme complexity must be avoided in the interest of "turning on a dime."
5. Recognition of situational differences. Excessive standardization must be avoided to capitalize on individual differences and unique situations.

In addition, many large organizations are becoming increasingly proactive toward the environment. In 1970 only a few corporations had a public affairs operation; by 1980, however, over 80 percent of the respondents to a survey of *Fortune* 500 firms had established such a department.[19]

Government, too, is becoming more and more the target of business influence. Many corporations maintain a Washington presence through trade association memberships, visits to legislators, and company offices in the nation's capital, as well as financial contributions to political action committees.[20]

Having acquired some appreciation of the organization-environment interface and the need for monitoring environmental relationships, we are now ready to examine a broader segment of the environment that is becoming increasingly important to management—the international environment.

SUMMARY

Organizations are *open systems;* that is, systems which interact with their environments. The *boundary* or *interface* between organizations and their environments is an area of importance, therefore, to the process of management. To be effective, managers of organizations must recognize environmental changes, opportunities, dangers, and constraints.

All organizations share a common *general* environment comprised of components, such as government, and conditions, such as inflation. Events occurring in the general environment often affect a particular organization's *specific* environment—those elements that directly influence the organization's operations. Managers sometimes fail to monitor these environments because of environmental complexity, managerial complacency, or a preoccupation with internal operating problems.

The economic system constitutes one important element of the general environment. Managers must be concerned with inflation, recession, productivity, economic growth, interest rates, energy resources, and materials shortages. Technological change and change in social institutions and values are likewise related to the operation of contemporary organizations. Of special significance to business organizations is the new wave of government regulation featuring environmental protection, consumer safety, and other efforts to improve the quality of life.

The most effective *boundary-spanning* managers actively engage in *environmental scanning;* that is, in gathering information about conditions and changes in the environment. The process of gathering information differs in the extent to which it is formalized, systematic, and continuing. The need for environmental scanning also varies with the degree to which an environment is stable or turbulent. After gathering relevant information about the organizational environment, managers must plan, organize, and direct in terms of environmental knowledge, a process described as *adaptive management.*

DISCUSSION QUESTIONS

1. What important point does the Timex Corporation example illustrate?
2. Identify some of the important elements in your college's or university's *general* environment. Also identify some of the major elements in its *specific* environment.
3. In spite of the several examples in the chapter of firms that failed to monitor their environments, some managers persist in operating their organizations as if they were closed systems. How can this behavior be explained?
4. What are some ways in which an energy shortage affects automobile manufacturers?
5. How is the "new style" of government regulation of business different from that which existed prior to the 1960s?
6. Define *environmental scanning.*
7. Which of the environmental systems—regulatory, economic, financial, social, technological, or marketing/industrial—would be of greatest concern to a furniture manufacturer? To an electric power company?
8. Why might managers be more concerned with understanding present environmental trends than with future trends?
9. How would the environmental scanning conducted by an office of consumer affairs differ from that conducted by a corporate economist? Which is more important for a major corporation?
10. What environmental "scanning devices" might be used by a business firm to assist in developing social objectives?
11. Define *adaptive management.* Does environmental scanning result in *adaptive management?*
12. Other than public affairs departments and Washington influence, can you think of other ways in which organizations behave proactively toward the environment?

NOTES

1. See William R. Dill, "Environment as an Influence on Managerial Autonomy," *Administrative Science Quarterly* 2 (March 1958): 409–43; Robert B. Duncan, "Characteristics of Organizational Environments and Perceived Environmental Uncertainty," *Administrative Science Quarterly* 17 (September 1972): 313–27; and Richard H. Hall, *Organizations: Structure and Processes* (Englewood Cliffs, N.J.: Prentice-Hall, 1972).

2. Robert H. Miles, *Macro Organizational Behavior* (Santa Monica, Calif.: Goodyear, 1980), p. 195.

3. "Japanese Heat on the Watch Industry," *Business Week*, 5 May 1980, pp. 92–100.

4. "A&P Looks like Tengelmann's Vietnam," *Business Week*, 1 February 1982, pp. 42–44.

5. Amitai Etzioni, "Why We Chose to Have Stagflation," *Business Week*, 27 February 1978, p. 18.

6. For an extensive discussion of the new regulation, see George A. Steiner, "New Patterns in Government Regulation of Business," *MSU Business Topics* 26 (Autumn 1978): 53–61; and Robert Crandall, "Is Government Regulation Crippling Business?" *Saturday Review*, 20 January 1979, pp. 31–34.

7. Paul W. MacAvoy, "The Existing Condition of Regulation and Regulatory Reform," in Chris Argyris et al., *Regulating Business: The Search for an Optimum* (San Francisco: Institute for Contemporary Studies, 1978), p. 4.

8. Liam Fahey and William R. King, "Environmental Scanning for Corporate Planning," *Business Horizons* 20 (August 1977): 67.

9. Neil H. Snyder, "Environmental Volatility, Scanning Intensity and Organization Performance," *Journal of Contemporary Business* 10 (2nd Quarter 1981): 16.

10. Ibid., p.5.

11. Dan Schendel, G. R. Patton, and James Riggs, "Corporate Turnaround Strategies: A Study of Profit Decline and Recovery," *Journal of General Management* 3 (Spring 1976): 3–11.

12. Ibid., p. 10.

13. Ibid., p. 11.

14. Edward H. Bowman, "Strategy and the Weather," *Sloan Management Review* 17 (Winter 1976): 49–62.

15. Ibid., p. 56.

16. The following study supports this proposition: Asterios Kefelas and Peter P. Schoderbek, "Scanning the Business Environment," *Decision Sciences* 4 (January 1973): 63–74.

17. Yezdi M. Godiwalla, Wayne A. Meinhart, and William D. Warde, "Environmental Scanning—Does It Help the Chief Executive?" *Long Range Planning* 13 (October 1980): 87–99.

18. A number of these features are mentioned by Michael J. Kami in "Planning in Times of Unpredictability," *Columbia Journal of World Business* 11 (Summer 1976): 32–33.

19. Gerald D. Keim, "Foundations of a Political Strategy for Business," *California Management Review* 23 (Spring 1981): 45.

20. Robert B. Dickie, "Playing the Government Relations Game: How Companies Manage," *Journal of Contemporary Business* 10 (3rd Quarter 1981): 108–10.

SUPPLEMENTARY READING

Cooper, Arnold C., and **Schendel, Dan.** "Strategic Responses to Technological Threats." *Business Horizons* 19 (February 1976): 61–69.

Dickie, Robert B. "Playing the Government Relations Game: How Companies Manage." *Journal of Contemporary Business* 10 (3rd Quarter 1981): 105–18.

Edrich, Harold. "Keeping a Weather Eye on the Future." *Planning Review* 8 (January 1980): 11–14.

House, William C. "Environmental Analysis: Key to More Effective Dynamic Planning." *Managerial Planning* 25 (January–February 1977): 25–29.

Humphries, George E. "Technology Assessment: A New Imperative in Corporate Planning." *Planning Review* 4 (March 1976): 6–9; 16.

Keim, Gerald D. "Foundations of a Political Strategy for Business." *California Management Review* 23 (Spring 1981): 41–48.

Lovdal, Michael L.; Bauer, Raymond A.; and **Treverton, Nancy H.** "Public Responsibility Committees of the Board." *Harvard Business Review* 55 (May–June 1977): 40–64; 178–81.

Nanus, Burt. "QUEST—Quick Environmental Scanning Technique." *Long Range Planning* 15 (April 1982): 39–45.

Preble, John F. "Corporate Use of Environmental Scanning." *University of Michigan Business Review* 30 (September 1978): 12–17.

Schendel, Dan; Patton, G. R.; and **Riggs, James.** "Corporate Turnaround Strategies: A Study of Profit Decline and Recovery." *Journal of General Management* 3 (Spring 1976): 3–11.

Simon, Michael E. "Government Regulation: Adding Up the Cost." *Journal of Contemporary Business* 9 (2nd Quarter 1980): 5–16.

Steiner, George A. "New Patterns in Government Regulation of Business." *MSU Business Topics* 26 (Autumn 1978): 53–61.

Terry, P. T. "Mechanisms for Environmental Scanning." *Long Range Planning* 10 (June 1977): 2–9.

Thomas, Philip S. "Environmental Analysis for Corporate Planning." *Business Horizons* 17 (October 1974): 27–38.

_____. "Environmental Scanning—The State of the Art." *Long Range Planning* 13 (February 1980): 20–28.

Wall, Jerry L. "What the Competition is Doing: Your Need to Know." *Harvard Business Review* 52 (November–December 1974): 22–38.

Weidenbaum, Murray L. *The Future of Business Regulation: Private Action and Public Demand.* New York: AMACOM, 1979.

Wilson, Ian H. "Business Management and the Winds of Change." *Journal of Contemporary Business* 7 (Winter 1978): 45–54.

4

INTERNATIONAL MANAGEMENT AND THE GLOBAL ENVIRONMENT

This chapter will enable you to

- *Describe the growth of the international business environment.*
- *Understand the political, legal, and cultural environment of international management.*
- *Identify the distinctive features of international management.*
- *Understand the Japanese system of management and the environment in which it operates.*

Many organizations saw their general and specific environments expand during the past decade to include *international* components and conditions. Because of the increasing importance of the global environment, an entire chapter will be devoted to examining it.

GROWTH OF INTERNATIONAL BUSINESS

Expansion of International Business

As part of the rapidly expanding international environment, American corporations are increasing exports and imports, establishing foreign subsidiaries, and creating international departments. The general broadening of American business commitments is indicated by the rise in U.S. direct investment abroad as shown in Figure 4–1. U.S. corporations increased their foreign investment by over 182 percent from 1970 to 1980.

The Competitive World

American industry must compete in world markets with industrial concerns of other nations. In recent years, this worldwide competition has been growing more severe, and the relative competitive strength of the United States has declined. The energy crisis, with increased prices for imported oil, has contributed to the problem as has our lagging productivity growth rate. During the past decade, for instance, the annual increase in productivity in the United States has fallen far behind the growth rates of such countries as Japan and West Germany. As a result

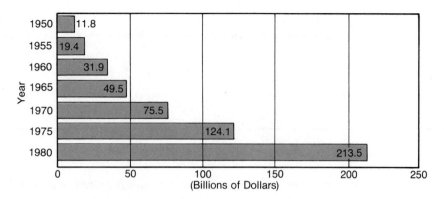

FIGURE 4–1 U.S. direct investment abroad
SOURCES: *Survey of Current Business* (February 1981): 50–51; (August 1981): 22.

of these forces, our country is no longer the one powerful nation in the international economy but is one of several powerful nations.

In spite of stiffening foreign competition, however, the United States has continued to expand its volume of international business. Continued expansion and improvement in competitive strength depend on the efficiency of American industry. Manufactured products must be priced competitively, and this type of competition demands continually rising productivity and declining unit labor costs. One specific ingredient in manufacturing productivity is automation, and many U.S. industrial managers have indicated that they will make increasing investments in automating their production processes over the next several years.

The Domestic Market

The American business firm has no monopoly on business transacted in the United States. German steel, Japanese autos, and French tires compete with American industry in its own home territory. Furthermore, foreign competition in the domestic market has expanded significantly during recent years, particularly in certain product areas. The increasing imports evident in Table 4–1 illustrate the intensifying competition some manufacturers face.

The pressure of foreign competition leads to demands for protective tariffs. Although these tariffs can provide direct protection against low-price imports, the indirect effects are often disastrous. By eliminating "undesirable" imports, we choke off the reciprocal market for other types of American exports.

A survey of six hundred executives in major U.S. corporations found that 72 percent believed that Japanese trade policies were unfair. Many thought that Japan's import policy was too restrictive and that the Japanese government was manipulating the value of the yen to lower the prices of its exports in order to increase foreign sales. Yet, in spite of the

TABLE 4–1   U.S. imports of selected commodities, 1970–1980

Commodity	1970 (Millions of Dollars)	1980 (Millions of Dollars)	Percent Increase
Automobiles and parts	5,068	24,015	374%
Motorcycles	307	1,149	274
Rubber tires and tubes	205	1,143	458
Iron and steelmill products	1,952	6,686	243
Clothing	1,269	6,427	406
Footwear	629	2,808	346
Clocks and watches	184	1,097	496

SOURCE: *Statistical Abstract of the United States,* 1981, pp. 852–53.

Japanese barriers to free trade, only 26 percent of the executives wished to see the U.S. government retaliate through regulation and control of foreign exports and imports. Because the revenue of many major U.S. companies depends partially on exports and because new U.S. tariff barriers could adversely affect trade with Europe, "U.S. executives have cast a resounding vote in favor of free trade."[1]

FREE TRADE AND JAPAN

To quell American and European fears over Japanese trade practices, the Japanese government created the Office of Trade Ombudsman in 1982. This office, with seventy-four reception areas in the United States, Canada, and Europe, was established to resolve complaints from companies having problems exporting merchandise to Japan. Reflecting the point of view of U.S. executives, the Japanese government stated in a two-page advertisement in *Business Week:* "As a nation that depends upon an open world-trading system, we believe we have an obligation to defend the principles of free trade."

SOURCE: *Business Week,* 7 June 1982, advertising insert.

Rise of the Multinational Corporation

Expansion of international business involves more than a conventional expansion of foreign trade. An important development has been the growth of *multinational corporations (MNCs)*—firms with operating components located in other countries.

The strength and vigor of multinational firms are due, in part, to their economic advantages. By operating across national boundaries, they can maximize operating efficiency in terms of the entire world. The MNC, for example, can take advantage of low labor costs in one part of the world, sell in countries of strong demand and higher costs, transfer managerial and professional skills from one country to another, and locate financial resources to minimize interest costs and taxes.

The International Business Machines Corporation is a good example of an MNC. In addition to its extensive facilities and operations in the United States, IBM operates in 124 other nations, does business in thirty languages and more than one hundred currencies, and operates twenty-three major manufacturing plants in fourteen countries. Its overseas growth rate increased from $51 million gross income in 1950 to $26.2 billion in 1980. In 1980, IBM's overseas business accounted for more than half of its gross income and net earnings.

The chairman and chief executive officer of the IBM World Trade Corporation—a part of IBM Corporation—described the interrelationships of world events and conditions within the MNC as follows:

> Despite the company's geographic dispersion, there is scarcely any event, however remote, that does not have some impact on the total company: currency devaluations and revaluations; a variety of international tensions; natural disasters such as floods and earthquakes; strikes; military coups; civil wars; and the like. In addition, a variety of business practices, customs, and national characteristics compound the complexity of our business environment. Since their beginnings, our operations abroad have been carried out by nationals in each of the countries in which we do business. In most countries, and certainly in all the larger ones, our people are local citizens, from the president down to the last clerk.[2]

American firms are not the only MNCs. During the 1970s, MNCs from other countries made dramatic gains to reduce the overall dominance of American corporations. Even though United States foreign investment has grown in absolute terms, American firms are facing increasing competitive pressure abroad, particularly from European and Japanese companies. In 1960, for example, seventeen American companies were among the world's twenty largest industrial firms. By 1980, the United States placed only twelve.[3]

Foreign corporations are also competing actively in the United States, as can be seen in Figure 4–2. Over half of the foreign direct investment in 1980 came from companies in Europe, the United Kingdom, and Canada, with the fastest growing investment rates attributed to Japan, West Germany, and France.[4] The major areas of foreign investment in the United States are in the manufacturing of chemicals, machinery, and petroleum, while trade and insurance make up the fastest growing areas.[5]

The U.S. economy is particularly attractive to foreign investors because it is politically stable and relatively homogeneous, and because

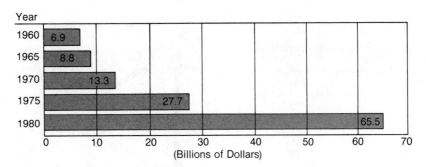

FIGURE 4–2 Foreign direct investment in the United States
SOURCE: *Statistical Abstract of the United States*, 1981, p. 834.

U.S. law treats foreign and domestic investors equally.[6] Some companies build plants in the United States (Volvo's auto assembly plant in Virginia, for example), while others enter the market by buying ownership in U.S. firms (Renault's investment in American Motors, for instance). Even the Soviet Union operates ten companies inside the United States.[7]

THE ENVIRONMENT OF THE MULTINATIONAL CORPORATION

Political and Legal Elements

As an organization's environment expands from domestic to international, management faces not only a larger number of environmental elements, but far greater environmental complexity. Rather than dealing with one legal system, management may find itself operating under dozens of sets of laws. Conflict among these diverse regulations is inevitable, and since each government controls only a portion of the MNC, the potential for conflict between the company and each nation also increases.

Each country, of course, has different regulations regarding requirements for local participation in ownership, labor unions, and distribution of products. This complexity is illustrated in Figure 4–3. The arrows in the figure indicate that the MNC's operations are constrained by both home and host governments. At the same time, however, the MNC may attempt to have various laws modified in its favor through lobbying and other acts of influence. In some cases, the U.S. government, through negotiations, may attempt to persuade the host country to modify certain restrictions, and vice versa. Meanwhile, various constituencies of the corporation in each country may attempt to influence its operations as the MNC, in turn, affects them. Constituencies unhappy with the

FIGURE 4–3   Legal and political
environment of the MNC

SOURCE: Adapted from Anant R. Negandhi, "Multinational Corporations
and Host Governments' Relationships:
Comparative Study of Conflict and
Conflicting Issues," *Human Relations*
33 (August 1980): 518.

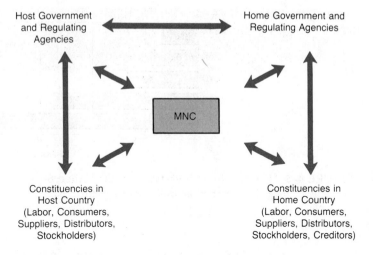

lack of responsiveness of the MNC to their concerns may turn to their
government for redress. Obviously, the MNC operates in a complex setting!

Host Country Relationships with Local Subsidiaries

As Figure 4–3 makes clear, the quality of the relationship between the
host country and the MNC is crucial. On the surface, it appears that both
parties in this relationship share mutual interests. If the MNC's local
subsidiary is able to operate profitably, the host country's economy will
be strengthened, employment will increase, the standard of living will
rise, and so on. In reality, however, this view is often not shared.

In a study of 124 subsidiaries of MNCs operating in six developing
countries, Negandhi found that host governments and MNCs "had, at
best, a most diffuse understanding of what they were expecting of each
other."[8] The MNC's decision to operate in a host country was based on
economic considerations; that is, optimizing the operations of the total
organizational system. The host country expected, on the other hand,
specific economic and social help from the MNC in the form of assistance to local entrepreneurs, the establishment of research and development facilities, and the introduction of products relevant to the local
economy. These desires were only noted by the MNC after the host
government had passed regulations to insure that the expectations
were met.[9]

Because the sales volume of some corporations exceeds the gross
national product of many host countries, local governments are highly
sensitive to displays of corporate power. Besides the obvious economic
effects of the MNC's operations, other social changes occur—migration
to urban areas, breakup of kinship and family, and change in social and
occupational status, for instance.

INTERNATIONAL COMPETITION AND ETHICS

As an example of the legal difficulties in international trade, consider the controversial U.S. Foreign Corrupt Practices Act of 1977. In an attempt to make the foreign practices of U.S. corporations more ethical, Congress made it a criminal offense for any U.S. business to offer a bribe to a foreign official, political party, or candidate for political office for the purpose of obtaining, retaining, or directing business to any person. This act made the United States unique on the international trade scene—it became the only country in the world to prohibit its own companies from bribing foreign officials.

Given the competitiveness of international trade, many U.S. managers felt that they were operating at a disadvantage. For example, prior to 1977, the United States was first in the world in the highly competitive construction industry but, by 1978, had fallen to fifth place. The government of Zaire informed the United States in 1979 that it would lose markets in that country if it persisted in diligently enforcing the new U.S. policies. The Joy Manufacturing Company of Pittsburgh lost a contract to build the pollution control equipment for the government-owned power company in Mexico after a Swedish firm made a payoff to Mexican officials.

SOURCE: Based on Sandra L. Caron, "Politics and International Business: The Impact of the Foreign Corrupt Practices Act," *Journal of Contemporary Business* 10 (3rd Quarter 1981): 17–28. For more discussion on this issue, see Suk H. Kim, "On Repealing the Foreign Corrupt Practices Act: Survey and Assessment," *Columbia Journal of World Business* 16 (Fall 1981): 16–21; and Jack Kaikati and Wayne A. Label, "The Foreign Antibribery Law: Friend or Foe?" *Columbia Journal of World Business* 15 (Spring 1980): 46–51.

In an attempt to maintain control over their own national economies, many host governments restrict the strategic freedom of local subsidiaries. For example, before allowing Ford Motor Company to establish production facilities in Spain, the Spanish government set certain conditions: Ford's sales volume was limited to 10 percent of the prior year's total auto market and its export volume had to equal at least two-thirds of its Spanish production. Additionally, Ford could not broaden its model line without government approval. Developing countries in South America, West Africa, and the Far East often require some local ownership of MNC subsidiaries in order to control their operations.[10]

The key to peaceful coexistence with the host government has perhaps best been expressed by Reginald H. Jones when he was chairman and chief executive officer of General Electric Company. Jones indicated that the relationship between an MNC and a host country develops over a period of years and is based on an understanding of the wants and needs of the host government. It is the responsibility of the corporation

---

A DIFFERENCE IN PERSPECTIVE

What is good for the host country may not necessarily be efficient for the MNC. Take the following example:

> In the fall of 1979, the Nigerian government notified French automobile manufacturer Peugeot that its recently expanded $100 million assembly plant would have to import all needed components and supplies through the underutilized port facilities in Lagos. Under this shipping plan, the parts and components had to be trucked across five hundred miles of bad road to the plant. Not only was such an operation more time-consuming and less reliable, it was more expensive than the previously employed daily cargo flights from France direct to the plant.

SOURCE: Yves L. Doz, Christopher A. Bartlett, and C. K. Prahalad, "Global Competitive Pressures and Host Country Demands: Managing Tensions in MNCs," *California Management Review* 23 (Spring 1981): 63.

---

to make its operations and products fit local needs and regulations. If this view predominates, then the probability of success increases because both parties want the venture to succeed.[11]

Social and Cultural Elements

When an organization operates outside its domestic boundaries, not only are legal and political problems compounded, but social and cultural differences also increase the complexity of managing. Each country has its distinctive culture—that is, its generally accepted values and patterns of behavior. These cultural differences interfere with the efforts of multinational managers to understand and communicate with those in other cultures. So that we can appreciate better the nature of cultural differences, we note some features of other cultures and the ways they differ from our own.

One important feature that varies from country to country is the prevailing attitude toward time. In the United States, for example, we are particularly time conscious, having long experience in using clocks and meeting deadlines. Close adherence to schedules is assumed, and promptness is expected in meeting appointments.

Managers in the Middle East, on the other hand, have only a vague concept of time. Before transacting business, they prefer to form a personal relationship with the other party by sitting down, having coffee, talking, and beginning to fashion a relationship based on trust.[12] Elsewhere, one of the major problems U.S. firms have in Latin America is persuading business customers to pay on time in a "mañana environment." Many U.S. companies have had to penalize heavily tardy payers, hire collections messengers, and build the cost of anticipated payment delays into the prices they charge.[13]

Successful operation abroad demands effective cultural adaptation of products, business practices, institutional arrangements, employment policies, and personal attitudes. Many U.S. firms which operate profitably in this country encounter frustration as they try to adapt their operations to other markets. Tandy Corporation, for example, built the highly successful chain of Radio Shack stores in this country but "stubbed its toe" in the European market.

> Tandy's disregard of host-country laws and customs has plagued its operations since it opened its first European store in 1973 at Aartselaar, Belgium. There, Tandy overlooked a law requiring a government tax stamp on window signs. In Germany, where Radio Shack has suffered some of its biggest losses, the company promoted its stores with giveaway flashlights. It was promptly hit with injunctions for violating German sales laws. Such freebies are one of Tandy's biggest come-ons in the U.S. In Holland, the company geared its first Christmas promotion to December 25, unaware that the Dutch exchange holiday gifts on St. Nicholas Day, usually celebrated on December 6.[14]

U.S. firms have been slow to introduce major changes in products or to create new products to meet unique foreign demands. Indeed, American business managers experience practical difficulty in thinking seriously of such products. Familiarity with the American culture apparently inhibits a manager's understanding of a radically different culture. For example, American manufacturers for many years did not produce small, low-priced, durable cars for non-Western cultures. The unconscious reference to one's own cultural values—the *self-reference criterion*—has been suggested as the cause of most international business problems overseas.[15]

One study in fact indicates that an important reason for our enormous trade deficit with Japan is not only tariffs and quotas, but our lack of understanding of how Japanese managers negotiate. Japanese sellers adjust their techniques to the culture in which they are selling while Americans make fewer adjustments. Since the Japanese believe that the seller is of lower status than the buyer—and should act with great respect for the buyer—they have been successful selling to Americans. But American sellers—expecting to be treated as equals by Japanese buyers—run into difficulty. The Japanese buyers find "this rather brash be-

INTERNATIONAL BLUNDERS

American refrigerator manufacturers entered the Japanese market without doing their homework and found that their products did not sell well. Japanese consumers live in small apartments and shop for groceries frequently. Hence, they do not need large, American-sized, refrigerators. Also, the Japanese are sensitive to electric costs and believe that American refrigerators consume too much electricity. Finally, since many Japanese sleep in a room separated from the kitchen by a mere paper screen, they dislike the noise made by U.S. refrigerators.

After a three-year, $2 million advertising campaign in Brazil, Campbell Soup Company lost $1.2 million in fiscal 1980 and began to curtail its operations there. Brazilian housewives preferred dehydrated soups over Campbell's vegetable and beef combinations. The dehydrated product allowed them to add their own ingredients. The homemakers felt that they were not fulfilling their role unless they could serve a soup that they could call their own.

A Betty Crocker cake mix designed by General Mills to be prepared in electric rice cookers flopped in Japan. The Japanese, who take pride in the purity of their rice, felt that it would be contaminated by the residue of cake flavor.

A baby food company which tried to sell its product with a baby on the label in a mostly illiterate African nation met with unexpected resistance. The prospective consumers believed the jars contained ground-up babies.

SOURCES: Based on Mike Sheridan, "Before Entering Japan Market, Know the Ropes, Execs Stress," *Houston Chronicle*, 10 June 1982; "Campbell Soup Fails to Make It to the Table," *Business Week*, 12 October 1981, p. 66; "Learning How to Please the Baffling Japanese," *Fortune*, 5 October 1981, p. 122; and "OSU Professor Knows How Not to Sell Baby Food," *Houston Post*, 2 November 1980.

havior in a lower status seller as inappropriate and lacking in respect. The Japanese buyer is made to feel uncomfortable, and he politely shuts the door to trade, without explanation."[16]

THE PROCESS OF INTERNATIONAL MANAGEMENT

Most business firms are affected by the trend toward operation on an international basis. Purely domestic concerns, for example, face competition from imports. For MNCs, however, the problems and challenges for management are numerous.

High Risk in International Business

A high degree of risk is involved in many ventures of the MNC. This risk is particularly true for firms in countries having an unstable political system, although problems of controls and taxation occur even in developed countries. In some countries, multinational firms face a danger of expropriation. Or the terms of the concession—for example, the price of oil—may suddenly change. The company may also be pressured to share ownership locally or be restricted in its freedom to transfer funds.

Assessment of political risks is extremely difficult, yet, of necessity, is rapidly becoming a part of multinational management. A survey of 193 U.S. firms with sales of at least $100 million in two or more countries indicated that over half had a formal group at corporate headquarters that reviewed overseas political and social factors when new investments were proposed. About the same number reported a group that monitored existing overseas operations. The most important aspects of the environment being assessed were political stability, foreign investment climate, profit remittances, exchange controls, and taxation. Most of the sources of information, however, were managers within the corporation and bankers. Hence, the analyses may suffer from a lack of objectivity.[17]

The U.S. government provides insurance for corporate assets through the Overseas Private Investment Corporation, established to encourage investment in less developed countries. This insurance covers loss of the firm's assets—not business losses from operations—due to expropriation, currency inconvertibility, war, revolution, or insurrection. To cover other losses, many corporations take out political risk insurance from private insurers. One estimate of the nation's five hundred largest MNCs suggests that over half have kidnap and terrorism insurance.[18] Additionally, managers can use such strategies as concentrating research and development facilities in the United States or selling a significant proportion of the overseas subsidiary's output to the parent corporation to stave off expropriation.[19]

Attitudes of Multinational Corporate Managers

Thinking and acting in a truly multinational fashion should eliminate bias in favor of particular countries, particularly the home country. Time and experience are required to develop a pattern of management thought that is conceptually "pure" in this way.

Three states of mind or attitudes of multinational managers have been identified:

1. *Ethnocentric (home-country oriented)*

   This attitude assumes a superiority of home country nationals over foreigners in headquarters or subsidiaries. Messages of instruction and advice go from headquarters to subsidiaries, and home standards are applied in judging performance.

2. *Polycentric (host-country oriented)*

This attitude recognizes variations in cultures and holds that local people understand local situations better than do foreigners. Foreign segments of the firm are given considerable latitude, and the corporation is held together by financial controls.

3. *Geocentric (world oriented)*

A world view is taken in deciding questions about raising money, building plants, conducting research, and so on. Foreign subsidiaries are parts of a whole whose focus is on worldwide objectives. A collaborative relationship exists between subsidiaries and headquarters.

The *geocentric* set of attitudes applies naturally to multinational firms. In practice, however, such attitudes are developed over time, and various obstacles interfere with their adoption. Until they accept such viewpoints, multinational managers may be more provincial than multinational. Patterns of thinking limit the development of international management skills.

A key dilemma faced by managers of MNCs is how much autonomy should be given to each foreign subsidiary. Some organizations let each subsidiary adjust to the demands of their host government, while others follow a worldwide business strategy with all foreign activities integrated and centrally managed. Since each strategy involves some important tradeoffs, a compromise between the two may be appropriate.[20]

For instance, a survey of management experts in thirty-nine countries strongly endorsed the concept of local autonomy—that is, expanding decision-making power in the host country subsidiary. According to these observers, conflicts are more likely to be resolved amicably by managers who are situated in host countries—managers possessing authority to deal with the issues in question.

To allow such local autonomy while still maintaining the advantages of centralized direction, the MNC must refine its planning process. Central headquarters must retain only those elements of planning that provide synergistic benefits.[21] In other words, the situation calls for sophisticated planning that creates just the right balance of power between central and host country management.

Management Development and Progression

The development and promotion of managers in MNCs are complicated by differences in national cultures. Unless managers are broadly experienced in various cultural settings, they tend to be ethnocentric in viewpoint and find it difficult, if not impossible, to appreciate the differing values of others. In addition to the necessary professional and technical qualifications, the ideal multinational manager should possess cultural empathy and adaptability.[22] Possession of these qualities is facilitated through knowledge of the culture and language of the host country, and an open attitude characterized by a willingness to listen to new ideas.

Although multinational firms regard themselves as multinational in management staffing, this is more fiction than fact at top executive levels. The headquarters of U.S.-based multinational corporations are staffed primarily with American managers. In offices located abroad, there is a mixture of American and other managers, but American managers still tend to hold the most influential positions. Exceptions exist, of course, and many executives recognize the desirability of developing a world-centered management team.[23]

Slowness in advancing foreign managers to corporate headquarters in the United States is not caused entirely by the restricted viewpoint of American executives. Some national managers prefer to stay in key management positions of subsidiaries rather than enter a foreign culture.

Use of foreign managers in overseas operations has proceeded much more rapidly. This practice is understandable in view of the national's background and ability to work in the local culture. American managers in overseas branches frequently encounter communications problems because they cannot speak a foreign language. In Japan, some firms—including International Business Machines Corporation, Fuji Xerox Company, Kellogg Company, and First National Bank of Chicago—have turned over top management positions to the Japanese.[24] These appointments have not only facilitated internal communications, but also have helped to "open doors a foreigner just can't enter."

Even in offices abroad, there are arguments for combining home country and foreign personnel in key management positions.[25] Company objectives must be understood overseas as well as at headquarters. Using some combination of nationalities, therefore, is one way to maintain cohesion as a business institution and, at the same time, use the knowledge of local needs and culture.

COMPARATIVE MANAGEMENT: JAPANESE PRACTICES

The study of comparative management seeks to identify and understand differences and similarities in managerial practices across cultures. If we can understand why some techniques are successful in certain cultural and political settings and others are not, then we have the means to improve the quality of management worldwide. This section focuses on the techniques of Japanese managers. This particular group was chosen because of the success of the Japanese in international business and because the American public and most of the world have recently become intrigued with Japanese managerial practices.[26]

In only thirty-five years, the Japanese have built the second largest economy in the free world. In the past two decades alone, Japan's growth in manufacturing productivity has been almost three times that of the United States. The following sections explore some of the reasons for this phenomenal success.

Japanese Management of Human Resources

Japanese management places heavy emphasis on the development and maintenance of its human resources.[27] Many large Japanese organizations prefer to hire individuals as they graduate from school.* These new workers are expected to accept the organization's goals and values, and they are constantly reinforced for doing so. Promotion is from within the organization with few—if any—individuals being hired from other companies. Employees are given extensive training and those who prove to be poor performers are retrained or transferred to areas more appropriate to their abilities. The chairman of Sony Corporation, for instance, indicates that one reason for his firm's diversification into such areas as spaghetti shops and cosmetics is to provide the widest possible latitude for the career paths of its young managers.[28]

Disruptive internal competition is discouraged by managerial emphasis on group—rather than individual—performance and by promotion based primarily on seniority. Personal relationships between superiors and subordinates are encouraged through numerous cultural and recreational activities in which the employees' spouses and children also participate. Even the introduction of new technology is not feared by workers who know that they enjoy employment security. If their jobs

A SENSE OF DUTY

Americans sometimes have difficulty understanding the Japanese worker's sense of duty. While the financial compensation of some U.S. chief executive officers increases as corporate profits decrease, Japanese executives routinely share pay cuts with their employees during business slumps. But the following, admittedly extreme, example clearly illustrates the differences between the two cultures:

> In September 1980, the captain of a Japanese ship carrying Subaru automobiles discovered upon docking in Los Angeles that two hundred of the cars had been damaged by water leaks. Considering himself responsible for the leaks, the captain killed himself.

SOURCE: Incident based on "An Industrial Nirvana," *Time*, 8 September 1980, p. 53.

---

*The organizations described in this section employ about 35 percent of the Japanese work force and comprise the sample which is most often publicized in the United States as representing "Japanese management."

are displaced by automation, they will simply be transferred to another area within the organization.[29]

Overall, Japanese employees perceive that their organization is committed to them and expects, in turn, loyalty from them. As a result, Japanese workers identify first with their employing organization and only secondly with their specific occupations. Their employment security encourages them to think of the success of their own careers and the success of their company as virtually synonymous. Hence, they are encouraged to take a long-range viewpoint and play an active role in participating in improving their firm's products and production process.

The most highly publicized report of Japanese managerial practices is contained in William G. Ouchi's best-selling book, *Theory Z: How American Business Can Meet the Japanese Challenge.*[30] A theory in only a loosely defined sense, "Z" refers to the style of management characteristic of large Japanese firms and exhibited by a few U.S. corporations such as Hewlett-Packard, IBM, Eastman Kodak, and Procter & Gamble. The characteristics of a Type Z organization are shown in Figure 4–4.

According to Ouchi, each Type Z organization has its own distinctiveness, yet all display features of Japanese firms. Although the total Japanese system of management (called Type J) cannot be wholly adapted to an American setting due to cultural differences, the Type Z characteristics are supposed to be compatible with an American setting.* The overall result is intended to be an organization which is a fully integrated system, having a clear philosophy and a common organizational culture shared by all employees.

Much of the evidence presented for the success of Theory Z is anecdotal in nature and lacks scientific, methodological rigor. Without such rigor, it is difficult to demonstrate that Type Z management is responsible for an organization's success. Despite its shortcomings, Theory Z has been well received by many U.S. managers who are eager to learn about Japanese management practices.[31]

The Environment of Japanese Management

Japanese success was not accomplished through managerial practices alone. The rebuilding of Japan after World War II was aided by a high degree of cooperation among government, labor, business, and financial interests.[32] Although conflict among these groups has appeared in recent years, the government continues to play a strong role in guiding the economy. The view is that what is good for Japan is good for business and labor alike.[33]

Since Japan spends only 1 percent of its gross national product on defense (the United States spends over 5 percent) and since one-third of total government spending is financed through borrowing (10 percent in

---

*Type J refers to the Japanese style of management practiced by Japanese firms as a whole. Type Z includes only Japanese firms that have the characteristics listed in Figure 4–4.

Type Z

1. *Long-term employment.* Individuals are employed effectively, although not officially, for their lifetime. Hence, turnover is low, individuals become very familiar with their organization and co-workers, employees are encouraged to develop a long-range viewpoint, and they understand that their own success and the success of their organization are intertwined.
2. *Consensual decision making.* No decision is made until all employees who will be affected by the decision have been able to offer their views. Although decisions are made slowly, they are likely to be understood and supported even though all employees may not feel the decision is best.
3. *Individual responsibility.* Although decision making is consensual, the individual manager is held responsible for the final decision. Holding the group responsible, as is done in Japan, cannot work in the United States because individual responsibility is such a central part of the national culture.
4. *Slow evaluation and promotion.* Slow promotion allows managers to become acquainted with the people and customs surrounding their jobs and permits better assimilation into the corporate culture. Performance evaluations are conducted infrequently and result from a process of agreement among all of the superiors who know the subordinate. The immediate supervisor, is freed from the need to be "objective" and can take a personal interest in the subordinate.
5. *Implicit, informal control with explicit, formalized measures.* Expectations of output and behavior—rather than being explicitly stated—are deduced from an understanding of the company's philosophy. There are formal accounting measures of performance, yet they do not dominate in major decisions.
6. *Moderately specialized career paths.* Individuals do not specialize in one functional area such as accounting or sales, but become familiar with several departments and functions within the firm. This process increases loyalty to the organization and impedes movement of individuals from one firm to another based on specialized expertise. Additionally, if all managers are familiar with large segments of the organization, coordination is smoother.
7. *Holistic concern, including family.* Work is considered an integral part of the employee's life. The relationship between the superior and subordinate is not confined only to work-related areas but includes all aspects of life. Family members interact frequently with other organization members and their families, and all feel an identification with the organization.

FIGURE 4–4   Characteristics of the Type Z organization
SOURCES: Adapted from William G. Ouchi, *Theory Z: How American Business Can Meet the Japanese Challenge* (Reading, Mass.: Addison-Wesley, 1981); and William G. Ouchi and Alfred M. Jaeger, "Type Z Organization: Stability in the Midst of Mobility," *Academy of Management Review* 3 (April 1978): 305–14.

the United States), taxes are relatively low. The resulting higher disposable income and numerous government tax incentives encourage a high savings rate among the Japanese. This savings base enables firms to borrow money to make large investments in developing new technology and products. Rather than having to show a quick return on their investments, Japanese managers are encouraged by their company's creditors to invest for long-range returns.[34]

Because of its small geographic size and its dependence on imported raw materials (particularly oil), the Japanese have long recognized the importance of world trade to their economy. Economies of scale have come from producing not only for Japanese consumers but the entire world. Numerous quotas and regulations protect their home market, while Japanese managers concentrate on their worldwide marketing and production effort and continue to lower costs and develop new technologies.[35] Additionally, the Japanese have become one of the most energy-efficient people in the world, able to produce one unit of gross national product at one-third of the energy cost needed in the United States.[36]

These and many other environmental elements have influenced Japanese managerial practices and labor's response to them. Because the cultural, governmental, and economic environment of Japan differs so greatly from that of the United States, American organizations cannot adopt in wholesale fashion Japanese management techniques. But careful study of what practices contribute to Japanese success and why these practices work can yield considerable benefits to American management.

SUMMARY

During the past decade, U.S. managers saw the general and specific environments of their organizations expand to include *international* elements. Foreign competitors became important overseas and at home. As part of this development, *multinational corporations* (MNCs) became the dominant business institution in world markets.

The MNC operates in a highly complex environment, conducting business across many conflicting *legal* and *political* systems. Because its operations are no longer coexistent with the jurisdiction of a single government, tensions often exist between the firm and its various *host governments*. The MNC's operations have both positive and negative consequences for its host countries; hence, those governments often place restrictions on the firm's freedom to operate. *Social* and *cultural* differences also compound the difficulty of doing business overseas. Knowledge of and adaptation to the various cultures is essential for effective performance.

Management of the multinational firm possesses certain distinctive features. The *political risk* in international business must be assessed and insured against. *Global strategy* must be formulated, and management should take a *geocentric* view of the corporation as a whole. *Management development and progression* involve special challenges, particularly in the promotion of nationals into key management positions in both the host countries and the headquarters' country.

Because the Japanese have enjoyed such phenomenal economic success since World War II, many U.S. managers have recently become interested in *Japanese management practices*. Japanese managers place heavy emphasis on the development of their human resources. In turn, they expect loyalty and dedication from their employees. Specific managerial techniques have been widely publicized as *Theory Z* management. But Japanese economic success depends on more than managerial techniques. Through close government-business cooperation and constant technological innovation, the Japanese have been able to expand their international markets while protecting their home front. Due to distinct cultural and political differences, American managers cannot adopt Japanese techniques in a wholesale fashion; however, they can learn by studying Japanese management practices.

DISCUSSION QUESTIONS

1. What has been the trend in U.S. direct investment abroad during recent years? What has been the trend in foreign investment in the United States?
2. What is the key to success for firms competing in international trade?
3. How does a multinational firm differ from an exporter? What are the customary distinguishing features of the multinational firm?
4. What unique problems of government regulation are presented by the multinational firm?
5. Why do the objectives of the host country and those of the MNC often differ? What problems do these differences create for management of the MNC?
6. In what ways do the background cultures of other countries appear to differ from U.S. culture? If you have traveled or lived abroad, give an example from your own experience.
7. What is the *self-reference criterion* and how can it lead to business problems for U.S. managers?
8. What are some of the *political risks* involved in operating overseas and how might they be protected against?
9. Explain the difference between an *ethnocentric* attitude and a *geocentric* attitude. How are they related to the multinational corporation?
10. How do you think the *Japanese management* emphasis on human resources has been instrumental in Japan's economic success?
11. What are some barriers to the wholesale adoption by U.S. managers of Japanese management techniques?

NOTES

1. "Still for Free Trade—But with Pressure on Japan," *Business Week*, 3 May 1982, p. 13.
2. Jacques G. Maisonrouge, "How a Multinational Corporation Appears to Its Managers," edited for The American Assembly by George W. Ball, *Global Companies: The Political Economy of World Business* (Englewood Cliffs, N.J.: Prentice-Hall, 1975), pp. 15–16.

3. *Fortune,* July 1961, p. 168; August 1961, p. 130; and 10 August 1981, p. 205.

4. *Survey of Current Business* (August 1981): 41.

5. A. D. Cao, "Foreign Acquisition in the U.S.: A Neomercantilist Challenge," *California Management Review* 22 (Summer 1980): 47–55.

6. Ibid.

7. David A. Heenan, "Moscow Goes Multinational," *Harvard Business Review* 59 (May–June 1981): 48.

8. Anant R. Negandhi, "Multinational Corporations and Host Governments' Relationships: Comparative Study of Conflict and Conflicting Issues," *Human Relations* 33 (August 1980): 534.

9. Ibid., pp. 534–35.

10. Yves L. Doz and C. K. Prahalad, "How MNCs Cope with Host Government Intervention," *Harvard Business Review* 58 (March–April 1980): 149–57.

11. "The Basic Formula for Business Success," *Harvard Business Review* 58 (November–December 1980): 155, as reprinted from Reginald H. Jones, "The Transnational Enterprise and World Economic Development," a speech delivered at Airlie, Va., July 10, 1980.

12. M. K. Badawy, "Styles of Mideastern Managers," *California Management Review* 22 (Spring 1980): 51–58.

13. "The Cost of Getting Paid Mañana," *Business Week*, 15 March 1982, p. 148.

14. "Radio Shack's Rough Trip," *Business Week*, 30 May 1977, p. 55.

15. For example, in 1978 over 40,000 Japanese visited the United States to study and acquire American technology. Only 5,000 Americans made such visits to Japan. Robert Ronstadt and Robert J. Kramer, "Getting the Most Out of Innovation Abroad," *Harvard Business Review* 60 (March–April 1982): 98.

16. John L. Graham, "A Hidden Cause of America's Trade Deficit with Japan," *Columbia Journal of World Business* 16 (Fall 1981): 9.

17. Stephen J. Kobrin, John Basek, Stephen Blank, and Joseph La Palombara, "The Assessment and Evaluation of Noneconomic Environments by American Firms: A Preliminary Report," *Journal of International Business Studies* 11 (Spring/Summer 1980): 32–47.

18. "Insuring Against Risk Abroad," *Business Week*, 14 September 1981, p. 62.

19. See the following for a discussion of these and other strategies: Alan C. Shapiro, "Managing Political Risk: A Policy Approach," *Columbia Journal of World Business* 16 (Fall 1981): 63–70; and Thomas A. Poynter, "Government Intervention in Less Developed Countries: The Experience of Multinational Companies," *Journal of International Business Studies* 13 (Spring/Summer 1982): 9–25.

20. Yves L. Doz, "Strategic Management in Multinational Companies," *Sloan Management Review* 21 (Winter 1980): 27–46.

21. William H. Newman, "Adapting Transnational Corporate Management to National Interests," *Columbia Journal of World Business* 14 (Summer 1979): 82–88.

22. Increasingly, U.S. firms are assigning women managers to overseas posts. See "A Rush of Recruits for Overseas Duty," *Business Week*, 20 April 1981, pp. 120–27.

23. For a discussion of this issue, see Howard V. Perlmutter and David A. Heenan, "How Multinational Should Your Top Managers Be?" *Harvard Business Review* 52 (November–December 1974): 121–32.

24. "A U.S. Turn to Native Talent in Japan," *Business Week*, 8 December 1980, pp. 56–58.

25. For one discussion of this topic, see Peter Kuin, "The Magic of Multinational Management," *Harvard Business Review* 50 (November–December 1972): 89–97.

26. An interesting discussion of the transference of U.S. managerial techniques to European managers can be found in "Europe's New Managers: Going Global with a U.S. Style," *Business Week*, 24 May 1982, pp. 116–22.

27. See Nina Hatvany and Vladimir Pucik, "Japanese Management Practices and Productivity," *Organizational Dynamics* 9 (Spring 1981): 5–21.

28. "Sony: A Diversification Plan Tuned to the People Factor," *Business Week*, 9 February 1981, pp. 88–89.

29. The massive introduction of robots is beginning to create a problem in this regard. See "The Robot Invasion Begins to Worry Labor," *Business Week*, 29 March 1982, pp. 46–47.

30. William G. Ouchi, *Theory Z: How American Business Can Meet the Japanese Challenge* (Reading, Mass.: Addison-Wesley, 1981).

31. For a highly critical view of Theory Z, see B. Bruce-Briggs, "The Dangerous Folly Called Theory Z," *Fortune*, 17 May 1982, pp. 41–53.

32. Roy C. Smith, "Japan as a Vulnerable No. 1," *Business Week*, 11 August 1980, pp. 13–14.

33. "Lessons from Japan, Inc.," *Newsweek*, 8 September 1980, p. 61.

34. Ibid., pp. 61–62.

35. Smith, "Japan as a Vulnerable No. 1," pp. 13–14; and Louis Kraar, "Inside Japan's 'Open' Market," *Fortune*, 5 October 1981, pp. 118–26.

36. Kyonosuke Ibe, "It Took the Japanese to Build Japan," *Business Week*, 6 October 1980, p. 17.

SUPPLEMENTARY READING

Amano, Matt M. "Organizational Changes of a Japanese Firm in America." *California Management Review* 21 (Spring 1979): 51–59.

Badawy, M. K. "Styles of Mideastern Managers." *California Management Review* 22 (Spring 1980): 51–58.

Ballon, Robert J. "A Lesson from Japan: Contract, Control, and Authority." *Journal of Contemporary Business* 8 (2nd Quarter 1979): 27–35.

Caron, Sandra L. "Politics and International Business: The Impact of the Foreign Corrupt Practices Act." *Journal of Contemporary Business* (3rd Quarter 1981): 17–28.

Doz, Yves L. "Strategic Management in Multinational Companies." *Sloan Management Review* 21 (Winter 1980): 27–46.

Doz, Yves L.; Bartlett, Christopher A.; and Prahalad, C. K. "Global Competitive Pressures and Host Country Demands: Managing Tensions in MNCs." *California Management Review* 23 (Spring 1981): 63–74.

Doz, Yves L., and Prahalad, C. K. "How MNCs Cope with Host Government Intervention." *Harvard Business Review* 58 (March–April 1980): 149–57.

Drake, Rodman L., and Caudill, Lee M. "Management of the Large Multinational: Trends and Future Challenges." *Business Horizons* 24 (May/June 1981): 83–91.

Drucker, Peter F. "Behind Japan's Success." *Harvard Business Review* 59 (January–February 1981): 83–90.

Graham, John L. "A Hidden Cause of America's Trade Deficit with Japan." *Columbia Journal of World Business* 16 (Fall 1981): 5–15.

Hatvany, Nina, and Pucik, Vladimir. "Japanese Management Practices and Productivity." *Organizational Dynamics* 9 (Spring 1981): 5–21.

Hout, Thomas; Porter, Michael E.; and Rudden, Eileen. "How Global Companies Win Out." *Harvard Business Review* 60 (September–October 1982): 98–108.

Killing, J. Peter. "How to Make a Global Joint Venture Work." *Harvard Business Review* 60 (May–June 1982): 120–27.

Puffer, Sheila M. "Inside a Soviet Management Institute." *California Management Review* 24 (Fall 1981): 90–96.

Reilly, Bernard J., and Fuhr, Joseph P., Jr. "Productivity: An Economic and Management Analysis with a Direction towards a New Synthesis." *Academy of Management Journal* 8 (January 1983): 108–17.

Ronstadt, Robert and Kramer, Robert J. "Getting the Most Out of Innovation Abroad." *Harvard Business Review* 60 (March–April 1982): 94–99.

Ryans, John K., Jr., and Shanklin, William L. "How Managers Cope with Terrorism." *California Management Review* 23 (Winter 1980): 66–72.

Shapiro, Alan C. "Managing Political Risk: A Policy Approach." *Columbia Journal of World Business* 16 (Fall 1981): 63–70.

Sullivan, Jeremiah J. "A Critique of Theory Z." *Academy of Management Review* 8 (January 1983): 132–42.

Tung, Rosalie L. "Patterns of Motivation in Chinese Industrial Enterprises." *Academy of Management Review* 6 (July 1981): 481–89.

PART TWO MANAGEMENT PLANNING AND DECISION MAKING

5

OBJECTIVES AND STRATEGIES

This chapter will enable you to

- *Understand the organization's mission, its various types of objectives, and the coalition of interests that is reflected in those objectives.*
- *Explain the significance of strategic planning and the various factors and elements involved in strategy formulation.*
- *Outline the steps involved in formulating organizational strategy.*

Organizations exist to accomplish objectives or goals.* This chapter, which opens our consideration of the *planning function*, explains the *nature of objectives* and the *organizational strategy* followed to achieve them.

ORGANIZATIONAL OBJECTIVES

Nature of Objectives

Organizations come into existence as a result of purposeful action by one or more individuals. It might seem, therefore, that organizational purpose would be obvious. *Organizational objectives* are often implicit, however, and require explicit formulation before they can be used for direction.

As Figure 5–1 indicates, objectives are an outgrowth of the organization's *mission statement*, "a broadly defined but enduring statement of purpose that distinguishes a business from other firms of its type and identifies the scope of its operations in product and market terms."[1] K mart Corporation, for instance, identifies itself as a general merchandise retailer that distributes a wide range of merchandise through a chain of discount department stores. To satisfy its broad array of customers, the company sells not only staple merchandise at low prices, but also a selective mix of national and designer brands. Although it is the second largest general merchandise retailer in the nation, "K mart is a local business to its customers. Each K mart store is planned, placed,

---

*The terms *objectives* and *goals* are used synonymously throughout.

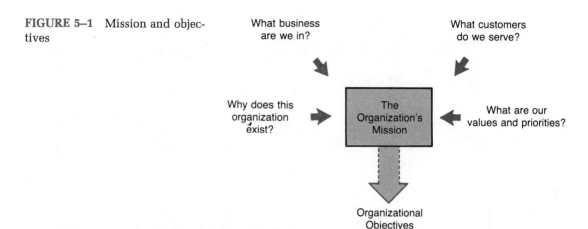

FIGURE 5–1   Mission and objectives

and operated as an individual unit, with regard for the economic, environmental and social circumstances of the community."[2] From such a "know thyself" statement, the organization's goals can be developed. An example of one organization's goals is shown in Figure 5–2.

Types of Organizational Objectives

Surveys indicate that most organizations have multiple objectives. One study of eighty-two large corporations found that the number of goals any one company set ranged from one to eighteen, with the average company having five to six.[3] Too few goals may result in neglect of critical areas in the environment, while too many may overly disperse the efforts of employees.[4]

Goals may be either *short-* or *long-range*. A survey of 228 companies headquartered in Texas indicated that the majority of firms established goals for three to five years into the future. Fewer than 7 percent set goals for periods in excess of ten years, and about 5 percent had no long-range goals at all (these were mostly small firms).[5] The planning horizon for an organization depends to a large extent upon its environment. Public utilities, which operate in a regulated, fairly predictable environment,

---

Objectives of First Interstate Bancorp, a multistate banking company headquartered in Los Angeles:

Profit Objective: To rank higher in earnings than in size and to consistently place in the first quartile in earnings growth among our peer financial institutions in the West.
Dividend Objective: To pay a competitive dividend.
Technology Objective: To maintain and enhance our competitive advantage in technology.
Marketing Objective: To provide a full spectrum of competitive financial services in both the retail and corporate marketplace.

FIGURE 5–2   An example of organizational objectives
SOURCE: First Interstate Bancorp, 1981 Annual Report, pp. 3–4.

often have longer-range goals than construction companies, which face more dynamic, unpredictable environments.

A distinction must be made between *official* and *operative* objectives.[6] Official objectives are those that management espouses publicly. A state university president, for instance, may state that a major goal of the university is to provide an education of the highest quality. The means to this end are termed operative goals—those objectives that the university actively pursues. These specify whether the university will emphasize the liberal arts or professional schools, whether resources will be allocated more heavily to graduate or undergraduate programs, and whether the faculty should emphasize teaching or research. Operative goals tell us what the organization is actually trying to do.

In some situations, operative goals may not be closely related to the organization's official statements. Take the public pronouncement of the university president above, for instance. In light of current enrollment trends, the overriding operative goal of the university may actually be to increase its enrollment, especially if its budget from the state is based on student head-count. This goal is unlikely to be highly publicized, particularly if its attainment requires a relaxing of admissions standards.

As is evident in Figure 5–2, organizations establish goals in several areas. These goals reflect the organization's various constituencies. For instance, many organizations set goals in such areas as customer service, return on stockholders' investment, treatment of employees, development of managers, and responsibility toward the local community.

Peter Drucker believes that objectives need to be set in all areas upon which the organization's survival depends. This, according to him, requires objectives in the key areas described below:

> A business must first be able to create a customer. There is, therefore, need for a *marketing objective*. Businesses must be able to innovate or else their competitors will obsolesce them. There is need for an *innovation objective*. All businesses depend on the three factors of production of the economist, that is, on the *human resource*, the *capital* resource, and *physical resources*. There must be objectives for their supply, their employment, and their development. The resources must be employed productively and their productivity has to grow if the business is to survive. There is need, therefore, for *productivity objectives*. Business exists in society and community and, therefore, has to discharge social responsibilities, at least to the point where it takes responsibility for its impact upon the environment. Therefore objectives in respect to the *social dimensions* of business are needed.
>
> Finally, there is need for *profit*—otherwise none of the objectives can be attained. They all require effort, that is, cost. And they can be financed only out of the profits of a business. They all entail risks; they all, therefore, require a profit to cover the risk of potential losses.[7]

Although non-business organizations have no profit objective, they must nevertheless deal with the efficient use of scarce resources. Hospital administrators, for example, are expected to avoid waste in providing the best possible health care with the limited resources they have available to them. Their efficiency objective is comparable to the profit objective of a business organization.

Values of Organizational Objectives

Identify Environmental Opportunities.   The environment presents both dangers and opportunities. By careful selection of objectives, management may exploit those opportunities and avoid those dangers. One value of organizational objectives, therefore, is proper orientation of the organization to its environment.

Guide Management Decisions.   Objectives also provide a focus for policy making and other management decisions. Business decisions and policies—in production, sales, finance, and so on—should be directed to the achievement of the firm's objectives. As an example, suppose that a chemical manufacturer desires to lead not only in the production of standard chemicals but also in research and the introduction of new products. The company's personnel policies and practices must provide for the recruitment and retention of creative scientists for its research laboratories. Financial planning must permit the investment of large amounts in research and facilities over a long period of time before a dollar is ever realized from these investments. Production planning must be sufficiently flexible and imaginative to adapt to new production techniques and to assist in the development of production processes for new products. Marketing personnel must be able to assess and develop markets to permit exploitation of new discoveries originating in the laboratory.

Facilitate Teamwork.   Clearly formulated objectives enable all parts of an organization to work toward the same goal. Production and sales departments need not work at cross purposes if there is a common objective. If production policies call for a product of high quality, advertising will not stress price to the exclusion of quality. Nor will prices be set on the basis of a competitor's inferior line of products.

Encourage Consistency.   Clear objectives also encourage a consistency in management, planning, and decision making over a period of time. Long-run goals provide caution against action that is merely expedient in the short run. Formulation of explicit objectives thus provides a stabilizing force in month-to-month and year-to-year management decisions. Merely implicit recognition of goals, however, involves the dangers of inconsistency, lack of coordination among departments, and temptation to compromise. If a student is not thoroughly committed to a college education, for example, the attraction of a good job or marriage may easily sidetrack that individual.

Organizations and Coalitions

In view of the numerous parties involved in the process of forming objectives, some writers have suggested that an organization should be thought of as a *coalition of interests*. In other words, organizational objectives in some way represent a consensus that has been hammered out in a manner acceptable to the various participants. Decisions are rarely the product of individual executives who have sufficient power to decide issues without regard for the views of others.

A variety of internal interests and external forces constrains the manager's choice of goals. It is unrealistic to think that a business manager sets objectives solely for the benefit of shareholders, totally apart from the consideration of other interests. This is simply impossible. Any manager who attempted to maximize profits by lowering wage rates or reducing quality would immediately experience severe opposition.

Managers, particularly top-level managers, play a unique role in the establishment of objectives. They must strike a balance among the various interests and participants. In other words, they must balance the pressures from the coalition members so that the continuing participation of each is assured.[8]

NATURE OF STRATEGIC PLANNING

While objectives are the ends that management hopes to attain, the means to those ends are the organization's *strategy*. Strategic planning is concerned with the development of broad or basic programs for the future, and it must be followed with planning of a more detailed and specific nature.

The Nature of Strategy

All types of organizations follow basic strategies. In government, public policy (strategy) emerges from a combination of legislative and administrative activity.[9] In its most general form, we recognize such strategies as our public energy policy, economic policy, environmental protection policy, and so on. Other nonprofit organizations such as churches, hospitals, educational institutions, and art museums show their individual strategies by the varied approaches they take to reaching their particular objectives.

In business firms, *strategic decisions* are concerned with such issues as breadth of product line, geographical scope, industry position, extent of vertical integration, and orientation toward growth. By strategic decision making, top management determines the position of the firm relative to its environment. At any given time, the firm's orientation to the environment may be described as its *strategic posture*. Changes in this posture require redeployment of the firm's assets into new configura-

OBJECTIVES AND STRATEGY

Top management of Lenox, the premier maker of china tableware in the United States, established a goal of doubling the company's annual sales within five years. The company's strategy is to diversify further into jewelry and giftware while acquiring an existing company that makes branded products in a field such as luggage or furniture, where the competition is not intense. Overall, management wishes to maintain the company's prestige image as it reduces its dependence on the slow-moving wedding sales field, its traditional area.

Increasing competition from Japanese makers of dinnerware has made jewelry and giftware attractive avenues of expansion to Lenox. It already owns the most recognized names in fashion jewelry— Keepsake and Art-Carved—and believes that the giftware market is recession-proof. Lenox's long-term debt is low (only 11.2 percent of its total capital), permitting it to expand easily.

SOURCE: Based on "Lenox: Capitalizing on Its Image to Launch New Luxury Lines," *Business Week*, 19 October 1981, pp. 141–44.

tions. Strategic decisions express the firm's basic purposes and the direction it wishes to take in relating to and serving the society of which it is a part.

Many large corporations have adopted strategic planning during recent years. A study of 104 large manufacturing firms revealed that 90 percent engaged in some form of long-range planning. Surprisingly, two-fifths of those organizations had not instituted their formal planning programs until after 1975.[10] As environmental complexity and instability continue to increase, so will the adoption of more formal long-range planning processes.[11]

Factors in Strategy Determination

Environmental conditions provide the background for strategic decisions. As changes occur in the environment, conditions become either more or less favorable for particular strategies. What may start as a shrewd strategy can wind up as a disaster if environmental conditions change suddenly.

For example, Braniff International applied for 624 new routes when the airline industry was deregulated in 1978. (By comparison, United Air Lines took only one new route.) Serving the new routes required more planes. These cost $925 million, much of it borrowed. Although risky, Braniff's strategy might have been successful except the environment intervened: the Iranian Revolution caused fuel prices to soar, and increased competition brought on by deregulation led to fierce fare reduction wars in the industry. Eventually Braniff found itself owing $733 million to creditors and selling seats at prices below cost. The company filed for bankruptcy in May 1982, eliminating over 9,000 jobs and stranding legions of passengers in airports all over the country.[12]

2 The resources of the firm comprise another important set of factors. Resources—whether they are financial, human, or other—may be used in various ways. In choosing a business strategy, the manager decides upon the environmental opportunities to which a particular combination of resources may be most profitably applied.

3 A third set of factors concerns the values and preferences of the firm's management. To some extent these reflect individual differences. Over the years, however, some organizations develop a particular ideology which attracts managers holding similar viewpoints. For example, particular firms may emphasize innovation, growth, customer service, high ethical standards, and so on.

Uncertainty and Judgment

Of all the types of decisions required in business operation, strategic decisions involve the greatest uncertainty. Their complexity grows out of the possibility of their changing the firm's relationship to the environment. More routine decisions are based on the framework of the firm as given and are less uncertain. The environment, with its changing patterns, at times almost defies prediction and intelligent forecasting.

This does not mean that the strategist lacks any data whatsoever. It does mean that the issues are typically fuzzy and the best strategy unclear. As a result, the top-level manager must use more subjective judgment in strategy decisions than is required for more routine decisions.

As a means of improving the quality of strategic decisions, some scholars have recommended the use of *dialectical analysis*.[13] This method involves tracing the strategic decision back to its underlying assumptions or premises. For example, the decision may be to open one hundred new retail outlets in the next three years. One of the assumptions underlying this decision is that economic growth and product demand will increase enough to make the new outlets profitable. The dialectic phase involves forming a set of assumptions opposite to those underlying the decision: economic growth and product demand will not increase sufficiently to make the new outlets profitable. This assumption, if plausible, would then be used to form a counter strategy. The two strategies are then combined to create a composite strategy. The three strategic alternatives are then judged on how well they fit the most logical set of assumptions. This technique helps to ensure that important aspects of the strategic situation are not overlooked and that a number of strategic alternatives are systematically examined.[14]

Elements of Corporate Strategy

Strategic decisions must be made in a number of different, but interrelated, areas. Underlying these decisions is the need for the organization to develop a *distinctive competence;* that is, the ability to do some things particularly well in comparison to its competitors.[15] One survey of 247 managers in eighty-eight companies indicated that "top managers make deliberate choices to develop strategies and distinctive competences quite different from those of competing organizations, even though the environmental demands faced by companies within the same industry may be generally similar."[16] Some of the areas in which an organization may develop a distinctive competence are discussed briefly in this section.

Product/Market Scope. One major facet of corporate strategy entails decisions concerning product/market scope. A firm may choose to concentrate its activities on a narrow range of products and markets—to be a specialist—or it may elect to diversify. Many degrees of diversification are possible. At the extreme, the firm may choose to enter a number of unrelated product fields. A wise choice of products and markets is essential for the firm's success.

Company resources constrain diversification. Unless financial and managerial resources are ample, the simplest plan is specialization. This plan places the least strain upon resources. One company, for example, that has capitalized upon its limitations is Charter Medical Corporation. Rather than competing for leadership in the hospital ownership field with such large firms as Hospital Corporation of America and Humana, Charter selected a niche in the underdeveloped market for psychiatric care. As Chairman William A. Fickling, Jr., put it:

> A leader in an industry always makes more money than an also-ran, and we will not take a backseat to anybody in psychiatric.[17]

Corporate Growth. In most cases, corporate management is interested in growth. Some managers feel, indeed, that growth is essential for survival—that a firm must either move ahead or fall backward. But there is a considerable range of growth attitudes and opportunities.

One possibility emphasizes the conservation and continued profitable use of present resources, rather than growth. Others may select moderate growth at some specific rate—for example, 5 percent or 10 percent per year—or a rate of growth comparable to that of the industry market.

Innovation. A firm may choose to be a leader or a follower in innovation. There are perils and rewards associated with either alternative. By choosing a path of leadership in innovation, the firm tends to maximize its research and development costs. It may reap the benefits of getting a

A NEGATIVE GROWTH STRATEGY

A number of tire manufacturers failed to anticipate the effects that long-lasting radial tires and high gasoline prices would have on tire sales. One such firm was Firestone Tire & Rubber Company, which not only failed to diversify into new markets but was simultaneously forced to spend $182 million to recall its defective Radial 500 tire.

After suffering a negative cash flow of $391.5 million in three years and accumulating debt of more than $1 billion, Firestone hired John J. Nevin from Zenith Corporation to become its chairman and chief executive officer. His first strategic decision was to nullify Firestone's decades-old strategy of trying to be the market leader in all lines of tires.

To implement his new strategy, Nevin made several moves: The company sold operations in five foreign countries and began reducing its ownership to a minority position in other foreign subsidiaries; and it shut seventeen tire plants in the United States and Canada and reduced the variety of tires it made from 7,300 to 2,600. Sales, which were $5.1 billion in 1979, dropped to an annualized rate of $3.6 billion by 1982.

Nevin's strategy is to concentrate on high-profit products such as Firestone radials for cars and light trucks and tractor tires, while transforming Firestone's 4,500 North American dealerships into auto maintenance and repair stations. The car repair business is particularly appealing since the involvement of gasoline stations in car repair has been steadily decreasing, and Firestone already has a well-established dealer system with the necessary physical plant in place.

SOURCE: Based on "Survival in the Basic Industries: How Four Companies Hope to Avoid Disaster," *Business Week*, 26 April 1982, pp. 74–76.

major share of a given market by getting there first, but this does not occur automatically.

Texas Instruments, for example, is well known for its strong emphasis on technological innovation. As one observer stated: "TIers think of themselves as shirt-sleeved pioneers who create new markets rather than exploiting existing ones."[18] This drive has enabled management to build a world-leading electronics firm virtually from scratch. Occasionally, the emphasis on technology, however, has been carried to extremes, overshadowing equally necessary emphases in marketing. In 1981, TI dropped its money-losing digital watch line. Although a pioneer in digital watches, TI virtually ignored fashion on styling (the watches had plastic cases and bands to keep the price low) and made little attempt to form good relationships with retailers.[19]

Geographic Scope. In this day of multinational corporations, only the earth itself sets the geographical limits. Many firms have chosen to cross international boundaries and to be multinational firms. Even here, however, there are alternatives in terms of which countries or areas of the world should receive primary interest.

A decade ago, the management of Continental Can Company (now The Continental Group) anticipated a leveling off in the domestic can market. In order to continue growing, management developed a two-pronged strategy to reduce Continental's dependence on this domestic market. On the one hand, the firm began to expand overseas by acquiring interests in firms in Brazil and Saudi Arabia. Simultaneously, Continental diversified domestically by purchasing companies in the insurance, financial, and gas fields, and by forming new businesses in pipelines, finance, and forest products. In five years, its profits more than doubled from $107.7 million to $224.8 million (on sales of $3.1 billion and $5.1 billion, respectively).

A firm obviously may choose a more geographically restricted market. It may operate as a purely local or regional firm, or it may operate primarily in one geographical area but sell in other areas of the country or the world.

STEPS IN STRATEGIC DECISION MAKING

Identify Opportunities and Risks

Assessment of environmental trends provides a starting point for the process of strategy determination shown in Figure 5–3. Environmental assessment should be part of the continuing monitoring process recommended in Chapter 3. Of particular concern are economic trends, new legislation, availability of resources, technological and social change, and new developments in markets and competition. Managers have two objectives in their environmental assessment: (1) to determine the risks

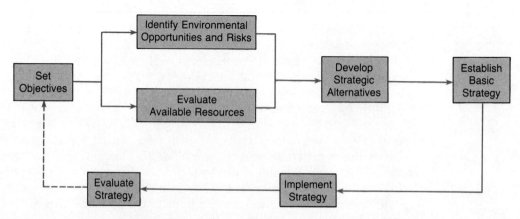

FIGURE 5–3   Strategic decision making

and threats that the organization faces or will face; and (2) to identify areas in which profitable opportunities exist.

This process is often quite difficult. Sometimes, for instance, management makes a serious mistake by overlooking a competitor.

> A visit to a pathology lab of the corporate hospital reveals as a common cause of death: killed by a competitor one did not know or did not take seriously. IBM, which did not make manual typewriters, destroyed Underwood's leadership position in the typewriter business with its electric typewriter. Yet for many years Underwood paid more attention to its traditional rivals, Smith-Corona and Royal-McBee. IBM was seen as a remote outsider with a special luxury product, not as a serious and dangerous challenger.[20]

Evaluate Available Resources

In evaluating available resources, the manager is concerned with strengths, weaknesses, and the extent to which resources are committed on a long-term basis. The evaluation, in most cases, will focus on the following key areas of the firm:

1. Financial capacity
2. Product/market position
3. Human resources
4. Physical plant and equipment
5. Technology base
6. Research and development programs
7. Production system
8. Marketing and distribution systems

The organization will have strengths in some of these areas, increasing the number of strategic alternatives available to it. In other areas, it may be weak, reducing its possible options. Of particular consideration is the extent to which the firm's resources are already committed. Even though a firm may be strong in some areas, a prior long-term commitment of its resources may severely limit its strategic alternatives.

During the last decade, many corporations have become more analytical in considering the deployment of their resources. One popular analytical approach has been developed by the Boston Consulting Group. This approach can be visualized in terms of the matrix display illustrated in Figure 5–4, which shows rate of growth for a market as a whole on the vertical axis and a company's share of that market on the horizontal axis.*

The market for computers, for example, is "fast growth," while the market for candy is "slow growth." A major corporation operating in several different industries may have some divisions or segments of its business in each of the four quadrants. A multi-product company, in other words, may simultaneously have "stars," "cows," "dogs," and "question marks."

FIGURE 5–4 The business portfolio matrix

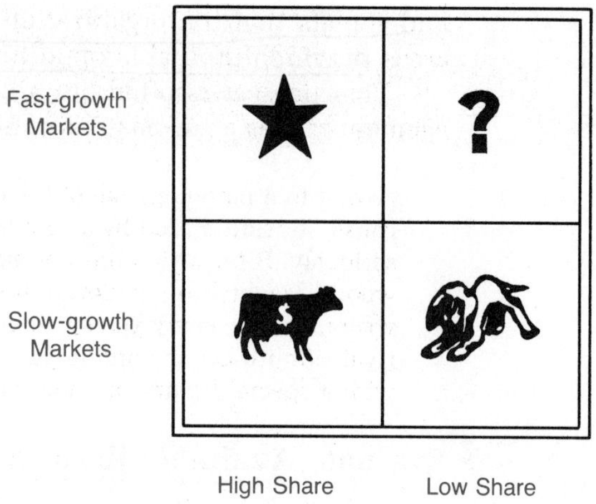

A firm would naturally prefer to have stars instead of dogs! In considering the deployment or redeployment of its resources in the four quadrants of the matrix, management might reason somewhat as follows:

- *Stars:* (High share of fast-growth market.) Inject additional money and attempt to gain an even larger share of the market.
- *Question Marks:* (Low share of fast-growth market.) Consider fighting for more market share but recognize danger of getting into a "cash trap."
- *Cows:* (High share of slow-growth market.) Milk the "cash cows"— that is, remove money and reinvest in stars or possibly question marks.
- *Dogs:* (Low share of slow-growth market.) Eliminate them.

The underlying idea holds that an increase in a company's volume leads to reduction of production costs. This results, in turn, from the operation of what Bruce Henderson has termed the "experience curve." Practice tends to make perfect, and production costs reportedly decline 20 to 30 percent in real terms whenever experience is doubled. As a result of these forces, a company which increases its volume by expanding market share and/or by concentrating in fast-growth markets may be able to increase its efficiency and profitability. Although this is only one of various analytical methods, it illustrates the systematic corporate evaluation of resource deployment.[21]

---

*The matrix described here was originally developed by Alan J. Zakon of the Boston Consulting Group and William W. Wommack, vice chairman of Mead Corporation, in 1967. The analytical approach described here has its critics. Many major corporations accept it, however, and the Boston Consulting Group has become the country's leader in business strategy consultation. For further reading on this and other analytical approaches, see Walter Kiechel, III, "Playing by the Rules of the Corporate Strategy Game," *Fortune*, 24 September 1979, 110–16.

THE STRATEGIC BUSINESS UNIT

Long recognized for its successful strategic planning, General Electric Company pioneered the concept of the strategic business unit (SBU). An SBU is an organizational subsystem which has a market, set of competitors, and mission distinct from the other subsystems in the firm. For example, one SBU at GE consists of departments which produce ranges, refrigerators, dishwashers, clothes washers and dryers, and so on. All share a common set of competitors, customers, markets, and mission, and are managed as a single business with its own objectives, strategies, and profit or loss figures. Each SBU requires its own type of managerial personnel, depending on its orientation, such as growth, generating cash flow, cost control, or so on.

In recent years, Japanese businesses have been turning to the SBU concept. Until energy costs began soaring in 1973, Japanese managers were more concerned with overall company profits than with the performance of each product line. Rapidly rising costs have created a new awareness of the relative profitability of individual products. Many Japanese companies are now sending managers to GE to learn how to implement SBUs. Toshiba Corporation, for instance, which organized into forty-three SBUs, boosted its sales from $3 billion to $8 billion in six years while reducing its payroll by 6 percent. Some of the cost reduction came from divesting product lines that failed to produce adequate profits.

SOURCE: Based on "Conversation with Reginald H. Jones and Frank Doyle," *Organizational Dynamics* 10 (Winter 1982): 44–48; and "A U.S. Concept Revives Oki," *Business Week*, 1 March 1982, p. 112.

Develop Strategic Alternatives

Development of strategic alternatives involves an integration of data concerning environmental risks and opportunities with data concerning available resources. In the case of the going concern, one alternative is to continue doing what it is already doing. This approach is the simplest and may be the best, but only for a time. A corporation must eventually modify its strategy because of the inevitable changes in the environment. Other alternatives are needed for serious consideration and comparison with the *status quo*.

The development of strategic alternatives is a creative process that requires a vision of the various possibilities for meeting the needs of the industry. Courage is required to propose a drastic change because of the great uncertainty involved. Also, proposed changes in strategy tend to conflict with existing strategy, the accepted way of doing things. Changes pose difficulties, even in contemplation, because of traditional and comfortable patterns of thinking and operation.

Establish Basic Strategy

The decision as to which strategy to adopt is difficult and requires much subjective judgment. The difficulty in making this choice arises from the fuzzy nature of the problem, the existence of unknowns that will become known in the future, and the paucity of available information.

Individual managers also possess personal values that inevitably affect strategy determination. One manager may wish to gain or hold a given share of the market. Another may emphasize product specialization or social values. The importance of individual leadership is evident as we think of companies that have shown the "stamp" of their leaders— Ford Motor Company, Polaroid, and IBM, for example. The opportunity and need for subjective judgment allow the introduction of personal values, philosophy, and ambitions.[22]

Whatever factors are included in the strategic decision, it is important that such a decision be made and that it be made clear to members of the organization. Otherwise, the company's direction is unclear, and the management team tends to move in various directions. Uncertainty appeared to characterize the W. T. Grant Company shortly before its collapse in 1975.

> Worse yet, early on Grant seemingly could not make up its mind what kind of store it was. "There was a lot of dissension within the company whether we should go the K-Mart route or go after the Ward's and Penney position," says a former executive. "Ed Staley and Lou Lustenberger were at loggerheads over the issue, with the upshot being we took a position between the two and that consequently stood for nothing."[23]

The strategic decision determines any changes to be made in the deployment of company resources. If a new strategy is to be followed, company assets must be recast into an appropriate mold for the new strategy. This often takes time because of the fixed nature of many assets, and rapid changes can be costly.

Redeployment of assets concerns more than financial and physical assets. Management groups, for example, have educational and experiential backgrounds that are related to existing strategy. Modification of that strategy may require changes in the management staff.

Implement Strategy

Strategy is implemented as the organization develops specific plans to carry out the overall strategy. If a firm decides to enter a regional market, for example, someone must set up the distribution system and see that it begins operation.

Middle and lower management put strategy into practice. Even though top management must decide overall strategy, because of the fundamental nature of the decision, they need the strong support of middle and lower management to make the strategy successful. Strategies may be operationalized on the basis of the following: departments, time frames, products/services, regions, or functions such as finance or personnel. Because of the importance of this topic, it will be explored further in the following chapter.

Evaluate Strategy

Periodic reevaluation of competitive strategy is necessary to prevent deterioration and obsolescence of the basic strategic approach. The environment changes in various ways, and continuing criticism of existing strategy helps to locate weaknesses in it at the earliest possible moment.

An evaluation process necessitates criteria, which brings us back to our earlier discussion of objectives. The firm's goals can be used for judging the effectiveness of strategic decisions as time goes by.

Some common criteria used to evaluate strategic performance are market share, sales growth, and profit objectives. In each area, management may use its own stated goal, past performance, or the record of competitors.

Quantitative goals alone are not sufficient, however; they must be accompanied by qualitative objectives. For example, in order to meet a goal of a 10 percent return on assets, some managers may be tempted to delay replacing old equipment with more expensive state-of-the-art machinery. If, however, management also has a goal of remaining current with technological advances, then this impulse would be controlled.

Logical Incrementalism

A somewhat different view of strategic planning can be found in the perspective termed *logical incrementalism*.[24] According to this view, because of a rapidly changing environment, managers often have insufficient time and information to undertake a full, formal analysis of all possible strategic alternatives. Hence, they deal with events in an incremental fashion, as illustrated in the following example:

> General Motors' top management only incrementally restructured its various car lines as it understood, step-by-step, the way in which the oil crisis and environmental demands would affect the viability of each existing divisional and dealership structure. In the aggregate these amounted to the greatest shift in balance and positioning among GM's automobile lines since Alfred P. Sloan. . . .[25]

The basic idea, of course, is that management sometimes does not know precisely its ultimate objective or its entire strategy. Bits and pieces of the strategy unfold incrementally as managers respond to a constantly changing environment. This incremental approach is necessitated by several factors, among them a lack of information about the environment, the difficulty of predicting the effect of various strategic decisions, and the resistance that major organizational changes usually encounter. Incremental movements allow the organization to experiment with various approaches, to learn, and to build awareness and commitment among those who must implement the decisions.

SUMMARY

An organization's *objectives or goals* are an outgrowth of its *mission statement*, which distinguishes it from other firms and identifies the scope of its operations. Management sets goals in a number of areas which reflect the organization's environment and constituencies. Establishing objectives benefits an organization in several ways. For example, objectives provide a basis for decision making and for teamwork among departments and individuals. To some extent, organizational objectives reflect a *coalition of interests,* a consensus among the various internal and external participants.

While objectives are the ends that management hopes to attain, the means to the ends are the organization's *strategy. Strategic planning* involves basic decisions affecting the very nature of an organization and its relationship to the environment. Strategic planning is based upon *environmental conditions, resources* available to the firm, and *managerial values.* Because of the unknowns, particularly in future developments, and the complex nature of these decisions, strategic decision making necessitates subjective judgment. But this judgment is consistently directed toward the development and maintenance of a *distinctive competence*— the ability of the organization to do some things better than its competitors. Strategic decisions involve choices concerning such factors as product/market scope, corporate growth, innovation, and geographic scope.

The determination of strategy for a firm involves a series of steps, the first of which is the identification of opportunities and risks in the environment. This step is followed by an evaluation of available resources and assessment of the firm's competitive strengths. Other steps include the development of strategic alternatives, commitment to a particular strategy, and later evaluation of the strategy as the basis for a subsequent round of strategy determination. During periods of rapid environmental change, management may follow a policy of *logical incrementalism,* that is, developing strategy in bits and pieces as they begin to understand the situation and secure the commitment of their subordinates.

DISCUSSION QUESTIONS

1. What is the relationship between the organization's *mission statement* and its *objectives?*
2. Distinguish between *official* and *operative* goals. Give an example.
3. Why is it necessary for business organizations to have more than a profit objective?
4. In what way does a clearly stated objective enable all parts of an organization to work effectively together?
5. Define *organizational strategy* and explain its relationship to objectives.

6. Explain the difference between *strategic posture* and *strategic plan*.
7. Why is it that a good strategy, selected carefully with proper consideration of all relevant variables, cannot be continued indefinitely?
8. In what ways are strategic decisions different from administrative, routine decisions?
9. What is meant by an organization's *distinctive competence*? Give examples of organizations which have attained distinctive competence in one or more areas.
10. In determining its product/market scope, a firm may choose to specialize or diversify. What are the primary factors that make it difficult to diversify?
11. How can the Boston Consulting Group's business portfolio matrix aid management in strategic decision making?
12. The problems of the W. T. Grant Company were used to illustrate management's failure to make a strategic decision. What causes firms to lose "by default" in this way?
13. Why are both quantitative and qualitative measures of strategic performance necessary?

NOTES

1. John A. Pearce III, "The Company Mission as a Strategic Tool," *Sloan Management Review* 23 (Spring 1982): 15.
2. K mart Corporation, 1981 Annual Report, p. 4.
3. Y. K. Shetty, "New Look at Corporate Goals," *California Management Review* 22 (Winter 1979): 74.
4. Ibid.
5. Kamal M. Abouzeid, "Corporate Goal Identification and Achievement," *Managerial Planning* 29 (November–December 1980): 17–22.
6. Charles Perrow, "The Analysis of Goals in Complex Organizations," *American Sociological Review* 26 (December 1961): 855.
7. Peter F. Drucker, *Management: Tasks, Responsibilities, Practices* (New York: Harper & Row, Publishers, 1973), p. 100. Reprinted by permission.
8. For a more extensive review of this topic, see the following: Richard M. Cyert and James G. March, *A Behavioral Theory of the Firm* (Englewood Cliffs, N.J.: Prentice-Hall, 1963); and Edwin A. Murray, Jr., "Strategic Choice as a Negotiated Outcome," *Management Science* 24 (May 1978): 960–72. A model of how coalitions influence strategy in organizations is provided by V. K. Narayanan and Liam Fahey, "The Micro-Politics of Strategy Formulation," *Academy of Management Review* 7 (January 1982): 25–34. They conclude that effective strategic management involves not only emphasis on the content of the strategy but equal attention to the internal political processes within the organization.
9. For a review of the strategic planning or policy process in government, see the following: Michael H. Moskow, *Strategic Planning in Business and*

Government. (New York: The Committee for Economic Development, 1978); Charles O. Jones, *An Introduction to the Study of Public Policy*, 2d ed. (Belmont, Cal.: Wadsworth Publishing Co., 1977).

10. Noel Capon, John U. Farley, and James Hulbert, "International Diffusion of Corporate and Strategic Planning Practices," *Columbia Journal of World Business* 15 (Fall 1980): 5–6.

11. William M. Lindsay and Leslie W. Rue, "Impact of the Organization's Environment on the Long-Range Planning Process: A Contingency View," *Academy of Management Journal* 23 (September 1980): 385–404.

12. "Braniff Makes a Crash Landing," *Newsweek*, 24 May 1982, pp. 62–65; and "A Braniff Revival is Only a Long Shot," *Business Week*, 31 May 1982, pp. 26–28.

13. Ian I. Mitroff and James R. Emshoff, "On Strategic Assumption-Making: A Dialectical Approach to Policy and Planning," *Academy of Management Review* 4 (January 1979): 1–12.

14. For a view opposing the use of dialectical analysis, see Richard A. Cosier, "Dialectical Inquiry in Strategic Planning: A Case of Premature Acceptance," *Academy of Management Review* 6 (October 1981): 643–48.

15. The meaning of this concept is summarized in Charles C. Snow and Lawrence G. Hrebiniak, "Strategy, Distinctive Competence, and Organizational Performance," *Administrative Science Quarterly* 25 (June 1980): 317–36. The term was first used by Phillip Selznick, *Leadership in Administration* (New York: Harper & Row, Publishers, 1957), and later refined by Kenneth R. Andrews, *The Concept of Corporate Strategy* (Homewood, Ill.: Richard D. Irwin, 1971).

16. Snow and Hrebiniak, "Strategy," p. 334.

17. "Charter Medical: Zeroing in on Neglected Areas in Psychiatric Care," *Business Week*, 26 July 1982, p. 76.

18. Bro Uttal, "Texas Instruments Regroups," *Fortune*, 9 August 1982, p. 41.

19. Ibid., p. 42.

20. Hugo E. R. Uyterhoeven, Robert W. Ackerman, and John W. Rosenblum, *Strategy and Organization: Text and Cases in General Management* (Homewood, Ill.: Richard D. Irwin, 1973), p. 31.

21. A popular alternative to this matrix is GE's nine-cell planning grid. A good discussion of this grid can be found in William F. Glueck, *Strategic Management and Business Policy* (New York: McGraw-Hill Book Co., 1980), pp. 164–66.

22. For a discussion of the effect of one aspect of the CEO's personality on the organization's strategy, see Danny Miller, Manfred F. R. Kets De Vries, and Jean-Marie Toulouse, "Top Executive Locus of Control and Its Relationship to Strategy-Making, Structure, and Environment," *Academy of Management Journal* 25 (June 1982): 237–53.

23. "How W. T. Grant Lost $175-Million Last Year," *Business Week*, 24 February 1975, p. 75.

24. James Brian Quinn, "Strategic Change: 'Logical Incrementalism,' " *Sloan Management Review* 20 (Fall 1978): 7–21; and "Managing Strategic Change," *Sloan Management Review* 21 (Summer 1980): 3–20.

25. Quinn, "Strategic Change," p. 10.

SUPPLEMENTARY READING

Bettis, Richard A., and **Hall, William K.** "Strategic Portfolio Management in the Multibusiness Firm." *California Management Review* 24 (Fall 1981): 23–38.

Chakravarthy, Balaji S. "Adaptation: A Promising Metaphor for Strategic Management." *Academy of Management Review* 7 (January 1982): 35–44.

"Conversation with **Reginald H. Jones** and **Frank Doyle.**" *Organizational Dynamics* 10 (Winter 1982): 42–63.

Hall, William K. "Survival Strategies in a Hostile Environment." *Harvard Business Review* 58 (September–October 1980): 75–85.

Hambrick, Donald C.; MacMillan, Ian C.; and **Day, Diana L.** "Strategic Attributes and Performance in the BCG Matrix—A PIMS-Based Analysis of Industrial Product Businesses." *Academy of Management Journal* 25 (September 1982): 510–31.

Harrigan, Kathryn Rudie. "Strategy Formulation in Declining Industries." *Academy of Management Review* 5 (October 1980): 599–604.

Kotter, John P. "Managing External Dependence." *Academy of Management Review* 4 (January 1979): 87–92.

Lenz, R. T. "Strategic Capability: A Concept and Framework for Analysis." *Academy of Management Review* 5 (April 1980): 225–34.

Mintzberg, Henry, and **Waters, James A.** "Tracking Strategy in an Entrepreneurial Firm." *Academy of Management Journal* 25 (September 1982): 465–99.

Mitroff, Ian I., and **Emshoff, James R.** "On Strategic Assumption-Making: A Dialectical Approach to Policy and Planning." *Academy of Management Review* 4 (January 1979): 1–12.

Narayanan, V. K., and **Fahey, Liam.** "The Micro-Politics of Strategy Formulation." *Academy of Management Review* 7 (January 1982): 25–34.

Naylor, Thomas H. "Strategic Planning Models." *Managerial Planning* 30 (July/August 1981): 3–11.

Ohmae, Kenichi. "Foresighted Management Decision Making: See the Options before Planning Strategy." *Management Review* 71 (May 1982): 46–55.

Pearce, John A. II. "An Executive-Level Perspective on the Strategic Management Process." *California Management Review* 24 (Fall 1981): 39–48.

———. "The Company Mission as a Strategic Tool." *Sloan Management Review* 23 (Spring 1982): 15–24.

Quinn, James Brian. *Strategies for Change: Logical Incrementalism.* Homewood, Ill.: Richard D. Irwin, 1980.

Schwartz, Howard, and **Davis, Stanley M.** "Matching Corporate Culture and Business Strategy." *Organizational Dynamics* 10 (Summer 1981): 30–48.

Shetty, Y. K. "New Look at Corporate Goals." *California Management Review* 22 (Winter 1979): 71–79.

6

MAKING OPERATING PLANS

This chapter will enable you to

- *Explain the relationship of operational planning to strategic planning and the way in which comprehensive business plans are prepared.*
- *Recognize the reasons for the growing use, as well as the frequent neglect, of business planning.*
- *Identify the most significant planning premises and show their implications for planning.*
- *Explain the nature of contingency planning and discuss the reasons for using multiple scenarios of the future.*
- *Recognize the distinctive planning contributions made by various organization members.*

Planning begins with decisions about objectives and strategy, but it does not end there. Management must distill these basic purposes into an interlocking set of long-range and short-range operating plans. In this chapter, we examine the planning process and the preparation of operating plans.

THE PLANNING PROCESS

Planning involves a series of steps, going from the general to the particular. As shown in Figure 6–1, *strategic planning* (the subject of Chapter 5) includes the establishment of objectives and the determination of

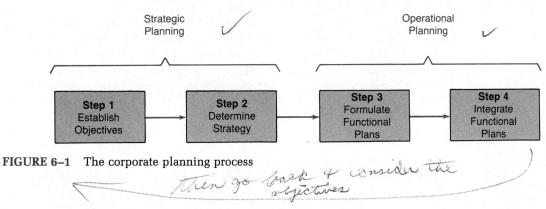

FIGURE 6–1 The corporate planning process

strategy. These steps identify the basic mission of the organization. Figure 6–1 also shows that *operational planning* (the primary focus of this chapter) includes the formulation and integration of functional plans. These plans identify the specific programs and activities necessary to reach the broader objectives.

Nature of Planning

Planning involves systematic thought and decision concerning a proposed course of action. It entails the selection of a given path to the future from the various possible alternatives. It is an intellectual process preceding the activity being planned.

Planning is a continuing activity of management. Managers never reach a point at which they stop planning. This does not mean, however, that they never complete work on specific plans. The budget for a given year may be adopted, but the manager who approves it must immediately turn to other planning and must soon begin consideration of the budget for the following year.

TOP PRIORITY: PLANNING

Threats to organizational health and survival quickly focus attention on those factors managers consider most crucial. When William R. Haselton (a Ph.D. in chemistry) was promoted to the position of chief executive of St. Regis Paper Company in 1979, he expressed embarrassment regarding St. Regis' mediocre performance—seventeenth of twenty-one companies in the forest products industry.

Haselton's prescription was a carefully developed five-year plan.

"What," the reader may ask, "is so special about five-year plans? Doesn't every big company have them?" Maybe so, but taking them seriously is another matter. Make no mistake: Haselton is taking this one seriously. On the surface, he's a soft-spoken, mild-mannered man, but nobody who has dealt with him can ignore the steely determination underneath.

Success for such a plan depends on many factors, some of which (such as general economic conditions) are beyond management's control. Haselton's approach, however, indicates the high priority given to planning as one critical factor in the company's success.

SOURCE: Adapted from Jean A. Briggs, "Woodsman, Spare That Company," *Forbes* 125, no. 3 (February 4, 1980): 37–38.

Plans require decision making, a topic treated in Chapter 8. Selection of a proposed course of action necessitates a decision in favor of this particular course of action and a rejection of other possibilities. Decision making is not synonymous with planning, however, because it is also required in other functions of management.

Plans are directed to the accomplishment of some objective or to the solution of some problem. Overall planning is concerned with broad company objectives and strategies. Functional and divisional planning is directed to the achievement of subsidiary goals which contribute to realization of the company's more fundamental objectives. At each level of the organization, some planning occurs, and it is concerned with the specific mission of the particular organizational component.

Preparation of Functional Operating Plans

Plans become more specific and shorter range as departmental managers engage in planning for their specific operations. As pictured in Figure 6–2, production managers prepare production plans, marketing managers prepare marketing plans, and so on. The goals of each functional department are derived from or related to the overall goals and plans for the entire organization.

Functional plans become more and more specific as they focus upon particular areas, rely upon quantitative measurement, and cover short time frames. One form of a detailed functional plan is a schedule which specifies actions for specific time periods. Another form is a budget which allocates specific sums for specific expenditures for specific time periods.

Integration of Plans: The Systems Concept

The open systems concept, explained in Chapter 2, is relevant to several aspects of planning. The various functional operating plans, for example,

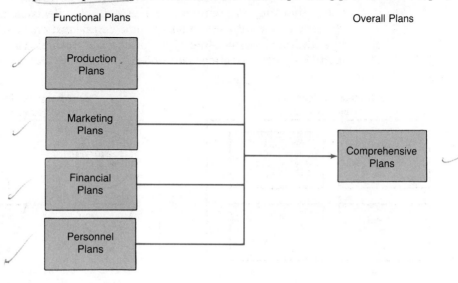

FIGURE 6–2   Functional plans and overall plans

should blend into an overall corporate plan or set of plans for a particular time period.

After functional and divisional plans are formulated, therefore, management must integrate them. This step produces a truly comprehensive plan rather than a set of contradictory plans. Each functional and divisional plan must be questioned as to its contribution to established objectives. Each must also be examined to determine its compatibility with other plans of the corporation. If each of six divisions proposes to spend $1 million and only $3 million is available, changes are imperative.

A second application of the systems concept is concerned with the relationship of operating plans—even well-integrated operating plans—to the basic objectives of the organization. The plans must "fit" the objectives, as illustrated in Figure 6–3. This may seem simple, but it does not happen automatically. Middle-level and lower-level managers sometimes follow plans that do not mesh with the "grand strategy" designed by top management.

As top-level managers attempt to implement new strategies, they often encounter difficulties with sales, engineering, or production. Functional specialists are familiar with or "locked into" other strategies and find it difficult to change.

> Advocates of bold new strategies have not recognized that they must first "uncouple" the functions from the viselike grip of past strategies *before* they can expect an appropriate response at lower organizational levels. The more that marketing, engineering, and manufacturing perfect their low-cost, efficient systems, the greater the likelihood that their operating plans will fail to discriminate among signals originating above them.[1]

Suppose, for example, that a corporation wishes to raise the quality level of the products it produces and sells or to sell custom-made products rather than standardized products. Such a decision may necessitate changes in recruitment, training, and compensation of sales personnel, in addition to many other types of change. Special effort is required to modify existing practices and policies which are well established.

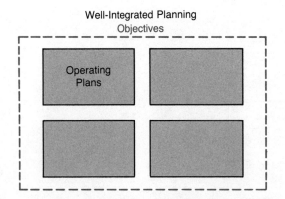
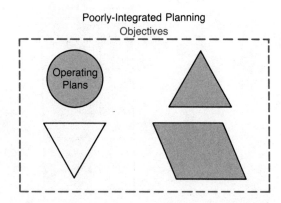

FIGURE 6–3   Degrees of integration in planning

Comprehensive planning produces an internally consistent hierarchy of plans, starting with the broad plans for the total enterprise and including the supporting specific and detailed operational plans.

The concept of *suboptimization* is pertinent to the practice of planning for the entire system. It is possible for a given department to optimize its output by reducing the efficiency of other departments or other functions. Simultaneous optimization of all departments may be impossible. The ideal combination of plans calls for optimization of company-wide operations. This often necessitates suboptimization—that is, operating at less than ideal conditions in particular departments—in order that the overall operations of the entire company might be optimized.

Time Spans in Planning

Time spans for planning may range from less than one year to more than twenty. Five-year plans are the long-range plans in most industries, but they are merely intermediate- or short-range plans in other industries. In electric and communication utilities, for example, it is often necessary to develop facilities and plans for service extending twenty or thirty years into the future, while lumber companies have reforestation plans covering a century.

The time span of planning tends to lengthen as one moves upward from lower to higher organizational levels. We do not expect credit managers, sales unit managers, machine shop managers, and other lower-level managers to develop long-range plans comparable to those for the organization as a whole. Instead, their planning is more tactical in nature and typically confined to meeting specific short-run objectives.

Figure 6–4 presents a planning model which makes a general distinction between the time frame for strategic planning and that for operational planning. A time horizon of three to fifteen years is suggested for the former and a time horizon of one to three years for the latter. The key element in determining the length of the operational planning cycle is the nature of the operating cycle. The operating cycle of a construction firm, for example, is much longer than the operating cycle of a food-processing firm.

Standing Plans

Not all plans are tied to specific calendar periods—either long-range or short-range. Organizational policies, for example, may be described as standing plans. Although policies are subject to modification over time, they have greater continuity than operating plans.

A policy might be defined as a *basic statement serving as a guide for administrative action.* By saying it is a guide, there is an implication that the policy does not usually specify detailed answers to particular problems. The manager has some degree of freedom.* As an example, a policy that says "No discrimination in hiring" does not indicate the em-

---

*In contrast, a *rule*—such as "no smoking"—permits no discretion regarding action to be taken.

FIGURE 6–4   Time frames for planning

SOURCE: John C. Camillus and John H. Grant, "Operational Planning: The Integration of Programming and Budgeting," *Academy of Management Review* 5 (July 1980): 375.

Cycle 1: Strategic Planning	
Level:	Corporate management
Focus:	Defining corporate mission, objectives in terms of rates of change in key parameters, strategies, and policies, articulating basic strategic assumptions
Horizon:	3 to 15 years (operating cycle plus redeployment time)

Cycle 2: Operational Planning	
Level:	Executive and operating management
Focus:	Defining quantitative goals in terms of financial statements, physical targets and time deadlines; generating action plans intended to achieve goals; developing contingent plans of action
Horizon:	1 to 3 years (depending on operating cycle)

ployment choice. It simply eliminates one factor as an element in the choice. It would still be desirable to analyze the ability of all candidates.

Some policies are particularly concerned with the "how" of administrative action.* By establishing an objective, as explained earlier, the organization determines its destination. Many policies are concerned with the route for reaching that destination. In other cases, objectives are given substance as they find expression in policies. Personnel objectives, for example, are abstract statements until they become embodied in policies.

Managerial Attitudes toward Planning

Growing Emphasis on Planning.   The increasing tempo of environmental change—from energy shortages to economic crises—has drawn attention to the need for anticipating developments and planning to meet them. Managers today face markets and competitive situations that are increasingly turbulent and changeable. A company and its management must "run fast" just to stay even with competition.

In striving for progress and even survival in such a fast-changing world, managers try to assess the future and to meet it as rationally as possible. Planning is a practice that becomes increasingly attractive with the growing uncertainties and perplexities in the environment. As might be expected, most large organizations engage in formal planning. A sur-

---

*A policy establishes general guidelines, in contrast to a procedure, which specifies the chronological sequence of steps or tasks.

vey of five hundred large U.S. corporations discovered that 94 percent had some type of documented long-range plans.[2] The major question is not whether to plan but how to plan most effectively.

PLANNING AS A RITUAL

In any given case, there is no guarantee that planning will improve performance. Only *good* planning can improve what would otherwise occur. And the planning must be translated into action. The possibility of bad or ineffective planning is evident in these comments of Russell L. Ackoff.

> A good deal of corporate planning I have observed is like a ritual rain dance; it has no effect on the weather that follows, but those who engage in it think it does. Moreover, it seems to me that much of the advice and instruction related to corporate planning is directed at improving the dancing, not the weather.

SOURCE: Russell L. Ackoff, *Creating the Corporate Future: Plan or Be Planned For* (New York: John Wiley and Sons, 1981), p. ix.

Historical Development of Business Planning.   Extensive business planning is a comparatively modern development. Early industrial and marketing organizations concentrated upon production and selling—upon doing rather than planning. This was partially a reflection of the size of industrial concerns. Small-scale operation permitted much planning to be done informally.

Various developments created a need for more extensive business planning. Growth in size made it difficult to operate without formalized planning. In the field of production management, the work of Frederick W. Taylor and the scientific management movement placed great stress upon detailed production planning. Periods of economic recession and the Great Depression of the 1930s in particular revealed the planning defects of marketers who were caught with shelves of high-priced inventory.

Since 1960, there has been a substantial increase in comprehensive planning. In earlier years, there was a tendency for planning to be performed on a departmental, piecemeal, fragmented basis. Planning was performed unevenly throughout the company, and the result was a collection of plans which controlled the operations of individual segments of the business but lacked overall unity. Hundreds of larger corporations have now adopted the practice of comprehensive corporate planning, regularly preparing formal long-range plans. Corporate planning staffs have also been established in numerous companies to coordinate planning at the top management level.

In the mid 1970s, some corporations extended their formal planning to include formulation of a set of alternative plans for use in situations involving much uncertainty. One of the alternative plans would presumably fit the specific situation as it unfolded. This practice, known as *contingency planning*, is discussed in a later section of this chapter.

Importance and Neglect of Planning.   Planning is necessary before any intelligent consideration can be given to building organizational relationships, directing and motivating behavior, or monitoring organizational performance. Although defective performance in any management activity is undesirable, planning errors go to the very heart of the organization. Serious mistakes or omissions in planning can hardly be offset by effective organizing or controlling.

In spite of its primacy, planning is perhaps the most easily neglected of all managerial functions. In a survey of long-range planning in multinational firms, executive respondents identified top management's preoccupation with current problems as having the greatest negative impact on planning effectiveness.[3] It is a rare manager who does not become too busy. The natural reaction is to devote time to those activities clamoring for attention.

James G. March and Herbert Simon have suggested a "Gresham's Law" of planning in which daily routine drives out planning.[4] During periods of recession, executives are frequently tempted to divert attention from managing to selling. Although direct participation in selling may be necessary, the neglect of planning is unfortunate. An example is found in the experience of Samuel B. Casey, Jr., president and chief executive officer of Pullman, who described the consequences as follows:

> "Most of my time should be spent on strategic planning," Casey notes. But with sales-related efforts now consuming 50% of his work day, twice as much as three years ago, "Planning has been pushed to the back burner," he says. "It's a tragedy."[5]

The negative effects of neglected planning are not always apparent in the short run. In fact, the organization may proceed from month to month and year to year with little outward indication of its weakness in planning. Eventually, however, management deficiencies in planning are revealed.

PLANNING PREMISES AND CONTINGENCY PLANS

Planning Premises

The planner is confronted with numerous uncertainties in the environment. Some are external to the organization and beyond the control of its management. The health of the economy represents one such factor.

Planning, of necessity, involves some consideration of these factors. What would be good planning based upon one premise becomes unwise planning if this premise proves to be wrong. Effective planning thus requires an accurate identification of the planning premises.

Classifying these as premises or assumptions does not indicate that they are accepted blindly or picked out of thin air. Premises involve predictions, and the predictions should be made as scientifically as possible. In some cases, of course, they can be little more than educated guesses.

Public Policy. Government fiscal policy has a direct impact on the economy and thus on most business concerns. The perception of planners concerning public policy trends, therefore, directly affects their plans. If public policy calls for a budget deficit, a stimulation of the economy is provided. Inflation may also be anticipated as a result of government fiscal policy, with an effect on business plans. Public monetary policy is likewise significant to business planners. The Federal Reserve Board has power through its control of interest rates, regulation of credit, and other measures to stimulate or retard business activity.

During the recession of 1982, concerns about these matters were evident as economists speculated on the speed and vigor of economic recovery. Central factors in their reasoning were the size of the budget deficit for the coming fiscal year and the policy of the Federal Reserve Board regarding the size of the money supply. The business press reported extensively on the political processes in Washington and the actions and statements of the Federal Reserve Board.

Tax legislation and changes in taxation of a more specific nature are likewise important in business planning. An expected rate of local property taxation, for example, is often one of the factors considered in choosing a business location. An investment tax credit makes investment in new facilities more attractive to many companies. Even methods of financing may be chosen on the basis of their respective tax advantages.

Economic Conditions. Planning must anticipate probable economic conditions in selecting the best course of action for the future. In fact, the planner's interest is not limited to short-run economic conditions. Long-run business prospects and the rate of economic growth for the economy and for specific industries are important to many decisions. Expansion plans involving major commitments, for example, must be based upon predictions of this type. The tremendous error of Sewell Avery of Montgomery Ward in financial and expansion policy following World War II is now a legend in the history of American business. While its competitor, Sears, Roebuck and Company, expanded, Montgomery Ward guarded its cash and waited for a depression.

Prospective economic conditions will affect production and inventory levels. The labor force and production facilities may be expanded if a period of prosperity is anticipated. A downturn calls for the opposite approach.

Financial planning similarly requires consideration of probable economic conditions. Borrowing may be reduced during a recession. Plans for working-capital loans may be needed when business recovery is imminent. New stock or bond issues must be appropriately timed to obtain a maximum price for the securities.

Other External Factors.   Among the many other external factors affecting business planning is that of *fashion trends*. The seriousness of this factor varies, obviously, from one type of business to another. Its influence often exists, however, in industries that have the appearance of immunity to fashion change. If the product being produced or sold is subject to rapid fashion obsolescence, an error in planning can be critical. The warehouse quickly may be filled with items that are no longer in style.

Competitors' plans and activities constitute another relevant factor for business planners. If a competitor succeeds in introducing an improved or a revolutionary new product, the market for conventional or unimproved items is clearly reduced. Sales promotion campaigns of one competitor may likewise take business away from other firms. By the same token, weaknesses in competition provide opportunities that may be exploited through planning.

Raw materials and labor markets are also significant in business planning. Anticipated price increases or shortages in raw materials, for example, may lead to planned stockpiling. Provisions being written into major labor contracts and general trends in personnel practices affect the expectations of personnel in most companies. Population trends and shifts to urban (or suburban) living likewise affect planning by many types of concerns.

No doubt numerous other factors having a significant effect on the planning process could be cited. These are merely suggested as some of the basic elements requiring attention by most concerns.

Contingency Planning

Difficulty in predicting future environmental conditions has led some companies to a practice known as *contingency planning*. To some extent, of course, planners have always experienced uncertainty, but the problem became increasingly serious during the 1970s. Planners found it incredibly difficult to formulate dependable assumptions. Unforeseen changes riddled their basic assumptions, and their plans became obsolete. Some management groups attempted to escape the dilemma by developing contingency plans—a set of plans for each of several circumstances. This process is portrayed graphically in Figure 6–5.

Planners develop *multiple scenarios* as they formulate a series of assumptions about the future. One scenario, for example, may specify

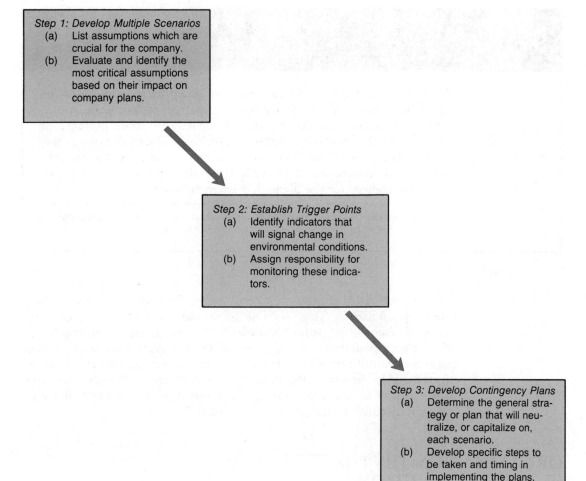

FIGURE 6–5   A contingency planning model

the economic conditions thought most likely to occur. Alternative scenarios might use a more optimistic assumption and a more pessimistic assumption. The use of multiple scenarios is not limited to assumptions about economic fluctuations, however. They may express differing assumptions about weather, political elections, environmental regulation, shortages of raw materials, strikes, and so on.

Plans must be prepared to cover the various conditions specified in the multiple scenarios. Although the term *contingency plans* suggests a complete set of plans "on the shelf" for use as needed, they are often developed somewhat informally. The contingency plans may be general statements of action to be taken without completely specifying the intended operational plan. Contingency plans that are properly developed specify *trigger points*—events that call for implementation of particular contingency plans.

**POSTAGE RATE
SCENARIOS**

"Scenarios for rather specialized subjects generally are developed because they have a direct bearing on a company's performance. A publishing corporation that spends $20 million a year on postage, for example, draws up several postage scenarios. The cost of postage for subscriptions is a critical factor in the profits of its magazine companies, and the realization of an unlikely possibility may present serious consequences for the plans that are developed."

SOURCE: Rochelle O'Connor, *Planning under Uncertainty: Multiple Scenarios and Contingency Planning* (New York: The Conference Board, 1978), p. 7.

One benefit of contingency planning is the broader outlook it provides for managers. They become more sensitive to various external forces. Probably the greatest drawback to contingency planning is the heavier administrative burden imposed on managers who must prepare not one but multiple sets of plans. If the firm's environment is extremely unpredictable, however, the benefits may well justify the cost. Because of the greater administrative load, the customary practice is to develop the various contingency plans in less detail.

ORGANIZATION OF THE PLANNING FUNCTION

All Management Personnel

Who should do the planning in an organization? Clearly, all management personnel must accept some planning responsibility. As a basic management function, planning is an inherent part of each manager's duties.

A distinction may be made, however, as to the relative amounts of planning to be performed by line managers in contrast to that performed by staff offices. By drawing upon the experience of operating management, top management achieves greater practicality in business plans. Operating managers know that at least some proposals will or will not work satisfactorily. Broad management participation is also necessary for genuine acceptance of adopted plans. Otherwise, a line manager is inclined to blame the plan if difficulty is experienced or to ignore it as much as possible.

EMERSON ELECTRIC'S CONTINGENCY PLANS

The Emerson Electric Company's budgeting system can be adapted to three different levels of sales volume.

> For each product, no matter how small, divisional management must come up with a five-year projection of sales and earnings. Once the projection is agreed upon by corporate and division chiefs, it is termed Budget A. Budget B is a contingency plan allowing for a 10% drop in projected sales, but it demands the same operating profit as Budget A. If sales drop 20%, Budget C goes into effect, but management is still committed to some profit.

SOURCE: "Emerson Electric's Rise as a Low-Cost Producer," *Business Week,* 1 November 1976, p. 47.

The need for broad management participation exists in public as well as private organizations. Agency heads and their top staff, because of the political nature of their positions, often have less longevity than middle- and lower-level managers.

> If career employees do not view the plan as realistic, it can be vitiated over time. This underscores the importance of involving career employees in the planning process.[6]

Top-management leadership is also essential if effective comprehensive planning is to be achieved. To be sure, organizational leaders cannot become involved in the detailed studies necessary in preparing forecasts and drawing up operating plans. Their concern and interest in such planning must be evident, however. Otherwise, plans are merely documents to prepare and file away before "getting back to work."

The Planning Staff

Many corporations, government agencies, and other organizations have established planning offices—called "planning coordinators," "directors of planning," and so on—to provide leadership in planning. For such staff offices, planning is not an activity that must be squeezed into an already busy operating schedule. As a result they can make more thorough investigations and analyses in devising, analyzing, and coordinating plans. Nevertheless, the direct involvement of line managers, including the chief executive, is essential for successful planning.

Work of the planning staff supplements, rather than replaces, planning by other managers. The major role of the planning staff is overall coordination of the total planning effort. This means that the planner gives line managers various types of assistance in planning. The planner, for example, may provide factual data—economic forecasts, projections of market demand, results of market research, information concerning competitive threats, and proposals for new ventures. The planner also reviews plans, notes omissions, questions premises, and proposes changes. Although planners act as initiators, educators, researchers, consultants, and reviewers, their primary role is that of coordinator of the entire planning program. The planner, as orchestrator of the entire planning process, typically arranges and schedules all planning cycle meetings. The agenda for one such planning conference is shown in Figure 6–6. In this meeting, the division chief must review strategic and operating plans for the division.

Contributions of Subordinates to Planning

Traditionally, we have viewed managers as the complete planners for their parts of the organization. Information was funneled to them, but they did the planning. According to the concepts of delegation and decentralization, however, planning should be pushed downward in the

INSUFFICIENT PLANNING AT LOWER LEVELS

Both chief executives and lower-level managers must take part in corporate planning in order to achieve a well-balanced set of corporate plans. Texas Instruments, one of the world's largest semiconductor companies, was striving in the early 1980s to improve planning at lower levels. Its problem was reflected in the critical comment of a former manager, "The corporate fathers don't have confidence in their people."

Even though TI used a noted Objectives-Strategies-Tactics planning system, lower-level managers apparently failed to contribute adequately to overall plans.

> The problem, Bucy [President J. Fred Bucy] feels, is that the planning system had "drifted out of alignment" with the operating system. Now TI is trying to make sure that operating managers get planning tasks that fall within the sphere of their immediate businesses.

SOURCE: Bro Uttal, "Texas Instruments Regroups," *Fortune* 106 (August 9, 1982): 40–45. © 1982 Time Inc.

FIGURE 6–6   Agenda for operating division plans presentation in a food products company
SOURCE: Rochelle O'Connor, *Company Planning Meetings* (New York: The Conference Board, 1980), p. 24.

A. [Division] Performance (20 Minutes)
  1. Year-to-date performance—12 month [Division] outlook.
  2. Identify major [Division] objectives:
    a. Objectives accomplished.
    b. Objectives *not* accomplished.
    c. Reason why/why not.
    d. Impact on [Division].

B. Division Strategic and Three-Year Plans (10 Minutes)
  1. Highlight *major* objectives and strategies of division strategic and three-year plans. (Brief, telegraphic review of key objectives and strategies—to provide linkage with [Division] annual plan.)

C. [Division] Annual Plan (1 Hour 45 Minutes)
  1. Basic assumptions used in development of the [Division] plan, and key issues having an impact on the [Division] plan.
  2. [Division] Annual Plan: Major programs and strategies in support of the plan—identifying linkage to strategic and three-year plans.
  3. Summary: [Division] objectives, net sales and operating income. (Net sales and operating income for [Division] against strategic and three-year plans projections—reasons and rationale for differences.)
  4. Identify those quantitative measures of performance, with supporting objectives, to be used by the division in evaluating performance—and manner in which measures will be tracked through the year (presented in a format which can be utilized in quarterly and operational reviews).

D. Break (15 Minutes)

E. Questions and Discussion (1 Hour)

F. Corporate Planning Committee Discussion (30 Minutes)

G. Closing Remarks (30 Minutes)

Total Time: 4 Hours 30 Minutes

---

organization. Specific plans should be formulated by the divisions and departments responsible for carrying out the work, within the framework of overall objectives and policies.

Involvement of line managers in planning requires careful formulation of the planning process to provide for their inputs. Unless the process is structured properly, the pressure of other work or other factors may cause the process to break down. Planning may even come to have such status implications that lower-level managers are excluded.

In a holding company headquartered in France with sales in the vicinity of three billion francs and multinational industrial operations, it turned out that the top managers of the main subsidiaries had never discussed with their own managers the formal plans they were preparing for the headquarters. For them, knowing about the formal plan content was a symbol of their involvement with the strategic issues of the corporation. As a consequence, they did not feel that their immediate subordinate line managers ought to be informed.[7]

If managers wish to draw extensively upon the thinking of subordinates in planning, they may arrange special ways to encourage such contributions. Subordinates may be asked to submit proposals or suggestions or to criticize tentative plans that have been drafted. They may also be appointed to serve on planning committees that work out plans for the entire organization.

SUMMARY

Planning consists of the activities involved in choosing courses of action to achieve organizational objectives. In keeping with the open systems concept, functional plans must be formulated and integrated to fit the overall strategy and objectives of the organization. Both long-range and short-range plans are necessary, and some types of plans such as policies are regarded as standing plans because of their continuing nature. In spite of the importance and growing emphasis in the use of planning, management pressures frequently lead to its neglect.

In planning, it is necessary for management to adopt certain assumptions or *premises*—particularly with regard to external factors—that serve as a background for the planning function. One major premise of this type involves *public policy* and the relationship of government to business. Prospective *economic conditions, fashion trends, competitive developments,* and *population trends* must also be considered in any attempt at intelligent planning.

Because of the growing difficulty of predicting future environmental conditions, some companies have adopted the practice of *contingency planning.* They develop *multiple scenarios* of the future and formulate a set of strategies and plans for each scenario.

Planning is a part of the activities of all management personnel. Some use is made of staff planners, however, who have the advantage of being able to devote their full attention to the analysis of business problems and the preparation of specific plans. Managers differ in the degree to which they use the thinking of subordinates in planning for the future of their organizations.

DISCUSSION QUESTIONS

1. "A good decision maker is also a good planner." Evaluate this statement.
2. Explain the relationship of the open systems concept to planning.
3. What determines the length of the future time period that should be covered by business planning?
4. In view of the uncertainties confronting most business organizations, how can you justify attempts at long-range planning?
5. Why is there a growing emphasis on planning?
6. Explain the concept of the greater importance of planning as compared with other managerial functions.
7. What is meant by *contingency planning*?
8. What are *multiple scenarios*? Why are they used?
9. Compare the effectiveness of planning performed by a staff office in contrast to that performed by line managers.

NOTES

1. John M. Hobbs and Donald F. Heany, "Coupling Strategy to Operating Plans," *Harvard Business Review* 55 (May–June 1977): 119–20.
2. James S. Ang and Jess H. Chua, "Long Range Planning in Large United States Corporations—A Survey," *Long Range Planning* 12 (April 1979): 99.
3. George A. Steiner and Hans Schöllhammer, "Pitfalls in Multi-National Long-Range Planning," *Long Range Planning* 8 (April 1975): 8.
4. James G. March and Herbert A. Simon, *Organizations* (New York: John Wiley & Sons, 1958), p. 185.
5. "Executive Suite Salesmanship," *Business Week*, 20 October 1975, p. 70.
6. Michael H. Moskow, *Strategic Planning in Business and Government* (New York: Committee for Economic Development, 1978), p. 44.
7. Xavier Gilbert and Peter Lorange, "Five Pillars for Your Planning," *European Business*, no. 42 (Autumn 1974): 62.

SUPPLEMENTARY READING

Allio, **Robert J.**, and **Pennington, Malcolm W.**, eds. *Corporate Planning: Techniques and Applications*. New York: American Management Association, 1979.

Banks, **Robert L.**, and **Wheelwright, Steven C.** "Operations vs. Strategy: Trading Tomorrow for Today." *Harvard Business Review* 57 (May–June 1979): 112–20.

Camillus, John C., and **Grant, John H.** "Operational Planning: The Integration of Programming and Budgeting." *Academy of Management Review* 5 (July 1980): 369–79.

Ellis, Darryl J., and **Pekar, Peter P., Jr.** *Planning for Nonplanners: Planning Basics for Managers.* New York: American Management Association, 1980.

Henry, Harold W. "Formal Planning in Major U.S. Corporations." *Long Range Planning* 10 (October 1977): 40–45.

Hobbs, John M., and **Heany, Donald F.** "Coupling Strategy to Operating Plans." *Harvard Business Review* 55 (May–June 1977): 119–26.

Hussey, D. E. *Introducing Corporate Planning.* 2d ed. New York: Pergamon Press, 1979.

Hussey, D.E., and **Langham, M.J.** *Corporate Planning: The Human Factor.* New York: Pergamon Press, 1979.

Jackson, John H., and **Adams, Susan W.** "The Life Cycle of Rules." *Academy of Management Review* 4 (April 1979): 269–73.

Kahalas, Harvey. "A Look at Planning and Its Arguments." *Managerial Planning* 30 (January–February 1982): 13–16.

Knisely, Gary, and **Matling, Stuart M.** "Profile of a Corporate Planner." *Planning Review* 8 (January 1980): 21–23.

Linneman, Robert E. *Shirt-Sleeve Approach to Long-Range Planning for the Smaller, Growing Corporation.* Englewood Cliffs, N.J.: Prentice-Hall, 1980.

Linneman, Robert E., and **Chandran, Rajan.** "Contingency Planning: A Key to Swift Managerial Action in the Uncertain Tomorrow." *Managerial Planning* 29 (January–February 1981): 23–27.

Mintzberg, Henry. "What Is Planning Anyway?" *Strategic Management Journal* 2 (July–September 1981): 319–24.

O'Connor, Rochelle. *Planning under Uncertainty: Multiple Scenarios and Contingency Planning.* New York: The Conference Board, 1978.

————. *The Corporate Planning Department: Responsibilities and Staffing.* New York: The Conference Board, 1981.

Reeser, Clayton. "Tactical Planning." *Managerial Planning* 30 (November–December 1981): 10–13.

Summers, Irvin, and **White, David E.** "Creativity Techniques: Toward Improvement of the Decision Process." *Academy of Management Review* 1 (April 1976): 99–107.

7

PLANNING TOOLS AND TECHNIQUES

This chapter will enable you to

- *Describe some of the planning tools and techniques available to managers.*
- *Explain management by objectives and point out its strengths and weaknesses.*
- *Identify some of the forecasting and budgeting techniques used by managers.*
- *Discuss how scheduling and coordinating activities are facilitated through network planning techniques.*
- *Demonstrate the applicability of break-even analysis to the planning process.*

Because planning is so essential to organizational effectiveness, a number of tools and techniques have been developed to make it more systematic. This chapter examines some of these aids to good planning—management by objectives, forecasting and budgeting procedures, network planning techniques, and break-even analysis. Although each is used under separate circumstances and for different purposes, the tools and techniques discussed in this chapter help the manager plan in a more systematic fashion. An orderly system of planning decreases the likelihood that the manager will neglect to plan or will set it aside indefinitely to deal with current operating problems.

MANAGEMENT BY OBJECTIVES

Management by objectives (MBO) is perhaps the most widely discussed planning technique in use today. Formulated in 1954 by Drucker, MBO is currently used in a wide variety of organizations—profit and non-profit, large and small.[1] Although its primary application is in planning, MBO concepts are also useful in motivation, management development, control, and performance appraisal. Some of these uses will be discussed later in the appropriate chapters.

The MBO Process

MBO is a planning technique which involves employees at lower levels in the organization in the process of goal setting. This approach is in sharp contrast to the more traditional approach in which the superior unilaterally establishes goals for his or her subordinates. The MBO process itself is comprised of the three basic steps illustrated in Figure 7–1.

Step 1. MBO begins with a meeting between the manager and subordinate in which the two discuss individual objectives for the subordinate. These objectives should be commensurate with the larger goals of the organization and the unit in which the subordinate works. Such meetings occur throughout the organization between all superiors and subordinates. The objectives which are discussed should be those which not only benefit the organization but also contribute to the professional development of the subordinate.

The systems approach indicates that individual goals must be set within the framework of unit and organizational goals since one manager's objectives may affect other individuals and units. Some theorists have carried this approach a step further by suggesting that the manager and subordinates act as a team in setting, first, group objectives and then individual objectives to increase cooperation and helping behavior within the unit.[2]

Step 2. In the second step, the manager and subordinate jointly establish specific objectives for the subordinate. These objectives may be six-month goals, yearly goals, or tied to the completion of a major project. Whatever the time frame, MBO focuses on defining desired end results; it does not simply describe job activities as does a formal job description. In some organizations, however, formal "action plans" are developed to guide subordinates in attaining their goals.

The objectives must be clearly stated and should be neither too difficult nor too easy to attain. Unreachable goals may cause the subordi-

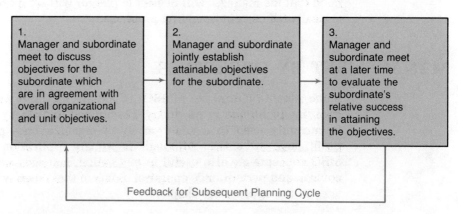

FIGURE 7–1   The MBO process

nate to give up in despair, while easy goals do not provide sufficient motivation or feelings of accomplishment once they have been reached. Each objective is usually assigned a weight—or priority—since the attainment of some goals may be more critical than others.

Each objective must be *verifiable*. That is, the manager and subordinate must be able to answer the question: "Has this goal been attained?" Hence, goals must be specified in exact terms. For instance, it would be inappropriate for a sales manager to set a goal of "increasing sales over the next six months." Instead, the manager might establish an objective of "increasing sales over the next six months by 8 percent while maintaining an average profit margin of 10 percent on all sales."

It is important that the goals be established jointly by the manager and subordinate. Goals dictated by the manager will not have full subordinate acceptance or commitment, and goals established without the manager's participation may be inappropriate to the unit. Also, nonparticipation by the superior may cause the subordinate to feel that the manager has little interest in the subordinate's development or in MBO in general.[3]

Step 3. If the mutually established objectives are clearly defined, verifiable, and reasonably attainable, the manager and subordinate should experience little difficulty in evaluating the subordinate's success in attaining the goals. The evaluation session should be constructive—not a forum for placing blame or finding fault. The emphasis should be on self-direction and self-control. The latter part of the session should be devoted to establishing goals for the next period.

Although established goals should not be changed without careful consideration, unforeseen environmental conditions can make some goals less realistic than they appeared earlier. In such cases, the goals should be modified by the manager and subordinate prior to the evaluation session. The evaluation must be based on the attainment of realistic goals.

Benefits of MBO

Our knowledge of the relative effectiveness of MBO is quite limited. Although most experts believe that full implementation of an MBO program requires two to five years, the longest experimental study to date lasted only three years.[4] A review of 185 studies of MBO concludes that those studies which used the least sophisticated research methods were the most likely to show that MBO was effective. More rigorous research studies were less likely to arrive at that conclusion.[5]

Advocates of MBO claim, however, that a properly designed and implemented program should yield a number of benefits. Perhaps the most important is that each manager in the organization is required to plan for the future in some detail. Through this process, individual plans are merged with unit and organization plans to yield a consistent and comprehensive plan for the organization, each unit, and each manager.

Another major benefit is the subordinate's stronger commitment to his or her job goals as a result of participation in setting the goals. This commitment, in turn, should lead to increased job satisfaction and, perhaps, superior performance since the individual knows exactly what is expected and in what direction to channel his or her activities. Job ambiguity, and perhaps even stress are, therefore, reduced.[6] Finally, communication between the manager and subordinate should be improved, and performance evaluation and control are facilitated by being conducted on a rational, objective basis.

Problems with MBO

Research has pinpointed a number of problems that arise in MBO programs.[7] A major complaint of managers, for instance, is that MBO increases the amount of paperwork required of them—to report progress toward goal attainment—and consumes considerable time in the counseling of subordinates. MBO may also be used as a "whip" to compel performance, and heavy emphasis may be placed on quantitative goals at the expense of equally important qualitative goals. In some cases, MBO has failed to provide adequate incentives to improve performance, and, in one study, the positive effects of MBO diminished over time in the absence of a program designed to "reinforce" the importance of MBO to the participants.

A major weakness in MBO may be found in its implementation. In some firms, for example, superiors simply assign goals to subordinates. Nonattainment of goals may be punished, so that MBO becomes "negative motivation"; that is, "either attain your goals or else." Or, superiors may not take the program seriously, and attainment of goals may not be properly rewarded. If all employees, regardless of performance, receive virtually the same percentage salary increase, they will perceive little relationship between goal attainment and rewards.[8]

Factors Essential to MBO Success

Perhaps the most crucial factor to the success of MBO is the wholehearted support of top management. Lower-level managers are unlikely to pay much attention to a program to which top executives give only lip service. Management can best demonstrate its support for MBO by introducing the program in a highly visible manner. The introduction should consist of a clear statement of the purposes of MBO, followed by detailed orientation and training in MBO concepts, including a workshop in which employees learn how to set moderately difficult, verifiable job goals. Top management can also reinforce the importance of the program periodically through group meetings, written support, refresher courses, and so on.

Another requirement is that the goals be acceptable to both superiors and subordinates. Goals must not be dictated. Goal setting and attainment should involve as little paperwork as practicable. And goal attainment must be rewarded. High performance which goes unrewarded is less likely to be repeated in the future.

MBO AT ALLIED

Allied Corporation uses a form of MBO for its managerial employees. As an example of "very demanding but obtainable objectives," the president of Allied Chemical Company, a division of Allied Corporation, had the following goals to meet by 1986:

1. Shift the current product mix away from a heavy emphasis on capital-intensive, cyclical commodity chemicals so that at least 25 percent of pretax income comes from specialty chemicals.
2. Top the industry average for 1986 in both profit growth and market share.
3. Make at least one significant acquisition.

SOURCE: Based on "The Hennessy Style May Be What Allied Needs," *Business Week*, 11 January 1982, p. 127.

FORECASTING AND BUDGETING

The *budget* is probably the most universal planning tool in existence today. As a plan of operation expressed in financial terms, the budget allocates resources in a manner intended to help the organization attain its objectives. Before this financial plan can be developed, however, a forecast of revenue is essential. Until the manager estimates how much money will be available to the organization, most expenditures cannot be planned.

Forecasting Techniques

Profit and nonprofit organizations alike must forecast the flow of incoming funds. This estimate, usually called the sales forecast in a business organization, can be developed through a number of different techniques.

Surveys. Surveys are used by some organizations to determine the demand for their product or service during an upcoming fiscal period. Using statistical sampling techniques, forecasters interview present and potential customers or clients over the telephone, in person, or through mailed questionnaires to determine their buying plans. This technique is useful in forecasting demand for consumer durable goods, such as automobiles or major appliances, or industrial goods, such as heavy equipment or machinery. In both cases, the buyer usually plans the purchase well in advance, because of its expense, and can estimate the probability of purchase with some accuracy. Some organizations conduct such surveys with their own personnel, while others hire research firms or use the results of national surveys such as those conducted by the Survey Research Center of the University of Michigan.

Sales Force Forecast. Using another technique, some organizations combine the forecasts of their sales representatives into an overall demand forecast. Management assumes that sales representatives should be able to predict future customer purchases since they maintain close contact with customers. Sales representatives, however, may not be fully informed of the organization's upcoming sales promotion and advertising plans or of environmental developments that might affect future sales. Also, if the organization uses forecasts to establish sales quotas, the submitted forecasts may be too low. Most firms which use this technique, therefore, adjust each individual forecast to reflect predicted environmental developments and past forecasting error on the sales representative's part before combining the adjusted forecasts.

Statistical Demand Analysis. Statistical techniques may be used to forecast future sales from past sales data. In one version of this technique, actual sales figures for the past several years are statistically related to "predictor variables" such as product price, advertising expenditures, and per capita disposable income in the sales area for those years. Using the analytical tool of multiple regression, the forecaster can derive an equation which will predict sales for the upcoming year using estimates of next year's product price, advertising expenditures, per capita income, and so on. The validity of this approach, of course, depends upon the similarity between past trends and future conditions. Any significant departure from historical trends will weaken the forecast dramatically.

Unfortunately, departures from historical trends seem to be occurring with increasing frequency. Because such departures are difficult to predict, one review of the evidence concludes that forecasts of two years or longer are "notoriously inaccurate."[9]

> Planning activities must accept the inaccuracy inherent in long-term forecasts. Even in the early seventies, for example, how many imagined the possibility of an oil embargo, a quadrupling of oil prices, severe shortage of raw materials, stagflation, high unemployment together with high inflation and interest rates, a near collapse of the stock market and two recessions in a period of less than five years?[10]

These techniques demonstrate some of the varied approaches available to forecasters. Use of more than one technique is recommended since a forecast based on two or more techniques has greater validity than one based on only a single estimate. Once the revenue forecast is developed, the organization can begin the budgeting process.

Budgeting Procedures

The revenue forecast is used to budget expenditures in such areas as production, direct labor, purchasing, and marketing. This process of planning future expenditures is essential to organizational goal attainment.

Most organizations use their fiscal year as the time period for budgeting. It is common practice to prepare the budget during the quarter preceding the start of the fiscal year, with final adoption just prior to the beginning of the new year. Before the beginning of each quarter, the budget for that quarter is often prepared in greater detail. During the year, the budget tends to become outdated because of changing conditions. For this reason, it is common practice to revise the budget periodically during the budgetary period. This technique, illustrated in Figure 7–2, is called a *rolling, or moving, budget*. Budgeting, in this sense, is a continuous process rather than a yearly event.

Some organizations use *variable*, rather than *static*, budgets. While static budgets are based on a specific forecasted level of sales, variable budgets attempt to match planned expenditures to varying revenue lev-

	Time Period			
	Quarter 1	Quarter 2	Quarter 3	Quarter 4
Activities	Final revision of Qtr. 3 budget	Final revision of Qtr. 4 budget	Final revision of Qtr. 1 budget	Final revision of Qtr. 2 budget.
	First revision of Qtr. 4 budget	First revision of Qtr. 1 budget	First revision of Qtr. 2 budget.	First revision of Qtr. 3 budget.
	Initial preparation of Qtr. 1 budget for next year.	Initial preparation of Qtr. 2 budget for next year.	Initial preparation of Qtr. 3 budget for next year.	Initial preparation of Qtr. 4 budget for next year.

FIGURE 7–2   Budgeting as a continuous process

els. For example, a lower-than-forecasted sales level is matched by a reduced budget and vice versa. When sales fluctuate considerably, variable budgets help the manager plan expenditures more accurately.

WHAT SHOULD FORECASTS INCLUDE?

Managerial forecasting has traditionally focused on financial and economic factors. In recent years, however, many managers have begun to realize that emphasizing these factors while ignoring social and political trends can be quite costly.

> General Motors Corp. and other auto makers paid dearly for failing to recognize early enough that Ralph Nader's objection to the Corvair model was a forerunner of a broad-based consumer movement for safer products and tougher liability standards. Similarly, by ignoring early warnings from environmentalists, hundreds of manufacturers were forced to retrofit plants with pollution-control gear that could have been incorporated more cheaply in the original plant design. More recently, Nestlé Co. faced a worldwide boycott of its products after it seemingly ignored the public outcry against its marketing of infant formula in underdeveloped countries where it was a far too expensive substitute for mother's milk.

Many firms now attempt to forecast major social and political changes and incorporate these predictions into their strategic and operating plans.

SOURCE: Based on "Capitalizing on Social Change," *Business Week*, 29 October 1979, p. 105.

Zero-base budgeting, first used by Texas Instruments in 1969[11] and later popularized by the Carter Administration, differs from the traditional *incremental budgeting process*. Incremental budgets are constructed on the foundation of past budgets; the costs and benefits of *new* activities are analyzed; and those activities with net benefits are added to the budget as are other increases required by inflation and other factors. Zero-base budgeting, on the other hand, begins with a "clean slate" each fiscal period. The cost and benefit of *all* activities—new and old—are examined,* and the activities are then ranked in terms of overall importance to the organization. The activities above a certain cut-off point are approved for the coming year.[12] In this manner, every dollar

---

*Zero-base budgeting is applicable to operations over which management has some discretion. In business organizations, such operations would include marketing, research, engineering, capital expenditures, and so on. Not included would be such areas as direct labor and direct materials; such costs are budgeted through standard costing procedures.

budgeted is justified in terms of attaining organizational goals, and major reallocations of resources can be made on a yearly basis. Planning is flexible rather than being "locked into" past activities and decisions.[13]

The results of a two-year experiment in three university computing centers give some indication that the center which used zero-base budgeting and integrated it into its planning process gave higher quality user service than did the two centers using incremental budgeting.[14] In any case, some scholars are beginning to recommend that organizations use both zero-base and incremental budgeting processes simultaneously for different subsystems in the organization. The former is recommended because of its ability to deal with a changing environment. The latter, on the other hand, is useful because it serves as one of the prime stabilizing processes in organizations.[15]

NETWORK PLANNING TECHNIQUES

Once the strategic and operating goals are set, whether through MBO or other processes, and budgetary resources are allocated, the manager may be able to use various *scheduling and network planning techniques* to make operational plans more precise. These techniques usually focus on the scheduling and coordinating of activities within a department, division, or a large project. Although they were originally designed for specific uses, experience has demonstrated their widespread applicability in diverse settings.

Scheduling Charts

The predecessor of present network techniques is the *Gantt Chart*, developed by Henry L. Gantt, one of the pioneers in scientific management. Originally devised to help in scheduling and controlling the work of particular machines, as shown in Figure 7–3, similar scheduling aids are used routinely today in a variety of organizational settings.

In Figure 7–3, the light lines and the job numbers above them show the jobs that have been scheduled for the current week. The production manager has had to plan which machines will be used for certain jobs at specific times. The heavy lines show the proportions of jobs completed, and the "V" at the top of the chart indicates the present date. In examining this chart, we can see that work on Machine A is running well ahead of schedule while work on Machine C has fallen behind. Hence, the chart also serves as a useful control tool.

With minor modifications, similar charts might be used to schedule sales representatives' calls on customers or the working hours and vacation times of employees in a department. A chart of this general type is provided to students at registration time at many universities. Students enter the courses they wish to take and schedule their outside work and social commitments by blocking out certain hours on various days to arrive at a schedule with no time conflicts.

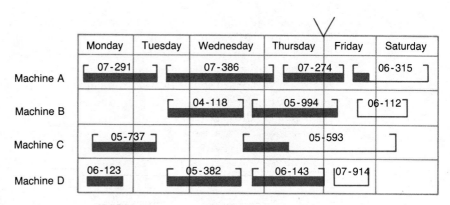

FIGURE 7-3   Gantt Chart
SOURCE: Robert H. Bock and William K. Holstein, *Production Planning and Control: Text and Readings* (Columbus, Ohio: Charles E. Merrill Publishing Co., 1963), p. 8.

Gantt and similar scheduling charts, however, were not designed for planning more complex projects comprised of a number of interrelated activities. To aid planners of these projects, a more sophisticated network technique—*Program Evaluation Review Technique* (PERT)—was devised.

Program Evaluation Review Technique

An elaboration of the scheduling concept discussed above, PERT was developed in 1958 as a system for planning and monitoring the development of the Polaris Ballistic Missile to be carried on nuclear submarines. The technique, widely credited with saving years of time in making the Polaris operational, was developed by the U.S. Navy in collaboration with Booz, Allen, and Hamilton—a management consulting firm—and Lockheed Aircraft Corporation. The focus of PERT is the scheduling and coordinating of the sequence and timing of activities within complex, nonroutine projects.*

The first step in using PERT is to construct the network of activities which must be completed for the project as a whole to be finished. The network shows what activities must await completion of other tasks and what activities can be performed concurrently with other tasks. In short, PERT represents an application of the systems concept to managerial planning.

The PERT network in Figure 7–4 shows in highly simplified form the basic steps that would be followed by a firm in marketing a new product. (The illustration assumes that the preliminary design work has

---

*PERT is similar to the Critical Path Method (CPM) devised by the Du Pont Company. The primary difference between the two techniques is that PERT was designed for planning and controlling new, nonroutine activities with which the planners had little previous experience. CPM, however, was intended for projects with which the planners did have prior experience. As a result, the time estimates for activities in PERT are probabilistic, while those in CPM are more exact. Our discussion will stress features that are common to both techniques.

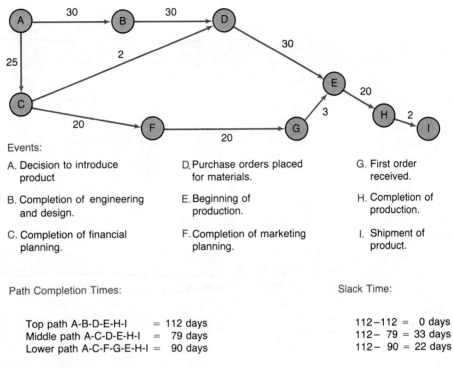

Events:

A. Decision to introduce product

B. Completion of engineering and design.

C. Completion of financial planning.

D. Purchase orders placed for materials.

E. Beginning of production.

F. Completion of marketing planning.

G. First order received.

H. Completion of production.

I. Shipment of product.

Path Completion Times:

Top path A-B-D-E-H-I = 112 days
Middle path A-C-D-E-H-I = 79 days
Lower path A-C-F-G-E-H-I = 90 days

Slack Time:

112−112 = 0 days
112− 79 = 33 days
112− 90 = 22 days

FIGURE 7–4 Simplified PERT Network to introduce new product

been completed and that a well-organized plant and distribution setup are available.) Activities, represented by arrows on the network diagram, are the tasks or operations that must be performed. The circles denote events, which mark the beginning or end of activities. Numbers on the arrows show the number of days estimated for each activity. These estimates are provided by the organizational departments which will be involved in the various activities. Note that the length of the arrows is not proportional to their time duration.

Proceeding from left to right, examination of the network reveals the total time it will take to complete the project. For example, the lower path requires 90 days for completion, the middle path will take 79 days, and the top path will require 112 days. The time required to complete the entire project is determined by the longest path. Although the middle path requires a time of only 79 days, it cannot be completed until activity B⟶D has first been finished. Even though the middle path can reach event D in only 27 days, the sequence of activities on the top path requires 60 days before event D is reached. Likewise, while the lower path can reach event E in 68 days, further work cannot proceed until sequence A⟶B⟶D⟶E is completed, which takes 90 days. Hence, the top path, requiring 112 days, constrains or prevents the earlier completion of the other two shorter paths. The top path, therefore, is termed the *critical path*. Any delay in this path will delay completion of the project. The other two paths have *slack* time, and it may be possible to divert personnel or other resources from these paths in order to speed up work on the critical path.

In actual practice, of course, the network would be infinitely more complex, requiring the use of a computer. Periodically, managers in charge of each activity would report on their progress, and the network would be recalculated to determine if the critical path had been altered.

PERT has several advantages. It requires the manager to take a systems view in planning all of the activities required for completion of a major project, and it helps the individuals involved to think in terms of the entire project, the task relationships, and their roles in the mission. Identification of the critical path allows the manager to shorten project completion time by adding resources—personnel, equipment, or overtime—to this path to decrease the time required to perform critical activities.

Because of its advantages, PERT is used extensively in planning construction projects, installing computer systems, manufacturing a variety of products, and establishing marketing and advertising campaigns for new products. One of the major users of PERT is the National Aeronautics and Space Administration (NASA) which has employed PERT to plan and coordinate such overwhelmingly complex projects as sending men to the moon and making the space shuttle operational. PERT, however, is not confined to large projects; its advantages in planning smaller undertakings are becoming increasingly evident. Many organizations place considerable value on this systematic, logical planning technique.

BREAK-EVEN ANALYSIS

Break-even analysis is a useful tool for managers who are planning to add new product or service lines to their current offerings or for potential entrepreneurs who plan to open their own businesses. This tool helps the manager determine what level of operations is required to break even, that is, to reach the point at which total revenue equals total cost.

Cost and Revenue Concepts

A knowledge of the following cost and revenue concepts is essential to the understanding of break-even analysis.

Fixed costs:	Costs that remain the same over the short run regardless of the organization's level of operations. Examples include property taxes, fire insurance premiums, and interest payments on debts.
Variable costs:	Costs that vary with the level of operations. Raw materials costs, sales commissions, and direct labor costs are examples.

Total cost:	Fixed costs plus variable costs.
Total revenue:	Total sales dollars, determined by multiplying product (or service) price by the quantity forecasted to be sold.
Break-even point:	Level of operations at which total revenue equals total cost.

Application of the Concepts

A simple example will demonstrate the usefulness of break-even analysis. Assume that you are considering opening a small "submarine sandwich" shop in a large office building currently under construction. Several hundred people will be working in the building once it opens, and many will no doubt be rushed for lunch and would like the idea of buying a sandwich without having to leave the building. After some investigation, you determine that fixed costs, such as space rental, salaries, and insurance, will be approximately $3,000 per month. The going price for submarine sandwiches is $3, and you estimate the cost of making the sandwich to be about $2. You plan to have the shop open for business five days a week from 10:00 A.M. to 4:00 P.M. How many sandwiches must be sold per month to break even?

The graphical analysis in Figure 7–5 demonstrates the relationships among the concepts defined above and reveals the break-even point.* Note that fixed costs are $3,000 no matter how many sandwiches are sold, while variable costs increase with the number of sandwiches sold. Hence, if there are no sales, total cost will be $3,000. If as many as 6,600 sandwiches are sold, total cost is $16,200 ($3,000 fixed costs plus $13,200 variable costs—that is, 6,600 sandwiches @ $2). Total cost for any level of monthly sales may be determined from the graph.

Total revenue ranges from zero at no sales to $19,800 at capacity (6,600 @ $3). The total revenue line intersects the total cost line at sale of 3,000 sandwiches. Sale of 3,000 sandwiches, then, will bring in just enough revenue to cover total cost; this is the break-even point. Monthly sale of less than 3,000 sandwiches will result in a loss since the total cost line is above the total revenue line, and sale of more than 3,000 sandwiches will result in a profit.†

This information must now be matched with a forecast of demand for the product to determine if sales of 3,000 per month are realistic.

---

*The monthly capacity of 6,600 sandwiches is based on selling a maximum of 50 per hour for six hours for twenty-two days per month.

†The same results can be determined by a simple formula:

$$\text{Break-even point in units} = \frac{\text{Fixed costs}}{\text{Unit price} - \text{Variable costs}}$$

This translates into

$$\frac{\$3,000}{\$3 - \$2} = 3,000 \text{ units}$$

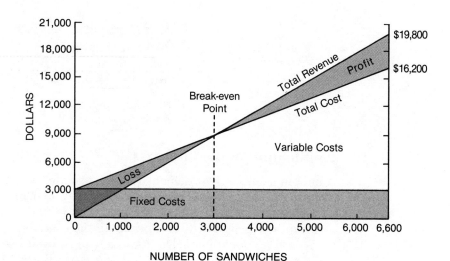

FIGURE 7–5   Break-even point chart

Remember also that any change in the estimated costs or the selling price will affect the break-even point.

This type of analysis can be used to experiment with different pricing policies to estimate the effect that varying prices will have on the break-even point. The effect of rising costs on operations can also be estimated with this tool. As the ratio of fixed costs to total cost increases, for example, the break-even point will move further to the right on the graph, forcing the organization to operate closer to capacity simply to break even. Industries with high fixed costs, such as the railroad or airline industries, are familiar with this problem. Finally, break-even analysis can help the manager determine when to drop a product or service that has been declining in sales volume.

CHRYSLER'S REVISED BREAK-EVEN POINT

After losing $3.5 billion over four years, Chrysler Corporation, under the leadership of Lee Iacocca, began to show a profit in 1982. Among other factors, the profit was made possible by lowering the firm's break-even point from an annual sales level of 2.4 million cars and trucks to about 1.2 million. The lower break-even point resulted from extensive white- and blue-collar layoffs, closing or consolidating twenty plants, and salary and benefit concessions from employees.

SOURCE: Based on "Chrysler? Profits? Iacocca Does It," *Newsweek*, 14 June 1982, p. 78.

Certainly, other factors in addition to selling price and cost functions must be considered in making the types of plans portrayed here. Competition and the effect of advertising, for instance, must also be taken into account. It should also be pointed out that break-even analysis is useful primarily in short-run planning under relatively stable conditions. Even with these limitations, however, break-even analysis can serve as a valuable input to the managerial planning process.

SUMMARY

Managers have available a number of tools and techniques to help them plan organizational operations. Perhaps the most widely discussed planning technique is *management by objectives* (MBO). MBO is an organization-wide program in which each manager and subordinate jointly establish job-related objectives for the subordinate. The objectives must be clear, verifiable, commensurate with overall organizational goals, and neither too easy nor too hard to attain.

Benefits claimed for MBO include improved planning, greater job commitment, increased job performance and satisfaction, and better superior-subordinate communication. Research, however, has revealed a number of problems; these may result from such factors as lack of top management support, failure to set goals jointly, or failure to provide adequate incentives for goal attainment.

Forecasting revenue and *budgeting* expenditures are almost universal planning tools. A forecast may be compiled through such techniques as surveys, sales force estimates, or statistical demand analysis. The forecast then serves as the base from which the budget is developed. *Rolling* budgets and *variable* budgeting techniques are particularly useful for organizations in dynamic environments. Some business and government organizations have turned to *zero-base budgeting* in recent years in an attempt to match planned expenditures to specific organizational goals and make the budgeting process more flexible.

Many organizations have found *network planning techniques* to be useful—and often essential—aids to scheduling and coordinating complex activities. *Scheduling charts,* based on the *Gantt Chart* concept, are used in a variety of settings to schedule work operations. A more sophisticated technique is *Program Evaluation Review Technique* (PERT), a modern application of the systems concept to managerial planning. Besides aiding the manager in scheduling and coordinating a complex series of activities, PERT helps to reduce the time required for project completion by helping the manager focus on the project's *critical path.*

Break-even analysis is used to determine the level of operations at which total revenue will equal total cost. This tool is useful to managers who are planning to add—or delete—product or service lines. The projected break-even point can be compared to a forecast of demand for the product or service to determine the feasibility of carrying the line.

DISCUSSION QUESTIONS

1. In a *management by objectives* program, what sort of objectives are the manager and subordinate supposed to establish?
2. Why should the manager and subordinate establish the objectives together?
3. What are some of the benefits of MBO to an organization?
4. What are some problems associated with MBO that management should attempt to avoid?
5. How might nonprofit organizations, such as churches or universities, *forecast* revenue?
6. How does *zero-base budgeting* differ from the traditional incremental budgeting process?
7. What types of organizations would find *network techniques* to be beneficial planning tools?
8. What is the *critical path* in PERT? What is its significance?
9. Develop a PERT chart for the folowing activities. Calculate the time required to complete the entire project. Identify the critical path and calculate slack time.

Activity	Days
A–B	3
B–C	5
B–D	6
C–E	2
D–E	4

Activity	Days
D–F	3
E–G	4
E–F	2
F–H	6
G–H	3

10. In what situations might *break-even analysis* be useful?
11. What are some of the limitations of break-even analysis?
12. The Herold Company makes trophies for bowling leagues. The company has fixed costs of $10,000 for its equipment and machinery. The company makes standard-sized trophies at a cost of $15 per unit and sells them for $25. With this information, construct a graph and determine the company's break-even point.

NOTES

1. Peter F. Drucker, *The Practice of Management* (New York: Harper & Row, Publishers, 1954). For a report on the development of MBO and its early usage at the General Electric Co., see Ronald G. Greenwood, "Management by Objectives: As Developed by Peter Drucker, Assisted by Harold Smiddy," *Academy of Management Review* 6 (April 1981): 225–30.

2. Rensis Likert and M. Scott Fisher, "MBGO: Putting Some Team Spirit into MBO," *Personnel* 54 (January–February 1977): 40–47.

3. See, for instance, John C. Aplin, Jr. and Peter P. Schoderbek, "MBO: Requisites for Success in the Public Sector," *Human Resource Management* 15 (Summer 1976): 30–36.

4. John M. Ivancevich, "Changes in Performance in a Management by Objectives Program," *Administrative Science Quarterly* 19 (December 1974): 563–74.

5. Jack N. Kondrasuk, "Studies in MBO Effectiveness," *Academy of Management Review* 6 (July 1981): 419–30.

6. James C. Quick, "Dyadic Goal Setting and Role Stress: A Field Study," *Academy of Management Journal* 22 (June 1979): 241–52.

7. See, for instance, Anthony P. Raia, "A Second Look at Management Goals and Controls," *California Management Review* 8 (Summer 1966): 49–58; Ivancevich, "Changes in Performance," pp. 563–74; and Perry D. Moore and Ted Staton, "Management by Objectives in American Cities," *Public Personnel Management* 10 (Summer 1981): 223–32.

8. An analysis of the ethical issues involved in the MBO process may be found in Charles D. Pringle and Justin G. Longenecker, "The Ethics of MBO," *Academy of Management Review* 7 (April 1982): 305–12.

9. Robin M. Hogarth and Spyros Makridakis, "Forecasting and Planning: An Evaluation," *Management Science* 27 (February 1981): 122.

10. Ibid.

11. Peter A. Pyhrr, *Zero-Base Budgeting* (New York: John Wiley & Sons, 1973).

12. For a summary of the problems involved in implementing zero-base budgeting programs in organizations, see Stanton C. Lindquist and R. Bryant Mills, "Whatever Happened to Zero-Base Budgeting?" *Managerial Planning* 29 (January–February 1981): 31–35.

13. Peter A. Pyhrr, "Zero-Base Budgeting: Where to Use it and How to Begin," *S.A.M. Advanced Management Journal* 41 (Summer 1976): 4–14.

14. James C. Wetherbe and John R. Montanari, "Zero Based Budgeting in the Planning Process," *Strategic Management Journal* 2 (January–March 1981): 1–14.

15. John J. Williams, "Designing a Budgeting System with Planned Confusion," *California Management Review* 24 (Winter 1981): 75–85.

SUPPLEMENTARY READING

Anderholm, Fred III; Gaertner, James; and **Milani, Ken.** "The Utilization of PERT in the Preparation of Marketing Budgets." *Managerial Planning* 30 (July/August 1981): 18–23.

Dean, Burton V., and **Cowen, Scott S.** "Zero-Base Budgeting in the Private Sector." *Business Horizons* 22 (August 1979): 73–83.

Frisbie, Gilbert, and **Mabert, Vincent A.** "Crystal Ball vs. System: The Forecasting Dilemma." *Business Horizons* 24 (September/October 1981): 72–76.

Greenwood, Ronald G. "Management by Objectives: As Developed by Peter Drucker, Assisted by Harold Smiddy." *Academy of Management Review* 6 (April 1981): 225–30.

Hogarth, Robin M., and **Makridakis, Spyros.** "Forecasting and Planning: An Evaluation." *Management Science* 27 (February 1981): 115–38.

Kahalas, Harvey. "A Look at Major Planning Methods: Development, Implementation, Strengths and Limitations." *Long Range Planning* 11 (August 1978): 84–90.

Kondrasuk, Jack N. "Studies in MBO Effectiveness." *Academy of Management Review* 6 (July 1981): 419–30.

Latham, Gary P., and **Locke, Edwin A.** "Goal Setting—A Motivational Technique That Works." *Organizational Dynamics* 8 (Autumn 1979): 68–80.

Lindquist, Stanton C., and **Mills, R. Bryant.** "Whatever Happened to Zero-Base Budgeting?" *Managerial Planning* 29 (January–February 1981): 31–35.

Locke, Edwin A.; Shaw, Karyll N.; Saari, Lise M.; and **Latham, Gary P.** "Goal Setting and Task Performance: 1969–1980." *Psychological Bulletin* 90 (July 1981): 125–52.

Makridakis, Spyros. "If We Cannot Forecast How Can We Plan?" *Long Range Planning* 14 (June 1981): 10–20.

Moore, Perry D., and **Staton, Ted.** "Management by Objectives in American Cities." *Public Personnel Management* 10 (Summer 1981): 223–32.

Pringle, Charles D., and **Longenecker, Justin G.** "The Ethics of MBO." *Academy of Management Review* 7 (April 1982): 305–12.

Rothermel, Terry W. "Forecasting Resurrected." *Harvard Business Review* 60 (March–April 1982): 139–47.

Spivey, W. Allen. "Forecasting: A Perspective for Managers." *Journal of Contemporary Business* 8 (3rd Quarter 1979): 61–78.

Wetherbe, James C., and **Montanari, John R.** "Zero Based Budgeting in the Planning Process." *Strategic Management Journal* 2 (January–March 1981): 1–14.

Wiest, Jerome D., and **Levy, Ferdinand K.** *A Management Guide to PERT/CM: With GERT/PDM/DCPM and Other Networks.* Englewood Cliffs, N.J.: Prentice-Hall, 1977.

Williams, John J. "Designing a Budgeting System with Planned Confusion." *California Management Review* 24 (Winter 1981): 75–85.

8

INFORMATION AND THE DECISION-MAKING PROCESS

This chapter will enable you to

- *Explain decision making and the types of decisions that managers face.*
- *Understand managerial decision-making styles and the effect of new contingency directions in decision making.*
- *Describe a computer-based management information system and show how distributed data processing aids managers in making decisions.*
- *Describe and analyze how managers actually make decisions and the constraints under which they must operate.*

Managers must be *decision makers*, because the *decision-making process* is a part of management. Decision making is not always easy or pleasant, however. In the executive suite, in fact, there is a tempting tendency to postpone decisions, to wait for further developments, to engage in additional study. Of course, such a procedure is often logical. There comes a time, however, when choice is necessary. Effective managers distinguish themselves by their ability to reach logical decisions at such times.

THE NATURE OF MANAGERIAL DECISION MAKING

What is Decision Making?

Managerial decision making involves a *conscious choice*. By making such a choice, a manager comes to a conclusion and selects a particular course of action from two or more alternatives. "The objective in making a decision . . . is to choose from among the most promising alternatives the one (or ones) that will produce the largest number of desirable consequences and the smallest number of unwanted consequences."[1]

In defining decision making, there is a tendency to focus upon the final moment in which the manager selects a course of action. A decision is announced, for example, that a new branch plant will be built in a particular city. Management has obviously made a decision. This concentration upon the final choice, however, tends to obscure the fact that decision making is in reality a process in which the choice of a particular solution is only the final step. The various stages of decision making, which are described in another section of this chapter, include steps of investigation and analysis as well as the final choice of alternatives.

Managers make decisions because they have been delegated the necessary authority to make choices of this type. They are presumed to have the right to make decisions pertaining to the organization and activities subject to their direction. Their decision-making authority is not absolute, however, with respect to subordinates. Their ability to make decisions affecting subordinates may be limited by the subordinates themselves.

Although most decisions are ultimately the responsibility of particular managers, discussing decision making as an individual task may be a bit misleading.* Behavioral scientists have stressed the numerous organizational influences at work in reaching a given decision. Many managers and even nonmanagerial personnel often affect the final choice. Herbert A. Simon refers to the *composite* decision and suggests that almost no decision made in an organization is the task of a single individual.[2]

Types of Decisions

A simple classification of decisions along a continuum ranging from routine to nonroutine—as shown in Figure 8–1—provides a useful distinction for study of managerial decision making. As can be seen, most decisions involve situations which contain both structured (that is, well-defined) and unstructured (that is, ill-defined) elements.

Decisions near the *routine* end of the continuum focus on well-structured situations. Such decisions recur frequently, involve standard decision procedures, and entail a minimum of uncertainty. Common examples include payroll processing, reordering standard inventory items, paying suppliers, and so on. The decision maker can usually rely upon policies, rules, past precedents, standardized methods of processing, or computational techniques. Probably 90 percent of management decisions are largely routine, although any manager's experience is significant in determining whether a specific decision is routine.

Decisions at the opposite—or *nonroutine*—end of the continuum deal with unstructured situations of a novel, nonrecurring nature. Their complexity is compounded by incomplete knowledge and the absence of accepted methods of resolution. Nonroutine decisions include not only the major corporate decisions, such as merger or acquisition, but also more restricted ones, such as adoption of a new advertising theme or purchase of a new labor-saving piece of equipment. A significant characteristic of such decisions is that no alternative can be proved to be the

---

*Specific techniques of group decision making are covered in Chapter 14.

FIGURE 8–1 Types of managerial decisions

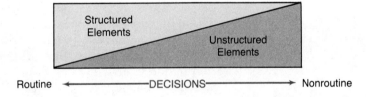

"best" possible solution to a particular problem. A much higher degree
of subjective judgment and even intuition are involved in nonroutine
decisions. In this chapter, nonroutine decisions are of primary concern.

RISKLESS DECISION MAKING?

Decision making and risk are inseparable partners, as the management of McDonnell Douglas Corporation was recently reminded.
McDonnell Douglas could have received the $3 billion order for sixty
jets that Delta Air Lines instead placed with Boeing Company in
1980. Reports indicated that Delta preferred McDonnell Douglas' proposed DC-11 to Boeing's 757, and that Delta felt it was important to
ensure that McDonnell Douglas had sufficient business to remain in
the commercial aircraft industry. Without McDonnell Douglas,
Boeing would have a virtual monopoly in that field, a situation that
Delta wished to avoid.

> But when it came to making a commitment, McDonnell Douglas was
> timid. Soured by a profitless decade for its commercial planes, the DC-9
> and DC-10, McDonnell Douglas insisted on finding a second carrier be-
> fore launching the DC-11—a tough job in a lean airline year. And it
> wanted fat progress payments, to help its cash flow, as Delta's 60 planes
> moved through production. "They wanted to launch a new plane with-
> out taking any risk," laments Robert Oppenlander, senior vice president
> of Delta. "That ain't the way it works."

SOURCE: "The Big Deal McDonnell Douglas Turned Down." Quoted from the December 1, 1980, issue of *Business Week* by special permission, p. 81.

Managerial Decision-Making Styles

A dozen managers, each faced with the same unstructured problem,
would likely use twelve widely divergent methods—or styles—to analyze the problem and formulate a solution. This variance in decision-
making styles reflects differences among managers in the way they perceive, organize, and understand their environment. These differences
stem from dissimilar work backgrounds, educational experiences, social
influences, value systems, and psychological attributes.

Decision-making styles have been classified in many different ways. One recent classification suggests the following four basic styles:[3]

1. *Decisive*—refers to a manager who processes a minimum amount of information to arrive at one firm conclusion. This individual is concerned with action, results, speed, and efficiency. Long, detailed reports will be sent back, ignored, or given to someone else to summarize.

2. *Flexible*—characterizes a manager who prefers concise reports containing a wide variety of briefly stated alternatives from which to choose. Rather than planning highly structured solutions, this manager prefers that solutions evolve as he or she gains acceptance from others.

3. *Hierarchical*—describes a manager who carefully analyzes large amounts of information to arrive at one "best" solution. He or she values perfection, precision, and thoroughness. Brief or summarized reports are viewed as inadequate.

4. *Integrative*—refers to a manager who uses masses of information to generate many possible solutions simultaneously (rather than sequentially as flexible managers do). This manager constantly alters and improves his or her plans and shuns brief reports in favor of complex analyses from varying points of view.

The effectiveness of any particular decision-making style depends on the specific situation the manager is facing.

Wickham Skinner and W. Earl Sasser, in their analysis of managerial decision-making styles, conclude that successful decision makers are inconsistent in the way they attack problems, varying their approach to fit the problem situation.[4] One problem, for example, may require analysis at a high conceptual level, while another may require a review of operational details. In one situation, a manager may consult his or her subordinates in solving a particular problem. In another situation, the same manager may arrive at the decision alone. Unsuccessful decision makers, on the other hand, generally approach each problem in the same predictable style. An adaptable style is apparently more effective than a single, unvarying approach to decision making.

Contingency Directions in Decision Making

The concept that successful decision makers vary their approach to fit the problem situation is consistent with the contingency viewpoint that characterizes much of management thought today. Two leaders in developing the contingency perspective in decision making, Lee Roy Beach and Terence R. Mitchell, propose that the manager's selection of the appropriate decision-making approach is influenced by the following factors (illustrated in Figure 8–2):[5]

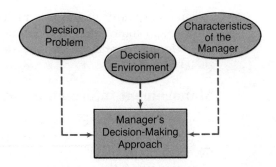

FIGURE 8–2   Influences on the manager's decision-making approach

1. The *decision problem*, which is comprised of the manager's familiarity with the problem, the problem's clarity and complexity, and the degree to which the problem's criteria, goals, and constraints change.
2. The decision *environment*, which includes the degree to which the decision can be reversed, the problem's significance, the accountability of the decision maker for results, and time and money constraints.
3. The *characteristics of the decision maker*, such as knowledge, ability, and motivation.

Familiar problems, for instance, may be solved by a knowledgeable manager simply through the use of habit. A complex problem which is highly significant to both the manager and the organization will be attacked through more analytical techniques, provided time and money permit and the manager has the requisite ability and knowledge. In some cases, the manager may request technical assistance in analyzing the problem. Ultimately, the selection of an approach is contingent upon a "compromise between the decision maker's desire to make a correct decision and his or her negative feelings about investing time and effort in the decision-making process."[6]

A model of this type requires years of testing to ascertain its *validity*; that is, its ability to help the practicing manager select the proper approach to a decision situation. Initial research results, however, have been promising.[7]

INFORMATION FOR DECISION MAKING

"It is a capital mistake to theorize before one has data," wrote Sir Arthur Conan Doyle in his *Adventures of Sherlock Holmes*. His statement could easily be applied today to the manager who is faced with a multitude of decisions. The importance of pertinent, timely information for decision making cannot be overlooked.[8]

Information has been called "the raw material of which decisions are made." And, just as in manufacturing, a direct correlation exists between the quality of the raw material and the quality of the resultant product. In today's world of giant conglomerates and far-flung overseas operations, a manager without adequate, reliable information is completely lost.

Management Information Systems

A manager receives the information needed for decision making through the firm's *management information system* (MIS). An MIS is just what the name implies—a system which collects data related both to internal operations and the external environment and then transforms the data into usable information.

Management information systems have existed, formally and informally, for centuries. Mintzberg reports that top managers rely on verbal interaction with other individuals for a major portion of their information.[9] But increasingly complex environments and organizational activities require more formal types of information systems. The development and widespread use of computers has provided the basis for such systems.

Before the computer, management was often forced to make decisions without adequate information because the problem of collecting and organizing relevant data was limited by the time and the personnel available. The value of the computer lies in its ability to record, organize, and classify data; to store and retrieve quickly vast amounts of information; and to make calculations that formerly took people months or even years to make.

The rapidly changing technology in this area has been reflected in a number of significant modifications to management information systems in just the past few years. Since the mid-1970s, the MIS in many organizations has become increasingly accessible and useful to the manager.

The Evolving Shape of Management Information Systems

Only a decade ago, most organizations had one or more large mainframe computers located in a centralized data processing center. The advent of minicomputers and microcomputers, however, led to a significant change in this arrangement. While mainframe computers commanded 80 percent of the computer market in 1976, these large computers will account for only slightly more than one-third of industry sales in 1985.[10]

The movement of computing power out of the hands of computer specialists and into the manager's own office is termed *distributed data processing*. The central data processing center continues to handle accounting, payroll, billing, and the like, but, more importantly, now serves as an "electronic librarian" for the storage of data banks. When these banks of data are stored together to serve one or more applications, the entire collection of data is known as a *data base*. This base can be accessed by individual managers using small computers in their own offices, as illustrated in Figure 8–3. This process eliminates the step in

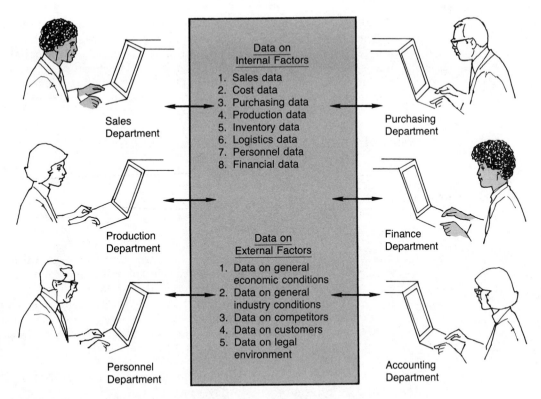

FIGURE 8–3 Simplified view of distributed data processing with a centralized data base

which managers had to describe their information requirements to a computer specialist who then later produced the desired results (or some variation thereof) in a printout.

A centralized data base allows managers of two separate departments to share the same information without having to store it in two different places. It also protects the integrity of the data by allowing only those managers who have been approved to have access to certain types of information.

The data in many organizations include not only detailed information on internal operations—by subsystems, time, and other variables—but also information on the environment. Organizations can compile, or purchase from service companies, industry statistics, abstracts of published literature, and information on major competitors and key customers.

The organization's small computers can also communicate with one another, allowing management to build such sophisticated systems as the one developed by Continental Illinois Bank:

Building on a network of interactive small-scale computers and a large central processing unit, Continental developed a central library containing the bank's vast data bank. So that bank managers could have a link to the office at home, at the airport, or in a hotel room, remote telephone dictating facilities were linked to the bank's word processing machines. An electronic mail system now allows managers to communicate without paper memorandums, and the messages are stored in an electronic filing cabinet. . . . Continental executives now have an office wherever there is a telephone. . . .[11]

The MIS and Managerial Decision Making

Distributed data processing allows the manager to have instant access to the latest data or reports on the status of key variables. But, more importantly, the computer can be used as an analytic tool.[12] Through access with a data bank, the manager can manipulate and extrapolate data to answer "what if" types of questions.

> The type of analysis performed differs from manager to manager. Some merely compute new ratios or extrapolate current trends into the future. Some graph trends of particular interest to gain an added visual perspective. Some work with elaborate simulation models to determine where capital investments will be more productive. All, however, enjoy a heightened ability to look at, change, extend, and manipulate data in personally meaningful ways.[13]

When used in this manner, the computer and its data bank are often referred to as a *decision support system*.

COMPUTER PHOBIA

Aside from recent graduates of business schools, many managers are unfamiliar with computer terminals and some are even afraid of them. In 1982, for instance, *Business Week* devoted three pages in one issue to helping managers conquer their fear of computers. According to that analysis, fear may stem not only from unfamiliarity, but also from failure to understand the benefits of the computer, anxiety about becoming "hooked" on the computer, and worry over one's job becoming obsolete.

Additionally, executives who do not know how to type are often intimidated by the keyboard. To overcome this obstacle, some computer companies have designed terminals which can be operated by moving a pointer to the right spot on the screen and then hitting a command key.

SOURCE: Based on "How to Conquer Fear of Computers," *Business Week*, 29 March 1982, pp. 176–78; and "Will the Boss Go Electronic, Too?" *Business Week*, 11 May 1981, p. 108.

Requirements for Successful Management Information Systems

Certain requirements are necessary for managers to use a distributed data processing system effectively. First, the manager must be willing to invest time and energy in learning the computer's capabilities and in defining what data are needed. Secondly, the organization must be willing to train managers in how to use computers, how to establish and update data bases, and how to perform analyses.[14]

A third requirement is that the system must meet the user's needs. Research has indicated that managers who are not involved in the design of the information system are not likely to understand it. This lack of understanding often results in little confidence in the system and even active resistance to much of its information.[15] Only the operating manager can define his or her information processing needs. These needs must be clearly communicated to the computer specialist who can then explain the technological—and cost—constraints and possibilities. By exposing computer specialists to the needs of operating managers and educating managers in computer concepts, an organization can attain a well-designed system that increases managerial effectiveness.

One source points out that the actual computer technology an organization uses is not as important as how the technology is used.[16] The system must be able to support each key manager's specific task and should mesh with the decision process each manager uses.[17] "This means that the application drives the technology and not, as too often before, the reverse."[18]

The firm's information system, it must be emphasized, is only one determinant of the quality of managerial decisions. The information provided must be absorbed, processed, and used by the manager as he or she proceeds through the decision-making process. In each of the steps in the decision-making model described below, managers will need various types and quantities of information to enable them to make effective decisions and to evaluate the relative success of the alternatives that they have chosen.

THE DYNAMICS OF DECISION MAKING

In Chapter 5, we examined the strategic decision-making process. Now we turn to a more generic analysis of managerial decision making. Although decisions are required in determining strategy, they are also necessary in many other managerial functions—leading, motivating, controlling, staffing, structuring, and so on.

Rational Decision Making

A rational approach to decision making involves a series of steps to reach a problem solution, as illustrated in Figure 8–4. Recognition and

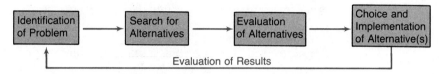

FIGURE 8–4   A model of the decision-making process

proper identification of a problem comprise the first step in decision making.

Identification of Problem.   A problem has often been defined as a discrepancy between that which exists and that which is desired. Problems requiring analysis and decision making surface in various ways.* As a result, we can never be sure that the most important problems are known or recognized at any one time.

Problems sometimes explode in the face of management. A key supervisor resigns, or a government contract is canceled. In other cases, imagination and perception are required to detect the problem because many problems do not appear in convenient forms. Experience is often useful in helping a manager discover problems. One study of thirty-three upper-level managers in major organizations indicated that 80 percent of them were aware of a problem's existence before such formal indicators as financial figures reflected it and before a superior or subordinate presented it to them.[19]

NEW DEVELOPMENT

The principle of the Polaroid Land camera resulted from a chance conversation between the inventor, Edwin H. Land, and his daughter, who asked about having some pictures developed which they had just taken. In a flash he saw here an opportunity to revolutionize photography with a process which would yield a finished print within moments after exposure. This set off the train of events which led finally to the picture-in-a-minute camera.

SOURCE: Based on Joseph D. Cooper, *The Art of Decision-Making*, (New York: Doubleday & Co., 1961), p. 16.

Occasionally, managers waste time developing solutions to "problems" which are only symptoms of deeper problems. What appears to be

---

*Chester I. Barnard has suggested the following origins of occasions for decision: (1) authoritative communications from superiors; (2) cases referred for decision by subordinates; and (3) cases originating in the initiative of the executive concerned. Chester I. Barnard, *The Function of the Executive* (Cambridge, Mass.: Harvard University Press, 1938), p. 190.

a problem may not be the problem at all. A high rate of employee turn-over, for instance, may be less a problem than a symptom of underlying defects in promotion policies, wages, or working conditions. Management must constantly strive, then, to sift from superficial difficulties the true problems that require investigation and solution. The way a decision maker perceives the problem is a major determinant of the alternative solutions that he or she will consider using.

Search for Alternatives. Consideration of the various possible solutions or alternative courses of action constitutes the second stage of decision making. Richard M. Cyert and James G. March theorize that managers begin their search for alternatives by identifying familiar alternatives which have been employed in previous decision situations. If these alternatives seem unsuitable, then search behavior becomes more active and less familiar possibilities are explored.[20] Nonroutine decisions, then, often require imagination and creative thinking.

In searching for solutions, decision makers face certain constraints that limit their spheres of discretion. These constraints are barriers which preclude certain choices that would otherwise be possible. The two most immediate constraints involve time and money. Decisions must generally be made by a specific date, and unlimited funds are not available for many otherwise desirable alternatives. Other constraints may be imposed by top management, government regulations, technological limitations, economic conditions, the abilities and interests of the firm's employees, and so on.

Evaluation of Alternatives. Evaluating the alternatives generated requires the manager to predict an uncertain future. Possible pros and cons must be considered. The manager may attempt to assign probabilities of future occurrence—based on past experience, formal forecasts, or subjective judgment—to the more pertinent factors.

At this stage, intuition may influence the decision process. Intuition "is that psychological function which transmits perceptions in an unconscious way."[21] This unconscious process helps the manager integrate ideas which do not appear at first to be related and to "grasp the meaning, significance, or structure of a problem without explicit reliance on analytical apparatus."[22]

During the evaluation stage, the manager must also realize that various alternatives may have differing impacts on various parts of the organization. Special interests of specific departments and individuals tend to interfere with the process by which facts are investigated and decisions reached. A decision which is favorable for the firm as a whole may strengthen or weaken the positions of different departments. To protect and enhance their various positions, therefore, rival managers often compete with each other, bargain, build alliances with others, and in sometimes devious ways attempt to influence outcomes. The evaluation process, then, includes the power struggles among various factions in the organization.

The manager must also be aware that decisions at higher levels in the organization automatically trigger the need for specific operational decisions to be made at lower levels. A hospital administrator's decision to open a new intensive care unit, for example, initiates a series of interactive decisions concerning what kinds of equipment will be needed, where it should be purchased, what types of personnel will be required, how these personnel will be organized, and so on.

Choice and Implementation of Alternative(s).   The climax of the decision-making process arrives when the manager exercises the final judgment. The manager may have gone step by step through an analysis of the problem and the proposed solutions, but the moment arrives when choice is necessary.

If the choice is based upon a careful analysis, we admire a decisive manager. Indecision often indicates an unwillingness to face the situation. By choosing, one commits oneself to a given position. In some decisions, a reputation is at stake, and the decision maker may risk disagreement and misunderstanding. Decision making can thus be a lonely, agonizing process to some managers.

The act of choice does not end the decision-making process. Forthright expression of the decision once it is made can help clear the air of uncertainty. Explanations to those affected may be desirable if the reasoning supporting the particular course of action is not clear. This step is often necessary to gain the requisite understanding and support.

Finally, the manager spends a great deal of time in *implementing* decisions—in seeing that they are carried out. This requires an ability to secure the cooperation of others in seeing that plans are followed. The success or failure of a decision is largely determined by how well it is implemented. Evaluation of the relative success of the implemented decision involves the managerial function of control.

Bounded Rationality

Even within the practical constraints discussed above, *objective rationality* in decision making is an unattainable goal. The manager, operating from a unique perceptual perspective—influenced by his or her training, education, and experience—often identifies and understands only part of a complex problem. Identification of possible alternatives is limited by the manager's habits, incomplete understanding of the organization's goals, deficiencies in knowledge, and inadequate information. The manager, then, operates under conditions of *bounded rationality*, viewing a complex situation in an oversimplified way, taking into account only those few factors of which he or she is aware, understands, and regards as relevant.[23]

Since neither the problem nor the alternative solutions are completely identified, it should not be surprising that the final decision does not—except by accident—yield a *maximum* return to the organization.

Managers must instead settle for a satisfactory return. In other words, they cannot maximize; they must *satisfice*.

> While economic man maximizes—selects the best alternative from among all those available to him; his cousin, whom we shall call administrative man, satisfices—looks for a course of action that is satisfactory or "good enough." Examples of satisficing criteria that are familiar enough to businessmen, if unfamiliar to most economists, are "share of market," "adequate profit," "fair price."[24]

SATISFICING

Problems are sometimes so overwhelming in their complexity that individuals, unable to analyze all possible alternatives, select a simplified solution. The following example of purchasing a plain-paper copier emphasizes this point:

> Given the plethora of brand names and model types—some 32 makers are marketing 148 plain-paper copiers in the U.S.—first-time buyers are often too confused to make a choice. So they frequently opt for the first machine they see or the one with the lowest price tag.

SOURCE: "The Squeeze on Copier Dealers," *Business Week*, 6 July 1981, p. 78.

Research in decision making, in fact, indicates that managers are often more action-oriented than contemplative. A study of managers in fourteen companies operating in four countries concludes that

> managing a response effectively requires that the manager get on with the job, rather than engage in a prolonged search for the ideal. Although managers found it difficult to interpret the uncertainties that surrounded them, they found that interacting with a problem was the most efficient route to a solution. This interaction lead to an increased understanding of the situation that was greater than that which could be achieved through deskwork alone.[25]

Encouraging Creativity in Decision Making

Creativity involves new ideas, new approaches, and new combinations of existing knowledge. In solving organizational problems through creative thinking, the individual mind is directed to an understanding of the problem and an imaginative search for a practical solution. Rather than taking an obvious explanation, the creative individual is always questioning, probing for a deeper understanding, and seeking a better way.

As an example, consider the Schwegmann Giant Supermarket chain of New Orleans. To expand from one small store in 1946 to its current domination of the city's supermarket business, Schwegmann needed financing. Rather than seeking it through such traditional means as banks, the store began selling bonds to its customers in denominations now ranging from $500 to $25,000. The bonds reflect the current market rate of interest (the low rates of interest on old bonds have even been increased to current market rates) and can be cashed in at any time with no penalty.[26]

Recruitment of personnel who have an unusually creative turn of mind is a first step in developing creativity in an organization, as shown in Figure 8–5. The employer is interested in the spark that distinguishes the imaginative from the routine employee. Identification of the particularly creative individual is difficult, and recruiters must look for something more than educational degrees and years of experience.

If an organization is to maximize the creative abilities of its members, it must also grant to them a considerable degree of freedom. This clearly rules out an insistence upon more than minimum conformity. Employees cannot be limited to following a set of rules and prescribed procedures. Rather, they may be encouraged to think about the work that is theirs to perform. Through delegation, they may receive freedom and responsibility in devising their own work methods.

It is also possible to grant creative individuals assistance in detailed and routine work. A professor may be given assistance in grading tests and thereby be permitted to engage in research. An engineer may be given assistance in drafting, filing, and typing. The problem is not so much the humble nature of routine work as it is the encroachment of detail upon time that should be devoted to achievement on a higher level.

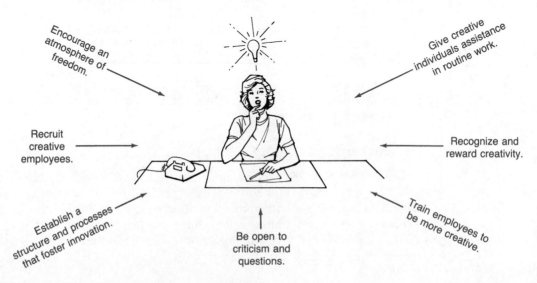

FIGURE 8–5 Fostering creativity in organizations

Stimulation of creative effort may also be attempted through continued recognition of achievement. This recognition includes financial rewards, but it is not limited to them. In fact, the symbolic significance of a financial reward may constitute its greatest value. It is recognition that the contribution itself is important, and this may require some financial reward. The promotional practices of the organization should likewise reflect the understanding and appreciation of management for the creative activities of particular individuals.

There is even some evidence that training can enhance creativity. After undergoing two days of intensive training in creative problem solving, a group of thirty-two engineers, engineering managers, and technicians in one study showed evidence of improved creativity. They spent more time in different modes of thinking, they were more open to different ideas, and they made fewer negative judgments on new ideas.[27]

An openness to criticism and tolerance of uncomfortable questions also contribute to an innovative atmosphere. A willingness to modify traditional organization structures and to change customary procedures is a part of this requirement. Although these characteristics are easy to specify, they are difficult to achieve. The status quo becomes accepted to the point that change is virtually impossible.[28]

This may explain why young organizations often (though not necessarily) display greater flexibility than older ones. But older, well-established organizations can take deliberate steps to encourage critical analysis on the part of their members.

Jay R. Galbraith suggests that organizations that want to innovate need a formal set of "roles, processes, rewards, and people practices that naturally lead to innovations."[29] For a new idea to have a chance, a middle management level "sponsor" is required to help fund its development and testing. Because new ideas are not neutral—they change careers, organizational structures and processes, and the allocation of resources—a top management "orchestrator" is needed to facilitate testing of the idea in the face of opposition. Additionally, the orchestrator should create incentives for both idea generators and sponsors to help attract, retain, motivate, and reward them.[30]

SUMMARY

Managerial decision making is an important, integral part of the management process. It involves a *conscious choice* from among two or more alternative courses of action. The decisions that managers face vary from *routine* to *nonroutine*, with the latter being characterized by incomplete knowledge and the absence of accepted methods of resolution. The approach—or style—used to solve such nonroutine problems varies among managers and depends upon each manager's background, perceptions, and psychological attributes.

Decision making is increasingly being analyzed from a *contingency viewpoint*. Although our understanding of this area is far from complete, it seems that the manager's selection of the proper approach to a problem situation may depend upon the particular problem being faced, the environment in which the problem exists, and the personal characteristics of the decision maker.

A manager receives the information needed for decision making through the firm's *management information system*, which provides data on internal operations and the external environment. Through recent innovations termed *distributed data processing*, managers now have immediate access to computing power. They may retrieve data and analyze and manipulate it as they attempt to understand situations and make decisions.

The decision-making process begins with the *identification of a problem* and then proceeds to a search for possible solutions or *alternative courses of action*. The selection of feasible alternatives is bounded by a number of practical and psychological constraints. The alternatives that are identified must be carefully *evaluated,* and the evaluation should lead logically to the *choice and implementation of one or more alternatives*. Because managers often have an incomplete understanding of the problem and its alternative solutions, decision makers, of necessity, *satisfice* rather than *maximize*. Organizations may stimulate *creativity* in decision making by recruiting particularly creative individuals, maximizing their freedom, providing assistance in detailed work, granting recognition for their achievements, training them to be more creative, tolerating criticism and questions, and establishing a structure and processes that foster innovation.

DISCUSSION QUESTIONS

1. What is the difference, if any, between *decision making* and *choosing a course of action?*

2. Explain how a *contingency approach* to decision making might apply in the decision to purchase a computer for use in a large business corporation.

3. Assume that your manufacturing company is faced with the decision of adding a new product line. You have been asked for your recommendation. What information would you need to make such a decision? How would a modern *management information system* help you?

4. What are the advantages to managers of having their own *decision support systems* rather than having to rely on a centralized data processing center?

5. What is meant by the statement that an effective MIS requires a strong commitment from both the organization and the users?

6. "Problems, problems—all I have is problems!" These words of one man-

ager indicate a sharp awareness of problems. In what way could *problem identification* be difficult?

7. What are the principal difficulties that hamper the development of *alternatives* in decision making?

8. If the preceding steps in decision making are taken, why is the final step of *choosing an alternative* difficult?

9. If a manager is effective as a decision maker, does this indicate that he or she is a good manager?

10. Why do not even the most thoroughly considered decisions yield *maximum returns* to the organization?

11. Explain how the concept of *satisficing* might apply in the decision to purchase a computer for use in a large business corporation.

NOTES

1. E. Frank Harrison, *The Managerial Decision-Making Process* (Boston: Houghton Mifflin Co., 1975), p. 32.

2. Herbert A. Simon, *Administrative Behavior* (New York: The Macmillan Co., 1957).

3. Phillip L. Hunsaker and Johanna S. Hunsaker, "Decision Styles—In Theory, in Practice," *Organizational Dynamics* 10 (Autumn 1981): 23–36. Another classification schema is identified in John C. Henderson and Paul C. Nutt, "The Influence of Decision Style on Decision Making Behavior," *Management Science* 26 (April 1980): 371–86.

4. Wickham Skinner and W. Earl Sasser, "Managers with Impact: Versatile and Inconsistent," *Harvard Business Review* 55 (November–December 1977): 140–48.

5. Lee Roy Beach and Terence R. Mitchell, "A Contingency Model for the Selection of Decision Strategies," *Academy of Management Review* 3 (July 1978): 439–49.

6. Ibid., p. 448.

7. See Daniel W. McAllister, Terence R. Mitchell, and Lee Roy Beach, "The Contingency Model for the Selection of Decision Strategies: An Empirical Test of the Effects of Significance, Accountability, and Reversibility," *Organizational Behavior and Human Performance* 24 (October 1979): 228–44; and James F. Smith, Terence R. Mitchell, and Lee Roy Beach, "A Cost-Benefit Mechanism for Selecting Problem-Solving Strategies: Some Extensions and Empirical Tests," *Organizational Behavior and Human Performance* 29 (June 1982): 370–96.

8. An intriguing analysis of other reasons for gathering information can be found in Martha S. Feldman and James G. March, "Information in Organizations as Signal and Symbol," *Administrative Science Quarterly* 26 (June 1981): 171–86.

9. Henry Mintzberg, *The Nature of Managerial Work* (New York: Harper & Row, Publishers, 1973).

10. "Moving Away from Mainframes," *Business Week*, 15 February 1982, p. 78.

11. Louis H. Mertes, "Doing Your Office Over—Electronically," *Harvard Business Review* 59 (March–April 1981): 127.

12. John F. Rockart and Michael E. Treacy, "The CEO Goes On-line," *Harvard Business Review* 60 (January–February 1982): 84–85.

13. Ibid., p. 85.

14. Ibid.

15. See Gary W. Dickson, James A. Senn, and Norman L. Chervany, "Research in Management Information Systems: The Minnesota Experiments," *Management Science* 23 (May 1977): 913–23; and Daniel Robey, "User Attitudes and Management Information System Use," *Academy of Management Journal* 22 (September 1979): 527–38.

16. Paul H. Cheney and Gary W. Dickson, "Organizational Characteristics and Information Systems: An Exploratory Investigation," *Academy of Management Journal* 25 (March 1982): 181.

17. Peter G. W. Keen, "Decision Support Systems: Translating Analytic Techniques into Useful Tools," *Sloan Management Review* 21 (Spring 1980): 41.

18. Ibid., p. 33.

19. Marjorie A. Lyles and Ian I. Mitroff, "Organizational Problem Formulation: An Empirical Study," *Administrative Science Quarterly* 25 (March 1980): 109.

20. R. M. Cyert and J. G. March, *A Behavioral Theory of the Firm* (Englewood Cliffs, N.J.: Prentice-Hall, 1963), pp. 120–22.

21. Carl G. Jung, *Psychological Types*, trans. H. Godwin Baynes (New York: Harcourt, Brace, 1924), p. 568.

22. Thomas S. Isaack, "Intuition: An Ignored Dimension of Management," *Academy of Management Review* 3 (October 1978): 919.

23. Herbert A. Simon, *Administrative Behavior*, 3d ed. (New York: The Free Press, 1976).

24. Herbert A. Simon, *Administrative Behavior* (New York: The Macmillan Co., 1957).

25. R. Jeffery Ellis, "Improving Management Response in Turbulent Times," *Sloan Management Review* 23 (Winter 1982): 3.

26. "Selling Steaks and Bonds," *Newsweek*, 25 January 1982, p. 58.

27. Min Basadur, George B. Graen, and Stephen G. Green, "Training in Creative Problem Solving: Effects on Ideation and Problem Finding and Solving in an Industrial Research Organization," *Organizational Behavior and Human Performance* 30 (August 1982): 41–70.

28. A discussion of the major factors that stifle innovation in organizations and how these might be overcome can be found in Edward E. Lawler and John A. Drexler, "Entrepreneurship in the Large Corporation: Is it Possible?" *Management Review* 70 (February 1981): 8–11.

29. Jay R. Galbraith, "Designing the Innovating Organization," *Organizational Dynamics* 10 (Winter 1982): 25.

30. Ibid., pp. 5–25.

SUPPLEMENTARY READING

Ackoff, Russell L. *The Art of Problem Solving: Accompanied by Ackoff's Fables.* New York: John Wiley & Sons, 1978.

Allen, Brandt. "An Unmanaged Computer System Can Stop You Dead." *Harvard Business Review* 60 (November–December 1982): 77–87.

Argyris, Chris. "Single-Loop and Double-Loop Models in Research on Decision Making." *Administrative Science Quarterly* 21 (September 1976): 363–75.

Basadur, Min; Graen, George B.; and **Green, Stephen G.** "Training in Creative Problem Solving: Effects on Ideation and Problem Finding and Solving in an Industrial Research Organization." *Organizational Behavior and Human Performance* 30 (August 1982): 41–70.

Carroll, Archie B. "Behavioral Aspects of Developing Computer-Based Information Systems." *Business Horizons* 25 (January/February 1982): 42–51.

Ellis, R. Jeffery. "Improving Management Response in Turbulent Times." *Sloan Management Review* 23 (Winter 1982): 3–12.

Feldman, Martha S., and **March, James G.** "Information in Organizations as Signal and Symbol." *Administrative Science Quarterly* 26 (June 1981): 171–86.

Galbraith, Jay R. "Designing the Innovating Organization." *Organizational Dynamics* 10 (Winter 1982): 5–25.

Kanter, Rosabeth Moss. "The Middle Manager as Innovator." *Harvard Business Review* 60 (July–August 1982): 95–105.

Keen, Peter G. W. "Decision Support Systems: Translating Analytic Techniques into Useful Tools." *Sloan Management Review* 21 (Spring 1980): 33–44.

Lawler, Edward E., and **Drexler, John A.** "Entrepreneurship in the Large Corporation: Is It Possible?" *Management Review* 70 (February 1981): 8–11.

Lyles, Marjorie A. "Formulating Strategic Problems: Empirical Analysis and Model Development." *Strategic Management Journal* 2 (January–March 1981): 61–75.

Lyles, Marjorie A., and **Mitroff, Ian I.** "Organizational Problem Formulation: An Empirical Study." *Administrative Science Quarterly* 25 (March 1980): 102–19.

Mertes, Louis H. "Doing Your Office Over—Electronically." *Harvard Business Review* 59 (March–April 1981): 127–35.

Mintzberg, Henry; Raisinghani, Duru; and **Theoret, Andre.** "The Structure of 'Unstructured' Decision Processes." *Administrative Science Quarterly* 21 (June 1976): 246–75.

Staw, Barry M. "The Escalation of Commitment to a Course of Action." *Academy of Management Review* 6 (October 1981): 577–87.

Takeuchi, Hirotaka, and **Schmidt, Allan H.** "New Promise of Computer Graphics." *Harvard Business Review* 58 (January–February 1980): 122–31.

Ungson, Gerardo Rivera; Braunstein, Daniel N.; and **Hall, Phillip D.** "Managerial Information Processing: A Research Review." *Administrative Science Quarterly* 26 (March 1981): 116–34.

9

MANAGEMENT SCIENCE: USING QUANTITATIVE METHODS IN DECISION MAKING

This chapter will enable you to

- *Define management science and explain how managers can use it to reduce the risk in decision making.*
- *Explain model building and discuss the advantages of using mathematical models to analyze problem situations.*
- *Describe specific management science techniques and illustrate their use in managerial decision making.*
- *Delineate the limitations of management science and discuss the prospects for its future use.*

In recent years, managers, managerial literature, and management theorists have emphasized the use of *quantitative techniques* in decision making. Some experts feel that the manager of the future who has an understanding of mathematical concepts will have a marked advantage over one who has little or no knowledge of such techniques. This chapter examines *quantitative methods,* some of the *specific techniques* used, and the *advantages and limitations of a quantitative approach to decision making.*

THE NATURE OF QUANTITATIVE METHODS

Development of Management Science

The use of quantitative techniques in management is not a recent development. In business, for instance, such factors as the rate of inventory turnover, quality control limits, and return on investment involve quantitative concepts for use in decision making, and all have been used for many years. However, the modern emphasis on quantitative methods involves a much different concept known as *management science,* or *operations research.*

Although these modern techniques are, in some cases, based on mathematical principles dating back as far as the eighteenth century, the specific body of knowledge known today as management science did not emerge until World War II. During the war, both British and American military leaders enlisted teams of scientists and mathematicians to aid them in solving complex military problems, such as assigning targets and scheduling bomb strikes or determining the safest method of transporting personnel and supplies across the oceans. The value of such systematic, mathematical analysis quickly became evident and, following the war, those who had served on, and worked with, operations research teams began to realize that the same basic concepts could be applied to other areas, such as managerial decision making.

Perhaps the major impetus to the growth of management science, however, was the invention of the electronic computer. Since management science is designed to deal with a complex set of interrelated factors, a tremendous amount of data is necessary for maximum effectiveness. Such large volumes of data can practicably be processed only by computer.

Definition and Scope of Management Science

The intent of management science is to improve organizational effectiveness by reducing the risk involved in decision making. Basically, it supplements the manager's experience and intuition with rigorous quantitative analysis. Many nonroutine decisions are so complicated that it would be quite difficult, or even impossible, for one person to visualize all of the significant interrelated factors. Without some sort of systematic, logical method of analysis, these problems would be solved in a basically subjective fashion. Management science, then, provides an objective supplement to the decision process, helping managers clarify their logic and thereby improve the quality of their decisions.

Management science is a mathematical application of the scientific method to the solution of organizational problems. Its primary distinguishing characteristics have been described as the following:

1. A systems view of the problem—a viewpoint is taken which includes all of the significant interrelated variables contained in the problem.
2. The team approach—personnel with heterogeneous backgrounds and training work together on specific problems.
3. An emphasis upon the use of formal mathematical models and statistical and quantitative techniques.

Few major nonroutine problems can be limited to only one functional area. Analysis of a complex production problem, for example, might involve not only the production department but also representatives from marketing and personnel—other functional areas interdependent with production. The team members, using statistical and quantitative methods, would develop a mathematical model of the relationships among the significant problem elements and would then arrive at decision recommendations based upon their analysis of the model.

This methodology can be profitably applied to a variety of organizational problems. The following list of practical applications, while not in any sense exhaustive, indicates the widespread usefulness of management science techniques:

1. Production scheduling
2. Warehouse and retail outlet location selection
3. Portfolio management
4. Product and marketing mix selection
5. Air and highway traffic control
6. Credit management
7. Hospital menu planning
8. Drug abuse treatment and rehabilitation.

A SYSTEMS VIEW

"There is an interesting story about an inventory manager who prided himself on *never* running out of stock. Only on rare occasions were any of his shelves empty. Late in his career a team composed of representatives from production, inventory control, finance, and marketing was asked to study this inventory system which had been so "successful" for 30 years. What they found was astonishing. His shelves were overflowing with stock. Millions of extra dollars were tied up in inventory for the purpose of preventing any possibility of an out-of-stock position. They quickly recommended a drastic reduction that would on occasion subject the organization to stockouts but would release much-needed funds for other investments. The team pointed out that the inventory manager viewed his function in very narrow terms and completely ignored the financial considerations of inventory control. Fortunately for the company, the team took a systems point of view."

SOURCE: Barry Shore, *Quantitative Methods for Business Decisions: Text and Cases* (New York: McGraw-Hill Book Co., 1978), pp. 7–8.

Management Science in Action

In addition to management science specialists, the problem-solving team should include representatives from the following areas: computer science, middle management, and the department which is being studied.[1] The large quantities of data often associated with management science studies require the expertise of someone familiar with the organization's computer system who can aid in collecting and processing the data.

Middle management must be included because the systems emphasis often requires the crossing of established functional lines of authority. The team, therefore, needs a member who understands the total system being analyzed and who has adequate authority to control the various functions involved in the study.

It is essential that the manager of the department being studied be included on the team. A manager who is not involved in the problem analysis and the subsequent formulation of the mathematical model is unlikely to have much confidence in the recommendations derived from the model. Proper implementation of a solution requires an operating manager who understands the solution and believes that it will work. Such an understanding can come only from close involvement with the team.

It must be emphasized that the team neither replaces the manager nor takes over managerial decision-making responsibility. The group merely attempts to formulate objective criteria upon which managers can base their decisions.

Managers do not need to be mathematicians to benefit from management science. However, they do need some understanding of quantitative tools—at least enough to enable them to appreciate the potential of quantitative analysis and to be aware of its limitations. Such an understanding will place them in a much better position to undertake the scientific analysis of problems. They also need some knowledge of quantitative techniques so that they may communicate intelligently with management science specialists.

> Quantitative methods impose a discipline that may at first be troublesome. Problems must be defined exactly and reduced to a conceptual framework. The relevant factors must be clearly identified, and assumptions about how each bears on the ultimate decision must be described independently and with recognition of interacting characteristics. Data must be selected to test out theories. Management has been performing these activities for years, of course, but to articulate them rigorously is a new demand. All this involves a more thorough understanding of *operations*, not of mathematics.[2]

THE METHODOLOGY OF MANAGEMENT SCIENCE

The Use of Models

The essence of the management science approach to decision making is *model building*. A model is basically a simplified representation of an actual situation or subject. Some types of models are quite common—model airplanes or automobiles built to scale are physical models; a road map is a geographic model; and the diagrams used in elementary economics textbooks to describe the concept of supply and demand are graphic models.

A model contains only the most important and basic features of the real system it represents. It is not necessary, for example, that a road map show houses, buildings, and trees. Such a map would be so large as to be completely unwieldy. However, a model can also be too abstract. A map showing only interstate highways would be of little use to a traveler going to a town located fifty miles from such a highway.

Mathematical Models

The models used in management science are mathematical, but their fundamental concept is no different from that of the road map—a simplified representation of a real system. The operations of any company, for instance, can be represented by a basic equation:

$$\text{Net Income} = \text{Revenue} - (\text{Expenses} + \text{Taxes})$$

The components of the equation can then be subdivided. Expenses, for example, can be broken down into manufacturing cost, selling cost, and administrative cost, and each could be further subdivided.

Mathematical models are constructed by devising a set of equations which represent the significant variables that must be considered and the relationships among those variables. Any important variable which would affect the decision must be included. Some models are highly complex and are, therefore, very difficult to construct. But underlying this complexity is always the basic equation that a measure of the system's overall performance (P) equals the relationship (f) between a set of significant controllable aspects of the system (C_j) and a set of uncontrollable aspects (U_j). Expressed symbolically, it would appear as follows:[3]

$$P = f\,(C_i,\ U_j)$$

Examples of controllable aspects of variables are product prices, the size and frequency of production runs, and departmental budgets. For the model to be realistic, limitations or constraints must be placed on these variables. Product prices, for instance, can fluctuate only within certain limits. A ridiculously high price would cause sales to drop to zero, and an extremely low price would fail to cover production costs. The uncontrollable variables—those not subject to the manager's control—would include such factors as competitors' prices, raw materials costs, and union wages.

Mathematical models may be either *deterministic* or *probabilistic*. In a deterministic model, all variables are assigned exact values. A product price, for instance, may be exactly $56, or the distance between two warehouses in a transportation problem may be 131 miles. In a probabilistic model, the values of some variables are uncertain. This uncertainty requires the use of probability concepts. The probability of striking oil when drilling, for instance, may be 10 percent. This figure might be based on past experience—the company, over a period of years, has discovered oil one of every ten times it has drilled.

Most business systems have a probabilistic element. Unfortunately, with probabilistic models a considerable amount of data must be collected in order to determine each probability distribution, and the analysis of models involving probability distributions is much more complicated. For these reasons a probabilistic system will often be represented by a deterministic model, each variable being given its average value.[4]

Advantages of Models

Construction of a model requires the manager and the management science team to consider carefully which aspects of the real system are significant, how much weight should be assigned to each, and how they are all interrelated. These preliminary decisions are valuable in themselves, because they force the manager to analyze in detail the problem situation.

Once the model is constructed, it may well be easier to understand than the real situation. The manager can then analyze, manipulate, and modify the model without disturbing the real system. To return to the road map example, a tourist planning to drive from St. Louis to Miami can select the shortest route by studying the map rather than by having to drive each possible route before deciding.

As in the physical sciences, the decision maker can hold some variables in the model constant while experimenting with others, attempting to determine how the real system would be affected by certain changes. Various alternatives can be analyzed without any interference with the actual system. Using the real system for experimental purposes could be extremely disruptive and costly.

Of course, such advantages depend upon the degree to which the model realistically represents the actual system. A drastically oversimplified model will certainly not be realistic, but one which attempts to duplicate the real system in every detail will be unmanageable. And some problems contain intangible and human factors which may be of paramount importance yet may be difficult, or impossible, to quantify and, therefore, to include in the model.

Steps in Quantitative Analysis

Synthesizing what has been said, we can enumerate a series of steps to be used in the quantitative analysis of business problems. These steps are as follows:

1. Formulate the problem—include the solution objective, the controllable and uncontrollable variables, and the pertinent constraints.
2. Construct a mathematical model—this should be a realistic, although somewhat simplified, representation of the real system.
3. Test and revise the model—test for realism by applying the model to historical data, if available, and locate and correct any errors.

THE NEW YORK TIMES MODEL

As a result of concern over declining market share and the future impact of the uncertain New York City economy on circulation and advertising, management of the New York Times Company began to design a corporate planning model in 1974. Since that time, models have been constructed for the newspaper itself, fifteen other newspapers owned by the corporation, *Family Circle* magazine, and two cable-television subsidiaries. The model of *The New York Times* newspaper is comprised of more than three hundred equations, and the models of the other businesses each contain twenty-five to thirty equations.

Management has been particularly pleased with the resulting forecasts of circulation and advertising expenditures. Both variables are linked, in the models, to the economies of New York City and the nation. The models have even been partially responsible for the change in format and layout of the newspaper.

SOURCE: Adapted from Thomas H. Naylor, "Effective Use of Strategic Planning, Forecasting, and Modeling in the Executive Suite," *Managerial Planning* 30 (January/February 1982): 9.

4. Derive a solution from the model—an optimal solution will depend upon the degree of accuracy with which the model represents the actual system.

5. Implement the solution—apply the model's solution to the real system, document its effectiveness, and continually update it.

SPECIFIC MANAGEMENT SCIENCE TECHNIQUES

Linear Programming

Linear programming is a deterministic model which aids the manager in deciding upon the optimal allocation of a firm's limited resources. Such resources would include money, capital equipment, raw materials, and personnel. Because they are limited, the manager wishes to use them in the most profitable combination; and their allocation is based upon an objective selected by management, such as maximum profit or minimum cost. Linear programming is one of the most widely used management science tools.

To be solvable by this technique, however, a problem must have the following characteristics:

1. A specified objective criterion.
2. Limited resources with alternative uses.
3. Quantitative measurement of the problem elements.
4. Linearity—all of the relationships in the problem must be precisely proportional. For instance, a 10 percent increase in shipping distance must cause a commensurate rise in shipping costs.

Once it is evident that the problem meets the linear programming requirements, the mathematical model can be formulated. Such a model is basically a set of linear equations describing the problem in mathematical terms. The equations are then solved simultaneously by a specific linear programming technique, such as the graphic method, simplex method, dual simplex method, or the modified distribution (MODI) method. The method selected would depend upon the nature of the problem.

A simple illustration will help to demonstrate the basic procedure. Assume that a company which has manufactured and sold box spring and mattress sets for years has recently decided to diversify its product line by manufacturing love seats.[5] The process used to produce love seats is similar to that employed in constructing box springs, and the profit margin for love seats is higher.

Management is now faced with a decision: How many mattress/box spring sets should it produce and how many love seats should it manufacture? Demand for both products appears high and relatively stable. Each mattress/box spring set sold contributes $100 to profit while each love seat sold will contribute $150. Each product must go through two processes: (1) framework construction with a total of 100 hours capacity per month, and (2) assembly with a total capacity of 80 hours per month.

Each love seat requires four hours in framework and two hours in assembly. Each mattress/box spring set requires two hours in framework and two hours in assembly. What combination of mattress/box spring sets and love seats should management produce in order to maximize its profits?

Summarizing the situation in tabular form, as shown in Table 9–1, helps one to visualize the problem more clearly.

The problem can now be transformed into the following mathematical model:

$$\text{Profit}_{max} = \$100M + \$150L$$

Subject to:

$$2M + 4L \leq 100 \text{ (Framework)}$$
$$2M + 2L \leq 80 \text{ (Assembly)}$$
$$\text{where } M, L \geq 0$$

TABLE 9–1 The linear programming problem

Processes	Hours Required/Product		Monthly Capacity in Hours
	Mattress/Box Spring Set	Love Seat	
Framework	2	4	100
Assembly	2	2	80
Contribution to profit	$100	$150	

The top line in the model is called the *objective function* and tells us that the goal or objective of this problem is to maximize profits in this situation in which each mattress/box spring set *(M)* contributes $100 to profits and each love seat *(L)* contributes $150.

This objective function is subject to the following *constraints*: the framework process has a maximum monthly capacity of 100 hours and each *M* requires 2 hours of this capacity while each *L* requires 4 hours; and in the assembly process, which has a total capacity of 80 hours, each *M* requires 2 hours and each *L* requires 2 hours. In no case can total production time in either process exceed the monthly capacity of the process although production time may be less than capacity (i.e., $\leq$). Finally, the designation "*M, L* $\geq$ 0" indicates that negative production (i.e., less than zero units) of either item is not possible.

We can now construct a graph of production combination possibilities, where the production of *M* is shown on the vertical axis and the production of *L* on the horizontal axis. Let us now graph the first constraint, which indicates the capacity of the framework process and the time required to construct the framework of both *M* and *L*:

$$2M + 4L \leq 100.$$

This simple function can be shown as a straight line on the graph in Figure 9–1.

FIGURE 9–1 The framework constraint

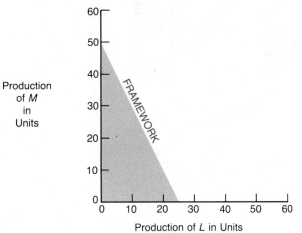

Production of *M* in Units

Production of *L* in Units

The shaded area is called the *feasibility space* because any production combination of M and L within this space is feasible (i.e., any combination of M and L within the shaded area can be produced without violating the capacity constraints of the framework process). Any production combination outside the feasibility space is not possible because it would violate the capacity constraints of the framework process.

Now we can add to the graph the second constraint—the assembly process—as shown in Figure 9–2:

$$2M + 2L \leqslant 80$$

Our feasibility space has now been reduced slightly. Although the framework process capacity permits construction of 50M, the capacity of the assembly process would be exceeded by that level of production. So the assembly process capacity has limited our feasible production combination possibilities.

The question now is: What is the most profitable combination within the feasibility space? Fortunately, we do not have to test all possible production possibilities within this space. In a two-dimensional problem like this, the optimum solution must always be at one of the corners of the feasibility space, as shown in Figure 9–3.

Each corner can now be tested using our objective function:

$$\text{Profit}_{max} = \$100M + \$150L$$

Test (M = 0, L = 0)	$100(0) + $150(0) = $0 profit
Test (M = 40, L = 0)	$100(40) + $150(0) = $4,000 profit
Test (M = 30, L = 10)	$100(30) + $150(10) = $4,500 profit
Test (M = 0, L = 25)	$100(0) + $150(25) = $3,750 profit

The optimum product mix then is to produce 30 mattress/box spring sets and 10 love seats every month, given current capacity. No other combination would yield more profit than $4,500.

FIGURE 9–2   The framework and assembly constraints

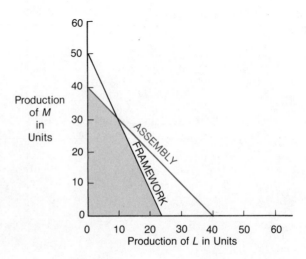

FIGURE 9–3   Possible solutions

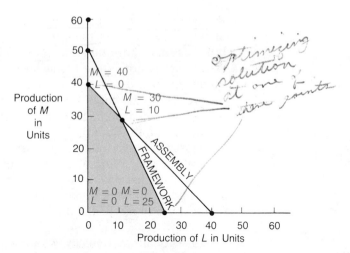

This simple example illustrates how to construct and solve a mathematical model. Even a problem containing a small number of variables, such as this one, is difficult to solve without the help of a systematic technique. Although realistic linear programming problems are considerably larger and more complex (requiring the use of a computer and a technique called the simplex method), the basic concepts used to solve such problems are similar to those shown in this example.

Although one illustration is based on a product mix problem, this is only one of the many applications of linear programming. Some of its other important uses are to determine distribution schedules to minimize transportation costs and to solve production scheduling, machine loading, and blending or mixing problems. Linear programming is also used to plan menus in university dormitories and hospitals. The objective is to minimize cost, and the various constraints relate to protein content, calories, cholesterol, and so on.

Although linear programming is applicable to a wide range of managerial problems, many problems do not fall within its requirements and cannot, therefore, be solved through this method.

> Such problems . . . may contain relationships which cannot be represented by linear functions, or may be characterized by probabilistic relationships or perhaps relationships which change over time. . . . To cope with complexities of this sort, several variations and extensions of linear programming have been developed. Quadratic programming and integer programming have been developed to attack problems of nonlinearity of functional relationships. Stochastic programming deals with problems containing probabilistic relationships. Dynamic programming can be adapted to problems in which time or the sequence of events is an important consideration.[6]

Probability Theory

The use of probabilistic models becomes necessary when the values of some variables are uncertain. In such situations, knowledge of probabil-

ity theory becomes quite useful. Probabilistic estimates of the occurrence of future events may be either *objective* or *subjective.* Objective probability estimates are derived from analyses of historical data, while subjective probabilities are based on the manager's intuition and often fall under the heading of formal "educated guesses." The more experienced managers are, the more nearly accurate their subjective probability estimates are likely to be. The concept of probability can best be illustrated by the use of an example.[7]

Assume that a company must make a decision whether to drill a wildcat oil well. Normally, this would be considered a type of decision involving a great deal of subjective judgment or intuition. However considering the problem in a systematic manner, the manager can formulate a procedure to aid in the decision by incorporating the following steps:

1. Identify alternative courses of action.
2. Determine the possible outcomes of each alternative.
3. Assign probabilities to the various outcomes.
4. Calculate the expected value of each alternative.
5. Choose the alternative with the highest expected value.

The first step reveals three alternatives: (1) drill; (2) don't drill; or (3) farm out for a royalty. Step 2 shows three possible outcomes or consequences of drilling or farming out: (1) dry hole; (2) small well; or (3) big well. The expected gain that would be associated with each outcome may then be estimated on the basis of past experience or the judgment of the oil operator.* In step 3, an estimate must also be made, on the basis of past experience or judgment, of the probability of experiencing each of three possible outcomes or consequences (dry hole, small well, big well). Figure 9–4 summarizes these factors and shows the expected value calculated for each alternative course of action.

It can be seen that the first alternative offers no prospects of gain or loss inasmuch as it is a decision not to drill. The second alternative, drilling, leads to a loss of $500,000 (cost of drilling) if no oil is found. A small well will produce $300,000 over and above drilling and operating costs. A big well will produce $9,300,000 on the same basis. If the drilling is farmed out (third alternative), a dry hole will avoid the $500,000 loss, but striking oil will produce a smaller return based on the royalty agreement.

The estimated probabilities appear below each outcome. The chances of hitting a dry hole, for example, are thought to be 6 out of 10. The expected value of each alternative is computed by adding the products of the probability and expected gain for each outcome or consequence. The alternative of drilling has an expected value of $720,000 in contrast to $162,500 and $0 for the other two alternatives. The solution

---

*In this illustration, the figures for gain in the event of success are really *present value* figures. The cash income from production will not be fully realized for many years, and the figures represent present value equivalents.

Alternatives	Outcomes			Expected Value
	Dry Hole	Small Well	Big Well	
	.6 Probability	.3 Probability	.1 Probability	
Don't Drill	$ 0	$ 0	$ 0	$ 0
Drill	−500,000	300,000	9,300,000	720,000
Farm Out	0	125,000	1,250,000	162,500

FIGURE 9–4   Payoff table (new values after costs)

is the alternative with the highest expected value—in this case, the decision should be to drill.

In this problem, then, the decision maker has reached a conclusion by assigning or assuming specific dollar values for each outcome and estimating the probability of each consequence. The process differs from one in which the decision maker is somewhat aware of differences but uses subjective judgment without trying to assign specific values for each variable. The same problem can be analyzed graphically in the form of a *decision tree*, as shown in Figure 9–5.

The rectangular node preceding the first three branches at the left of the decision tree indicates a decision situation. The manager must choose one of the three possible alternatives. The circular nodes to the right indicate the possible outcomes of each alternative decision.

Probability theory is increasingly being put to practical uses in industry. The Grocery Products Division of The Pillsbury Company, for instance, uses decision trees to aid in making marketing decisions at the

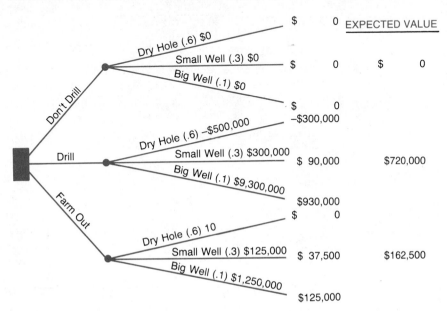

FIGURE 9–5   Decision tree analysis

middle- and top-management levels. At General Electric, all investment requests of more than $500,000 must be supported by a probabilistic assessment of the rate of return on the investment and other key measures. Ford, General Mills, and Du Pont are other prominent companies which use probability theory to aid in their decision-making processes.[8]

Simulation

Our discussion thus far has been primarily concerned with determining the optimal solution to a business problem. In some cases, however, the actual situation may be so complex that an optimal solution may be either impossible or inordinately expensive to derive. At such a time, the manager may turn to the technique of *simulation*.

This method involves the construction of a mathematical model which simulates the operation of the real system by describing the behavior of individual components of the system and the effects of their interaction. With the aid of a computer, such a model can be used by the manager to experiment with literally dozens of alternative decisions on the simulated system to determine which decision will yield the best results. Although the optimal solution may not be derived because of the impracticability of trying out all possible alternative decisions, a workable, satisfactory solution can be found.

The operation of an entire firm or a single department, such as the production department, can be simulated. Or the computer can simulate a selected geographic or demographic market to determine probable customer reaction to a change in marketing strategy, such as packaging or advertising. In effect, simulation gives the manager a laboratory in which he or she can observe the interaction of the significant factors in a problem while varying some and holding others constant.

Through simulation, the manager can experiment without affecting the real system. Automobile manufacturers can test design modifications, for instance, by simulating collisions on a computer rather than having to crash expensive cars on test tracks. Traffic systems—including the proportion of cars to trucks, peak congestion hours, and bus routes—can be simulated so that city planners can test new speed limits, road widths, traffic signals, and road patterns, all without ever leaving the office.[9]

As mentioned earlier, several years of operations can be simulated within a few minutes. The manager can experiment with a number of alternatives, testing each to see which will offer the best results over a period of time. The computer can print out the results of each alternative decision in the form of pro forma financial statements and share-of-the-market figures. Such a technique may well be easier for the nontechnical manager to understand than the more rigorous mathematical techniques.

Another major advantage of simulation is that it provides excellent managerial training. A manager's decision-making ability can be greatly enhanced by dealing with simulated situations involving different aspects of the job. In a few weeks or months, a manager can observe problem situations which would ordinarily occur over a period of years.[10]

One of the most widespread uses of simulation is the *business game*, developed in the mid-1950s, and now used extensively in university schools of business and management training programs. The basic concept in business gaming is that the participants must make corporate strategy decisions that are most likely to yield maximum profits in a competitive environment. The decision maker, for instance, may be able to increase the firm's share of the market by lowering prices or increasing advertising expenditures or both. However, the manager does not know what competitors may do or what changes may occur in the overall economic environment. Certain assumptions are required, therefore, as a basis for action. Such a technique may be used profitably for training managers.

A survey of 346 corporations in the United States and Canada indicates that the number of firms using simulation has increased significantly since 1969. Although most of these companies are relatively large (over $500 million in yearly sales), an increasing number are smaller firms (annual sales under $100 million). The most common uses of simulation models are in the financial, marketing, or production areas.[11]

GE'S BUSINESS GAME

General Electric has devised such a method—C.A.S.E. (Computer Assisted Simulation Exercises)—to accelerate the growth of "general managers." The participants are assigned to specific management positions in one of two competing companies—Basic or Universal.

Each participant receives a five-year history of the firm and a functional package. The participant selected to act as marketing manager, for instance, receives data primarily on the marketing function. This requires close cooperation with those participants who have received data on engineering, personnel, finance, and production. The management team then plans, makes decisions, receives the results, plans again, and makes more decisions.

SOURCE: Based on William E. Rothschild, "The C.A.S.E. Approach—A Valuable Aid for Management Development," *California Management Review* 14 (Fall 1971): 31–38.

Simulation, however, for all of its advantages, is not without limitations. Because it may be easier for the manager to undestand than the more precise mathematical models, there is a danger that simulation may be used even when a more analytical technique can, and should, be applied. The manager should recognize that optimal solutions are not necessarily provided through simulation. And even a satisfactory solution requires a large number of experiments and computations. The survey reported above indicated that the average number of mathematical equations in a simulation model was 545, with some models containing several thousand equations. The average time required for development was 18 months.[12]

Finally, it is important to remember that simulation must be based on actual data and must accurately represent, although in a simplified form, the real world. Simulation cannot be used when the necessary data are not available.

Other Management Science Tools

Queuing theory, or waiting line theory, is a management science technique which aids the manager in making decisions involving the establishment of service facilities, such as determining the optimal number of tellers in a bank at certain hours, checkers in a grocery store, clerks in a tool crib, or loading docks at a warehouse. A policy of maintaining a large number of service facilities, such as check-out counters in a supermarket, can be quite costly. Although the supermarket customers will experience little waiting time to have their grocery bills totaled, several of the checkers will be idle for long periods during the day. On the other hand, maintaining only one or two check-out counters will result in lengthy waiting lines, impatient and angry customers, and the eventual loss of business to competitors. Both extremes involve costs—the cost of idle checkers versus the cost of lost business; queuing theory helps the manager balance these two costs.[13]

A technique useful in solving problems for which precise mathematical models are not feasible is *heuristic programming*. This method is used in analyzing large, relatively unstructured problems. A heuristic process is basically a rule-of-thumb or computational procedure which directs the computer to limit the number of different alternatives to be analyzed. Rather than taking all alternatives into account, some are ignored to reduce the size of the problem. In fact, very large problems are broken down into smaller subproblems, which can be solved more easily. The solution is found through a process analogous to trial-and-error reasoning.

EVALUATION OF MANAGEMENT SCIENCE

Use and Limitations of Management Science

The use of management science is increasing, particularly in small organizations. An extensive survey of 492 firms which use it indicates that 46 percent of the companies with fewer than 10,000 employees have established management science departments since 1970. Larger organizations generally have longer histories of management science usage—66 percent of the firms with over 50,000 employees set up such departments before 1965.[14]

Managers are aware, however, that management science is not a panacea for all organizational problems. Its practical use in decision making is subject to a number of constraints. Perhaps the chief limitation is that some variables in business decisions are simply not quantifiable. Yet, to use management science properly, all variables must be assigned quantitative weights. This holds true even for the less rigorous techniques of simulation and heuristic programming—computers "think" only in mathematical terms. If a variable, such as creativity, cannot be expressed mathematically, it cannot be subjected to a management science approach.[15]

A NONQUANTIFIABLE VARIABLE

"One bus company carried out a major routing exercise and as a result closed down a number of its routes and started several new ones. The company believed that this would lead to a substantial reduction in total costs while still maintaining the same level of service. They did not take full account of the resistance to change of existing bus users. As a result of public pressure one of the closed routes had to be started up again. This wiped out most of the predicted savings."

SOURCE: John Hull, John Mapes, and Brian Wheeler, *Model Building Techniques for Management* (Westmead, England: Saxon House, 1976), p. 170.

A further limitation is the gap that exists between the manager and the management scientist. The manager may have little knowledge or appreciation of sophisticated mathematical techniques, while the management science specialist has little knowledge of the problems the manager faces. This limitation, however, is being gradually overcome by training management students in quantitative techniques and by assigning line managers to management science teams. Indeed, the survey mentioned above reports that one-third of the academic degrees held by management scientists are now in either business administration or management science.[16] Organizations might also include quantitative training in their management development programs, while introducing management science specialists to the concepts of organization theory and behavior.

Another problem is the spurious accuracy that may be associated with quantitative analysis. The use of numbers and equations gives an appearance of scientific accuracy. The resulting willingness to place too much confidence in quantitative methods may be dangerous. Too often we are more concerned with numbers than with the reality the numbers are supposed to represent. There is an "all-important difference between *precision* (which is a measure of how many zeroes and decimal places the number has) and *accuracy* (which is how correct the number is)."[17]

For instance, one manager admits that he has "many times" modified the value of probability estimates in decision analysis in order to justify to corporate headquarters an alternative that he and his superiors desired.[18] If unrealistic estimates are used in making a decision, the results will be undependable. Yet managers often hesitate to question quantitative reports generated by computers for fear of revealing their own ignorance. Many executives still automatically assume that work done on a computer is correct.[19]

Finally, the more sophisticated forms of quantitative analysis are both elaborate and costly. Large, complex problems can be economically subjected to analysis in this way, but many smaller problems and minor decisions cannot justify such refinements in their solution. Management cannot afford to shoot every sparrow with a cannon.

We should note also that the use of quantitative tools is concerned with only one phase of the decision-making process. Quantitative analysis is not ordinarily used to identify the problem or to develop the alternative possibilities that are open. It is only after groundwork of this nature has been performed that the adoption of quantitative analysis becomes appropriate. It does not, therefore, constitute a substitute for the entire decision-making process according to traditional methods.

THE DIFFERENCE BETWEEN PRECISION AND ACCURACY

A tragic example of quantitative estimates gone awry was the abortive rescue attempt of the U.S. hostages in Iran in April 1980. The rescue mission involved eight Sea Stallion helicopters which were to journey over eight hundred miles from the carrier Nimitz to a point just southeast of Teheran. Military planners had determined that the mission required a minimum of six helicopters. They calculated that there was a .965 probability that if eight helicopters were sent, at least six would make it to the rendezvous point outside Teheran.

Long before the rendezvous point was reached, however, two helicopters had broken down and another had been forced to return to the Nimitz because of instrument malfunctions. The second helicopter to break down did so because of the loss of its second-stage hydraulic pump. No spare pump had been brought along because an actuarial study of the parts most likely to break down concluded that the need for a spare pump was marginal.

SOURCE: The probability estimates are based on David C. Martin, "New Light on the Rescue Mission," *Newsweek*, 30 June 1980, pp. 18–20.

Future of Management Science

The field of management science is steadily developing. How rapidly new techniques and new applications will be devised can only be surmised, but the outlook is optimistic. As computer technology improves, new quantitative methods probably will be designed to enable the manager to attack even poorly structured business problems and to analyze the results of thousands of alternatives combining complex relationships.

The current state of knowledge is already such that many of the present routine decision-making activities of lower and middle managers, such as inventory control and production and distribution scheduling, can be programmed.

> Once the problem has been programmed, it is no longer necessary for the manager to give as much time and thought in reaching decisions on the firm's problems. Instead of being bogged down with the routine decisions of his department, he can now relegate these to a management information computer system. Thus lower and middle management can now spend time planning for their respective areas, training their personnel, and perhaps for the first time, getting their respective jobs "under control."[20]

As planning and decision making become more complex in an increasingly dynamic environment, well-managed companies will tend to rely more heavily on scientific methods of analysis to help reduce the concomitant risk and uncertainty. One need not fear, however, that the process of decision making will be taken over by computers and mathematicians.

> [Management science] is to the manager what the telescope is to the astronomer and the microscope to the biologist. Astronomers, before they had telescopes, had to work in a very halting fashion. The provision of the telescope did not mean that we no longer required astronomers but rather that it gave them an extra insight into their particular subject and hence led them into much more difficult areas.[21]

Management science, then, will become increasingly valuable to managers, but it will certainly never replace them.

SUMMARY

The application of quantitative techniques to managerial decision making can aid greatly in reducing the risk and uncertainty managers must confront daily. Although managers have used some quantitative tools for decades, the emphasis in recent years has been on *management science*—a concept which emerged during World War II. Used in conjunction with the computer, management science is the *mathematical ap-*

plication of the scientific method to the solution of business problems.

At the center of this approach is the *mathematical model*—a set of equations representing the actual problem situation. The model is constructed by a *team* composed of management science and computer specialists and managers representing the departments being studied. The specific techniques used to construct and solve the model depend upon the nature of the problem.

Linear programming, for instance, is used to determine the optimal allocation of a firm's limited resources. *Probability theory* is a systematic and logical method of solving a problem which would otherwise involve substantial judgment. Satisfactory solutions to problems that are too complex for precise mathematical techniques can be derived through *simulation*. The most profitable number of service facilities for an organization can be computed through the use of *queuing theory*, and *heuristic programming* is a technique that aids in the analysis of large, unstructured problems.

Management science does have definite limitations, the major one being that some aspects of decisions are simply not quantifiable. But the field is still relatively new and its practical applications are already numerous. Although management science will certainly never replace the manager or eliminate the manager's decision-making responsibility, it will become an increasingly valuable management tool.

DISCUSSION QUESTIONS

1. Management science occasionally has been called "quantitative common sense." Do you agree with this designation? Why or why not?

2. What are some advantages of the *team approach* to management science?

3. What problems might arise in the relationship between the manager and the management science team?

4. Since the manager cannot affect *uncontrollable variables*, why should these variables be included in the *mathematical model* of the problem?

5. Is management science more useful in making routine or nonroutine decisions?

6. Would a decision tree be considered a deterministic or probabilistic model? Explain why.

7. In your opinion, why is management science not being more widely used in business decision-making today?

8. What steps might organizations take to increase the use of quantitative techniques in decision making?

9. Do you feel that the manager of the future who has an understanding of management science will have a marked advantage over one who has little knowledge of such concepts?

10. Company A wishes to maximize its profit by manufacturing two products,

Model A and Model B. A wholesaler has signed a contract promising to purchase at a predetermined price all the company can manufacture over the next 30 days. The basic question is how many units of each product to manufacture. Information concerning the production of the two products is as follows:

Processes	Labor Hours Required/Product Model A	Model B	Labor Hours Available Next 30 Days
Manufacturing	15	10	15,000
Painting	1	1	1,200
Assembly	3	2	3,000
Contribution to profit	$400	$300	

11. A public official must select only one of four available options (choosing more than one option would make too many political "waves") for controlling urban air pollution: (1) ban outdoor fires, (2) restrict auto traffic, (3) close coal-burning power plants, or (4) reroute aircraft takeoffs. Each of these alternatives will provide a given number of Air Quality Points (AQPs) assuming certain climatic conditions are present. A higher AQP rating means better air. The AQPs for the various conditions have been estimated as below:

Decision Alternatives	States of Nature Inversion	Onshore Wind	Calm	Fog
Ban fires	12	9	6	14
Restrict traffic	14	15	5	10
Close plants	3	11	9	9
Reroute aircraft	18	2	8	6

Determine the appropriate decision if the weather bureau certifies the probability of inversion as .2, onshore wind as .3, calm as .4, and fog as .1.

NOTES

1. Barry Shore, *Quantitative Methods for Business Decisions: Text and Cases* (New York: McGraw-Hill Book Co., 1978), pp. 435–36.
2. Robert F. Vandell, "Management Evolution in the Quantitative World," *Harvard Business Review* 48 (January–February 1970): 92.
3. Russell L. Ackoff and Patrick Rivett, *A Manager's Guide to Operations Research* (New York: John Wiley & Sons, 1963), pp. 24–26.

4. John Hull, John Mapes, and Brian Wheeler, *Model Building Techniques for Management* (Westmead, England: Saxon House, 1976), p. 12.

5. The product mix problem seems appropriate because production planning receives more management science emphasis than any other function in U.S. corporations according to Stanley J. PoKempner, *Management Science in Business*, A Research Report from the Conference Board's Division of Management Research (New York: The Conference Board, 1977), p. 18.

6. Barry E. Cushing, "The Application Potential of Integer Programming," *Journal of Business* 43 (October 1970): 457. Copyright © by the University of Chicago, 1970.

7. This example is adapted from material prepared by Dr. C. Jackson Grayson, Jr., and is used with his permission.

8. Rex V. Brown, "Do Managers Find Decision Theory Useful?" *Harvard Business Review* 48 (May–June 1970): 81–83.

9. "Mapping with a Computer," *Newsweek*, 11 September 1978, p. 87.

10. Roger I. Hall, "A System Pathology of an Organization: The Rise and Fall of the Old *Saturday Evening Post*," *Administrative Science Quarterly* 21 (June 1976): 185–211, has simulated the dynamic relationships among the parts of a publishing system to analyze the reasons for the success—and eventual failure—of the old *Saturday Evening Post*.

11. Thomas H. Naylor and Horst Schauland, "A Survey of Users of Corporate Planning Models," *Management Science* 22 (May 1976): 927–37.

12. Ibid., p. 932.

13. A detailed description of the steps needed to construct a model which simulates alternative queuing systems and configurations of inspection stations for customs inspectors in international airports is presented in Eugene Richman and Dennis Coleman, "Monte Carlo Simulation for Management," *California Management Review* 23 (Spring 1981): 82–91.

14. PoKempner, *Management Science in Business*, p. 7.

15. See Russell L. Ackoff, "On the Use of Models in Corporate Planning," *Strategic Management Journal* 2 (October–December 1981): 358.

16. PoKempner, *Management Science in Business*, p. 29.

17. John Cobbs, "A Misplaced Faith in Numbers," *Business Week*, 19 November 1979, p. 17.

18. F. L. Harrison, "Decision Making in Conditions of Extreme Uncertainty," *Journal of Management Studies* 14 (May 1977): 172.

19. "How Personal Computers Can Backfire," *Business Week*, 12 July 1982, pp. 58–59.

20. From *Decision Making through Operations Research*, p. 536, by Robert J. Thierauf. Copyright © 1970 by Robert J. Thierauf. By permission of John Wiley & Sons, Inc.

21. Ackoff and Rivett, *Operations Research*, p. 97.

SUPPLEMENTARY READING

Ackoff, Russell L. "On the Use of Models in Corporate Planning." *Strategic Management Journal* 2 (October–December 1981): 353–59.

Anderson, John C., and **Hoffmann, Thomas R.** "A Perspective on the Implementation of Management Science." *Academy of Management Review* 3 (July 1978): 563–71.

Arnoff, E. Leonard. "Managers Should Marry Models." *Planning Review* 4 (July 1976): 11–14.

Brightman, Harvey, and **Noble, Carl.** "On the Ineffective Education of Decision Scientists." *Decision Sciences* 10 (January 1979): 151–57.

Fuller, Jack A., and **Atherton, Roger M.** "Fitting in the Management Science Specialist." *Business Horizons* 22 (April 1979): 14–17.

Gaither, Norman. "The Adoption of Operations Research Techniques by Manufacturing Organizations." *Decision Sciences* 6 (October 1975): 797–813.

Graham, Robert J. "The First Step to Successful Implementation of Management Science." *Columbia Journal of World Business* 12 (Fall 1977): 66–72.

Grayson, C. Jackson, Jr. "Management Science and Business Practice." *Harvard Business Review* 51 (July–August 1973): 41–48.

Green, Thad B.; Newsom, Walter B.; and **Jones, S. Roland.** "A Survey of the Application of Quantitative Techniques to Production/Operations Management in Large Corporations." *Academy of Management Journal* 20 (December 1977): 669–76.

Hertz, David B. "Does Management Science Influence Management Action?" *Columbia Journal of World Business* 12 (Fall 1977): 105–12.

Levitt, Theodore. "A Heretical View of Management 'Science.'" *Fortune*, 18 December 1978, pp. 50–52.

Naylor, Thomas H. "Effective Use of Strategic Planning, Forecasting, and Modeling in the Executive Suite." *Managerial Planning* 30 (January–February 1982): 4–11.

Neuhauser, John J. "Business Games Have Failed." *Academy of Management Review* 1 (October 1976): 124–29.

Richman, Eugene, and **Coleman, Dennis.** "Monte Carlo Simulation for Management." *California Management Review* 23 (Spring 1981): 82–91.

Sullivan, William G. "The Use of Decision Trees in Planning Plant Expansion." *Advanced Management Journal* 40 (Winter 1975): 29–39.

Ulvila, Jacob W., and **Brown, Rex V.** "Decision Analysis Comes of Age." *Harvard Business Review* 60 (September–October 1982): 130–41.

Whitehouse, Gary E., and **Wechsler, Ben L.** *Applied Operations Research: A Survey.* New York: John Wiley & Sons, 1976.

Zand, Dale E., and **Sorensen, Richard E.** "Theory of Change and the Effective Use of Management Science." *Administrative Science Quarterly* 20 (December 1975): 532–45.

PART THREE
ORGANIZING FOR
EFFECTIVE
PERFORMANCE

10
CREATING THE ORGANIZATION STRUCTURE

This chapter will enable you to

- *Understand the nature of organizing, the values of good organization, and the potential dangers in organization planning.*
- *Identify and explain the underlying situational forces influencing the shape of organizations.*
- *Distinguish the various patterns for grouping jobs and/or activities and explain the reasons for using particular patterns in particular situations.*
- *Recognize the impact of personal goals and motivations on organizing decisions.*

The manager's organizing decisions involve the formal structuring of relationships among jobs, people, and activities. Given an assortment of jobs, how shall they be related or grouped? This chapter examines *structural aspects of organizational life*—specifically, the *process of creating organizations, underlying forces which influence their shape, patterns of grouping jobs and activities,* and *human factors in structural decisions.*

NATURE AND IMPORTANCE OF ORGANIZING

To integrate the contributions of many individuals, a manager must devise some pattern which relates each of them to the others. Without some such pattern of coordination, results would be chaotic. In this section, we examine the nature, benefits, and criticisms of *formal organization,* the structure that is intended to provide coordination.

Formal Organization

Social scientists developed a theory of *formal organization* that stressed the rational nature of this formal organization and applied the name *bureaucracy* to it. According to this theory, the formal organization is visualized as a pyramid of officials who direct and coordinate the work of specialists by use of formal procedures. It is considered important that roles be carefully defined and rules for interaction clearly delineated.

The formal organization or bureaucracy, therefore, consists of the management-specified framework of relationships. This formal organization makes up the skeleton for the social system and is supplemented by informal relationships that develop spontaneously among organization members without explicit definition by management.

Basic Parts of Organizations

To understand better the nature of organizing, consider a generalized description of organizations and their component parts. Think in terms of a medium or large organization—whether it be a business firm, university, hospital, or some other type of institution. Figure 10–1 presents a sketch of such an organization and its basic parts as visualized by Henry Mintzberg. This sketch of basic parts should not be confused with an organization chart. It merely shows the broad segments of activity which all organizations have in common.

At the bottom of the diagram is the *operating core*. It consists of the people who produce the primary goods and/or services of the organization. These are, for example, the assemblers in a manufacturing plant, the faculty in a university, and the nurses in a hospital. Apart from the contribution of the operating core, the organization has no reason for existence.

Coordination of work in the operating core is provided by two management groups. The *strategic apex* is the top management group, and the term emphasizes the strategy-determining role which relates the organization to its environment. Within the strategic apex is the chief executive officer who serves as the ultimate coordinating unit in the organization.

FIGURE 10–1   Basic parts of an organization

SOURCE: Henry Mintzberg, *The Structuring of Organizations,* © 1979, p. 20. Reprinted by permission of Prentice-Hall, Inc., Englewood Cliffs, N.J.

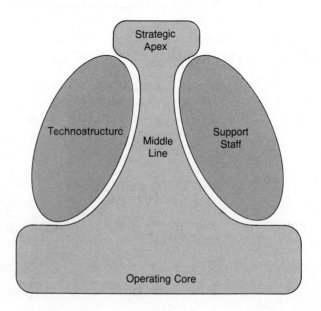

The *middle line* links the operating core with the strategic apex. Divisional managers, department heads, foremen, and supervisors are all part of this middle line.

Two types of auxiliary functions are identified. One of these, the *technostructure*, includes analysts who assist the middle line and the strategic apex in performance of their managerial functions. Accountants, production schedulers, and corporate planners are all part of the technostructure. Another type of assistance is provided by the *support staff*. Their contributions include such activities as housekeeping services, cafeteria operation, public relations, and payroll preparation. In contemporary organizations, staff offices often combine activities of both a technostructure and support staff nature.

Creation of an organization structure is often considered synonymous with the preparation of organization charts. The chart is a device used to portray formal organizational relationships, but we must recognize that the chart is only a picture. The chart is no more the organization itself than any symbol is the thing it represents. The real organization structure is the total pattern of human relationships that exists.

Benefits of Proper Organization

The benefits of good organizing are those related to what a theorist calls *sound organization*. Charting an organization, for example, brings to light and helps eliminate weaknesses, including gaps in responsibility, overlapping of functions, duplication of effort, and working at cross purposes. At best, patterns of relationships in large organizations are extremely complex.

The organizer attempts to create a logical structure—that is, a structure designed to work efficiently through careful work specialization, a well-defined hierarchy, and a set of rules and procedures. In addition, a clearly outlined organization structure provides the incumbent of a position with a clearer understanding of management expectations. It also stresses unity of command, thus eliminating confusion and identifying the line of responsibility for each individual. The planned organization also specifies the authority assigned to each position, so that the incumbent will know the scope and limits of authority in the position.

Critical Views of Detailed Organization Planning

Administrators and scholars do not agree on the desirability of extensive organization planning. Critics argue that some flexibility in relationships and procedures is desirable. They feel that excessive detail in specifying responsibilities is stifling and that efficient operation can be achieved without extensive organization planning and without its paraphernalia, including charts and manuals.

In general, critics of the carefully planned organization object to rigid chains of command and organization charts that become ends in themselves. Bureaucracy is replaced by *bureaupathology* in which red tape triumphs and means become ends.[1] These critics condone some leapfrogging over supervisory echelons and crossing over organization lines to reach into other departments with ideas, suggestions, and criticisms.

Both advocates and critics of organization planning have a point. It *is* desirable to study and structure organizational relationships. At the same time, some flexibility is necessary in practical, day-to-day organizational life.

BUREAUCRACY AND BUREAUPATHOLOGY

"The true bureaucrat is any individual who has lost sight of the underlying purpose of the job at hand, whether in government, industry—or a bank. The purpose of a library, for example, is to facilitate the reading of books. Yet to a certain type of librarian, perfection consists of a well-stocked library with a place for every book—and every book in its place. The reader who insists on taking books home, leaving empty spaces on shelves, is this librarian's natural enemy.

"It is a cast of mind invulnerable even to the vicissitudes of war. We see it in James Jones's novel *From Here to Eternity* when American soldiers under surprise attack by Japanese planes at the outbreak of World War II rush to the arsenal for weapons, only to find the door barred by a comrade-in-arms loudly proclaiming that he cannot pass out live ammunition without a written request signed by a commissioned officer.

"One of these custodians forgot the purpose of a library, the other, the purpose of an army. Both illustrate how, in institutionalized endeavors, means have a way of displacing the ends they are originally designed to serve. In fact, it is one of the bureaucrat's distinguishing features that, for him or for her, the means *become* the ends."

SOURCE: "The Bureaucrat," *Citiviews* (New York: Citicorp, undated).

The Systems Approach to Organizing

In the light of systems theory, organizing may be visualized as a design function—creating the structure or framework of the system. Managers establish those relationships among component parts that will provide the most effective system.

If managers approach organizing without a systems point of view, however, they may adopt organizational rules of thumb or follow conventional practice with little regard for the unique requirements of the particular system. An innovative organization, for example, must be designed differently from an operating organization. As Jay R. Galbraith points out, operating organizations "are designed to efficiently process the millionth loan, produce the millionth automobile, or serve the millionth client."[2] If a corporation also wishes to design new products and bring them to market, it may need a different type of organization—one which protects innovators and their ideas from operating managers whose quest is efficiency in processing the millionth loan, producing the millionth automobile, or serving the millionth client.

Organizing on a systems basis logically begins with a consideration of the nature of the system—its activity or function or purpose. What is it expected to do and how should it operate? A sound systems-organizing approach has been suggested by Peter F. Drucker. He stresses the importance of identifying key activities as a basis for building the organization structure.[3] Questions that help identify these key activities are the following:

1. In what area is excellence required to obtain the company's objectives?
2. In what area would lack of performance endanger the results, if not the survival, of the enterprise?
3. What are the *values* that are truly important to us in this company?[4]

After the key activities provide the basic framework, the organizer uses *decision analysis* and *relations analysis* to group tasks. *Decision analysis* asks questions about the types of decisions that must be made and the levels at which they appropriately can be made. Can the system function more effectively by delegating broad decision-making authority to lower levels of management? *Relations analysis* examines the points of contact among activities and personnel. The structure must facilitate cooperative relationships among people whose functions are intertwined. Once again, the focus is upon the working relationship of components of the system.

UNDERLYING FORCES THAT SHAPE ORGANIZATIONS

Contingency Theory and Organization Structure

The dynamic nature of modern organizations produces repercussions in organizational relationships. For example, business firms which diversify their product line may find it necessary to modify their structure in order to produce and sell the new products efficiently. If the products are drastically different from those in the existing line, completely new departments may be required. Decentralization may similarly be justified by changes of this type.

Personnel changes also lead to organization changes. This is particularly true of replacements at the top-management level. Personal abilities differ among executives, and modifications of organization are made to accommodate the strengths or weaknesses of particular executives. New executives also have their own ideas of organization, and these frequently differ from those of their predecessors.

Since organization structures reflect the functions and purposes of organizations, it is not surprising to find that structures differ because of the basic differences among organizations.

Contingency theory stresses the unique nature of situations and the impact of situational variables on management and organizational performance. It thus helps to explain variations in structure. We would not expect a church, a business corporation, and a college football team to use identical patterns of organization and management. Nor would we expect an organization to retain the same structure over time while it was changing in other ways.

No doubt many aspects of organizational situations logically call for variations in structure. Situations are so complex, however, that scholars find it difficult to isolate the most important variables and to understand their implications for design of organizations. The factors discussed in the following sections—technology, size, environment, and strategy—seem important on the basis of research to date. Nevertheless, they should be taken as tentative explanations of differences in structure, subject to refinement as they are studied further.

Technology and Structure

A few decades ago, writers generally assumed that organizational concepts were universally applicable. Today, however, this assumption is questioned by those who emphasize the drastic differences in industrial technology. (Technology, in this case, refers to methods of operation including both the machinery and related techniques or methods.)

Perhaps the best-known research in this area was the study of about one hundred British manufacturing plants conducted by a university research team and reported by Joan Woodward.[5] The researchers gathered extensive data about the features of formal organization of each plant but experienced difficulty in discerning a logical pattern. The type of organization structure did not initially appear to be significant in explaining differences in degrees of success.

Organization differences became sharp, however, when the plants were grouped according to type of production technology. Eleven classes of technology were established involving various kinds of unit production, batch production, mass production, and process production.

When the plants were divided into the eleven categories, organization patterns were immediately apparent. The patterns included such traditional features as span of control and uses of line and staff.

> Among the organizational characteristics showing a direct relationship with technical advance were: the length of the line of command; the span of control of the chief executive; the percentage of total turnover allocated to the payment of wages and salaries; and the ratios of managers to total personnel, of clerical and administrative staff to manual workers, of direct to indirect labor, and of graduate to non-graduate supervision in production departments.[6]

Within technological groupings, the study also revealed a connection between type of structure and successful performance. Thus, it appeared that given types of structures were more appropriate for given technologies. In other words, there tended to be an optimal type of organization.

The Woodward study has been extended and its results corroborated to some extent in other settings. In spite of the investigations to date, however, knowledge about the nature of the technology-organization relationship and its implications is limited.[7]

The Woodward study was quite broad in relating the structure of entire manufacturing plants to the technology of those plants. However, given organizations frequently use many different technologies in their operation. More recent studies, therefore, have extended this concept and increased its practicality by focusing upon the technology of individual units and the structure of those individual units.[8]

Size and Structure

The size of organizations also appears to affect their structure. In general, research studies have compared organizations of varying size in terms of a number of organizational variables. One such variable is "formalization"—the extent to which rules, procedures, and instructions are written. Another variable is "concentration of authority"—that is, the degree to which authority for given types of decisions is concentrated at higher levels or delegated to lower levels.

One of the early and most famous studies was conducted by the "Aston group," a group of scholars associated with the University of Aston in Birmingham, England.[9] They concluded that organization size played an important role in determining structure, especially when compared to technology. The correlation of organization size with specialization, standardization, formalization, and centralization was consistently stronger than the correlation of technology with these same factors.

Other studies have subsequently investigated the relationship of size and structure, and the findings have varied.[10] Although size has been rather consistently related to structure in these studies, the precise nature of the relationship is unclear. And even the Aston study did not suggest that size was the only variable affecting structure. It appears that organizational size influences its structure, but the precise nature of this influence remains a question.

Environment and Structure

Organizations exist in different environments. We recognize, for example, that steel producers, residential builders, private universities, and public utilities face substantially different external situations. Some environments are described as stable and predictable, whereas others are characterized by shifting conditions, uncertainty, and difficulty in predicting the course of events. Uncertainty in a business environment is created by the existence of many competitors and competitive products, broad price ranges and price instability, numerous changes in product design, frequent innovations, and rapid growth in the underlying body of knowledge. Do such differences in environments affect organization structure? The answer is yes, although research is only slowly unraveling the nature of the environment-organization relationship.[11]

As one example of environment-organization research, Lorsch and Morse examined differences in the environments of selected manufacturing plants and research laboratories.[12] They found the environments of manufacturing plants to be relatively stable and certain. Once production was scheduled, the automated nature of plant facilities took over. Rate of change in knowledge was slow. New products required only minimal changes in manufacturing and assembly operations. Feedback was immediate, with regular inspection of product quality during the manufacturing process and prompt reports of customer dissatisfaction. Strategic concerns centered on cost, quality, and delivery.

Managers of the industrial research laboratories, on the other hand, faced uncertain and rapidly changing environments. Problems could be approached in a variety of ways with various possible solutions. Information necessary to work out research problems was ambiguous, open to varied interpretations, and apt to become obsolete. Knowledge was changing rapidly, and feedback was long term—for example, five years from laboratory idea to manufacturing success.

The research of Lorsch and Morse indicated that the more successful manufacturing organizations emphasized formal structure, using formal job descriptions, rules, procedures, detailed control systems, and greater centralization of decision making. The high-performing laboratories, on the other hand, displayed greater flexibility in management with only general job descriptions, a minimum of rules, reliance on self-discipline, and greater participative decision making.

In summary, research has shown that environmental differences are significant in shaping organization structures. Successful performance seems to require an appropriate fit between the type of external environment and the type of formal organization. Successful firms operating in dynamic environments, for example, tend to be more decentralized than those in more stable environments.[13]

Strategy and Structure

As environments change, organizations devise new strategies and adapt their structures to pursue those strategies. To discover the influence of strategy on organization, one must analyze the organization changes that accompany or follow strategy changes. A major study by Alfred D. Chandler, Jr., demonstrated the connection between business strategy and organization structure.[14]

Chandler examined the administrative histories of almost one hundred large industrial enterprises, and he analyzed in detail the organizational development of Du Pont, General Motors, Standard Oil (New Jersey), and Sears, Roebuck. His general thesis may be stated as follows:

> Strategic growth resulted from an awareness of the opportunities and needs—created by changing population, income, and technology—to employ existing or expanding resources more profitably. A new strategy required a new or at least refashioned structure if the enlarged enterprise was to be operated efficiently. The failure to develop a new internal structure, like the failure to respond to new external opportunities and needs, was a consequence of overconcentration on operational activities by the executives responsible for the destiny of their enterprises, or from their inability, because of past training and education and present position, to develop an entrepreneurial outlook.[15]

A practical example is found in RepublicBank Corporation's organizational adaptation to meet the competition of brokerage firms, savings and loan associations, and others in a rapidly changing environment.[16] Bank managers sensed that dramatic changes were occurring in the banking industry. They identified environmental factors affecting the banking industry as shown in Figure 10–2.

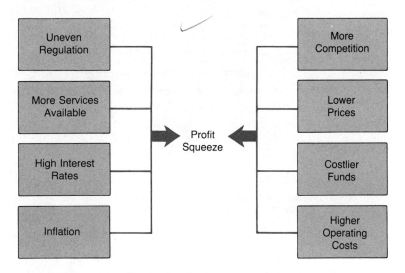

FIGURE 10–2   Environmental forces impacting the banking industry

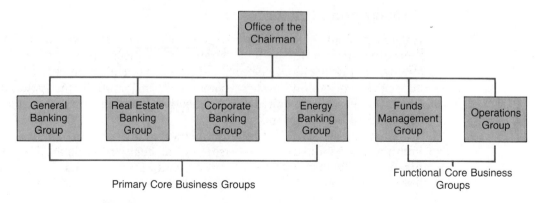

FIGURE 10–3   RepublicBank's organizational structure

To meet the challenges, RepublicBank adopted the form of organization shown in Figure 10–3. In rationalizing the formation of these primary groups, bank managers pointed directly to the bank's strategy. The energy banking and real estate banking groups will enable them, in their words, "to take bold action in these two areas of special RepublicBank strength." The corporate banking group will permit them "to adapt our corporate strategies for successful competition with non-banks, foreign banks and money center banks."

The value of this example lies in the explicit linkage between strategy and structure. In effect, the managers of this bank said, "Here are important changes we see in our environment, and here is how we can organize to deal strategically with this changing environment."

Raymond Miles and Charles Snow have reported studies of strategy and structure in four industries: college textbook publishing, electronics, food processing, and hospitals.[17] They found it possible to classify organizations in these various industries according to their strategic orientation—"defenders," "prospectors," "analyzers," and "reactors"—and to predict with some reliability the structural characteristics associated with a given strategy. "Defenders," for example, tend to rely on functional organization structures which group specialists with similar skills into similar units. They also tend to use an extensive division of labor and a high degree of formalization. Miles and Snow's research has thus supported the connection between strategy and structure.

Underlying Forces and Management Design

Some contingency theorists believe that one or more of the underlying forces described above virtually dictate the type of organization that should or must be used. They use the term *imperative*—such as the "technological imperative"—to convey this idea of some factor acting as a powerful determinant of structure. As we have noted in the discussion,

FIGURE 10–4 Underlying forces and managerial choice of structure

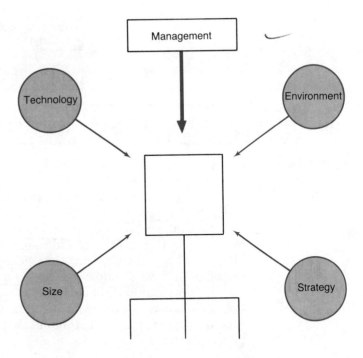

however, the evidence is still spotty. Research results have conflicted.

Managers, therefore, have much discretion. As portrayed in Figure 10–4, the structure is directly affected by various underlying forces, but the significance of each of these forces and their interrelationships is not fully understood. They do not lead directly and obviously to specific organization structures, so managers must still choose what they perceive to be the best structure.

PATTERNS OF ORGANIZATION

This section explains the way in which individual jobs—machine operators, engineers, accountants, sales representatives, and so on—are grouped for purposes of management. We accept the jobs themselves as given and concentrate upon relationships among them. In Chapter 16, we will examine the content of jobs, the problems involved in highly specialized work, and other aspects of job design.

Choosing a Pattern

Managers have options in grouping jobs into departments. At the top level are two basic structural patterns. Perhaps the best known is the *functional pattern in which* the type of activity or function serves as the organizing principle. The tax office at city hall or the sales organization of a small manufacturer are examples of functional departments.

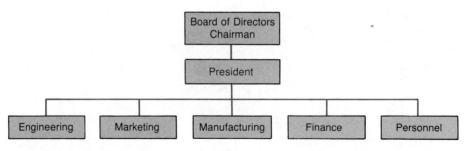

FIGURE 10–5   Functional pattern of organization

The major alternative to the functional pattern is *divisional* organization, and it has two varieties.* The most popular form, *product* divisionalization, brings together activities related to a given product line—for example, manufacturing and sales activities related to Frigidaire appliances. Other organizations—the Federal Reserve banking system, for example—use *geography* as the basis for divisional grouping.†

Divisionalization frequently goes hand in hand with decentralization of authority. Major segments of the General Motors Corporation, for example, operate somewhat autonomously under general direction by the corporation.

Function as the Pattern

Small manufacturing enterprises find the functional pattern particularly appropriate. This pattern is not limited to the top level of the organization, however. Within the manufacturing department (a functional department), work may be further subdivided on the basis of function. Organizational components at this level may include drilling, grinding, painting, and so on. Different office units similarly may perform typing, filing, and messenger service. An example of the functional pattern is shown in Figure 10–5.

Efficiency and economy are among the more important advantages of functional organization, especially for relatively small companies. All selling, for example, is concentrated in one department. A potential weakness in the functional pattern is its tendency to encourage a narrowness of viewpoint. It is easy for functional executives and personnel to look at problems from the standpoint of selling or manufacturing or some other functional specialty rather than seeing them from the standpoint of the company as a whole.

Growth in an organization may produce strains on the functional organization. Extreme product diversification and widespread territorial

---

*Even though they are frequently interrelated, *divisionalization* is not synonymous with *decentralization*. As explained in Chapter 11, p. 000, decentralization emphasizes the level of decision making in organizations.

†Within major functional or divisional components, still other patterns may be used. Sales forces, for example, may be subdivided according to the type of customers they serve.

expansion, in particular, contribute to the difficulty of successfully operating according to a simple functional pattern.

Product as the Pattern

Product patterns are used not only at the top level (product divisionalization) but also at lower levels. In a functional sales department, for example, sales personnel may be specialized on the basis of product lines. Similarly, the grouping of college professors into such departments as English, philosophy, and economics provides an example in the field of education. An example of the product pattern in a business corporation is presented in Figure 10–6.

The advantages of product divisionalization are particularly significant in the case of a highly diversified product line. The work of manufacturing or sales personnel in a consumer products division, for example, is drastically different from the work of similar personnel in an atomic power division. Product patterns permit specialization in terms of the product or group of products.

Executive development is another attractive feature of product organization. In the functional organization, executives are trained in functional areas and imbued with a functional viewpoint. Only by position rotation or service in different functional areas do they acquire experience outside their own field of specialization. In contrast, the general manager and assistant manager of a product department are responsible for dealing with problems in various functional areas—including production, sales, and research and development.

The Geographic Pattern

Some organizations use geographic divisions, rather than product divisions, as their primary pattern. This includes some business corporations, even though most divisionalized business firms follow the product pattern.

The geographic-division structure of the Prudential Insurance Company of America is shown in Figure 10–7. Each of Prudential's nine regional home offices is headed by a president who directs operations, including the selling and servicing of individual and group insurance, in his or her territory. The actuarial staff in each regional office has the freedom to underwrite new business within actuarial standards set by the corporate office. All regional home offices have their own staff and service divisions in public relations, advertising, methods, research, and personnel administration.

Geographic divisionalization has certain advantages in common with the product pattern. Breadth of managerial experience is secured in the administration of regional areas. Financial control of operations is also facilitated, because managers can prepare a separate income statement for each geographic area and determine its contribution to corporate profits.

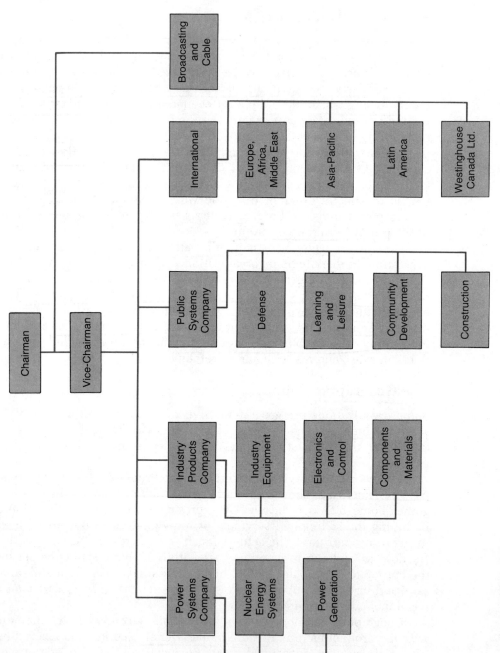

FIGURE 10-6 Westinghouse Electric Corporation: Product divisional pattern
SOURCE: Company Records (1982). This simplified chart does not show all of the staff offices and activities of the corporation.

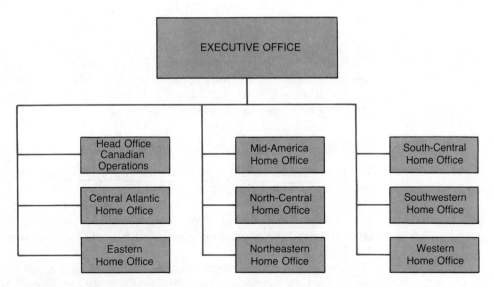

FIGURE 10–7   Regional office organization of the Prudential
Insurance Company of America
SOURCE: Company records (1982).

The locational format is also used at lower levels—in organizing sales activities, for example. Adaptation to local situations and knowledge of customer needs peculiar to a given area are facilitated by the locational pattern.

HUMAN FACTORS IN STRUCTURAL DECISIONS

Personal and Organizational Goals

As with other phases of business enterprise, decisions about organization structure affect both the organization and its members.[18] These effects are not necessarily the same for all parties. What is good for the organization is not necessarily good for the individual.

One study of these varied goals is that of Paul R. Lawrence in his analysis of changing organizational patterns.[19] Lawrence discusses the values involved in organization change in terms of three *dimensions*. The change, if it is to be an ideal change, must be beneficial when measured along each of these dimensions.

1. Achievement of organizational purpose
2. Achievement of self-maintenance and growth
3. Achievement of social satisfactions

These concepts will furnish the framework for the following discussion.

Achievement of Organizational Purpose

A structural change is typically introduced because of its presumed benefit for the particular organization. Formal evaluation of a proposed change is made almost exclusively in terms of this particular value. Few changes have a chance for adoption if they cannot be shown to have positive advantages in terms of this dimension.

Individual Growth and Development

Members of organizations are also concerned with organization change for purely personal reasons. As Jeffrey Pfeffer and Gerald Salancik have observed, "Organizational decisions are made by real managers interested in their own career advancement who operate with the blinders derived from their particular backgrounds, training, and organizational positions."[20]

Almost any organization change could have quick and profound repercussions in terms of an individual's status and opportunity for growth. Jobs may be eliminated, departments trimmed in size, and the future possibilities for any individual greatly circumscribed or enhanced as a result of the change. Threats to the status of existing departments and positions, therefore, may arouse major opposition. The executive who led General Electric's shift from a functional to a product pattern, Ralph J. Cordiner, spoke of the hostility evoked by the change.

> There were lots of objections from the functional people. We had a functional operation in those days—engineering, manufacturing, sales, finance. The functional people had tremendous power. They weren't about to let go of it.[21]

Social Satisfactions

Employees derive social satisfactions from the work group. They feel themselves a part of a social group and enjoy the contacts and friendships involved in their association with others.

A change of organization may disturb the social group and social relationships of affected employees. It is apparent that the change might be viewed as negative and threatening to existing satisfactory social relationships. Or, the changed situation might be welcomed because of a promised improvement in social relationships.

To illustrate the concept, suppose that production employees worked in small groups with each employee assigned to and a part of a closely integrated team. Suppose also, for technological reasons, that the nature of work arrangements was changed to break up the work teams that existed. If these employees were removed from their original groups, scattered as individual members along an assembly line, and denied an opportunity for close social relationships with other employees, they might be less satisfied. Measured along this dimension, then, organization change prompted by considerations of organizational efficiency might, at the same time, be damaging to the personal social satisfaction of employees.

SOCIAL SATISFACTION IN COAL MINING

Traditionally, miners functioned as a part of small primary work groups, called "marrow groups," in what was known as *single place mining*. A coal face of six to eleven yards in length, called a "place," was worked on any particular shift by one, or possibly two, men. Each miner was a complete miner, performing all necessary tasks at the face—not only removing coal but also setting roof supports, taking up stone in the floor, and so on. The primary work group consisted of the men who worked the same place on the same or different shifts—a maximum of six in a two-man, three-shift group. Individual workers formed their own groups by choosing fellow workmen of similar skill and working capacity. (Earnings were determined by group performance.)

Introduction of belt conveyors led to *longwall mining*—a method that differed greatly from the single place tradition. For example, work roles became specialized and the small marrow groups were replaced by specialized task groups differing from one another in status and attractiveness. This type of work organization led to a number of substandard results—productivity lower than potentially possible, inflated costs, poor management-labor relations, low job satisfaction, and high absenteeism. Subsequent modification of the work organization into a *composite longwall* method, in which there was no rigid division of labor, resulted in substantial improvements, thus demonstrating the relationship between organization structure and the social satisfactions of work.

SOURCE: E. L. Trist et al., *Organization Choice* (London: Tavistock Publications, 1963). The study was part of a research project conducted by England's Tavistock Institute of Human Relations.

Reconciling the Various Goals

It would be desirable to create such changes in organization structure in such a way that they would meet satisfactorily all three goals or dimensions. Unfortunately, this may not always be possible, but Lawrence's tentative conclusion was that the goals are not necessarily irreconcilable.[22]

In reasoning about organization changes and considering the possibility of undertaking organization change, an awareness of the different goals permits analysis of alternatives with full consideration of the different aspects of the case. It may help also in understanding the nature of difficulties or objections that arise in connection with a proposed change in organization.

The Challenge of Parkinson's Law

A few years ago, C. Northcote Parkinson wrote satirically on organization and administration. In his famous "law," he stated that "work expands so as to fill the time available for its completion."[23] Parkinson's suggestion is that organizations do not grow in a logical fashion merely to care for increased workloads. In other words, one can draw no conclusion about the magnitude of the work performed on the basis of the size of the organizations. "The rise in the total of those employed," said Parkinson, "is governed by Parkinson's Law and would be much the same whether the volume of the work were to increase, diminish, or even disappear."[24]

CHALLENGING PARKINSON'S LAW

Parkinson's Law suggests that the growth of corporate bureaucracies may be inevitable. Victor Kiam, who bought Sperry Corporation's Remington shaver division in 1979, evidently feels that flabby corporate bureaucracies are *not* inevitable. At the time of purchase, Remington had piled up losses of $30 million over five years. Kiam proceeded to fire seventy executives the first week. He also lowered prices and stepped up advertising.

Kiam's efforts have been successful as Remington earned profits on increased sales and regained market share. "We don't need a lot of chiefs," Kiam says. "We need people who can produce."

SOURCE: "Smooth Performance: Remington's Shaver Turnaround." *Fortune* 105 (January 11, 1982), p. 11. © 1982 Time Inc.

If there is a measure of truth in the writing of Parkinson (and as a satirist, of course, Parkinson overstates his case), it would appear that personal considerations are influential in the determination of organization design. Those in a position to influence decisions regarding organization may act on the basis of "what's best for me" rather than "what's best for the organization." The term *empire building* has been applied to situations of this kind, and those thought to be building organizations for the primary purpose of increasing personal or departmental prestige have been denounced as *empire builders*.

This idea of Parkinson's goes beyond mere recognition that organization changes affect people either favorably or unfavorably. Far from being mere pawns, the individuals in the organization manipulate the structure to maximize personal benefits. In a study of organizational power in a university, a team of British scholars found that much "politicking" and "jostling for power" resulted from the competing internal interests of various departments.[25] "Each department," they wrote, "protects and advocates its own 'product' of teaching and research in certain subjects."[26] Success or failure in jostling for limited resources obviously leads to organizational growth or decline. The extent to which personal and departmental considerations may thus directly affect organization planning is unknown. The widespread interest in Parkinson's Law on the part of practicing administrators indicates that the possibility may be less remote than sometimes believed. It is probably a subtle influence where it does occur and thus may not be recognized except by those who are unusually perceptive in their observations of administrative behavior.

SUMMARY

Organizing involves the grouping of jobs into a *framework* for coordination and direction. This organizational framework, the *formal organization*, may be portrayed by use of an *organization chart*. Although careful structuring of the organization is thought to be beneficial in terms of clarifying lines of command and eliminating gaps and overlaps, some critics argue that extremely detailed organization structures may be dysfunctional.

The systems approach to organizing emphasizes the essential relationships of component parts of the organization. The organizer must begin with a consideration of the nature of the system—its function or purpose. Key activities, decisions, and relations must be analyzed in the process of designing the organization structure.

Contingency theory helps explain variations in organization structure by emphasizing situational differences among organizations. Some of the underlying forces that shape organizations include the firm's *technology, size, environment,* and *strategy.*

Once job content is determined, jobs and activities must be grouped to devise an overall structure. At the top organizational level are two basic alternatives—a *functional* pattern or a *divisional* (either *product* or *geographic*) pattern. Divisionalized organizations typically adopt the organizational philosophy of *decentralization.*

Decisions affecting organization structure involve *values* and *goals* for both the organization and its individual members. Although personal organizational goals may conflict, they are not necessarily irreconcilable. Paul R. Lawrence has suggested that organization changes be evaluated in terms of the following three dimensions: (1) *achievement of organizational purpose,* (2) *achievement of self-maintenance and growth,* and

(3) *achievement of social satisfactions*. Ideally, a change would produce positive effects along all three dimensions.

According to the argument of *Parkinson's Law*, personal considerations directly affect the design of organizations. Individual managers (*empire builders*) are believed to manipulate the structure in order to maximize results for themselves.

DISCUSSION QUESTIONS

1. In what sense is an organization chart symbolic?

2. What specific benefits should result from good organization?

3. Speaking of formal organization planning, is it true that if you "put a person in a square" you limit him or her? What would be the nature of this limitation, and how serious would it be?

4. How does the systems point of view affect the manager's organizing function?

5. Give several examples, including some based upon your own observations, of organization changes caused by the dynamic nature of organizations.

6. How is *contingency theory* related to variations in organization structure? What are the major factors involved in a contingency view of organizations?

7. What is meant by the *pattern* of organization? Why is a mixture of patterns customary?

8. What is the meaning of *divisionalization*?

9. What advantages are found in the *product pattern* of organization that do not exist in the *functional pattern*?

10. In the study of a proposed change in organization, will participation by the individuals who are involved impede or contribute to the study?

11. Contrast the basic ideas involved in the Lawrence and Parkinson studies of organization change.

NOTES

1. See Victor A. Thompson, *Bureaucracy and the Modern World* (Morristown, N.J.: General Learning Press, 1976), Chapters 4 and 5, for an excellent discussion of this topic.

2. Jay R. Galbraith, "Designing the Innovating Organization," *Organizational Dynamics* 10, no. 3 (Winter 1982): 6.

3. Peter F. Drucker, *Management: Tasks, Responsibilities, Practices* (New York: Harper & Row, Publishers, 1974), Chapters 42 and 43.

4. Ibid., pp. 530–31.

5. Joan Woodward, *Industrial Organization: Theory and Practice* (London: Oxford University Press, 1965). By permission of the Clarendon Press, Oxford.

6. Ibid., p. 51.

7. For a review of this topic, see Louis W. Fry, "Technology-Structure Research: Three Critical Issues," *Academy of Management Journal* 25 (September 1982): 532–52.

8. W. Alan Randolph, "Matching Technology and the Design of Organization Units," *California Management Review* 23 (Summer 1981): 39–48.

9. David J. Hickson, D. S. Pugh, and Diana C. Pheysey, "Operations Technology and Organization Structure: An Empirical Reappraisal," *Administrative Science Quarterly* 14 (September 1969): 378–97.

10. See John R. Kimberly, "Organizational Size and the Structuralist Perspective: A Review, Critique, and Proposal," *Administrative Science Quarterly* 21 (December 1976): 571–97; and John H. Jackson and Cyril P. Morgan, *Organization Theory: A Macro Perspective for Management* (Englewood Cliffs, N.J.: Prentice-Hall, 1978), Chapter 7.

11. One of the widely acclaimed statements of theory in this area appears in James D. Thompson, *Organizations in Action* (New York: McGraw-Hill Book Co., 1967), Chapter 6.

12. Jay W. Lorsch and John J. Morse, *Organizations and Their Members* (New York: Harper & Row, Publishers, 1974). The research project described here also examined the significance of personal characteristics of organization members as related to environment and internal organization.

13. For further reading, see Robert Duncan, "What Is the Right Organization Structure? Decision Tree Analysis Provides the Answer," *Organizational Dynamics* 7 (Winter 1979): 59–80; Stephen M. Shortell, "The Role of Environment in a Configurational Theory of Organizations," *Human Relations* 30 (March 1977): 275–302; and John W. Slocum, Jr. and Don Hellriegel, "Using Organizational Designs to Cope with Change," *Business Horizons* 22, no. 6 (December 1979): 65–76.

14. Alfred D. Chandler, Jr., *Strategy and Structure* (Cambridge: The MIT Press, 1962).

15. Ibid., pp. 15–16.

16. See *Strategy for Managing Change,* pamphlet issued by RepublicBank Corporation (Dallas, Tx.) in 1982, p. 5. The change is also reported in "RepublicBank's Texas-size Gamble," *Business Week,* no. 2752 (16 August 1982), pp. 96–97.

17. Raymond E. Miles and Charles C. Snow, *Organization Strategy, Structure, and Process* (New York: McGraw-Hill Book Co., 1978).

18. For a discussion of the impact of structure on attitudes, see Donald J. Vredenburgh and Joseph A. Alutto, "Perceived Structure in Relation to Individual Attitudes and Performance," *Organization and Administrative Sciences* 8 (Summer/Fall 1977): 255–72.

19. Paul R. Lawrence, *The Changing of Organizational Behavior Patterns: A Case Study of Decentralization* (Boston: Harvard Business School, Division of Research, 1958), Chapter 10.

20. Jeffrey Pfeffer and Gerald R. Salancik, "Organizational Design: The Case

for a Coalitional Model of Organizations," *Organizational Dynamics* 6 (Autumn 1977): 17.

21. "An Interview with Retired GE Chairman Ralph Cordiner," *Forbes*, 15 October 1967, p. 31.

22. Lawrence, *Organizational Behavior Patterns*, p. 217.

23. C. Northcote Parkinson, *Parkinson's Law* (Boston: Houghton Mifflin Company, 1957), p. 2. Used by permission of Houghton Mifflin Company and John Murray (Publishers) Ltd.

24. Ibid., p. 4.

25. Richard J. Butler et al., "Organizational Power, Politicking and Paralysis," *Organization and Administrative Sciences* 8 (Winter 1977/1978): 45–59.

26. Ibid., p. 54.

SUPPLEMENTARY READING

Bobbitt, H. Randolph, Jr., and **Ford, Jeffrey D.** "Decision-Maker Choice as a Determinant of Organization Structure." *Academy of Management Review* 5 (January 1980): 13–23.

Cherns, Albert. "The Principles of Sociotechnical Design." *Human Relations* 29 (August 1976): 783–92.

Child, John. "Organizational Design and Performance: Contingency Theory and Beyond." *Organization and Administrative Sciences* 8 (Summer–Fall 1977): 169–83.

Dalton, Dan R.; Todor, William D.; Spendolini, Michael J.; Fielding, Gordon J.; and **Porter, Lyman W.** "Organization Structure and Performance: A Critical Review." *Academy of Management Review* 5, no. 1 (January 1980): 49–64.

Davis, Louis E. "Evolving Alternative Organization Designs: Their Socio-technical Bases." *Human Relations* 30 (March 1977): 261–73.

Duncan, Robert. "What Is the Right Organization Structure? Decision Tree Analysis Provides the Answer." *Organizational Dynamics* 7 (Winter 1979): 59–80.

Ford, Jeffrey D., and **Slocum, John W., Jr.** "Size, Technology, Environment and the Structure of Organizations." *Academy of Management Review* 2 (October 1977): 561–75.

Fry, Louis W. "Technology-Structure Research: Three Critical Issues." *Academy of Management Journal* 25, no. 3 (September 1982): 532–52.

Huber, George P.; Ullman, Joseph; and **Leifer, Richard.** "Optimum Organization Design: An Analytic-Adoptive Approach." *Academy of Management Review* 4, no. 4 (October 1979): 567–78.

Jackson, John H., and **Morgan, Cyril P.** *Organization Theory: A Macro Perspective for Management.* Englewood Cliffs; N.J.: Prentice-Hall, 1978.

Kilmann, Ralph H. "On Integrating Knowledge Utilization with Knowledge Development: The Philosophy Behind the MAPS Design Technology." *Academy of Management Review* 4, no. 3 (July 1979): 417–26.

Lorsch, Jay W. "Organizational Design: A Situational Perspective." *Organizational Dynamics* 6 (Autumn 1977): 2–14.

Lorsch, Jay W., and **Morse, John J.** *Organizations and Their Members: A Contingency Approach.* New York: Harper & Row, Publishers, 1974.

Miles, Raymond E.; Snow, Charles C.; Meyer, Alan D.; and **Coleman, Henry J., Jr.** "Organizational Strategy, Structure, and Process." *Academy of Management Review* 3 (July 1978): 546–62.

Mintzberg, Henry. *The Structuring of Organizations.* Englewood Cliffs, N.J.: Prentice-Hall, 1979.

_____. "Structure in 5's: A Synthesis of the Research on Organization Design." *Management Science* 26, no. 3 (March 1980): 322–41.

_____. "Organization Design: Fashion or Fit?" *Harvard Business Review* 59, no. 1 (January–February 1981): 103–116.

Parkinson, C. Northcote. "Parkinson's Law of the Vacuum (or Hoover for President)." *Forbes* 125, no. 10 (12 May 1980): 135–40.

Randolph, W. Alan. "Matching Technology & the Design of Organization Units." *California Management Review* 23, no. 4 (Summer 1981): 39–48.

Shortell, Stephen M. "The Role of Environment in a Configurational Theory of Organizations." *Human Relations* 30 (March 1977): 275–302.

Slocum, John W., Jr., and **Hellriegel, Don.** "Using Organizational Designs to Cope with Change." *Business Horizons* 22, no. 6 (December 1979): 65–76.

Woodward, Joan. *Industrial Organization: Theory and Practice.* London: Oxford University Press, 1965.

11

AUTHORITY IN ORGANI-ZATIONAL RELATIONSHIPS

This chapter will enable you to

- *Understand the nature of authority and identify a number of reasons that organization members accept managerial authority.*
- *Recognize the reasons for establishing and adhering to a chain of command and the conditions that may justify short-circuiting this chain.*
- *Recognize and explain the significance of major variables that affect the optimum size of the span of control.*
- *Define delegation of authority and outline the benefits of delegation and barriers to delegation.*
- *Explain the factors leading to decentralization and the advantages and difficulties associated with decentralization.*

In a formal organization, *authority* flows through a *chain of command*. By issuing orders, managers provide direction and coordination necessary for organized endeavor. This official chain does not control every aspect of organizational activity, of course, because individual members can respond to directions in many ways. Nevertheless, the order-giving system has a great deal to do with what happens in organizations. In this chapter, we examine the *nature of authority* and such related topics as *chain of command, span of control, delegation,* and *decentralization.*

THE NATURE AND USE OF AUTHORITY

What Is Authority?

Authority may be defined as a superior's capacity, on the basis of formal position, to make decisions affecting subordinates. Authority is evident in all areas of society. In the family, the parent makes decisions for minor children. At a busy intersection, a police officer gives directions to motorists. In football, the quarterback calls plays. In organizational life, managers act as decision makers.

Authority might be called *institutionalized power* to emphasize its connection with the formal organization and to distinguish it from other types of power. This does not imply that it is absolute power, but authority must have some means of enforcement to be recognized as authority. Otherwise, it is a hollow, meaningless, "paper" right of command.

In contrast to authority, *power* requires no formal position to be recognized as power. It refers to the ability to make things happen, to get results. Only a part of the total power is institutionalized. This means that others besides managers have power. Output quotas, for example, may be established and enforced by informal work groups.

Determinants of Acceptance of Authority

The behavior of subordinates shows that they accept the claims of authority by superiors. Why do they subordinate themselves in this way? A number of factors are involved in fostering respect for authority.

One factor is our culture and its embodiment of the roles of order giving and order receiving. Throughout their lives, members of organizations have been conditioned to accept authority. Therefore, some tendency to accept orders comes naturally for most people. In fact, an individual openly defiant of general managerial authority would encounter disapproval from most members of an organization.

Rewards and penalties also foster acceptance of authority. Employee A or Manager A may be fired if his or her challenge to official policy becomes too outspoken. Similarly, this individual may expect the rewards of advancement and other benefits to accompany cooperation with the programs of superiors.

Belief in, or identification with, the purpose of the organization is another reason to accept authority, particularly in the case of cooperative organizations. Members accept authority as part of getting the job done.

Further explanation of subordinate acceptance of authority is found in the superior knowledge or expertise of the superior. The element of technical skill or professional competence is particularly important in managing personnel who attach great importance to such qualities— for example, in managing skilled craftsmen, scientists, or college professors.

The factor of personal leadership also affects the acceptance of authority. Some subordinates respond to the orders of superiors because of the subordinates' admiration for their superiors as individual leaders.

Another validating factor is the desire to avoid responsibility. It seems easier for some to accept directions than to make decisions, particularly if the task is not unpleasant or if the decision lies outside the experience and competence of the subordinate.

In any particular instance, authority may be recognized as legitimate because of a combination of these factors. There is no need, however, for *all* factors to be present in establishing authority. In a given case, just one factor (such as disciplinary sanctions) may be of primary importance in making the executive position a powerful one.

Limits to the Exercise of Formal Authority

Citizens of a country do not always obey its statutes. Motorists, for example, often ignore the 55 mile-per-hour speed limit. Members of organizations may also choose to resist managerial authority. In a notable challenge to traditional views, Chester I. Barnard drew attention to the possibility of a subordinate's rejection of direction by higher authority. "It is surprising," said Barnard, "how much that in theory is authoritative, in the best of organizations in practice lacks authority—or, in plain language, how generally orders are disobeyed."[1] Acceptance of the order, then, becomes an important step or part of making the authority of the order-giver effective. Following is a more explicit statement of Barnard's position:

> If a directive communication is accepted by one to whom it is addressed, its authority for him is confirmed or established. It is admitted as the basis of action. Disobedience of such a communication is a denial of its authority for him.[2]

This reasoning does not mean that subordinates automatically resist all authority. Many directions are accepted without question. In fact, Barnard suggests the existence of a *zone of indifference* that determines which orders will be accepted.

> The phrase "zone of indifference" may be explained as follows: If all the orders for actions reasonably practicable be arranged in the order of their acceptability to the person affected, it may be conceived that there are a number which are clearly unacceptable, that is, which certainly will not be obeyed; there is another group somewhat more or less on the neutral line, that is, either barely acceptable or barely unacceptable; and a third group unquestionably acceptable. This last group lies within the "zone of indifference." The person affected will accept orders lying within this zone and is relatively indifferent as to what the order is so far as the question of authority is concerned.[3]

The point of this reasoning is that the authority of a superior's order is seldom so absolute that the subordinate has no choice whatever. As Herbert Simon has expressed it, "the leader, or the superior, is merely a bus driver whose passengers will leave him unless he takes them in the direction they wish to go."[4]

The fact that subordinates possess power does not eliminate authority as a management right. Managers do have power and must use it as necessary for the good of the organization. An understanding of subordinate power should not render managers impotent but rather contribute to good judgment in their decisions and to an avoidance of orders that might be difficult to enforce.

Forms of Resistance to Authority

On rare occasions, subordinates openly defy official orders, and a condition of mutiny exists. In other cases, employees are represented by a union and voice opposition in the form of grievances and union demands.

If resistance of subordinates were limited to cases of these types, the problem would be greatly simplified. As a matter of fact, resistance usually takes a more subtle form. Subordinates resist without forcing a showdown. They may go through the motions of compliance but fail to follow through with the behavior desired by the superior. It is this type of challenge to authority that is most baffling and troublesome for administrators.

Rules that presumably control subordinates are also weapons in the hands of subordinates. An overly zealous observance of rules may be dysfunctional. The following incident illustrates the limitation that rule keeping may impose upon management power:

> Train crews in a marshaling yard were handling 150 trains a day. Through shortcuts (often violating safety rules) they were able to finish their work in six hours. The rest of the time they could sleep or read.
>
> Then management decided that since the men had so much free time they could handle 200 trains. Immediately the men began to follow all the rules. They would never move a train even a few feet without having someone to go to the rear and wave a red flag. As a result, the men put in a full day's work, but productivity fell to 50 trains a day. Soon management gave up its demands for 200.[5]

The ability of subordinates to thwart executive authority varies greatly with the social context. In military organizations, for example, compliance with official orders is more nearly automatic than is customary with business organizations. Most business firms, in turn, possess greater authority than organizations of a voluntary nature.

THE CHAIN OF COMMAND

What Is the Chain of Command?

In its simplest form, a *chain of command* is the relationship between a superior and a subordinate. Starting at the top with the chief executive, we may visualize a series of lines connecting the executive with the next layer of management. An organization chart diagrams these organizational relationships with lines fanning out from the chief executive and increasing in number at lower levels of the organization.

The phrase "chain of command" implies an authoritative relationship, but the chain has at least three distinguishable characteristics, namely, *authority, responsibility*, and *communication*. In an authoritative chain, the manager's status is that of order-giver. The chain is an *official* channel, and the superior's communications are authoritative (Figure 11–1).

The chain of command is also a line of responsibility which holds subordinates accountable for their performance. If satisfactory perfor-

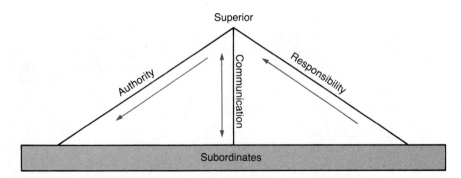

FIGURE 11–1   Features of the chain of command

mance is the rule, there may be little or no mention of accountability. In many cases, however, managers conduct formal performance reviews in which they evaluate and discuss the performance of subordinates.

Classical management theory says that authority should be commensurate with responsibility. This means that there is a basic unfairness involved in holding an individual responsible for that which he or she lacks authority to accomplish. Unfortunately, higher management sometimes fails to see the limitations confronting a subordinate or neglects to confer upon him or her the necessary authority. Even in well-managed organizations, however, authority is seldom spelled out as carefully as implied by traditional management theory. In practice, employees are expected to "get the job done" as well as possible even though their authority may be limited or unclear.

Difficulties in Adhering to the Chain of Command

In practice, adherence to the chain of command can never be complete. Almost any manager is known personally and evaluated by two or three levels of supervision. Relationships of this type are not confined to *joint conferences* in which several layers of management are present but also include "leapfrogging" that runs counter to the chain-of-command concept.

Several forces contribute to this flexibility of the chain of command. One is the need for speed in communications. Clearing a communication through several levels of management is time consuming even if the matter is given reasonably prompt treatment. For example, if D (in Figure 11–2) wishes to communicate with G through channels, D must go through C, B, A, E, and F.

FIGURE 11–2   Communication
through the chain of command

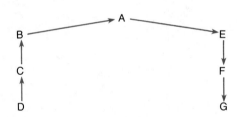

Furthermore, strict adherence to the chain of command can block a superior's understanding of the organization below and the "bright young people" who are there. The more rigidly that higher-ranking executives follow the chain of command, the less they can see lower-ranking personnel in action. They see only their immediate subordinates. In practice, however, they get acquainted by relaxing their adherence to the chain of command—for example, by casual conversations and by direct supervision when intermediate managers are away.

Some short-circuiting by subordinates is also justified as a protection against unfairness in supervision. Although managers may be reasonable and fair most of the time, they occasionally take arbitrary and harsh administrative action. In such cases, the subordinate has little recourse except to "go over the head" of the superior. IBM, from its earliest days, has followed an "open-door" policy that permits individuals to bring problems of unfair treatment to top management.

> The Open Door exists today as it did then. I'm sure that a policy of this kind makes many a traditional manager's blood run cold. He probably sees it as a challenge to his authority or, worse yet, as a sharp sword hanging over his head. But the fact remains that in IBM it has been remarkably effective, primarily because—by its mere existence—it exercises a moderating influence on management. Whenever a manager makes a decision affecting one of his people, he knows that he may be held accountable to higher management for the fairness of that decision.[6]

Dangers in Short-Circuiting the Chain of Command

Short-circuiting the official chain of command quickly undermines the position of a bypassed manager. In contacts between the bypassed manager and that manager's subordinates, the effectiveness of leadership is impaired. Subordinates may well reason, "If the boss does not take our supervisor seriously, why should we?" These subordinates are also subjected to multiple supervision and to the probable unpleasantness involved in such an arrangement.

Short-circuiting is more or less serious depending upon circumstances. Emergency situations, for example, lead to greater tolerance of contacts outside the chain of command. No one considers it necessary to shout "Fire" through channels! In the absence of emergencies, the willingness of intermediate management levels to tolerate leapfrogging depends upon such factors as the importance of subject discussed, the nature of the contact (whether it is confined to discussion or involves decisions), and the extent to which intermediate levels are kept fully informed.

Administrative finesse is required in keeping out-of-channels contacts harmless to the organization structure and positive in their contribution to organizational purposes. There is a fine line, for example, between discussions of an informational nature and discussions in which advice is given or implied.

Unity of Command

The concept of unity of command holds that no individual should be subject to the direct command of more than one superior at any given time. In practice, this precept is often violated. In some cases, a subordinate reports to two or more superiors of approximately equal status. In other situations, one manager exercises *administrative* control, while another manager provides *technical* control over work. Sometimes organizational relationships are vague, and the subordinate finds that two or more superiors are behaving as though the subordinate reports to each of them.

The reasoning supporting the desirability of unity of command is that two or more superiors are unlikely to agree perfectly in their instructions to the same subordinate. The individual subject to multiple supervision is also subject to intersender role conflict and likely to be dissatisfied with the supervisory situation.[7] The subordinate is in a strategic position, furthermore, to play off one supervisor against another, inasmuch as neither superior has complete knowledge of the total assignment.

THE SPAN OF CONTROL

Thus far, we have looked at authority and its exercise through the chain of command. A related question concerns the breadth of a manager's reach—that is, the number of subordinates that he or she can effectively manage.

Spans and Echelons

The *span of control* refers to the number of immediate subordinates reporting to a given manager. If the president gives orders to only one executive vice-president, the president's span of control is one.

The size of the span of control is inversely related to the number of echelons, or layers, in an organization. As the span is broadened, there is a tendency to flatten the structure. In Figure 11–3 we can see that a span of two would require four echelons to direct eight operative employees, whereas a span of four would require only three echelons.

Limiting or Expanding the Span of Control

The reason for limiting the span of control is plain enough. The strength and time of any manager are limited. One manager, for example, could not personally direct the work of a thousand employees. The logic supporting smaller spans is sometimes extended far beyond the obvious case. A manager who can in some way direct the activities of twelve subordinates, it is reasoned, should be able to direct eight or six or four even more effectively. Extremely small spans are costly, however, and may also be defective by encouraging overly close supervision.

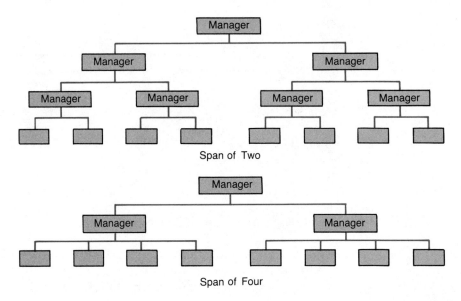

Span of Two

Span of Four

FIGURE 11–3   Spans of different sizes

Enlarging the span, as noted earlier, produces a flatter organization by reducing the number of echelons. This facilitates vertical communication by eliminating organizational levels that can become communication bottlenecks.

By broadening the span of control, organizations may also experience an increase in morale. The evidence is far from conclusive, however. A well-known study of this type concerns Sears, Roebuck and Company.[8] In this company, some managers were assigned relatively large numbers of subordinates. These managers were unable to direct and control their subordinates in a detailed manner. Sears's management concluded that the flat organization with a wider span of control resulted in "not only a higher level of accomplishment but, at the same time, a more satisfying type of supervision and a higher level of employe morale."

In another study, Lyman Porter and Edward Lawler measured the job satisfaction of almost 2,000 managers in companies of various sizes.[9] They found no overall superiority of flat over tall organizations in providing need satisfaction for managers. Another study of 467 trade salespeople from three large national organizations has shown a relationship between flatness and organizational behavior.[10] Trade salespeople in the flat organization perceived more self-actualization, more autonomy satisfaction, and lower amounts of stress and performed more efficiently than salespeople in medium and tall organizations. However, another study of sales representatives indicated that role conflict and role ambiguity increased as the span of control widened.[11] From these studies, it is evident that the relationship between flatness and morale is not clear.

Another obvious advantage of the larger span of control is the reduction of administrative overhead cost. By having each manager direct a larger number of subordinates, the necessary number of management officials is substantially reduced in any sizable organization.

SPANS AND ECHELONS IN THE AUTO INDUSTRY

The U.S. auto industry's problems of profitability and productivity may be caused, in part at least, by tall structures and narrow spans of control. Ford, for example, has twelve layers of organization from the factory floor to the chairman's office. Toyota, in contrast, has only seven layers. At Toyota, a foreman reports directly to a plant manager, whereas a Ford foreman must go through three levels of management to reach the plant manager.

SOURCES: Based on "Japan's Edge in Auto Costs," *Business Week,* 14 September 1981, p. 97; and "Ford's Financial Hurdle," *Business Week,* 2 February 1981, p. 62.

Variables Affecting Optimum Size Span

The diversity in existing sizes of spans might be explained, at least partially, by variations in the managerial situation. A number of possible variables can be easily identified. Unfortunately, most of these variables are merely hypotheses, and more extensive research is required to be sure of their validity.[12]

Nature of Work. It seems likely that the type of work has some bearing in determining the appropriate span. The similarity of functions managed, for example, affects the nature of problems coming to the manager's attention. A study by Jon Udell supports the presumed relationship between similarity of functions supervised and span of control.[13]

Intuitively, we can also see a logical connection between various other aspects of work and the manager's span. For example, the importance of the work seems significant, because managers are more personally involved in the most important projects. And the inherent difficulty of work may affect the number of type of managerial problems—for example, time-consuming complex problems might well arise in a research and development project. Even the geographical spread of managed activities may limit the span size, because it seems more difficult and time consuming to manage dispersed activities and personnel.

The Manager. In analyzing the optimum span of control, we should not overlook the executive as an individual. All managers do not have the same physical, mental, and emotional characteristics.

Some individuals are tougher physically and more resilient in react-ing to the demands of their offices. Some might be described as "easy-going," while other are "ulcer-prone." The mental ability of some indi-viduals also equips them to size up situations and reach decisions more quickly than is possible for others. Such individual differences are recognized among college students in that, to achieve the same grade, some students spend long hours studying while other barely "crack a book."

Methods of Management.   A number of management practices facilitate direction by managers and thus seemingly contribute to their capacity to manage a larger number of subordinates. One of these is the delegation of authority. If managers delegate substantial amounts of authority, they free themselves from work that is burdensome and that consumes a great deal of time.

Other managerial techniques affecting the size of the span include the use of budgetary control systems. A manager who approves a course of action in the officially adopted budget is relieved of the necessity of evaluating subsequent actions that fall within the scope of that budget. Similarly, a higher-level executive may, through a framework of policies, establish guidelines for lower levels of management. In this way, the executive can rule in advance on general problems and avoid the need for minute examination of specific issues. However, the Udell study found no evidence to prove that the use of written policies affected span size.[14] Therefore, we must regard the impact of formal policies as hypo-thetical, not yet demonstrated by research.

Executives are also able to broaden their span of control by the use of staff assistants. A staff specialist can provide another set of legs and eyes and ears for the executive. The empirical evidence cited by Udell supports this hypothesis.[15]

Capacity and Training of Subordinates.   The manager who has tal-ented, competent subordinates can minimize time spent in control of their activities. Competent, well-trained personnel are less prone to make errors and require less correction and counseling from their supe-riors. In addition, the ability of subordinates may manifest itself in read-ily identifying problem areas and in devising solutions to these prob-lems.

This difference in the capacity and training of subordinates is sig-nificant at any level of the organization. At the higher levels, it involves greater capacity for dealing with broad administrative problems. At op-erative levels, competent workmanship can simplify the task of a first-line supervisor by eliminating errors and minimizing the need for de-tailed instruction. Udell found that the span of control was related to length of experience of subordinates.[16] His findings are thus consistent with the proposition that capable subordinates permit a manager to use a broader span.

DELEGATION OF AUTHORITY

The Nature of Delegation

Having established a chain of command, an organizer should then determine the vertical level at which decisions of various types will be made. To the extent that decision making is passed downward from superior to subordinates, the manager is practicing *delegation of authority*.

Delegation of authority involves an assignment of responsibility and authority by a superior to a subordinate. Through delegation, a manager is given the right to plan the activities of a unit, direct the work of subordinate personnel, and make other decisions pertinent to the operations of the organization. If authority is delegated to an operative employee, the right is that of deciding various details of the work and using property and supplies belonging to the employer.

Granting authority need not involve a "blank check" to be classified as delegation. Even in similar lines of work, managers differ in the degree of freedom extended to subordinates. It is less a matter of *delegation versus nondelegation* than it is a matter of *more or less* delegation. Many managers, however, go through the motions of delegating authority, subscribe to the principle in theory, and believe they are delegating, but fail to delegate in a significant way.

When authority is delegated, an obligation is thereby placed upon the subordinate. For example, a department manager in a retail store who is granted authority to purchase goods sold in the department is expected to exercise authority in such a way as to bring profit to the company. The manager is rewarded for success and penalized for failure in achieving this objective.

Although a manager may delegate authority to a subordinate, the manager doing the delegating does not escape responsibility to higher management. Instead, delegation creates an additional relationship of obligation between subordinate and superior (Figure 11–4).

A coach may delegate to a quarterback the right to call a series of plays during a football game. If the quarterback comes up with a poor series of calls, the coach must still shoulder the coaching responsibility. Irate fans would hardly be impressed with the coach's explanation that the responsibility was really that of the quarterback and not that of the coach!

Barriers to Delegation

Organizational Barriers. Some organizations are traditionally democratic in allowing decisions to be made far down in the organization structure. In other organizations, control and decision making are tightly centralized. For example, educational institutions typically operate in a decentralized manner. A military organization provides an example in the opposite direction of tightly controlled and centralized management.

Most business institutions are inclined, because of the forces affect-

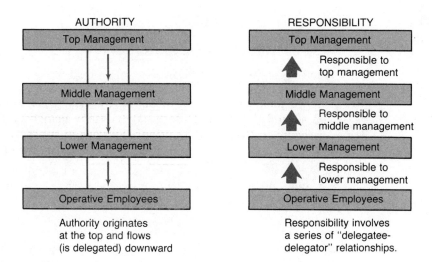

FIGURE 11–4   Authority and responsibility

ing their operation, to fall somewhere between these extremes. Individual companies also differ considerably in their philosophies concerning delegation of authority. During the same years in which Henry Ford I personally directed and controlled the Ford Motor Company, General Motors was developing its system of decentralized management.

Given a particular cultural environment, the degree of delegation still depends upon individual factors. One of these is the type of function or work being managed. A manager may find it impossible to "stay on top" of work performed by subordinates if the subordinates experience much variation in their required duties. The manager's only recourse may be to allow them greater freedom. One study compared the predictability of hospital work—the extent to which unexpected events disturb work routine—with closeness of supervision.[17] A strong, positive correlation was discovered between predictable work and close supervision. Apparently, managers were unable to follow closely those jobs having unexpected variations in their day-to-day content.

The manager is also limited by the training and ability level of subordinates. If employees are so inexperienced that their work is subject to frequent error and requires constant checking, it is almost impossible to delegate extensively. If employees, on the other hand, are well qualified in terms of education and experience, the manager can delegate more freely.

Psychological Barriers.   Some of the most persistent problems in delegation are psychological. Many managers experience difficulty in adopting a delegation-of-authority approach to management. Frequently, the manager has developed a practice of supervision that makes little use of delegation and that keeps the manager in personal contact with all phases of the work. This approach may have been developed over a period of many years and may involve a deeply ingrained habit pattern.

Another psychological barrier derives from the feeling of importance attached to the exercise of power. The egos of managers are involved, and they can sense their own importance as subordinates come to them with questions and refer problems to them for decision. Their importance and significance are less apparent when decision-making power is turned over to others.

A manager's feeling of insecurity may likewise make it difficult to be a good delegator. Unfortunately, many managers do find themselves insecure in their own positions. Surveys of supervisory and managerial attitudes have shown that a substantial percentage of management personnel, even in well-managed organizations, are quite unsure where they stand with their immediate superiors and the company which employs them.

This feeling of insecurity may affect delegation in different ways. The insecure manager feels it necessary to keep in close touch with work for which he or she is responsible. The manager is fearful of the consequences if all responsibilities are not carefully discharged. It is difficult, with this attitude, to allow a subordinate to take part of the work and perform it without careful scrutiny.

Barriers of the Delegatee.   Not all barriers to delegation are found in the delegator. Frequently, we visualize subordinates as eagerly reaching out to grasp any decision-making authority that is proffered them. Unfortunately, the real-life situation reveals many subordinates who are apathetic and lack motivation. Others are apprehensive about accepting authority. Some employees apparently wish to have decisions made by those above them and find the task of reaching their own decisions uncomfortable.

Advantages of Delegation

A major advantage of delegating authority is that it relieves the delegator of certain time-consuming work. Delegation also locates decision making closer to the work being performed and, as a result, often leads to more practical decisions. Delegation thus contributes directly to the improvement of productivity.

Another value of delegation is its contribution to development of subordinates. One does not learn to play tennis by reading a book. Obviously, it is possible to acquire some knowledge of the rules of the game and certain of the fundamentals in this way. But development of tennis-playing skills requires months and years of swinging a racket on a tennis court. In much the same way, one must develop management ability by managing. In other words, one learns to make decisions by making decisions. The implications for delegation of authority are clear. By forcing a subordinate to assume responsibility and to make decisions, the superior is insisting upon the subordinate's "practicing management."

It is also widely believed that personnel respond to delegated authority with favorable attitudes, that they enjoy the greater responsibilities. Obviously, this generalization could not apply to all operative employees or even to all managers. Some individuals—and they can be found in any sizable organization—like the security associated with detailed supervision. It seems likely, however, that most employees—particularly those in management positions—respond positively toward delegated authority.[18]

INCREASING DELEGATION AT BURROUGHS

In recent years, the Burroughs Corporation has been directed by two dynamic chairmen whose management styles differed dramatically. Until 1978, tough, domineering Ray W. Macdonald led the computer company in a period of highly successful growth. Macdonald's leadership style was described as follows:

> Macdonald ran Burroughs with iron-fisted control, choosing—and sometimes even designing—the products that the company would market. Insiders say the most trivial decisions were made by Macdonald. . . .

Because of this failure to delegate, however, the company failed to keep pace with the industry and to develop senior management talent.

In 1980, following an interim chairmanship, the chief executive position was handed to W. Michael Blumenthal, former chairman of Bendix Corporation and former U.S. treasury secretary. Blumenthal immediately launched a massive reorganization to decentralize Burrough's marketing and product development operations. His reasoning was expressed as follows:

> "This company has functioned in the past on a very centralized basis," Blumenthal went on. "I will want to establish more profit centers, and move the profit-and-loss responsibility down to the lowest possible levels in the company. . . ."

The reorganization, announced in 1981, placed greater responsibility on lower levels of management. This chief executive's prescription of delegation was intended to correct an organizational weakness and to restore the firm's momentum.

SOURCES: "The Burroughs Syndrome," *Business Week*, 12 November 1979, pp. 82–88; "Executive Suite: Will a Shake-up Revive Burroughs? *Business Week*, 4 May 1981, pp. 53–54; and "Shape Up, or Else," *Forbes*, 27 October 1980, pp. 38–40.

DECENTRALIZATION

Growth of Decentralization

As organizations grow, they become more difficult to manage. When they become huge—with tens of thousands or hundreds of thousands of employees—they become unwieldy and require new types of organizational and management practices.

About 1920, General Motors pioneered an approach to management of large organizations that was to become famous. Introduced by Alfred P. Sloan, Jr., this management approach became known as *decentralized management*. Decentralization facilitated, or at least permitted, the tremendous growth that made General Motors one of the leading industrial concerns in the world with more than 650,000 employees and sales of $60 billion.

Decentralized management basically involves the subdivision of a large organization into components of more manageable size. The key to decentralization, however, is the autonomy accorded to separate divisions. They are directed by divisional heads who function much like chief executives. Decentralization thus necessitates delegation of authority, but it is not synonymous with delegation. Even in more centralized organizations, individual managers may delegate freely. Decentralization

DECENTRALIZING BRITISH STEEL CORPORATION

Decentralization can work even in a government-owned company. In 1980, Ian MacGregor was lured out of retirement to head the British Steel Corporation, which was losing more than $4 million a day. MacGregor quickly turned the company around and headed it toward financial health. His first order of business was to restore the morale of middle management, and he sought to accomplish this by building up their independence and responsibility. Some of MacGregor's philosophy is evident in the following account:

> "There's a tendency for companies under government control to become organized like the government itself, in a bureaucratic mode with centralized decision-making. I felt if we reversed that we would see some improvement in performance."
>
> He called in Roger Morrison, head of the London branch of McKinsey & Co., the consulting firm, and they drew up a reorganization that was put into effect within three months. The corporation was broken up into units according to product lines, and the executives heading the units were given responsibility for procuring their own supplies and raw materials, as well as for marketing their finished goods.

The decentralization remedy has won acclaim throughout the corporation. Even union representatives have expressed commendation for MacGregor's performance.

SOURCE: Robert Lubar, "An American Leads British Steel Back from the Brink," *Fortune* 104, no. 6 (21 September 1981): 97. © 1981 Time Inc.

occurs when delegation is practiced systematically throughout an organization by the creation of relatively autonomous divisions.

Decentralization of authority and decision making is often centered about product or territorial divisions that receive grants of authority from company headquarters. As noted in Chapter 10, such organization structures are described as *divisionalized*. It should be noted, however, that decentralization is not the same as divisionalization. In a company organized along functional lines, lower-level officials may be granted either substantial or minor authority. And even in a company having product or territorial divisions, there is no guarantee that divisions are free from close headquarters control.

Advantages of Decentralization

The advantages cited earlier for delegation of authority apply to decentralization as well. By decentralizing, the company may, for example, develop managerial ability throughout the organization. Another significant advantage of decentralized corporate management is the *profitcenter* principle. The division manager who is given freedom in management can be held responsible for the profitable operations of the division.

Managers of profit centers can be highly motivated to operate profitably. Their effectiveness or ineffectiveness is no longer obscured by blending the operating results of all divisions into one overall financial report. The value of this strong incentive is evident in the experience of Dawson International (manufacturer of cashmere sweaters in Scotland). When the earnings of this company sagged in the early 1970s, Chairman Alan Smith removed the top executives and set up a decentralized system. Smith is quoted as follows:

> "We're almost fanatical about decentralization," he says. "Each of our 24 subsidiaries is a profit center. I tell the managers, 'It's your business, get on with it and make money.' "[19]

Creation of the decentralized profit centers evidently provided a powerful incentive, because Dawson's pretax profit increased from a mere 1.2 percent of sales in 1975 to a very healthy 16 percent.

Decentralization also facilitates product diversification. It is difficult, if not impossible, for a company having a highly diversified line of products to operate with tightly centralized management. Centralized control over the units of a food chain, for example, is simpler than centralized control of a company producing such diverse equipment as water heaters, electronic equipment, and farm implements.

In some cases, at least, lower-level decisions are also better than higher-level decisions. The manager on the "firing line" is close to the problem and often has insights that higher-level management lacks. In addition, the immediate manager is in a position to move quickly if not required to check constantly with headquarters. One research study has shown that firms facing strong competitive pressures, with the accompanying market turbulence, tend to use more decentralization and more participative decision making.[20]

Difficulties in Decentralizing

Centralization of some functions encourages economy of operation. Consider, for example, the college recruitment program of a large corporation having numerous branch plants. If the personnel function were completely decentralized, each branch plant should prepare brochures, contact universities, and arrange to interview prospective graduates. This would add unnecessarily to the cost of operation.

Also, in some decentralized organizations, autonomous divisions have used their freedom unwisely, making costly mistakes. In the banking industry, for example, loans involving excessive risk have been made by divisions of banks eager to improve divisional performance. When the Penn Square Bank of Oklahoma City failed in 1982, many larger banks such as Continental Illinois National Bank and Trust Company of Chicago, Seattle-First National Bank, and New York's Chase Manhattan Bank were affected. These larger banks suffered because they had joined with Penn Square Bank in some of its loans. Penn Square Bank was recognized, belatedly at least, as a high-flying energy lender, a "go-go bank." How could more conservative banks become involved in such loans?

> Decentralization could well explain Chase's difficulties. The bank's Institutional Banking Div., says one former Chase employee, aggressively hunted for quick profits. It failed to have the Penn Square participation reviewed by Chase's highly respected energy lending group. . . .[21]

In this case, the practice of decentralization permitted autonomous divisions to function without adequate control. Perhaps a stronger control system could have been established at the divisional level. Nevertheless, this incident shows another potential danger in decentralization.

Lack of capacity of lower-level personnel may also limit the ability of top management to decentralize. This may be a vicious circle, however, with the lack of ability an effect as well as a cause of failure to decentralize. If so, it spotlights a serious weakness in higher-level management.

Some types of functions are also more easily decentralized than others. Manufacturing has traditionally been one of the first to be decentralized, while finance has remained centralized even in many large companies that are otherwise decentralized.

SUMMARY

Authority is defined as the capacity to make decisions affecting the behavior of subordinates. It may also be described as *institutionalized power,* and it differs from *influence,* in which the recipient exercises individual critical faculties in determining personal behavior. Authority is established by a number of different factors such as the general culture, rewards and penalties, belief in the organization's purpose, expertise, personal leadership, and the desire of some to avoid responsibility.

Limitations exist in the extent to which formal authority is accepted by subordinate members of an organization. Chester I. Barnard has suggested the concept of a *zone of indifference* within which employees are willing to accept orders. Forms of resistance include not only open defiance but also subtle disobedience.

Adherence to the *chain of command* strengthens the organization by preserving the status of management officials and avoiding confusion among subordinate personnel. Subordinates often find it distressing to receive multiple supervision, whether this results from short-circuiting the chain of command or from conflict with the concept of *unity of command.*

Although there are difficulties in extending the size of the span of control, some have found advantages, particularly in terms of communication, productivity, and morale, in the use of broader spans that result in flatter organizations. Some of the variables affecting the desirable size of the span of control include the nature of the work, the qualities of the manager, managerial methods and procedures, and the capacity of subordinates.

By *delegation of authority,* a manager conveys to a subordinate the right to make decisions that would otherwise be made by the delegator. Barriers to delegation include both *organizational barriers* and *psychological barriers.* Inexperience of personnel, for example, constitutes an organizational barrier. Psychological barriers reflect such factors as deeply ingrained habit patterns, sense of individual importance, feeling of insecurity, and enjoyment of exercising power. Another barrier to delegation takes the form of the subordinate's reluctance to assume delegated authority. Among the advantages of delegation are the relief of the delegator from time-consuming work, development of subordinate personnel, and improvement of morale.

Decentralization occurs when delegation is used systematically and extensively throughout an organization. Decentralization aids control through use of the *profit-center* principle, facilitates product diversification, and improves some decisions by permitting them to be made closer to the problem level. Difficulties in decentralizing include uneconomical duplication of some operations and limited capability of lower-level personnel.

DISCUSSION QUESTIONS

1. How does the concept of *authority* differ from that of *power?* From that of *influence?*

2. Explain the reasons for acceptance of authority. In what way is our culture associated with this?

3. What is the *zone of indifference* suggested by Barnard, and how is this related to a superior's authority?

4. If subordinates are inclined to resist authority, what forms may their resistance take?

5. What pressures encourage short-circuiting of the chain of command? Do these factors constitute valid reasons or are they merely excuses for short-circuiting?

6. Suppose a top-level executive feels it is necessary to go outside channels in contacting a manager two or three levels below. How can adverse effects be minimized?

7. How is the span of control related to the number of echelons in an organization?

8. What seems to be the greatest advantage resulting from expanding the span of control?

9. Distinguish between *delegation* and *decentralization.*

10. How can a feeling of insecurity act as a barrier to delegation?

11. Discuss the relationship of delegation of authority and morale of employees. Do subordinates really want authority and the responsibility that accompanies it?

12. What advantages do *decentralization* and *divisionalization* have in common?

13. Have you ever worked for a supervisor who delegated very little authority? For one who delegated extensively? Describe as carefully as possible your reactions and the reactions of your fellow employees to either or both types of supervision.

NOTES

1. Reprinted by permission of the publishers from Chester I. Barnard, *The Functions of the Executive,* Cambridge, Mass.: Harvard University Press. Copyright, 1938, by the President and Fellows of Harvard College, 1966, by Grace F. Noera Barnard, p. 162.

2. Ibid., p. 163.

3. Ibid., pp. 168–69.

4. Herbert A. Simon, *Administrative Behavior,* 3d ed. (New York: The Free Press, 1976), p. 134

5. George Strauss and Leonard R. Sayles, *Personnel: The Human Problems of Management,* 2d ed. (Englewood Cliffs, N.J.: Prentice-Hall, 1967), p. 189.

6. Thomas J. Watson, Jr., *A Business and Its Beliefs* (New York: McGraw-Hill Book Co., 1963), p. 20.

7. Confirmation of this negative attitude effect of multiple supervision in bureaucratic organizations is reported in Martin J. Gannon and Frank T. Paine, "Unity of Command and Job Attitudes of Managers in a Bureaucratic Organization," *Journal of Applied Psychology* 59 (June 1974): 392–94.

8. James C. Worthy, "Organizational Structure and Employe Morale," *American Sociological Review* 15 (April 1950): 169–79.

9. Lyman W. Porter and Edward E. Lawler III, "The Effects of 'Tall' Versus 'Flat' Organization Structures on Managerial Job Satisfaction," *Personnel Psychology* 17 (Summer 1964): 135–48.

10. John M. Ivancevich and James H. Donnelly, Jr., "Relation of Organizational Structure to Job Satisfaction, Anxiety-Stress, and Performance," *Administrative Science Quarterly* 20 (June 1975): 272–80.

11. Lawrence B. Chonko, "The Relationship of Span of Control to Sales Representatives' Experienced Role Conflict and Role Ambiguity," *Academy of Management Journal* 25, no. 2 (June 1982): 452–56.

12. One carefully designed research study, using a small sample, is reported in Jon G. Udell, "An Empirical Test of Hypotheses Relating to Span of Control," *Administrative Science Quarterly* 12 (December 1967): 420–39.

13. Ibid., p. 428.

14. Ibid., p. 431.

15. Ibid., p. 425.

16. Ibid., p. 435.

17. Gerald D. Bell, "The Influence of Technological Components of Work upon Management Control," *Academy of Management Journal* 8 (June 1965): 127–32.

18. For a research study that supports this position, see J. Kenneth White and Robert A. Ruh, "Effects of Personal Values on the Relationship between Participation and Job Attitudes," *Administrative Science Quarterly* 18 (December 1973): 506–14.

19. "Mongolian Connection," *Fortune* 102, no. 9 (3 November 1980): 19. © 1980 Time Inc.

20. Pradip N. Khandwalla, "Effect of Competition on the Structure of Top Management Control," *Academy of Management Journal* 16 (June 1973): 285–95.

21. "The Stain from Penn Square Keeps Spreading," *Business Week* 2 August 1982, p. 62.

SUPPLEMENTARY READING

Alper, S. William. "The Dilemma of Lower Level Management: Freedom versus Control." *Personnel Journal* 53 (November 1974): 804–8.

Briggs, Jean A. "Easing Into High Gear." *Forbes* 128, no. 5 (31 August 1981): 91–95.

Carlisle, Arthur Elliott. "The Golfer." *California Management Review* 22, no. 1 (Fall 1979): 42–52.

Chonko, Lawrence B. "The Relationships of Span of Control to Sales Representatives' Experienced Role Conflict and Role Ambiguity." *Academy of Management Journal* 25, no. 2 (June 1982): 452–56.

Dubin, Robert. *Human Relations in Administration*, 4th ed., Chapters 12 and 13. Englewood Cliffs, N.J.: Prentice-Hall, 1974.

Gabarro, John J., and **Kotter, John P.** "Managing Your Boss." *Harvard Business Review* 58 (January–February 1980): 92–100.

Ivancevich, John M., and **Donnelly, James H., Jr.** "Relation of Organizational Structure to Job Satisfaction, Anxiety-Stress, and Performance." *Administrative Science Quarterly* 20 (June 1975): 272–80.

Kotter, John P. "Power, Dependence, and Effective Management." *Harvard Business Review* 55 (July–August 1977): 125–36.

Krein, Theodore J. "How to Improve Delegation Habits." *Management Review* 71, no. 5 (May 1982): 58–61.

Laurent, André. "Managerial Subordinancy: A Neglected Aspect of Organizational Hierarchies." *Academy of Management Review* 3 (April 1978): 220–30.

Limerick, David C. "Authority Relations in Different Organizational Systems." *Academy of Management Review* 1 (October 1976): 56–58.

Mackenzie, Kenneth D. *Organizational Structures.* Arlington Heights, Ill.: AHM Publishing Corp., 1978.

Montana, Patrick J., and **Nash, Deborah F.** "Delegation: The Art of Managing." *Personnel Journal* 60, no. 10 (October 1981): 784–87.

Oncken, William, Jr., and **Wass, Donald L.** "Management Time: Who's Got the Monkey?" *Harvard Business Review* 52 (November–December 1974): 75–80.

Perrow, Charles. "The Bureaucratic Paradox: The Efficient Organization Centralizes in Order to Decentralize." *Organizational Dynamics* 5 (Spring 1977): 3–14.

Shetty, Y. K. "Managerial Power and Organizational Effectiveness: A Contingency Analysis." *Journal of Management Studies* 15 (May 1978): 176–86.

Vancil, Richard F. "Managing the Decentralized Firm." *Financial Executive* 48, no. 3 (March 1980): 34–43.

Van Fleet, David D., and **Bedeian, Arthur G.** "A History of the Span of Management." *Academy of Management Review* 2 (July 1977): 356–72.

12

INTER-
DEPARTMENTAL
RELATIONSHIPS

This chapter will enable you to

- *Understand the importance of lateral relationships and the forms of interdepartmental collaboration.*
- *Explain the nature of line and staff functions, the traditional view of authority relationships between them, and the types of limitations placed on line authority.*
- *Understand the reasons for using a matrix organization structure and the nature of interdepartmental relationships within such a structure.*
- *Outline the major reasons for interdepartmental conflict and recognize practices that contribute to cooperation.*

Earlier chapters have emphasized the vertical structure or chain of command as the method for achieving coordination. In contrast, this chapter examines horizontal or lateral relationships which supplement chain-of-command decision making. Although departments deal with other departments through vertical channels, they also relate to each other directly without using the linkage of higher-level managers. (The word *department* is used here in a general sense and includes the many types of horizontal and diagonal relationships among units, branches, offices, divisions, and so on.) This chapter treats the general nature of *lateral* relationships among departments, the special features of *line and staff* relationships, the modern *matrix structure,* and the problem of *interdepartmental conflict.*

LATERAL RELATIONSHIPS AMONG DEPARTMENTS

Need for Lateral Relationships

A department typically interacts with a number of other departments, although the pattern and volume of interaction is not uniform. A sales department, for example, may interact with manufacturing, personnel, advertising, accounting, legal, research, and other departments. Many of

FIGURE 12–1   Horizontal coordination

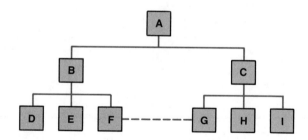

these interactions involve direct contacts, as sales personnel and sales managers confer directly with their peers in other departments.

To function effectively, therefore, organizations must use horizontal forms of communication and decision making.* They can avoid an overload in the chain of command by working directly with other departments at the same level in solving problems and coordinating their respective activities. If every difficulty or point of friction between departments were taken upward to a mutual superior, that superior would need to devote an unreasonable amount of time to peacemaking and integrative activities.

Suppose that Departments F and G in Figure 12–1 experience a problem that affects their respective operations and overall organization performance. Department F, for example, may encounter delays which affect the flow of output from Department F to Department G. If this problem can be resolved laterally, it avoids delays and also minimizes the managerial burden placed on managers of A, B, and C.

The extent of horizontal coordination varies with the nature of work operations and particularly the degree of task uncertainty. Task uncertainty refers to variability in work—for example, the sameness of work from day to day, the number of exceptions, frequency of delays in deciding how to solve problems, and so on. One research study has shown that as tasks increase in uncertainty, more horizontal communication and group meetings are used in lieu of the chain of command.[1]

Forms of Horizontal Decision Making

Collaboration among departments takes various forms. The simplest approach involves *direct contact* between managers who have a mutual problem. Suppose, for example, that two departments in a university school of business prepare tentative schedules that would overload limited facilities or that would offer required seminars at the same hour. Instead of referring such problems upward to the dean for resolution, the

---

*Management theorists have long recognized the need for horizontal communication and decision making, but, in earlier years, treated it as a limited, exceptional relationship needing careful control. The noted French writer, Henri Fayol, emphasized the need for supervisory authorization prior to lateral contacts and prompt reporting of any lateral agreements to higher-level supervisors. See Henri Fayol, *General and Industrial Management*, trans. Constance Storrs (New York: Pitman Publishing Corp., 1949).

department chairpersons can simply get together and work out a solution.

In some organizations, the volume of interdepartmental contacts is so great that a special *liaison role* is created to assist in coordination. This may be illustrated by the product design and process design groups of a manufacturing plant.[2] The product design group prepares new product designs, and the process design group works out the manufacturing processes necessary to produce them. To aid in coordination, a group of process designers is physically stationed in the product design area. This liaison group performs a variety of integrative activities such as working with product designers to find design alternatives which allow less costly manufacturing processes. In addition, close contact with product designers enables the process designers to schedule their own manufacturing process design work efficiently. They have discovered that design of a new product does not need to be 100 percent complete before the manufacturing process design can begin.

LATERAL RELATIONS— ENGINEERING AND TESTING

In a laboratory testing facility, mechanics and electronics technicians make test set-ups and conduct tests. They work under the direction of an operations supervisor who visits the area once or twice daily to check on work progress. Technical direction for their work, however, comes from test engineers who report to a different chain of command.

Testing work is scheduled jointly by the operations supervisor and director of test engineering. For smooth operation, engineers and technicians must cooperate fully, and the two managers must also coordinate their work closely. The managers must respond immediately in the event of difficulty. Conflicts in equipment and personnel requirements must be resolved by the engineers, technicians, or the two managers. Only in rare and difficult cases are conflicts taken upward to a mutual superior in the chain of command.

As long as the spirit of teamwork prevails, the jobs sail through to completion. Such day-to-day collaboration by test operators, engineers, and first-line managers illustrates the practical value of lateral relationships and their superiority to reliance on the chain of command.

As more general problems arise or projects become more complex, management may create a *task force* or *team* of representatives from various departments to provide coordination. A task force might be created within a college or university, for example, to coordinate efforts to achieve academic accreditation. Formation of teams has also been proposed as a mechanism for guiding market research projects.[3] These teams would bring together personnel from such diverse areas as manufacturing, finance, accounting, advertising, sales, product planning, and market research to define market research needs and guide research projects.

As lateral decisions become increasingly important, a need for still stronger leadership often arises. This leads to the creation of an integrating role.[4] Someone is assigned specific leadership responsibility for integrating or coordinating interdepartmental efforts. These integrative positions carry such titles as product manager, program coordinator, business manager, project leader, and so on. A product manager, for example, becomes the representative for a given product in all departments having any relationship to that product. If this type of structure continues to grow and the coordinator acquires formal authority, it becomes the matrix structure described later in this chapter.

LINE AND STAFF RELATIONSHIPS

The particular type of lateral relationship between line and staff departments deserves special attention. Even though scholars have debated the usefulness of a line-staff classification, the concept has figured prominently in management writings and is used extensively in practice.

The Nature of Line and Staff Functions

In most organizations, a simple distinction can be made between activities that accomplish the basic purposes of the organization and activities that are indirectly helpful. In colleges and universities, for example, the teaching faculty provides educationl services, whereas student financial aid offices contribute indirectly by helping students to finance their education. In manufacturing plants, production departments make products for customers, whereas personnel offices recruit employees for production and other departments. In department stores, selling departments sell merchandise to customers, whereas credit departments evaluate the financial capacity of customers.

From an operational point of view, *line activities are those that contribute directly to accomplishment of the organization's primary objective.* The primary or line functions of a manufacturing concern, for example, include producing and selling a product. The firm exists to make and sell products, and customers pay for this service. Employees in production and sales, accordingly, are line personnel, and the manufacturing and sales departments are line departments of the enterprise. In basic economic terms, line departments produce "time, place, and form" utility for customers.

Staff functions, on the other hand, are *supporting functions*. Their performance facilitates the accomplishment of primary objectives by line departments. The nature of staff work is often described as advisory to other departments. In addition, the staff may be used for investigation, fact gathering, and service. In fact, many nonline departments provide a combination of advice and service.

One weakness of this classification is that it does not distinguish between important and unimportant activities. We can, for example, classify finance or accounting as a staff function, but it is dangerous to assume that either is unimportant. In classifying specific functions as line activities, therefore, we must avoid the error of considering staff functions as unimportant.

One useful distinction in types of staff is that of *personal staff* and *specialized staff*.[5] The personal staff is an individual who serves one particular superior. Personal staff assignments may be specialized or may involve a sort of generalized troubleshooting which ranges across a broad subject area. The assistant to the president of a firm is an example of this type of staff position. In contrast, the specialized staff serves an entire organization. It also has a special area of competence in which it is expected to be proficient. Such activities as personnel or labor relations, public relations, and legal counsel are examples of specialized staff functions.

Traditional View of Line Authority

Much of the line and staff problem in a typical organization centers about the question of authority between line and staff departments or personnel. Who decides questions of mutual interest to both line and staff departments? According to the traditional view of management writers, line managers are the proper decision makers, and their authority must be maintained. And, to preserve unity of command, staff must be denied command authority. Only in this way, presumably, can line managers be held responsible for results.

How then can staff managers perform the functions for which they are responsible? Although they may seek to enforce their judgment by appealing to the chain of command, they cannot expect higher-level managers to solve all their problems for them. For the most part, they must use lateral relationships and provide advice and service which is perceived by the line to be competent and practical. Figure 12–2 illustrates the relationship between line and staff departments.

Discussion of the traditional staff role and the degrees of staff authority tends to understate its extensive influence—an influence that often exceeds its formal authority. Some reasons for the power of staff are identified in the following statement:

> Since they are experts in their respective areas, staff people can withhold valuable advice or slow down service to pressure a manager to heed their

FIGURE 12–2 Line-staff organization

EXPLANATORY NOTE: According to the traditional view, staff has a "dotted-line" or advisory relationship (not a command relationship) to other departments.

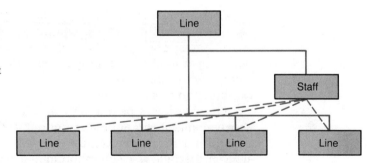

influence attempts. A cooperative staff can be an important asset, but because staff people are experts in areas in which line managers are not, they can sometimes overwhelm the line manager with their specialized knowledge. They may have more influence with higher levels of line management because these managers depend on them to provide information about line performance.[6]

Increasing Staff Authority

The supposedly ideal authority relationships between line and staff are difficult to observe. Situations arise in which it appears desirable from the standpoint of the organization as a whole to delegate to staff some degree of decision-making authority. A deliberate decision may place certain issues or decisions in the hands of staff.

Various degrees or types of staff authority have been established.[7] One type, *compulsory staff consultation*, requires operating managers to confer with appropriate staff personnel before taking action. They are not required to follow the advice but presumably must listen before acting.

Another type of staff authority, *concurrent authority*, substantially increases the power of staff. The line manager must obtain staff agreement before taking action. By requiring concurrent authority, the organization makes sure that staff knowledge is used in reaching a decision. As an example, the line manager may be required to get the concurrence of the legal department before signing a contract.

It is common for some staff offices to possess authority of this type. In the Eli Lilly Company, for instance, Chief Executive Officer Richard D. Wood described it as follows:

> It's very hard in our company to distinguish between line and staff. The line sometimes jokes that the staff really has line authority over their activities, and in some ways that really is correct. For example, the line would never adopt a financial policy that the chief financial officer said was inappropriate. And although the personnel man is not the final absolute authority, he certainly has at least an equal voice in important decisions relating to people.[8]

STAFF THREATS TO
LINE AUTHORITY

To function as contemplated in traditional theory, the staff must tread softly to avoid threats to line authority. Accordingly, a chief executive officer who builds up the power of staff offices makes life difficult for line managers. Harold S. Geneen's almost legendary managerial style as CEO of International Telephone and Telegraph Corporation (until his retirement in 1977) created intense pressure for line managers. Part of this pressure was exerted through the ITT staff whose surveillance was described as follows:

> An equal source of managerial terror in the Geneen years was the mammoth corporate staff. Line managers worked with the unsettling knowledge that they were being scrutinized by teams at headquarters who could advance their own careers by finding problems and perhaps exaggerating their importance. Like most bureaucracies, the staff in time became bloated and unwieldy. But Geneen stuck faithfully to the system.

A later CEO cut back the huge staff, thereby changing the balance of power—a move widely applauded by ITT's operating managers.

SOURCE: Geoffrey Colvin, "The De-Geneening of ITT," *Fortune* 105 (11 January 1982): 34–39. © 1982 Time Inc.

An even greater limitation is placed on the authority of line managers by granting *functional authority* to staff. This gives staff some specified authority over line activities. One of the most common forms of functional authority is the assignment to specialized staff of controls pertaining to their own areas. Often these are of a routine or procedural nature—"how to do it" rather than "what to do." The accounting office establishes accounting procedures, and the personnel department specifies personnel procedures. As another example, a dangerous industrial production process may require functional authority for safety inspectors. Although safety management is a staff function, management may grant the safety inspector authority to shut down an operation in order to insure adequate safety for personnel and equipment.

We can see from the examples of an attorney's approval of contracts and a safety inspector's approval of safety conditions that staff authority is limited to particular issues or conditions. Such arrangements restrict the line manager's independence in specific areas, but they do not create full-fledged dual or multiple lines of command. This difference should be apparent as we proceed to discussion of the *matrix organization* in the following section.

MATRIX ORGANIZATION STRUCTURE

The growing complexity of environments, markets, and technology has led to the development of a special form of organization called the *matrix structure*. This type of organization originated in the project management system used in the aerospace industry in the 1950s and is currently used in such areas as government, banking, insurance, hospitals, and higher education.

What Is a Matrix Organization?

A matrix structure involves a dual line of command, forsaking the unity-of-command concept advocated by traditional management theory. This departure from the unified command principle is prompted by a complexity of operations which requires decisions incorporating both functional and project thinking.

An example will clarify this concept. Figure 12–3 presents an outline of a matrix structure in the aerospace industry. The traditional departments of production, engineering, materials, and accounting continue to exist and are headed by managers whose primary orientation lies in their respective functional specialties. A second line of command appears, however, as project managers are appointed to coordinate work

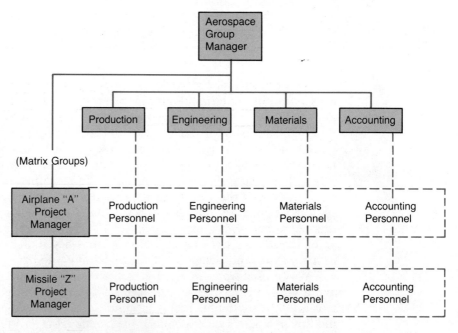

FIGURE 12–3   Matrix organization structure

on particular projects. The Airplane "A" project manager, for example, oversees production, engineering, and other work of Airplane "A" and has some measure of control over those activities. Some personnel within functional departments, therefore, report to both a functional manager and a project manager.

The dual line of command is imposed because management wishes to emphasize particular projects as well as functional specialties. Production specialization and expertise are important, but concentration on production problems and production efficiency may lead to neglect of project priorities. What is most logical in terms of the production function is not necessarily most logical in terms of the Airplane "A" or Missile "Z" projects.

In traditional structures, project coordination is performed by the general manager who oversees the various functional departments. In a matrix organization, however, the general manager delegates a part of his or her coordinating function to the various project managers. The project managers can give much more detailed attention to the many specific projects than can one general manager.

Changed Organizational Relationships

The matrix structure modifies the relationships that exist among managers in a traditional line and staff organization.[9] The key positions involved in matrix organizations, as shown in Figure 12–4, are the *general manager* (top leadership), *matrix manager,* and *2-boss manager.*

The authority of the *general manager* is basically similar to that of a manager in a traditional structure.[10] The special demands imposed on this position by the matrix structure are those of getting the participation and cooperation of lower-level personnel in nontraditional roles.

The *matrix manager*, on the other hand, shares power with other matrix managers. The functional manager—in production or engineer-

FIGURE 12–4   Key positions in matrix organizations

SOURCE: Paul R. Lawrence, Harvey F. Kolodny, and Stanley M. Davis, "The Human Side of the Matrix," *Organizational Dynamics,* Summer 1977 (New York: AMACOM, a division of American Management Associations, 1977), p. 44.

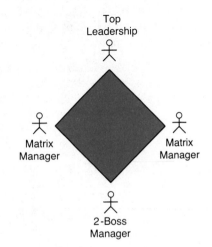

ing, for example—can no longer unilaterally establish work priorities, assign subordinates to particular projects, or evaluate employee performance. These management decisions are shared with one or more other matrix managers. Consultation on such matters is essential, and many matrix structures require dual "sign-offs" on performance evaluations and on pay and promotion decisions. In view of the strong emphasis upon lateral relationships and the need for negotiations and trade-offs in reaching decisions, matrix managers must exercise skills that are less essential in traditional organizations. This poses problems for matrix managers, especially for those who have worked in traditional organizations and who sense a loss of control and status as they become matrix managers.

The role of the *2-boss manager*, the one who must take orders from two or more matrix managers, is also difficult. Theoretically, matrix managers should achieve such excellent coordination that their subordinates, the 2-boss managers, face no conflicting demands. In practice, however, such perfection in management is unlikely to occur. Consequently, 2-boss managers must somehow deal with the frustrations of trying to reconcile directions coming from the dual lines of supervision. As it becomes necessary in specific cases to choose between legitimate but competing interests, the 2-boss manager may face rejection or even punishment from the "losing" side of the matrix.

Problems in Matrix Organizations

It is hardly surprising that some organizations have experienced problems in using the matrix structure. The severity of such problems is a matter of conjecture, because they are frequently intertwined with other types of problems. This makes it difficult to know how much of the blame belongs with the matrix.

One example relates to Intel Corporation, a manufacturer of semiconductors, which uses a matrix type of organization. After rapid growth in the 1970s, Intel experienced slower growth in the early 1980s and suffered the loss of a number of key managers and engineers.[11] Difficulty with the matrix structure was apparently one factor in Intel's problems.

> . . . Intel has tried to keep control of its sprawling organization with a matrix management scheme that gives managers multiple bosses, each with specialized functions. That system worked well when the company was smaller, but it has been strained by Intel's growth. "A matrix contributes to uncertainty if people don't understand the relationships," comments one former employee.[12]

Another company which has experienced matrix problems is Ebasco Services. This company, which uses a matrix organization in its engineering and consulting work, has experienced a measure of conflict in the functioning of this type of organization.[13] On major projects, such as construction of a nuclear power plant, general managers must constantly work at reducing tension among key personnel. To promote harmony, Ebasco has devised a variety of training and troubleshooting programs, such as seminars to explain matrix organization and team-building sessions to help personnel who are experiencing conflict.

Problems of the type described above arise because the matrix organization is much more complex than traditional structure. The various managerial roles involve greater ambiguity and conflict, requiring increased skill in lateral relationships. Such an intricate structure is used, in spite of such difficulties, because of the complexity of modern organizations and the need to focus attention simultaneously on various facets of their operations.

Varieties of Matrix Organizations

As indicated earlier, the matrix organization has moved from its birthplace in the aerospace industry into many institutional settings. To show the diverse applications of matrix organization, we briefly note a few examples.

Higher Education. In a school of business, faculties are typically grouped in departments such as marketing, accounting, and finance. Direction of the graduate program cuts across these departmental lines. The director of the MBA program and department heads, for example, may both exercise some degree of control over course offerings and class schedules. Their relative amounts of power will differ, based on the traditions of the school and the extent to which it has moved toward a mature matrix.

Multinational Corporations. In many multinational corporations, area managers concentrate upon the company's relationship to the economic, political, and cultural features of the country or region. At the same time, product and functional managers give some direction to activities in the various geographic areas.

> Consider how this worked in such a company that was deciding to build a new facility in what we'll call country Z. From the point of view of manufacturing, the new facility should have been a mass-production facility large enough to serve the entire Asian market and ensure economies of scale. But product management wanted a separate facility for their most technical products to ensure good engineering. In the interest of maintaining their "charter" to operate in country Z, the area manager got both to modify their plans and agree to place a smaller, high-technology plant in Z—which was insisting that it did not want to be simply a cheap labor contractor.[14]

Court Administration. At the urging of Chief Justice Warren Burger, local, state, and federal courts began to use court administrators.[15] Their task is to integrate the parts of the criminal justice system—law enforcement, prosecution, probation, and so on. The court administrators work with the various units to persuade them to modify their practices adequately to meet the overall needs of the criminal justice system.

Product Management. In some types of manufacturing, specific managers are designated to coordinate production and marketing of individual products. A product manager, for example, might have responsibility for a particular toothpaste, shampoo, or facial tissue. Such product managers must cross many functional lines in working with product development, marketing strategy, sales promotion, advertising, pricing, production, and other areas.

These examples are cited to convey some idea of the range of possible uses of matrix organization. Although this form has gained in popularity and usage during the last two decades, its applications are still varied and its forms diverse. No doubt many matrix organizations have simply evolved from line and staff structures. Nevertheless, it is a distinct form of organization with apparent advantages in dealing with the administration of complex activities and interests.

INTERDEPARTMENTAL CONFLICT

Even though organization structures are designed to promote collaboration, most organizations experience internal conflicts. Although some conflicts are constructive, many of them hamper effective performance. Many such conflicts involve segments of the organization—group against group or department against department.

Examples of Interdepartmental Conflict

Although the existence of interdepartmental conflict is obvious to those experienced in modern organizational life, two examples will be cited.

In a manufacturing concern, conflict occurred between a small research and development group and first-line production foremen. The four managers in the R and D group held college degrees, but foremen complained that they lacked practical experience. Foremen charged that the engineers did not provide enough detailed information in their drawings, that they lacked an adequate understanding of equipment capacity, that they specified impractical materials based on some salesperson's suggestion, and that they created unnecessary production interruptions to try out new techniques. On the other hand, the engineers felt that line foremen were unwilling to change production methods and that they lacked an adequate education to comprehend broader responsibilities and to understand explanations of engineers. The result was a running battle between the engineering and production functions.

In a retail establishment, the department managers experienced constant tension and occasional conflict with two auxiliary departments—credit and auditing. These managers felt the credit department was in-

flexible in approving credit, rejecting credit applications of worthy customers because of "red tape." The audit department served as the control
arm of higher management and, in the eyes of department managers,
displayed an amazing lack of understanding in their "snooping." The
fact that a department manager had aggressively sought to obtain an item
for the past six months was no excuse for being sold out. Also, department managers were required to document completely any error charged
to auditing, but auditors simply conveyed a "we-don't-make-mistakes"
attitude. One department head described his view of staff personnel as
follows:

> I would classify staff men in one of three ways—(1) those I never saw,
> (2) those who put their own interests above mine, and (3) those who genu-
> inely wanted to help. It seldom took more than one encounter to decide
> how to classify a particular man. Once I decided he belonged to group 2, I
> took evasionary tactics to keep him in the dark.

Benefits of Conflict

Even though conflict can be disruptive to the organization, we cannot
categorically denounce all conflict as destructive. Some social scientists
speak of "conflict management" as an opportunity for benefiting the corporation.

One potential benefit from conflict is the improved thinking that
may emerge from competition among departments. As happens in competitive sports, weaknesses are detected and strengths are revealed. In
academic circles, the interaction of minds and thinking is seen as a
means of protecting truth and exposing error. In the business organization, likewise, manufacturing departments may point out weaknesses in
sales programs, and industrial engineering departments may turn up
weaknesses in manufacturing operations. Or, a dispute over two alternatives may stimulate a search for a mutually acceptable, better, third
alternative.

Unfortunately, there is often a "fallout" of hostility and ill will from
conflict situations. Negative feelings offset the benefits that might otherwise result from such conflict. This suggests the importance of controlling conflict situations sufficiently to avoid dysfunctional consequences.
As Ross Webber has summarized it, "The emerging thesis is that too
little expressed conflict leads to stagnancy, but uncontrolled conflict
threatens chaos."[16]

Causes of Interdepartmental Conflict

Although managers should adopt a systems view of the total organization, they often limit their view to their immediate departments. From
the standpoint of the organization as a whole, of course, such narrowness of interests is irrational. Nevertheless, it happens. Department managers, either consciously or subconsciously, come to think of their departments as their territory or their "turf."

Territorial encroachment is a threat to narrowly focused department managers. These managers remain alert for intruders or "poachers" in their territorial preserves. Line managers, for example, may fear that personnel specialists are infringing on their jobs. Managers of one department can easily see representatives of other departments as "meddling" or interfering with internal department operations.

Operating department managers may expect purchasing agents to act as little more than order placers. Department managers in production or sales may likewise resist advice from personnel advisors on how to manage their employees. "Don't tell me how to run my business!"

Conflicts between departments may easily involve more substantial issues, however. Departmental interests may simply be incompatible. One cannot win without the other losing. Two departments, for example, may compete for their own shares of a limited capital budget. Funds allocated to one department are not available for another department.

Conflicts among departments are also encouraged by differences between the types of personnel assigned to two different departments. Melville Dalton's well-known study of line and staff relationships discovered that staff personnel in the plants he examined were younger, better educated, and better dressed than line managers. The latter were experienced in the practical aspects of work and followed a different life style than the staff specialists.[17] The heterogeneity seemed to increase problems between the two groups.

Individual differences in the way people look at problems may also contribute to the intensity of conflict. In other words, the perceived conflict may be greater than the underlying conflict of interest. If a line manager visualizes a qualified well-meaning staff specialist as a threat, the possibilities for conflict exist.

In summary, interdepartmental conflicts have both rational and emotional bases. Conflicts in interest and territorial encroachments may create a situation in which both parties cannot win. In addition, these conflicts may be stimulated by differences in personal characteristics and perceptions.

Methods of Conflict Resolution

To avoid an impasse, organizational conflicts must somehow be resolved. A number of approaches to settlement of disputes are discussed in this section.

Appeal to the Chain of Command. The organizational system is so designed that all individuals, groups, and departments have some common superior. One obvious method of resolving a point of contention, therefore, is to take it to the appropriate manager.*

---

*Etzioni argues for settlement of disputes at a relatively low level in the chain of command, thereby minimizing the administrative burden on higher-level officials. See Amitai Etzioni, *Modern Organizations* (Englewood Cliffs, N.J.: Prentice-Hall, 1964), p. 27.

Appeal to the chain of command has its limitations, however. The most knowledgeable decision makers may be the disputants themselves. Higher-level managers, moreover, cannot possibly be involved in all the details of operations at lower levels. Consequently, taking a dispute to a higher-level manager does not guarantee the best judgment in all cases. Furthermore, a manager who hears constant appeals from subordinates becomes burdened with a heavy load of conflict resolution and comes to view subordinates as incapable of solving their own problems.

Dominance of the Stronger Party.   Conflicts may also be settled as one party or the other gains the upper hand and wins. If a dispute is permitted to continue and if disputants have unequal power, the stronger will win. If the position of the stronger contestant in organizational struggles is favorable for the system as a whole, this method of resolution is productive.

Allowing settlement of disputes by dominance produces the problem of defeated or wounded managers. If the defeat is severe, the vanquished manager may permanently withdraw by resignation or transfer. In other cases, the defeated party may accept the defeat, stay on, and wait for a more opportune time to fight again. If more than two parties are involved in the conflict, dominance may be achieved by means of majority rule or even by a coalition of aggressive minority interests.

Bargaining between Competitors.   The bargaining method has been widely used in resolving labor disputes. However, this approach also applies to other types of conflict, as department heads, for example, attempt to resolve any dispute through the give and take of negotiations.

Settlements achieved through negotiation often involve compromise. In compromise settlements, both parties lose something, and no distinct winner emerges. Union representatives, for example, may give up the right to decline overtime work, and management may offer a higher wage settlement in return.

In some cases, the bargaining approach to resolving conflicts is blended with an appeal to the chain of command. A common superior oversees the bargaining process.

> . . . I have found that one of the most successful ways to manage conflict is to get all key parties in the same room simultaneously from time to time. There is no better therapy than to thrash out the major issues together with an executive in charge to draw conclusions that everybody hears at the same time and the same way.[18]

Modifying Organizational Relationships.   In some cases, organizational arrangements are dysfunctional and lead to conflict. Established work patterns impose a strain on relationships. A good example of this problem is the secretary or secretarial pool that provides service for a number of administrators or professionals. The difficulty of pleasing many supervisors bothers the subordinate, and the need to compete for the time of the subordinate bothers the supervisors.

If changes can be made in faulty organization structure, conflict may be dissipated. In a well-known case in the restaurant industry, a spindle was inserted between low-status waitresses and higher-status countermen to whom they gave orders.[19] Waitresses simply placed the written tickets on the spindle, from which countermen removed them. This arrangement depersonalized the relationship and reduced the conflict.

Problem-Solving Approach to Conflict Resolution. The *problem-solving, or integrative decision-making,* approach to conflict resolution directs attention to the controversy itself and away from the parties in conflict. To the extent that the controversy has been created by poor communication, it can be resolved by discussion. By concentrating upon the issue, furthermore, instead of personalities, the interchange can avoid emotional overtones that make communication difficult. Both sides are committed to the same goal, finding a solution for the mutual problem.

A person using the problem-solving approach is, according to Alan Filley, saying the following three things to other involved parties:

1. "I want a solution which achieves your goals and is acceptable to both of us."
2. "It is our collective responsibility to be open and honest about facts, opinions, and feelings."
3. "I will control the process by which we arrive at agreement but will not dictate content."[20]

The problem-solving approach has been described as a *win-win* method, in contrast to *win-lose* and *lose-lose* methods. Both parties, in other words, can be winners by imaginatively working out a mutually satisfactory solution. This method contrasts with a *lose-lose* compromise situation in which both parties give up something for a settlement. A major advantage of the problem-solving method is the shared commitment of both parties to the solution. Problem solving also provides a strong foundation for further collaboration and resolution of future conflicts.

Developing Strong Interdepartmental Relationships

Much undesirable conflict can be avoided by building strong interdepartmental relationships. In a sense, positive action to encourage cooperation is "preventive maintenance," eliminating disputes before they can arise. Sales and manufacturing departments, for example, have mutual concerns as well as competitive interests. A continuing emphasis upon total system goals and a continuing encouragement toward collaboration can be useful in minimizing conflict.[21]

ENCOURAGING A PROBLEM-SOLVING APPROACH

Attainment of a problem-solving approach is sometimes hampered by hostilities resulting from earlier conflict, inadequate communication, and tendency to blame the other party. Departments at swords' points with each other have combative rather than problem-solving attitudes.

In one company, the marketing and engineering departments were fighting more than cooperating. To change their attitudes, management brought the two groups together for discussion and then enforced two "rules of the road":

1. Skipper your own ship.
2. Stick to what is happening now, not yesterday or tomorrow.

(The former was designed to avoid telling the other department how to operate and the latter to minimize remembered hurts or projected wrongs.)

Teams were assembled from each department and asked, in separate work sessions, to list five things the other department was doing that made life difficult in their own department. For example, marketing said that engineering changed project manager assignments without telling them who was in charge of what. By subsequent discussion of the two lists, observing the two "rules of the road," the two departments were able to adopt a problem-solving approach and deal with their mutual problem in a rational manner.

SOURCE: The problem-solving sessions cited here are described by Donald G. Livingston, "Rules of the Road: Doing Something Simple about Conflict in the Organization," *Personnel* 54 (January–February 1977): 23–29.

Corporate efforts to improve interdepartmental relationships are illustrated by the actions of Dun and Bradstreet Corporation. To keep its services attuned to the rapidly changing environment of its customers, this company is attempting to stimulate cooperation by strengthening interdepartmental communication.

But most important, interdepartmental communications have become the driving force behind D&B's management approach. D&B's staff of some 70 in-house trainers now offer crash courses on technology and on the art of listening, says Charles J. Wielgus, senior vice-president for human resources. Managers of D&B's 130 profit centers are meeting with a frequency that was previously unheard of.[22]

Dun and Bradstreet also fosters collaboration through such practices as rotating managers from one division to another and providing incentives for joint ventures between divisions.

Perhaps the most critical determinant of cooperation is the quality of interdepartmental communication. An industrial engineering staff, for example, must be aware of the processing problems encountered in manufacturing operations. Department managers can contribute positively to this goal as they keep in close touch with other departments. In addition, higher-level managers can see that all interested departments are represented in discussions, meetings, and decisions in which they have a legitimate concern.

SUMMARY

Lateral relationships are necessary to achieve interdepartmental coordination without overloading the chain of command. They take such forms as *direct contact, liaison role, task force, team,* and *integrating role*.

Line functions, those directly concerned with the accomplishment of an organization's primary objectives, are aided by *staff functions* and staff personnel. The staff may be visualized as providing support for line activities in the form of service and advice. One classification of staff functions distinguishes between *personal* staff and *specialized* staff. According to traditional theory, staff should generally occupy an advisory rather than a command relationship to line. As a practical matter, however, staff is frequently granted some authority, such as *compulsory staff consultation, concurrent authority,* or *functional authority*.

The *matrix structure* has evolved as a result of complex environments, markets, and technology and is used in such varied organizations as government, manufacturing, banking, hospitals, and higher education. It involves dual lines of command and creates difficult managerial roles, particularly for the *matrix manager* and the *2-boss manager*.

Conflicts among groups and departments often disrupt organizational relationships and operations. Although some conflicts are beneficial to the organization, many are dysfunctional. Causes of such conflicts include the *territorial encroachments* of one department on another and *conflicts in interest* between two or more departments. *Conflict resolution* may be achieved in a number of ways, including *appeal to the chain of command, dominance* of the stronger party, *bargaining* between competitors, *structural modifications,* and *problem solving*. Steps to avoid conflict by developing strong interdepartmental relationships are desirable, particularly among key line and staff departments.

DISCUSSION QUESTIONS

1. What difficulties are likely to occur if an organization relies primarily on *vertical* rather than *lateral relationships*?

2. Explain the nature of a *liaison role* in *lateral relationships*.

3. What limitation or inaccuracy may be involved in viewing staff offices as having merely an *advisory* relationship to line functions?

4. Suppose the chief executive of a growing company employs an attorney and designates him or her as the "legal department." Is this an example of a *personal* staff or *specialized* staff?

5. If the staff lacks authority, how can it provide any guidance or control? Won't its suggestions be disregarded by line managers? Should it, therefore, be given some degree of authority?

6. Explain the concept of *functional authority*. What are its weaknesses?

7. How does a *matrix* structure differ from a *line* and *staff* structure?

8. What special difficulties are experienced by *matrix managers* and *2-boss managers* in a *matrix* structure?

9. What is the difference between an interdepartmental conflict that is beneficial and one that is destructive?

10. Give an example of an interdepartmental conflict based on a real *conflict of interest*, if there is such.

11. What steps can be taken to strengthen interdepartmental relationships and thereby minimize interdepartmental conflict?

NOTES

1. Andrew H. Van de Ven, André L. Delbecq, and Richard Koenig, Jr., "Determinants of Coordination Modes within Organizations," *American Sociological Review* 41 (April 1976): 322–28.

2. This example is cited by Jay R. Galbraith, *Organization Design* (Reading, Mass.: Addison-Wesley Publishing Co., 1977), p. 194.

3. William B. Locander and Richard W. Scamell, "A Team Approach to Managing the Market Research Process," *MSU Business Topics* 25 (Winter 1977): 15–26.

4. Paul R. Lawrence and Jay W. Lorsch, "New Management Job: The Integrator," *Harvard Business Review* 45 (November–December 1967): 142–51.

5. Louis A. Allen, *The Management Profession* (New York: McGraw-Hill Book Co., 1964), p. 222.

6. John H. Jackson and Cyril P. Morgan, *Organizational Theory: A Macro Perspective for Management* (Englewood Cliffs, N.J.: Prentice-Hall, 1978), p. 145.

7. For a fuller discussion of various types of staff authority, see Jackson and Morgan, *Organizational Theory*, pp. 144–45.

8. "Conversation with Richard D. Wood," *Organizational Dynamics* 9 (Spring 1981): 28.

9. An explanation of the way in which most matrix structures evolve from traditional forms of organization is presented in Harvey F. Kolodny, "Evolution to a Matrix Organization," *Academy of Management Review* 4 (October 1979): 543–53.

10. For an excellent discussion of the various managerial roles in a matrix structure, see Paul R. Lawrence, Harvey F. Kolodny, and Stanley M. Davis, "The Human Side of the Matrix," *Organizational Dynamics* 6 (Summer 1977): 43–61.

11. "Why They're Jumping Ship at Intel," *Business Week*, 14 February 1983, pp. 107–8.

12. Ibid., p. 108.

13. "How Ebasco Makes the Matrix Work," *Business Week*, 15 June 1981, pp. 126–31.

14. Leonard R. Sayles, "Matrix Management: The Structure with a Future," *Organizational Dynamics* 5 (Autumn 1976): 9.

15. Ibid.

16. Ross A. Webber, *Management: Basic Elements of Managing Organizations* (Homewood, Ill.: Richard D. Irwin, 1975), p. 583.

17. Melville Dalton, "Conflicts between Staff and Line Managerial Officers," *American Sociological Review* 15 (June 1950): 342–51.

18. R. F. Good in "Letters to the Editor," *Harvard Business Review* 55 (November–December 1977): 47.

19. For Whyte's report on his classic study of the restaurant industry, see William Foote Whyte, *Human Relations in the Restaurant Industry* (New York: McGraw-Hill Book Co., 1948), Chapter 6.

20. Alan C. Filley, *Interpersonal Conflict Resolution* (Glenview, Ill.: Scott, Foresman and Co., 1975), pp. 27, 29, 30.

21. For a study of the usefulness of superordinate goals in reducing conflict, see J. David Hunger and Louis W. Stern, "An Assessment of the Functionality of the Superordinate Goal in Reducing Conflict," *Academy of Management Journal* 19 (December 1976): 591–605.

22. "How D&B Organizes for a New-Product Blitz." Quoted from the November 16, 1981 issue of *Business Week* by special permission, © 1981 by McGraw-Hill, Inc., pp. 87–90.

SUPPLEMENTARY READING

Browne, Philip J., and **Cotton, Chester C.** "The Topdog/Underdog Syndrome in Line-Staff Relations." *Personnel Journal* 54 (August 1975): 443–44.

Browne, Philip J. and **Golembiewski, Robert T.** "The Line-Staff Concept Revisited: An Empirical Study of Organizational Images." *Academy of Management Journal* 17 (September 1974): 406–17.

Cleland, David J. "The Cultural Ambience of the Matrix Organization." *Management Review* 70 (November 1981): 24–28; 37–39.

_____. "Matrix Management (Part II): A Kaleidoscope of Organizational Systems." *Management Review* 70 (December 1981): 48–56.

Cosier, Richard A., and Ruble, Thomas L. "Research on Conflict-Handling Behavior: An Experimental Approach." *Academy of Management Journal* 24 (December 1981): 816–31.

Davis, Stanley M., and Lawrence, Paul R. *Matrix.* Reading, Mass.: Addison-Wesley Publishing Co., 1977.

Filley, Alan C. *Interpersonal Conflict Resolution.* Glenview, Ill.: Scott, Foresman and Co., 1975.

Greiner, Larry E., and Schein, Virginia E. "The Paradox of Managing a Project-Oriented Matrix: Establishing Coherence within Chaos." *Sloan Management Review* 22 (Winter 1981): 17–22.

Kolodny, Harvey F. "Managing in a Matrix." *Business Horizons* 24 (March/April 1981): 17–24.

Lawrence, Paul R.; Kolodny, Harvey F.; and Davis, Stanley M. "The Human Side of the Matrix." *Organizational Dynamics* 6 (Summer 1977): 43–61.

Morrison, Ann M. "The General Mills Brand of Managers." *Fortune* 103 (12 January 1981): 99–107.

Nossiter, Vivian. "A New Approach toward Resolving the Line and Staff Dilemma." *Academy of Management Review* 4 (January 1979): 103–6.

Patton, Arch. "Industry's Misguided Shift to Staff Jobs." *Business Week,* 5 April 1982, pp. 12–15.

Phillips, Eleanor, and Cheston, Ric. "Conflict Resolution: What Works?" *California Management Review* 21 (Summer 1979): 76–83.

Sayles, Leonard R. "Matrix Management: The Structure with a Future." *Organizational Dynamics* 5 (Autumn 1976): 2–17.

Shapiro, Benson P. "Can Marketing and Manufacturing Coexist?" *Harvard Business Review* 55 (September–October 1977): 104–14.

Smith, H. R. "A Socio-Biological Look at the Matrix." *Academy of Management Review* 3 (October 1978): 922–26.

13

ORGANI-ZATIONS AS SOCIAL SYSTEMS

This chapter will enable you to

- *Explain the human side of organization and the nature of organizations as social systems.*
- *Understand the nature of informal power and the political processes involved in building and exercising such power.*
- *Analyze the effect of culture on the functioning and management of organizations.*
- *Describe the nature of status differences and contributions of status systems to organizational life.*

An organization can be visualized as a series of productive operations and activities that are integrated by the *organization structure*. This is a correct but incomplete notion of organized behavior. Although the formal structure specifies important relationships, it is merely the skeleton of the organization. The organization is a *social system*, and all formal and informal human relationships are important parts of the system. In this chapter, we broaden our view of organizations to emphasize various aspects of human relationships which supplement the formal structure. Special attention is given to the *informal, power-oriented behavior* of managers and also to the concepts of *culture* and *status* as they relate to organizational life.

THE SOCIAL STRUCTURE OF ORGANIZATIONS

The Human Side of Organizations

An organization requires people to provide the mental and physical services necessary to accomplish its objectives. The official responsibilities and relationships of these people are indicated in a general way by an organization chart. The lines on such a chart represent *interpersonal* relationships, and these relationships provide the skeleton for the social structure. When we say that a laboratory supervisor reports to a department manager, this involves more than one box on a chart reporting to

FIGURE 13–1   Formal and informal relationships

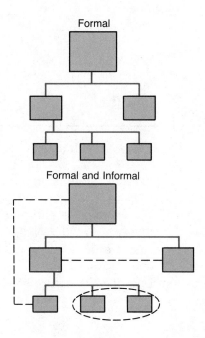

another box. It means that the individuals in these positions personally
interact, with varying degrees of cooperation, conflict, and respect.

The *social structure* of an organization encompasses more than the
formal superior-subordinate relationships, however. Any member of the
organization also has contact with other members of the same organization. Two employees work side by side in a shop or share adjoining
desks in an office. All of these informal relationships, if they continue
over time, are a part of the social structure of the organization (Figure 13–1).

An organization, therefore, is more than a collection of individuals.
To understand its nature, we must recognize social relationships and
their significance.[1] The highly personal nature of organizations became
painfully clear to one college student on a summer job.

> I was employed as a forklift driver for one long, frustrating summer. Soon
> after being introduced to my work group, I knew I was in trouble. A clique
> had formed and, for some reason, resented college students. During lunch
> breaks and work breaks, I spent the whole time by myself. Each morning I
> dreaded going to work. The job paid well, but I was miserable.

Fortunately, most interpersonal relationships are less unpleasant, and
many contribute positively to attainment of organizational goals.

The Organization as a Social System

The effect of the Hawthorne Studies, described in Chapter 2, was to turn
a spotlight on the social structure of organizations. Using the insights of
these experiments and of much subsequent research, management theorists now visualize organizations as *social systems*. According to this

view, the social system of a hospital, store, or university has as its component parts the employees of those organizations. The component parts—that is, the people—function or work together through patterns of interaction that develop among the members. One part of an organization—say a drafting room or typing pool—is a social system, and the entire organization is also a social system. In other words, there are subsystems within social systems.

A formal organization structure, if it were sufficiently detailed to include all employees, would show all component parts of the social system—that is, all personnel. It would also indicate the approximate formal relationships of these parts to each other. A manual or job description might detail the activities expected from a particular position and describe the intended relationships and methods of working with others. Functioning of the system is only partially prescribed by the statement of formal organization, however. Employees devise arrangements and procedures that supplement or conflict with the formally prescribed structure.

Job assignments typically require an employee to interact with other people and also permit incidental interactions with still other members of the organization. Consequently, most employees function as members of small groups—work teams, committees, lunch groups, and so on. Both formally and informally, such groups contribute to the attainment of organizational goals and to the social satisfactions of group members.*

The use of power in a social system also varies, to some degree, from that prescribed by the official chain of command. The exercise of formal authority is supplemented by highly personal efforts, many of which may be described as *political*. The next section of this chapter examines this relatively uncharted area of informal organizational power.

As social systems, organizations also embody two other features common to all social systems: *culture* and *status*. The relationship of these two factors to organizations and their effectiveness is discussed in the latter sections of this chapter.

POWER AND POLITICS

Empirical investigations of organizations have revealed the existence of unofficial power; that is, power which exists outside the formal organization. A review of the social structure is incomplete, therefore, without reference to informal power and politics.

Sources of Power

Many members of the organization—not just managers—possess power to some degree. This section of the chapter explores why some people have more power than others. One well-known classification of the

---

*In view of the obvious importance of group relationships, Chapter 14 is devoted to an extended treatment of this dimension of the social system.

sources of power indicates that an individual can derive power from one or more of the following bases:[2]

1. *Reward power*—an individual can influence the behavior of others because he or she has the ability to reward them for their cooperation.
2. *Coercive power*—others cooperate with an individual because they fear that he or she will punish them for not cooperating.
3. *Legitimate power*—cooperation occurs because the individual has been formally appointed or elected as the leader, and the followers have been conditioned to accept orders from the formal leader. The title of manager or supervisor automatically confers legitimate power (also known as authority) upon an individual.
4. *Referent power*—an individual's charismatic personality is instrumental in causing others to cooperate because they admire the individual and wish to identify with him or her.
5. *Expert power*—others cooperate with an individual because they believe that he or she is more expert or knowledgeable about a task than they are.

Subsequent additions to this list include the following: (6) power that is derived from one's access to important individuals and information;[3] (7) power through exchange (such as ingratiation or praise); (8) power by manipulation (where the recipient is not aware of being influenced); (9) power from persistence or assertiveness; and (10) power by banding together to form a coalition.[4]

Examination of this list indicates that power, unlike authority which is reserved for managers only, can be accumulated by virtually anyone in the organization. A computer programmer or secretary may, under some conditions, have considerably more power than a divisional manager. Regardless of who is wielding the power, the more bases of power that individual can draw upon, the greater will be his or her ability to influence the behavior of others.

A Contingency View of Power

A somewhat more complex explanation of the origins of power is known as *strategic-contingencies theory*.[5] This view holds that the power of an individual or of a particular department or unit within an organization is contingent upon the problems and uncertainties facing the organization as a whole. According to this theory, power accrues to individuals and organizational components which cope with critical organization problems.

> In its simplest form, the strategic-contingencies theory implies that when an organization faces a number of lawsuits that threaten its existence, the legal department will gain power and influence over organizational deci-

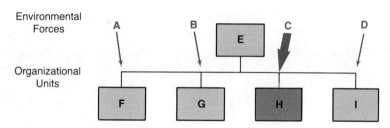

FIGURE 13–2   The impact of critical contingencies
EXPLANATORY NOTE: The impact of environmental forces varies,
and some create more critical threats than others. If force C constitutes
the most critical threat, unit H, which must cope with force C, will
tend to obtain necessary scarce resources and wield much power.

sions. . . . In time, the head of the legal department may become the head
of the corporation, just as in times past the vice-president for marketing
had become the president when market shares were a worrisome problem
and, before him, the chief engineer, who had made the production line run
as smooth as silk.[6]

In Figure 13–2, the greatest threat is posed by environmental force
C, and the organization's resources and power will flow to Unit H which
must deal with this threat. To the extent that power develops as suggested by the *strategic-contingency theory*, therefore, the various parts
of an organization become more or less powerful.

In the insurance industry, for instance, the dominant environmental
requirement is product/market adjustment and innovation. Insurance executives who are in marketing or product development have been found
to have relatively great power within their management teams. By contrast, hospital executives who are in accounting, process improvement,
or operations have relatively great power because they are situated to
cope with their firm's dominant environmental requirement of effi-
ciency/cost control.[7]

The Managerial Power Structure

The combination of formal structure and the informal, power-oriented
activities of managers creates centers of power or influence in an organization. The framework incorporating these centers of influence might
be called the *power structure*.

The power structure differs from the formal organization structure
to the extent that the influence of particular units and individuals does
not correspond perfectly to the formal structure. In view of variations in
both structural and personal factors, some such discrepancy between formal position and power is to be expected. Rarely would six vice-
presidents each have precisely the same influence over company policy.

Differences in relative power are readily recognized by people who
work in, or who are closely associated with, various organizations. People generally agree regarding those who are most powerful. The follow-

ing comments reflect the view of two researchers who have analyzed perceptions of organizational power:

> So far we have studied over 20 very different organizations—universities, research firms, factories, banks, retailers, to name a few. In each one we found individuals able to rate themselves and their peers on a scale of influence or power. . . . Their agreement was unusually high. . . .[8]

One of the classic studies of organizational power is Melville Dalton's analysis of the political activities and power structure in the Milo Fractionating Center, a fictitiously named industrial organization having 8,000 employees.[9] As a part of his study, Dalton rated the relative influence of various members of the management team. Their influence did not always correspond to their formal positions. As an example, he found that the assistant plant manager (Hardy) held power equal to that of his boss, the plant manager (Stevens). Following is Dalton's explanation of the Hardy-Stevens relationship:

> In executive meetings, Stevens clearly was less forceful than Hardy. Appearing nervous and worried, Stevens usually opened meetings with a few remarks and then silently gave way to Hardy who dominated thereafter. During the meeting most questions were directed to Hardy. While courteous, Hardy's statements usually were made without request for confirmation from Stevens. Hardy and Stevens and other high officers daily lunched together. There, too, Hardy dominated the conversations and was usually the target of questions. This was not just an indication that he carried the greater burden of minor duties often assigned to assistants in some firms, for he had a hand in most issues, including major ones. Other items useful in appraising Hardy and Stevens were their relative (a) voice in promotions, (b) leadership in challenging staff projects, (c) force in emergencies, (d) escape as a butt of jokes and name-calling, (e) knowledge of subordinates, (f) position in the firm's social and community activities.[10]

Dalton's study of the Milo plant reveals conditions of influencing organizational behavior that, to some extent, exist in every organization. The positions of power are not always evident on the surface and cannot be read with assurance from the organization chart. Careful observation of the functioning of the organization, however, reveals the true power centers and the extent to which they differ from the formal organization structure. One author's view of some of the indicators of an individual manager's power is shown in Figure 13–3.

Power-Oriented Behavior and Job Dependency

Managers engage in various types of power-oriented behavior to augment their official authority. Their activities are often described as *political*. Unfortunately, the word *politics* has a connotation of unstatesmanlike conduct. As used here, however, political activity is concerned with the manner in which positions of power are established and influence is exerted in the administrative process. There is nothing to indicate the use of power for undesirable ends.

To what extent a manager can—
- Intercede favorably on behalf of someone in trouble with the organization
- Get a desirable placement for a talented subordinate
- Get approval for expenditures beyond the budget
- Get above-average salary increases for subordinates
- Get items on the agenda at policy meetings
- Get fast access to top decision makers
- Get regular, frequent access to top decision makers
- Get early information about decisions and policy shifts

FIGURE 13–3 Some common symbols of a manager's organizational power (influence upward and outward)

SOURCE: Reprinted by permission of the Harvard Business Review. An exhibit from "Power Failure in Management Circuits" by Rosabeth Moss Kanter (July/August 1979). Copyright © 1979 by the President and Fellows of Harvard College; all rights reserved.

The extent to which personnel engage in political activity depends upon their own vulnerability. The nature of such dependency is not always evident. The following account by a manager describes his own feelings of dependency on others:

> In retrospect (after a year and a half on the job), it is hard to believe how little I really did know. For example, Helen Wagner wasn't in any picture book or on any organization chart, but she is about as important as anyone to the success of the acquisition that I'm working on now. Helen is (Executive VP) Phil Peter's secretary. Phil is my boss on this project. A variety of key decisions that I have to clear through him come up occasionally and demand a reasonably quick or very quick response. Phil's office is in Manhattan in our headquarters building, and so my access to him on the phone or by memo is through Helen. And as you can imagine, he is very busy and gets lots of phone calls and mail. Helen is responsible for making judgments regarding priorities. She's got the power to make my life very difficult.[11]

Managers who are highly dependent on many others for success must spend more time building relationships and "mending fences" than managers who can personally control their own resources. In Figure 13–4, John Kotter has portrayed the contrasting circumstances of a plant manager X with few dependencies and a hospital manager Y with many dependencies.

The two managers differed sharply in the time they spent to make sure that others "cooperated" with them.

> Whereas Y spent close to 80 percent of her day in activities that related directly to acquiring and maintaining power or to using it to influence others, X spent about 25 to 30 percent of his time in those activities.[12]

Kotter has concluded that "the larger the number of job-related dependencies, the more time and energy the management incumbent tends to put into power-oriented behavior to cope with those dependencies."[13]

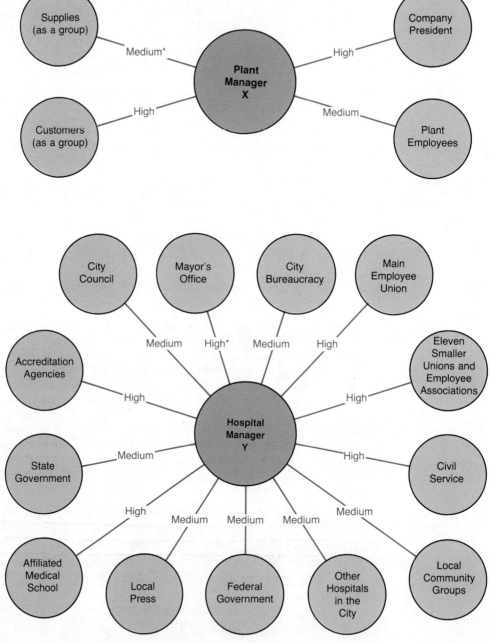

*The manager's level of dependence on other individuals or groups.

FIGURE 13–4 Dependence inherent in two managerial jobs
SOURCE: Reprinted, by permission of the publisher, from "Power, Success, and Organizational Effectiveness," John P. Kotter, *Organizational Dynamics* 6 (Winter 1978). © 1978 by AMACOM, a division of American Management Associations, p. 29. All rights reserved.

Techniques of Building and Using Political Power

Managers use various methods of building power and exerting that power to achieve their goals. For example, they create obligations by doing favors for others.

> "Most of the people here would walk over hot coals in their bare feet if my boss asked them to. He has an incredible capacity to do little things that mean a lot to people. Today, for example, in his junk mail he came across an advertisement for something that one of my subordinates had in passing once mentioned that he was shopping for. So my boss routed it to him. That probably took 15 seconds of his time, and yet my subordinate really appreciated it. To give you another example, two weeks ago he somehow learned that the purchasing manager's mother had died. On his way home that night, he stopped off at the funeral parlor. Our purchasing manager was, of course, there at the time. I bet he'll remember that brief visit for quite a while."[14]

Not all favors are personal favors. The manager's role in the organization may involve the provision of official services—the personnel manager who recruits capable personnel, for example. Such services may be performed in such a way that the recipient correctly perceives his or her dependence upon the personnel manager. In various ways, a manager may "take care" of others who will respond with feelings of loyalty.

A manager's political activities may be directed toward control of subordinates, colleagues, and even superiors. Other managers at approximately the same level constitute potential competitors or allies, and the manager typically seeks to exert as much influence as possible in matters of mutual interest.

Once power is established, it is exerted in various ways. For example, managers engage in face-to-face discussions to persuade others concerning a "correct" course of action. Or they encourage an influential, trusted third party to present a desired point of view. Many indirect methods of influencing organizational behavior exist.

Managers engage in various forms of informal activity, therefore, to supplement the power of their organizational positions. These informal power-oriented activities are frequently described as 'political." Managers' total power, then, involves a combination of their formal power and their unofficial power developed and exerted in less obvious, informal ways.

Informal Power and Organizational Effectiveness

Informal power-oriented activities of managers can contribute to, or interfere with, the achievement of organizational goals. Authority is granted to those in positions of leadership so they can function effectively in coordinating organizational activities. Informal power may be used for the same purpose and thereby contribute to organizational effectiveness.

DEMONSTRATING ONE'S POWER

When young Tim Babcock was put in charge of a divison of a large manufacturing company and told to "turn it around," he spent the first few weeks studying it from afar. He decided that the division was in disastrous shape and that he would need to take many large steps quickly to save it. To be able to do that, he realized he needed to develop considerable power fast over most of the division's management and staff. He did the following:

He gave the division's management two hours' notice of his arrival.

He arrived in a limousine with six assistants.

He immediately called a meeting of the 40 top managers.

He outlined briefly his assessment of the situation, his commitment to turn things around, and the basic direction he wanted things to move in.

He then fired the four top managers in the room and told them that they had to be out of the building in two hours.

He then said he would personally dedicate himself to sabotaging the career of anyone who tried to block his efforts to save the division.

He ended the 60-minute meeting by announcing that his assistants would set up appointments for him with each of them starting at 7:00 A.M. the next morning.

Throughout the critical six-month period that followed, those who remained at the division generally cooperated energetically with Mr. Babcock.

SOURCE: Reprinted by permission of Harvard Business Review. Excerpt from "Power, Dependence, and Effective Management" by John P. Kotter (July-August 1977). Copyright © 1977 by the President and Fellows of Harvard College; all rights reserved.

On the other hand, informal power may damage organizational relationships and reduce overall effectiveness. The company politician may be more concerned with the advancement of personal interests than those of the organization.[15] To prevent such situations from getting out of hand to the extent that political activities dominate rather than supplement normal management processes and personal ambition supplants organizational goals, top management must sense and prevent extreme or self-seeking forms of political action. A program and practice of objective evaluation of subordinates is one essential safeguard against the destructive company politician. Political intrigue that subordinates organizational goals to narrow personal objectives must be rejected. The climate must prevent an abuse of political power. This is difficult to accomplish, of course, because political action is often carefully camouflaged and rationalized.

ORGANIZATIONAL CULTURE

The way organizations function is affected not only by the power of managers but also by underlying cultural forces. Organizational culture regulates the way in which the firm's members go about their work and even the way in which managers build and exercise power.

What Is Culture?

In its general sense, *culture* consists of the behavior patterns and values of a social group. These are patterns of belief and behavior that have been learned from other members of the society. They are, as the cultural anthropologist would say, *socially transmitted*.

An organization functions within the cultural system of the society in which it is located. The expectations of the surrounding community with regard to the establishments located within it are based upon the community's cultural traditions. Employees also bring into the firm the cultural values they have assimilated from the community. Both the community and the employees are inclined to expect, therefore, some conformity to prevailing cultural values.

But organizational culture is more than simply a reflection of broader social values and expectations. Organizations within the same industry and city often exhibit distinctly different ways of operating.

> All one has to do to get a feel for how the different cultures of competing businesses manifest themselves is to spend a day visiting each. Of course there are patterns in the trivia of variations in dress, jargon, and style—but there is something else going on as well. There are characteristic ways of making decisions, relating to bosses, and choosing people to fill key jobs.[16]

Over time, each organization evolves its own culture. This set of values, beliefs, and behaviors is passed down to succeeding generations of employees to become the generally accepted mode of operation.

A key value at PepsiCo, for instance, is winning. New employees quickly learn that the fastest path to success lies in beating their competition—both inside and outside the company. A "creative tension" is fostered among departments, and "careers ride on tenths of a market share point." "Consistent runners-up find their jobs gone. Employees know they must win merely to stay in place—and must devastate the competition to get ahead."[17]

By contrast, prior to 1982, a key value at J. C. Penney Company was building long-term loyalty.

Customers know they can return merchandise with no questions asked; suppliers know that Penney will not haggle over terms; and employees are comfortable in their jobs, knowing that Penney will avoid layoffs at all costs and will find easier jobs for those who cannot handle more demanding ones. Not surprisingly, Penney's average executive tenure is 33 years while Pepsi's is 10.[18]

CORPORATE CULTURE

Corporate traditions sometimes differ to the point that communication and mutual understanding become difficult. Itel Corporation, which was founded in 1967, grew rapidly and developed what has been termed an "opulent" style with company-paid January extravaganzas—Caribbean cruises and Acapulco vacations—for hundreds of employees. When Itel "fell on hard times" in 1979, it appealed to National Semiconductor Corporation, an austere supplier, to reduce deliveries. But the gulf in values between the two companies made agreement difficult.

> The two companies, remarkably different in corporate culture, were at each other's throats. Says one ex-Itel officer, "Dealing with them is like dealing with cavemen. When they came over from their cinder-block offices in Santa Clara and saw all our Persian rugs, they were sure we were ripping them off."

SOURCE: Bro Uttal, "The Lease Is Up on Itel's Lavish Living," *Fortune*, 8 October 1979, p. 113.

Implications of Culture in Management

Organizational culture can facilitate or hinder the firm's strategic actions. Because culture reflects the past, periods of environmental change often require significant modification of the organization's culture. General Foods Corporation, for example, whose past emphasis on cost control and earnings improvements has been instrumental in its success, has found it necessary to develop a new strategy emphasizing diversification and growth. ". . . the question is whether [CEO James L. Ferguson] can change the corporation's culture from one that stresses strict conservatism to one that fosters the type of entrepreneurial spirit that the new goals require."[19] To facilitate the change, the organization has revised its compensation system (to link bonuses to increases in sales volume rather than just to increased earnings); decentralized decisions on spending for new products, advertising, and some capital investments; increased its emphasis on product development; and sent its managers to marketing and product seminars.[20]

It is essential that significant changes in strategy be accompanied by corresponding modifications in organizational culture. Otherwise the strategy is likely to fail. Conservative organizations do not become aggressive, entrepreneurial firms simply because they have formulated new goals and plans. J. C. Penney, for instance, is finding that, to operate effectively in their inceasingly competitive industry, they must change their "comfortable" culture to a more "enterprising" orientation.

Culture can even provide an excuse for inaction. Joseph W. Whorton and John A. Worthley suggest that the culture of management in the public sector is comprised of "if-onlys" and "thems." These may be offered as excuses for nonperformance or as explanations of failure.[21] Such excuses and explanations reflect the numerous constraints under which managers in government operate. "If-onlys" are illustrated by such statements as

- "If only I could fire Jones, then we could get this department in shape" (reflects Civil Service constraints).
- "If only the budget division would stop setting expenditure ceilings" (reflects legislative constraints).

"Thems" refer to the "adversaries" of public managers—that is, those groups which influence or set the constraints. These include politicians, the press, consumer groups, and so on.

> [If onlys and thems] foster an elaborate myth that insulates the organization from its environment by creating the expectancy that performance will always be something less than it could be.
>
> When fully institutionalized as part of the culture, if-onlys and thems can produce a wholly negative focus and become defense mechanisms for resisting change and denying the possibility that new technologies might improve organizational performance.[22]

Continuing organizational performance and success depend heavily upon the organizational culture which is appropriate to the current environment. What was, at one time, a facilitative culture vis-à-vis the environment, may, because of changing conditions, become a barrier to continued organizational effectiveness.

THE NATURE AND FUNCTIONS OF STATUS

One aspect of culture involves judgments of the relative importance of various individuals, roles, and groups.

What Is Status?

Status is concerned with a person's prestige or standing within a group (or the standing of a group within a larger society). Status suggests that one is relatively better or more important than another. Deference is generally shown to the person with higher status.

Different people naturally use different weights or values in their individual judgments regarding status. Technically, therefore, there are as many different status systems as there are individuals making judgments of this variety. We often simplify this process, however, by making generalizations about status. These generalizations express a general consensus regarding the status of particular individuals, positions, occupations, or groups.

Status Differences in Organization

Two kinds of status systems have been suggested by Chester I. Barnard.[23] The first of these, *functional status,* is based upon the type of work or activity performed. The professional, whether an engineer, attorney, or otherwise, enjoys greater prestige than nonprofessional members of the organization. The craftsman has a higher status than the unskilled employee.

Scalar status, on the other hand, is concerned with the level in the organization's hierarchy or chain of command. In a position that is high in the organizational pyramid, the incumbent is considered an important executive or a "wheel."

The two types of status suggested by Barnard—functional status and scalar status—are both descriptive of the position, regardless of the incumbent. These types of status are supplemented by a third variety that might be designated as *personal* status. Although formal position, by virtue of its scalar and functional qualities, goes a long way in determining an individual's status, this status may be augmented or reduced by the individual's personal characteristics. When a brilliant or distinguished person replaces a lackluster incumbent, the replacement enjoys higher status even though the position may be unchanged. In a business organization this would be true whether the position is that of executive, supervisor, craftsman, scientist, or engineer. In a university, the same would be true of a new president, dean, department chairman, professor, or coach.

Functions of the Status System

Status systems often appear undemocratic. They are a reality in organizations, however, and we sometimes overlook their constructive role. Two of their positive contributions relate to communication and motivation.

Maintaining Effective and Authoritative Communication. The existence of a status system makes possible effective and authoritative communication. Someone must provide direction and coordination to members of work organizations. The status system permits understanding concerning who is to lead and who is to follow.

Providing Incentives for Advancement. The status system and symbols of status that pervade our society also provide strong motivation. Few individuals are content with the status quo, and their aspirations are often linked with conceptions of status as much as they are with hopes of purely material advancement. Most people think it is important to live in the "right" section of the city and drive a type of car befitting their positions.

The rise in our standard of living may have changed the nature of the status symbols, but it has hardly eliminated status distinctions. No matter how much we may disparage status differences, we must recognize their powerful influence as a motivational force. Achievement in our society results from such motivation. In criticisms of status factors, therefore, we should consider the alternatives in terms of motivational power.

Symbols of Status

Status levels are indicated by various indicators closely connected with the individual. These *symbols* permit an observer to understand the prestige level of the person in question.

Vice-presidents have offices that are not only private, but larger than those of lower officials. Office furnishings similarly reveal status distinctions. At some level, offices are carpeted, and metal desks give way to wooden desks. Draperies at the window and paintings on the wall are also symbolic of prestige. Potted plants, lounge chairs, private washrooms, intercom boxes, and adjoining private conference rooms all suggest the prestige of the person occupying the office.

In addition to material trappings, privileges indicate the status level of the incumbent. Many employees, for example, punch a time clock, while higher-level employees are not required to do so.

Status symbols communicate the facts regarding status to members of the organization. By communicating such information, they contribute to the values inherent in the status system itself.

Problems of Status

Although status performs constructive functions as noted, it also has disadvantages. Indeed, some are so conscious of its weaknesses that they refer to the *pathology* of status. One important negative feature concerns the *social distance* between organization levels. When social distance is great, a subordinate may feel that the superior is detached or aloof or "living in another world." Even though some authoritative communication is desirable, organization levels must work together in achieving the objectives of the organization. It is possible, consequently, that status distinctions may be emphasized to the point that active cooperation is reduced. The subordinate may follow orders but find it difficult to work closely with higher levels. An individual may also become so preoccupied with status symbols that the entire system is run into the ground. Getting a private office or a staff assistant or a desktop computer becomes important in and of itself, and little regard is paid to the intrinsic need for these symbolic trappings.

OFFICES AT THE WHITE HOUSE

Perhaps nowhere are the trappings of office more important than at the highest reaches of government. In the following excerpt, John Dean, former counsel to President Nixon, recounts his impressions of the office as a status symbol:

> Success and failure could be seen in the size, decor and location of offices. Anyone who moved to a smaller office was on the way down. If a carpenter, cabinetmaker or wallpaper hanger was busy in someone's office, this was a sure sign he was on the rise. Every day, workmen crawled over the White House complex like ants. Movers busied themselves with the continuous shuffling of furniture from one office to another as people moved in, up, down, or out. We learned to read office changes as an index of the internal bureaucratic power struggles.

SOURCE: John W. Dean III, *Blind Ambition: The White House Years*, pp. 29–30 © 1976 by John W. Dean. Reprinted by permission of Simon & Schuster, a Division of Gulf & Western Corporation.

Members of an organization may also experience feelings of anxiety as a result of status considerations. One's status may appear undesirable, and the person may feel powerless to change it. Whatever the reason, the inability to improve one's status may produce a sense of frustration within that individual. This feeling may be described as *status anxiety*. *Status inconsistency* may also lead to anxiety. The title of the position may be right, for example, but the incumbent may lack a private office that seems appropriate for the particular level. Status anxiety may have adverse physical effects, such as producing ulcers. More frequently, such status problems simply create individual unhappiness and reduce organizational efficiency.

SUMMARY

The Hawthorne Studies increased our understanding of the social nature of business organizations. These experiments demonstrated that organizations are *social systems* in which relationships among people are extremely significant in determining organizational behavior. As social systems, organizations include not only *formal* groups and relationships but also *informal* groupings and relationships that supplement the formally prescribed structure.

Formal authority conferred by the organization is supplemented by informal, power-oriented activity of organization members. Not only do managers possess power to varying degrees, but nonmanagerial members may also accumulate power. The more bases of power an individual can draw upon, the greater will be his or her ability to influence the behavior of others. According to the *strategic-contingencies theory,* the greatest organizational power accrues to individuals and organizational components which cope with the most critical threats or problems confronting organizations.

The *power structure* of an organization may be similar to the formal organization, but differences exist in the case of those who hold more or less power than the formal structure confers upon them. Organizational power is derived not only from a formal position of authority, but also from informal and political relationships and activities.

Organizational culture reflects not only societal values and expectations but also the unique set of values, beliefs, and behaviors that characterizes each organization. Organizational culture can facilitate or hinder the firm's strategic actions. Because culture reflects the past, periods of environmental change often require significant modification of the organization's culture.

Status refers to gradations in standing or rank that exist in any group. Status is *scalar, functional,* and *personal* and is determined by a combination of organizational and personal factors. The status system performs useful functions in organizations and in society generally. Status levels are communicated by means of *symbols,* which include not only official titles but also such privileges and physical trappings as private offices and lunch room privileges. Although it performs useful functions, the status system also involves problems of *social distance* between organizational levels, preoccupation with status symbols, and *status anxiety.*

DISCUSSION QUESTIONS

1. Refer to some organization with which you are familiar. Describe both its formal structure and informal structure.
2. Explain the concept of an organization as a *social system.*
3. Explain how a nonmanagerial member of an organization might accumulate *power.* Is there any base of power not available to a nonmanager?
4. How does *strategic-contingency theory* explain the relative power of various organization components?
5. What is the *power structure,* and why may it differ from an accurately drawn organization chart?
6. Describe an "organization politician." What practices does such an individual typically follow?
7. Explain carefully the concept of *organizational culture.*

8. What is the relationship between organization *strategy* and *culture*?

9. When the president, in a well-known novel, told a younger executive to call him "Tony," the young man went home in great excitement. Both he and his wife considered it a cause for celebration. How would you interpret this incident in the light of this chapter?

10. What is the basic distinction between *functional* status and *scalar* status?

11. Do you believe that the average American works more for money (and the goods and services that money will buy) or for status and the symbols that signify status?

NOTES

1. For a discussion of one aspect of social relationships, see Carl E. Pickhardt, "Problems Posed by A Changing Organizational Membership," *Organizational Dynamics* 10 (Summer 1981): 69–80.

2. John R. P. French, Jr., and Bertram Raven, "The Bases of Social Power," in *Studies in Social Power*, ed. D. Cartwright (Ann Arbor, Mich.: University of Michigan Press, 1959): pp. 150–67.

3. David Mechanic, "Sources of Power of Lower Participants in Complex Organizations," *Administrative Science Quarterly* 7 (December 1962): 353.

4. For an overview of the literature in this area, see Warren K. Schilit and Edwin A. Locke, "A Study of Upward Influence in Organizations," *Administrative Science Quarterly* 27 (June 1982): 304–16.

5. D. J. Hickson et al., "A Strategic Contingencies Theory of Intraorganizational Power," *Administrative Science Quarterly* 16 (June 1971): 216–29.

6. Gerald R. Salancik and Jeffrey Pfeffer, "Who Gets Power—And How They Hold On To It: A Strategic-Contingency Model of Power," *Organizational Dynamics* 5 (Winter 1977): 5.

7. Donald C. Hambrick, "Environment, Strategy, and Power within Top Management Teams," *Administrative Science Quarterly* 26 (June 1981): 253–75.

8. Salancik and Pfeffer, "Who Gets Power," p. 4.

9. Melville Dalton, *Men Who Manage* (New York: John Wiley & Sons, 1959).

10. Ibid., p. 23.

11. Reprinted, by permission of the publisher, from "Power, Success and Organization Effectiveness," John P. Kotter, *Organization Dynamics* 6 (Winter 1978). © 1978 by AMACOM, a division of American Management Associations, p. 31. All rights reserved.

12. Ibid., p.30.

13. Ibid.

14. Reprinted by permission of Harvard Business Review. Excerpt from "Power, Dependence, and Effective Management" by John P. Kotter (July–August 1977). Copyright © 1977 by the President and Fellows of Harvard College; all rights reserved.

15. For an examination of the ethics of organizational politics, see Gerald F. Cavanagh, Dennis J. Moberg, and Manuel Velasquez, "The Ethics of Organizational Politics," *Academy of Management Review* 6 (July 1981): 363–74.

16. Howard Schwartz and Stanley M. Davis, "Matching Corporate Culture and Business Strategy," *Organizational Dynamics* 10 (Summer 1981): 30.

17. "Corporate Culture: The Hard-to-Change Values That Spell Success or Failure," *Business Week*, 27 October 1980, pp. 148; 151; 154 (quotes are from pp. 151 and 148).

18. Ibid., p. 148.

19. "Changing the Culture at General Foods," *Business Week*, 30 March 1981, p. 136.

20. Ibid., pp. 136; 140.

21. Joseph W. Whorton and John A. Worthley, "A Perspective on the Challenge of Public Management: Environmental Paradox and Organizational Culture," *Academy of Management Review* 6 (July 1981): 359–60.

22. Ibid., p. 360.

23. Chester I. Barnard, *Organization and Management* (Cambridge: Harvard University Press, 1948), pp. 209–10.

SUPPLEMENTARY READING

Alexander, C. Norman, Jr. "Status Perceptions." *American Sociological Review* 37 (December 1972): 767–73.

Allen, Robert W.; Madison, Dan L.; Porter, Lyman W.; Renwick, Patricia A.; and Mayes, Bronston T. "Organizational Politics: Tactics and Characteristics of Its Actors." *California Management Review* 22 (Fall 1979): 77–83.

Bacharach, Samuel B., and Lawler, Edward J. *Power and Politics in Organizations.* San Francisco: Jossey-Bass Publishers, 1980.

Blackburn, Richard S. "Lower Participant Power: Toward a Conceptual Integration." *Academy of Management Review* 6 (January 1981): 127–31.

Buss, Martin D. J. "Making It Electronically." *Harvard Business Review* 60 (January–February 1982): 89–90.

Cavanagh, Gerald F.; Moberg, Dennis J.; and Velasquez, Manuel. "The Ethics of Organizational Politics." *Academy of Management Review* 6 (July 1981): 363–74.

Evan, William M. "Culture and Organizational Systems." *Organization and Administrative Sciences* 5 (Winter 1974/1975): 1–16.

Farrell, Dan, and Petersen, James C. "Patterns of Political Behavior in Organizations." *Academy of Management Review* 7 (July 1982): 403–12.

Kanter, Rosabeth Moss. "Power Failure in Management Circuits." *Harvard Business Review* 57 (July–August 1979): 65–75.

Kotter, John P. *Power in Management.* New York: AMACOM, 1979.

Murray, Victor, and **Gandz, Jeffrey.** "Games Executives Play: Politics at Work." *Business Horizons* 23 (December 1980): 11–23.

Nadler, David A., and **Tushman, Michael L.** "A Model for Diagnosing Organizational Behavior." *Organizational Dynamics* 9 (Autumn 1980): 35–51.

Saunders, Carol Stoak. "Management Information Systems, Communications, and Departmental Power: An Integrative Model." *Academy of Management Review* 6 (July 1981): 431–42.

Schneider, Benjamin. "Organizational Climates: An Essay." *Personnel Psychology* 28 (Winter 1975): 447–79.

Schwartz, Howard, and **Davis, Stanley M.** "Matching Corporate Culture and Business Strategy." *Organizational Dynamics* 10 (Summer 1981): 30–48.

Silverzweig, Stan, and **Allen, Robert F.** "Changing the Corporate Culture." *Sloan Management Review* 17 (Spring 1976): 33–49.

Whorton, Joseph W., and **Worthley, John A.** "A Perspective on the Challenge of Public Management: Environmental Paradox and Organizational Culture." *Academy of Management Review* 6 (July 1981): 357–61.

Wiley, Mary Glenn, and **Eskilson, Arlene.** "The Interaction of Sex and Power Base on Perceptions of Managerial Effectiveness." *Academy of Management Journal* 25 (September 1982): 671–77.

14

GROUP PROCESSES AND COMMITTEES

This chapter will enable you to

- *Identify the types of groups in organizations and the functions they perform.*
- *Understand the major attributes of organizational groups.*
- *Explain the reasons for the formation of committees and the dangers inherent in their use.*
- *Recognize the strengths and weaknesses of group decision-making techniques.*

Much of the work in organizations is accomplished through group effort. Departments, committees, and task forces are collections of individuals who interact to accomplish some common objective. An understanding of how groups affect organizational performance and individual behavior is essential to management.

NATURE OF GROUPS

A group is composed of two or more individuals who interact to a significant degree in the pursuit of a common goal. As they interact, the individuals are "psychologically aware of one another" and "perceive themselves to be a group."[1]

Types of Groups

As the previous chapter indicated, groups in organizations can be classified as *formal* or *informal*. A formal group is created by management and charged with the responsibility of contributing to the organization. An informal group is a natural outgrowth of human interaction and develops without formal management sanction.

Formal Groups. The most common formal group is the *command group*, composed of a manager and his or her immediate subordinates. Command groups are often formally designated as departments or work units. The purpose of such groups is "to perform some task more efficiently through the pooling and coordination of the behavior and resources of a collection of individuals."[2]

Apathetic Groups—Consistently indifferent to managerial decisions; little group cohesion.

Erratic Groups—Vacillation between cooperative and antagonistic behavior; often highly centralized leadership in the group.

Strategic Groups—Continuous pressure against management; high degree of internal unity.

Conservative Groups—Mostly cooperative; moderate internal unity.

FIGURE 14–1   Sayles's classification of work groups
SOURCE: Leonard R. Sayles, *Behavior of Industrial Work Groups*
(New York: John Wiley & Sons, 1958), Chapter 2.

Another formal group is the *problem-solving group,* which combines the knowledge and resources of several individuals to solve a problem or exploit an opportunity. The most common problem-solving group is the *committee,* a relatively permanent collection of individuals who are responsible for specific assignments or activities. A *task force* is a less permanent form of problem-solving group, often established to deal with a particular problem that cuts across functional or departmental lines.

> [Formal] work groups activities are guided both by the goals of the group and the goals of the larger organization. These goals include concern for the members of the group, but have work performance as their primary focus. . . .Work groups must be considered as components of a larger organization. . . .Each work group interfaces with several other groups, and members may have multiple group affiliations. In addition, most industrial work groups or management teams exist in a hierarchical structure and have a formally designated leader.[3]

Informal Groups.   Informal groups arise spontaneously throughout the organization and are found at all hierarchical levels. "Whenever individuals associate on a fairly continuous basis there is a tendency for groups to form whose activities may be different from those required by the organization."[4] Such groups may form because individuals receive satisfaction from their association with others or because they wish to advance some common interest.

Although our concern in this chapter is the formal group, such groups cannot be studied in isolation. Formal interaction is inevitably modified by informal activities and attitudes. As an example, consider Leonard Sayles's classification of work groups, shown in Figure 14–1. Although the groups are formal work groups, their behavior reflects their members' informal attitudes toward management.

Functions of Groups

The primary function of a formal group is to *attain some goal or goals which contribute to overall organizational effectiveness.* These goals, of course, vary from group to group. One group may have the responsibility of keeping accurate accounting records, another planning future strategy, and still another training and developing managers. The rationale underlying group formation is termed *synergy;* that is, the whole is greater than the sum of its parts. In other words, people working together, combining their diverse talents and perspectives and exchanging varied ideas and methods, can accomplish significantly more than could the same individuals working alone.

Formal and informal groups also *provide satisfaction for the social needs of members of the organization.* Opportunity for social interaction and satisfaction can make a job or organization bearable even though it may also have undesirable features. Membership in groups not only provides opportunities for enjoyable social interaction but also contributes to the emotional well-being of employees. Employees are aided in maintaining their emotional equilibrium, particularly in times of crisis or difficulty, by the support they receive from fellow workers.

Group membership also *helps to satisfy other needs.* Group members who are accepted by their peers may feel more *secure* than isolated individuals. Group membership also provides a form of *recognition and identity* far more personal than that bestowed upon the individual by the organization. Finally, membership in an elite group helps fulfill a person's need for *esteem.*

GROUP LOYALTY

Under extreme circumstances, the desire to be with the members of one's group exceeds even the desire for physical safety. As one officer in the Royal Air Force during World War II wrote:

> Everyone looked forward to the completion of his tour, but so strong was the crew spirit in the Bomber Command that it was not an uncommon occurrence for a man to volunteer to do as many as 10 extra trips so that he and his crew could finish together. . . .

SOURCE: D. Stafford-Clark, "Morale and Flying Experience: Results of a Wartime Study," *Journal of Mental Science* 95 (January 1949): 15.

ATTRIBUTES OF GROUPS

Activities, Interactions, and Sentiments

One approach to understanding work group behavior draws attention to three attributes which characterize virtually any group: *activities, interactions, and sentiments.*[5] Activities are those physical acts the employee is required to engage in to perform the job, such as driving a truck, typing invoices, or mapping out an advertising campaign. These

FIGURE 14–2   Activities, interactions, and sentiments

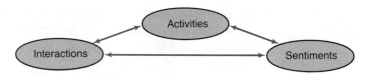

activities typically require the employee to engage in interactions with other people during the work day, such as consulting with a superior or coordinating one's work with the work of other employees. Sentiments are the feelings and attitudes the employee has about his or her job, peers, supervisor, the organization's policies, the meaning of work, and so on.

As employees engage in these required activities and interactions, nonrequired activities and interactions emerge. Interaction between some employees, for instance, may lead to sentiments of liking which result in the taking of breaks together, talking with each other on the job more than is required, and so on. Activities such as football pools or horseplay may likewise emerge. Similarly, sentiments of dislike may emerge, causing employees to avoid interaction, even though it may be required.

Hence, activities, interactions, and sentiments are interrelated, as shown in Figure 14–2. Required activities and interactions, along with existing sentiments, may lead to the emergence of new activities, modified interactions, and changes in sentiments, all of which could result in still further modifications.

As an illustration of these factors in a practical situation, consider a change in production technology that takes employees out of small work teams and distributes them along an assembly line. In all probability, the scope of the job (required activities) would be narrowed. Furthermore, a reduction in interactions would occur. As a result of changes in activities and interactions, sentiments would likewise be affected. If the individual enjoys interaction and the opportunity for performing a varied job, as would be true of most employees, the change to assembly line work would create dissatisfaction and possibly bitterness. This, in turn, might affect activities (the way work is performed or the quality of work) and interactions (with the line supervisor, for example).

Norms

Over time, the interrelationships among activities, interactions, and sentiments within a group result in the evolution of group norms. A *norm* is a generally agreed-upon standard of behavior to which every member of the group is expected to adhere. The strongest norms are related to those forms of behavior that are considered most significant by the group members. The workers in the Bank Wiring Observation Room in the Hawthorne Plant, referred to in Chapter 2, established a daily production norm and enforced that norm through a number of informal means. Peripheral norms may also evolve to provide guidelines for less important behaviors.

A faculty group, for example, may develop powerful norms in the areas of research and teaching. The norms may indicate that each faculty member is expected to engage in empirically based research and to publish the results in certain quality journals. In the teaching area, a norm might dictate that professors should not assign the grade of "A" to more than 10 percent of their students. Peripheral norms may also develop, such as one which implies that faculty members should avoid casual clothing and "dress well" when teaching. Professors who ignore the norms on research and teaching may find themselves isolated—excluded from interaction (both professional and social) with other faculty members. However, an instructor who insists on wearing a sweat shirt and jeans to class may be viewed askance, but will generally be accepted by the faculty group if his or her research and grading activities comply with the norms.

Norms allow the group to control some of the more important aspects of member behavior, thereby increasing predictability and order within the group. The success and continuity of a group may well depend upon member adherence to norms. Groups without strong norms are unlikely to be as stable, long-lasting, or as satisfying to their members as are groups with well-developed norms receiving strong member support.

Conformity

Adherence to group norms as a result of perceived group pressure is termed *conformity*. Since significant nonconformity threatens the group's standards, stability, and longevity, the pressure placed on a member to conform to important norms can be intense. Persistent nonconformity may be punished in a variety of ways, the most common being social rejection resulting in isolation.*

Conformity takes two forms: (1) *compliance*—a change in behavior resulting in closer adherence to group norms, and (2) *private acceptance* or *internalization*—a change in both behavior and belief to conform more closely to group norms. Most work group norms apply primarily to behavior, although a statement of beliefs may be required for acceptance by certain groups, such as religious or charitable organizations. Compliance is emphasized heavily because behavior is visible—while beliefs are not—and it is often necessary that a group behave in a united way if it is to succeed.

Not all individuals conform to the same extent. Individuals with low status in the group, for instance, are more likely to conform closely to all of the group's norms in order to be accepted by the other members. Persons with low self-confidence are more likely to conform since they

---

*For the story of a crane operator whose fellow workmen refused to speak to him for 367 days as punishment for working during a one-day strike, see George A. Lundberg, Clarence C. Schrag, and Otto N. Larsen, *Sociology*, 3d ed. (New York: Harper & Row, Publishers, 1963), p. 70.

may feel that the group's decisions are superior to their own. Individuals are also likely to conform when they perceive that the group's goals are similar to their personal goals. Conformity increases in ambiguous situations (when individuals are not certain how to behave and must look to the group for guidance) and during crises (when the stability of the group is threatened).

Cohesiveness

Cohesiveness refers to how closely the group members "stick together" and act as a single unit rather than as individuals. A cohesive group is attractive to its members, causing them to desire to maintain their membership in the group. As a group becomes more attractive to members, therefore, it becomes more cohesive. Dorwin Cartwright proposes that a person's attraction to a group is determined by four interacting sets of variables:

(a) his *motive base for attraction,* consisting of his needs for affiliation, recognition, security, money, or other values that can be mediated by groups;

(b) the *incentive properties of the group,* consisting of its goals, programs, characteristics of its members, style of operation, prestige, or other properties of significance for his motive base;

(c) his *expectancy,* the subjective probability, that membership will actually have beneficial or detrimental consequences for him; and

(d) his *comparison level*—conception of the level of outcomes that group membership should provide.[6]

If a group provides its members with outcomes they value and is more successful in providing these outcomes than are alternative groups, the members are likely to become cohesive over time. Cohesive group members derive considerable satisfaction from their interactions and activities.

Cohesiveness also may have powerful effects on group performance. Since membership in a cohesive group is valued by its members, conformity to group norms will be high, reflecting the desire of the members to remain in the group. Hence, if the group develops low work performance norms, the members will produce at a low level, and the opposite behavior will occur in groups with high performance norms. The level of a cohesive group's production norms may reflect the group's sentiments toward management.[7] A situation of mutual trust between management and the work group, fostered by members' perceptions of fair treatment by management, is likely to be more conducive to high performance goals than are conditions characterized by distrust and a "we-versus-them" attitude.

As Figure 14–3 indicates, every manager should be aware of the group attributes discussed in this section. A new manager, particularly, must attempt to determine how cohesive his or her subordinates are, what norms they consider important, and how closely they conform to

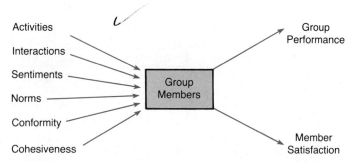

FIGURE 14–3 Some factors affecting group performance and member satisfaction

those norms. Without prior assessment of the group's interactions, activities, and sentiments, a new manager might change the group's structure or work methods and, in the process, inadvertently violate the group's central norms. In such situations, the puzzled manager may be faced with resistance to the change or even outright rebellion.

As we have seen, groups can have both positive and negative effects on organizational performance. Unfortunately, "there are still major gaps in our understanding of the reasons why some groups function effectively—and why others turn out to be a source of continual difficulty and dismay for both group members and organizational management."[8]

Autonomous Work Groups

A movement intended to harness the positive aspects of group behavior and improve both member satisfaction and organizational performance is the trend toward *autonomous work groups*. This movement is an outgrowth of the *sociotechnical* systems approach to designing jobs and organizations. The aim is to mesh fulfillment of the workers' needs for social satisfaction with the technical requirements of the organization.

Basically, an autonomous work group is a small team that is given the responsibility for planning and carrying out a whole task. A group of coal miners, for instance, might be given responsibility for an entire geographic section of a mine. The duties of the foreman would be assumed by the group, which would be responsible for its own production. Each miner might be required to learn all of the tasks involved in mining coal so that the members could switch jobs whenever an individual became tired or bored or was absent.[9] Compensation and feedback about performance would be based on the group's accomplishments, rather than on individual contributions.

J. Richard Hackman has suggested the following conditions under which a "self-managing" group design is appropriate:[10]

- when the best possible job design for individuals would involve only a narrowly defined task;
- when the setting requires high interdependence among workers;
- when the workers have strong needs for social interaction; and
- when the motivating potential of the jobs is expected to be considerably higher if arranged as a group task rather than as a set of individual tasks.

Autonomous groups are inappropriate if the individuals' tasks are not interdependent, if the individuals have higher needs for personal growth and development than for social interaction at work, or if the potential for conflict within or between groups is high.

The research results on the effectiveness of autonomous work groups are mixed.[11] Hence, a wholesale movement to the use of such groups is not recommended. Instead, such self-managing teams should be placed selectively into those situations that are known to be appropriate until it is better understood how to install and maintain them.[12]

THE USE OF COMMITTEES

Aside from the command group—composed of a manager and immediate subordinates—the most common formal group in many organizations is the committee. A *committee* involves a meeting of two or more individuals who are officially drawn together to consider issues pertinent to the organization or to function in a certain capacity.

Nature of Committees

Committees have multiplied as organizations have grown in size and complexity. In large governmental, educational, charitable, and business institutions, committees have become an integral part of the administrative structure. In the business·field, they are not limited to large corporations but are also found in relatively small concerns. Nor are they limited to top management levels, but they function at middle and lower levels of the organization as well.

Committees are almost infinite in their variety. In duration, for example, there are standing committees maintained permanently and *ad hoc* (or special purpose) committees appointed to serve only temporarily. In their time requirements, they range from those that meet rarely to those that meet regularly on a weekly and, in some cases, even a daily, basis.

With respect to purpose, committees may be policy making, administrative, executive, innovative, informational and so on. The subjects they consider are as varied as the organization itself, including general management, engineering, product design, research, safety, capital spending, advertising, collective bargaining, public relations, and many others.

Committees also may be distinguished as to their power within the organization. Top echelon committees have greater power or influence than do minor committees existing far down in the same organization. The influence of a committee also differs on the basis of its status as an advisory or decision-making committee.

The highest-level committee within most organizations is its board of directors. This group acts as a policy-making committee, working through appointed managers, but it may also overlap the top administrative levels of the concern through the use of an executive committee. (That is, the membership of an executive committee may include individuals who serve as both directors and managers of the corporation.)

Reasons for Use of Committees

For decades, the strengths and weaknesses of committees—illustrated in Figure 14–4—have been debated. In spite of their weaknesses, however, the general consensus among administrators is that committees are essential in managing large organizations and often useful in managing smaller groups. Supporters of committees give a number of reasons for their use.

Better Decisions through Group Deliberation. The committee can be used to pull together the different abilities and knowledge of its members. No two individuals approach solution of a complex problem in precisely the same way, and varied analytical abilities may, through committee deliberation, be brought to bear upon the same problem. The various departments and functional areas of the organization also involve different points of view which may be discovered and applied to the question at hand.

Committee analysis or review of a problem represents a kind of insurance against a decision based upon faulty reasoning or personal bias. This implies, of course, that the committee is more than a rubber stamp and that members can speak out on issues under consideration. (A cartoon has depicted the chairperson putting the question to vote with "All who object, say 'I resign.'") It also implies that the committee chairperson is sufficiently honest and alert to recognize personal bias when a challenge is voiced in the committee and is willing to act accordingly.

Coordination of Work. Specialization of work, both operative and managerial, makes the problem of synchronization of activities difficult. Many functions of one department are intertwined with those of other departments. As an example, a decision in the area of research and development may have repercussions affecting sales, production, finance, personnel, public relations, the legal department, and other activities.

Strengths	Weaknesses
Better decisions through group deliberation	Waste of time and money
Coordination of work	Danger of compromise
Securing cooperation in execution	Difficulty in placing responsibility
Training of participants	Delay and indecision
	Domination by one individual

FIGURE 14–4   Strengths and weaknesses of committees

In the organization that has become too large for personal observation by its members, the left hand does not always know what the right hand is doing unless active steps are taken to achieve this objective. The committee provides one way to achieve coordination of effort.

Securing Cooperation in Execution.   Certain barriers interfere with effective implementation of plans and policies. Among these are misunderstanding of a given plan or policy and also the feeling that one must follow a policy or plan without an opportunity to express opinions about it. The difficulties may occur in terms of both knowledge and desire.

A committee may be used as a means of attacking both problems. For example, discussion in a committee meeting can bring to light mistaken ideas and answer questions concerning the matter under consideration. A committee member who is involved in the discussion of a problem and its solution is more likely to be aware of why certain alternatives were rejected and others accepted. This knowledge is likely to lead to better understanding of the decision.

Likewise, a member's resistance to a committee decision with which he or she does not agree is likely to be lessened if the member is allowed to express objections to the decision. Even if some members disagree with the committee's final decision, it is difficult for them to oppose the decision as violently as they might if it were simply handed to them without explanation or opportunity for comments.

Training of Participants.   Development of personnel for all levels of management is one of the important responsibilities of administrators. By serving as committee members, participants are exposed to ideas and knowledge outside their usual areas of responsibility. In addition, committee members may engage in study in the process of preparing for committee participation, particularly if they are given some special responsibilities in connection with committee projects and performance. Perhaps the greatest training value comes from the give-and-take of committee sessions. In this atmosphere, committee members gain experience in speaking before a group, expressing ideas, and defending points of view.

Dangers and Difficulties in Use of Committees

Committees have their detractors. Remember the suggestion that a camel is a horse that was put together by a committee? Such comments refer to the dangers inherent in committee use.

Waste of Time and Money.   One criticism of committees is that they waste managerial time and thus dollars. Committee action may be wasteful because there are too many committees, because a committee is too large, because a committee meets too frequently, or because a committee operates inefficiently.

Committees often waste time on subjects of negligible importance or subjects that could be disposed of by one individual without difficulty. C. Northcote Parkinson has formulated what he calls the *law of triviality* which holds that "the time spent on any item of the agenda will be in inverse proportion to the sum involved."[13] His discussion suggests that committees are prone to engage in interminable discussion of items of little significance.

A major cause of wasted time is what Norman R. F. Maier has identified as a "conflicting secondary goal—winning the argument":

> When groups are confronted with a problem, the initial goal is to obtain a solution. However, the appearance of several alternatives causes individuals to have preferences, and once these emerge the desire to support a position is created. Converting those with neutral viewpoints and refuting those with opposed viewpoints now enters into the problem-solving process.
> More and more the goal becomes that of winning the decision rather than finding the best solution. This new goal is unrelated to the quality of the problem's solution and therefore can result in lowering the quality of the decision.[14]

Danger of Compromise. One of the greatest potential weaknesses of committees is their tendency toward compromise decisions. One hears such statements as "Committee solutions simply represent the lowest common denominator of the thinking of the members on that committee." The general thought is that the group lacks the will or forcefulness to reach the same sound conclusion that might be achieved by one individual acting alone.

Recent reviews of the evidence lend some support to this position. Although the quality of group judgments is generally superior to the quality of the judgments made by the average member of the group, group decisions are often inferior to the decisions of the most competent group member.[15] Even though most of the research has been conducted in artificial laboratory settings rather than in organizational committee meetings, these findings suggest potential weaknesses in using interacting groups for decision making.

Compromise is often the result of conformity. An individual who disagrees with the majority may well decide to comply—and vote with the majority—rather than risk alienating the other members for the sake of a losing cause. Irving L. Janis has coined the term "groupthink" to refer to an excessive type of conformity.

> The symptoms of groupthink arise when the members of decision-making groups become motivated to avoid being too harsh in their judgments of their leaders' or their colleagues' ideas. They adopt a soft line of criticism, even in their own thinking. At their meetings, all the members are amiable and seek complete concurrence on every important issue, with no bickering or conflict to spoil the cozy, "we-feeling" atmosphere.[16]

Another pressure that contributes to a spirit of compromise is the personal work load of committee members. Because these executives typically have full schedules, they attempt to reach a committee decision quickly in order to resume their regular responsibilities. Also, most committee members do not wish to embarrass other members of the same committee. To save face for all participants, the group may accept a conclusion or solution that is not violently opposed by any of the members.

Difficulty in Placing Responsibility.   Committee activity can be a shield behind which an individual manager can take refuge. Holding any one manager responsible for the group's decision becomes difficult. Proceeding against a group of executive personnel is almost impossible. As a result, responsibility may be diffused through committee activity in such a way that it is difficult to say that any one individual assumes full responsibility.

Delay and Indecision.   Committee action takes time. Individual committee members must assemble, and meetings require reconciliation of time demands of the committee with the personal schedules and other official responsibilities of the members. Speed of action in a business organization is important, particularly if it is not achieved at the expense of a proper evaluation of alternatives. Business opportunities may be lost by failure to act quickly. Smaller concerns are often recognized as having advantages over larger competitors for this very reason. An organization honeycombed with committees moves more slowly than a streamlined organization acting on the basis of individual judgment and decision.

Domination by One Individual.   Occasionally a committee operates under the thumb or domination of one person. This person's reaction provides the key to action by the group. An expression of disapproval, for example, whether verbal or by facial expression, may start the entire group on a negative approach or evaluation. In its most extreme form, such domination results in a committee that constitutes a form of window dressing to approve some pet idea of the dominant individual.

This deterioration of the committee function contrasts sharply with the values that are believed to exist in committees. Committees are presumably characterized by the give-and-take of equals. Committee deliberation represents a pooling of ideas in an atmosphere of mutual respect and tolerance. One member builds upon suggestions of another member. All participants sense a freedom to correct, to question, and to suggest modifications to the ideas and purposes of others.

The dominant individual is ordinarily the chairperson of the committee. Frequently, this person is also the superior of other members of the committee. The committee may, therefore, be inclined to show deference for this reason alone. If the chairperson is a driving, dominant type of leader, it is difficult to change the atmosphere when the scene shifts to a committee room.

Committee Management

In spite of the problems associated with committees, the difficulties inherent in management of the typical large organization have led a growing number of firms to supplement individual leadership with committee management at the top level of the administrative structure. One of the earliest formal top-management committees in a major corporation was established in 1921 when Irénée du Pont, president of E. I. du Pont de Nemours & Company adopted a committee system to deal with the problem of product diversification.[17]

COMMITTEE MANAGEMENT AT J. C. PENNEY

One organization that recently made the switch to committee management is the J. C. Penney Company. Adopted during the tenure of Chairman and CEO Donald V. Seibert, Penney's top management committee consists of fourteen executives who are involved in decisions ranging from strategic planning to personnel.

In fact, committees permeate the entire structure at Penney's. Permanent subcommittees deal with different key parts of the organization and ad hoc task forces are formed to deal with specific issues that arise.

Each member of the top management committee not only sits on the subcommittee in his or her functional area—merchandising, personnel, strategic planning, and so on—but also is an active member of subcommittees in a number of other areas. As one manager comments, "It's made me a much broader-gauged manager. You get a mixture of people who are authorities on a subject and of others who can lend a broader view. It's a real learning experience."

SOURCE: "Teamwork Pay Off at Penney's," *Business Week*, 12 April 1982, p. 107.

The increasing complexity of management in large-scale enterprise encourages adoption of the team approach to corporate management, in which the organization is managed by a committee. While there has been no widespread adoption of this general management committee approach, a number of companies—among them Bank of America and J. C. Penney Company—have taken significant steps in this direction.

Committee management, however, has not worked well in all cases. Aetna Life & Casualty, the first insurance company to adopt team management, abolished the system after four years because committee management "tended to lead to delays or impede the decision-making process on occasion."[18] Contingency theory, of course, implies that committee management would not be equally effective in all organizations or situations.

Quality Circles

Much publicity has been given recently to *quality circles*, which consist of formal groups (or committees) of employees who meet regularly to devise means of improving productivity and product or service quality. Most quality circles include both managerial and nonmanagerial employees. Estimates indicate that over 1,500 U.S. companies now use quality circles.[19]

Unlike members of managerial committees, members of quality circles often receive training. The leader of the group may enroll in a one-

QUALITY CIRCLES IN JAPAN

Hitachi Corporation of Japan has a highly developed quality circle program. Quality-circle-type groups operate in twenty-seven of its factories in the following fashion:

1. 29 percent of the groups work on improving and controlling product quality;
2. 67 percent focus on improving and refining operations management; and
3. 4 percent concentrate on improving work safety.

A typical group is comprised of eight to ten people. Participants include production workers, clerical and support personnel, and certain managerial personnel.

In Hitachi's Musashi Semiconductor Works plant, for instance, each group commits itself to filing a certain number of improvement proposals per month and is asked to submit a monthly review of its activities. The program began in 1977. In 1978, 26,543 proposals were submitted. Over 112,000 suggestions were filed in the last six months of 1980 alone, for an average of 45 proposals per group each month. Of those proposals, almost 88 percent were implemented. Over 25 percent of those were suggestions on how to reduce standard times at individual work stations, 27 percent dealt with reducing inventory, almost 25 percent with increasing office efficiency, and 6 percent with safety improvements and overhead cost savings.

SOURCE: Based on William H. Davidson, "Small Group Activity at Musashi Semiconductor Works," *Sloan Management Review* 23 (Spring 1982): 3–14.

to-two-week training course, and the circle members may receive several hours training in problem-solving techniques. In any case, an absolute prerequisite for the use of quality circles is an organizational guarantee that worker layoffs will not result from work-improvement suggestions made by the circles.[20] Without workers' trust, quality circles are unlikely to exist for long, much less be effective.[21]

GROUP DECISION-MAKING TECHNIQUES

Members of problem-solving groups usually engage in extensive inter-action as they attempt to arrive at a decision. As we have seen, certain strengths and weaknesses are associated with this interaction. Two tech-niques have been developed in recent years which attempt to overcome some of the weaknesses while simultaneously enhancing the strengths of group decision making.

Nominal Group Technique

The nominal group technique (NGT) is used to identify problems and devise solutions to them.[22] The term nominal refers to a group of people working in the presence of one another without interacting. This defini-tion is modified somewhat in actual practice, however, as we will see.

Implementation of the technique typically involves a group of six to nine people sitting together at a table. If, for instance, the session is one of problem solving, each person would be asked to formulate alternative solutions to the problem and to write each of them down on a card. During this phase, the members are not allowed to speak to one another. The purpose is to stimulate "creative tension" within the group members by placing them in the presence of others who are silently working. If one observes other members industriously writing down alternative so-lutions, then he or she will be psychologically encouraged to formulate a list of solutions also. Since the members are not allowed to interact, no prejudgment of ideas can occur and the individuals are not likely to "fall into a rut" and think only along the lines suggested by the more verbal members of the group.

In the next stage, a person who serves as a recorder asks each group member, one at a time, to read aloud the alternatives that he or she has written on the card. Each alternative is recorded on a blackboard or tear sheet as it is read aloud. No comments are permitted as the alternatives are read and recorded. This procedure allows all members to participate to the extent of their abilities while not allowing one person to dominate the session. It also eliminates the distraction of arguments among mem-bers wishing to defend their own alternatives.

Only after these two stages are completed are the members permit-ted to interact by discussing the alternatives on the board. They may request clarification or elaboration and are allowed to defend their own ideas and attack the ideas of others. At the end of the discussion period, each member votes, by secret ballot, for those alternatives that he or she considers to be the best solutions to the problem. Secrecy reduces the pressure to conform to the voting patterns of others and permits each person to support only those alternatives perceived to be the "best." The results of the secret vote comprise the group's decision.

The most frequent use of the nominal group technique has been in complex program-planning situations in business and other areas such as health and education. But the technique could be used within a department, division, or a small organization to identify important problems and arrive at feasible solutions.

Delphi Technique

The *Delphi Technique*[23] involves even less group interaction than the nominal group technique. In this process, the group members never meet face-to-face and communicate only through writing.

The group is composed of individuals who are knowledgeable about a certain field of thought. Each person is mailed a questionnaire asking for his or her judgments regarding a particular topic within that field. The respondents fill out the questionnaires, without communicating with each other, and return them to a monitoring team.

The team compiles the results and sends a summary of the results to each respondent along with a second questionnaire. After reviewing the summary and observing the other group members' judgments, each respondent then fills out and mails in the second questionnaire. Some respondents will alter their judgments on this questionnaire (compared to their earlier responses) as a result of reviewing the judgments of the other members. This process of responding-receiving feedback-responding continues until some group consensus is reached.

Evaluation of Group Decision-Making Techniques

The objective of these techniques is to minimize the weaknesses of group decision making while enhancing the strengths. Both techniques appear to reduce such problems as conformity, argument, and domination by one person. The NGT achieves this through a highly structured process which permits verbal interaction only after ideas and suggestions have been generated by the group members. The Delphi technique accomplishes it by eliminating all direct interaction. Both techniques, then, emphasize task goals while deemphasizing the social needs of the participants.

Less structured interaction, of course, is often essential—when coordination is required, when decisions are complex and involve change in the status quo, or when people desire to interact for social psychological reasons. Nevertheless, both of the techniques discussed above can be useful.[24] The NGT may be used to generate ideas or facts without the initial distraction of socioemotional interaction, while the Delphi technique may be employed in areas where uncertainty is high, interaction is not required, and time is not a major constraint. Most work groups would not use these techniques as part of their normal operations but might employ them occasionally—for example, to generate solutions to a new or difficult problem.

Planning the Decision-Making Process

Although reams have been written on *how* to conduct a group decision-making meeting, there are few guidelines on how to design the group *prior* to the meeting. "Yet the decisions a manager makes in designing a judgmental decision-making . . . group may substantially affect the quality and character of its judgments."[25] Not only should the mode of group functioning—nominal, interacting, Delphi, and so on—be planned, but consideration should also be given to the types of members—experts, representatives of constituent groups, department members, and so on—who are likely to be most effective in certain situations. Additionally, the manager should determine what criteria—decision quality, acceptance by affected parties, originality, and so on—should be used to evaluate the group's decision.[26]

The point, of course, is that the manager cannot wait until the group convenes to decide how to proceed. There is some evidence that managers who fail to plan the decision-making process may "unknowingly reduce the potential for the group to reach an effective decision."[27] Other evidence indicates that, under some conditions, the group members' attempts to implement the decisions they have already reached are affected by the way the decision process is structured.[28]

SUMMARY

Groups are essential to the accomplishment of organizational goals. In fact, the organization chart illustrates the *formal* grouping of individuals who are charged with the responsibility of contributing to the organization's goals. Within these formal groups arise *informal* collections of individuals who interact to satisfy their social needs or advance some common cause.

Group behavior may be analyzed by examining the *activities, interactions,* and *sentiments* of the group members. The interrelationships among these variables over time result in the evolution of group *norms.* Members are expected to *conform* to these norms in order to preserve the group's order, stability, and existence. Groups with a high rate of conformity are termed *cohesive.* Members of cohesive groups derive satisfaction from their group membership and often develop important norms regarding work performance. A movement intended to harness the positive aspects of group behavior and improve both member satisfaction and organizational performance is the trend toward *autonomous work groups*. These are small teams that are given the responsibility for planning and executing a whole task.

Committees have become an integral part of the administrative structure of most modern organizations. Advantages resulting from the use of committees include the improvement of decisions through group deliberation, coordination of work, facilitation of cooperation in the execution or application of plans and policies, and training of participants. Among the offsetting dangers and limitations are the waste of time and money, danger of undesirable compromise in decision making, difficulty in placing responsibility for decisions, delays and indecision in administrative action, and domination of the committee by one person. *Quality circles* are special types of committees which attempt to improve productivity and quality.

To overcome some weaknesses of group interaction, two group decision-making techniques have been devised. The *nominal group technique* requires members to formulate their ideas in silence, without interacting. Only later are they permitted to discuss their ideas with each other. This interacting phase is then followed by another noninteracting phase in which the members use a secret ballot to vote on the best ideas. The *Delphi technique* goes a step further, eliminating all interaction. Group members respond to questionnaires soliciting their expert judgments on a particular topic. Although these techniques eliminate many of the liabilities associated with interaction, they also lose some of the important advantages. The necessity for planning the decision-making process is evident.

DISCUSSION QUESTIONS

1. Explain this statement: "*Formal group* interaction is inevitably modified by *informal* activities and attitudes."
2. What are the implications of the statement in Question 1 for the manager of a formal work group?
3. Think of a group to which you belong. What are the central *norms* which govern behavior in the group? What functions do these norms perform?
4. In the area of *conformity*, why do most groups require only *compliance*, rather than *private acceptance*, from their members?
5. Is it better for a supervisor to deal with subordinates as individuals or to encourage development of a *cohesive* work group? Explain.
6. Under what conditions might the formation of *autonomous work groups* be appropriate?
7. Which of the suggested dangers or difficulties in the use of committees appears most serious? What is the basis for your answer?

8. Under what conditions might management of an organization by a *committee*, rather than a single chief executive officer, be successful?

9. How do *quality circles* differ from the traditional type of committee?

10. Compare the advantages and disadvantages of the following decision-making techniques: (a) a group in which the members *interact* freely, (b) a group using the *nominal group technique*, and (c) a group using the *Delphi technique*.

NOTES

1. Edgar Schein, *Organizational Psychology*, 2d ed. (Englewood Cliffs, N.J.: Prentice-Hall, 1970), p. 69.

2. Dorwin Cartwright and Alvin Zander, eds., *Group Dynamics: Research and Theory*, 3d ed. (New York: Harper & Row, Publishers, 1968), p. 54.

3. J. Stephen Heinen and Eugene Jacobson, "A Model of Task Group Development in Complex Organizations and a Strategy of Implementation," *Academy of Management Review* 1 (October 1976): 99–100.

4. James L. Gibson, John M. Ivancevich, and James H. Donnelly, Jr., *Organizations: Behavior, Structure, Processes*, 3d ed. (Dallas: Business Publications, 1979), p. 138.

5. William Foote Whyte, *Organizational Behavior: Theory and Application* (Homewood, Ill.: Richard D. Irwin and The Dorsey Press, 1969), Chapters 4 and 5, and George Homans, *The Human Group* (New York: Harcourt, Brace, 1950).

6. Dorwin Cartwright, "The Nature of Group Cohesiveness," in *Group Dynamics*, 3d ed., ed. Cartwright and Zander, p. 96.

7. A classic study of the effects of cohesiveness on group performance and member satisfaction is reported in Stanley E. Seashore, *Group Cohesiveness in the Industrial Work Group* (Ann Arbor, Mich.: University of Michigan Press, 1954). Another excellent discussion of this topic is available in Rensis Likert, *New Patterns of Management* (New York: McGraw-Hill Book Co., 1961), Chapter 3.

8. J. Richard Hackman, "The Design of Self-Managing Work Groups," in *Managerial Control and Organizational Democracy*, ed. B. King, S. Streufert, and F. Fiedler (Washington , D.C.: V. H. Winston & Sons, 1978), p. 62.

9. See Melvin Blumberg, "Job Switching in Autonomous Work Groups: An Exploratory Study in a Pennsylvania Coal Mine," *Academy of Management Journal* 23 (June 1980): 287–306.

10. Hackman, "The Design of Self-Managing Work Groups," pp. 85–87.

11. See Melvin Blumberg, *Job Switching in Autonomous Work Groups: A Descriptive and Exploratory Study in an Underground Coal Mine* (Palto Alto, Calif.: R & E Research Associates, 1978); and Andrew D. Szilagyi, Jr., and Marc J. Wallace, Jr., *Organizational Behavior and Performance*, 2d ed. (Santa Monica, Calif.: Goodyear Publishing Co., 1980).

12. Hackman, "The Design of Self-Managing Work Groups," pp. 88–89.

13. C. Northcote Parkinson, *Parkinson's Law* (Boston: Houghton Mifflin Co., 1957), p. 24.

14. Norman R. F. Maier, "Assets and Liabilities in Group Problem Solving: The Need for an Integrative Function," *Psychological Review* 74 (July 1967): 242.

15. Gayle W. Hill, "Group versus Individual Performance: Are $N + 1$ Heads Better Than One?" *Psychological Bulletin* 91 (May 1982): 517–39; and John Rohrbaugh, "Improving the Quality of Group Judgment: Social Judgment Analysis and the Delphi Technique," *Organizational Behavior and Human Performance* 24 (August 1979): 73–92.

16. Irving L. Janis, "Groupthink," *Psychology Today* 5 (November 1971): 43.

17. M. R. Lohmann, *Top Management Committees*, AMA Research Study 48 (New York: American Management Association, 1961): 5.

18. "Aetna: Where Group Management Didn't Work," *Business Week*, 16 February 1976, p. 77.

19. "Will the Slide Kill Quality Circles?" *Business Week*, 11 January 1982, p. 108.

20. Ibid., pp. 108–9.

21. For a discussion of various obstacles to establishing successful quality circle programs in U.S. organizations, see Gerald D. Klein, "Implementing Quality Circles: A Hard Look at Some of the Realities," *Personnel* 58 (November-December 1981): 11–20.

22. The nominal group technique was devised by Andrew H. Van de Ven and André L. Delbecq. The technique is described in a number of sources; one of the clearest statements may be found in Van de Ven and Delbecq, "Nominal versus Interacting Group Processes for Committee Decision-Making Effectiveness," *Academy of Management Journal* 14 (June 1971): 203–12. A more extensive reference is Delbecq, Van de Ven, and David H. Gustafson, *Group Techniques for Program Planning* (Glenview, Ill.: Scott, Foresman and Co., 1975).

23. Norman C. Dalkey, *The Delphi Method: An Experimental Study of Group Opinion* (Santa Monica, Calif.: The Rand Corporation, 1969).

24. The research results in this area are mixed and are largely based on experimental studies in laboratory settings. Three representative studies are Van de Ven and Delbecq, "The Effectiveness of Nominal, Delphi, and Interacting Group Decision Making Processes," *Academy of Management Journal* 17 (December 1974): 605–21; Thad B. Green, "An Empirical Analysis of Nominal and Interacting Groups," *Academy of Management Journal* 18 (March 1975): 63–73; and Frederick C. Miner, Jr., "A Comparative Analysis of Three Diverse Group Decision Making Approaches," *Academy of Management Journal* 22 (March 1979): 81–93.

25. Stephen A. Stumpf, Dale E. Zand, and Richard D. Freedman, "Designing Groups for Judgmental Decisions," *Academy of Management Review* 4 (October 1979): 589.

26. Stephen A. Stumpf, Richard D. Freedman, and Dale E. Zand, "Judgmental Decisions: A Study of Interactions among Group Membership, Group Functioning, and the Decision Situation," *Academy of Management Journal* 22 (December 1979): 765–82.

27. Ibid., p. 779.

28. Sam E. White, John E. Dittrich, and James R. Lang, "The Effects of Group Decision-Making Process and Problem-Situation Complexity on Implementation Attempts," *Administrative Science Quarterly* 25 (September 1980): 438.

SUPPLEMENTARY READING

Alderfer, Clayton P. "Improving Organizational Communication through Long-Term Intergroup Intervention." *Journal of Applied Behavioral Science* 13 (April-May-June 1977): 193–210.

Blumberg, Melvin. "Job Switching in Autonomous Work Groups: An Exploratory Study in a Pennsylvania Coal Mine." *Academy of Management Journal* 23 (June 1980): 287–306.

Burton, Gene E., and Pathak, Dev S. "Social Character and Group Decision Making." *S.A.M. Advanced Management Journal* 43 (Summer 1978): 12–20.

Cartwright, Dorwin, and Zander, Alvin, eds. *Group Dynamics: Research and Theory.* 3d ed. New York: Harper & Row, Publishers, 1968.

Davidson, William H. "Small Group Activity at Musashi Semiconductor Works." *Sloan Management Review* 23 (Spring 1982): 3–14.

Delbecq, André L., and Van de Ven, Andrew H. "A Group Process Model for Problem Identification and Program Planning." *Journal of Applied Behavioral Science* 7 (July-August 1971): 466–92.

Fotilas, Panagiotis N. "Semi-autonomous Work Groups: An Alternative in Organizing Production Work?" *Management Review* 70 (July 1981): 50–54.

Hackman, J. Richard. "The Design of Self-Managing Work Groups." In *Managerial Control and Organizational Democracy,* edited by Bert King, Siegfried Streufert, and Fred E. Fiedler. Washington, D.C.: V. H. Winston & Sons, 1978, pp. 61–91.

Heinen, J. Stephen, and Jacobson, Eugene. "A Model of Task Group Development in Complex Organizations and a Strategy of Implementation." *Academy of Management Review* 1 (October 1976): 98–111.

Hoffman, L. Richard. "Applying Experimental Research on Group Problem Solving to Organizations." *Journal of Applied Behavioral Science* 15 (July-August-September 1979): 375–91.

King, Corwin P. "Decision by Discussion: The Uses and Abuses of Team Problem Solving." *S.A.M. Advanced Management Journal* 41 (Autumn 1976): 31–38.

Klein, Gerald D. "Implementing Quality Circles: A Hard Look at Some of the Realities." *Personnel* 58 (November-December 1981): 11–20.

Maier, Norman R. F. "Assets and Liabilities in Group Problem Solving: The Need for an Integrative Function." *Psychological Review* 74 (July 1967): 239–49.

Nadler, David A. "The Effects of Feedback on Task Group Behavior: A Review of the Experimental Research." *Organizational Behavior and Human Performance* 23 (June 1979): 309–38.

Shambaugh, Philip Wells. "The Development of the Small Group." *Human Relations* 31 (March 1978): 283–95.

Stumpf, Stephen A.; Zand, Dale E.; and **Freedman, Richard D.** "Designing Groups for Judgmental Decisions." *Academy of Management Review* 4 (October 1979): 589–600.

Van de Ven, Andrew H. "Problem Solving, Planning, and Innovation. Part I. Test of the Program Planning Model." *Human Relations* 33 (October 1980): 711–40.

Van de Ven, Andrew H., and **Delbecq, André L.** "The Effectiveness of Nominal, Delphi, and Interacting Group Decision Making Processes." *Academy of Management Journal* 17 (December 1974): 605–21.

PART FOUR
MANAGING
HUMAN
RESOURCES

15

HUMAN RESOURCE MANAGEMENT

This chapter will enable you to

- *Explain the process of human resource planning and recruiting.*
- *Comprehend the process organizations use to select and hire new employees, and the role management plays in orienting newcomers to their surroundings and in helping them become integral parts of the organization.*
- *Understand the purpose of performance appraisal and the contributions and limitations of certain appraisal techniques.*
- *Identify the various methods of management development.*

A competent, motivated team of organization members can make the difference between an effective and an ineffective organization. Building and maintaining this team require careful management of the organization's human resources. This process begins with *human resource planning* and the subsequent *recruitment* of job applicants. Through a process involving a number of hurdles such as application blanks, background checks, tests, and interviews, qualified applicants are *selected* for positions within the organization. These new employees must be appropriately compensated, oriented to their jobs and surroundings, and socialized into organizational membership. *Performance appraisal* not only helps new employees understand organizational expectations, but measures how effectively the organization's human resources are being used. Finally, any effective organization must have an able, competent cadre of managers. Building such a team requires a well-planned *management development* program.

HUMAN RESOURCE PLANNING AND RECRUITING

Nature of Planning

Determining the firm's human resource requirements is the first step in staffing the organization. The process of *personnel forecasting* enables management to answer such questions about the future as the following:

1. How many additional personnel will we require over the next year? The next five years?
2. What types of positions must we fill?
3. What qualifications are required for these positions?

In estimating staff requirements, a number of factors must be considered. Probable losses from retirements, deaths, resignations, and other reasons must be calculated. Estimates of this kind require attention to age distribution of present staff, historical rate of attrition, and so on. Any expansion plans of the business similarly affect estimated requirements. This factor requires a forecast of future trends, as discussed in earlier chapters.

Human resource planning has become increasingly important in recent years. Rapid technological change, combined with an uncertain economy, has made planning more necessary, yet more difficult, than ever. Additionally, federal Equal Employment Opportunity (EEO) programs have caused management to plan and develop more rational career paths and job requirements, and more objective procedures for matching candidates with jobs. Some EEO regulations that affect management are shown in Figure 15–1.

In spite of the importance of planning, formal human resource planning programs are not as common as one might expect. A survey of 195

Title VII of Civil Rights Act (1964, amended in 1972)—applies to all private employers with at least fifteen employees, governments at all levels, and labor unions with at least fifteen members. States that *race, religion, national origin, sex,* or *color* may not be used to

1. refuse to hire or to discharge an individual or discriminate against a person with respect to pay, conditions of employment, or privileges of employment;
2. classify employees in such a way as to deprive anyone of employment opportunities; or
3. refuse entrance into training programs or apprenticeship programs.

Executive Order 11246 (1972)—established an *affirmative action program* which applies to all organizations with federal contracts or subcontracts. Goes further than the Civil Rights Act by stating that an employer can no longer be passive, but must actively attempt to reduce unequal employment opportunities through recruitment, selection, placement, performance evaluation, wage programs, and so on. In short, all personnel activities must foster affirmative action.

FIGURE 15–1   Major equal employment opportunity requirements for organizations

NOTE: Although the Civil Rights Act and the Affirmative Action Program have had the greatest impact on organizational staffing, other acts prohibit discrimination on the basis of age or require federal contractors and the federal government to practice affirmative action toward the physically or mentally handicapped and veterans. An excellent discussion of EEO programs may be found in Michael R. Carrell and Frank E. Kuzmits, *Personnel: Management of Human Resources* (Columbus, Oh.: Charles E. Merrill Publishing Co., 1982), Chapter 5.

of the largest 1,000 companies in the United States indicated that, while 80 percent had formal personnel planning programs, 20 percent did not. Only 30 percent of the formal programs included all positions within the company, while the remaining 70 percent encompassed only managerial and technical personnel. In the area of planning for managerial succession, fewer than 10 percent of the programs planned six or more years in advance, 84 percent planned one to five years ahead, and 11 percent planned less than a year in advance, if at all.[1]

Job Analysis

Effective personnel planning requires detailed knowledge of the positions in the organization. The process of compiling this information is termed *job analysis*. A job analysis includes two elements: (1) a *job description*, which contains the specific duties and responsibilities of the position; and (2) a *job specification*, which defines the education, experience, skills, and behaviors required of the position holder. A representative job description and specification for the personnel manager of a plant are shown in Figure 15–2.

Besides its obvious use in human resource planning, the job analysis document has a number of other important uses, including the following:[2]

1. It serves as the basis for recruitment advertisements in newspapers and other publications.
2. It helps interviewers match applicants to job openings.
3. It is used in orienting and training new employees.
4. It serves as a basis for performance appraisal.

Since jobs change as the organization changes, frequent updating of job descriptions and specifications is required. Although the initial job analysis is usually performed by the personnel department, it is the responsibility of line managers to notify the personnel department of changes in the jobs under their supervision.

Process of Recruiting

Once management has determined the number and types of positions to be filled over some span of time, the process of recruiting qualified applicants to fill those positions begins. In some cases, job seekers initiate the process themselves by walking in and filling out applications or by mailing unsolicited résumés to the personnel department. Current employees may even recommend individuals they know to fill particular job openings. Although these are inexpensive means of garnering a pool of applicants, it is unlikely that unsolicited applications will match the organization's specific needs. Then, too, most organizations are required to conduct an objective recruiting process in order to comply with EEO guidelines.

TITLE OF POSITION: **Personnel Manager, Plant**

Basic Purpose

To develop and maintain an employee relations climate that creates and permits a stable and productive workforce. To manage and coordinate all functions of employee relations, including employment, labor relations, compensation and benefit services, manpower planning, training and development, affirmative action, and security.

Duties and Responsibilities

1. Selects, trains, develops, and organizes a subordinate staff to perform and meet department responsibilities and objectives effectively.

2. Provides leadership in the establishment and maintenance of employee relations that will assist in attracting and retaining a desirable and productive labor force.

3. Manages the interpretation and application of established corporate and division personnel policies.

4. Directs the preparation and maintenance of reports necessary to carry out functions of the department. Prepares periodic reports for the Plant Manager; Director, Employee Relations; Manager, Labor Relations; and/or Manager, Compensation and Benefits, as necessary or requested.

5. Directs and maintains various activities designed to achieve and maintain a high level of employee morale.

6. Plans, implements, and maintains a program of orientation for new employees.

7. Provides and serves as the necessary liaison between the location employees and the location Plant Manager.

8. Supervises the labor relations staff in administration of the labor agreements and interpretation of contract language and ensures that the Supervisor, Labor Relations is well informed to administer the provisions effectively and in accordance with management's philosophy and objectives.

9. Strives to establish an effective working relationship with union representatives to resolve and minimize labor problems more satisfactorily and to avoid inefficient practices and work stoppages.

10. Determines, or in questionable cases recommends, whether grievance cases appealed to the arbitration stage should be settled by concessions or arbitrated. Prepares and presents such cases or supervises subordinates in same.

11. Manages and coordinates planning for plant labor contract negotiations; ensures that labor cost aspects are defined and that major position papers are prepared. Supervises the preparation and publication of contract language and documentation. Serves as chief spokesman or assists in negotiations at the operating unit level.

12. Establishes operative procedures for ensuring timely compliance with notice, reporting, and similar obligations under agreements with labor organizations.

13. Supervises the compensation and benefits staff in the administration and/or implementation and communication of current and new compensation and benefit programs, policies, and procedures.

14. Directs the development and implementation of approved location affirmative action plans to achieve and maintain compliance in accordance with the letter and intent of equal employment opportunity laws and executive orders.

15. Plans, implements, and maintains supervisory and management development activities.

16. Provides leadership in the establishment and maintenance of a plant security force.

17. Represents the company in the community and promotes the company's goodwill interests in community activities.

Organizational Relationships

This position reports directly to the Plant Manager and functionally to the Director, Employee Relations. Directly supervises Supervisor, Labor Relations; Supervisor, Employment; Supervisor, Compensation and Benefits; and Supervisor, Security; and indirectly supervises additional nonexempt employees. Interfaces daily with management and division employee relations.

Position Specification

Bachelor's Degree, preferably in Personnel Management or equivalent plus 6–8 years related experience, including supervisory/managerial experience in a wide range of employee relations activities. Must possess an ability to understand human behavior and be able to lead and motivate people. Must have mature judgment and decision-making ability.

FIGURE 15–2 Sample job description and specification

SOURCE: Reprinted, by permission of the publisher, from *Job Descriptions in Manufacturing Industries* by John D. Ulery, pp. 24–26. © 1981 by AMACOM, a division of American Management Associations, New York. All rights reserved.

Most organizations, then, must proactively seek job applicants, usually from a number of sources. Each source, of course, has its own advantages and disadvantages.[3] As an example, consider three common sources of applicants for entry-level managerial positions—colleges and universities, other organizations, and the organization itself.

College Recruiting. Most large firms, many government agencies, and some small companies send recruiters to college campuses on annual or semiannual quests for job candidates.[4] This process allows organizations to choose to recruit only from those colleges with academic programs that fit their needs and to specify the types of applicants—by major field of study or degree—that they will interview. Some organizations even indicate that they will not interview students who have cumulative grade point averages below a certain point.

On the other hand, campus recruiting is an expensive means of forming an applicant pool. The direct cost of recruiting and selection is relatively high. The recruiter must travel to the campus to interview between eight and twelve applicants. Out of the eight to twelve applicants, only one or two may actually meet the organization's needs. And since these one or two individuals may also receive competing job offers from other firms, the company may actually hire only one individual after recruiting at, say, ten different universities. Figure 15–3 indicates some major reasons why graduates reject college job offers as well as some reasons why companies do not offer jobs to certain graduates. The expected turnover rate of these employees is also great. One source indicates that, within 3-1/2 years, 32 percent of engineering majors and 27 percent of accounting/business administration majors had quit their first job.[5]

Recruiting from Other Organizations. Other organizations—often competitors—also may be used to train or supply managerial talent. Employees of other organizations have been seasoned by experience and, hence, may be superior to employees of the same caliber without work experience. Some factors contributing to this increasingly common practice are the trend toward professional management (with an emphasis on administrative ability and loyalty to the profession as well as the employer), and the emergence of specialized executive recruiting firms. Unfortunately, some organizations known for their excellent managerial training programs are often used as "training grounds" by other organizations. A recent college graduate, after completing the expensive training provided by one organization, may be recruited by other organizations lacking quality training programs.

Internal Recruiting. The organization itself is another source of executive personnel. In filling vacancies, many corporations emphasize promotion from within. This has the advantage of rewarding outstanding performance on the part of the existing staff. It also secures executive

---

Reasons Why Graduates Reject Company Offers

- Company location—size of community
- Salary
- Type of work—job assignment
- Wants faster promotion—desires more responsibility
- Not interested in industry
- Reluctance to travel or relocate
- Seeks greater opportunity for graduate study

Reasons Why Employers Do Not Offer Jobs to Certain Graduates

- Negative personality or poor impression: More specifically, lack of motivation, ambition, maturity, aggressiveness or enthusiasm
- Inability to communicate—poor communication skills
- Lack of competence—inadequate preparation
- Low grades—poor grades in major field
- Unidentified goals
- Unrealistic expectations
- Lack of interest in the type of work
- Unwillingness to travel or relocate
- Poor preparation for the interview
- Lack of work experience

FIGURE 15–3   Reasons for rejections (ranked by frequency of mention)
SOURCE: Frank S. Endicott, *The Endicott Report 1980* (Evanston, Ill.: The Placement Center/Northwestern University), pp. 7–8. Reprinted by permission.

personnel who have experience with the organization and its methods of operation. Some organizations maintain computerized *skills inventories* for this purpose. Such an inventory can provide detailed information on the present performance, strengths, weaknesses, and potential for promotion of each of the organization's employees.

Assessment centers may also be used to locate potential managerial talent within the organization. According to the typical format, one or more six-person groups are brought together to participate in group exercises for two or three days. During this time, they take part in interviews, psychological tests, and simulation exercises such as in-basket tests.* A trained staff of line managers, personnel specialists, and psychologists observes the applicants during the exercises. Results of assessment evaluations in selecting the prospects with management poten-

---

*An in-basket test is a simulated situation in which the candidate is given a set of memoranda, telephone messages, letters, notes, and requests that he or she must organize and respond to within a limited period of time. The exercise tests the individual's ability to set priorities, relate items, request additional information, make decisions, and so on.

tial are encouraging, but, to date, there is no clear evidence that assessment center predictions are significantly more accurate than those based on biographical data, peer nominations, or supervisory ratings.[6]

A danger in internal recruitment, or at least in extensive reliance upon this source, is the inbreeding that may occur. This is particularly serious in positions requiring originality and new ideas.

SELECTION AND ORIENTATION

Overview of Selection

One a pool of applicants is available, the process of selecting individuals to fill the appropriate positions begins. Many organizations use a *multiple-hurdles* model of selection such as the one illustrated in Figure 15–4. Under this system, the size of the applicant pool diminishes after each step or hurdle. Only those applicants who pass all of the hurdles may be offered jobs. Each hurdle should help distinguish between individuals who are likely to perform well and those who probably will not.

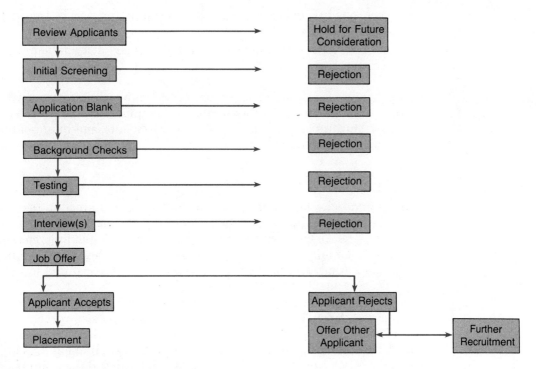

FIGURE 15–4   Selection process steps

SOURCE: Adapted from Michael R. Carrell and Frank E. Kuzmits, *Personnel: Management of Human Resources* (Columbus, Oh.: Charles E. Merrill Publishing Co., 1982), p. 206.

Application Blank/Résumé

The first step in the selection process for individuals applying for operative work is filling out an application blank. Candidates for managerial jobs are usually screened through information on their résumés, and those who appear qualified are often asked to complete a standardized application blank.

This initial step in the selection process, as is true of subsequent steps, must be conducted in such a way as to minimize the possibility that the organization will discriminate against applicants. For instance, organizations usually cannot request such information from job applicants as the following:

1. Race, national origin, or religion (although these data must be gathered to meet EEO/affirmative action requirements, they should be kept separate from the applicant's file)
2. A photograph of the individual (it can identify the individual's sex, race, or national origin)
3. Height or weight (unless they are bona fide occupational qualifications)
4. Date of birth or age (except when a minimum age is required by child work laws)
5. Marital status or number of children (may discriminate against women

Application blanks and résumés not only give the organization pertinent data on applicants' qualifications and background, but also "test the candidates' abilities to write, to organize their thoughts, and to present facts clearly and succinctly."[7]

Background Checks

Background checks are necessary to validate the information the candidate has given on the application blank. If sufficient lead time is available, the checks may be made through the mail. Telephoning references, however, not only provides greater speed but also a higher probability of eliciting a frank response since the reference is not required to put his or her assessment of the candidate in writing.

If the candidate has previous work experience, the most useful references are likely to be previous supervisors and even coworkers. Again, legal restrictions on requesting information apply. It is legal, however, for an employer to release the following information about ex-employees: dates of employment; job progression; job titles, duties, and responsibilities; performance appraisals by employees' supervisors; or other objective measures of employee performance such as absenteeism, quantitative production, or sales.[8]

LIES ON RÉSUMÉS?

After four years as a tennis bum, Nick Lawrence, 35, was broke and needed a job again. His résumé detailing his work as a high-level computer systems analyst was first rate. His references were even better.

The result of his brief job search was a bidding war for his services between a major bank and a computer company. There were offers and counteroffers.

Lawrence chose the bank, even though the computer company offered more money, because he figured he could get lost more easily in the bank's executive structure.

Why was that important? Lawrence's résumé was a fake. He had never been more than a low-level computer operator.

One friend wrote the phony résumé. Another, who owned a computer company, lied about Lawrence's work from an employer's perspective. Still another friend claimed falsely to be a satisfied client of Lawrence.

The bank found him out a year later and he was asked to resign. Sound far-fetched?

While the name is fictional, the story is true, according to William Lewis, president of Career Blazers, one of New York's largest employment agencies. Lewis says that between 25 percent and 40 percent of all résumés contain some kind of false material, such as incorrect employment dates.

SOURCE: "Résumé Lies Common, Agency Says," *The Houston Post*, 22 November 1981. Reprinted by permission.

Tests

Many organizations use some form of testing in their selection process because they believe that it introduces a needed element of objectivity into what is essentially a subjective process. Tests may attempt to measure such characteristics as the applicant's general intelligence or aptitudes. To ensure that tests do not discriminate against certain groups of applicants, organizations must validate their tests. A valid test is one that measures the individual's ability or potential ability to perform in a particular type of job. Organizations that use tests are generally pleased with the results; one estimate indicates that 95 percent of the employers who have tried applicant testing continue to use this process.[9]

Interviews

Although interviews may be used at various stages of the selection process, job candidates are inevitably interviewed after all of the previous hurdles have been cleared. Although it is, by far, the most widely used selection tool, interviewing is at best an inexact "science."

The essence of the interview's basic subjectivity is portrayed in Figure 15–5. In this conceptualization, the outcome of an interview depends upon three factors: (1) the applicant's experiences, background, characteristics, perceptions, and behavior; (2) the situation, which includes variables ranging from current economic conditions to the physical setting of the interview; and (3) the interviewer's own experiences, background, characteristics, perceptions, and behavior. It is the unique interaction of these variables, which will differ from one interview to the next, that determines the outcome. From this perspective, it is not surprising that the interview is unscientific.

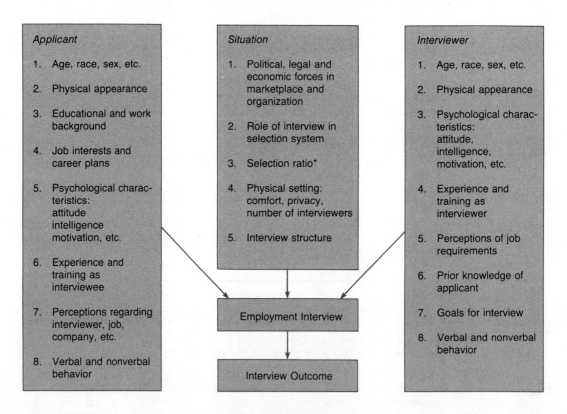

*Selection ratio refers to the number of candidates for a job per number of jobs available.

FIGURE 15–5   The employment interview
SOURCE: Richard D. Arvey and James E. Campion, "The Employment Interview: A Summary and Review of Recent Research," *Personnel Psychology* 35 (Summer 1982): 283.

In spite of its subjectivity, however, the interview continues to be widely used. It is, for instance, the only way management has to judge an applicant's verbal fluency and ability to present his or her ideas to others. It is also the primary means the organization has of selling itself to applicants who may have alternative job opportunities.

Two recently developed techniques hold some promise for making the interview more objective. One is the *panel interview* in which the applicant is interviewed by a panel of individuals. It may be that "sharing different perceptions with the different interviewers forces interviewers to become more aware of irrelevant inferences made on non-job related variables."[10]

The second development is the *situational interview* comprised of objectively scored questions derived from a systematic job analysis. The questions are composed by the job supervisors themselves and require applicants to indicate how they would behave in representative job situations. For example, in developing questions for individuals applying for sawmill worker positions, supervisors wrote the following question:

> Your spouse and two teenage children are sick in bed with a cold. There are no relatives or friends available to look in on them. Your shift starts in 3 hours. What would you do in this situation?

Based on their own experience, the supervisors devised the following three benchmark responses to evaluate the application:

> I'd stay home—my spouse and family come first (1 point).
> I'd phone my supervisor and explain the situation (3 points).
> Since they only have colds, I'd come to work (5 points).[11]

Compensation

Decisions to hire an applicant must be coupled with decisions concerning the applicant's compensation. In its broadest sense, compensation refers not only to the individual's salary or wages but also to group benefits such as health, life, and dental insurance; pension plans; vacation time; food services; profit sharing; and stock options.

Compensation systems should not simply evolve; they should be carefully planned. Because they represent a significant portion of the organization's total cost of doing business (perhaps as high as 40 percent in manufacturing organizations to over 70 percent in service organizations) and because pay is one of the most important job factors to individual employees, management must decide on the goals of its compensation system.[12] Among the more common objectives are the following:[13]

1. *Attract employees*—organizations must pay competitive salaries to attract qualified applicants.
2. *Retain good employees*—although high-quality employees may leave the organization for a number of reasons, the most frequent cause is inadequate compensation.

A WEEK IN THE LIFE
OF A JOB APPLICANT

A student reports that he had widely varying experiences during his first week of interviews with job recruiters in the university placement center. At the first interview, the recruiter monopolized the entire twenty-five minutes with a monologue describing the company and its products, structure, and career paths. With no time remaining, the recruiter asked the student: "Do you have any questions?"

By contrast, the second recruiter began the interview by hurling the following question at the student before he was even seated: "If you were suddenly made president of this company, what two changes would you make first?" The question, of course, tested the student's knowledge of the company, preparation for the interview, and his ability to think quickly and articulate a response.

The third interview was virtually unstructured. The recruiter began by conversing about the university's football team and other non-job-related matters. Finally turning to the task at hand, the recruiter asked two questions: "What can you tell me about yourself?" and "What would you like to know about our company?"

3. *Motivate employees*—although pay has limited value in motivating all employees (see Chapter 19), management can help encourage high job performance by tying financial rewards to employee performance levels.

4. *Meet legal requirements*—federal (and some state) laws govern such areas of compensation as minimum wages, overtime pay, and equal pay for men and women who do equal work on jobs requiring equal skill, responsibility, and effort being performed under similar working conditions.

Wages and salary levels are usually set through the process of *job evaluation*—the systematic analysis of jobs to determine their relative worth to the organization. Job evaluation systems usually assign points to all the jobs in the organization, based on such variables as working conditions and the responsibility the job involves. These points are then converted into pay scales for each job in the organization. Jobs which are less important to the company receive lower levels of compensation that those that are more important. The characteristics of the person holding the job (such as skill level or educational attainment) may be used to adjust the pay rate of some individuals.

Edward E. Lawler III argues that, in some cases, such *job content-based evaluation systems* have dysfunctional consequences.[14] If, for instance, evaluation systems measure responsibility rather than skills, individuals may be encouraged to seek supervisory jobs, even though they lack managerial skills. Or they may attempt to increase the size of their budget and their span of control.

On the other hand, *person-based job evaluation systems,* which pay individuals according to their skill levels, can encourage individuals to learn new skills and further develop the ones they already possess. This system can be useful, for instance, in encouraging technical specialists to remain in their specialization by providing attractive levels of compensation to them. Currently, for instance, engineers in many chemical companies must eventually enter the managerial ranks if they expect to advance significantly in compensation and career standing because these forms of advancement are based on budgetary and people responsibilities.

COMPENSATION AT KODAK

Few companies have so recognized the importance of their total compensation system as has Eastman Kodak Company, the giant of the photographic products industry. For over seventy years, Kodak has not only paid relatively high salaries, but has also paid annual bonuses to all employees. The bonus, paid each March, can amount to several thousand dollars even to production workers.

Its recreation and sideline benefits are perhaps the most extensive in the United States. Employees can borrow cameras and other equipment, buy film at a discount, and use company darkrooms. Both employees and retirees are eligible for discounted vacation trips and company-sponsored sports and entertainment events. Kodak shows first-run movies at lunchtime, provides bowling alleys, and even has its own savings and loan association.

The results? Kodak's management feels that it has been able to retain its most creative employees and that its work force possesses unusual *espirit de corps.* Not incidentally, it remains one of the country's largest nonunionized employers.

SOURCE: Based on "Kodak Fights Back," *Business Week,* 1 February 1982. pp. 53–54.

Orientation

Once an individual has accepted a job offer, the employing organization has the responsibility of orienting the newcomer to the new surroundings and helping him or her become a part of the organization. These

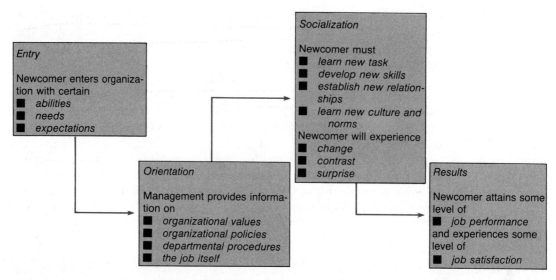

FIGURE 15–6   Orientation and socialization

processes, illustrated in Figure 15–6, are respectively referred to as *orientation* and *socialization*.

Some organizations, mostly large ones, conduct formal orientation programs for new employees, while other organizations orient the employee more informally. Whatever form it may take, orientation should focus on two levels—(1) information about the organization in general, such as its values and policies, and (2) information concerning the newcomer's own department and job. Some of this information may even be conveyed during earlier job interviews. Evidence indicates that a modest but significant reduction in turnover among new employees can be achieved by giving them a "realistic job preview" during the interview stage.[15]

Socialization

The socialization process, culminating with the employee's transformation from "outsider" to organizational "insider," may require anywhere from a month to a year, depending on the particular organization and individual. Socialization encompasses such formal and informal activities as learning the job and developing appropriate skills, forming new interpersonal relationships, and accepting the organization's culture and norms.

Meryl Reis Louis suggests that three features characterize the newcomer's entry experience:[16]

1. Change—the external, objective differences in moving from one organization to another (e.g., a change in such factors as physical location, title, and salary).

2. *Contrast*—differences between prior and present experiences the newcomer regards as personally significant (e.g., recent college graduates may contrast the frequent and relatively objective feedback about their performance in college courses with the less frequent and relatively subjective performance appraisals in their first job).

3. *Surprise*—the difference between the newcomer's expectations about the new organization and job and what he or she actually experiences in the new setting.

Surprises are often interpreted in the light of the newcomer's prior experience, which may be inappropriate to the new setting. Yet these interpretations, correct or incorrect, can lead to feelings of commitment to the organization or alienation from it. Individuals who expect to be competent job performers and perceive that they are not may experience considerable dissatisfaction with their job, the new organization, and even themselves. On the other hand, individuals who perceive themselves to be competent performers but who are disappointed with other aspects of the organizational milieu may spend more energy looking for a new employer than performing well on their job.

Such dysfunctional consequences for the newcomer and organization alike can be lessened through appropriate supervisory behavior. As Daniel C. Feldman points out, "The supervisor can make or break a newcomer's early career in an organization."[17] The supervisor, for instance, can facilitate socialization by training newcomers in job specifics; fostering links between newcomers and their coworkers; buffering newcomers from demands outside the work group so they can learn the job more quickly; and conducting early and frequent performance appraisals which give newcomers accurate assessments of their performance and help them channel their efforts in the proper direction.[18]

PERFORMANCE APPRAISAL

Nature of Performance Appraisal

Aside from its obvious utility in helping new employees understand the expectations of their supervisor and the organization, *performance appraisal* measures how effectively the organization's human resources are being used. As such, it is a form of control which compares measured performance with an established standard, resulting in corrective action, if necessary. Specifically, performance appraisal should

1. Provide feedback to each individual in the organization on his or her job performance. Most of us desire to know exactly "where we stand" and how our job performance is rated by our supervisor.

2. Link rewards, such as promotions or merit raises, to actual performance. In this vein, performance appraisal serves as a motivational tool.

3. Show the employee how to improve his or her performance. This use of performance appraisal has applications in training and developing the organization's human resources.

4. Help the organization comply with EEO programs.* EEO actions and judicial decisions have emphasized the need for organizations to maintain "accurate, objective records of employee performance to defend themselves against possible charges of discrimination in discharges, promotions, and/or salary increases."[19]

In most organizations, the immediate supervisor conducts a formal, systematic performance appraisal of subordinate employees. Some organizations supplement this evaluation, however, with appraisals by other managers familiar with the subordinate's performance or by the subordinate's peers in an attempt to reduce subjectivity.

The performance of most employees is evaluated on an annual basis. Although organizations should, logically, make the evaluation follow the completion of a major project—so that the appraisal is tied naturally to task completion—many schedule performance evaluations on arbitrary dates because it is more convenient. Hence, all employees may be evaluated after their first three months on the job and, thereafter, at yearly intervals.

Techniques of Performance Appraisal

The specific techniques of appraisal vary from organization to organization. Usually the appraisal is recorded on a form and shown to the employee. In some organizations, the superior and subordinate discuss the evaluation; in others, the subordinate simply signs the form, acknowledging having seen it. Some of the more widely discussed techniques of appraisal are examined below.

Conventional Rating Scale. The oldest and most often used appraisal technique is the *conventional rating scale,* illustrated in Figure 15–7. Although the exact form varies among organizations and among departments within an organization, the conventional rating scale usually contains a list of qualities, characteristics, or traits upon which the employee is to be rated on a scale ranging from "poor" to "outstanding." A common example is the instructor evaluation form filled out by students at the end of each term at most universities. The instructor may be rated

---

*One analysis of sixty-six court cases involving alleged discrimination in performance appraisal indicates that successful defenses of the charges were enhanced if the appraisal criteria were based on a job analysis; specific, objective performance criteria were used; specific written instructions had been given to the supervisors who conducted the appraisals; and the supervisors personally reviewed the appraisal results with the employee. See William H. Holley and Hubert S. Feild, "Will Your Performance Appraisal System Hold Up in Court?" *Personnel* 59 (January–February 1982): 61–63.

	(5) Outstanding	(4) Good	(3) Satisfactory	(2) Fair	(1) Poor	Not Observed
Job Knowledge						
Quality of Work						
Relationships with Subordinates						
Initiative						
Personal Appearance						
Cooperation						
Reliability						
Career Potential						

Name_____   Position_____

FIGURE 15–7   Example of a conventional rating scale

on such qualities as "presentation of material" and "preparation for class."

The major advantage of the conventional rating scale is the ease of developing it. The scale may be designed by the raters themselves, consultants, or the personnel department. Obviously, the qualities upon which the individual is to be rated must be directly related to effective performance. Personal appearance or initiative, for instance, are not equally important in all positions and may not even be necessary for effective performance in some jobs.

Aside from the difficult problem of deciding which qualities are essential to effective job performance, conventional rating scales are subject to a number of *rater weaknesses*. Raters, for instance, differ in their interpretations of "outstanding" and the standards they mentally establish for evaluating subordinates. Some may be lenient, much as the teacher who assigns "A"s to 40 percent of the class, while others may be "tough graders." If the rating period is one year, some raters may evaluate based on only the past few weeks' or months' performance (the *recency effect*). Some may fall victim to the *halo effect*, assigning the same rating to each quality being assessed.

Ranking.   To overcome some of these difficulties, some organizations have turned to *ranking*, a technique that requires the rater to rank his or her subordinates from highest to lowest, based on some criterion. The criterion, for instance, may be job performance, promotion potential, or ability to relate to clients. This technique makes it impossible for the rater to assign all subordinates an "outstanding" or an "average" rating. In others words, the rater is forced to compare subordinates and differentiate among them.

The use of this technique makes it difficult to give concrete feedback to employees, however. It may be hard to explain to an individual why he or she is ranked eighth instead of fifth. Also, the technique gives no consideration to the extent of differences between ranks. Is the difference between the top two employees the same as the difference between the ninth and tenth? Finally, ranking makes it difficult to compare employees in department A with those in department B. The top employee in department A, for example, might rank only fourth if he or she were in department B.

Behaviorally Anchored Rating Scales. In recent years, a new technique termed *behaviorally anchored rating scales* (BARS) or *behavioral expectation scales* (BES) has been devised to measure actual specific job behavior.[20] The scales are devised by the raters themselves and are intended to reduce subjective rater judgment. To develop the scales, the raters give examples of subordinate job behavior which is particularly effective or ineffective. Then specialists place these "critical incidents" into a smaller number of job dimensions. Another group of raters is then asked to categorize the incidents within each dimension from highly effective to grossly ineffective forms of behavior.[21] An example of the incidents within the dimension "meeting day-to-day deadlines" for a department manager in a retail store is shown in Figure 15–8. When numerically scaled, the behavior might range from one at the bottom to nine at the top.

The advantages of this technique are as follows:

1. BARS possesses the distinct legal strength of being based on an extensive job analysis.
2. The scales refer to actual observable job behavior which is related to effective performance.
3. The scales make clear what effective performance is and, hence, can be used to help employees improve their performance.
4. The scales are designed by the raters themselves and, therefore, should be more acceptable to them.

Additionally, there is some evidence that employees whose performance is evaluated on BARS scales view the appraisal process more favorably than do those who are rated on conventional rating scales.[22]

Unfortunately, BARS is expensive to develop (costing as much as $3,000 for a single job category[23]) and requires a substantial number of employees performing the same job (for instance, department managers in a large retail chain) before the technique becomes cost feasible. Research to date indicates that the extra cost may not be warranted for many organizations since the accuracy of BARS over other techniques has not yet been clearly demonstrated.[24]

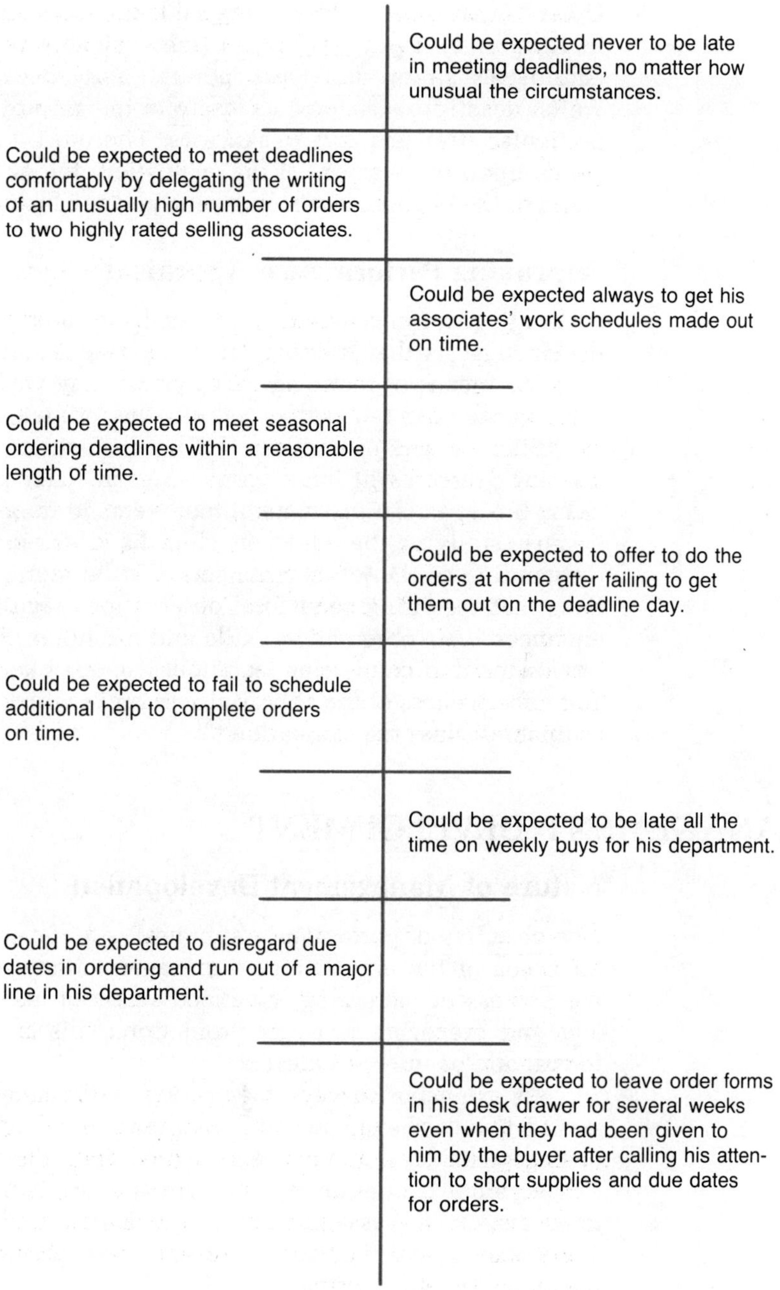

Could be expected never to be late
in meeting deadlines, no matter how
unusual the circumstances.

Could be expected to meet deadlines
comfortably by delegating the writing
of an unusually high number of orders
to two highly rated selling associates.

Could be expected always to get his
associates' work schedules made out
on time.

Could be expected to meet seasonal
ordering deadlines within a reasonable
length of time.

Could be expected to offer to do the
orders at home after failing to get
them out on the deadline day.

Could be expected to fail to schedule
additional help to complete orders
on time.

Could be expected to be late all the
time on weekly buys for his department.

Could be expected to disregard due
dates in ordering and run out of a major
line in his department.

Could be expected to leave order forms
in his desk drawer for several weeks
even when they had been given to
him by the buyer after calling his attention to short supplies and due dates
for orders.

FIGURE 15–8   Department manager job behavior rating scale
for the dimension, "Meeting Day-to-Day Deadlines"
SOURCE: John P. Campbell et al., *Managerial Behavior, Performance,
and Effectiveness* (New York: McGraw-Hill Book Co., 1970), p. 122.

Other Techniques.   Other appraisal techniques include *MBO* (discussed in Chapter 7), *essay evaluation* (the evaluator is asked to describe the employee's strong and weak points), and *checklist* (the rater checks which descriptive statements apply to the employee). Each has its own particular strengths and weaknesses. The most appropriate method depends upon the purpose of the evaluation, the nature of the job, preferences of the organization's members, and the history of the organization.

Improving Performance Appraisal

Although most organizations do not have rater training programs, evidence suggests that training improves rater accuracy. In fact, the most effective means of reducing rating errors may well be to concentrate on training the rater rather than refining the rating instrument. Alerting raters to the dangers of leniency and halo effect, for instance, leads to significant decreases in these forms of error. Rater participation in developing the appraisal instrument, too, seems to improve accuracy, perhaps because studying the job to develop the scales increases the rater's understanding of the job components. Furthermore, some supervisors believe that recording behavioral observations regularly in a formal diary enhances their observation skills and retention. Finally, training in interviewing and counseling techniques seems likely to improve the tone and effectiveness of the appraisal session in which the superior and subordinate discuss the evaluation.[25]

MANAGEMENT DEVELOPMENT

Nature of Management Development

One objective of performance appraisal is to determine the developmental needs of the organization's managers. *Management development* is the process of increasing the effectiveness of managers in their present jobs and preparing them for promotion. This is accomplished through formal and/or informal means.

An extensive survey of fifty-nine well-managed business firms revealed that, although no two companies used identical approaches to management development, most agreed that "the vast majority of actual development occurs on the job, through the handling of progressively more responsible assignments and problems under fire."[26] The respondents also agreed that formal development programs are valuable supplements to job experience.

Organizations can provide opportunities for management development, but cannot actually develop managers. The managers themselves must accomplish their own development. Sending a manager to a training conference, for example, is no guarantee of improved performance. If any real development is to occur, managers must assume some responsibility for their own progress. Of course, the organization can create the proper atmosphere, provide opportunities for development, and encourage interest in activities of this kind.

Management Development Methods

Job-Centered Training.   As we have seen, the most basic or fundamental approach to management development is that of managerial experience. The manager learns to manage by managing. Such experience may be more or less productive depending upon the type of direction and guidance provided by higher management. Extensive delegation of authority, for example, seeks to maximize development through managerial experience. A manager who has no opportunity to make significant decisions has little opportunity to develop decision-making ability.

Job Rotation.   One method of expanding direct job experience is to broaden that experience through a system of rotation. Such a job rotation plan seeks to maximize experience by shifting managers periodically from one job to another. Individuals selected for such programs are moved at the end of a stipulated period—say one year—and the positions they hold at any given time are viewed as training positions.

A less formalized variation of job rotation is also used by many organizations. In promotion and transfer decisions, an attempt is made to move individuals to facilitate their development. This system does not operate on a calendar basis, however, and there is no planned series of steps or transfers. A manager, for example, may fill a position in engineering for two or three years. If a vacancy occurs in sales or production management at the end of that time, consideration is given to shifting the engineering manager into such a position.

Supervisory Coaching.   The supervisory manager is expected to provide guidance to subordinates and serve as their role model. This function is considered so important that 92 percent of the firms in the survey mentioned above evaluate their middle- and upper-level managers on their abilities to develop subordinates.[27]

If coaching can be conducted in the right atmosphere, it provides an excellent type of developmental experience. Its major limitation is its dependence upon the skills of the coach. It has the practical advantage of being centered in the "real world"—the manager's work activities—and provides guidance from the one best able to evaluate performance and to supply help—the employee's superior. The requirement poses a problem for the superior, however, in that appraising and coaching may easily be viewed as critical and destructive rather than as helpful and motivating to the subordinate.

Training Conferences.   Managerial personnel are often brought together for training conferences. The purpose of such conferences is to impart knowledge or to improve skills of participants through lectures, case

studies, role playing, and videotaped simulations which allow participants to view and critique their own behavior. Conferences of this type
are particularly appropriate in cases in which a number of managers
have similar training needs.

Outside Developmental Activities.   Some organizations use outside activities or schools in supplementing inside development or in providing
training not available within the firm. Of particular interest are the management development programs conducted by university schools of business. These programs typically range from one to six or eight weeks in
length and deal with general aspects of administration. Many of them
use the case method of instruction extensively.

MANAGEMENT DEVELOPMENT BY COMPUTER

CBS operates its own management school to develop both upper-
level and entry-level managers. Part of the training for the latter
group, comprised of individuals who have little or no managerial decision-making experience, includes a number of simulated decision
situations based on actual occurrences in various CBS divisions. The
participants might be faced with decisions on how to allocate work
loads, how to set production quotas, how to determine pay raises for
subordinates, and so on.

Seated at computer terminals, the management trainees read the
facts of a particular situation and are then given several decision options to choose from. After they enter their decision into the computer, they are immediately given the outcome of their decision and
a new list of alternatives from which to choose.

For example, a trainee placed in the position of a regional sales
manager for a CBS magazine must decide what to do when a star
sales representative has been offered a higher salary by a competitor.
If the trainee decides to meet the competitive offer, the computer indicates that, although the sales representative stays with CBS, other
sales representatives will begin to demand more money. The trainee
must now decide whether to continue giving raises. Had the trainee
decided not to meet the competitive offer, the computer would indicate that the sales representative leaves CBS and that a replacement
must now be chosen from among three applicants.

At the end of each day, the trainees receive print-outs showing
how their decisions reflected their abilities to plan, set goals and
priorities, organize work, manage time, and supervise.

SOURCE: Based on "A Surprise CBS Morale-Booster," *Business Week*, 20 October
1980, p. 125.

Professional associations also provide training conferences for professional management personnel. Some are limited to such technical fields as engineering or accounting, whereas others deal with general problems of management. Participation in such conferences exposes a manager to current thinking and also provides contact with personnel from other organizations with similar problems.

Evaluating Development Programs

A recent survey of some of the largest companies in the United States indicates that the most common means of evaluating the effectiveness of development programs in forty-seven firms involved, in order, the following: (1) the judgment of higher-level management; (2) the judgment of participants either *after the program was over*, or (3) *at* the program's conclusion; and (4) the measurement of changes in on-the-job behavior or performance.[28] Although the judgments of upper-level managers and the perceptions of program participants are useful in evaluating program effectiveness, more objective job performance-related criteria are desirable. Participants can "feel good" about a program, yet fail to change their behavior on the job. Development is worth its cost if the job performance of the program participants improves significantly or if the participants are better prepared for promotion. Management needs to develop evaluation techniques which reflect the extent of these changes.

SUMMARY

Building an effective organizational team requires planning and control of its human resources. This process begins with a forecast of the organization's future personnel needs based upon an *analysis* of its job requirements, projections of turnover, and plans for growth. Once management has determined the number and types of positions to be filled over some span of time, the process of *recruiting* qualified applicants from a variety of sources to fill those positions begins. From the resulting applicant pool, those individuals estimated (through application blanks, background checks, tests, and interviews) to have the appropriate ability or potential ability are *selected*. Applicants are offered a certain level of *compensation*—salary and benefits—reflecting the relative worth of their jobs to the organization.

Once an individual has accepted the job offer, the employing organization is responsible for *orienting* the newcomer to the job and new surroundings and helping him or her become a part of the organization. The individual's *socialization* process can be aided through appropriate managerial actions, many of which depend upon the skill of the newcomer's supervisor.

Performance appraisal is a control technique designed to measure how effectively the organization's human resources are being used. Specifically, it provides feedback to employees concerning their performance and how it may be improved. A number of appraisal techniques are available to organizations. These include *conventional rating scales, ranking, behaviorally anchored rating scales,* and *MBO*—each with its own advantages and disadvantages.

Once the developmental needs of the organization's managers have been determined through performance appraisal, *management development,* the process of increasing managerial effectiveness and preparing managers for promotions, is begun. The most fundamental type of development is that which occurs in the actual performance of managerial duties. Regardless of what formal training opportunities may be provided by management, development must ultimately be *self-development.*

DISCUSSION QUESTIONS

1. What role does *job analysis* play in *human resource planning*?
2. Compare the advantages and difficulties in *recruiting* managerial personnel from competitive organizations.
3. Explain the *multiple-hurdles* model of *selection*.
4. Why is *interviewing* a subjective process? How can this subjectivity be reduced?
5. Besides paying employees "a fair day's wage for a fair day's work," what ends do organizations seek to attain through their *compensation* systems?
6. Distinguish between *orientation* and *socialization*. What role might the immediate supervisor play in facilitating both processes?
7. What are the purposes of performance appraisal?
8. How do *conventional rating scales* and *behaviorally anchored rating scales (BARS)* differ?
9. How might performance appraisal be improved?
10. Explain the reasoning underlying the concept or principle of *self-development* in managerial growth.
11. Describe the ideal conditions for effective on-the-job management development.

NOTES

1. Guvenc G. Alpander, "Human Resource Planning in U.S. Corporations," *California Management Review* 22 (Spring 1980): 24–32.

2. Based on Michael R. Carrell and Frank E. Kuzmits, *Personnel: Management of Human Resources* (Columbus, Oh.: Charles E. Merrill Publishing Co., 1982), p. 88.

3. There is some evidence to indicate that the source from which an employee is recruited is related to the employee's subsequent job performance, absenteeism, and work attitudes. See James A. Breaugh, "Relationships between Recruiting Sources and Employee Performance, Absenteeism, and Work Attitudes," *Academy of Management Journal* 24 (March 1981): 142–47.

4. For a review of the literature concerning student perceptions of college recruiters, see Sara L. Rynes, Herbert G. Heneman III, and Donald P. Schwab, "Individual Reactions to Organizational Recruiting: A Review," *Personnel Psychology* 33 (Autumn 1980): 529–42.

5. Frank S. Endicott, *The Endicott Report 1980* (Evanston, Ill.: The Placement Center, Northwestern University, 1979), p. 8.

6. See, for instance, John R. Hinrichs, "An Eight-Year Follow-up of a Management Assessment Center," *Journal of Applied Psychology* 63 (October 1978): 596–601; and Richard J. Klimoski and William J. Strickland, "Assessment Centers—Valid or Merely Prescient," *Personnel Psychology* 30 (Autumn 1977): 353–61.

7. George Strauss and Leonard R. Sayles, *Personnel: The Human Problems of Management*, 4th ed. (Englewood Cliffs, N.J.: Prentice-Hall, 1980), p. 371.

8. Carrell and Kuzmits, *Personnel*, p. 213.

9. Ibid., p. 215.

10. Richard D. Arvey and James E. Campion, "The Employment Interview: A Summary and Review of Recent Research," *Personnel Psychology* 35 (Summer 1982): 293.

11. Gary P. Latham, Lise M. Saari, Elliott D. Pursell, and Michael A. Campion, "The Situational Interview," *Journal of Applied Psychology* 65 (August 1980): 424.

12. Edward E. Lawler III, *Pay and Organization Development* (Reading, Mass.: Addison-Wesley Publishing Co., 1981), pp. 4–5, 31.

13. Carrell and Kuzmits, *Personnel*, pp. 426–35.

14. Lawler, *Pay and Organization Development*, pp. 34–35.

15. Paula Popovich and John P. Wanous, "The Realistic Job Preview as a Persuasive Communication," *Academy of Management Review* 7 (October 1982): 577.

16. Meryl Reis Louis, "Surprise and Sense Making: What Newcomers Experience in Entering Unfamiliar Organizational Settings," *Administrative Science Quarterly* 25 (June 1980): 226–51.

17. Daniel C. Feldman, "A Socialization Process That Helps New Recruits Succeed," *Personnel* 57 (March–April 1980): 22.

18. Ibid; and Louis, "Surprise and Sense Making," p. 247.

19. Alan H. Locher and Kenneth S. Teel, "Performance Appraisal—A Survey of Current Practices," *Personnel Journal* 56 (May 1977): 245.

20. A technical variation of this technique is known as behavioral observation scales (BOS). For an explanation of the differences, see Gary P. Latham, Charles H. Fay, and Lise M. Saari, "The Development of Behavioral Observation Scales for Appraising the Performance of Foremen," *Personnel Psychology* 32 (Summer 1979): 299–311.

21. A more complete and detailed description of the formulation of BARS may be found in John P. Campbell et al., *Managerial Behavior, Performance, and Effectiveness* (New York: McGraw-Hill Book Co., 1970), pp. 119–23.

22. John M. Ivancevich, "A Longitudinal Study of Behavioral Expectation Scales: Attitudes and Performance," *Journal of Applied Psychology* 65 (April 1980): 139–46.

23. "Appraising the Performance Appraisal," *Business Week*, 19 May 1980, p. 153.

24. Rick Jacobs, Ditsa Kafry, and Sheldon Zedeck, "Expectations of Behaviorally Anchored Rating Scales," *Personnel Psychology* 33 (Autumn 1980): 630; and Paul O. Kingstrom and Alan R. Bass, "A Critical Analysis of Studies Comparing Behaviorally Anchored Rating Scales (BARS) and Other Rating Formats," *Personnel Psychology* 34 (Summer 1981): 263–64.

25. For a discussion of rater training, see the following: Jacobs et al., "Expectations of Behaviorally Anchored Rating Scales," pp. 595–640; Frank J. Landy and James L. Farr, "Performance Rating," *Psychological Bulletin* 87 (January 1980): 71–107; and John M. Ivancevich, "Longitudinal Study of the Effects of Rater Training on Psychometric Error in Ratings," *Journal of Applied Psychology* 64 (October 1979): 502–8.

26. Lester A. Digman, "How Well-Managed Organizations Develop Their Executives," *Organizational Dynamics* 7 (Autumn 1978): 68.

27. Ibid.

28. Lester A. Digman, "How Companies Evaluate Management Development Programs," *Human Resource Management* 19 (Summer 1980): 9–13.

SUPPLEMENTARY READING

Arvey, Richard D., and Campion, James E. "The Employment Interview: A Summary and Review of Recent Research." *Personnel Psychology* 35 (Summer 1982): 281–322.

Beer, Michael. "Performance Appraisal: Dilemmas and Possibilities." *Organizational Dynamics* 9 (Winter 1981): 24–36.

Bernardin, H. John, and Buckley, M. Ronald. "Strategies in Rater Training." *Academy of Management Review* 6 (April 1981): 205–12.

Bluedorn, Allen C. "Managing Turnover Strategically." *Business Horizons* 25 (March/April 1982): 6–12.

Brinkerhoff, Derick W., and **Kanter, Rosabeth Moss.** "Appraising the Performance of Performance Appraisal." *Sloan Management Review* 21 (Spring 1980): 3–16.

Cederblom, Douglas. "The Performance Appraisal Interview: A Review, Implications, and Suggestions." *Academy of Management Review* 7 (April 1982): 219–27.

Coulson, Robert. "The Way It Is—Rules of the Game—How to Fire." *Across the Board* 19 (February 1982): 30–48.

Dalton, Dan R., and **Todor, William D.** "Turnover: A Lucrative Hard Dollar Phenomenon." *Academy of Management Review* 7 (April 1982): 212–18.

Dipboye, Robert L. "Self-Fulfilling Prophecies in the Selection-Recruitment Interview." *Academy of Management Review* 7 (October 1982): 579–86.

Feldman, Daniel C. "A Socialization Process That Helps New Recruits Succeed." *Personnel* 57 (March–April 1980): 11–23.

Holley, William H., and **Feild, Hubert S.** "Will Your Performance Appraisal System Hold Up in Court?" *Personnel* 59 (January–February 1982): 59–64.

Hollmann, Robert W. "Managing Troubled Employees: Meeting the Challenge." *Journal of Contemporary Business* 8 (4th quarter 1979): 43–57.

Kaye, Beverly L., and **Krantz, Shelley.** "Preparing Employees: The Missing Link in Performance Appraisal Training." *Personnel* 59 (May–June 1982): 23–29.

Lawler, Edward E. III. *Pay and Organization Development.* Reading, Mass.: Addison-Wesley Publishing Co., 1981.

Louis, Meryl Reis. "Surprise and Sense Making: What Newcomers Experience in Entering Unfamiliar Organizational Settings." *Administrative Science Quarterly* 25 (June 1980): 226–51.

Porras, Jerry I., and **Anderson, Brad.** "Improving Managerial Effectiveness through Model-Based Training." *Organizational Dynamics* 9 (Spring 1981): 60–77.

Schwartz, Stanley J. "How to Dehire: A Guide for the Manager." *Human Resource Management* 19 (Winter 1980): 22–25.

Skinner, Wickham. "Big Hat, No Cattle: Managing Human Resources." *Harvard Business Review* 59 (September–October 1981): 106–14.

Wanous, John P. *Organizational Entry: Recruitment, Selection, and Socialization of Newcomers.* Reading Mass.: Addison-Wesley Publishing Co., 1980.

16

JOBS, STRESS, AND THE QUALITY OF WORKING LIFE

This chapter will enable you to

- *Point out the reasons for job specialization and the problems associated with highly specialized jobs.*
- *Explain public concern with quality of working life and the contribution made by the redesign of jobs.*
- *Understand the nature of work-related stress and approaches to stress management.*
- *Outline the types of role conflict and the approaches useful in minimizing such conflict.*

Job design—deciding what activities will constitute individual jobs—is a basic part of the management of human resources. In this chapter, we focus on job content and consider the features of jobs that make them productive and enjoyable. This exploration leads to two related issues—stress and role conflict.

JOBS AND THE QUALITY OF WORKING LIFE

In designing jobs, managers must keep their eyes on two goals. First, they must create jobs which permit the organization to be productive. Second, they must create jobs that provide a suitable quality of working life—jobs which employees perceive as meaningful and satisfying.

Specifying Job Content

By deciding the duties to be included in a specific job, the manager specifies the role of the individual selected to fill that job. A *role* may be defined as the behavior or set of activities expected of a particular individual, the *focal* person. A typist, for example, may be expected to type letters, answer the telephone, obtain supplies for the office, and perform other specified duties. The technology of the organization and its overall structure and policies have much to do with the nature of individual jobs.

As a matter of fact, there are expectations of many groups and individuals, the *role set*, concerning the behavior of any one person. Figure

FIGURE 16–1 Role set and role
expectations

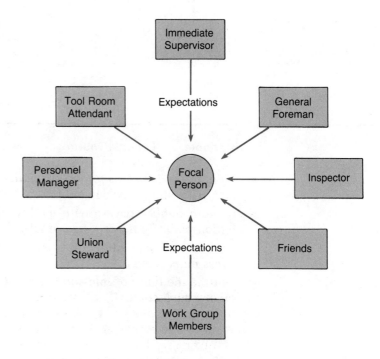

16–1 shows these relationships. Fellow employees and subordinates, for example, also expect the focal individual to behave in particular ways.

Management's definition of job requirements, then, establishes the formal organizational expectations concerning the focal person. This becomes a critical type of expectation as far as the employee's relationship with the employer is concerned. The employee must presumably fulfill these role requirements in some reasonable degree in order to continue employment and receive the normal rewards for satisfactory performance.

Job Descriptions

Organizations differ in the extent to which they formally specify duties. Duties are typically expressed in some detail in written form called a *job description*. Supervisors place their own interpretations on formal statements of expectations, however, so supervisory expectations are seldom completely specified by the job description. Others also develop individual expectations of appropriate behavior. We must beware of assuming that informal expectations are unimportant. Expectations of peers, for example, are often powerful determinants of individual behavior.

Technology and Job Design

As a small organization grows, some division of duties and specialization of work occur spontaneously. The efficiency derived from specialization of labor greatly impressed the famous economist Adam Smith as he observed the relatively simple process of manufacturing pins. Following is his well-known description of production in the pin factory:

> One man draws out the wire, another straights it, a third cuts it, a fourth points it, a fifth grinds it at the top for receiving the head; to make the head requires two or three distinct operations; to put it on is a peculiar business; to whiten the pins is another; it is even a trade by itself to put them into the paper. . . . I have seen a small manufactory of this kind where ten men only were employed, and where some of them consequently performed two or three distinct operations. But though they were very poor, and therefore but indifferently accommodated with the necessary machinery, they could, when they exerted themselves, make among them about twelve pounds of pins in a day. There are in a pound upwards of four thousand pins of a middling size. Those ten persons, therefore, could make among them upwards of forty-eight thousand pins in a day. . . . But if they all wrought separately and independently, . . . they certainly could not each of them have made twenty, perhaps not one pin in a day. . . .[1]

The scientific management movement also strongly emphasized work standardization. The employee was expected to perform the task in precisely the same way each time, using the method considered most efficient by a methods analyst. It was thought that employees would almost invariably follow less efficient methods if they were allowed to introduce innovations of their own.

The modern assembly line is an excellent example of the continued use of the principle of division of labor. Each employee has only one or a few minor functions in the assembly process to perform. It is this type of specialization in modern industry that has made possible its impressive growth in productivity.

Impact of Specialization on Employees

Historically, as managers sought to improve productivity, they divided jobs into smaller and smaller segments. Duties were grouped to provide homogeneity in the work of each individual. More difficult features were removed from the job and turned over to specialists. A setup specialist, for example, took over the more demanding duties of the machine operator, while the operator became a machine "tender."

While work specialization and standardization greatly increased productivity, as expected by the writers cited earlier, a number of negative results were also experienced.[2] From the standpoint of many workers, jobs became less attractive. Performing only a very specialized task gave them less feeling of accomplishment than they had enjoyed previously.

The extent of work dissatisfaction in America is not entirely clear, however, and it may be exaggerated somewhat in popular thinking. Individuals can adapt to various circumstances, including repetitive work, and many appear to be reasonably contented. A substantial percentage of the work force, in fact, consistently report being "satisfied" with their jobs.[3]

The definition of "satisfied," however, is not always clear. Many reportedly "satisfied" employees are far from enthusiastic about their work. Many such apparently contented employees may be unchallenged and underused, and they might respond positively to more meaningful work. Professionals, managers, and highly skilled personnel express more satisfaction that clerical and unskilled employees.[4] Even though the problem of dissatisfaction may be overstated, much dissatisfaction does exist, particularly in such cases as the highly routine assembly line.

Automobile assembly work has long been recognized as a prime example of extreme specialization—what some critics call "dehumanized work." In general, most automobile assembly jobs lack challenge, diversity, or opportunity for significant decision making. At the General Motors' plant in Lordstown, Ohio, one worker was quoted as follows:

> My former job at a steel mill was hot and dirty, but I felt like a man there. Here I feel like nothing.[5]

VIEWS OF WORK

Eric Hoffer:

"I can still savor the joy I used to derive from the fact that while doing dull, repetitive work on the waterfront, I could talk with my partners and compose sentences in the back of my mind, all at the same time."

B. C. Forbes:

"Whether we find pleasure in our work, or whether we find it a bore, depends entirely upon our mental attitude toward it, not upon the task itself."

Poem—"On Walking Through the Gate":

Easy, tedious work—
50 thousand ashtray doors and
100 thousand screws!
Childish, foolish, serious banter
As monotonous as the line—
Are these men—and women—
These workers of the world?
Or is it an overgrown nursery—
This factory—this automobile mill—

SOURCES: Eric Hoffer, *In Our Time* (New York: Harper & Row, Publishers, 1976), p. 6. "Thoughts on the Business of Life," *Forbes*, 1 September 1974, p. 104. "On Walking Through the Gate," *Life and Work* 14 (Winter 1974): 1.

The repetitive nature of specialized jobs becomes particularly objectionable to many employees. A given job may involve one operation, requiring only a few minutes or possibly just a few seconds, and be repeated over and over again. In addition, many such jobs are subject to continuous pacing by the assembly line. The problem is less one of physical fatigue than of boredom and pressure. The following comments are critical of the repetitive nature of highly routinized jobs:

> The casings were on rollers, so I merely pulled one in front of me, screwed in the plug, and pushed the casing on to the next worker. This process was repeated, as I recall, from 400 to 600 times daily. Although I could see at least 50 workers from my station, the noise was so great I had to yell to be heard by my nearest co-worker who was about eight feet away. These conditions made for a pretty lonely work day. I was constantly trying to devise some way to keep from getting overly bored. The work was completely dull, and effective communication was zero.

Not all employees experience such negative feelings about repetitive work, however. Some appreciate undemanding jobs which provide freedom for social interaction and opportunity to think about subjects unrelated to work. Feelings of employees about routine work apparently range from extremes of "intense dislike" to "appreciation." Between these extremes falls a substantial group who tolerate routine work, report "satisfaction," but lack enthusiasm for the job. The proportion of those who are bored and those who are "satisfied" but unchallenged seems large enough to justify the efforts of management to make work as meaningful as possible.

Work That Motivates Performance

As noted above, the influence of modern technology has led to many jobs which are boring and lacking in challenge. Public concern about the quality of working life is sometimes framed in terms of a right to *meaningful work*. Some jobs are seen as demeaning and inconsistent with the individual's worth and need for development.

What is it about work and people that result in a dispirited work force? What, in contrast, is necessary to make work both productive and satisfying? A stimulating analysis of this problem area has been conducted by J. Richard Hackman and Greg R. Oldham.[6] Their model of job characteristics and performance motivation is shown in Figure 16–2.

The middle section of Figure 16–2 deals with three important psychological states. The model suggests that these states must be present if there is to be high internal motivation. First, the work must be perceived as meaningful in terms of the individual's background and values. Second, the individual must feel some responsibility for the work. Third, there must be some knowledge of results. Hackman and Oldham illustrate these states by explaining the role of a college professor:

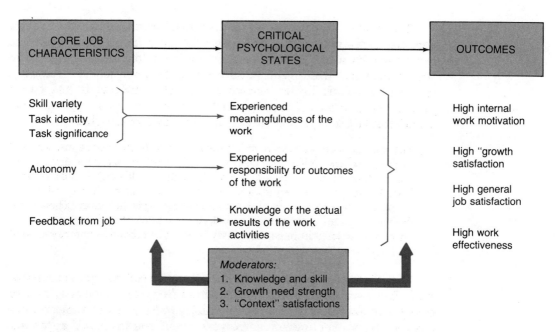

FIGURE 16–2   The complete job characteristics model
SOURCE: J. Richard Hackman and Greg R. Oldham, *Work Redesign.*
Addison-Wesley, Reading, Mass. Pp. 73 & 90. Reprinted with permission.

One of your authors, like many college teachers, finds that his day is made or broken by how well the morning lecture goes. The task is meaningful to him (he finds lecturing challenging and believes it to be important); he feels that the quality of the lecture is *his* responsibility (he's never quite learned how to attribute responsibility for a bad class to the students); and his knowledge of results is direct and unambiguous (undergraduates are expert in using subtle cues—and some not so subtle, such as newspaper reading—to signal how much they feel they are learning from the day's class). So all three of the psychological states are present in the lecturing task, and internal motivation to do well is very high indeed.[7]

As shown in the section of Figure 16–2 entitled "Core Job Characteristics," certain properties of the work itself contribute to these psychological states. Research has shown that three characteristics (skill variety, task identity, and task significance) are related to meaningfulness of work, that autonomy is related to feelings of responsibility, and that feedback is necessary for knowledge of actual results. The relationship of autonomy and feelings of responsibility is illustrated by Ian MacGregor's efforts, cited on page 237, to revitalize the British Steel Corporation. As the new chief executive officer, MacGregor sought to rebuild the morale of middle management by substantially increasing their authority.

Because people differ, they do not respond identically to core job characteristics. As shown in Figure 16–2, these differences ("moderators") relate to individual variations in knowledge and skill, growth need strength, and "context" satisfactions. The latter are concerned with the work environment—for example, the physical working conditions.

Evidence for the validity of the model is somewhat tentative. Hackman and Oldham believe that the available evidence shows the model to be more right than wrong.[8] However, they recognize its limitations and suggest it is best viewed as a guide for further research and as an aid in planning for changes in work systems.

Job Enrichment

As an offset to any technical gains through job specialization, we have seen that workers find the monotony and reduction of skill unpleasant. These are undesirable consequences for both the employee and the manager. In deciding the extent to which specialization should be carried, then, the manager must consider the matter from the standpoint of both engineering and human behavior.

Considerations of this type have led to efforts to restore variety and, more importantly, responsibility and self-determination to specialized jobs—in short, to despecialize them. This process became known as *job enlargement* or *job enrichment*. The latter term is preferable in emphasizing an increase in difficulty and responsibility in contrast to an increase in variety only. Job enrichment seeks to provide core job characteristics of the type proposed by the Hackman-Oldham model shown in Figure 16–2.

The American Telephone and Telegraph Company is one of the companies that has studied the practicality of job enrichment. The following account describes a job enrichment project in a subsidiary company:

> Through changing the work modules, Indiana Bell Telephone Company scored a striking success in job enrichment within the space of two years. In Indianapolis, 33 employees, most of them at the lowest clerical wage level, compiled all telephone directories for the state. The processing from clerk to clerk was laid out in 21 steps, many of which were merely for verification. The steps included manuscript reception, manuscript verification, keypunch, keypunch verification, ad copy reception, ad copy verification, and so on—a production line as real as any in Detroit. Each book is issued yearly to the customers named in it, and the printing schedule calls for the appearance of about one different directory per week. . . .
>
> In a workshop, the supervisors concluded that the lengthy verification routine, calling for confirmation of one's work by other clerks, was not solving the basic problem, which was employee indifference toward the tasks. Traditional "solutions" were ineffective. They included retraining, supervisor complaints to the employees, and "communicating" with them on the importance to customers of error-free listing of their names and places of business in the directories. As any employee smart enough to be hired knows, an incorrect listing will remain monumentally wrong for a whole year.

The supervisors came up with many ideas for enriching the job. The first step was to identify the most competent employees, and then ask them, one by one, if they felt they could do error-free work, so that having others check the work would be pointless. Would they check their own work if no one else did it?

Yes, they said they could do error-free work. With this simple step the module dropped from 21 slices of clerical work to 14.[9]

Employees were subsequently given their own books and performed all 14 remaining steps without verification unless they themselves arranged it. The new arrangement became so efficient that some clerks had charge of more than one book, and each clerk expressed satisfaction with having control over a complete module of work—"a book of my own."

Although instances of job enrichment have been well publicized, the total number of workers affected to date is relatively small. And not all employees want enriched jobs.

Six Detroit auto workers were flown to Sweden and spent a month working as engine assemblers in a Saab plant. At the end of the month, five of the six workers reported that they preferred the U.S. assembly line.[10]

Furthermore, some attempts at job enrichment have failed. In one insurance company, for example, results of the job enrichment program were so disappointing that management abandoned the project one year after implementing it.[11] A primary cause was management's failure to compensate employees adequately for their increased responsibilities. Clearly, job enrichment is no panacea and requires the same type of

VOLVO'S USE OF JOB ENRICHMENT

One of the most widely reported examples of assembly line reorganization is that of Volvo, the Swedish auto manufacturer. Starting with the construction of its new Kalmar factory, Volvo broke up the assembly line system in which employees are paced by the line. The work was organized so that each work group was responsible for a particular, identifiable portion of the car—electrical systems, interiors, doors, and so on. Each work group, furthermore, had its own buffer areas for incoming and outgoing cars and could pace itself and organize its work internally as it wished. Although the new plants are a little more costly to build, Volvo reports that they have shown good productivity, and they expect productivity to increase.

SOURCE: One of many accounts of Volvo's work reorganization is Pehr G. Gyllenhammar, "How Volvo Adapts Work to People," *Harvard Business Review* 55 (July–August 1977): 102–13.

management commitment, diagnosis, and patient discussion as that required in other types of organizational change.

In deciding the extent to which job enrichment will be used, managers must consider the following factors:

1. Education and experience of employees.
2. Employee readiness for participation and need for autonomy.
3. Technology of the work process.
4. The organization's management philosophy and extent to which it accepts a participative approach.

The job enrichment efforts described above were directed at the improvement of individual jobs. Managers and researchers seeking to enhance the quality of working life have also discovered the importance of autonomous work groups in making working life more attractive. This adds the improvement of interpersonal relationships as a supplement to the improvement of individual job components. The topic of work group design was discussed in Chapter 14.

Flexitime and the Compressed Work Week

Another approach to improving the quality of working life involves the modification of traditional work schedules. *Flexitime*, for example, substitutes individual work schedules for one uniform schedule applicable to all personnel. Even on the same shift, some employees may begin work at 7:00 A.M., some at 8:00 A.M., some at 9:00 A.M., and so on. Normally, there is a central period of the day during which all personnel are present.

In contrast to flexitime, the *compressed work week* requires longer work days but fewer days per week. Four ten-hour days, for example, may be substituted for the traditional five eight-hour days.

Some types of work obviously lend themselves to flexible scheduling much more than others. Flexitime, for example, could not be used in cases where a number of employees must constantly work together as a team. Also, the four-day week may create problems for organizations which must remain open and service customers five days per week.

These systems of work scheduling have met with some success, particularly in terms of employee attitudes. Research studies of flexitime, though limited in number, have reported favorable employee reactions (for example, easier travel and less need for unpaid absences) and possible (but unproven) improvement in productivity.[12] Studies of the compressed work week similarly indicate that employee attitudes have been favorable. Performance results are ambiguous, however, as they are with flexitime. Some studies show an improvement in productivity, but others show no effect or even detrimental effects.[13] Fatigue seems to be the primary negative aspect of the longer day.

STRESS MANAGEMENT

One feature of most jobs is the pressure they create for incumbents. Employees are impelled, either by themselves or by supervisors, to fulfill work assignments and to respond to time deadlines. The effect of these and other tension-producing aspects of work results in a condition called *stress*. Although stress is not a new phenomenon, its human and economic cost is becoming increasingly apparent.

The Nature of Stress

Stress is a part of any productive life, and everyone experiences a degree of tension as a part of living and working. In some cases, of course, the tension becomes so great as to be harmful. Our response to the minor and major pressures of life—the tension we feel—constitutes stress.

Some, but not all, stress is centered in the individual's work life. It may also be caused by events and circumstances related to family, friends, and the outside world. An employee, for example, may be sensitive to supervisory pressure to meet output quotas, fearful of a child's involvement with drugs, and troubled by the prospect of nuclear war. The resultant feelings, with all of the psychological and physiological aspects, are the stress felt by that employee. (In this discussion, we are particularly concerned with job stress.) Stress occurs when one's equilibrium is disturbed. The initial response to danger has been described by many as a fight-or-flight reaction. The person who meets a tiger in the jungle has only two options. Adrenalin flows, and the problem is quickly resolved in one of these ways. But the person who meets a "tiger" in the office often faces a more complex situation. Stress builds up, because it is difficult either to fight or to flee.

The consequences of job stress are both physiological and psychological. Numerous physical disorders are related to stress, including cardiovascular disease, gastrointestinal problems, headaches, backaches, skin disorders, and so on. The psychological consequences include feelings of depression, anxiety, and nervousness.

Stress at Work

Some stress is clearly beneficial. The stress produced by a college test, for example, may contribute to learning. If the stress is not too extreme, in other words, it can stimulate motivation and achievement. Figure 16–3 shows the relationship of stress to efficient performance. It is the right-hand half of the curve that involves danger—the extreme stress that is dysfunctional in leading to less effective performance.

Employees who are working under extreme stress cannot function effectively. They may lose interest in work, experience difficulty in making decisions, become forgetful, find it difficult to concentrate, and/or resort to alcohol or tranquilizers. Eventually, they may reach a condition described as *burnout*. In burnout, the stress becomes so severe that the

FIGURE 16–3   Relationship of
stress to performance

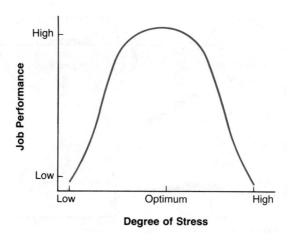

victim becomes virtually incapacitated. The following account describes such a situation:

> A vice president of a large corporation who didn't receive an expected promotion left his company to become the CEO of a smaller, family-owned business, which was floundering and needed his skills. Although he had jumped at the opportunity to rescue the small company, once there he discovered an unimaginable morass of difficulties, among them continuous conflicts within the family. He felt he could not leave; but neither could he succeed. Trapped in a kind of psychological quicksand, he worked nights, days, and weekends for months trying to pull himself free. His wife protested, to no avail. Finally, he was hospitalized for exhaustion.[14]

Causes of Stress

A *stressor* is the external agent which disturbs the individual's equilibrium. Stress, as explained earlier, is the individual's response to such an external threat. If your supervisor says, "I want that project completed by tomorrow, or I want to know the reason why," he or she places you in a stressful situation. Individual differences are obviously important in determining the significance of particular stressors. A supervisory comment like that above will be taken much more seriously by an insecure, timid employee than by a self-confident, outgoing type.

Figure 16–4 pictures some of the many types of stressors operating within the organization. Some, such as noise, are related to the physical environment. Others, such as dual supervision, entail role conflict. A number, such as heavy work load, are related to the individual job. In summary, potential stressors are found in all aspects of work, including job demands, group relationships, and organizational policies. In addition, there are many outside sources of stress such as those associated with family life.

Although there are numerous sources of stress in modern life, job-related factors are apparently among the most important causes. In a study of 196 senior managers in England, 57 percent of those experienc-

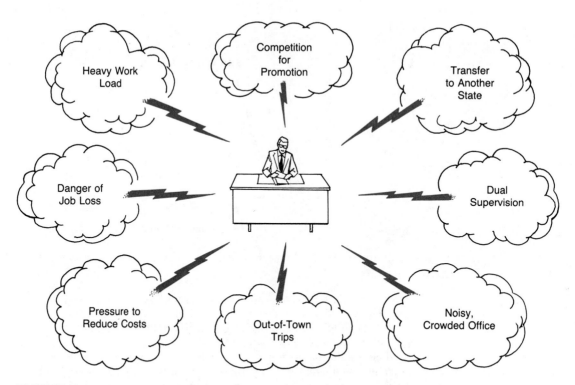

FIGURE 16–4   Stressors at work

ing stress cited work as the primary cause.[15] Family problems were cited by 45 percent of those experiencing stress. We can readily see the possibility that work problems and family problems may affect each other.

Managing Stress

Some steps to minimize stress must be implemented by the individual—for example, physical exercise. (Even though exercise must be accomplished by the individual, many employers provide gymnasiums and/or encourage exercise in other ways.) A variety of relaxation techniques such as transcendental meditation, yoga, and biofeedback have also been suggested as stress-reduction methods. One chief executive, George F. Bennett of State Street Investment Corporation, was quoted in *Harvard Business Review* regarding his personal approach to meditation:

> "I have been an evangelical Christian all my life. I believe in prayer and reading the Bible daily. I realize the strength and the peace and tranquility you can get from taking your eye off the business ball for just a few minutes by praying or reading the Bible."[16]

Other types of stress-reduction methods would involve management. Control of noise and temperature, for example, may require modification of physical facilities. Many practices that might be labeled as good management—such as minimizing role conflict, providing for effective communication, and outlining career development plans—would reduce substantially the level of stress in many organizations.

THE PROBLEM OF ROLE CONFLICT

One of the important sources of stress is role conflict. Research has shown that individuals subjected to role conflict tend to experience stress and job dissatisfaction.[17] The following discussion presents a number of types of role conflict and provides suggestions for limiting such conflict. A more extended discussion of conflict resolution was given in Chapter 12.

Individual-Role Conflict

Managers try to match employees to jobs—to get a good fit between employee capacity, interests, and values on the one hand and job requirements on the other. This task is not easy to accomplish, however. As shown in Figure 16–5, employees may be overqualified or underqualified, and either condition produces a poor fit.

An unchallenging, boring job leads to one type of *individual-role conflict.* Such jobs require so little ability that employees perceive themselves as underused. On the other hand, an individual may lack necessary skills for a particular job. Vocational or other personal interests may also conflict with the attributes of particular jobs. Another variety of this type of conflict occurs when organizations encroach on the personal life and values of the individual—for example, demanding that a manager sign contracts or engage in behavior that violates the manager's own code of ethics.

Designing jobs to fit individual talents provides one type of solution to individual-role conflict. Although this solution has been applied in many individual instances, it demands more organizational flexibility than is commonly found. Some adaptation of job requirements to meet personal needs is possible, but some adaptation of individuals to meet job demands is also expected. Job enrichment attempts to upgrade the level of work generally on the assumption that most jobs are far below the talents of the typical employee.

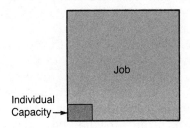
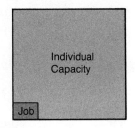

FIGURE 16–5   Individual-role conflict

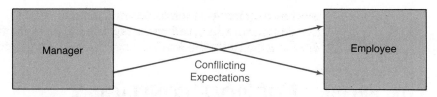

FIGURE 16–6   Intrasender role conflict

Intrasender Role Conflict

Management expectations regarding employee behavior are not always consistent. Individual employees may simply be asked to go in two directions at the same time or to perform in two contradictory ways, as shown in Figure 16–6. In such cases, the job is irrationally designed so that a qualified individual cannot fill it satisfactorily. The inconsistencies may not be recognized by managers, but they are painfully clear to role incumbents.

An employee's supervisor, for example, may expect performance results that are simply impossible—such as an output rate that can be achieved only by dropping quality below an acceptable level. In a college or university context, a board of trustees may hold a president responsible for improving the quality of instruction while simultaneously holding the line on expenses. In other words, the president may be denied the financial resources necessary to accomplish what the board demands. Such discrepancies in expectations are no doubt overlooked or rationalized in some way by managers.

Correction of this inconsistency in management expectations requires managers to impose self-discipline in their own expectations regarding the performance of subordinates. Managers often wish to be "tough minded" and to obtain high levels of performance. They feel they cannot afford to be overly lenient, therefore, and to tolerate a soft and flabby organization. There is a difference, however, between tough-mindedness and inconsistent expectations. The latter is, at best, irrational. A job should be defined with internal consistency.

Intersender Role Conflict

In some cases, the incumbent may receive supervision or direction from two or more managers, as portrayed in Figure 16–7. For example, a technical or professional employee may receive "technical" directions from a technical specialist and "general" directions from an administrative manager. Or, an employee may receive directions directly from two or more levels of management.

Intersender role conflict may develop in many ways. A classic case is that of the first-line supervisor, who has frequently been described as "the man in the middle." Subordinates look to the supervisor to represent them to higher levels of organization and expect the supervisor to "go to bat" for them at times. Higher levels of management, however, see

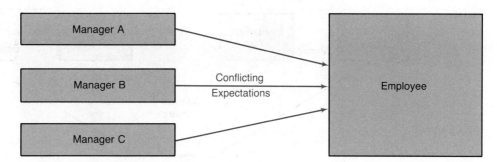

FIGURE 16–7   Intersender role conflict

the first-line supervisor as their representative in dealing with and occasionally "laying down the law" to indifferent employees.

A general manager of a corporate division faces a similar dilemma of conflicting expectations. The following situation in an international company illustrates the problem:

> Headquarters restricted the freedom of one division manager to purchase from the outside, an order which threatened to undermine his authority as a general manager. He was torn between the dilemma of (a) asserting his authority with his subordinates by ignoring or fighting headquarters' orders, or (b) weakening his image as a superior by following headquarters' orders. Being a good subordinate would have weakened him as a superior; yet, by being a strong superior, he would have been a disloyal subordinate. As it turned out, the general manager held prolonged negotiations with a peer in the pooled sales force to arrive at a mutually satisfactory solution, but this made the general manager appear inconclusive and indecisive to his subordinates.[18]

"Boundary" roles, that is, those jobs at the interface of two or more organizations, are more likely to be conflict ridden.[19] The incumbent is subject to tugging or pressure from more than one direction and to a sense of being in the middle. An example of a boundary role is that of a purchasing agent who must work with production personnel on the inside of a company and with vendors on the outside.

Part of the solution to the problem of intersender role conflict is found in careful organizational design. Supervision of jobs can be structured to minimize multiple lines of command. Other cases require a better understanding of organizational complexity—such as the interfacing "boundary" role of a first-line supervisor or division general manager—and an agreement on organizational goals.[20] Some, but not all, of the intersender role conflict, in other words, may be avoided by careful designing of jobs and proper structuring of organizational relationships.

Interrole Conflict

Any employed individual fills more than one role. An individual may simultaneously fill the role of manager, husband or wife, civic leader,

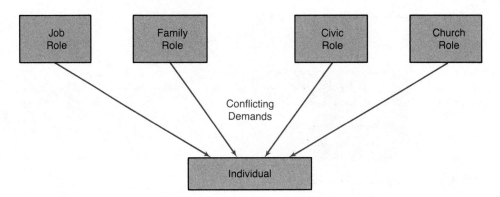

FIGURE 16–8   Interrole conflict

and church official. At times, demands from these different roles conflict as illustrated in Figure 16–8. A frequent clash, for example, occurs between demands of the organization and demands of the family. Even within an employing organization, an individual may occasionally be expected to fill more than one role—for example, professor and department chairman in a college or university.

The issues of *interrole conflict* obviously go beyond the boundaries of any one organization. In general, we are concerned with the balance between organizational commitment and other interests of the individual. The job designer must exercise some discretion in the extent of demands upon the total life of the individual.

Clarity in Job Demands

A related problem is that of *role ambiguity*. An individual may not quite know what is expected of him or her. Students often protest that teachers give confusing assignments, and employees find that their supervisors are less than crystal clear.

Studies have shown significant relationships between role clarity and such factors as general job interest and job tension.[21] Role clarity is particularly helpful to employees having a high need for role clarity in making them more innovative, more satisfied, less tense, and less inclined to leave. Such research confirms the commonsense notion that some individuals would experience great discomfort with extreme vagueness in job requirements. This does not prove the need for preparing job descriptions with maximum detail, but it does suggest the danger of excessive looseness in role specification, especially with employees who need more clarity.

Proper stipulation of job requirements should reduce the ambiguity in any particular job. Much of the haze surrounding jobs results from management carelessness in job design.

SUMMARY

By creating jobs and specifying job content, management creates organizational *roles*. These are the sets of behaviors or activities expected of individual members of the organization. The underlying technology and quest for efficiency tend to force an oversimplification of jobs, a reduction in the range of duties, and a lowering of skill demands.

The extreme forms of specialization and the standardization of work create monotony, boredom, and reduced job satisfaction for employees. In response to dissatisfaction of this type, employees naturally seek a higher *quality of working life*. Scholars have identified key characteristics of attractive jobs (as in the Hackman-Oldham model), and many managers have used *job enrichment* programs in an attempt to restore desired job characteristics. *Flexitime* and the *compressed work week* have also been introduced to improve further the quality of working life.

Jobs frequently involve pressures which cause tension or *stress*. Some stress is productive, but excessive stress is harmful to the individual and the organization. Many elements of the job and workplace act as *stressors* on the individual. Reduction of stress is possible through such individual efforts as physical exercise and through such organizational efforts as reducing role conflict.

Creation of jobs also involves a problem of *role conflict* and *role ambiguity*. Individual members of organizations often face conflicting or vague role expectations. These take such forms as *individual-role conflict*, *intrasender role conflict*, *intersender role conflict*, *interrole conflict*, and *role ambiguity*. Some of these difficulties may be minimized, if not eliminated, by careful formulation of job requirements.

DISCUSSION QUESTIONS

1. Explain and give examples of the meaning of the following terms: *role, focal person, role set.*
2. If a job description exists, is the role of the job incumbent completely defined by this description?
3. What explains the historic trend toward narrowing the scope of industrial jobs?
4. How is the thinking of Adam Smith, an economist, related to organizational theory?
5. Why are automobile manufacturers interested in the "quality of working life"?
6. Evaluate the impact of work specialization upon employees.
7. What generalizations can be made about the extent of worker dissatisfaction in America?
8. Explain the following concepts as they relate to the Hackman-Oldham

model of job characteristics in Figure 16–2 (p. 348): *core job characteristics; critical psychological states; outcomes;* and *moderators.*

9. What is the purpose of job enrichment and how does it differ from job enlargement?
10. What are *flexitime* and the *compressed work week?* How do they relate to job enrichment?
11. How is stress related to job performance?
12. Identify a number of *stressors* that exist in most work organizations.
13. Explain the concept of individual-role conflict and give an example.
14. What is intrasender role conflict, and how can it possibly exist in rational organizations?
15. How does the foreman provide a good example of intersender role conflict?
16. Explain the meaning of interrole conflict.

NOTES

1. From Adam Smith: *The Wealth of Nations, Representative Selections,* edited by Bruce Mazlish, copyright © by The Bobbs-Merrill Co., Inc., p. 5. Reprinted by permission of the Liberal Arts Press Division.
2. For a stimulating discussion of the seriousness of this problem and the extent to which employees *need* involvement in their work, see Robert Dubin, *Human Relations in Administration,* 4th ed. (Englewood Cliffs, N.J.: Prentice-Hall, 1974), pp. 125–29.
3. See J. Richard Hackman, "The Design of Work in the 1980s," *Organizational Dynamics,* Summer 1978, pp. 3–5; and Sar A. Levitan and William B. Johnston, *Work Is Here to Stay Alas* (Salt Lake City: Olympus Publishing Co., 1973), p. 70.
4. Sar A. Levitan and William B. Johnston, *Work Is Here to Stay Alas,* pp. 70–75.
5. "The Spreading Lordstown Syndrome," *Business Week,* 4 March 1972, p. 69.
6. J. Richard Hackman and Greg R. Oldham, *Work Redesign* (Reading, Mass.: Addison-Wesley Publishing Co., 1980).
7. Ibid., p. 73.
8. Ibid., pp. 95–97. See also Ricky W. Griffin, "A Longtitudinal Investigation of Task Characteristics Relationships," *Academy of Management Journal* 24 (March 1981): 99–113; and Karlene H. Roberts and William Glick, "The Job Characteristics Approach to Task Design: A Critical Review," *Journal of Applied Psychology* 66 (April 1981): 193–217.
9. Robert N. Ford, "Job Enrichment Lessons from AT&T," *Harvard Business Review* 51 (January–February 1973): 97.
10. Hackman, "The Design of Work in the 1980s," p. 4.
11. Paul J. Champagne and Curt Tausky, "When Job Enrichment Doesn't Pay," *Personnel* 55 (January–February 1978): 30–40. Also see William A. Pas-

more, "Overcoming the Roadblocks in Work-Restructuring Efforts," *Organizational Dynamics* 10 (Spring 1982): 54–67; J. Richard Hackman, "Is Job Enrichment Just a Fad?" *Harvard Business Review* 53 (September–October 1975): 129–38; and Noel M. Tichy, "When Does Work Restructuring Work? Organizational Innovations at Volvo and GM," *Organizational Dynamics* 5 (Summer 1976): 63–80; George W. Bohlander, "Implementing Quality-of-Work Programs: Recognizing the Barriers," *MSU Business Topics* 27 (Spring 1979): 35–40.

12. See William D. Hicks and Richard J. Klimoski, "The Impact of Flexitime on Employee Attitudes," *Academy of Management Journal* 24 (June 1981): 333–41; and Jay S. Kim and Anthony F. Campagna, "Effects of Flexitime on Employee Attendance and Performance: A Field Experiment," *Academy of Management Journal* 24 (December 1981): 729–41.

13. Simcha Ronen and Sophia B. Primps, "The Compressed Work Week as Organizational Change: Behavioral and Attitudinal Outcomes," *Academy of Management Review* 6 (January 1981): 61–74.

14. Harry Levinson, "When Executives Burn Out," *Harvard Business Review* 59 (May–June 1981): 74.

15. Cary L. Cooper, *Executive Families under Stress: How Male and Female Managers Can Keep Their Pressures Out of Their Homes* (Englewood Cliffs, N.J.: Prentice-Hall, 1981), p. 20.

16. Herbert Benson and Robert L. Allen, "How Much Stress Is Too Much?" *Harvard Business Review* 58 (September–October 1980): 92.

17. See, for example, Thomas W. Johnson and John E. Stinson, "Role Ambiguity, Role Conflict, and Satisfaction: Moderating Effects of Individual Differences," *Journal of Applied Psychology* 60 (June 1975): 329–33.

18. Hugo E. R. Uyterhoeven, "General Managers in the Middle," *Harvard Business Review* 50 (March–April 1972): 77.

19. See Daniel Katz and Robert L. Kahn, *The Social Psychology of Organizations*, 2d ed. (New York: John Wiley & Sons, 1978), p. 210.

20. For further reading, see Roberta G. Simmons, "The Role Conflict of the First-Line Supervisor: An Experimental Study," *American Journal of Sociology* 73 (January 1968): 482–95.

21. John M. Ivancevich and James H. Donnelly, Jr., "A Study of Role Clarity and Need for Clarity for Three Occupational Groups," *Academy of Management Journal* 17 (March 1974): 28–36.

SUPPLEMENTARY READING

Alber, Antone F. "The Real Cost of Job Enrichment." *Business Horizons* 22 (February 1979): 60–72.

Alber, Antone F., and **Blumberg, Melvin.** "Team vs. Individual Approaches to Job Enrichment Programs." *Personnel* 58 (January–February 1981): 63–75.

Brousseau, Kenneth R. "Toward a Dynamic Model of Job-Person Relationships: Findings, Research Questions, and Implications for Work System Design." *Academy of Management Review* 8 (January 1983): 33–45.

Cooper, Cary L., and **Davidson, Marilyn J.** "The High Cost of Stress on Women Managers." *Organizational Dynamics* 10 (Spring 1982): 44–53.

Davis, Louis E. "Job Design: Overview and Future Direction." *Journal of Contemporary Business* 6 (Spring 1977): 85–102.

Griffin, Ricky W.; Welsh, Ann; and **Moorhead, Gregory.** "Perceived Task Characteristics and Employee Performance: A Literature Review." *Academy of Management Review* 6 (October 1981): 655–64.

Hackman, J. Richard. "The Design of Work in the 1980's." *Organizational Dynamics* 7 (Summer 1978): 3–17.

Hackman, J. Richard, and **Oldham, Greg R.** *Work Redesign.* Reading, Mass.: Addison–Wesley Publishing Co., 1980.

Herzberg, Frederick, and **Zautra, Alex.** "Orthodox Job Enrichment: Measuring True Quality in Job Satisfaction." *Personnel* 53 (September–October 1976): 54–68.

Ivancevich, John M., and **Matteson, Michael T.** "Optimizing Human Resources: A Case for Preventive Health and Stress Management." *Organizational Dynamics* 9 (Autumn 1980): 5–25.

———. *Stress and Work: A Managerial Perspective.* Glenview, Ill.: Scott, Foresman and Co., 1980.

Kim, Jay S., and **Campagna, Anthony F.** "Effects of Flexitime on Employee Attendance and Performance: A Field Experiment." *Academy of Management Journal* 27 (December 1981): 729–41.

Levinson, Harry. "When Executives Burn Out." *Harvard Business Review* 59 (May–June 1981): 73–81.

Miles, Robert H., and **Perreault, William D., Jr.** "Organizational Role Conflict: Its Antecedents and Consequences." *Organizational Behavior and Human Performance* 17 (October 1976): 19–44.

Oldham, Greg R.; Hackman, J. Richard; and **Pearce, Jone L.** "Conditions Under Which Employees Respond Positively to Enriched Work." *Journal of Applied Psychology* 61 (August 1976): 395–403.

Pasmore, William A. "Overcoming the Roadblocks in Work–Restructuring Efforts." *Organizational Dynamics* 10 (Spring 1982): 54–67.

Pearce, Jone L. "Bringing Some Clarity to Role Ambiguity Research." *Academy of Management Review* 6 (October 1981): 665–74.

Poza, Ernesto J., and **Markus, M. Lynne.** "Success Story: The Team Approach to Work Restructuring." *Organizational Dynamics* 8 (Winter 1980): 3–25.

Runcie, John F. "By Days I Make the Cars." *Harvard Business Review* 58 (May–June 1980): 106–15.

Sailer, Heather R.; Schlacter, John; and **Edwards, Mark R.** "Stress: Causes, Consequences, and Coping Strategies." *Personnel* 59 (July–August 1982): 35–48.

Schuler, Randall S. "Role Conflict and Ambiguity as a Function of the Task-Structure-Technology Interaction." *Organizational Behavior and Human Performance* 20 (October 1977): 66–74.

Sell, Mary Van; Brief, Arthur P.; and **Schuler, Randall S.** "Role Conflict and Role Ambiguity: Integration of the Literature and Directions for Future Research." *Human Relations* 34 (January 1981): 43–71.

Smith, Howard R. "The Half-Loaf of Job Enrichment." *Personnel* 53 (March–April 1976): 24–31.

_____. "The Uphill Struggle for Job Enrichment." *California Management Review* 23 (Summer 1981): 33–38.

Terkel, Studs. *Working: People Talk about What They Do All Day and How They Feel about What They Do.* New York: Pantheon Books, 1974.

Whetten, David A. "Coping with Incompatible Expectations: An Integrated View of Role Conflict." *Administrative Science Quarterly* 23 (June 1978): 254–71.

17

ORGANIZATION CHANGE AND DEVELOPMENT

This chapter will enable you to

- *Understand the pressures and opportunities that create the need for organizational change.*
- *Identify and discuss the steps involved in a program of planned organizational change.*
- *Explain organization development, a type of change program that focuses on human behavior and interaction.*
- *Become familiar with the concept of organizational effectiveness.*

As anyone who has lived through the turbulent times of the past two decades can attest, change resulting from an increasingly dynamic environment is an inescapable part of our lives. Organizations, of course, are affected by the same forces and must change in order to remain effective. This chapter examines the *forces* that provide the impetus for organizational change and the *programs* for introducing such changes. The third section of this chapter introduces you to the field of *organization development* and the role it plays in planned organizational change. Finally, we examine the ultimate goal of planned change—maintaining the organization's *effectiveness.*

FORCES FOR CHANGE

A number of basic forces, individually or in combination, can lead to significant change within an organization. One broad set of forces consists of pressures or opportunities which arise from outside the firm. Another set is comprised of internal pressures or opportunities. This section examines both of these forces. Figure 17–1 illustrates many of the major external and internal forces for change that affect contemporary organizations.

External Forces

The purpose of monitoring the environment is to help management detect events which require some form of organization change. In some cases, environmental *pressures* adversely alter the "fit" between the organization and its environment. At one time, for example, the matrix

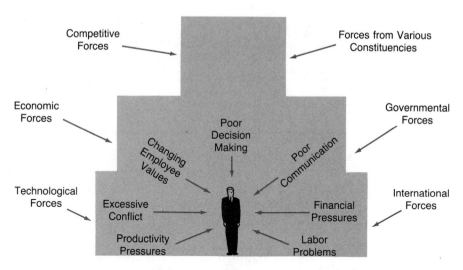

FIGURE 17–1   Internal and external forces for change

management structure and corporate planning system of Texas Instruments were the envy of its competitors. By 1982, however, TI had lost its long-time sales leadership position in the U. S. semiconductor market to Motorola, had seen profits decline for six consecutive quarters, and had experienced delayed product introductions and missed opportunities. An analysis of its way of operating led top management to modify the organization. The extensive changes included establishing new profit centers, each encompassing a complete business, and decentralizing decision making by giving the profit center managers complete control over their resources (rather than having to borrow them from centralized functional areas). Management felt that such extensive changes were necessary to enable TI to meet the competition.[1] Actions such as these are termed *reactive change*. The organization reacts, or responds, to environmental pressures.

In other situations, management's monitoring activities may reveal environmental *opportunities which* can be exploited. In such cases, management initiates change by leading the organization in new directions to maintain its competitive edge. Such actions reflect a strategy of *proactive change*.

Any number of external forces can lead to reactive or proactive organizational change. Undeniably, one of the most prominent forces in recent years has been technology. Increasing knowledge and technological advances in semiconductors and microcircuitry, for instance, have provided the opportunity for enterprising inventors and entrepreneurs to create a new industry in personal computers. This development, in turn, is enabling progressive banks, retail stores, and real estate agencies to devise means by which their customers can transfer funds, make purchases, or shop for new houses without having to leave their homes. Technological change, in some cases, has proceeded with unbelievable rapidity.

PROACTIVE CHANGE

For almost 140 years, Dun & Bradstreet Corporation, a wide-ranging information services company, has been a financially successful firm. Among its many products and services, D&B provides financial and credit information; collection services; market research and electronic data processing systems development; group insurance to small businesses; "Yellow Pages" sales representation; management, marketing, and information processing consulting; "Official Airline Guides"; encyclopedias; and trade and professional magazines. The firm has successfully weathered business cycles and wars, and today dominates many of its markets.

Some companies in such an enviable position might relax and become complacent: Not Dun & Bradstreet. As Harrington "Duke" Drake, chairman and CEO, explains:

> "Our goal is to be in a state of continuous transition so we can always accommodate the changing environment of our clients,". . . . "Instead of concentrating on new ways to package and sell information we happen to have on hand, we are beginning to look at the changing needs of the marketplace and to devise ways to fill those needs."

SOURCE: "How D&B Organizes for a New-Product Blitz," *Business Week*, 16 November 1981, p. 87.

One firm built a new plant to make transistors and moved in a work force from another location but was forced to close the plant six months later because the "bottom had fallen out" of the transistor market due to newly developed microminiature circuitry.[2]

There are numerous other environmental forces which influence organizational change. Depressed economic conditions have provided the impetus for significant organizational changes in some industries during the past few years. Of course, a constant force for managers in virtually any organization is competitive pressure. And, as we saw in earlier chapters, government, the international arena, and pressures from various constituencies such as consumer interest groups, the community, and stockholders all create forces for organizational change.

Internal Forces

Events occurring within the organization can also create change. Labor problems such as strikes, high grievance rates, or the threat of unionization often cause management to modify its personnel policies. High turnover among employees or excessive absenteeism are also instrumental in causing management to reassess its operations. Such "people" pressures may result in changes in job design, organization structure, wage rates, hiring, policies, supervisory styles, and so on.

Over the past decade, managers have been particularly concerned about the problems of stagnant productivity and changing employee values. The search for ways to improve productivity has led to the adoption of new forms of technology, motivation systems, and participative decision making. Increasing participation in decision making, for instance, is not only an attempt to improve productivity, but is also a response to demands by employees that they be permitted a voice in decisions that affect their work.

Motivation to Change

Most organizational change is probably reactive rather than proactive. Few organizations, for reasons we shall examine shortly, are likely to create significant change on their own in the absence of any immediate pressure to modify their operations. As Michael Beer has pointed out: "If there is one thing of which researchers are very certain, it is that organizations do change when they are under pressure and rarely when they are not."[3]

Beer believes that crisis is often required to get the attention of top management. Although all organizations do not require crisis to change, it is undeniably a powerful force. Its key role may be to raise "dissatisfaction with the status quo [in order] to overcome resistance caused by the costs of change to organizational members."[4]

We strongly believe, however, that managers should place more emphasis on proactive change strategies. The assumption that pressure is required for organizations to change should be altered to create a new emphasis. Rather than simply reacting to environmental change that has already occurred, managers should be encouraged to *create* change. These changes often generate pressures to which other organizations must then respond. Certainly, some organizations practice proactive change. The best examples are often pioneers in emerging industries—such companies as Wang Laboratories in the word processing field or Apple Computer in the personal computer market. But managers in any organization in any field have the opportunity to create change. What is required is creativity and a major modification in management's way of thinking about organizational-environmental relationships.

THE PROCESS OF CHANGE

Once management's monitoring activities have detected significant pressures for—or opportunity to—change, management can begin the necessary process of modifying the organization. This section examines *planned organizational change*, a procedure that consists of the sequence of steps illustrated in Figure 17–2.

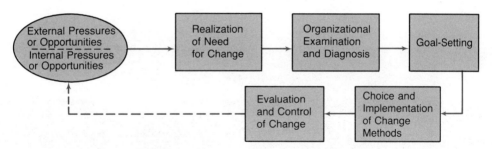

FIGURE 17–2   Planned organizational change

Realization of Need for Change

Even intense forces for change do not automatically lead to organizational adaptation. The reason for this delay in management's response is illustrated in Figure 17–3. Although the forces for change may be great, the forces opposing change may be equally powerful.[5]

Reasons for Resisting Change.   Change, of course, is not always resisted. Few of us would refuse a gift of a million dollars even though accepting it would likely lead to significant changes in our life style. But often change is not viewed positively, either because the benefits of the proposed change are unclear or because organization members perceive that the benefits of the change are outweighed by its costs. Such costs include the following:

1. Many individuals resist change because they fear it may adversely affect their *job security*. In truth, organizational changes in recent years have often involved extensive layoffs as organizations attempted to cut costs and increase operating efficiency. The problem, of course, is that what is good for the organization is not necessarily good for each of its members.

2. Since change, by definition, alters the status quo, some individuals are likely to lose *political power* or *status* while others stand to gain. Even such simple changes as moving individuals from one set of offices to new quarters in another part of the same building can create considerable anxiety.

3. Organizational change usually modifies the organization's *informal network* of relationships. The introduction of new technology or the transfer of personnel can break up cohesive work groups and threaten friendships and norms. Few of us are anxious to change familiar, comfortable ways of working with others.

4. Some individuals resist change because they fear that they will be unable to acquire the necessary *new skills* and *behaviors*. This fear is particularly prevalent in organizations undergoing technological change.[6]

FIGURE 17–3   Forces for—and
against—change

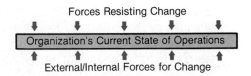

Forces Resisting Change

Organization's Current State of Operations

External/Internal Forces for Change

POLITICAL RESISTANCE TO CHANGE

After a number of years of rapid growth, the president of an organization decided that its size demanded the creation of a new staff function—New Product Planning and Development—to be headed by a vice president. Operationally, this change eliminated most of the decision-making power that the vice presidents of marketing, engineering, and production had over new products. Inasmuch as new products were very important in this organization, the change also reduced the vice presidents' status which, together with power, was very important to them.

During the two months after the president announced his idea for a new product vice president, the existing vice presidents each came up with six or seven reasons the new arrangement might not work. Their objections grew louder and louder until the president shelved the idea.

Resistance to change may not always be conscious. Organizational culture, a concept discussed in Chapter 13, can make change difficult even for those individuals who desire to change. For example, the Electronic Devices Division of Rockwell International Corporation, after dismal operating results, attempted to carve out a niche for itself in 1982 in the high-growth and high-profit-margin markets of the semiconductor industry. These markets, however, are characterized by "fever-pitch" competition, an environment that differs considerably from Rockwell's traditional military electronics market. "Some former Rockwell executives doubt that the conservative parent corporation will provide the kind of entrepreneurial environment necessary for the division to blossom."[7]

Reducing Resistance to Change.   Figure 17–3 indicates that resistance to change can be overcome either by increasing the forces for change or by reducing the forces resisting change. Organizational change specialists generally prefer the latter approach because increasing the forces for change often leads to a strengthening of the resistance to change. In practice, however, both approaches are used to "unfreeze" resistant attitudes and behaviors. The following discussion presents a sample of various methods for overcoming, or reducing, resistance to change:[8]

1. If the resistance is based on poor or misleading information, a program of *education and communication* concerning the purpose and benefits of the change may help reduce the resistance. Such a program obviously requires that the resistors trust top management. Additionally, it may be necessary for management to guarantee organization members that neither their job security nor their income will be adversely affected by the change.[9]

2. Resistance can sometimes be reduced by encouraging the resistors to become *involved* in the change program and to *participate* in designing and implementing it. In many cases, such participation can lead to increased member commitment to the change program.

3. Management can sometimes *facilitate* the change by offering *support* such as training employees in the new technology or aiding them in developing the behavioral skills that will be required. Such support can reduce the anxieties that cause resistance to certain types of change.

4. Because all three of these forms of reducing resistance can be time consuming, management may turn to *coercion*. In this case, organization members are *forced* to change through threats (of job loss, for instance), firings, or transfers of resistors. The outcomes of this strategy may include anger and lingering bitterness. "But in situations where speed is essential and where the changes will not be popular, regardless of how they are introduced, coercion may be the manager's only option."[10]

Certainly the appropriate approach depends upon the magnitude and type of change, the characteristics of the members who will be affected, the expected time frame, and the reasons for opposition to the change. The wise manager analyzes the situation carefully before deciding upon a means of reducing or overcoming resistance. As Kurt Lewin, one of the pioneers of organizational change theory, pointed out:

> Managers rushing into a factory to raise production by group decisions are likely to encounter failure. In social management as in medicine, there are no patent medicines and each case demands careful diagnosis.[11]

Organizational Examination and Diagnosis

Once organizational attitudes are "unfrozen" and members realize that change is needed, it is necessary to examine the organization in order to diagnose the specific areas that require change. Some organizations term this phase *self-study*. Often, a consultant, or *change agent*, is brought in

A MONUMENTAL TASK OF "UNFREEZING"

What some people have described as "the biggest single planned organizational change in the country in the second half of the century" is presently occurring at American Telephone & Telegraph Company. In 1982, the company and the U.S. Justice Department agreed that the firm might provide deregulated products and services if it divested itself of its Bell System telephone companies.

Changing from a fully regulated mode of operation to a partly regulated (long-distance network)/partly unregulated operation requires tremendous change for a firm of this size (over one million employees and $125 billion in assets prior to the break up). Charles L. Brown, chairman of the board, has pointed out just one of the many areas of significant change that is required:

> A deep and complex problem is posed by the need to change employee work habits and methods that are almost instinctive. In other words, the business procedures that get the job done are going to have to change and it's not easy to do that. I think it's a major problem that almost surmounts most of the others. We have an immense "book" of "correct" procedures that aren't so correct anymore.

SOURCE: "Conversation with Charles L. Brown," *Organizational Dynamics* 11 (Summer 1982): 30,33.

from outside the organization to aid in the examination and diagnosis. Although the organization's own managers can—and do—serve as change agents, an outside consultant may be able to view the organization more objectively. Management must be aware, however, that a consultant often arrives with his or her own set of biases and selective ways of viewing organizational problems. Hence, it is advisable for the consultant, after collecting information on the organization's operations, to compare his or her problem definition with that of management's. Both organization members and consultants are likely to understand the problems better by comprehending how and why the other arrived at a particular diagnosis.

Optimally, the focus of the self-study is each of the organization's four major subsystems and their interactions, as shown in Figure 17–4. Change may be required in the organization's *technology* (how it changes inputs into outputs), its *tasks* (the way specific jobs are designed), its *structure* (the way the tasks are grouped), or its *people* (the way in which organization members behave and interact). By taking a systems view, management will realize that a change in any one of these subsystems will affect the others.

FIGURE 17–4 Interactions among organizational subsystems
SOURCE: From Harold J. Leavitt, "Applied Organizational Change in Industry: Structural, Technological and Humanistic Approaches," in James G. March, ed., *Handbook of Organizations.* Copyright © 1965 by Rand McNally College Publishing Co., p. 1145.

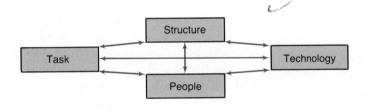

Goal Setting

Upon completion of the self-study, organization members must formulate the goals they wish to establish for the change program. In other words, they must explicitly answer the question, What changes do we desire in our organization?

David A. Nadler and others emphasize the importance of communicating a clear image of the future to organization members.[12] Change programs are likely to be more effective if those involved have a clear idea of the direction in which they are going and what their ultimate destination will be.

> While there is no concrete future state on which to focus, some picture of the future can be constructed and communicated. In this case, it is more likely to be a vision or a set of principles or guidelines for doing business than a concrete structure or set of organizational arrangements. It may simply be a statement of "what we will be and what we won't be," or a description of "why we are where we are, and where (in general terms) we're headed".[13]

Certainly the foundation for the journey—why the organization must change and how its members will be affected by the change—should have already been communicated.

Choice and Implementation of Change Methods

Once the goals of the change program are established, the specific methods to be used must be selected. The techniques available to management, as implied by Figure 17–4, may focus upon changing the following: the task (through job enrichment, for example), structure (by developing profit centers, for instance), technology (through increasing the level of computerization, for example), people (such as reducing destructive intergroup conflict), or any combination of these.

There is some evidence that a shared approach—one involving individuals at all levels of the hierarchy in choosing and implementing change methods—is characteristic of successful programs.[14] Participation, of course, requires much time and the relinquishing of managerial control, and can create new problems such as conflict. In some cases, however, these costs are overshadowed by the benefits. A recent study of change in a public utility in which the employees were represented by two labor unions serves as an example. Those employees who directly participated in planning and implementing the change perceived themselves as having more influence over work-related decisions, were more likely to feel that their contributions were accepted by those above them, and had more favorable attitudes toward their jobs and the organization than did employees who did not directly participate. These results were maintained over a three-year period.[15]

Certainly this step in the change process must be carefully managed. Otherwise, managers may fall into the trap of focusing most of their attention on the future state they desire while assuming that the implementation stage simply involves mechanical or procedural details. Such assumptions are likely to result in a disappointing failure of the change program.

Evaluation and Control of Change

Evaluation of the change involves frequent monitoring of organizational performance and employee performance and attitudes to ensure that the change is proceeding as planned. Such monitoring requires the development of feedback mechanisms to provide the necessary information.

> There is a huge amount of anecdotal data about senior managers ordering changes and assuming those changes were made, only to find out to their horror that the changes never occurred. Such a situation develops because managers lack feedback devices to tell them whether actions have been effective or not. During stable periods, effective managers develop various ways of eliciting feedback. During the transition state, however, these mechanisms often break down because of the turbulence of the change or because of the natural avoidance of providing "bad news." Thus it becomes important for transition managers to develop multiple, redundant, and sensitive mechanisms for generating feedback about the transition.[16]

Feedback is essential because organization change programs, even though successful, often have side effects—the creation of new problems. As Gerald I. Susman puts it, "We never quite solve our problems, rather we navigate through sets of interdependent problems guided by the vision of a more desirable future."[17] Certainly, a perspective which evaluates the change from a systems viewpoint is required.

Finally, it is important to realize that significant change takes time. "Refreezing" individuals into the new ways of working and interacting requires a new reward system. Since people are likely to behave in ways that lead to the rewards they desire, rewards such as pay increases and promotions should be linked to the types of behavior that are required to make the organization change effective.

ORGANIZATION DEVELOPMENT

This section examines more closely one particular approach to organization change which has been widely adopted in recent years. Long-term, systemwide organization change that focuses primarily on the ways that organization members behave and interact is termed *organization development* (OD). Encompassing a wide range of programs, OD attempts to improve organizational relations and encourage teamwork.

Definition of OD

The field of OD is still somewhat nebulous, and practitioners do not agree on a definition of its scope. The following statement by Richard Beckhard provides a useful, working definition:

> Organization development is an effort (1) *planned,* (2) *organization-wide,* and (3) *managed* from the *top,* to (4) increase *organizational effectiveness* and *health* through (5) *planned interventions* in the organization's "processes," using *behavioral-science* knowledge.[18]

OD is *planned* in the sense of involving (1) a systematic diagnosis of the way an organization functions and (2) a prescription of certain organization development methods to improve its functioning. The analysis involves an *entire organization,* although this may be a corporation, an autonomous division, or even a local unit.

In saying the development is *managed from the top,* Beckhard is stressing the desired commitment of top leaders to it. Increasing *effectiveness and health* of an organization would entail improvements in intergroup and interdepartmental collaboration, development of undistorted communication, identification of shared values, and reduction of interpersonal friction.

By *planned intervention,* managers and other organizational members step back and analyze the way the organization is functioning and look at alternative ways of working together. The *behavioral science* knowledge deals with such features of organizations and management as "motivation, power, communications, perception, cultural norms, problem-solving, goal-setting, interpersonal relationships, intergroup relationships, and conflict management."[19]

A central figure in most types of organization development is the change agent who provides the technical or professional leadership necessary to improve the functioning of the organization. The change agent must inspire confidence, which, in turn, requires an ability to understand and diagnose organizational problems as well as a knowledge of behavioral science and OD methodology. The client organization, however, must accept responsibility for the program and for its implementation if the program is to be taken seriously.

Assumptions underlying OD

The basic assumption underlying OD is that it is possible for "the goals and purposes of the organization [to be] attained at the same time that human values of individuals within the organization are furthered."[20] Human beings are viewed as desiring growth, development, and the opportunity to contribute to organization goals if permitted. Such human development requires effectively functioning work groups and an organization characterized by a high degree of interpersonal trust, support, and cooperation.[21]

Beyond this basic assumption, the field of OD is founded on other fundamental beliefs, which include the following:[22]

1. The level of interpersonal trust, support, and cooperation is lower than is desirable in most organizations.

2. Most people wish to make—and are capable of making—a greater contribution to organization goal attainment than the organization's environment permits.

3. People wish to be accepted by others and to interact with them in groups. Work effectiveness increases through joint problem solving and task collaboration.

4. The culture in most organizations suppresses the feelings people have about each other, and these suppressed feelings adversely affect problem solving, personal growth, and job satisfaction.

5. Viewing personal feelings as important to the organization can open up avenues for improved goal setting, leadership, communications, problem solving, intergroup collaboration, and job satisfaction.

6. Organization structure and job design can be modified to meet the needs of individuals, groups, and the organization better.

OD Methods

In addition to such change techniques as MBO, job enrichment, and various conflict resolution tools, OD researchers and consultants have developed a number of unique methods to change individuals, groups, and organizations. A sampling of these methods is presented below.

Individual Change. An example of a method developed to change individuals is *sensitivity (or T-Group) training*. Its purpose is to develop interpersonal skills of organization members. Through participation in group projects and exercises, managers are taught to look at themselves and their behavior as it may affect others and to attempt to understand the behavior and attitudes of others. Emphasis is placed on the way that individuals "come across" in their face-to-face interactions with others. An analysis of thirty-five OD studies over a sixteen-year period indicated that almost one-fourth of those programs focused on individual change, using sensitivity training or other similar "laboratory" training techniques.[23]

Group Change. *Team-building* conferences are intended to improve the functioning of groups or work teams. Activities of this type begin with a review of team purposes and priorities, and areas in which im-

OD AT EBASCO

Ebasco Services, a builder of power plants and a subsidiary of Enserch Corporation, firmly believes in the effectiveness of organization development. The company turned to this form of organizational change several years ago when it was experiencing operating problems with its matrix management system and was increasingly being underbid for lucrative projects by its competitors.

To increase its understanding of the company's problems, top management commissioned a survey in which each of three hundred managers was interviewed for ninety minutes or more. The results of these interviews yielded enough information to fill 40,000 index cards and 515 pages of data analysis. Among other findings, the study revealed widespread uncertainty about individual futures in the organization and considerable confusion concerning the matrix structure.

To allay managers' concerns over their career progression, the company made several changes. One of the most important was the development of "potential appraisals" which outline each manager's likely career path in the organization. Ebasco also devised a computerized career-tracking program to match employee skills with projected staffing needs and promotions. And, to aid first-level managers, the firm instituted a development program which helps supervisors learn to handle the types of problems that they are likely to face.

To reduce misunderstanding about the matrix structure, Ebasco's OD staff held over one hundred seminars to explain the system to its employees. The company's performance appraisal program was revised to reflect the fact that employees who report to two bosses should have their performance evaluated by both of those managers. Additionally, about sixty team-building sessions were held in which a "facilitator" met with conflicting matrix personnel. Each individual was first asked for his or her perception of the conflict and its causes, and then confrontation sessions were held to reduce the conflict. Although all matrix-related problems have not disappeared, tensions have decreased considerably.

SOURCES: Based on "When Bosses Look Back to See Ahead," *Business Week*, 15 January 1979, pp. 60-61; and "How Ebasco Makes the Matrix Method Work," *Business Week*, 15 June 1981, pp. 126, 131.

provement may be helpful. After the self-diagnosis, group members attend several sessions, guided by the change agent, in which they discuss possible ways of solving problems and making their group function more effectively. Team building was utilized as the primary intervention technique in 40 percent of the studies referred to above.

> Team-building methodology is based on what behavioral scientists call an action research paradigm. This paradigm directly applies Kurt Lewin's three-stage process of change (i.e., unfreezing, changing, and refreezing). The key aspects include collection of data, diagnosis of problems, feedback to the work group, discussion of the data by the work group, action planning, and action. The sequence tends to be cyclical, with the focus on new or advanced problems as the group learns to work together more effectively. . . .[24]

Organization Change. One of the most widely discussed means of changing organizations is Robert Blake and Jane Srygley Mouton's *Grid organization development*.[25] The *Managerial Grid®*, a key tool in this program, shows managerial orientation in terms of two variables—concern for people and concern for production (Figure 17–5).

A series of exercises is used to permit managers to analyze their own positions on the Grid and to work toward the ideal 9,9 position. The

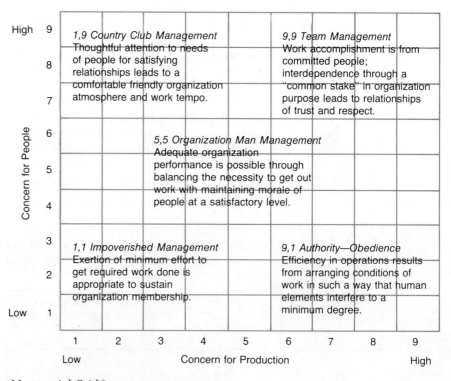

FIGURE 17–5   *The Managerial Grid®*
SOURCE: The Managerial Grid figure from *The New Managerial Grid*, by Robert R. Blake and Jane Srygley Mouton (Houston: Gulf Publishing Company). Copyright © 1978, page 11. Reproduced by permission.

complete Grid program involves additional steps designed to carry the Grid approach to all parts of the organization. The Managerial Grid was used by 11 percent of the thirty-five organizations referred to above that carried out OD studies.[26]

The Role of Survey Feedback. As the first step, many OD techniques require collecting data through questionnaires which explore the feelings and attitudes of all organization members toward their jobs, their supervisors, their peers, and the organization in general. The results of the survey are then presented to the organization members as a starting point in the change process to aid in diagnosing where change is needed. This feedback process occurs in a session attended by the supervisor, his or her subordinates, and the change agent who acts as a facilitator. The primary differences between survey feedback and the traditional employee survey process are shown in Figure 17–6.

	Traditional Approach	Survey Feedback or OD Approach
Data collected from:	Rank and file, and maybe foreman	Everyone in the system or subsystem
Data reported to:	Top management, department heads, and perhaps to employees through newspaper	Everyone who participated
Implications of data are worked on by:	Top management (maybe)	Everyone in work teams, with workshops starting at the top (all superiors with their subordinates)
Third-party intervention strategy:	Design and administration of questionnaire, development of a report	Obtaining concurrence on total strategy, design and administration of questionnaire, design of workshops, appropriate interventions in workshops
Action planning done by:	Top management only	Teams at all levels
Probable extent of change and improvement:	Low	High

FIGURE 17–6 Two approaches to the use of attitude surveys
SOURCE: Wendell L. French, Cecil H. Bell, Jr., *Organization Development: Behavioral Science Interventions for Organization Improvement*, 2d Edition, © 1978, p. 153. Reprinted by permission of Prentice-Hall, Inc., Englewood Cliffs, New Jersey.

OD: A Critique

Most of the evidence on the effectiveness of OD is anecdotal rather than research-based. From their own experiences, change agents have attempted to form general principles of OD which have not been rigorously tested for the most part.[27] Research, when it has been conducted, has often been incomplete. Many research efforts to assess the effectiveness of a particular OD program have focused on organizational performance in only the first year of the program, even though many change efforts require two to three years before results are detectable.[28]

An analysis of fifty-two OD studies between 1965 and 1980 indicated that those studies characterized by low methodological rigor were more likely to report successful outcomes for the OD program than were more rigorous studies.[29] "Ideally, evaluation data should provide a sound empirical base that managers and consultants can use to make informed decisions regarding the choice, continuance, expansion, or curtailment of OD programs."[30]

Perhaps deficient research is inevitable in a new, rapidly growing field. But if OD is to fulfill its potential of helping organizations interact more effectively with their environment, then its results must be more clearly documented. This requires that the goals of the change effort be explicitly stated before the change program begins, that multiple short- and long-term measures of effectiveness be used, and that cause-and-effect relationships be fully documented.

THE GOAL OF CHANGE: ORGANIZATIONAL EFFECTIVENESS

We have seen that the purpose of organizational change is to ensure that the organization operates effectively. Precisely, what is an effective organization? As is the case with a number of thorny issues, the exact definition of *organizational effectiveness* is the focus of considerable debate and could be the subject of several chapters.[31] Many theorists and practitioners, however, would probably agree that an effective organization is one that attains its goals, if goals are defined broadly. Such goals are of two basic types:[32]

1. Primary goals—those tied directly to satisfying the needs of the organization's primary client group (those people the organization was established to serve).
2. Secondary goals—those tied to the satisfaction of the needs of secondary beneficiary groups (organization members, the general public, suppliers, creditors, regulating agencies, and so on).

The actual weight, or importance, assigned to these various goals by top management will vary over time and across situations. Also, we must realize that the goals may conflict with one another.

This conceptualization of organizational effectiveness is useful for profit and nonprofit organizations alike. A business, for instance, must satisfy the needs of its customers (primary client group) without ignoring the needs and requirements of its employees, stockholders, bondholders, suppliers, OSHA, EPA, IRS, and so on (secondary beneficiary groups). A company which is able to perform adequately in the eyes of each of these groups is considered more effective than one which does not. And it seems probable that an effective business organization is a profitable one. Profitability in itself, however, does not indicate effectiveness. Profit may be attained by polluting the environment or selling illegal products. Effectiveness, then, encompasses considerably more than profitability.

A nonprofit organization, such as a university, must satisfy the needs of its students (primary clients) for education and personal development as well as such secondary beneficiary groups as faculty, administration, community, EEOC, the state legislature, employees, and so on. Although no well-accepted measure such as profit exists, the university is effective to the extent it satisfies these various and often conflicting needs.

Management's task, then, is to make the organization effective and maintain that effectiveness over time. To attain this end, managers must take a balanced, systems view of their organization, realizing that its multiple goals may conflict and that emphasis on particular goals may change or fade as conditions change. Effectiveness, once attained, is not a constant state. Careful and continued monitoring of the organization and its environment will enable management to plan and carry out the organization changes that are required to maintain effectiveness.

SUMMARY

A number of basic forces may create the need for significant change within an organization. These precipitating factors consist of *external forces*—environmental *pressures* or *opportunities*—and/or *internal forces*—events occurring within the organization. Although most organizational change is a reaction to these forces, many organizations could improve their performance by emphasizing proactive strategies which create—rather than simply respond to—environmental change.

The process of *planned organization change* begins with the realization of the need for change. Organization members often resist change because the benefits of the proposed change are unclear or because they perceive that the benefits of the change are outweighed by its costs. Even the culture of some organizations makes change difficult. Change can be facilitated either by increasing the forces for change or reducing the forces resisting change.

Once organizational attitudes are "unfrozen" and members realize that change is needed, it is necessary to examine the organization in order to diagnose the specific areas that require change. Upon completion of this *self-study*, organization members must formulate the goals they wish to establish for the change program. Then, the specific methods to be used in attaining these ends must be selected and implemented. Finally, the change program must be evaluated—through feedback mechanisms—and controlled by "refreezing" individuals into the new ways of working and interacting.

One popular approach to changing organizations that focuses primarily on the ways in which organization members behave and interact is termed *organization development* (OD). This approach assumes that it is possible for organization goals to be attained at the same time that human values of organization members are being furthered. OD change techniques may concentrate on changing individuals, as with sensitivity training, for instance; on changing groups, as in team building; or on changing the entire organization system, by using the Managerial Grid, for example. To date, the research evidence on the effectiveness of OD has been characterized by low methodological rigor and, hence, is largely inconclusive.

The purpose of organization change is to improve *organizational effectiveness*. An effective organization is one that attains its goals, where goals are broadly defined. These include the organization's *primary* goals (those tied directly to satisfying the needs of the people the organization is established to serve) and *secondary* goals (those tied to the satisfaction of the needs of various secondary beneficiary groups such as organization members, the general public, owners, suppliers, creditors, regulating agencies, and so on).

DISCUSSION QUESTIONS

1. Identify some *external* and *internal forces* that could create the need for change in your university.
2. Distinguish between *pressures* and *opportunities* for change.
3. What are some of the reasons why organization members *resist* change even when it is needed?
4. How might resistance to change be *reduced* or *overcome*?
5. What is an organization *self-study* and what is its purpose?
6. What are the advantages and disadvantages associated with using a participative approach to organization change?
7. What is the *OD* approach to changing organizations?
8. How does *survey feedback* differ from the traditional employee attitude survey?
9. What do we know to date about the effectiveness of OD?
10. Reply to the question: "Is your university an effective organization?" Justify your answer based on the definition of *organizational effectiveness* presented in this chapter.

NOTES

1. "An About-Face in TI's Culture," *Business Week*, 5 July 1982, p. 77.

2. Edgar F. Huse, *Organization Development and Change*, 2d ed. (St. Paul, Minn.: West Publishing Co., 1980), p. 19.

3. Michael Beer, *Organization Change and Development: A Systems View* (Santa Monica, Calif.: Goodyear Publishing Co., 1980), p.47.

4. Ibid.

5. Kurt Lewin, *Field Theory in Social Science: Selected Theoretical Papers*, ed. D. Cartwright (New York: Harper & Row, Publishers, 1951).

6. For an analysis of organizational resistance to the new information technology, see Shoshana Zuboff, "New Worlds of Computer-Mediated Work," *Harvard Business Review* 60 (September–October 1982): 142–52.

7. "Rockwell's New Formula for Cashing in on Chips," *Business Week*, 6 September 1982, p. 59.

8. This discussion is based on John P. Kotter and Leonard A. Schlesinger, "Choosing Strategies for Change," *Harvard Business Review* 57 (March–April 1979): 109–12.

9. For an account of an organization change program that attempted to maintain the organization's effectiveness during a time of retrenchment and layoffs, see Leonard Greenhalgh, "Maintaining Organizational Effectiveness during Organizational Retrenchment," *Journal of Applied Behavioral Science* 18 (1982): 155–70.

10. Reprinted by permission of Harvard Business Review. Excerpt from "Choosing Strategies for Change" by John P. Kotter and Leonard A. Schlesinger (March–April 1979). Copyright © 1979 by the President and Fellows of Harvard College; all rights reserved.

11. Kurt Lewin, "Studies in Group Decision," in *Group Dynamics*, ed. D. Cartwright and A. Zander (New York: Row, Peterson, 1953), p.300.

12. David A. Nadler, "Managing Organizational Change: An Integrative Perspective," *Journal of Applied Behavioral Science* 17 (April–May–June 1981): 202.

13. David A. Nadler, "Managing Transitions to Uncertain Future States," *Organizational Dynamics* 11 (Summer 1982): 44.

14. Larry E. Greiner, "Patterns of Organization Change," *Harvard Business Review* 45 (May–June 1967): 119–28.

15. Aaron J. Nurick, "Participation in Organizational Change: A Longitudinal Field Study," *Human Relations* 35 (May 1982): 413–29.

16. Nadler, "Managing Organizational Change," p.294.

17. Gerald I. Susman, "Planned Change: Prospects for the 1980s," *Management Science* 27 (February 1981): 150.

18. Richard Beckhard, *Organization Development: Strategies and Models* (Reading, Mass.: Addison-Wesley Publishing Co., 1969), p. 9.

19. Ibid., p. 13.

20. Wendell L. French and Cecil H. Bell, Jr., *Organization Development: Behavioral Science Interventions for Organization Improvement* (Englewood Cliffs, N.J.: Prentice-Hall, 1973), p. xiii.

21. Ibid., Chapter 6.

22. This discussion is based on Huse, *Organization Development and Change*, pp. 29–30; and Wendell L. French, "Organization Development Objectives, Assumptions, and Strategies," in *Organization Development: Theory, Practice and Research*, ed. W. L. French, C. H. Bell, Jr., and R. A. Zawacki (Dallas: Business Publications, 1978), pp.28–29.

23. Jerry I. Porras, "The Comparative Impact of Different OD Techniques and Intervention Intensities," *Journal of Applied Behavioral Science* 15 (April–May–June 1979): 156–78.

24. S. Jay Liebowitz and Kenneth P. De Meuse, "The Application of Team Building," *Human Relations* 35 (January 1982): 3.

25. Robert Blake and Jane Srygley Mouton, *The New Managerial Grid* (Houston: Gulf Publishing Co., 1978).

26. The basic goal of the Grid—developing a 9,9 style of management—has been criticized by many scholars. The contingency approach to leadership, presented in Chapter 20, indicates that under certain circumstances, a behavioral pattern emphasizing both concern for people and production may not always be ideal or desirable. An argument for the 9,9 style may be found in Robert R. Blake and Jane Srygley Mouton, "A Comparative Analysis of Situationalism and 9,9 Management by Principle," *Organizational Dynamics* 10 (Spring 1982): 20–43.

27. Porras, "The Comparative Impact," pp. 156–78.

28. Jerry I. Porras and Per Olaf Berg, "Evaluation Methodology in Organization Development: An Analysis and Critique," *Journal of Applied Behavioral Science* 14 (April–May–June 1978): 151–73.

29. David E. Terpstra, "Relationship between Methodological Rigor and Reported Outcomes in Organization Development Evaluation Research," *Journal of Applied Psychology* 66 (October 1981): 541–43.

30. Ibid., p. 541.

31. For a clear discussion of the major approaches to evaluating organizational effectiveness, see Kim Cameron, "Critical Questions in Assessing Organizational Effectiveness," *Organizational Dynamics* 9 (Autumn 1980): 66–80.

32. This classification is based on B. J. Hodge and William P. Anthony, *Organization Theory: An Environmental Approach* (Boston: Allyn and Bacon, 1979): pp. 199–203.

SUPPLEMENTARY READING

Ackerman, Linda S. "Transition Management: An In-Depth Look at Managing Complex Change." *Organizational Dynamics* 11 (Summer 1981): 46–66.

Beer, Michael. *Organization Change and Development: A Systems View.* Santa Monica, Calif.: Goodyear Publishing Co., 1980.

Burke, W. Warner. "Organization Development and Bureaucracy in the 1980s." *Journal of Applied Behavioral Science* 16 (July–August–September 1980): 423–37.

Cameron, Kim. "Critical Questions in Assessing Organizational Effectiveness." *Organizational Dynamics* 9 (Autumn 1980): 66–80.

"A Dialogue with Warren Bennis. . . Organization Development at the Cross-roads." *Training and Development Journal* 35 (April 1981): 19–26.

Greenhalgh, Leonard. "Maintaining Organizational Effectiveness during Organizational Retrenchment." *Journal of Applied Behavioral Science* 18 (1982): 155–70.

Hall, Richard N. "Effectiveness Theory and Organizational Effectiveness." *Journal of Applied Behavioral Science* 16 (October–November–December 1980): 536–45.

Huse, Edgar F. *Organization Development and Change.* 2d ed. St. Paul, Minn.: West Publishing Co., 1980.

Kanter, Rosabeth Moss. "Dilemmas of Managing Participation." *Organizational Dynamics* 11 (Summer 1982): 5–27.

Kotter, John P., and **Schlesinger, Leonard A.** "Choosing Strategies for Change." *Harvard Business Review* 57 (March–April 1979): 106–14.

Liebowitz, S. Jay, and **De Meuse, Kenneth P.** "The Application of Team Building." *Human Relations* 35 (January 1982): 1–18.

March, James G. "Footnotes to Organizational Change." *Administrative Science Quarterly* 26 (December 1981): 563–77.

Nadler, David A. "Managing Organizational Change: An Integrative Perspective." *Journal of Applied Behavioral Science* 17 (April–May–June 1981): 191–211.

Pasmore, William, and **Friedlander, Frank.** "An Action-Research Program for Increasing Employee Involvement in Problem Solving." *Administrative Science Quarterly* 27 (September 1982): 343–62.

Porras, Jerry I. "The Comparative Impact of Different OD Techniques and Intervention Intensities." *Journal of Applied Behavioral Science* 15 (April–May–June 1979): 156–78.

Sheldon, Alan. "Organizational Paradigms: A Theory of Organizational Change." *Organizational Dynamics* 8 (Winter 1980): 61–80.

Susman, Gerald I. "Planned Changes: Prospects for the 1980s." *Management Science* 27 (February 1981): 139–54.

Umstot, Denis D. "Organization Development Technology and the Military: A Surprising Merger?" *Academy of Management Review* 5 (April 1980): 189–201.

Woodworth, Warner; Meyer, Gordon; and **Smallwood, Norman.** "Organization Development: A Closer Scrutiny." *Human Relations* 35 (April 1982): 307–19.

Zuboff, Shoshana. "New Worlds of Computer-Mediated Work." *Harvard Business Review* 60 (September–October 1982): 142–52.

18

MANAGEMENT OF PROFESSIONAL CAREERS

This chapter will enable you to

- *Appreciate the importance of career planning and understand the steps necessary in preparing such a plan.*
- *Outline the stages of professional careers and point out the distinctive features of each stage.*
- *Understand the significance of mentor-protégé relationships in career progression.*
- *Recognize the special problems involved in family-career conflicts, dual-career marriages, and career planning for women.*
- *Understand the importance of time management in professional careers and the practical steps involved in managing one's time.*

As you prepare for a professional career, you can readily appreciate the difficulty as well as the seriousness of career choices. The many decisions involved in commitments to work life are too important to be left to chance. In this chapter, therefore, we discuss the process of *professional career planning* and the issues related to such planning.

THE CAREER MANAGEMENT PROCESS

Nature of Career Planning

Professional work careers begin as students leave college and enter organizational life. *Career planning* or *career management* refers to the decisions involved in career choices such as entry into the world of work, new job assignments, transfers, promotions, moves to other organizations, and the like. In brief, it concerns the planning of one's life work.

Although entry into organizational life is the career beginning, it is *only* the beginning. Choices and planning are required as the individual starts as a trainee, gains sufficient experience to act independently, often moves on to direct others, accepts broader responsibilities, weathers mid-career crises, moves laterally and/or upwardly, and eventually withdraws and retires.

Both the individual and the employing organization participate in the career planning system. First the individual and/or organization

FIGURE 18–1   Elements of career management

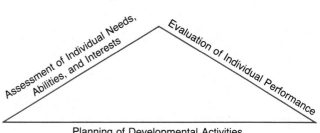

Planning of Developmental Activities

must assess his or her own abilities and interests—a continuing process. Second, the organization and the individual must evaluate on-the-job performance—again a continuing activity. Third, the individual and/or the organization must plan activities that will develop the individual for projected positions, a lifelong process (Figure 18–1).

The degree of aggressiveness in career planning varies. Some individuals accept life as it comes and take promotions if and when they come. And some organizations simply assume that "the cream will rise to the top." In contrast, the concept of career planning emphasizes the purposeful mapping of career moves and the proper preparation for those moves. Although little research has been conducted in this area, some evidence indicates that extensive career planning is related to an effective career.[1]

Mutual Interests in Career Planning

The professional may do his or her own career planning without the collaboration of an employing organization. Because of their mutual interests, however, both the individual and the employing organization may become involved in career planning. As shown in Figure 18–2, both the individual and the employing organization must exercise judgment and make choices at all critical points throughout the professional career.

Some organizations ignore career management, and others approach it systematically with formal development programs. One survey of organizational practices discovered the following types of career development activities:[2]

1. Career counseling during the performance appraisal session.
2. Special career counseling for high-potential employees.
3. Career pathing to help managers acquire experience for future jobs.
4. Rotating first-level supervisors through various departments to prepare them for upper-management positions.
5. Job posting of open positions and consideration of individual bids.
6. In-house advanced management development program.
7. Tuition reimbursement program.
8. Career counseling and job rotation for women and minorities.
9. Preretirement counseling.

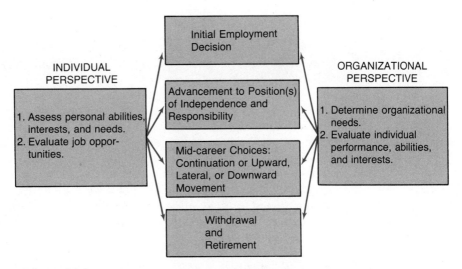

FIGURE 18–2 Career decisions

Organizations conduct career management programs in order to increase their operating efficiency. By assessing future needs for professional personnel and monitoring the progression and development of individuals, they attempt to provide a competent staff and avoid shortages in professional talent that might otherwise occur.

One risk of career-management programs is that of unrealistic expectations. If career planning programs create strong aspirations and if the organization cannot deliver the necessary opportunities, professional employees may experience dissatisfaction and anxiety. People who cannot achieve career goals within the organization may become embittered or seek fulfillment in other organizations.

Importance of Personal Goal Setting

Career management involves personal goal setting—the identification of job goals and planning to reach those goals. People who plan their careers in this way can accelerate their development and seize opportunities as they become available.

Everyone has at least vague goals for employment and career. Clear identification of goals and a strong commitment to them, however, can pay rich dividends in career progress. A goal-directed person usually attains more than the person lacking a sense of direction. The implications are clear for the person beginning a career: You can "go further" and enjoy greater personal satisfaction in your achievements by setting and periodically updating career goals.

Setting career goals provides a target and encourages the planning of personal development necessary to goal attainment. In addition, goal setting provides a sound basis for decisions. A person with a goal can better evaluate alternative opportunities as they appear and avoid total reliance on a quick weighing of pros and cons.

Preparing a Career Plan

A person can develop his or her career plan with or without the help of the organization. We can sketch here only the general approach to formulating such a plan. (For further assistance, you should consult one of many guides to career planning.*)

Step one involves the identification of your long-range career objectives. In view of your abilities, preparation, background, and interests, where do you hope to go professionally? This step requires a balancing of professional goals with those in other areas—family, religious, recreational, and so on. As a student, you may find that career goals are vague because of your lack of knowledge of opportunities coupled with an inadequate basis for evaluating your own potential. Fortunately, your career plans need not be "set in concrete" but can be revised periodically throughout your career.

Step two calls for the establishment of more immediate, short-run goals, goals that might be realized within one to five years. At the time of employment, for example, you might specify completion of the probationary period as one goal, followed perhaps by some assignment of greater independence and responsibility. Precise description of such a goal would depend on the field of employment and the type of assignments young professionals might receive in their first few years of employment.

The *third step* entails establishment of a timetable for the intermediate goals and even for other more distant points on the route to the ultimate career goal. For example, you might aspire to become comptroller or vice president by the age of 35. Timetables must obviously be expressed in flexible terms, because much of your progress lies beyond your personal control. Nevertheless, establishing a timetable enables you to monitor your progress. If extensive delays are encountered, you may need to reevaluate career goals, seek employment elsewhere, or take other appropriate action. The important idea is that you should take responsibility, as far as possible, for your own career rather than allowing it to meander along without direction.

As a *fourth step*, you should decide what activities are necessary to prepare for the next targeted position. In some cases, further education is desirable. In other cases, the best preparation is realized through diligent performance in the present job, supplemented perhaps by reading of professional and trade journals. Establishing these preparatory steps in measurable terms allows you to obtain reinforcement through achievement of specific goals.

---

*Three books offering career-planning assistance are Richard Nelson Bolles, *What Color Is Your Parachute?* (Berkeley, Calif.: Ten Speed Press, 1982); Edmond Billingsley, *Career Planning and Job Hunting for Today's Student: The Nonjob Interview Approach* (Santa Monica, Calif.: Goodyear Publishing Co., 1978); and Marilyn A. Morgan, *Managing Career Development* (New York: D. Van Nostrand Co., 1980).

Getting Started: Selecting a Profession

Career planning properly begins with the choice of profession. Speaking of occupational "choice" is somewhat misleading. Rather than a choice at a certain point in time, one's vocational selection is actually a developmental process spanning the years from late childhood to early adulthood. During this process, the individual eliminates some occupational alternatives and retains others. Even after entering a career, many individuals will eventually find their work unsatisfactory, their opportunities shrinking, or their interests changing, and feel compelled to make a shift.

Among the various theories which attempt to explain why we choose the occupations we do are the following:

> People choose work environments that match their personalities—that is, environments which let them exercise their skills and abilities, express their attitudes and values, and take on agreeable problems and roles.[3]

> A person's occupational choice depends upon: (1) factors over which the individual has no control (state of the economy, family background, and chance); (2) the individual's marital status; (3) characteristics specific to the individual (physical and intellectual characteristics, temperament and personality, interests and values, and the individual's sex); and (4) learned skills of various sorts.[4]

> A person selects an occupation which reflects his or her self-concept. That is, individuals will choose an occupation which expresses their ideas of the kinds of people they are.[5]

Selecting a field of work necessitates self-evaluation—a determination of who you are and what you want. You must consider what you enjoy doing, evaluate your skills or potential abilities, and think about your basic values. Manuals are available to help you think about vocational choice and suggest steps to follow in selecting a profession.*

Even after you make a choice, however, you are subject to change it. Edgar H. Schein suggests that an individual's basic career "anchor" or orientation is developed gradually over several years of work experience. As people move through their careers, they develop knowledge about their own abilities and talents, motives and needs, and values. This increasing self-awareness enables them to stabilize and guide their careers. Hence, an individual may well change careers after a few years in an attempt to secure a match between career and his or her self-perception.[6]

---

*The three books cited above—Bolles, *What Color Is Your Parachute?*; Billingsley, *Career Planning*; and Morgan, *Managing Career Development*—offer practical how-to-do-it guidance.

Getting Started: Selecting an Organization

For those seeking employment—and even for entrepreneurs, for that matter—the first choice pertains to industry. You must decide whether your interests lie in retailing, banking, oil, utilities, professional services, steel, publishing, education, government, or elsewhere. Some are growing industries, and some offer better average salary levels than others. Retailing and utilities, for example, reportedly offer lower salaries on the average, although the average obviously does not set limits in the individual case.

In selecting a specific organization, the quality of management is more important than the beginning salary. An organization with a well-developed career management program, therefore, is an attractive prospective employer. A growing, thriving organization has more to offer most individuals than a faltering organization in the process of retrenchment.

One often-overlooked possibility is to form your own organization, to go into business for yourself.[7] Entrepreneurship or launching new ventures offers rich rewards to those with the requisite ability, interest, and courage. In the last decade, many business schools have launched courses in entrepreneurship and new venture management at both the graduate and undergraduate levels.

STAGES IN PROFESSIONAL CAREERS

In her best seller, *Passages,* Gail Sheehy describes the predictable crises and stages of adult life.[8] This idea of stages can be applied specifically to working life and can assist in our understanding of career development.

The Concept of Stages

At different points in one's working life, a person faces drastically different situations. The neophyte's situation, for example, contrasts sharply with that of the peaked performer at mid-career or the executive awaiting retirement. Different interests, relationships, goals, responsibilities, and emotional responses reflect the varied positions of individuals on career paths. In thinking about career planning, therefore, it is helpful to examine the features of careers at various stages.

Identification of career stages is necessarily arbitrary, and writers differ in the number of stages they recognize. In this discussion, we shall think in terms of three stages: early career, mid-career, and late career (Figure 18–3).

Stage 1: Early Career Period

The early career period begins with entry into the organization and continues through initial training and also through a time of broadening

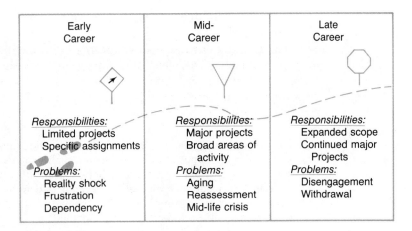

Early Career	Mid-Career	Late Career
Responsibilities: Limited projects Specific assignments	*Responsibilities:* Major projects Broad areas of activity	*Responsibilities:* Expanded scope Continued major Projects
Problems: Reality shock Frustration Dependency	*Problems:* Aging Reassessment Mid-life crisis	*Problems:* Disengagement Withdrawal

FIGURE 18–3   Career stages

work experiences. While the length of the period varies, we may think of it as lasting roughly until the age of 30 to 35 for a person who graduates from college at the usual age.

After the new employee joins the organization, he or she typically works under the close supervision of a more experienced employee. The work itself is generally routine, often a part of a larger project or broader area of responsibility.

The routine and sometimes monotonous nature of initial work assignments often proves frustrating to the person who enters the organization expecting to receive glamorous work assignments, to solve difficult problems, and to make his or her mark in the world. The phrase "reality shock" has been used to describe the beginner's experience of reconciling preemployment expectations and dreams with the realities of the work organization. Some managers see this period as a necessary time to get the new employee's head out of the clouds and to acquaint him or her with the "real world." The disillusionment reported by a young professional illustrates this point:

> My first year here was frustrating. I had a good record in graduate school. I was ready to go to work and make a contribution. But for a year, no one paid much attention to my suggestions. I almost left. It took me a year to realize that I didn't yet understand the complexity of the problems we were working on. Now I try to take enough time with new people to help them understand the dilemma of that first year.[9]

Even though entry level jobs contain less responsibility than higher-level positions, some organizations attempt to make initial job experiences challenging. This practice apparently contributes to career progress. A study of managerial careers in American Telephone and Telegraph Company has shown a strong connection between job challenge and career achievement. At the time of the study, almost six out of ten men who had experienced high job challenge had reached middle management. However, fewer than one out of ten who had low job challenge had done so.[10]

The newcomer must also adapt to a relationship of dependency. He or she is closely supervised and dependent on a more experienced employee for training and guidance. There is a new world of organizational relationships to learn, and this is also a part of the beginning employee's "reality shock."

> For many new employees, particularly those who entered in staff or managerial roles (as opposed to hourly work), reality shock consisted of the discovery, among other things, that other people in the organization were a roadblock to what they wanted to get done. Others in the organization did not seem as smart as they should be, seemed illogical or irrational, or seemed lazy, unproductive, or unmotivated.[11]

After completing initial training and beginning to "learn the ropes," the trainee often achieves a position of greater independence. He or she may be given responsibility for particular projects or a particular area of responsibility, and supervision becomes less detailed.

Work experiences in the early years following the break-in period enable the person to develop professional abilities. Frequently, this period involves specialization. By specializing, the professional develops a strong foundation for service to the organization, but there is the danger of being "trapped" in a specialized area. This period of development is an important part of the career, however, and danger is involved in trying to escape this stage too quickly because of impatience.

> Time after time our study, we encountered first-level managers who were not effective in their positions because they did not understand the technical aspects of the work they were supervising. This tended to undermine the manager's self-confidence as well as the confidence of his subordinates.[12]

As John Kotter, in his study of general managers, points out, the correct criterion for how rapidly one should advance is not the number of functional areas worked in or the number of training courses completed, but growth in business knowledge and in interpersonal and intellectual skills.[13]

Young managers, as might be expected, change jobs more frequently than do older executives. One survey of almost 1,200 managers in three major U.S. corporations reveals that the greatest job mobility occurs when managers are under thirty-two years of age.[14] Contrary to popular belief, however, the managers who changed employers made no higher— and, in many cases, lower—salaries than did managers who remained with the same company. It is only when these mobile executives reach mid-career that their jobs in various companies and their background of diversified corporate experience begin to pay off financially.[15]

SUCCESS SYNDROME

The successful [general managers—that is, managers with some profit center and multifunctional responsibility] I have known typically rose quickly in their organizations. Indeed, early in their careers most developed what might be called a "success syndrome"—that is, their careers followed this pattern:

1. They did well in an early assignment.
2. That success led to a promotion or a somewhat more challenging assignment.
3. That reinforced (or even increased) their self-esteem and motivation and led to greater formal or informal power and more opportunities to develop greater power. The more challenging jobs also stretched their abilities and built their skills.
4. That in turn led to an increase in their relevant relationships (including one or more with a mentor in top management), greater relevant knowledge, and improved interpersonal and intellectual skills.
5. All of the foregoing helped them perform well in their jobs.
6. That led to another promotion or a more challenging assignment.
7. And the pattern repeated itself, again and again.

SOURCE: Reprinted, by permission of the publisher, from "General Managers Are Not Generalists" by John P. Kotter, *Organizational Dynamics*, Spring 1982. © 1982 by AMACOM, a division of American Management Associations, New York. All rights reserved.

Stage 2: Mid-Career Period

Some people remain, by virtue of ability or choice, at the professional level described in Stage 1. They continue to serve as competent, independent performers of significant work. During the Stage 2 years, however, many professionals move on to assume broader responsibilities. This period runs from roughly thirty or thirty-five to fifty or fifty-five years of age. Typically, the increased responsibilities involve leadership or direction, formally or informally, of the work of others in the organization.

The Stage 2 professional may also be an "idea person" as indicated by this statement by a Stage 2 scientist:

> I sell ideas. I would describe myself as an innovative scientist. When I work on a problem, it starts to bug me. At some time, I will read something

and apply it back to solve the original problem. Others often come to me with problems they cannot solve. Generally I can pull some information from my experience or reading and give them a direction to follow in solving the problems.[16]

Often, during Stage 2, the professional moves into or upward in the managerial ranks. It is also a period of reassessment—coming to terms with "aging" and facing the disparity between dreams and accomplishments. Some have referred to it as a "mid-life crisis." It may lead to adjustment in career goals or job changes and possibly to problems in family relationships. If properly coped with, it can also lead to feelings of inner calm.

Stage 3: Late Career Period

The career directions established in Stage 2 may continue through the final years of a working career. Some persons, however, move on to a more advanced level of career responsibilities. We might think of this period as running from roughly fifty or fifty-five years of age until retirement. Gene W. Dalton, Paul H. Thompson, and Raymond L. Price have described these individuals ("Stage IV" in their frame of reference) as influencing the direction of the organization or some major segment of it.

> A stereotype of organizations pictures this influence as being exercised by only one person—the chief executive officer. But this influence is in fact more widely distributed among key people than is commonly thought. They exercise this influence in a number of ways: negotiating and interfacing with the key parts of the environment; developing the new ideas, products, markets, or services that lead the organization into new areas of activity; or directing the resources of the organization toward specific goals.[17]

For many, the late career period is a period of relative stability. During this period, of course, the person must face the prospect and eventually the experience of retirement. The details of this period are difficult to summarize because of the highly diverse career patterns that have developed. At some point, the professional must begin a process of disengagement and withdrawal that may require time. The higher the organizational level, the more difficult it is for the employee simply to "lay down his or her tools" and walk off into retirement.

SPECIAL ISSUES AND RELATIONSHIPS IN CAREER MANAGEMENT

Career management involves a number of significant internal and external relationships. Internally, the functions of the mentor are important to career progress. Externally, the professional must balance his or her professional life with family life—an especially challenging task for women professionals and members of dual-career families.

Mentor Relationships

In the early-career period, young professionals are often aided by older, experienced individuals. These teachers, who also function as protectors and advocates, are known as *mentors*. In some cases, they are immediate supervisors, but in other cases, they are merely senior employees. The following account of early job experiences describes first a weak and then a strong mentor.

> In my first two years in the company I was unhappy with my job. I worked for a man that I disliked and did not respect. He provided very little assistance or guidance. As a result, I made little or no progress. Then I began to work with another engineer who could get things done; he protected me from the flak coming down from above. He provided a climate that I enjoyed and he was willing to go to bat for me. When he became a formal group leader, I insisted on being transferred into his group, where I became the informal leader. Later, he recommended me for a supervisory position.[18]

For the young professional, the implications of mentor relationships are clear. By observing and listening to the mentor, he or she discovers how the system works and gains the practical judgment that is not learned in a formal professional education. A survey of 1,250 executives revealed that nearly two-thirds reported having had a mentor, with most of those relationships beginning during the first five years of the individual's career. Those executives who had mentors earned more money at a younger age and were more likely to follow a career plan than were those who did not have a mentor.[19]

Professional Lives and Family Lives

The stereotype of the fast-track, workaholic manager who sacrifices family for professional success may not be accurate, but it expresses a widespread concern about conflicts between work and family life. Those in professional careers face the problem of integrating these two areas of life. How does the professional, for example, maintain a strong family life while faced with excessive hours, frequent travel, and job worries that do not disappear at night?

One question concerns the relative importance of family versus profession. One might assume that problems occur because career-minded individuals simply forget about their families and place relatively less value on family relationships. This does not seem to be the case, however, with most executives. A study of 532 executives by Fernando Bartolomé and Paul Evans has revealed the dual orientation of most executives.[20] While 7 percent were dominantly career centered and

14 percent were dominantly family centered, an impressive 79 percent expressed a dual orientation. In effect, this majority said that *both* career and family were important and satisfying, though in different ways.

EMOTIONAL SPILLOVER

In studying the private and professional lives of over 2,000 managers, Fernando Bartolomé and Paul A. Lee Evans have found that some very successful executives have meaningful private lives while others do not.

What *does* distinguish the two groups is this: the executives whose private lives deteriorate are subject to the negative effects of what we call emotional spillover; work consistently produces negative feelings that overflow into private life. In contrast, the other group of executives have learned to manage their work and careers so that negative emotional spillover is minimized, and thus they achieve a balance between their professional and private lives.

SOURCE: Fernando Bartolomé and Paul A. Lee Evans, "Must Success Cost So Much?" *Harvard Business Review* 58 (March-April 1980): 137.

Even though most executives attach a high value to family life, they have difficulty in successfully integrating the two areas. In the study cited above, Bartolomé and Evans found that only about one-half of the managers were satisfied with their relative investment of time and energy in professional and family life. This suggests the problem is serious and deserving of serious effort in reconciling the conflicting demands of profession and family.

Dual-Career Marriages

A potentially more serious conflict of professional and family life occurs in the case of dual-career marriages. In such a family, their careers are a top priority matter for both husband and wife. The situation differs from that of family units in which the wife works merely to supplement family income. The problems in a dual-career marriage are quite different because the two careers must be reconciled with each other and with family demands. If there are young children, the conflicts obviously become even more severe. As one consultant so aptly puts it, "The two-career family is always fighting time, since there is no full-time person at home to tend to household chores and other necessities."[21]

Job location and transfer often provide particular difficulties for the dual-career couple. The location that provides the best opportunity for one may not provide the best opportunity for the spouse. And, a reloca-

Issue	Percentage of Companies That Favor	Percentage of Companies That Practice
Flexible Work Hours	73%	37%
Flexible Work Places	35	8
Cafeteria (Pick and Choose) Fringe Benefits	62	8
Financial Support for Child-Care Facilities	54	19
Paternity Leaves for the Father	80	Almost nonexistent

FIGURE 18–4   The gap between beliefs and practice: Results of a survey of 374 large companies
SOURCE: "Corporations and Two-Career Families: Directions for the Future," compiled by Catalyst, a resource center for professional women, as reported in Marilyn Hoffman, *The Houston Post*, 11 October 1981.

tion necessary for the advancement of either the husband or the wife obviously threatens the career of the other. In fact, a survey of 310 women in training and development positions indicated that these respondents felt their career should not be secondary to their husbands' jobs. The higher the woman's income level, the more strongly she believed that her husband should be willing to move with her if she were transferred, and the less likely she would be to move with her transferred husband if the move would adversely affect her career.[22]

Employers have shown greater flexibility in their personnel policies in recent years as dual-career marriages have become more common. Nevertheless, the husband and wife must still do most of the adjusting and reconciling of conflicting interests (Figure 18–4). An attitude of cooperation is essential, of course, for finding successful solutions.

The coping mechanisms that may be used are varied and often prosaic. Outside help may be obtained, for example, for cleaning and babysitting, and conflicting demands may be resolved at times by careful planning. The process of time management, discussed later in the chapter, can also be of help in solving dual-career problems.

Professional Careers for Women

Entry of women into professional careers has accelerated rapidly in recent years. Many organizations that were male enclaves in the 1950s and 1960s first admitted a few token women and then moved on to open the professional ranks to widespread participation by women.

Women now hold one-fourth of the managerial and administrative jobs in private industry.[23] As you have probably noticed, this trend is reflected in business and professional school enrollments. For instance, one-fourth of MBA students are female, compared to 3.5 percent in 1971,

PORTRAIT OF A DUAL-CAREER MARRIAGE

Consider another couple. Bea and Don get up at 6:30 A.M. each morning, shower, dress, and start breakfast by 7:00, when their two children awake. By 7:30 they are all at the breakfast table, checking schedules for the day. At 8:00 the kids make lunches and leave for school. Bea begins her drive into the city. Traffic is heavy and she usually doesn't arrive at her desk until 9:00. Don takes the train to his job. If it's a normal, uneventful day, Bea and Don leave at 5:00 P.M. and are home by 6:00. More often than not, unexpected problems delay their arrival until 7:00 or later.

A part-time housekeeper arrives at 3:30 to be with the children and begin dinner. Whoever arrives first drives her home. When Bea and Don are both home, the family eats together. If not, the kids eat first and the parents "survive on lukewarm leftovers." Not having regular meals together is one source of stress they report. The family does dishes together. At this point, Bea and Don shift into their parent roles. Helping the children with homework, going to school meetings, shopping for Scout uniforms or Halloween costume materials, or listening to one of them practice a band instrument takes up the evening, often until 10:00. "Sometimes I don't even get to check the mail," Bea reports. At this point she gets ready for the next day, listing instructions for the housekeeper, checking the children's after-school schedule, and so forth. If either of them has work to do, it gets done after 10:00. They try to be in bed by midnight, although both admit it doesn't always happen.

On weekends, the shopping and errands take up most of Saturday, with their son's sports sandwiched in between. The family goes to church on Sunday and, adds Bea, "That is the only afternoon you could even call 'free.'" Her major complaint? "No break in it all. I'm always working, doing something. If I'm not going, going at the office, then I'm coping with something that's come up at home. I almost went nuts when our son became a Cub Scout. There was no way he was ever going to pass his achievements without scheduling that into our evenings. The problem is that there's always something. If it isn't Scouts, it's a broken clarinet, or discovering at 8:00 A.M. that there's nothing in the house for the kids' lunches."

Bea and Don seem to have their roles well balanced, although they have little leisure time to relax—a common problem for most couples. Balancing home, work, and family demands not only produces stress, it also creates a situation that prevents people from doing the very thing that would help them manage stress—taking time to rest and play.

SOURCE: Francine S. Hall and Douglas T. Hall, *The Two-Career Couple.* © 1979, Addison-Wesley, Reading, Mass., pp. 96–97. Reprinted with permission.

and the proportion of advanced accounting degrees earned by women rose from 7 percent in 1969 to 28 percent in 1980.[24]

Women, too, are appearing in areas once felt to be the exclusive preserve of men.

> [In 1980] one-third of the students at General Motors Institute—the respected school of engineering and administration that produces a large number of GM managers—were women. One recent female GMI graduate, Adele E. Heinz, learned how to machine lathe a rocker arm and negotiate with unions during her five-year course and is now forecasting overseas diesel sales for GM. Heinz says the process was invaluable in preparing her for the work world. "I don't think that women are really being done a favor when they're promoted too soon into positions that perhaps they're not ready for," she says.[25]

Yet, in spite of the impressive gains of the past decade, female managers have still not been fully assimilated into the management structure.

> . . . Those women who have achieved executive rank tend to be clustered in areas traditionally more open to females: public relations, personnel and other staff jobs, or the media and service industries. Partly because they lack the profit-and-loss responsibility of line jobs, women executives also earn less than men with the same background.[26]

A recent poll of six hundred top-level executives from the twelve hundred largest U.S. firms indicated that "women in responsible corporate jobs are routinely accepted by top executives in major corporations, and many of the traditional prejudices appear to be disappearing."[27] Yet, 41 percent of the executives agreed that "it has been harder to promote women to high-level positions than we thought it would be" (52 percent disagreed with that statement), and 41 percent believed that "men don't like to take orders from women" (49 percent disagreed).[28]

Social change inevitably takes time, but the rapid strides made by women into managerial ranks within the past decade or so are noteworthy. The achievements of current women managers combined with the increasing number of women earning business degrees indicate that women more and more will be entering the ranks of top management.

TIME MANAGEMENT IN PROFESSIONAL CAREERS

This chapter concludes with a practical section on time management. Time management concepts are directly relevant to one's professional career, but they may be learned and used during one's student days as well. The discussion, therefore, concentrates on time management practices that are applicable to student life.

WOMEN AND MOBILITY

Despite the vast scope of American businesses' multinational operations, virtually no female managers were given overseas assignments for years. Now, that has begun to change.

Previously, companies simply assumed that foreign businessmen, accustomed to more patriarchal cultures, would shy away from doing business with U.S. women and that these women would decline to make the sacrifices involved in spending time in strange lands once they discovered the reality of those sacrifices. But when companies responded to the social pressures that have moved women into almost all aspects of corporate life and acceded to the growing number of requests for overseas assignments, they discovered that they had been wrong on both counts. Most women stuck to their new posts, and most foreign businessmen were no more reluctant to do business with an American woman than with an American man.

Even within the United States, most companies—and most women—have resisted the geographical transfer of female managers. But, this too has changed.

It appears that, sometime since 1975, enough women achieved corporate rank to enable women managers to behave normally by corporate standards without risking social disapproval. A choice dictated by ambition was no longer an admission of unfemininity but a proof of commitment. . . .

Says E. Jill Hayosh, personnel planning manager for women on the corporate personnel and organization staff of the Ford Motor Co. in Detroit: "When we interview on college campuses, there's an understanding that career paths in sales and marketing will involve moving, and there just isn't any sex difference in the response."

SOURCE: "A Rush of Recruits for Overseas Duty," *Business Week,* p. 120. Quoted from the 20 April 1981 issue of *Business Week* by special permission; and "Now Eager to Accept Transfers," *Business Week,* p. 153. Quoted from the 26 May 1980 issue of *Business Week* by special permission.

The Problem of Time Pressure

"How am I ever going to get all of this done?"
"There simply aren't enough hours in the day!"
These are frequent comments from managers, college students, and people from every walk of life. We have all experienced the stress that comes with the realization that we have more work to do than we have

time available in which to do it. Many of us leave the office, classroom, or library wondering where the time has gone and why we accomplished so little during that time.

To deal with these problems, the field of *time management* has developed during the past decade. Some selected time management tools are presented here to help you manage your time more wisely.

Begin Each Day with a Written Plan

Set aside the last few minutes of each working day to plan the activities of the following day. One way of doing this is to construct a written list of everything you need to accomplish the next day. These activities can be written down in random order as they occur to you.

Analyze each item on the list and assign it a priority. Not all activities are equally urgent or important, and, in some cases, activities can be delegated to someone else or need not be done at all. If you have a major exam in two days and have not yet begun to study, that item should obviously be given the number one priority. Getting your hair cut or having your car oil changed could probably be postponed until you feel more comfortable about your test preparation. These two items, then, would be assigned low priorities.

In any case, the point is to assign a relative priority to each activity and then begin the following day by attacking the #1 priority item on your list, then #2, and so on. This is hardly a revolutionary idea, but it is a significant improvement over the unorganized way in which many of us start each day. We move aimlessly from one activity to another, giving attention to items that seem interesting or to whatever our gaze happens to fall on. A list of activities with assigned priorities provides a systematic daily plan.

Avoid Procrastination

Most of us delay unpleasant or difficult tasks as long as possible. Two consultants contend that anxiety over having to perform difficult tasks causes us to retreat to more familiar and less threatening activities.[29] We justify engaging in these trivial or more interesting activities by telling ourselves that we are getting those items out of the way in order to concentrate solely on the difficult task. Too often, at the end of the day, we find that we have accomplished nothing of consequence and have never gotten to the major task!

Instead, try dividing the dreaded task into small manageable subtasks. Assign each a high priority. Each subtask alone will seem less unpleasant, and the feeling of accomplishment derived from completing part of the project may make it easier to work on the remaining parts. Remember that further procrastination only leads to more anxiety and frustration.

Use Your Productive Time Wisely

Each of us has certain times during the day when he or she is more productive than at other times. Some students, for instance, find that they study best after 9:00 P.M., while others prefer early morning hours. The hours when you feel fresh, alert, and energetic are the hours you should use to work on those high priority items. Unfortunately, we often waste these productive times by taking coffee breaks, going through the mail, working on trivial matters, or socializing with others. Then, when we finally do begin to work, we find that our energy level is lower and that we just cannot bring ourselves to face item #1 on our list.

Productive time should be devoted to accomplishing high priority items, and it must be kept as free from interruptions as possible. Your concentration and efficiency are higher when you are able to work without having to stop and attend to other matters. For this reason, some persons have developed the habit of arriving at work or school significantly earlier than anyone else. You can probably accomplish more in two uninterrupted hours at the beginning of the day (provided those are productive hours for you) than in all the hours that follow.

Applying Time Management

Professional personnel who manage their time carefully should accomplish more and make better progress on their career paths than those who merely react to the pressures of the moment. One word of caution, however: time management requires considerable self-discipline. One consulting firm that charges managers a hefty fee to help them learn to manage their time found that one-fourth of their past clients had fallen back into their old habits.[30] As a student, you can master the art of time management and improve your career prospects. The time to start is now!

SUMMARY

Professional *career planning* or *career management* refers to the decision making involved in choosing and moving through one's working career. The process requires assessing individual needs, abilities, and interests; evaluating work performance; and planning developmental activities. Both the individual and the employing organization have vital interests in career decisions.

During their early career years, professionals frequently experience some degree of "reality shock"—a clash of preemployment expectations with the "real world." After beginners progress beyond a training period and acquire expertise, often involving some years of specialization, they move into a mid-career period of expanding responsibilities. Frequently, they also experience a "mid-life crisis," a time of reassessment and reconsideration of career plans established earlier. The third stage of a career, the late career period, culminates in a time of withdrawal and eventually in retirement.

Mentors play a significant role in the socialization and development of young professionals. They are senior employees (often supervisors) who guide beginners and look out for their interests.

Family interests and professional interests involve some conflict, and many executives experience feelings of frustration in reconciling them. *Dual-career marriages* provide an especially difficult set of competing interests. Professional careers for women have become much more common in recent years, as females increasingly enter managerial occupations. In spite of their impressive gains, however, female executives are still more likely to be found in staff—rather than line—positions. But their achievements, combined with increasing numbers of women earning business degrees, indicate that they will more and more be filling line positions and entering the top management ranks.

Management of time is important to successful performance and advancement in a career. As students moving toward professional careers learn to plan and effectively manage their use of time, they acquire a skill that will be useful throughout their professional lives.

DISCUSSION QUESTIONS

1. How does *career planning* differ, if at all, from simply finding a job?
2. What is the risk of "unrealistic expectations," and how is this related to career planning?
3. Outline the steps necessary in preparing a career plan.
4. Explain the meaning of "reality shock" as applied to careers. Is it helpful or harmful?
5. What are the values of early career specialization, and what is the danger of being "trapped" in a specialized area?
6. What is the "mid-life crisis," and how does it affect a career?
7. How does a *mentor* contribute to the career development of a young professional?
8. How well do executives appear to reconcile their career and family interests?
9. Identify some of the major problems involved in dual-career marriages.
10. Explain how a written plan may contribute to effective time management.

NOTES

1. Sam Gould, "Characteristics of Career Planners in Upwardly Mobile Occupations," *Academy of Management Journal* 22 (September 1979): 539–50.

2. Marilyn A. Morgan, Douglas T. Hall, and Alison Martier, "Career Development Strategies in Industry—Where Are We and Where Should We Be?" *Personnel* 56 (March–April 1979): 13–30.

3. John L. Holland, *Making Vocational Choices: A Theory of Careers* (Englewood Cliffs, N. J.: Prentice-Hall, 1973).

4. Anne Roe, "Perspectives on Vocational Development," in *Perspectives on Vocational Development*, ed. J. M. Whiteley and A. Resnikoff (Washington, D. C.: American Personnel and Guidance Association, 1972), pp. 61–82.

5. Donald E. Super, "Vocational Development Theory: Persons, Positions, and Processes," in *Perspectives on Vocational Development*, ed. J. M. Whiteley and A. Resnikoff (Washington D. C.: American Personnel and Guidance Association, 1972), pp. 14–33.

6. Edgar H. Schein, *Career Dynamics: Matching Individual and Organizational Needs* (Reading, Mass.: Addison-Wesley Publishing Co., 1978).

7. For an extended treatment of this possibility, see Gordon B. Baty, *Entrepreneurship: Playing to Win* (Reston, Va.: Reston Publishing Co., 1974); Clifford M. Baumback and Joseph R. Mancuso, *Entrepreneurship and Venture Management* (Englewood Cliffs, N. J.: Prentice-Hall, 1975); or Karl H. Vesper, *New Venture Strategies* (Englewood Cliffs, N. J.: Prentice-Hall, 1980).

8. Gail Sheehy, *Passages* (New York: E. P. Dutton and Co., 1976).

9. Gene W. Dalton, Paul H. Thompson, and Raymond L. Price, "The Four Stages of Professional Careers—A New Look at Performance by Professionals," *Organizational Dynamics* Summer 1977 (New York: AMACOM, a division of American Management Associations, 1977), p. 25.

10. Douglas W. Bray, Richard J. Campbell, and Donald L. Grant, *Formative Years in Business: A Long-Term AT&T Study of Managerial Lives* (New York: John Wiley & Sons, 1974), p. 74.

11. Schein, *Career Dynamics*, p. 95.

12. Dalton, Thompson, and Price, "Four Stages of Professional Careers," p. 28.

13. John P. Kotter, "General Managers Are Not Generalists," *Organizational Dynamics* 10 (Spring 1982): 18.

14. John F. Veiga, "Do Managers on the Move Get Anywhere?" *Harvard Business Review* 59 (March–April 1981): 28.

15. Ibid., p. 36.

16. Dalton, Thompson, and Price, "Four Stages of Professional Careers," p. 30.

17. Ibid., p. 32.

18. Ibid., p. 24.

19. Gerard R. Roche, "Much Ado about Mentors," *Harvard Business Review* 57 (January–February 1979): 14–15, 20.

20. Fernando Bartolomé and Paul A. Lee Evans, "Professional Lives versus Private Lives—Shifting Patterns of Managerial Commitment," *Organizational Dynamics* 7 (Spring 1979): 3–29.

21. "Reducing Stress in Two-Career Families—Expert's Advice," *U.S. News & World Report*, 2 November 1981, p. 89.

22. Joe A. Cox and Kris Moore, "Whither Thou Goest. . . Well, We'll See: Relocations and the Dual-Career Marriage," in Southwest Division, Academy of Management *Proceedings*, 1981, p. 131.

23. "Women and the Executive Suite," *Newsweek*, 14 September 1981, p. 65.

24. Ibid.; and "The Lasting Changes Brought by Women Workers," *Business Week*, 15 March 1982, p. 64.

25. "Women and the Executive Suite," p. 68. Copyright 1981 by Newsweek Inc. All rights reserved. Reprinted by permission.

26. Ibid., p. 65.

27. "How Executives See Women in Management," *Business Week*, 28 June 1982, p. 10.

28. Ibid.

29. Ronald N. Ashkenas and Robert H. Schaffer, "Managers Can Avoid Wasting Time," *Harvard Business Review* 60 (May-June 1982): 99.

30. Marlys Harris, "Getting Organized," *Money* 11 (August 1982): 90.

SUPPLEMENTARY READING

Conarroe, Richard R. "Climbing the Corporate Success Ladder: A Self-Marketing Program for Executives." *Management Review* 70 (February 1981): 24–28; 42–44.

Davis, Stanley M., and **Gould, Roger L.** "Three Vice Presidents in Mid-Life." *Harvard Business Review* 59 (July–August 1981): 118–30.

De Long, Thomas J. "Reexamining the Career Anchor Model." *Personnel* 59 (May–June 1982): 50–61.

Evans, Paul, and **Bartolomé, Fernando.** *Must Success Cost So Much? The Human Toll of Corporate Life.* New York: Basic Books, 1981.

Figler, Homer R. *Overcoming Executive Mid-Life Crisis.* New York: Wiley-Interscience, 1978.

Gabarro, John J., and **Kotter, John P.** "Managing Your Boss." *Harvard Business Review* 58 (January–February 1980): 92–100.

Halcomb, Ruth. "Mentors and the Successful Woman." *Across the Board* 17 (February 1980): 13–18.

Hall, Douglas T. *Careers in Organizations.* Pacific Palisades, Calif.: Goodyear Publishing Co., 1976.

Hall, Francine S., and **Hall, Douglas T.** *The Two-Career Couple.* Reading, Mass.: Addison-Wesley Publishing Co., 1979.

Korman, Abraham K., with **Rhoda W. Korman.** *Career Success/Personal Failure.* Englewood Cliffs, N. J.: Prentice-Hall, 1980.

Kotter, John P.; Faux, Victor A.; and **McArthur, Charles C.** *Self-Assessment & Career Development.* Englewood Cliffs, N. J.: Prentice-Hall, 1978.

Louis, Meryl Reis. "Managing Career Transition: A Missing Link in Career Development." *Organizational Dynamics* 10 (Spring 1982): 68–77.

Luthans, Fred, and Davis, Tim R. V.. "Behavioral Self-Management—The Missing Link in Managerial Effectiveness." *Organizational Dynamics* 8 (Summer 1979): 42–60.

Morgan, Marilyn A.; Hall, Douglas T.; and Martier, Alison. "Career Development Strategies in Industry—Where Are We and Where Should We Be?" *Personnel* 56 (March–April 1979): 13–30.

Morris, J. Stephen, and Tapper, Michael M. "Dealing with the Career in Crisis." *Personnel* 59 (May–June 1982): 62–69.

Near, Janet P.; Rice, Robert W.; and Hunt, Raymond G. "The Relationship between Work and Nonwork Domains: A Review of Empirical Research." *Academy of Management Review* 5 (July 1980): 415–29.

Schein, Edgar H. *Career Dynamics: Matching Individual and Organizational Needs.* Reading, Mass.: Addison-Wesley Publishing Co., 1978.

Stringer-Moore, Donna M. "Impact of Dual Career Couples on Employers: Problems and Solutions." *Public Personnel Management* 10 (Winter 1981): 393–401.

Veiga, John F. "Do Managers on the Move Get Anywhere?" *Harvard Business Review* 59 (March–April 1981): 20–38.

Webber, Ross A. "Career Problems of Young Managers." *California Management Review* 18 (Summer 1976): 19–33.

PART FIVE
LEADING
AND
MOTIVATING

19

MOTIVATION AND JOB SATISFACTION

This chapter will enable you to

- *Understand the concept of motivation and identify the primary elements of a motivational system.*
- *Explain the major theories of motivation and recognize how each can be applied to human behavior in organizations.*
- *Become familiar with the concept of job satisfaction and understand its relationship to organizational effectiveness.*

A major responsibility of managers at all organizational levels is to direct and inspire the work of others. High performing employees can make the difference between a marginal organization and a highly effective one. To fulfill this responsibility, the manager should understand individual and group behavior and be able to motivate, lead, and communicate. This chapter begins our section on the interpersonal processes involved in management by examining the topic of *motivation* and the related concepts of *individual needs and job satisfaction.*

NATURE OF MOTIVATION

Definition of Motivation

Motivation refers to (1) the *direction* of an individual's behavior; that is, what one chooses to do when several alternatives are available; (2) the *strength* of the behavior once the choice is made; and (3) the *persistence* of the behavior.[1] For an organization to be effective, its members must direct their behavior toward high job performance in a strong, persistent way. How management can encourage this type of behavior is the subject of much of this chapter.

Systemic Elements of Motivation

A number of elements enter into the motivational process and affect the usefulness of any particular motivational approach. Because of the interrelationships among such elements, we recognize that motivation is more complex than often assumed. The three general elements of a mo-

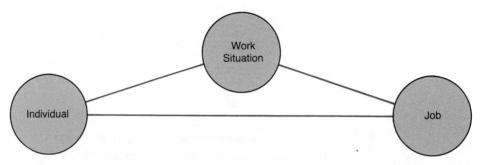

FIGURE 19–1   Elements of a motivational system

tivational system, as portrayed in Figure 19–1, are (1) the individual being motivated, (2) the job, and (3) the work situation.

The Individual.   *Individual differences* are a fact. Organization members, whether managerial or nonmanagerial, differ in intelligence, ability, attitudes, and needs. Hence, they are unlikely to react uniformly to particular motivational forces.

The Job.   The discussion of job design in Chapter 16 noted the variation in job requirements and attractiveness. Some highly routinized jobs become dull and unpleasant to many employees. Other jobs are challenging and a source of enjoyment and pride. Once again, individual differences interact with job design to determine job attractiveness. Not all employees desire challenging jobs. One major motivational difficulty, however, appears to lie in the abundance of highly standardized jobs.

The Work Situation.   The third category of variables affecting work motivation involves the situational background or environment of the work. Many aspects of the work situation appear significant. Relationships with other members of the work group or organization, depending on the circumstances, may stimulate or retard performance because of the individual's adherence to group norms or a desire to obtain peer approval. Supervisory behavior is likewise relevant in the establishment of work standards, regulation of work processes, and dispensation of rewards.

   The concept of *organizational climate* denotes that part of the overall work environment which is described as organization "atmosphere" or "culture." The organizational climate is generally defined as the *perceived* quality of the organizational environment.[2] The climate, developed by the day-to-day administration of the organization, includes such factors as the perceived consistency and equity of the reward system, the perceived structure (including rules, procedures, and "red tape"), the perceived emphasis on rewards or punishment, and so on. The organizational climate might be described as "open," "supportive," "stressful," or "impersonal." Although organization climate affects motivation, its precise impact is not yet clear.

The interaction of the three sets of factors—the individual, the job, and the work situation—produces the motivational appeal to individual members of the organization. As we realize that each of these three sets of factors might be broken into still more specific elements, we can gain an appreciation of the overall complexity of work motivation.

Managerial Assumptions underlying Motivation

Motivational plans and approaches reflect an underlying set of managerial assumptions about the nature of people and their probable response to various types of motivation. The best-known classification of assumptions was provided by Douglas McGregor under the labels of *Theory X* and *Theory Y*.[3] Although these concepts are often regarded as leadership approaches, they are more appropriately described as assumptions.

Theory X represents a relatively pessimistic view of human nature and holds that most people, and employees in particular, tend to be lazy, lack ambition, and require supervision to "keep them moving." The opposite assumptions of Theory Y may be explained as follows:

> Theory Y states, in essence, that man is capable of integrating his own needs and goals with those of the organization; that he is not inherently lazy and indolent; that he is by nature capable of exercising self-control and self-direction, and that he is capable of directing his efforts toward organizational goals.[4]

Although the assumptions are not in themselves leadership approaches, they tend to produce differences in motivational efforts. Theory X managers tend to rely to a greater extent on disciplinary methods and penalties, while Theory Y managers tend to place more emphasis on positive motivation and self-management. A manager's view of the nature of human beings obviously influences his or her methods of motivating subordinates.

Overview of Motivation

Because motivation is an unobservable concept—we can observe only an individual's job performance but not the reasons underlying the level of performance—various theories have been developed to explain it. Even a perfunctory discussion of each of these theories is far beyond the scope of a single chapter.[5] Hence, the following presentation of selected motivational theories focuses on those ideas which are most likely to continue to influence management practice in the 1980s.

THEORIES OF MOTIVATION

Motivation theories may be divided into two groups.[6] *Content theories* emphasize the specific factors that motivate an individual. These factors may reside within the individual (human needs, for instance) or within the individual's environment (job characteristics, for example). *Process theories*, on the other hand, focus on the dynamics of motivation, from the initial energization of behavior, through the selection of behavioral alternatives, to actual effort.

Content Theories

Need Hierarchy.   One of the earliest and most enduring content theories is the need hierarchy proposed by A. H. Maslow.[7] The stairstep diagram in Figure 19–2 ranks five categories of human needs in accordance with Maslow's theory.

If needs are viewed in this way, it is the physiological needs—inherited drives directly connected with the physical body—that must be satisfied first.* The hungry individual seeks food rather than companionship in work. Once these needs are reasonably well satisfied, the next level—the need for safety and security—assumes priority. Only after our physical and safety needs are being met do we begin to desire companionship and close interpersonal relationships. Partial satisfaction of the belongingness needs activates the need to respect ourselves and to have others think well of us. Finally, if all four of these needs are reasonably satisfied, we are then driven by the need to self-actualize—to fulfill our potential.

Although some have questioned Maslow's assertion that needs are arranged in a hierarchy,[8] Maslow appropriately emphasized that much human behavior is directed toward the satisfaction of unfulfilled needs. Furthermore, it seems likely that Maslow is at least partially correct, particularly in distinguishing between lower-level needs—that is, the physiological and security needs—and higher-level needs.

> There is a strong evidence to support the view that unless the existence needs are satisfied none of the higher-order needs will come into play.
> There is also some evidence that unless security needs are satisfied, people will not be concerned with higher-order needs. . . . There is, however, little evidence to support the view that a hierarchy exists once one moves above the security level.[9]

A two-level hierarchy can, therefore, be supported on the basis of present knowledge.

---

*There are at least two other well-known need theories. One identifies three basic drives which vary from individual to individual: (1) the need for *achievement*, (2) the need for *power*, and (3) the need for *affiliation*. Another classifies human needs into three basic categories: (1) *existence* needs (material and physiological desires), (2) *relatedness* needs (relationships with significant others), and (3) *growth* needs (desires to create and produce). For information on the former, see John W. Atkinson and Joel O. Raynor, *Personality, Motivation, and Achievement* (Washington, D.C.: Hemisphere Publishing Corp., 1978) and David C. McClelland and David H. Burnham, "Power Is the Great Motivator," *Harvard Business Review* 54 (March-April 1976): 100–10. The latter is described in Clayton P. Alderfer, *Existence, Relatedness, and Growth: Human Needs in Organizational Settings* (New York: The Free Press, 1972).

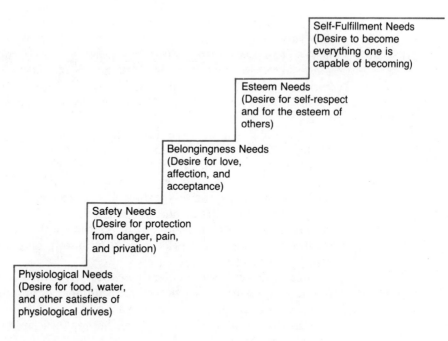

FIGURE 19-2   Maslow's need hierarchy

Contemporary organizations satisfy needs in varying degrees. Physiological and safety needs are at least partially satisfied for many U.S. workers through wages and salaries, medical and life insurance benefits, retirement plans, safety regulations, and so on. In some organizations, labor unions have provided additional need satisfaction through seniority protection clauses, strike benefits, and cost of living allowances. The lack of fulfillment of higher-level needs poses a significant problem for millions of employees, however.

Two-Factor Theory.   Perhaps the most widely discussed content theory is Frederick Herzberg's *two-factor theory* of motivation.[10] Herzberg proposed that two major categories of job factors—*hygiene factors* and *motivators*—affect employee attitudes and behavior, as suggested in Figure 19–3.

Hygiene factors are associated with the job *context* or environment and serve to keep employees from becoming dissatisfied. Examples are

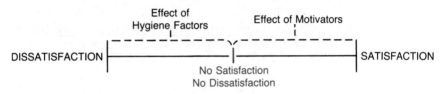

FIGURE 19-3   Two-factor theory

organizational policy and administration; interpersonal relationships with superiors, peers, and subordinates; job security; and salary. If employees feel that the organization's policies are appropriate, that their salaries are fair, that they have adequate job security, and that their working relationships are pleasant, they are unlikely to be dissatisfied. These factors, however, are insufficient to satisy them or to motivate them to high performance.

The motivational role is filled by the second type of job factor. Examples of motivators are achievement, recognition, responsibility, and advancement. These factors are associated with the job *content* and, if present, make individuals satisfied with their jobs and help to motivate them. According to Herzberg, then, if management can enrich employees' jobs by giving them more responsibility, a chance to advance, and feelings of achievement and recognition, the employees will perform better. In other words, job enrichment should help employees satisfy their upper-level needs.

Research evidence on Herzberg's theory is mixed, and the theory's foundations have been criticized on a number of grounds.[11] The theory has, however, had a significant impact on job design. Much of the recent work in job enrichment, reported in Chapter 16, is an outgrowth of Herzberg's earlier efforts.

A Process Theory: Expectancy Theory

A motivational formulation which explicitly accounts for individual differences is *expectancy theory*,[12] which, unlike Maslow's or Herzberg's conceptualizations, is a process theory. Expectancy theory hypothesizes that motivation begins with a desire for something—perhaps self-actualization, higher status, a feeling of accomplishment, or more leisure time. The degree to which an individual desires a particular *outcome* is termed the *valence* (or psychological importance) of that outcome. Outcomes may be either *extrinsic*—external rewards such as pay or promotion—or *intrinsic*—internal rewards such as feelings of increased self-esteem or self-actualization.

The individual seeks to determine how the desired outcomes can be attained. Feelings of accomplishment, for instance, may be attained in a variety of ways—performing well on one's job, going to work for another organization, or even engaging in off-the-job activities. Management, of course, hopes that the employee will engage in high job performance. But the means the employee will use to gain the desired feelings of accomplishment depends upon the factors illustrated in Figure 19–4.

Expectancy is the individual's estimate of the likelihood that his or her effort will result in performance. Effort is not the same as performance, as any student who has studied all night for an exam only to make a "D" will testify. Performance depends not only upon effort but also the individual's (1) having the appropriate abilities and traits, and (2) channelling his or her behavior in the proper direction, rather than

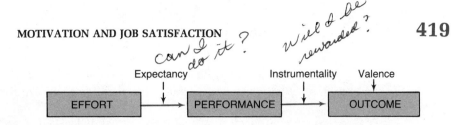

FIGURE 19-4   Expectancy theory

engaging in unfocused effort. *Instrumentality* is the relationship the individual perceives between performance, once it is attained, and the desired outcome.

Assume that the employee mentioned above desires a greater feeling of accomplishment and feels there are two possible means of attaining it: performing well on his or her present job or taking a new job with another organization. The individual will first estimate the probability that effort will lead to high performance on the present job and will compare this estimate with the expectancy that effort directed toward finding a new job (another type of performance) will result in an appropriate position. Next, the individual will assess the likelihood that job performance will lead to feelings of accomplishment and compare this with the probability that a job change will result in the desired feelings of accomplishment.

The alternative the employee will choose is a multiplicative function of valence, instrumentality, and expectancy, as shown in Figure 19–5. In the situation illustrated, the employee is likely to quit his or her present position to go to work for another organization. Why? Because he or she places a high value (10, say, on a scale of 10) on accomplishment and perceives a job change as being highly instrumental (.8 probability) in attaining the desired outcome and believes that his or her job-seeking efforts are reasonably likely (.6 probability) to lead to a new job. Although the probability of performing well on the present job is higher (.8 probability), the present job is not seen as being instrumental (.2 probability) in attaining feelings of accomplishment.

Expectancy theory, then, accounts for individual differences by showing that each of us is motivated by differing outcomes to which we assign our own valences. Additionally, our perceptions of instrumentality and expectancy are also likely to differ. In the example given above, for instance, job enrichment would probably be beneficial for that em-

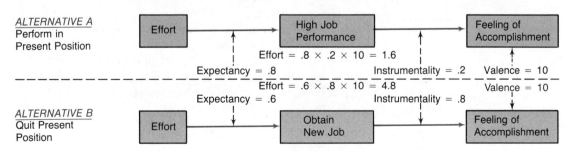

FIGURE 19–5   Assessment of behavioral alternatives

ployee because it should increase the employee's estimate of the instrumentality between performance and feelings of accomplishment.

Management's Role. Management's task is to (1) ensure that employees perceive high instrumentalities between job performance and the outcomes they desire, and (2) increase employee expectancies that effort will result in performance. The first requires management to learn what outcomes employees value, since the outcomes that motivate one individual may differ from those that motivate another person. This may be done through questionnaires or interviews. It also requires managers to be alert and consistent in providing such extrinsic rewards as recognition and salary increases. The second—increasing expectancies—can be accomplished through training and development programs which improve employee abilities, well-designed MBO programs, or even job descriptions, which help employees channel their efforts in the proper direction. The more certain employees are of their expectancy and instrumentality estimates, the more likely is expectancy theory to predict their behavior accurately.[13]

When an individual is relatively certain that his or her effort will result in high performance and is equally certain that performance will

INSTRUMENTALITY IN UNIVERSITIES

Managers of organizations must ensure that they reward the type of performance they desire. As Steven Kerr has so aptly pointed out, some universities *hope* that their professors will teach well, but *reward* them for research and publications.* Hence, many instructors are more likely to spend time writing than preparing for class because they perceive a low instrumentality between teaching well and the outcomes they desire, such as promotions, pay raises, and national recognition. Administrative encouragement of excellent teaching will have little effect until a higher instrumentality is perceived between teaching and rewards.

In spite of this reward system, some professors at those universities teach well. Why? Because they perceive a high instrumentality between their performance and the particular set of outcomes that they desire—helping students learn, being recognized as one of the school's premier teachers, fulfilling the need for esteem and self-satisfaction, and so on.

*Steven Kerr, "On the Folly of Rewarding A, While Hoping for B," *Academy of Management Journal* 18 (December 1975): 769–83.

be rewarded with desirable outcomes, that person is likely to be a high performer, according to expectancy theory. Conversely, when individuals perform well, but observe that their rewards do not differ significantly from employees who are poor performers, their estimates of instrumentality and, hence, their efforts, are likely to decrease in the future. If an organization rewards seniority rather than performance, it can scarcely hope to have a work force composed of high performers.

Assessment of Expectancy Theory.   The complexity of expectancy theory poses a problem for researchers and practitioners alike.[14] Research findings have been mixed, partially because of varying methods of measuring the theory's concepts. Implementation of the theory in an organization requires that motivational programs be tailored to individual needs and that they recognize that these needs change over time.* A manager who is aware of his or her subordinates' needs and the outcomes they desire can use expectancy theory concepts to motivate those subordinates, provided the manager has control over the necessary rewards.

The value of expectancy theory lies in its emphasis on individual differences and its explication of how one's goals and desires influence one's behavior. Human beings are viewed as thinking individuals who reason and make conscious behavioral choices based on their expectations about the future.

A Process Theory: Behavior Modification

A considerably different philosophy of motivation is derived from *behavior modification* principles, based upon operant conditioning theory.[15] A well-established area of study in psychology, operant conditioning has only recently been applied formally to human behavior in organizations.[16]

Operant behavior—unlike instinctual behavior such as sneezing—is behavior that is followed by an event (called *reinforcement*) which affects the probability that the behavior will occur again in the future. The closer the reinforcement follows the behavior, the greater the likelihood that future behavior will be affected. The major types of reinforcement available to the manager are defined below:

1. *Positive reinforcement* increases the probability that the behavior will be repeated in the future. An employee who has just performed some task superbly may be praised, recognized publicly, given a raise or promotion, or handed an attractive job assignment.

2. *Negative reinforcement* or *avoidance* strengthens behavior by pro-

---

*Some organizations have recently begun to offer flexible "cafeteria" benefit plans, which allow employees to choose benefits to suit their own needs. The benefits, however, are rarely tied to high performance, negating much of their motivational potential.

viding an avenue of escape from an unpleasant event. In this case, an individual might perform well to avoid being chewed out by the boss.

3. *Punishment* decreases the probability that undesirable behavior will be repeated. An employee who arrives at work late may be reprimanded by the boss or have his or her pay docked.

4. *Extinction* is also used to reduce undesirable behavior. In this case, positive reinforcement is withheld following the behavior. An individual's inane comments at a meeting may simply be ignored.

"The objective of each of the four reinforcement types is to modify an individual's behavior so that it will benefit the organization."[17] Of course, the effectiveness of a given form of reinforcement upon behavior may vary from individual to individual. Praise, for instance, is not positively reinforcing for all people.

Probably the most common form of reinforcement used by managers is positive reinforcement. When desirable behavior is positively reinforced each time it occurs, a *continuous reinforcement* schedule is being used. *Partial reinforcement* occurs when the desired behaviors are reinforced occasionally rather than continuously. In practice, most reinforcement is partial, since continuous reinforcement is often impractical. Salary, for instance, is paid on a *fixed interval* schedule, such as monthly or weekly. Praise is often bestowed at *variable intervals*, that is, not at regularly scheduled times.

Operant conditioning theory hypothesizes that partial reinforcement is more effective in sustaining behavior than is continuous reinforcement. Particularly effective is a *variable ratio* schedule under which behavior is reinforced, on the average, following every x number of desired responses.[18] If the average is ten, for example, reinforcement might occur after three responses, then after twenty responses, then after seven, for an average of ten. (Gambling is a common example of variable ratio reinforcement, and the gambling habit is notoriously hard to break.) Results of controlled research on variable ratio reinforcement in organizations, however, are not clear.[19]

Punishment, although used frequently in organizations, has been examined less than positive reinforcement.[20] Based on a review of the evidence, Richard D. Arvey and John M. Ivancevich generated a number of propositions to suggest how certain conditions might influence the effectiveness of punishment.[21] They suggest, for instance, that punishment is usually more effective when

1. It occurs immediately after the undesirable behavior occurs.
2. It is moderate in intensity, rather than low or high.
3. The punisher has relatively close and friendly relationships with the employee being punished.
4. It occurs consistently after every undesired response.

BEHAVIOR MODIFICATION IN ORGANIZATIONS

Emery Air Freight. At Emery Air Freight, positive reinforcement practices have become the major motivational tool used by managers. All of the firm's managers have been trained in reinforcement techniques through self-instructional programmed texts. The primary reinforcer, when the program began, was praise. Although the original intent was to use praise on a variable ratio scale, it gradually became more of a continuous reinforcer. As such, its effect was dulled and it even became an irritant to some recipients.

> To counter this potential difficulty, Emery managers and supervisors have been taught and encouraged to expand their reinforcers beyond praise. Among the recommended reinforcers have been formal recognition such as a public letter or a letter home, being given a more enjoyable task after completing a less enjoyable one, invitations to business luncheons or meetings, delegating responsibility and decision making, and tying such requests as special time off or any other deviation from normal procedure to performance.
>
> Emery Air Freight's program has been perhaps the most well-publicized illustration of organizational behavior modification. The company reports cost savings of millions of dollars, increased job performance, and significant revenue increases, which it attributes to the behavior modification program.

Department Store. Sales clerks in eight departments in a large department store were positively reinforced for engaging in the following behaviors:

- Being present in the department.
- Assisting a customer within five seconds (or if already waiting on a customer, acknowledging the new customer's presence and promising assistance momentarily).
- Keeping the display shelves at least 70 percent filled.

Those who behaved in the desired fashion received time off with pay, or the cash equivalent, and an opportunity to compete in a drawing for a paid week's vacation for two.

Their performance showed a significant improvement compared to the performance of clerks in eight other departments whose undesired behavior was punished but whose desired behavior was ignored (extinction).

SOURCES: Adapted from W. Clay Hamner and Ellen P. Hamner, "Behavior Modification on the Bottom Line," *Organizational Dynamics* 4 (Spring 1976): 11–15 (quote is from p. 15); Fred Luthans, Robert Paul, and Douglas Baker, "An Experimental Analysis of the Impact of Contingent Reinforcement on Salespersons' Performance Behavior," *Journal of Applied Psychology* 66 (June 1981): 314–23.

5. It is administered consistently across different employees by the same manager, and different managers are consistent in punishing the same undesired response.

6. The reason for the punishment is clearly communicated to the employee.

Differences between Expectancy Theory and Behavior Modification. The primary, and highly significant, difference between expectancy theory and behavior modification is the relative emphasis placed upon the internal thought processes of the individual. Expectancy theory is firmly based on the view that one's present behavior is a function of his or her expectations about the future and the connection he or she perceives between present behavior and future outcomes. In other words, we choose to act as we do because we believe our actions will result in some desirable future outcome.

Behavior modification, on the other hand, proposes that our present behavior results from our past experiences. We engage in certain behaviors because they have been positively reinforced, and we avoid actions that have been punished.

> Notice that there are no references to any internal cognitive processes. Reinforcers do not feel good or bad, they simply change the frequency of the behavior. The true behaviorist believes that operant behavior is caused by environmental events. This philosophy is called *environmental determinism*. It is our past history of reinforcement that causes our current behavior.[22]

Similarities between Expectancy Theory and Behavior Modification. Although both theories explain present behavior in considerably different ways, both strongly emphasize the essential linkage between performance and rewards. Behavior desired by management must be rewarded while undesirable behavior should not be rewarded.

> Indeed, it may be that the two models are not entirely incompatible. Combining . . . [behavior modification] and . . . [expectancy theory] influences on effort and performance may increase our ability to structure rewarding environments to the benefit of both organizations and their employees.[23]

Issues in Motivation

The Opportunity to Perform. Of the three systemic elements in motivation identified earlier in this chapter—the individual, the job, and the work situation—most of the emphasis in motivational research has been on the individual and job design. Only recently have scholars begun to emphasize the importance of broader situational factors.[24]

It is the manager's responsibility to provide an *opportunity* for willing and able subordinates to perform well. "In many work situations, persons who are both willing and able to successfully accomplish a task may be either inhibited in or prevented from doing so due to situational characteristics beyond their control."[25] Creating a facilitative environment requires an analysis of such factors as the organization's (or subsystem's, depending on the manager's level in the hierarchy) technology, planning/scheduling systems, and delegation practices. For instance, improvements in performance brought about through technological change are probably more dramatic than are increases resulting from emphasis on rewards or job design. Also, efficient planning for the delivery of raw materials and parts and for the scheduling of workflow and coordination of activities provides the opportunity for higher performance than does an inefficient planning system. Even delegation of challenging and important tasks to able individuals helps them realize their full potential and is likely to pay dividends in higher performance. Additionally, such actions as placing able newcomers into a formal work group of high performers, and the sponsorship of aspiring managers by higher-level executives in a mentor relationship can encourage high performance.[26] These suggestions are by no means all-inclusive—they are simply suggestive ways in which management can increase the opportunity for subordinates to perform.

Role of Pay in Motivation. Although the precise effect of pay on individual motivation is debated, pay can motivate under certain conditions.[27] The primary requirement for strong motivation is that pay be explicitly tied to individual job performance. But this condition, unfortunately, is not as simple as it appears. Performance must be directly, objectively measurable. Even if performance is measurable, the individual must be able to control those aspects of performance on which he or she is to be evaluated. (Profit-sharing plans typically fail to meet this criterion, for instance, because the work of one individual has so little impact on overall profit performance.) If the foregoing conditions are met, management must then ensure that the pay increases awarded to high performers are sufficiently large to be meaningful.* Unless all of these conditions are met—and in many situations, they cannot be—pay is unlikely to encourage more than average performance.

Ethical Considerations in Motivation. The use of motivational techniques prompts a number of ethical considerations. For instance, does motivation at some point become manipulation?[28] To what extent do managers have the right to control the behavior of subordinates? Since we have only limited knowledge of human motivation, is management's application of such concepts as expectancy theory or behavior modifi-

---

*During times of inflation, organizations often give across-the-board pay increases to their employees to help them cope with the rising cost of living. The Hay Compensation Comparison (conducted by Hay Associates, a management consulting firm) indicates that the difference between the percentage salary increase given to an employee rated "outstanding" versus one rated "satisfactory" dropped from 6 percent to 3.9 percent between 1971 and 1981.

cation premature? If so, what are the dangers of premature application? Further, some motivation systems—such as expectancy theory—require the probing of employee values relating to the desirability of various outcomes. How far should management go?

> Most people are sensitive to the privacy of individual values in the context of other social behaviors such as voting, yet no one seems bothered by the possibility that the worker may not want his or her values explored, or that line supervisors may not be competent to perform such an assessment accurately.[29]

The answers to issues such as these are neither easy nor simple. But managers must be aware of the issues. Programs intended to enhance organizational effectiveness must not disregard the individual's freedom, dignity, and right to privacy.

JOB SATISFACTION

As suggested earlier, motivation, performance, and job satisfaction are intertwined. In this final section, we will look specifically at the nature of job satisfaction and its relationship to motivation.

The Nature of Job Satisfaction

Job satisfaction is a multidimensional concept, encompassing the attitudes an individual has toward such important dimensions as the following:

- the organization
- immediate supervision
- financial rewards
- fellow employees
- the job

Employees also have attitudes related to the work environment, job security or uncertainty, prestige of the product or department, and organization location. Their attitudes toward these factors are indicative of their apathy or enthusiasm toward the activities and objectives of the organization. Specific attitudes, moreover, need not be uniformly favorable or unfavorable. An employee, for example, may feel proud of the company and its contribution to society but dislike the monotony of work.

Job Satisfaction and Performance

A perplexing question concerning job satisfaction is the extent of its relationship to performance or efficiency. Intuitively, we are inclined to expect a strong positive correlation. Yet, a moment's reflection reminds us that a happy, sociable employee may spend time socializing rather than working, and a college student may be satisfied with his or her part-time job because the task is not demanding and allows the student to study on the job. In short, little substantive evidence supports the idea that a "happy worker is a hard worker."

DECLINE IN JOB SATISFACTION

Although job satisfaction among U.S. workers remained relatively steady for over thirty years, the results of the most recent national survey indicate that job satisfaction declined significantly during the 1970s. As one survey put it, "A consensus is emerging that there has been a shift in the attitudes and values of the U.S. work force and that this shift has been accompanied by increased dissatisfaction with many aspects of work."

The decline is evident in a number of areas, among them dissatisfaction with treatment at work, with job surroundings, and with the amount of information and authority available to get the job done. The average worker feels that his or her job is less interesting than workers did in previous decades, and many feel that their skills are underused and they have insufficient control over the days they work and their job assignments. As might be expected, clerical and hourly workers register lower on the satisfaction scale than do managers.

Employees feel that their companies should attempt to remedy their problems and complaints, yet less than a fourth of the hourly and clerical employees in one large survey believed that their companies were responsive to their feelings.

SOURCE: Data from the "Quality of Employment Survey," University of Michigan Survey Research Center; Work in America Institute Inc., reported in John Hoerr, "A Warning That Worker Discontent is Rising," *Business Week*, 4 June 1979, p. 152; and M. R. Cooper, B. S. Morgan, P. M. Foley, and L. B. Kaplan, "Changing Employee Values: Deepening Discontent," *Harvard Business Review* 57 (January-February 1979): 117–25 (quote is from p. 117).

Recent evidence suggests that both satisfaction and performance are related to rewards.[30] Rewards provide satisfaction to the subordinate if he or she values those particular rewards and if they are provided in sufficient magnitude. But the rewards are not likely to influence performance unless the subordinate perceives that his or her effort will result in high performance and that the performance will be rewarded. If a subordinate who performs poorly is rewarded with the same salary increase as that given to high performers, the subordinate is likely to be satisfied with the reward, but little improvement in his or her performance is likely. "A properly designed reward system . . . dissatisfies low performers because it doesn't give them the rewards they want."[31]

It is then the manager's responsibility to help them translate their dissatisfaction into improving their effort and performance.

Effects of Job Satisfaction

Even though it appears that favorable job satisfaction may not inspire high productivity, other beneficial effects occur. Favorable employee attitudes, according to different studies, are associated with a lower rate of personnel turnover and less absenteeism.[32] In view of this fact, job satisfaction could significantly affect organizational effectiveness. A high rate of turnover, for example, tends to increase recruitment and training costs.

A high morale level probably also represents a "plus" in terms of public relations. In addition to general benefits accruing from a favorable public relations image, recruitment may be easier. A favorable public attitude encourages the best applicants to apply, and this is particularly significant in times of short labor supply.

Union relationships may also be helped or hindered by the general attitudes of personnel. Grievances and work stoppages can result from negative attitudes. No doubt the task of supervision is also less burdensome if job satisfaction is high. A manager, therefore, has a number of reasons for seeking positive attitudes.

ACROSS THE BOARD

The recession of the early 1980s, enormous increases in jet fuel prices, and the competition brought about by deregulation of the industry combined to create very serious financial problems for U.S. airline companies. One particularly hard-hit firm was Trans World Airlines. Among the cost-reduction measures that top management ordered was a 10 to 25 percent cut in the salaries of eight hundred TWA managers on that portion of their annual pay exceeding $35,000.

> The newly enforced efficiencies at TWA have also produced some hidden costs. [TWA President C. E. Meyer, Jr.], for example, is already walking a tightrope in handling employee morale. He contends that the across-the-board pay cuts at TWA will produce no ill effects on work performance, and he even maintains that five pilots recently laid off have called him to say they understand the reasons. But of the pay cuts, another airline industry executive remarks: "If I were running the company and decided to cut the budget by 15%, I would get rid of the deadwood and give everyone else a raise. You ought to be motivating them."

SOURCE: "Trans World Corp.: The Strategy Squeeze on the Airline," *Business Week*, 19 May 1980, p. 106–7 (quote is from p. 107).

SUMMARY

The topics of *motivation* and *job satisfaction* are central to organizational effectiveness. Motivation refers to the direction, strength, and persistence of an individual's behavior. The motivation process is complex, involving three major groups of variables: the individual, the job, and the work situation.

Early ideas about motivation took the form of *content theories*, focusing on the specific factors that motivate people. Two of the better-known theories in this area are Maslow's *need hierarchy*, and Herzberg's *two-factor theory*. Maslow suggests that individuals are motivated by the desire to fulfill needs and that these needs range, hierarchically, from physiological needs to self-fulfillment needs. Herzberg proposes that factors associated with the job context (*hygiene factors*) can keep employees from becoming dissatisfied while factors associated with the job content (*motivators*) are capable—through job enrichment—of making individuals satisfied with their jobs and motivated.

Worker's maturity

A more complex formulation that recognizes the differences among individuals is *expectancy theory*. This theory hypothesizes that individuals will direct strong effort toward their jobs when (1) they believe that high performance will lead to outcomes they desire, and (2) when they expect that their efforts will indeed result in high performance. Human beings are viewed as thinking individuals who make conscious behavioral choices based on their expectations about the future.

Mgr's use of power

A significantly different view of motivation is based on *behavior modification* principles, derived from operant conditioning theory. These principles predict that behavior which is *positively reinforced* is likely to be repeated in the future, while behavior which is *punished* is likely to decrease in occurrence. Present behavior, then, is a function of past reinforcement experiences. Although this is nearly the opposite view presented by expectancy theory, both ideas emphasize the essential linkage between performance and rewards.

Although most of the emphasis in motivational research has been on the individual and job design, managers are also responsible for providing an *opportunity* for willing and able subordinates to perform well. Creating a facilitative environment requires an analysis of factors such as technology, planning/scheduling systems, delegation practices, placement, and mentorship.

Pay can be used to motivate employees if (1) the pay is explicitly tied to the individual's job performance, (2) the performance is objectively measurable, (3) the individual can control those aspects of performance which are being evaluated, and (4) the pay increases awarded to high performers are large enough to be meaningful.

Job satisfaction is a multidimensional concept composed of the attitudes a person has toward such task dimensions as the organization, immediate supervision, financial rewards, fellow employees, and the job. Although many individuals expect job satisfaction and performance to be positively related, there is no necessary relationship between the two. Evidence suggests that both are influenced by rewards. Valued rewards can increase employee satisfaction but will influence performance only if they are directly tied to performance criteria.

DISCUSSION QUESTIONS

1. What is meant by the *systemic* elements of motivation, and what are the major components in a motivational system?

2. Explain the distinction between *Theory X* and *Theory Y* and indicate the type of leadership or motivation that might be associated with each.

3. Explain carefully the concept of a *hierarchy of needs*. What is the significance of this concept in terms of motivation?

4. What is the difference between a "hygiene factor" and a "motivator"? Specifically, how are individuals motivated, according to the *two-factor theory*?

5. Define the following concepts: *outcome, valence, instrumentality,* and *expectancy,* and explain how individuals are motivated according to *expectancy theory.*

6. How does *expectancy theory* account for individual differences?

7. Explain how *behavior modification* may be used to motivate individuals to high performance.

8. What is the major difference between *expectancy theory* and *behavior modification*? How are they similar?

9. Explain how a properly trained, highly motivated employee may not be able to perform well due to a lack of *opportunity.*

10. What are some of the difficulties involved in using pay as a tool for *motivation?*

11. Is a "happy worker" likely to be a "hard worker"? Why or why not?

12. What types of benefits may result from favorable employee attitudes?

NOTES

1. John P. Campbell et al., *Managerial Behavior, Performance,* and *Effectiveness* (New York: McGraw-Hill Book Co., 1970), p. 340.

2. See, for example, George H. Litwin and Robert A. Stringer, Jr., *Motivation and Organizational Climate* (Boston: Harvard University Graduate School of Business Administration, 1968).

3. Douglas McGregor, *The Human Side of Enterprise* (New York: McGraw-Hill Book Co., 1960).

4. Edgar H. Schein, "In Defense of Theory Y," *Organizational Dynamics* 4 (Summer 1975): 20.

5. An excellent source for an overview of this area is Richard M. Steers and Lyman W. Porter, eds., *Motivation and Work Behavior*, 2d ed. (New York: McGraw-Hill Book Co., 1979).

6. Campbell et al., *Managerial Behavior*, p. 341.

7. A. H. Maslow, "A Theory of Human Motivation," *Psychological Review* 50 (July 1943): 370–96.

8. John Rauschenberger, Neal Schmitt, and John E. Hunter, "A Test of the Need Hierarchy Concept by a Markov Model of Change in Need Strength," *Administrative Science Quarterly* 25 (December 1980): 654–70; and Mahmoud A. Wahba and Lawrence G. Bridwell, "Maslow Reconsidered: A Review of the Research on the Need Hierarchy Theory," *Organizational Behavior and Human Performance* 15 (April 1976): 212–40.

9. Lyman W. Porter, Edward E. Lawler III, and J. Richard Hackman, *Behavior in Organizations* (New York: McGraw-Hill Book Co., 1975), p. 43.

10. Frederick Herzberg, Bernard Mausner, and Barbara Block Snyderman, *The Motivation to Work* (New York: John Wiley & Sons, 1959). A succinct discussion of Herzberg's theory with an accompanying practical application may be found in Frederick Herzberg, "One More Time: How Do You Motivate Employees?" *Harvard Business Review* 46 (January–February 1968): 53–62.

11. See, for instance, Robert J. House and Lawrence A. Wigdor, "Herzberg's Dual-Factor Theory of Job Satisfaction and Motivation: A Review of the Evidence and a Criticism," *Personnel Psychology* 20 (Winter 1967): 369–89.

12. Two of the better-known formulations are found in Victor H. Vroom, *Work and Motivation* (New York: John Wiley & Sons, 1964) and Lyman W. Porter and Edward E. Lawler III, *Managerial Attitudes and Performance* (Homewood, Ill: Richard D. Irwin, 1968).

13. Kenneth R. Ferris, "Perceived Environmental Uncertainty as a Mediator of Expectancy Theory Predictions: Some Preliminary Findings," *Decision Sciences* 9 (July 1978): 379–90. A discussion of the criteria for a successful incentive program may be found in Robert D. Pritchard, Philip J. DeLeo, and Clarence W. Von Bergen, Jr., "A Field Experimental Test of Expectancy-Valence Incentive Motivation Techniques," *Organizational Behavior and Human Performance* 15 (April 1976): 355–406.

14. A representative review of the research on expectancy theory may be found in Terence M. Mitchell, "Expectancy-Value Models in Organizational Psychology," in *Expectancy, Incentive and Action*, ed. N. Feather (Hillsdale, N.J.: Erlbaum and Associates, 1980).

15. See B. F. Skinner, *Science and Human Behavior* (New York: The Free Press, 1953); and C. B. Ferster and B. F. Skinner, *Schedules of Reinforcement* (New York: Appleton-Century-Crofts, 1957).

16. A review of behavior modification applications in organizations may be found in Harold W. Babb and Daniel G. Kopp, "Applications of Behavior Modification in Organizations: A Review and Critique," *Academy of Management Review* 3 (April 1978): 281–92.

17. Andrew D. Szilagyi, Jr., and Marc J. Wallace, Jr., *Organizational Behavior and Performance*, 2d ed. (Santa Monica, Calif.: Goodyear Publishing Co., 1980), p. 125.

18. An interesting application of variable ratio reinforcement in a small manufacturing plant is described in John G. Carlson and Kenneth D. Hill, "The Effect of Gaming on Attendance and Attitude," *Personnel Psychology* 35 (Spring 1982): 63–73.

19. Robert D. Pritchard et al., "The Effects of Varying Schedules of Reinforcement on Human Task Performance," *Organizational Behavior and Human Performance* 16 (August 1976): 205–30; and Robert D. Pritchard, John Hollenback, and Philip J. De Leo, "The Effects of Continuous and Partial Schedules of Reinforcement on Effort, Performance and Satisfaction," *Organizational Behavior and Human Performance* 25 (June 1980): 336–53.

20. For an extensive review of the variables that affect the supervisor's use of rewards and punishments, see Philip M. Podsahoff, "Determinants of a Supervisor's Use of Rewards and Punishments: A Literature Review and Suggestions for Further Research," *Organizational Behavior and Human Performance* 29 (February 1982): 58–83.

21. Richard D. Arvey and John M. Ivancevich, "Punishment in Organizations: A Review, Propositions, and Research Suggestions," *Academy of Management Review* 5 (January 1980): 126–29.

22. Terence R. Mitchell, *People in Organizations: Understanding Their Behavior* (New York: McGraw-Hill Book Co., 1978), p. 167.

23. Steers and Porter, eds., *Motivation and Work Behavior*, 2d ed., p. 213.

24. Melvin Blumberg and Charles D. Pringle, "The Missing Opportunity in Organizational Research: Some Implications for a Theory of Work Performance," *Academy of Management Review* 7 (October 1982): 560–69; and Lawrence H. Peters and Edward J. O'Connor, "Situational Constraints and Work Outcomes: The Influences of a Frequently Overlooked Construct," *Academy of Management Review* 5 (July 1980): 391–97.

25. Peters and O'Connor, "Situational Constraints," pp. 391–92.

26. Blumberg and Pringle, "The Missing Opportunity," pp. 567–68.

27. Edward E. Lawler III, *Pay and Organizational Effectiveness: A Psychological View* (New York: McGraw-Hill Book Co., 1971); and Edward E. Lawler III, "Merit Pay: Fact or Fiction?" *Management Review* 70 (April 1981): 50–53.

28. These and other issues are raised in Craig C. Pinder, "Concerning the Application of Human Motivation Theories in Organizational Settings," *Academy of Management Review* 2 (July 1977): 384–97.

29. Ibid., p. 386.

30. Charles N. Greene and Robert E. Craft, Jr., "The Satisfaction-Performance Controversy—Revisited," in *Motivation and Work Behavior*, 2d ed., ed. Steers and Porter, pp. 270–87.

31. Lloyd Baird, "Managing Dissatisfaction," *Personnel* 58 (May–June 1981): 18.

32. The most often-referenced review in this area is found in Vroom, *Work and Motivation*, 1964. Also see Daniel Katz and Robert L. Kahn, *The Social Psychology of Organizations*, 2d ed. (New York: John Wiley & Sons, 1978), pp. 414–17.

SUPPLEMENTARY READING

Arvey, Richard D., and **Ivancevich, John M.** "Punishment in Organizations: A Review, Propositions, and Research Suggestions." *Academy of Management Review* 5 (January 1980): 123–32.

Baird, Lloyd. "Managing Dissatisfaction." *Personnel* 58 (May–June 1981): 12–21.

Blumberg, Melvin, and **Pringle, Charles D.** "The Missing Opportunity in Organizational Research: Some Implications for a Theory of Work Performance." *Academy of Management Review* 7 (October 1982): 560–69.

Deci, Edward L. "The Hidden Costs of Rewards." *Organizational Dynamics* 4 (Winter 1976): 61–72.

Dowling, William. "Are Workers Pigeons?" *Across the Board* 15 (November 1978): 26–33.

Hamner, W. Clay, and **Hamner, Ellen P.** "Behavior Modification on the Bottom Line." *Organizational Dynamics* 4 (Spring 1976): 3–21.

Haynes, Robert S.; Pine, Randall C.; and **Fitch, H. Gordon.** "Reducing Accident Rates with Organizational Behavior Modification." *Academy of Management Journal* 25 (June 1982): 407–16.

Kearney, William J. "Pay for Performance? Not Always." *MSU Business Topics* 27 (Spring 1979): 5–16.

Lawler, Edward E. "Merit Pay: Fact or Fiction?" *Management Review* 70 (April 1981): 50–53.

Locke, Edwin A. "The Myths of Behavior Mod in Organizations." *Academy of Management Review* 2 (October 1977): 543–53.

Mawhinney, Thomas C. "Operant Terms and Concepts in the Description of Individual Work Behavior: Some Problems of Interpretation, Application, and Evaluation." *Journal of Applied Psychology* 60 (December 1975): 704–12.

Mayes, Bronston T. "Some Boundary Considerations in the Application of Motivation Models." *Academy of Management Review* 3 (January 1978): 51–58.

Mitchell, Terence R. "Motivation: New Directions for Theory, Research, and Practice." *Academy of Management Review* 7 (January 1982): 80–88.

Peters, Lawrence H., and **O'Connor, Edward J.** "Situational Constraints and Work Outcomes: The Influences of a Frequently Overlooked Construct." *Academy of Management Review* 5 (July 1980): 391–97.

Podsahoff, Philip M. "Determinants of a Supervisor's Use of Rewards and Punishments: A Literature Review and Suggestions for Further Research." *Organizational Behavior and Human Performance* 29 (February 1982): 58–83.

Porter, Lyman W., and **Lawler, Edward E., III.** *Managerial Attitudes and Performance.* Homewood, Ill.: Richard D. Irwin, 1968.

Steers, Richard M., and **Porter, Lyman W.,** eds. *Motivation and Work Behavior.* 2d ed. New York: McGraw-Hill Book Co., 1979.

Vroom, Victor H. *Work and Motivation.* New York: John Wiley & Sons, 1964.

20

MANAGERIAL LEADERSHIP

This chapter will enable you to

- *Understand the manager's leadership function and identify the various leadership styles that managers use.*
- *Recognize the situational nature of leadership by identifying situations in which certain leadership styles are more appropriate than others.*
- *Discuss participative leadership and indicate the conditions under which it is most effective.*

Organizational performance is closely related to quality of *leadership*. Although competent leadership is not the only important ingredient for successful operation, it is an essential one. A bungling leader can wreck morale and destroy efficiency. Strong leadership, on the other hand, can transform a lackluster group into a strong, aggressive, successful organization. This chapter examines *leadership* and its contribution to organizational performance.

THE MANAGER'S LEADERSHIP FUNCTION

Through *leadership*, a manager secures the cooperation of others in accomplishing an objective. Managers at all hierarchical levels have a leadership role to perform. Although some people equate leadership with management, the two concepts differ significantly. A number of management activities—such as determining strategy, budgeting, or monitoring environmental information—are not directly related to leadership. Leadership is more properly viewed as a *managerial function*. The activities of a leader are directed toward getting effective work from team members. Leadership is a social talent, that of getting the best effort of the organization's employees.

Leadership Traits

Early theorists believed that the primary factors in leadership effectiveness were the leader's personal characteristics or *traits*. In other words, these theorists explained leadership ability in terms of some property possessed in different amounts by different people. Effective leaders were, at one time or another, hypothesized to be intelligent, tall, self-confident, and so on.[1] From such a perspective, leadership exists primarily in the characteristics of the leader.

TRAGIC TRAITS

Unfortunately, the most dramatic leader of modern times was probably Adolf Hitler. Although not very imposing physically, he seems to have mesmerized audiences with "his ability to sense what a given audience wanted to hear and then manipulate his theme in such a way that he would arouse the emotions of the crowd."

There is something almost magical about the power of his oratory. . . . When he is at a climax and sways to one side or the other his listeners sway with him; when he leans forward, they, also, lean forward, and when he concludes, they are either awed or silent or on their feet in a frenzy.

SOURCES: Walter C. Langer, *The Mind of Adolf Hitler: The Secret Wartime Report* (New York: Basic Books, 1972), p. 46; and Stanley High, "The Man Who Leads Germany," *The Literary Digest*, 21 October 1933, p. 42.

A leader's effectiveness, however, usually depends upon considerably more than his or her personal characteristics. For instance, Fred Fiedler and Albert Leister propose that the weak relationships found between leader intelligence and group task performance result from a "screening process."[2] The effect of the leader's intelligence on the group's performance may be "screened" by such variables as the leader's motivation to complete the task successfully, the leader's prior experience with this type of task, how the leader relates to his or her superior, and the leader's relationship with the work group. A very intelligent leader with little motivation or experience may perform less effectively than one who is less intelligent but highly motivated and enjoys the close cooperation of group members.

Leadership Style: The Ohio State and Michigan Studies

The inability of trait concepts to account adequately for leadership effectiveness led to a focus on the leader's behavior or *leadership style*. In other words, the emphasis shifted from the personal qualities of the leader to how the leader behaved.

Although a number of leadership classification schemes have been developed, the most widely accepted schema distinguishes between leadership behavior which focuses primarily on task accomplishment and behavior which emphasizes building a strong relationship between the leader and his or her subordinates. This classification is based upon more than three decades of research from the Ohio State University and the University of Michigan.

Researchers at the Ohio State University have termed these two dimensions of leader behavior *initiating structure and consideration*.[3] Initiating structure concerns the leader's actions that define leader-follower relationships, establish definite standards of performance, specify standard operating procedures, and determine who does what. Consideration is related to the leader's attitude toward followers, the warmth of personal leader-follower relationships, the leader's willingness to listen, and the degree of mutual trust between leader and followers. Since the two dimensions are relatively independent, a leader's behavior may be characterized by either or both. Figure 20–1 indicates four possible combinations of the two dimensions.

The late Rensis Likert and his associates at the University of Michigan Institute for Social Research have distinguished between *job-centered* supervision and *employee-centered* supervision.[4] The former type of supervision devotes primary attention to the work to be performed, whereas the latter places the primary emphasis upon development of effective work groups. The same research distinguished between managers who supervise closely versus those who supervise generally.

There is considerable similarity among the leadership styles described above. There are technical variations, however, which lead to some differences in research results.[5]

Intuitively, we expect employee-centered, considerate leadership to be better than task-centered leadership in producing superior group performance. To date, however, research results have been disappointing. Some studies have reported significant correlations, but they are offset by other studies with conflicting findings. No consistent pattern of research results can be used to establish this relationship with any certainty. It seems that significant relationships are being obscured by situational differences in various studies. Under particular circumstances, one leadership approach may lead to higher productivity, while in other circumstances, a different type of leadership may be necessary for maximizing performance. Evidence indicates that the relative effectiveness

FIGURE 20–1   Four possible leadership styles

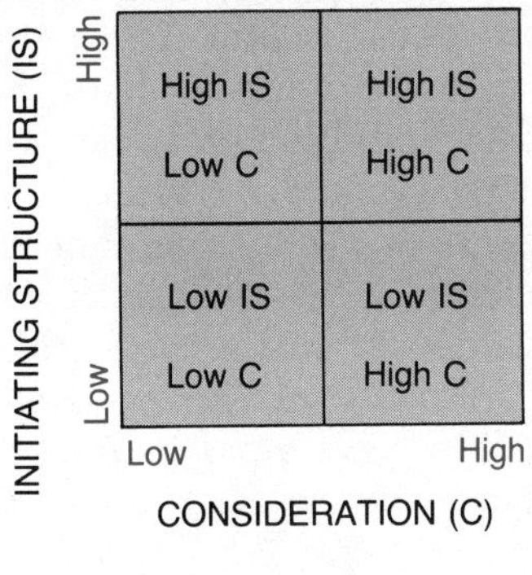

of consideration and initiating structure depends on such situational factors as the type of organization, the size and cohesiveness of the group, the attitudes of subordinates, and how much influence the leader has with higher-level executives.[6]

LEADERSHIP STYLES

"The right way to run this place is to hire smart people, point them in the right direction and get out of the way."

—The research vice president of Bell Laboratories

"A totally democratic form of leadership has no place aboard a ship. . . . At best, a captain is a benevolent despot."

—Captain of a U.S. Navy destroyer

"I am very demanding . . . won't tolerate laziness. . . . If you aren't prepared to bust your ———, you had better find another job."

—Chairman and CEO of a large manufacturing corporation

"I would rather have an army of rabbits led by a lion, than an army of lions led by a rabbit."

—Attributed to Napoleon

SOURCES: "Ma Bell's Dream Factory," *Newsweek*, 25 January 1982, p. 68; Barnard Collier, "The Navy Shapes Up," *Parade*, 27 September 1981, p. 25; and Hugh D. Menzies, "The Ten Toughest Bosses," *Fortune*, 21 April 1980, p. 65.

A positive correlation does seem to exist between employee-oriented, considerate leadership and employee morale, but even this relationship does not hold in all situations. In those cases showing positive correlations between person-centered leadership and productivity or satisfaction, we are often unsure which is the "chicken" and which is the "egg." It may be that the leader is merely responding positively to effective performance of subordinates. George Farris cites a delightful cartoon picturing two rats in a Skinner box. Said one rat to the other: "I've really got this psychologist conditioned. Every time I press the bar, he gives me a pellet of food."[7] Similarly, it may be followers who condition leaders to respond in a particular way, rather than vice versa.

There is some evidence to indicate, for instance, that low performing subordinates cause their superior to behave less considerately, more punitively, and more autocratically toward them. Conversely, high subordinate performance results in greater consideration and less task-orientation on the part of the leader.[8] Overall, most such studies show that a leader's behavior and attitudes vary as a function of the subordinates' performance and that the behavior and attitudes of subordinates reflect the leader's behavior.[9] This phenomenon might be termed *reciprocal causation*.

Leadership Substitutes

Another complicating factor in any analysis of the effect of leadership style on group performance and member satisfaction is a phenomenon known as leadership *substitutes*. These substitutes are variables that weaken the leader's ability to improve or retard the performance or satisfaction of subordinates.[10] The extensive training and experience of subordinates, for example, may make a leader's task-oriented behavior irrelevant.[11] Similarly, such factors as a task which is intrinsically satisfying or the interaction among cohesive group members may eliminate the need for employee-centered behavior by the leader.

The point, of course, is that leadership style is not equally important in all situations. Some situations appear to contain variables that influence subordinate performance or satisfaction more strongly than does the leader's behavior.

SITUATIONAL FACTORS IN LEADERSHIP

In an attempt to incorporate the complexities of situational variables into our understanding of leadership effectiveness, current theorists have turned to contingency theories. This section discusses the two major attempts in this direction.

Contingency Model of Leadership

The most ambitious effort to date is Fred Fiedler's *contingency model of leadership*.[12] Fiedler and his associates propose that the most effective leadership style depends upon the particular situation. Situations are classified in terms of their "favorableness" for the leader; that is, the degree to which the situation permits the leader to influence the behavior of group members.

Situational Factors.   The following three factors define the situation:

1. *Leader-member relations:* The most important factor in a situation is the relationship between the leader and the group members. The trust and confidence members place in their leader depend, to a

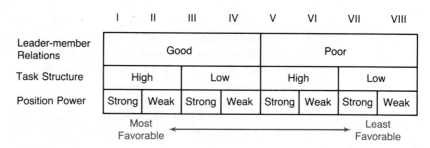

FIGURE 20–2   The situational favorableness dimension
SOURCE: From *Leadership and Effective Management* by Fred E.
Fiedler and Martin M. Chemers. Copyright © 1974 by Scott, Foresman
and Company. Reprinted by permission.

large extent, upon the leader's expert and referent power, as discussed in Chapter 13.

2. *Task structure:* The degree to which the requirements of the subordinates' task are clearly specified.

3. *Leader position power:* The extent of the leader's legitimate, reward, and coercive powers.

The most favorable situation combines close leader-member relations, well-defined tasks, and strong formal position power. Various combinations of these factors yield eight possible leadership situations which range from highly favorable to highly unfavorable, as shown in Figure 20–2.

Leadership Style.   Fiedler classifies leadership styles into the traditional task-oriented and relationship-oriented categories with one important difference: these two styles of leadership are considered to be opposite ends of a single continuum rather than independent dimensions, as the Ohio State theorists suggest. Leadership style, according to Fiedler, reflects an individual's underlying need structure which consistently motivates his or her behavior in various leadership situations. Consequently, one's leadership style depends upon his or her personality and cannot be readily changed. Leadership style is measured by the leader's responses to a test instrument called the *least-preferred coworker* scale. This short questionnaire requires the leader to think of the person at work with whom he or she can work *least well* and to describe that person along such dimensions as the following:

pleasant   _____ unpleasant
           8   7   6   5   4   3   2   1

supportive   _____ hostile
           8   7   6   5   4   3   2   1

Individuals who describe their least-preferred coworker in relatively favorable terms (that is, pleasant, supportive, and so on) are relationship-oriented leaders. Task-oriented leaders, those who obtain major satisfaction from completing the task successfully, give their least-preferred coworker a relatively unfavorable description.[13]

Combining Leadership Style and the Situation. Fiedler's findings, based on three decades of research, are summarized in Figure 20–3. Task-motivated leaders are more effective (in terms of group performance) in the "most favorable" and "least favorable" situations. Relationship-oriented leaders perform best in "mixed situations"—those which are moderately favorable or unfavorable.

In other words, Fiedler's results indicate that task-oriented leaders are likely to have high-performing groups when the leader has either a great deal of influence (octants I, II, and III) or very little influence (octants VII and VIII). In these situations, a leader who concentrates primarily on the task is required. In situations (octants IV, V, and VI) in which the leader has only moderate influence, a leader who focuses on interpersonal relationships is more likely to have a high-performing group.[14]

Relationship-motivated leaders perform better →

Task-motivated leaders perform better →

Leader-Member Relations	Good	Good	Good	Good	Poor	Poor	Poor	Poor
Task Structure	Structured		Unstructured		Structured		Unstructured	
Leader Position Power	Strong	Weak	Strong	Weak	Strong	Weak	Strong	Weak
	I	II	III	IV	V	VI	VII	VIII

FIGURE 20–3 How the style of effective leadership varies with the situation

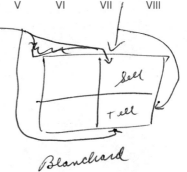

LEADERSHIP STYLE
AND THE SITUATION

The importance of matching the style of the leader to the situation is illustrated by the following experiences of corporate executives who left industry for academia. One individual, who went from a position as chairman and CEO of a railroad to become dean of a business school, found that his leadership style was not transferable. Accustomed to giving unquestioned orders, he discovered that trying to rule independent faculty members by fiat did not work. The faculty and students became so alienated by his autocratic style, along with other factors, that he resigned a year later.

By contrast, the former CEO of a large corporation who became dean at another business school used his "thoughtful and participatory management style" to make a number of major curriculum changes with little faculty resistance.

SOURCE: Based on "Executive Suite: A Rough Ride through Academia," *Business Week*, 17 August 1981, p. 37.

Leadership Training. These conclusions influence Fiedler's recommendations concerning leadership training. If a leader's style is dependent upon his or her personality, then changing a leader's style would require a personality change. Fiedler contends it is more feasible to alter the situation to fit the leader's style.

This may be accomplished through a self-administered, programmed technique which requires the leader to complete the least-preferred coworker scale and determine his or her leadership style. Then the leader is shown how to diagnose a situation and change or modify the factors so that the situation is matched to the leader's style.

> These changes in situational control might involve requests by the leader to be given routine assignments or to be given the less structured and unusual tasks; the leader might attempt to develop a closer, more supportive relationship with subordinates or to maintain more formal and distant relations; the leader might try to be "one of the gang" or emphasize rank and prerogatives.[15]

Fiedler believes that the *Leader Match* program is cost-effective because it requires no instructor time and only four to six hours of the trainee's time. Initial results indicate that the performance ratings of leaders two to six months after their training are significantly higher than those of leaders who did not receive the training.[16]

Assessment of the Contingency Model. The contingency model has weaknesses. The three situational factors proposed by Fiedler are probably only a partial listing of important variables. Such factors as the organization's reward system, the cohesiveness of the group, and the skill and training of group members may affect group performance. Secondly, while the model predicts the conditions under which a given leadership style will be effective, it fails to provide a clear explanation of the leadership process. And, finally, from a practical standpoint, altering situational factors to match a leader's style may be difficult.

> Leadership effectiveness cannot be the only concern of administrators as they make decisions about job assignments. They must consider other aspects of the organization's operations which may conflict with their attempts to make good use of leadership talent. Some characteristics of the job, task, or organization simply may not be subject to change, at least in the short run.[17]

Despite its limitations, the contingency model has emphasized the situational nature of leadership and helped us realize that almost anyone can succeed—or fail—as a leader. Leadership involves more than a person's traits or behavior. Contemporary leadership theories must consider not only the leader, but also the leader's subordinates and the task to be accomplished.

Path-Goal Theory of Leadership

A second effort to characterize leadership is the *path-goal theory of leadership* which grew out of attempts to explain the mixed findings of the Ohio State studies.[18] At its outset, this theory deviates from the contingency model by stating that the traditional means of characterizing leadership style as either task-oriented or relationship-oriented is insufficient. Instead, the same leader can engage in any of the following leadership styles:

1. *Directive leadership*—lets subordinates know what is expected of them and how the task should be accomplished.
2. *Supportive leadership*—shows concern for the needs of subordinates, makes the work more pleasant, and is friendly and approachable.
3. *Participative leadership*—consults with subordinates and takes their suggestions into consideration when making decisions.
4. *Achievement-oriented leadership*—emphasizes excellence in performance and displays confidence that subordinates will assume responsibility and accomplish challenging goals.

The most appropriate style is the one that has the greatest impact on the subordinates' performance and satisfaction.

> . . . The motivational functions of the leader consist of increasing the number and kinds of personal payoffs to subordinates for work-goal attainment and making paths to these payoffs easier to travel by clarifying the paths,

reducing road blocks and pitfalls, and increasing the opportunities for personal satisfaction en route.[19]

The major situational variables to be considered are (1) *the subordinates' personal characteristics, and (2) the environmental pressures and demands with which subordinates must cope to accomplish work goals and attain satisfaction.* Both variables must be taken into account by the leader in determining the most appropriate leadership style.

Research Results.   As an example of subordinates' personal characteristics, research indicates that individuals who believe that they control their own destiny (internals) are more satisfied under a participative leadership style than are individuals who are more fatalistic (externals). Conversely, externals are more satisfied under directive leadership than are internals.[20] In other words, a person with a strong internal locus of control prefers situations where he or she has some voice in decision

A CHANGING LEADERSHIP SITUATION

As organizations change, so do their leadership requirements. Such changes in the leadership situation may even make the incumbent leader obsolete. The Colgate-Palmolive Company grew from a stodgy soap and detergent marketer into a diversified conglomerate, which more than tripled its sales volume between 1971 and 1979. As the company grew, the board became increasingly dissatisfied with the managerial style of CEO David Foster and eventually replaced him with Keith Crane.

It is no accident that the directors' choice to succeed Foster stands a world apart from him in temperament and style. Unlike the flamboyant Foster, Keith Crane is low-key and shuns publicity. Crane delegates authority briskly, whereas Foster ran a one-man show. Crane piles up mountains of evidence before making a decision, while Foster relied heavily upon instinct.

The architect of the company's growth, David Foster, created a system that demanded a style of leadership that differed from his own. His style apparently did not fit the changed situation.

He finds it a touch ironic that he himself began the process of building Colgate into too large a complex to be managed by one-man rule—since his own inability to adjust to that fact made him pay the ultimate price personally.

SOURCE: Adapted from Hugh D. Menzies, "The Changing of the Guard at Colgate," *Fortune,* 24 September 1979, pp. 92–100.

445

making, while those who feel that their behavior is externally determined are more likely to feel comfortable under directive leadership.

In the area of environmental demands, the most studied variable has been task structure. Research has indicated that when the task is ambiguous and unstructured, a directive leadership style is most effective because it imposes structure upon the task, thereby permitting subordinates to deal with it more successfully.[21] Supportive leadership is most effective when subordinates are working on stressful, frustrating tasks and, hence, need the understanding and concern of their boss.

Assessment of Path-Goal Theory. Although path-goal theory and the contingency model both emphasize the situational nature of leadership, they also differ significantly. The most obvious difference—that path-goal theory proposes that a leader can engage in more than one style of behavior—was noted earlier.

Another major difference is that, unlike the contingency model, path-goal theory does not attempt to identify all of the variables that influence a leadership situation. The theory states that the major situational variables are subordinate characteristics and environmental demands, but this statement provides a research direction rather than a guideline for practitioners. Specific characteristics and demands have been identified by research and incorporated into the theory, and future studies will doubtless modify the theory further.[22]

Finally, as path-goal theory evolves, it not only proposes the most effective style of leadership for a particular situation, but it also explains the reasons underlying the proposition. Unlike the contingency model, which primarily *predicts* the best style for a given situation, path-goal theory attempts to *predict* and *explain*.

To date, only a few of the path-goal theory's possible predictions have been tested. The results have been "only moderately supportive."[23] One explanation for the mixed results is that not only are the variables difficult to measure, but various studies measure them in different ways, reducing comparability of the results. Then, too, leadership substitutes, which negate the need for certain leader behaviors, may be present in some situations.[24]

Each of the schools of thought that we have examined approaches leadership from a somewhat different perspective.* Each has its supporters and its detractors. "Because at least some empirical support is

*Another view of situational leadership is provided by Paul Hersey and Kenneth H. Blanchard. According to this perspective, a manager should employ a task-oriented style with subordinates who are not "mature" in relation to the specific task they are to perform (that is, they have low willingness or ability to take responsibility for the task, and/or they lack the necessary experience or education to perform it). As subordinates mature, the leader's behavior should change in the following sequence: (1) high-task/low-relationship orientation; (2) high-task/high-relationship orientation; (3) low-task/high relationship orientation; and (4) low-task/low-relationship orientation. Hence, highly motivated and well-trained subordinates need neither strong direction nor strong supportive behavior. See Paul Hersey and Kenneth L. Blanchard, *Management of Organizational Behavior: Utilizing Human Resources*, 4th ed. (Englewood Cliffs, N.J.: Prentice-Hall, 1982), pp. 150–75.

available for each perspective, leadership appears to be a far more complex set of cause-and-effect relationships than suggested by any one of the comparatively simple theoretical models offered to date."[25] Although we have learned much, much remains to be learned.

PARTICIPATIVE LEADERSHIP

A leadership style that has received considerable attention in recent years is *participative leadership*. In general, a program of participation attempts to involve subordinates—sometimes managerial subordinates and sometimes the rank and file—more directly in some aspects of their superior's decision making—an activity that would not be expected, or even tolerated, in many organizations.*

The continuum of leadership behavior, shown in Figure 20–4, illustrates various degrees of participative leadership. To the left of the continuum, the manager makes a decision unilaterally, without allowing subordinates to participate. Toward the other end, the manager uses less authority while granting subordinates a greater voice in decision making.

Benefits of Participation

Much work, even in some supervisory positions, seems monotonous and uninspiring. An opportunity for participation provides a contrast to such unchallenging assignments and is welcomed by many employees. From a psychological point of view, there is a vast difference between *activity* and *participation*. Participation may add meaning to work and permit employees to become *identified with it*. In contrast to a system in which all important thinking is limited to the superior, participative management places subordinates on an entirely different footing. Soliciting the assistance of subordinates assumes they have something valuable to offer and that their opinions have significance. This adds dignity to the jobs and to the incumbents. Egoistic needs, you may recall, may be satisfied by a sense of accomplishment in work. The possible contribution of participation to one's sense of accomplishment is substantial.

Benefits of participation are not limited to the employees. In tapping the thinking of employees, management gets the benefit of their contributions as well as their enthusiastic work. Also, in introducing changes, participation can help to minimize employee resistance. In fact, some changes occur in direct response to employee participation.

From the standpoint of both morale and organizational efficiency, therefore, participative management apparently has much to recommend it. Some caution is still necessary, however. Even though many studies have shown that productivity improvements have resulted from employee participation, conflicting evidence exists.

---

*In contrast to delegation of decision-making authority to a subordinate, the concept of participation is primarily concerned with a sharing of the decision-making process between a superior and a subordinate or subordinates.

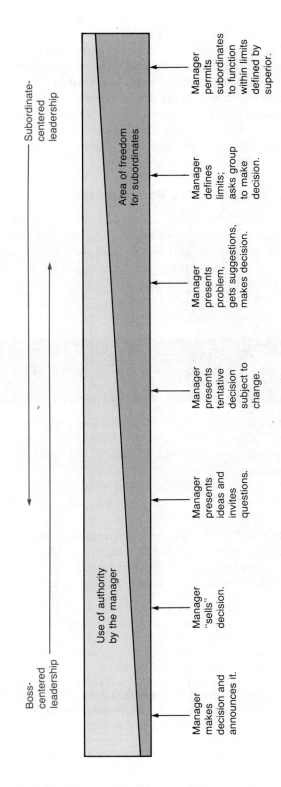

FIGURE 20-4 Continuum of leadership behavior

SOURCE: Robert Tannenbaum and Warren H. Schmidt, "How to Choose a Leadership Pattern," *Harvard Business Review* 36 (March–April 1958): 96. Reprinted with permission. Also see the authors' "Retrospective Commentary," *Harvard Business Review* 51 (May–June 1973): 166–68.

Participative leadership does not appear to be effective in all situations or for all groups. Personality differences, for instance, may make followers more or less interested in participation. There is also a danger in overdoing participation. In a study of project engineers, John Ivancevich found that engineers who were asked to participate more than they desired shared certain characteristics—low performance and high stress—with engineers who were not allowed to participate as much as they desired.[26] The optimal level of participation evidently varies from individual to individual.

Prerequisites for Participation

It seems likely that participation may function more successfully in some settings than in others. The type of subordinates, for example, is one significant variable. Participation assumes that subordinates *can* contribute something worthwhile, but their contribution depends upon their ability and background. If subordinates lack the proper educational background or if the problem at hand is beyond them, little can be achieved through participation.

PARTICIPATION: A THREAT?

Most research on participative leadership has focused on the resultant satisfaction and performance of the subordinates. But other factors also influence the relative effectiveness of participative approaches.

In the early 1970s, General Foods Corporation opened a pet-food plant in Kansas, which was designed around the concept of participative leadership. Semiautonomous work groups, working with a "coach," made their own management decisions and rotated jobs among themselves. Members even voted on pay raises for coworkers.

The economic indicators of effectiveness were predominatly favorable, but human problems arose in the system.

> The problem has been not so much that the workers could not manage their own affairs as that some management and staff personnel saw their own positions threatened because the workers performed almost too well. One former employee says the system—built around a team concept—came squarely up against the company's bureaucracy. Lawyers, fearing reaction from the National Labor Relations Board, opposed the idea of allowing team members to vote on pay raises. Personnel managers objected because team members made hiring decisions. Engineers resented workers doing engineering work.

SOURCE: Adapted from "Stonewalling Plant Democracy," *Business Week*, 28 March 1977, p. 78.

Effective participation also requires a set of necessary psychological conditions. Subordinates must be capable of becoming psychologically involved, possess some intelligence, and be in touch with reality. They must favor participation and not feel that the boss always knows best. They must also see the relevance of the problem to their own lives and be able to express themselves satisfactorily.

PARTICIPATIVE MANAGEMENT IN EUROPE

Participative management practices in Europe are termed *industrial democracy*, which refers to a formal arrangement of worker representation in organizational decision making. Some examples:

- *Sweden:* Since 1946, representatives of management and the workers in firms with over fifty employees have met regularly to solve problems and exchange information. In a number of factories, autonomous work groups have the responsibility for manufacturing an entire product and do their own inspecting and controlling.

- *Germany:* A system of *co-determination* exists in which publicly owned companies have two boards: (1) a supervisory board of directors which makes long-range strategic decisions and sets company policy; and (2) a management board which operates the company on a daily basis. In firms which employ more than two thousand persons, membership on the supervisory board is divided evenly between shareholders' representatives and representatives of the workers. In somewhat smaller companies (those having between 500 to 2,000 employees), the supervisory board is composed of two-thirds shareholders' representatives and one-third worker representatives.

Some companies have gone even further than required in increasing worker participation. Rosenthal A. G. of West Germany, a manufacturer of fine china and glassware, encourages worker ownership as well as participation. Shares of stock have been distributed as bonuses to employees, and the firm offers a type of mutual fund to its workers. Today, nine out of ten workers in the company own shares of its stock. The head of the company contends, "We have less illness, fewer strikes, less trouble and more contribution from our workers than the average."

SOURCE: Adapted from Bernard M. Bass and V. J. Shackleton, "Industrial Democracy and Participative Management: A Case for a Synthesis," *Academy of Management Review* 4 (July 1979): 393–95; and Jean A. Briggs, "Is This an Answer?" *Forbes,* 7 June 1982, pp. 52–55 (quote is from p. 55).

The atmosphere of the organization also must be conducive to participation. If highly autocratic management prevails throughout an organization, a particular manager may have difficulty in adopting a participative approach.

> . . . Research shows that the people with power are the ones who are apt to value it the most. A number of articles and books have pointed out that people who rise in modern business organizations tend to have strong interests in and needs for power. Thus the people who (participation) proponents expect to run the risks entailed in relinquishing power are the very people who hold power most dear. Strategies that depend on these people giving power away voluntarily are not apt to be implemented.[27]

The existence of a labor union may affect the nature and extent of possible participation. If the union feels that management's attempts to stimulate employee participation threaten the workers' loyalty to the union, opposition can be expected. Responsible, mature thinking on the part of both management and the union is required for effective participation in such situations.

Other prerequisites for effective participation are also important, such as the availability of time. Emergency conditions may not permit consultation. The financial cost of participation may also exceed its potential values. The various prerequisites serve as limitations, then, in managerial use of the participative approach.

Model of Participative Decision Making

A model intended to clarify when subordinates should be allowed to participate in decision making has been developed by Victor Vroom and Philip Yetton.[28] Depending upon the situation, a leader may make a decision alone or may involve subordinates in the decision process to varying degrees, as shown in Figure 20–5.

The relevant situational variables are defined by seven questions, shown in the top of Figure 20–6. The first three questions focus on the quality of the decision, while the last four are concerned with the acceptance of the decision by the subordinates.

The lower part of Figure 20–6 presents a decision tree (or flowchart) the manager may use to determine which decision method or methods are appropriate for a given situation. As an example, look at the lowest branch of the decision tree. This represents a situation in which:

A. the problem has a quality requirement;
B. the manager does not have sufficient information to make a high-quality decision;
C. the problem is unstructured;
D. subordinate acceptance of the decision is important for effective implementation;

AI.	You solve the problem or make the decision yourself, using information available to you at the time.	CII.	You share the problem with your subordinates as a group, obtaining their collective ideas and suggestions. Then you make the decision, which may or may not reflect your subordinates' influence.
AII.	You obtain the necessary information from your subordinates, then decide the solution to the problem yourself. You may or may not tell your subordinates what the problem is in getting the information from them. The role played by your subordinates in making the decision is clearly one of providing the necessary information to you, rather than generating or evaluating alternative solutions.	GII.	You share the problem with your subordinates as a group. Together you generate and evaluate alternatives and attempt to reach agreement (consensus) on a solution. Your role is much like that of chairman. You do not try to influence the group to adopt "your" solution, and you are willing to accept and implement any solution which has the support of the entire group.
CI.	You share the problem with the relevant subordinates individually, getting their ideas and suggestions without bringing them together as a group. Then *you* make the decision, which may or may not reflect your subordinates' influence.		A = autocratic C = consultative G = group

FIGURE 20–5 Decision methods for group problems
SOURCE: Reprinted from *Leadership and Decision-Making* by Victor H. Vroom and Philip W. Yetton by permission of the University of Pittsburgh Press.© 1973 by University of Pittsburgh Press.

E. if the manager makes the decision alone, he or she cannot be reasonably certain that it will be accepted by the subordinates;

F. the subordinates do not share the organizational goals to be attained in solving the problem.

In this situation, the manager should use decision method CII (Figure 20–5)—share the problem with subordinates in a group meeting, obtaining their ideas and suggestions, and then make the decision alone.

As may be seen from the chart in Figure 20–6, some situations permit a choice of alternative decision methods. In those cases, the choice would depend upon the leader's personality, the subordinates' qualifications, and the time available.

Research on the model has been fairly encouraging.[29] Vroom and Arthur Jago, using self-report measures, found that, of 181 actual decisions made by 96 managers, 68 percent of the decisions conforming to the model were successful while only 22 percent of the decisions failing to conform to the model were successful.[30] Another study of 47 owners of small franchises and 241 of their employees found that employees of managers who made decisions in accordance with the model were more "satisfied with supervision" and had higher productivity than employees of managers whose decisions failed to conform to the model.[31]

A. Does the problem possess a quality requirement?
B. Do I have sufficient information to make a high quality decision?
C. Is the problem structured?
D. Is acceptance of the decision by subordinates important for effective implementation?
E. If I were to make the decision by myself, am I reasonably certain that it would be accepted by my subordinates?
F. Do subordinates share the organizational goals to be attained in solving this problem?
G. Is conflict among subordinates likely in preferred solutions?

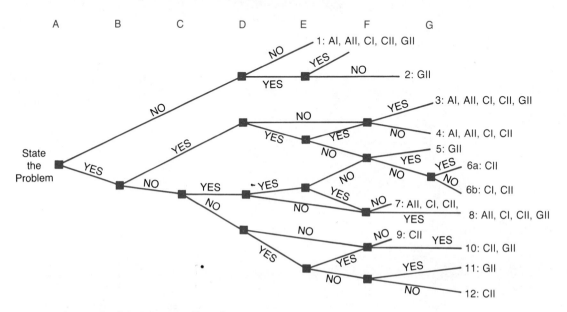

FIGURE 20–6   Decision process flowchart

The Vroom-Yetton model deals with only one aspect of leadership, participative decision making. But it, like the contingency model and the path-goal theory, emphasizes the situational nature of the leadership function. An effective leader is one who is able to match his or her style to the situation in an appropriate way.

SUMMARY

Through the function of *leadership,* a manager secures the effort and teamwork of organization members. Early theorists believed that the leader's *traits* or personal characteristics induced others to follow him or her. But the inability of trait concepts to account adequately for leadership effectiveness led to a focus on the leader's *style* or behavior. Most of this research, often referred to as the Ohio State and Michigan studies, has examined the effects of task-oriented styles versus relationship-oriented styles on group performance and satisfaction. Mixed findings have resulted, indicating that leadership effectiveness cannot be understood through analysis of the leader's style alone.

Current theories take a broader approach by including the interaction between the leader's style and various situational factors. The most complete formulation to date is Fiedler's *contingency model of leadership* which predicts the leader style that is most effective depending upon the particular combination of three situational factors: *leader-member relations, task structure,* and *leader position power.* A different approach is taken by the *path-goal theory,* an attempt to explain which of four leadership styles is most effective, depending upon the *subordinates' personal characteristics* and the *environmental pressures and demands with which subordinates must cope to accomplish work goals and attain satisfaction.*

One of the most widely discussed leader behaviors is *participative leadership,* a style which involves subordinates in the managerial decision-making process. Although participative leadership is not effective in all situations or for all groups, research indicates a positive relationship between participative leadership and employee productivity and satisfaction in many cases. The *Vroom-Yetton model* attempts to clarify situations in which participative leadership can be used effectively.

DISCUSSION QUESTIONS

1. Why are "trait theories" insufficient explanations of leadership effectiveness?

2. Distinguish between a *job-centered* supervisor and an *employee-centered* supervisor. On the basis of your own experience, describe the leadership approach of one manager (or teacher) in each category.

3. Disregarding situational factors, what general relationship exists between leadership style and group effectiveness? What is the most obvious explanation for this relationship?

4. In those cases which do show a positive correlation between employee-centered leadership and productivity, how can one know which is the cause and which is the effect?

5. Is *leadership style* important in all situations? Why or why not?

6. What is the significance of the *leadership situation* in choosing a pattern of leadership?

7. Explain Fiedler's *contingency model of leadership*.

8. Compare and contrast the *contingency model of leadership* with the *path-goal theory of leadership*.

9. Does evidence show that *employee participation* contributes to productivity?

10. How might the *Vroom-Yetton model of leadership* be useful to a practicing manager?

NOTES

1. Studies in organizations have consistently shown that the leader's sex has little effect on the way subordinates perceive leader behavior or on subordinate satisfaction. See M. M. Petty and Nealia S. Bruning, "A Comparison of the Relationships between Subordinates' Perceptions of Supervisory Behavior and Measures of Subordinates' Job Satisfaction for Male and Female Leaders," *Academy of Management Journal* 23 (December 1980): 717–25; and Richard N. Osborn and William M. Vicars, "Sex Stereotypes: An Artifact in Leader Behavior and Subordinate Satisfaction Analysis?" *Academy of Management Journal* 19 (September 1976): 439–49.

2. Fred E. Fiedler and Albert F. Leister, "Leader Intelligence and Task Performance: A Test of a Multiple Screen Model," *Organizational Behavior and Human Performance* 20 (October 1977): 1–14.

3. Bernard M. Bass, *Stogdill's Handbook of Leadership: A Survey of Theory and Research*, rev. ed. (New York: The Free Press, 1981), pp. 358–92.

4. See Rensis Likert, *New Patterns of Management* (New York: McGraw-Hill Book Co., 1961), Chapter 2.

5. Ralph M. Stogdill, *Handbook of Leadership: A Survey of Theory and Research* (New York: The Free Press, 1974), p. 403.

6. Bass, *Stogdill's Handbook of Leadership*, pp. 382–90.

7. George F. Farris, "Chicken, Eggs and Productivity in Organizations," *Organizational Dynamics* 3 (Spring 1975): 10.

8. Arthur G. Jago, "Leadership: Perspectives in Theory and Research," *Management Science* 28 (March 1982): 321.

9. Aaron Lowin and James R. Craig, "The Influence of Level of Performance on Managerial Style: An Experimental Object-Lesson in the Ambiguity of Correlational Data," *Organizational Behavior and Human Performance* 3 (November 1968): 440–58; and David M. Herold, "Two-Way Influence Processes in Leader-Follower Dyads," *Academy of Management Journal* 20 (June 1977): 224–37.

10. Steven Kerr and John M. Jermier, "Substitutes for Leadership: Their Meaning and Measurement," *Organizational Behavior and Human Performance* 22 (December 1978): 375–403. Results of a test of this concept can be

found in Jon P. Howell and Peter W. Dorfman, "Substitutes for Leadership: Test of a Construct," *Academy of Management Journal* 24 (December 1981): 714–28.

11. An intriguing leadership substitute is known as subordinate "self-management." A description of this concept and how it might be developed is found in Charles C. Manz and Henry P. Sims, Jr., "Self-Management as a Substitute for Leadership: A Social Learning Theory Perspective," *Academy of Management Review* 5 (July 1980): 361–67.

12. This theory of Fred E. Fiedler is widely discussed in the literature. For one comprehensive source, see Fred E. Fiedler and Martin M. Chemers, *Leadership and Effective Management* (Glenview, Ill.: Scott, Foresman and Co., 1974).

13. Controversy continues to rage over the meaning and interpretation of the least-preferred coworker scores. Two representative analyses can be found in Chester A. Schriesheim, Brendan D. Bannister, and William H. Money, "Psychometric Properties of the LPC Scale: An Extension of Rice's Review," *Academy of Management Review* 4 (April 1979): 287–90; and Robert W. Rice, "Reliability and Validity of the LPC Scale: A Reply," *Academy of Management Review* 4 (April 1979): 291–94.

14. One analysis of 145 tests of the validity of Fiedler's model revealed strong statistical support for the model's predictions of group performance. See Michael J. Strube and Joseph E. Garcia, "A Meta-Analytic Investigation of Fiedler's Contingency Model of Leadership Effectiveness," *Psychological Bulletin* 90 (September 1981): 307–21. For a report of an unsuccessful test of the contingency model, see Robert P. Vecchio, "An Empirical Examination of the Validity of Fiedler's Model of Leadership Effectiveness," *Organizational Behavior and Human Performance* 19 (June 1977): 180–206.

15. Albert Leister, Donald Borden, and Fred E. Fiedler, "Validation of Contingency Model Leadership Training: Leader Match," *Academy of Management Journal* 20 (September 1977): 466.

16. See Jago, "Leadership," p. 323; and Fred E. Fiedler and Linda Mahar, "The Effectiveness of Contingency Model Training: A Review of the Validation of Leader Match," *Personnel Psychology* 32 (Spring 1979): 45–62.

17. Chester A. Schriesheim, James M. Tolliver, and Orlando C. Behling, "Leadership Theory: Some Implications for Managers," *MSU Business Topics* 26 (Summer 1978): 38.

18. The path-goal theory is explained in a number of sources. One of the most complete discussions can be found in Robert J. House and Terence R. Mitchell, "Path-Goal Theory of Leadership," *Journal of Contemporary Business* 3 (Autumn 1974): 81–97.

19. Ibid., p. 85.

20. Terence R. Mitchell, Charles M. Smyser, and Stan E. Weed, "Locus of Control: Supervision and Work Satisfaction," *Academy of Management Journal* 18 (September 1975): 623–31.

21. An elaboration on this finding and some exceptions to it may be found in H. Kirk Downey, John E. Sheridan, and John W. Slocum, Jr., "The Path-Goal Theory of Leadership: A Longitudinal Analysis," *Organizational Behavior and Human Performance* 16 (June 1976): 156–76. See also Chester A. Schriesheim and Angelo S. De Nisi, "Task Dimensions as Moderators of

the Effects of Instrumental Leadership: A Two-Sample Replicated Test of Path-Goal Leadership Theory," *Journal of Applied Psychology* 66 (October 1981): 589–97.

22. An interesting theoretical modification of path-goal theory is presented in Ricky W. Griffin, "Task Design Determinants of Effective Leader Behavior," *Academy of Management Review* 4 (April 1979): 215–24.

23. Janet Fulk Schriesheim and Chester A. Schriesheim, "A Test of the Path-Goal Theory of Leadership and Some Suggested Directions for Future Research," *Personnel Psychology* 33 (Summer 1980): 350.

24. Ibid., pp. 367–68.

25. Jago, "Leadership," p. 330.

26. John M. Ivancevich, "An Analysis of Participation in Decision Making among Project Engineers," *Academy of Management Journal* 22 (June 1979): 253–69.

27. Walter R. Nord and Douglas E. Durand, "What's Wrong with the Human Resources Approach to Management?" *Organizational Dynamics* 6 (Winter 1978): 17.

28. Victor H. Vroom and Philip W. Yetton, *Leadership and Decision-Making* (Pittsburgh: University of Pittsburgh Press, 1973).

29. A critique of the Vroom-Yetton model may be found in R. H. George Field, "A Critique of the Vroom-Yetton Contingency Model of Leadership Behavior," *Academy of Management Review* 4 (April 1979): 249–57; and a response to the critique may be found in Arthur G. Jago and Victor H. Vroom, "An Evaluation of Two Alternatives to the Vroom/Yetton Normative Model," *Academy of Management Journal* 23 (June 1980): 347–55.

30. Victor H. Vroom and Arthur G. Jago, "On the Validity of the Vroom-Yetton Model," *Journal of Applied Psychology* 63 (April 1978): 151–62.

31. Charles Margerison and Richard Glube, "Leadership Decision-Making: An Empirical Test of the Vroom and Yetton Model," *Journal of Management Studies* 16 (February 1979): 45–55.

SUPPLEMENTARY READING

Barnes, Louis B. "Managing the Paradox of Organizational Trust." *Harvard Business Review* 59 (March–April 1981): 107–16.

Bass, Bernard M. *Stogdill's Handbook of Leadership: A Survey of Theory and Research,* rev. ed. New York: The Free Press, 1981.

Bass, Bernard M., and **Shackleton, V. J.** "Industrial Democracy and Participative Management: A Case for a Synthesis." *Academy of Management Review* 4 (July 1979): 393–404.

Davis, Tim R. V., and **Luthans, Fred.** "Leadership Reexamined: A Behavioral Approach," *Academy of Management Review* 4 (April 1979): 237–48.

Fiedler, Fred E. *A Theory of Leadership Effectiveness.* New York: McGraw-Hill Book Co., 1967.

_____. "The Leadership Game: Matching the Man to the Situation." *Organizational Dynamics* 4 (Winter 1976): 6–16.

Field, R. H. George. "A Critique of the Vroom-Yetton Contingency Model of Leadership Behavior." *Academy of Management Review* 4 (April 1979): 249–57.

Gordon, Gil E., and Rosen, Ned. "Critical Factors in Leadership Succession." *Organizational Behavior and Human Performance* 27 (April 1981): 227–54.

Halal, William E., and Brown, Bob S. "Participative Management: Myth and Reality." *California Management Review* 23 (Summer 1981): 20–32.

House, Robert J. "A Path-Goal Theory of Leadership Effectiveness." *Administrative Science Quarterly* 16 (September 1971): 321–38.

Jago, Arthur G. "Leadership: Perspectives in Theory and Research." *Management Science* 28 (March 1982): 315–36.

Karmel, Barbara. "Leadership: A Challenge to Traditional Research Methods and Assumptions." *Academy of Management Review* 3 (July 1978): 475–82.

Manz, Charles C., and Sims, Henry P., Jr. "Self-Management as a Substitute for Leadership: A Social Learning Theory Perspective." *Academy of Management Review* 5 (July 1980): 361–67.

McConkey, Dale D. "Participative Management: What It Really Means in Practice." *Business Horizons* 23 (October 1980): 66–73.

Melcher, Arlyn J. "Participation: A Critical Review of Research Findings." *Human Resource Management* 15 (Summer 1976): 13–21.

Nystrom, Paul C. "Managers and the Hi-Hi Leader Myth." *Academy of Management Journal* 21 (June 1978): 325–31.

Pfeffer, Jeffrey. "The Ambiguity of Leadership." *Academy of Management Review* 2 (January 1977): 104–12.

Sashkin, Marshall. "Changing toward Participative Management Approaches: A Model and Methods." *Academy of Management Review* 1 (July 1976): 75–86.

21

THE PROCESS OF COMMUNI-CATION

This chapter will enable you to

- *Explain the communication process and identify various methods of transmitting messages.*
- *Understand an organization's formal and informal channels of communication.*
- *Analyze the major barriers to effective communication.*
- *Become familiar with some techniques for developing effective communication.*

The *process of communication* is an integral part of the functioning of any organization. Leadership is exerted and coordination is achieved through communication. As managers improve their understanding of communications problems and increase their skill in communication, therefore, organizational performance will become more effective.

NATURE OF COMMUNICATION

Management through Communication

The manager's world is a *world of words*. Much, perhaps most, of his or her time is spent in communicating with others. On the basis of various studies of managers in action, we know that most managers show a strong preference for verbal over written communication. Henry Mintzberg's observation of chief executive behavior revealed that 78 percent of their time was devoted to verbal interaction.[1] Figure 21–1 shows the relative importance of various types of interaction.

Any type of organized activity, in fact, demands communication. The direction of the communication may be downward (such as giving instructions or passing along policy changes), upward (as in reporting results or asking for additional information), or horizontal (such as coordinating the activities of two or more departments). The need for good communication permeates every activity and department in an organization.

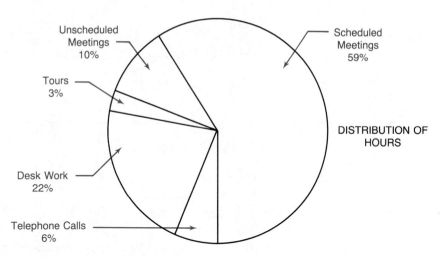

FIGURE 21–1   Distribution of hours
SOURCE: Adapted from (upper portion) Figure 4 (p. 39) in *The Nature of Managerial Work* by Henry Mintzberg. Copyright © 1973 by Henry Mintzberg. Reprinted by permission of Harper & Row, Publishers, Inc.

Definition of Communication

Communication is an interactive process between two or more people, as illustrated in Figure 21–2. A *sender* initiates the process by transmitting a message to a *receiver* or group of receivers. The message conveys not only facts but also the sender's feelings and attitudes about those facts and, often, the sender's feelings and attitudes toward the receiver. The receiver is not passive; he or she often transmits a return message through a nod, a frown, a question, or some other form of behavior to indicate reception and understanding of the message. Feelings and attitudes, of course, may also be conveyed by this return message. Ideally, this "sending-receiving-sending" process continues until both parties fully understand the messages that have been transmitted.

Without reception, communication does not occur, but this fact is not as obvious as it seems. The manager who writes several memos per week to a subordinate believes that he or she is communicating even though the subordinate may routinely discard the messages without reading them. The personnel manager who posts a written explanation,

FIGURE 21–2   The communication process

full of legal jargon, of the changes in the organization's health insurance policy is not communicating, since many employees may never see the notice and those who do are unlikely to expend the time and effort required to read it. The goal of the sender should be to transmit a message which is received, so that it may be understood and acted upon.

Methods of Communication

Messages are transmitted in a variety of forms. We all know that language—written and spoken—provides tools for communication. What we sometimes overlook is that language may be supplemented by other less obvious forms of communication. Nonverbal behavior may well be more important than words in conveying meaning.

Consider the physical expression of a speaker, for example. What can the listener detect from this? If a supervisor scowls, the subordinate discovers the supervisor's unhappiness or displeasure. This may lead to various conclusions about the real meaning of the scowl, such as "She's unhappy about my performance, and my future is clouded." If the supervisor wears a smile, the same message may carry quite a different meaning. Almost instinctively, a subordinate picks up and interprets such signals. By looking at the boss, a subordinate knows whether the time is ripe to ask for a raise or to request a day off.

Not only physical expressions and gestures but also voice inflections may tell the listener more than the words themselves reveal. The term *paralanguage* refers to an individual's "tone and quality of voice, pitch, pacing of speech, and sounds such as sighs or grunts," which add meaning to the spoken word.[2] The tone of voice for instance, can transform words of praise into sarcasm. Even silence, the absence of language, can communicate! If an employee performs exceptionally well or completes a project in an outstanding manner, he or she might logically expect some word of commendation. Silence, however, communicates indifference or disrespect, whether intended or not.

Perhaps the most forceful method of communication is not language at all. There is an old saying that "Actions speak louder than words." We observe an individual's behavior and infer something about the person. Even the choice of a meeting place can communicate:

> When a boss and a subordinate meet, whose office do they use? If the boss is sensitive to place as territory, the purpose of the meeting will decide the question. To conduct an adversary discussion, to emphasize hierarchy and authority, or to give direction, the boss should hold the meeting in his or her office. If, however, the boss wants to reach out to the subordinate—to have a conversation more on the other's terms—he or she might well consider traveling to the subordinate's office.[3]

From the standpoint of employees, such actions provide the most eloquent expression of management policy and values.

Communication and the Systems Viewpoint

The organization has been pictured throughout this text as a system of interrelated parts functioning together to accomplish certain objectives. Such organizations are not only energy systems in which physical materials are changed by the application of human and other energy but also informational systems. In fact, communication provides the means for directing and blending all system and subsystem activities. Information flow becomes more and more significant as one moves from the area of physical processing to areas emphasizing managerial decision making.

The process of communication may be visualized as the functioning of an organizational subsystem. The formal communications system or network is a decision-making system in that it brings problems and related information to managers who must make decisions in solving those problems. The communication system also takes overall system plans and objectives, as formulated by top management, and carries them downward through the various echelons to the operative level. In fact, the organization structure is an elaborate system for gathering, evaluating, and disseminating information.

COMMUNICATING EXPECTATIONS

A manager's expectations of subordinates' job performance may be communicated in a variety of ways. John Gabarro reports the impressions of a corporate vice-president observing the behavior of the firm's newly appointed president:

"I knew immediately, the first day, he was going to be different from [his predecessor]. Everyone knew he was going to be more demanding. A lot of little things—he spends no time on small talk and whenever someone else does he changes the subject back to business. He sat behind his desk while [his predecessor] always sat in the easy chair. [His predecessor] was very informal, vague, kind of a 'good Joe' seat-of-the-pants-type guy. [The new president] was prepared to the teeth. We all knew it was the start of a new era."

Even a manager's working hours communicate expectations to his or her subordinates. A subordinate, observing his boss' work schedule, comments:

"He was the first one in the office. His car was in the lot by 7:00 every morning, and he never left before 6 P.M. That told people a lot about what he expected from us."

SOURCE: John Gabarro, "Socialization at the Top—How CEOs and Subordinates Evolve Interpersonal Contracts," *Organizational Dynamics* 7 (Winter 1979): 14.

The total communications system is not limited to the formal network, however. The informal organization, or grapevine, is a part of the system even though it is less susceptible to control. Design of the formal organization structure provides a set of officially established and approved communication channels. An officially designated communication network is always supplemented to some degree, however, by informal channels.

The systems viewpoint stresses the critical role of communication in the functioning of the total system and the importance of a free flow of information throughout the firm. Although we focus here on the organization's internal communication system, the open systems view also includes external communication channels. Through these channels the organization communicates with its environment. Advertising and public relations would be common examples of external communication.

CHANNELS OF COMMUNICATION

Formal Channels of Communication

Every organization has a formally sanctioned communication structure—or network of channels—through which messages move from senders to receivers. These channels may be *downward, upward or horizontal,* as shown in Figure 21–3. The entire network of formal channels within an organization is depicted by the firm's organization chart.

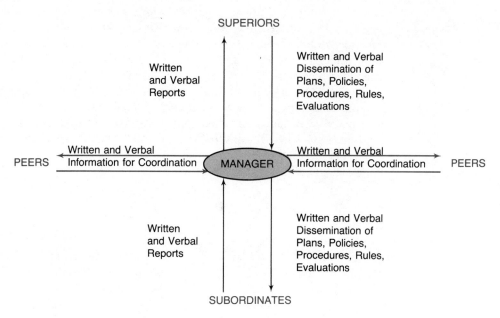

FIGURE 21–3   Formal channels of communication

Downward Communication Channels. Effective downward communication—from superior to subordinate—is crucial to an organization's success. Plans, policies, and procedures originating at upper management levels must be communicated accurately to lower levels of the organization to ensure effective performance. Daniel Katz and Robert Kahn enumerate five basic types of downward communication:

1. Specific task directives: *job instructions.*
2. Information designed to produce understanding of the task and its relation to other organizational tasks: *job rationale.*
3. Information about organizational *procedures and practices.*
4. *Feedback* to the subordinate about his or her performance.
5. Information of an ideological character to inculcate a sense of mission: *indoctrination of goals.*[4]

Overall, the intent of downward communication is to increase the subordinate's understanding of the organization and his or her job. "If people know the reasons for their assignment, this will often insure their carrying out the job more effectively; and if they have an understanding of what their job is about in relation to their subsystem, they are more likely to identify with organizational goals."[5]

Downward communication may take a number of different forms. The most direct method consists of face-to-face verbal interaction. Although less personal, written instructions, explanations, and evaluations are commonly used to reach a wider audience or to provide a permanent record of the message. Many organizations also use periodicals or newspapers (known as "house organs"), employee manuals, public address systems, and bulletin boards to communicate downward.

Research indicates that managers do not communicate with their subordinates as well as they believe they do. Although subordinates desire information from their superiors, a dramatic reduction in information content occurs as messages are transmitted from higher to lower organization levels. Superiors, however, are unaware of this decline in information content and consistently overestimate the amount of information their subordinates have received.[6] The reasons for these and other organizational communication problems will be examined in a later section of this chapter.

Upward Communication Channels. Upward communication consists of reports from lower level participants about their job performance, their problems, the performance of others, and their attitudes toward organizational policies and procedures. Without such information, upper management could not accurately monitor organizational performance and make decisions about future organizational programs and activities. Upward communication, of course, also provides feedback through which the superior can determine whether downward communication has been received and understood. Finally, some forms of subordinate-superior communication, such as participative management or management by objectives, encourage subordinates to participate in organizational planning and decision-making processes, thereby strengthening their commitment to the organization.

The most basic form of upward communication, the performance report to higher levels, is the most troublesome. Problems in this area are rooted in the unique nature of the superior-subordinate relationship. The subordinate occupies a position of dependency with respect to his or her superior, making the relationship much more than a casual one. To a great extent, the subordinate's future depends upon the superior's judgment. If the subordinate is to advance, earn pay increases, or receive choice work assignments, the decision must be that of the superior.

In view of the critical importance of the superior's opinion, it is only natural for the subordinate to wish to control all factors serving to influence supervisory judgment. In communication, therefore, the subordinate desires to transmit a message and *also* to influence the superior favorably. Achieving the goal of favorably influencing the supervisor may require some alteration of the communication itself. In its extreme

THE NEED FOR
UPWARD COMMUNICATION

Without open upward communication, top management becomes increasingly divorced from operational reality. One of the most graphic examples of this process is found in the Iranian overthrow of Shah Mohammed Reza Pahlavi in January 1979.

Over a period of years, the Shah, who more and more came to believe in his own infallibility, lost touch with the people he governed. By 1978, he had even stopped consulting his closest advisors.

> He often would brook no contradiction, nor, it seemed, bad tidings of any sort. Over dinner at the palace one night, the wife of one of the Shah's nephews said, "Did you hear about the trouble at the bazaar over food prices?" The Shah pretended not to hear, and someone next to her intoned sharply, "No bad news at the dinner table, please." At last, even SAVAK [his secret police] watered down its reports to please him. "No one dared to conceal the truth from his father," said a West European intelligence officer. "No one dared to tell the truth to the Shah."
>
> Having cut himself off from his country, he had no way of knowing the extent of the growing opposition. . . . Even in June 1978, when there was rioting in Teheran, the Shah still had no inkling of the bloody revolution to come. In July, he went off on his annual vacation to the Caspian Sea.

SOURCE: "The Man Who Meant Well," *Newsweek*, 4 August 1980, p. 41. Copyright © 1980 by Newsweek, Inc. All rights reserved. Reprinted by permission.

form, this could involve misrepresentation of facts. But, perhaps more likely, this simply involves a subtle, perhaps almost unconscious, adaptation of the subordinate's communication. If the communication goes upward through several levels, it may become increasingly rosy and at the same time farther and farther from reality.

Research indicates that subordinates may be more open and honest with managers who are strongly relationship-oriented.[7] Such openness may also be more common in organic (that is, flexible, decentralized) settings than in mechanistic (that is, less flexible, centralized) structures.[8] Other studies report that openness of communication is enhanced when the subordinate trusts his or her supervisor,[9] and evidence indicates that modifications to important messages are unlikely to occur when the subordinate knows that the superior can obtain the correct information from another source.[10]

Horizontal Communication Channels.   Although vertical communication channels have received greater emphasis in management theory than have horizontal channels, both are equally important to organizational effectiveness. Lateral flows of information help to

1. coordinate the activities of different departments through dispersal and sharing of pertinent information;
2. solve interdepartmental problems and conflicts by providing a direct means of communication; and
3. provide emotional and social support to employees through interaction focusing on common task concerns.

The horizontal flow of information also serves to reduce the strain on vertical communication channels. If the production manager wishes to communicate with the marketing manager, he or she may do that directly without first going through their common superior, the vice president of operations, unless it is necessary that the latter be involved. This "short-circuiting" of the chain-of-command avoids some of the problems involved in vertical communication, such as distortion and slowness.

As organizations become more diversified and their employees more specialized, the need for coordination, and, hence, horizontal communication, increases. Many organizations have responded to this need by creating committees composed of representatives from different departments and areas of specialization. The interchange of information among the committee members often results in greater awareness and understanding of the functions and problems of other areas.

Informal Channels of Communication

Much of the communication within organizations is transmitted through nonformal channels. "Nonofficial" messages comprise the organization's informal communication system, often referred to as the *grapevine*.

Activities in the formal system are systematic and preplanned, and communication tends to be authority-laden, planned, and documented. Informal or emergent system activities are ad hoc and spontaneous. Therefore, communication in the [informal] system is typically not planned or documented. It is of a face-to-face, interpersonal nature. People communicate to one another directly because the nature of their own psychology, situational circumstances, and their relationships with others cause them to "want to communicate," not because the organization "tells them to communicate."[11]

Functions of the Grapevine. The grapevine involves a normal, rather than an abnormal, set of relationships. Informal communication occurs naturally wherever individuals are thrown together in work or social contacts. Such spontaneous communication can help *satisfy the social needs* of many individuals.

In addition, the *grapevine is often more informative* than the formal communication system. Official channels may report that the organization's president has resigned for "reasons of health," or "family and personal considerations," but the grapevine supplements this pronouncement by reporting the "inside"· details of the resignation. A third function of the informal communication system is that *messages may be transmitted more rapidly* through the grapevine than through formal channels.[12]

Accuracy of the Grapevine. Occasionally, one gets the impression that only false rumors are circulated by the grapevine. It is true that rumors occur and that wild ones may be rapidly transmitted through informal channels. But other, more substantial information is also conveyed in this way. As a matter of fact, research indicates that rumors occur relatively infrequently and that most of the information transmitted through informal channels is fairly accurate.[13]

The grapevine may be so accurate because of configuration of informal communication channels. The grapevine is often visualized as a long chain, with A telling B, who in turn passes it on so that it eventually reaches Z. Such a pattern of transmission would clearly maximize the chances for error. Studies of the grapevine, however, have provided evidence that conflicts somewhat with this concept. The general pattern, as discovered by one researcher, is that of the *cluster chain,* illustrated in Figure 21–4.[14] One link in the communication network informs a number of people instead of just one person. One or two of each cluster of receivers, in turn, pass the communication on to another group.

Occasional rumors or errors require corrective action. If a manager discovers an unfounded rumor among subordinates, for example, he or she may simply call them together and discuss the matter with them. Whether the facts will be accepted as such depends upon management's reputation for accuracy and candor in previous communication.

Some organizations have established special programs to detect rumors, asking employees to bring them to the attention of management.

FIGURE 21–4   The grapevine

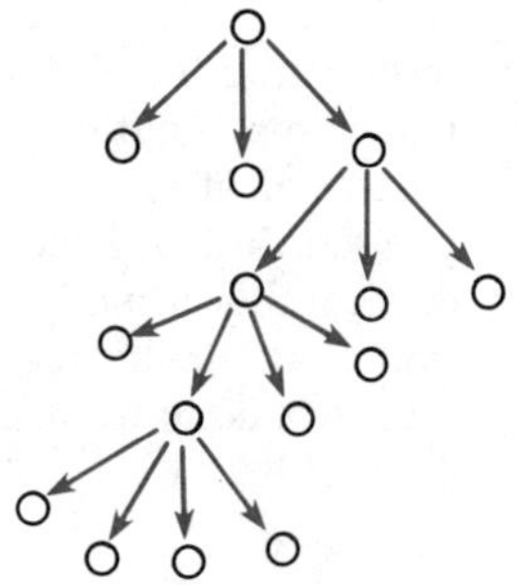

The rumor is then presented along with the facts. The employee newspaper and bulletin boards, among other media, have been used for this purpose.

Constructive Value of the Grapevine.   Unless managers wish to multiply their own communication efforts many times, they cannot channel all information through the official chain of command. Informal communications supplement and amplify those emanating from official sources. Much information about work assignments and company policy, for example, is picked up from fellow employees. Also, the grapevine supplies the manager with information about subordinates and their work experiences, thereby increasing the manager's understanding and effectiveness.

A constructive approach to dealing with the grapevine begins with the effort to furnish complete and accurate information. In addition, a manager may recognize the informal communication leaders. By keeping them well-informed, the manager can come closer to assuring the accuracy of information entering the grapevine. Also, listening to the grapevine as much as possible will keep the manager in closer touch with the thinking of subordinates.

Communication Channels within Groups

Over the past thirty years, researchers have experimented with small group communication networks. The results indicate that the pattern of communication a group uses to solve task problems affects the group's performance and the satisfaction of its members.

Three of the more common communication networks which have been studied are illustrated in Figure 21–5. In the *wheel* network, each member can communicate only with the individual in the center, who, in turn, may communicate with any of the other members. The *circle* allows each individual to communicate with two other individuals—those on either side. Any member of the *all-channel* network can communicate with any other member.

The following conclusions indicate the effects communication networks have on group performance and member satisfaction:[15]

FIGURE 21–5 Small group communication networks

Wheel   Circle   All-Channel

1. Simple problems are solved most rapidly by the wheel network. Information is channeled to the central individual in the wheel who then combines the information to solve the problem.

2. The all-channel and circle networks are able to solve complex problems more rapidly. Such problems require considerable two-way communication—answering questions, confirming facts, and seeking additional information.

3. The satisfaction of members with their tasks is higher in the circle and all-channel networks. Within the wheel network, however, the satisfaction of the individual occupying the central position is much higher than that of the peripheral members. Evidently members of the two "decentralized" networks and the central figure in the wheel feel greater freedom and independence in their positions, while the wheel's peripheral members feel that their behavior is controlled by the central member.

4. The central individual in the wheel invariably emerges as the group leader, whereas no leader appears consistently in the circle or all-channel networks. The leader of the wheel has greater access to information and the opportunity to coordinate the activities of the other members. The leader, however, often suffers from information overload—particularly in complex problem situations.

Because this research on group communication networks has been conducted in laboratory (that is, artificial) settings, the degree to which the findings can be generalized to actual organizations is debatable. In the experimental settings, each group is viewed as an independent system. However, our earlier discussion of systems theory indicates that groups within organizations are not independent. They are connected to other work groups, to supervisors, to incentive systems, and to informal communication channels. Hence the research in this area has taken a rather narrow view of groups. On the other hand, the results strongly indicate that a group's communication network affects both performance and satisfaction.

Some of these findings have been replicated in field studies of ongoing organizations. For example, a study of forty-four project groups in a research and development laboratory in a large corporation found that project groups with higher performance levels had evolved communication structures appropriate to their tasks. Effective groups dealing with nonroutine or complex tasks used decentralized communication patterns involving extensive peer contact and peer decision making in a form roughly similar to the all-channel network described above. Groups that dealt effectively with more routine tasks evolved centralized communication patterns much like the wheel.[16]

BARRIERS TO COMMUNICATION

Perfect communication would accurately transmit an idea from one mind to another. Unfortunately, transmission is often imperfect. The message received by Person B differs from the message transmitted by Person A, a situation illustrated in Figure 21–6. The circle on the left represents the message (the facts, feelings, and attitudes) that A sends to B. The circle on the right indicates the facts, feelings, and attitudes that B perceives are being transmitted. The overlapping shaded area between the two circles indicates the only part of A's message that is actually understood by B.

The problem, of course, is that A believes that B understood the entire message that was sent, and B thinks that he or she understood the message transmitted by A. Both may now proceed on the assumption that perfect communication has occurred, yet both are operating on incorrect premises. This section explores some of the reasons why communication is often imperfect.

Perceptual Barriers

Considerable differences exist in the way individuals perceive, organize, and understand their environment. These differences stem from different job experiences, educational backgrounds, value systems, and so on. It is not surprising, then, that these differences influence interpretation of messages. A person receives a message and interprets it in the light of previous experiences.

Past experiences may cause an individual to have preconceived ideas of what others are trying to say. If so, it is difficult for the individual to hear anything that differs from his or her preconceptions. Suppose the boss commends a subordinate who is convinced that the supervisor is prejudiced and unfair. The subordinate may think, "The boss must be trying to pull a fast one."

The subordinate in this case is guilty of attributing inaccurate meaning to the boss's message. Individuals often infer that something is being communicated when it is not. This inference then becomes a "fact" upon which the person proceeds. Attributing unwarranted meaning to another's message can be hazardous unless the receiver is conscious of the

FIGURE 21–6 Imperfect communication

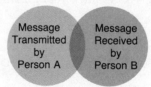

differences between the facts transmitted by the message and the meaning he or she attributes to those facts. Inferences should be made only in probabilistic terms; that is, "the boss *possibly* commended me because. . . ."

Semantic Barriers

Organizations, departments, functional areas, and members of the same occupational group often devise their own "language" or *jargon* to facilitate communication among members of the same unit. Although such specialized language may increase communication accuracy and understanding among these individuals, jargon is often a source of dismay to "outsiders." Individuals use jargon so often that they forget that clients or members of other units or occupations may not understand their special terminology. Consider the dilemma of a recently employed production assembler who might receive the following type of instruction from her supervisor:

DIFFERENT PERCEPTIONS

People interpret the same stimulus in different ways, depending on their previous experience. Take the case of a supervisor who is watching a group of employees laughing.

1. To the manager who believes that work must be painful in order to be productive, the laughter communicates to him or her that time is being wasted, and perhaps assignments are too easy.
2. To the manager who believes that contented employees work harder, the laughter communicates that he or she is succeeding as a manager.
3. To the manager who is personally insecure, the laughter communicates that the employees are ridiculing him or her.

SOURCE: Adapted from George Strauss and Leonard R. Sayles, *Personnel: The Human Problems of Management*, 2d ed. (Englewood Cliffs, N.J.: Prentice-Hall, 1967), p. 227.

Alice, I would like you to take the sixth yellow chair on this assembly line, which is in front of bonding machine #14. On the left side of your machine you will find a wiring diagram indicating where you should bond your units. On the right-hand side of your machine you will find a carrying tray full of 14-lead packages. Pick up the headers, one at a time, using your 3-C tweezers and place them on the hot substrate below the capillary head. Grasp the cam actuator on the right-hand side of the machine and lower the hot capillary over the first bonding pad indicated by the diagram. Ball bond to the pad and, by moving the hot substrate, loop the wire to the pin indicated by the diagram. Stitch bond to this lead, raise the capillary, and check for pigtails. When you have completed all leads, put the unit back in the carrying tray.

Your training operator will be around to help you with other details. Do you have any questions?[17]

Another semantic barrier to communication is that the same words do not always carry the same meaning for both parties. A supervisor, for example, may intend to commend subordinates by commenting upon "satisfactory" performance. Subordinates may take offense at such commendation, however, because they know they are "superior" and not merely "satisfactory"! Similarly, the boss's statement to a subordinate to do something "as soon as possible" may mean that the subordinate should perform the required activity immediately. The subordinate, however, may interpret the request to mean that the required task should be taken care of after everything else the subordinate has to do is completed!

Serial Transmission Barriers

Perceptual and semantic barriers can easily distort communication between two individuals. Imagine then the potential for distortion that exists when a message is transmitted through a series of individuals. This *serial transmission effect* is illustrated to most of us at an early age through the game of "rumor." A child at one end of a line of children communicates a message verbally to the next child. The receiver then transmits the message to the next child, and so on until the last one in line has received the message. The original message is then compared to the message received by the last person in line. The two usually differ significantly.

In organizations, serial transmission may be either vertical or horizontal. The first receiver may misunderstand or ignore parts of the message, reinterpret parts, or omit some portions of the message that seem irrelevant before transmitting the message to the next "link" in the chain. If the next receiver likewise modifies the message, the end result will be considerably distorted. The greater the number of links in the chain, the greater the potential for distortion and misunderstanding.

Information Overload

Communication systems often become defective by providing or permitting a greater volume of communication than the organization can handle—a condition termed *information overload*. Managers are not only informed, but deluged with information. A communication network is capable of carrying only so much information, and a manager has only so much time available for reading letters, studying reports, talking on the telephone, and conferring with others. Beyond some point, an attempted increase in communication volume may contribute to inefficiency rather than performing its intended function.

SERIAL TRANSMISSION DISTORTION

A reporter was present at a [Vietnamese] hamlet burned down by the U.S. Army's 1st Air Cavalry Division in 1967. Investigation showed that the order from the division headquarters to the brigade was: "On no occasion must hamlets be burned down."

The brigade radioed the battalion: "Do not burn down any hamlets unless you are absolutely convinced that the Viet Cong are in them."

The battalion radioed the infantry company at the scene: "If you think there are any Viet Cong in the hamlet, burn it down."

The company commander ordered his troops: "Burn down that hamlet."

SOURCE: James G. Miller, "Living Systems: The Organization," *Behavioral Science* 17 (January 1972): 149, as reprinted from H. Faas and P. Arnett, "Civilians Fear My Lai Is U.S. 'Achilles Heel'," *Cleveland Plain Dealer*, 8 December 1969, p. 6.

The nature of the manager's job is a major cause of information overload. Managers are required to make decisions and coordinate the activities of others. These role prescriptions demand extensive communication with other subsystems and with individuals and organizations outside the manager's organization. "What seems like a reasonable flow of information from each subsystem or network can easily become a flood when all of these subsystem networks of information converge at one point to form the too often swollen river of information.[18]

This flow of information increases significantly when major changes occur in the organization's environment. An unexpected drop in sales causes management to request information concerning the decline. The resulting statistical data, analyses, and suggested solutions for the problem may amount to a deluge of information, which by its very volume delays processing of the information by the overloaded manager. One study of information overload in two different settings found that overloaded individuals had lower job performance than did employees who reported that they had insufficient information for proper job accomplishment.[19]

DEVELOPING EFFECTIVE COMMUNICATION

Whatever the level of communication in an organization, managers can increase its effectiveness by attention to the factors discussed in this section. Underlying each suggestion is the need for the sender to empathize with the receiver. Admittedly, a manager may find it difficult to identify with the values or career orientation of subordinates or of more technically oriented individuals. But the more the manager understands the receiver's job and role in the organization, the more likely the manager will be able to communicate appropriately and effectively.

Two-Way Communication

Management literature often emphasizes the importance of two-way communication. An interchange of messages that permits discussion back and forth between two persons, superior and subordinate, for example, presumably communicates with greater effectiveness than a one-way flow. Managers who engage in two-way communication do more than *tell* their subordinates. They *tell* and *listen* or, in other words, engage in conversation with subordinates by encouraging feedback.

Two-way communication offers several advantages, possibly the most significant being greater accuracy. The receiver can check on any unclear matter by asking questions. The give-and-take of discussion may also clarify issues in a general way. In the case of superior-subordinate communication, furthermore, the subordinate gains a sense of greater involvement and self-respect through two-way communication.

The following comments by Harold Leavitt point out strengths and imply weaknesses of a one-way communication flow:

> If speed alone is what is important, then one-way communication has the edge. If appearance is of prime importance, if one wishes to look orderly and businesslike, then the one-way method again is preferable. If one doesn't want one's mistakes to be recognized, then again one-way communication is preferable. Then the sender will not have to hear people implying or saying that he is stupid or that there is an easier way to say what he is trying to say.[20]

Although two-way communication is usually preferable, it does not occur automatically. The manager must work at it to make sure it happens.

The Listening Side of Communication

As noted, communication involves both transmission and reception. Much of the study of communication has stressed the transmitter and has tended to ignore the receiver. As we have discovered, however, the listener is not completely passive. Listening requires the active participation of the receiver; it is not simply hearing. A major cause of poor listening centers around the fact that while the average person speaks at a rate of one hundred to two hundred words per minute, the average listener can process at least four hundred words per minute.[21] This excess listening capacity permits the mind to wander instead of concentrating on the speaker's message.

An active listener, however, learns to use this excess capacity to increase his or her understanding of what the speaker is saying. The

ENCOURAGING TWO-WAY COMMUNICATION

Some organizations are attempting to make two-way communication a permanent part of their vertical communication system. Through a climate survey—questionnaires focusing on individual departments within an organization—employees are encouraged to tell their supervisors what they think of them, their fellow workers, and their organization. The results of the questionnaire study are discussed at a "feedback session" attended by the supervisor, the subordinates, and a person involved in the survey analysis. Obviously, the success of the survey depends upon the anonymity of individual responses and a willingness by supervisors to discuss the problems raised by subordinates.

> *Successful Results.* [General Electric Company] found that more than half the respondents to one survey were unhappy with the information and recognition they received, as well as with their opportunities for advancement. So the unit's manager instituted regular monthly meetings, brought in experts to answer questions, and started a newsletter. A year later, those unhappy with the information they received dropped from 50% to none. And the number unhappy with the opportunities for promotion fell from more than 50% to 20% even though not one person was promoted or changed jobs. "But they understood the situation," points out Thomas D. Holman, manager of personnel research, "and that made the difference."

SOURCE: Adapted from "A Productive Way to Vent Employee Gripes," *Business Week*, 16 October 1978, pp. 168–71. Quoted from the 16 October 1978 issue of *Business Week* by special permission.

following suggestions, for instance, may help you become a more effective listener:[22]

1. Attempt to identify the main points or central idea that the speaker is trying to impart.
2. Use the time lag between speaking and listening rates to review mentally the points the speaker has already made.
3. Search for deeper meanings than you received upon hearing the message for the first time by analyzing words for secondary or connotative meanings.
4. Anticipate what the speaker will say next in order to compare the actual message being transmitted with what you predicted. This mental activity helps reinforce the speaker's ideas in your mind and focuses your attention upon the message.

5. Do not be distracted by the speaker's unique speaking style; listen for content, not delivery.
6. Ask questions when you do not understand what is said.
7. Compensate for emotionally charged words by trying to determine objectively what meaning those words hold for the speaker.
8. Withhold evaluation of the message until the speaker is finished and you are certain that you understand what was transmitted.
9. Be flexible in your views. Even ideas that you cannot totally accept may have some merit.

Becoming an active listener, then, requires both concentration and practice. One cannot be an effective communicator without giving conscious attention to the act of listening.

LISTENING AT SPERRY CORPORATION

Perhaps no organization has done more to emphasize the importance of listening than Sperry Corporation, a manufacturer of machinery, computers, and flight and navigation control systems. Its long-running advertising campaign based on the slogan, "We understand how important it is to listen," stressed the significance of listening as an essential managerial skill. Effective listening enables Sperry's employees to respond appropriately to people who have direct interest in the products and performance of the company.

According to Sperry Corporation, listening is the communication skill that we use most but are taught least. Believing that active listening can be learned, Sperry designed five courses in listening—one for each major organizational division, to reflect each division's environment. By the early 1980s, about 10,000 of Sperry's 90,000 employees had completed a course in how to become an "active listener."

SOURCE: Adapted from *Your Personal Listening Profile,* a pamphlet (Sperry Corporation); and John Louis DiGaetani, "The Sperry Corporation and Listening: An Interview," *Business Horizons* 25 (March/April 1982): 34–39.

Aggressively Sharing Information

In the typical situation, managers transmit to subordinates those messages that seem necessary in the regular course of business operations. If subordinates need directions or information, the necessary instructions are given. There is no particular attempt to hold back the facts. Rather, the attention is simply upon those communications that are essential to the operation.

As long as an organization is small and the operation simple, this approach may work reasonably well. Through personal observation, subordinates can supplement that which they learn through formal channels. As the organization grows, however, it may become so compartmentalized that the individual has a very narrow view of the overall operation.

In such situations, an *aggressive willingness to share information* is required.[23] A survey of 695 employees in a large public utility firm revealed that those employees who had positive feelings about the sharing of information within the organization also had positive feelings regarding the organization's interpersonal milieu, management in general, and the way employees identify with the organization. Conversely, the withholding of important information by management was negatively related to job satisfaction.[24]

Need for Honesty and Sincerity

A communications program is occasionally used as a type of propaganda effort. An attempt is made to sell or convince employees of some point of view. Of course, attempts at persuasion need not involve deceit. In fact, presentation of the organization's point of view may be justified. An organization or supervisor may slip into the habit of using information as a technique for manipulation, however. Rather than being forthright and open, information is tailored or withheld to produce the desired effect—"What they don't know won't hurt them."

Such an attitude toward communication is insulting to subordinates, and employees are quick to detect such insincerity. Attempts to manipulate subordinates, therefore, will typically be rejected and produce a negative reaction as well. The intelligence of employees should not be underestimated.

Trust and openness on the part of the sender lead to more open, accurate communication since such qualities usually evoke a positive response from the receiver. Likewise, lack of trust or deception on the sender's part may cause the receiver to be cautious and nonsupportive. Effective communication cannot exist in a relationship without trust.

Channel Selection

A manager has available a variety of communication channels and methods. Some use the written word, in such varied forms as policy statements, official letters, memos, personal notes, bulletin board announcements, newspaper articles, and employee handbooks. Even oral communications differ greatly in nature and formality. The manager may make a formal address, talk with a colleague over a cup of coffee, hold a committee discussion, or talk on the telephone.

Some channels and methods work better for a given type of communication than do others. An announcement of a change in the retirement program would normally be written rather than being transmitted via the grapevine. In seeking support of a colleague for a proposed policy change, a manager would probably rely on informal discussion rather than send a formal letter. The channel and method are properly tailored to the communication. Errors in choice of channel and method may produce friction within the organization. For example, formal confrontation in a staff meeting prior to informal discussion of a controversial matter may create hostility and invite open opposition.

Other factors, of course, such as the quality of interpersonal relationships and interaction patterns among organization members as well as the speed and provisions for feedback among various channels must also be weighed. Consideration of these various factors should impress us with the complexity of the communication process and the need for skillful channel selection to maximize the manager's effectiveness.

SUMMARY

Communication is an integral aspect of management. Through communication, information, facts, feelings, and ideas are transmitted from one person to another. The communications network, including the formal organizational structure and the supplementary informal channels, may be visualized as an informational system used to direct and coordinate the activities of the various parts (subsystems) of the firm. Communication is accomplished not only through language, but also through voice inflections, physical expressions and gestures, silence, and behavior.

Management establishes a network of *formal communication channels* through which official messages move downward, upward, and horizontally throughout the organization. *Downward channels* transmit plans, policies, and procedures from upper management to lower levels in order to increase subordinates' understanding of their organization and jobs. *Upward channels* carry reports from lower levels which enable managers at higher levels to monitor organizational performance for future decision-making activities. The actions of various departments are coordinated and conflict among the departments resolved through *horizontal channels.*

The grapevine, or *informal communication network,* supplements the formal communication channels. This informal network emerges spontaneously to help satisfy the social needs of organizational participants and to provide information not carried through official channels.

Evidence indicates that particular configurations of group communication networks are more appropriate in certain situations than in others. Simple, routine problems are solved more rapidly by the *wheel* network, while complex, nonroutine tasks should be dealt with through the *all-channel* and *circle* networks.

Communication barriers prevent perfect transmission from a sender to a receiver. The sender's *perceptual world*, for instance, may differ considerably from the receiver's. Organizational or departmental *jargon* hinders accurate communication, as does the *serial transmission effect*. And many managers suffer from *information overload*, a condition in which the volume of information received by the manager is greater than his or her capacity to absorb and use it.

An effective communication program requires the manager to engage in *two-way communication* with subordinates, superiors, and peers. The ability to *listen* must be carefully cultivated, and the manager must attempt to *share information aggressively*. Adequate communication does not develop naturally without effort. In view of the employee's ability to detect insincerity, *openness* and *honesty* are also prime features of effective communication. The proper *channel* and method for most effective communication depend upon the nature of the communication and other factors.

DISCUSSION QUESTIONS

1. Communication includes more than the transmission of facts. What are the other aspects of communication? Of these, which is most difficult to transmit in writing?

2. "Without reception, communication does not occur." How can a manager determine whether subordinates are receiving the message that he or she is sending?

3. Suppose a state governor or the president of the United States personally inspects a flood-stricken area. Explain the significance of such a visit from the standpoint of communication.

4. What are the purposes of *downward communication? upward communication? horizontal communication?*

5. Why do superiors overestimate the amount of information their subordinates receive?

6. What is the basic reason for distortion in performance reports to higher levels?

7. What are the functions of the informal communication system (the *grapevine*)?

8. Why is the *wheel* network inappropriate for solving complex, nonroutine problems?

9. Explain the major barriers to effective communication.

10. How does one become a more effective listener?

11. What philosophy of management is implied by the phrase *aggressive sharing of information?*

NOTES

1. Henry Mintzberg, *The Nature of Managerial Work* (New York: Harper & Row, Publishers, 1973), p. 38.

2. Michael B. McCaskey, "The Hidden Messages Managers Send," *Harvard Business Review* 57 (November–December 1979): 147.

3. Ibid., p. 138.

4. Daniel Katz and Robert L. Kahn, *The Social Psychology of Organizations*, 2d ed. (New York: John Wiley & Sons, 1978), p. 440.

5. Ibid., p. 443.

6. This research is summarized in John E. Baird, Jr., *The Dynamics of Organizational Communication* (New York: Harper & Row, Publishers, 1977), p. 269.

7. J. C. Wofford, P. J. Calabro, and Alan Sims, "The Relationship of Information Sharing Norms and Leader Behavior," *Journal of Management* 1 (Fall 1975): 23.

8. Jerald W. Young, "The Subordinate's Exposure of Organizational Vulnerability to the Superior: Sex and Organizational Effects," *Academy of Management Journal* 21 (March 1978): 119-20.

9. These studies are summarized in Jerry C. Wofford, Edwin A. Gerloff, and Robert C. Cummins, *Organizational Communication: The Keystone to Managerial Effectiveness* (New York: McGraw-Hill Book Co., 1977), pp. 376–77; and Janet H. Gaines, "Upward Communication in Industry: An Experiment," *Human Relations* 33 (December 1980): 929–42.

10. George Huber, "Organizational Information Systems: Determinants of Their Performance and Behavior," *Management Science* 28 (February 1982): 138–55.

11. Wofford et al., *Organizational Communication*, p. 389.

12. Katz and Kahn, *Social Psychology of Organizations*, p. 449.

13. A brief review of the literature in this area is provided by Baird, *Dynamics of Organizational Communication*, p. 275.

14. Keith Davis, *Human Relations at Work*, 3d ed. (New York: McGraw-Hill Book Co., 1967), p. 225.

15. Excellent reviews of the literature in this area may be found in Baird, *Dynamics of Organizational Communication*, pp. 277–85; Wofford et al., *Organizational Communication*, Chapter 16; and Everett M. Rogers and Rekha Agarwala-Rogers, *Communication in Organizations* (New York: The Free Press, 1976), pp. 118–23.

16. Michael L. Tushman, "Work Characteristics and Subunit Communication Structure: A Contingency Analysis," *Administrative Science Quarterly* 24 (March 1979): 82–98.

17. Earl R. Gomersall and M. Scott Myers, "Breakthrough in On-the-Job Training," *Harvard Business Review* 44 (July–August 1966): 66.

18. Richard K. Allen, *Organizational Management through Communication* (New York: Harper & Row, Publishers, 1977), p. 80.

19. Charles A. O'Reilly III, "Individuals and Information Overload in Organizations: Is More Necessarily Better?" *Academy of Management Journal* 23 (December 1980): 684–96.

20. Harold J. Leavitt, *Managerial Psychology*, 3d ed. (Chicago: The University of Chicago Press, 1972), p. 118.

21. This and other research findings on oral communication are summarized in Richard C. Huseman, James M. Lahiff, and John D. Hatfield, *Interpersonal Communication in Organizations: A Perceptual Approach* (Boston: Holbrook Press, 1976), p. 107.

22. These suggestions are based on Larry L. Barker, *Listening Behavior* (Englewood Cliffs, N.J.: Prentice-Hall, 1971), pp. 73–78; and Huseman et al., *Interpersonal Communication*, pp. 112–15.

23. A recent technological innovation in sharing information is the "in-house newscast." The purpose of this videotape presentation is to inform employees of external developments which may affect their organization and to share information about internal operations. See "TV That Competes with the Office Grapevine," *Business Week*, 14 March 1977, pp. 49–54 for a more complete discussion.

24. Paul M. Muchinsky, "Organizational Communication: Relationships to Organizational Climate and Job Satisfaction," *Academy of Management Journal* 20 (December 1977); 592–607.

SUPPLEMENTARY READING

Baskin, Otis W., and **Aronoff, Craig E.** *Interpersonal Communication in Organizations.* Santa Monica, Calif.: Goodyear Publishing Co., 1980.

Cross, Gary P. "How to Overcome Defensive Communications." *Personal Journal* 57 (August 1978): 441–456.

Di Gaetani, John L. "The Business of Listening." *Business Horizons* 23 (October 1980): 40–46.

————. "The Sperry Corporation and Listening: An Interview." *Business Horizons* 25 (March/April 1982): 34–39.

Gabarro, John. "Socialization at the Top—How CEOs and Subordinates Evolve Interpersonal Contracts." *Organizational Dynamics* 7 (Winter 1979): 3–23.

Hatfield, John D., and **Huseman, Richard C.** "Perceptual Congruence about Communication as Related to Satisfaction: Moderating Effects of Individual Characteristics." *Academy of Management Journal* 25 (June 1982): 349–58.

Ilgen, Daniel R.; Fisher, Cynthia D.; and **Taylor, M. Susan.** "Consequences of Individual Feedback on Behavior in Organizations." *Journal of Applied Psychology* 64 (August 1979): 349–71.

Josefowitz, Natasha. "Management Men and Women: Closed vs. Open Doors." *Harvard Business Review* 58 (September–October 1980): 56–62.

Katz, Daniel, and **Kahn, Robert L.** *The Social Psychology of Organizations.* 2d ed. Chapter 14. New York: John Wiley & Sons, 1978.

Kikoski, John F. "Communication: Understanding It, Improving It." *Personnel Journal* 59 (February 1980): 126–31.

"Listening and Responding to Employees' Concerns: An Interview with A. W. Clausen." *Harvard Business Review* 58 (January–February 1980): 101–14.

McCaskey, Michael B. "The Hidden Messages Managers Send." *Harvard Business Review* 57 (November-December 1979): 135–48.

Roberts, Karlene H., and **O'Reilly, Charles A., III.** "Some Correlations of Communication Roles in Organizations." *Academy of Management Journal* 22 (March 1979): 42–57.

St. John, Walter. "In-House Communication Guidelines." *Personnel Journal* 60 (November 1981): 872–78.

Sanderlin, Reed. "Information Is Not Communication." *Business Horizons* 25 (March/April 1982): 40–42.

Schein, Edgar H. "Improving Face-to-Face Relationships." *Sloan Management Review* 22 (Winter 1981): 43–52.

Tortoriello, Thomas R.; Blatt, Stephen J.; and **De Wine, Sue.** *Communication in the Organization: An Applied Approach.* New York: McGraw-Hill Book Co., 1978.

Wilkins, Paul L., and **Timm, Paul R.** "Perceived Communication Inequity: A Determinant of Job Dissatisfaction." *Journal of Management* 4 (Spring 1978): 107–19.

PART SIX
CONTROLLING
PERFORMANCE

22

THE PROCESS OF CONTROL

This chapter will enable you to

- *Understand the purpose of control and explain each of the steps in the control process.*
- *Discuss how the control process is applied to the financial area of the organization.*
- *Identify some of the dysfunctional consequences of control and suggest how they may be overcome.*

Organizations seldom function perfectly in executing plans. As a result, a manager must monitor operations to discover deviations from plans and to be sure the organization is functioning as intended. Management activities that check on performance and correct it when necessary are a part of the *managerial control function.*

AN OVERVIEW OF CONTROL

Definition of Control

Henri Fayol succinctly summarized the control process over sixty-five years ago in the following statement:

> In an undertaking, control consists in verifying whether everything occurs in conformity with the plan adopted, the instructions issued, and principles established. It has for object to point out weaknesses and errors in order to rectify them and prevent recurrence. It operates on everything, things, people, actions.[1]

Although the language is somewhat archaic, Fayol's definition emphasizes that (1) *the functions of planning and control are closely related;* (2) *the purpose of control is to ensure that the organizational system operates effectively;* and (3) *the focus of control is broad, encompassing all of the organization's resources—human, material, and financial.*

The interrelated steps which make up the control process are shown in Figure 22–1. These activities may be visualized as an essential subsystem of the total operating system. In brief, the purpose of managerial

THE ORGANIZATIONAL SYSTEM

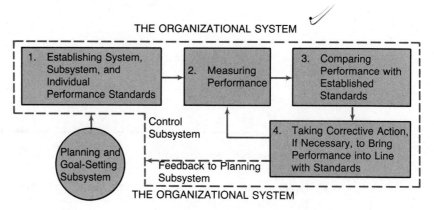

FIGURE 22–1   The control process

control is to assure the coordination and effective performance of all other subsystems (for example, production, sales, finance, and personnel) so that organizational plans are properly implemented and organizational goals achieved. We will examine each of the steps in the control process.

Establishing Standards

The first step in the control process, establishing standards, emphasizes the inseparability of planning and control, for it is through planning and goal setting that control standards are established.

Goals at various organizational levels are translated into standards by making them measurable. An organizational goal to increase market share, for example, may be translated into a top management performance standard to increase market share by 8 percent within a twelve-month period. This standard then serves as the basis upon which a middle management performance standard, such as "increase sales within the southwest region by $13,000,000 within twelve months," is established. Further down the ladder, the standard at the individual sales representative's level might become "increase sales in your district by $400,000 within twelve months." In many cases, these yearly standards will be broken down into quarterly standards so that corrective action may be taken early should performance begin to fall below the standard.

Although this example illustrates growth and sales standards, standards must be established in all areas of the organization. In manufacturing, for example, product specifications provide predetermined standards that regulate the manufacturing process. A given dimension may be specified as fifteen inches with a tolerance of plus or minus one-fourth inch. Likewise, a university should have standards controlling the quality of students entering the university, the quality of instruction, graduation requirements, financial expenditures, lobbying activities at the state legislature, the quality of student services, fund raising, the type and amount of research conducted by the faculty, and so on.

Superordinate System	Criteria
Stockholders	Price appreciation of securities
	Dividend payout
Labor force	Wage levels
	Stability of employment
	Opportunity
The market: consumers	Value given
The market: competitors	Rate of growth
	Innovation
Suppliers	Rapidity of payment
Creditors	Adherence to contract terms
Community	Contribution to community development
Nation	Public responsibility

FIGURE 22–2   Systems criteria for judging company performance

SOURCE: Reprinted by permission of the *Harvard Business Review.*
Exhibit from "The Manager's Job: A Systems Approach" by Seymour
Tilles (January–February 1963). Copyright © 1963 by the President
and Fellows of Harvard College; all rights reserved.

Control, then, requires a systems view. An organization must develop *sets of criteria*, each of which corresponds to some wider system of which the organization is a part. Figure 22–2 presents some suggestions concerning appropriate criteria for a business organization with respect to various superordinate systems.

Quantification of the objective or standard is sometimes difficult. Consider the goal of product leadership, for example. In evaluating its product leadership, an organization compares its products with those of competitors and determines the extent to which it pioneers in the introduction of basic products and product improvements. Such standards may exist even though they are not formally and explicitly stated. Inability to quantify the output standard, however, does not indicate the absence of some conception as to what constitutes reasonable or standard output or performance. This conception, in effect, constitutes a standard for controlling.

Measuring Performance and Comparing It to Standards

Performance measurement occurs at various stages of the operations process, as indicated in Figure 22–3. Performance may be measured at the input stage (to determine the quality of materials purchased, for example), during the process stage (to determine if the product being manufactured meets quality standards, for instance), or at the output stage (perhaps to determine how well the product is selling).

Some controls, such as those at the input stage, are *preventive controls.* They measure performance and compare it to standards before the

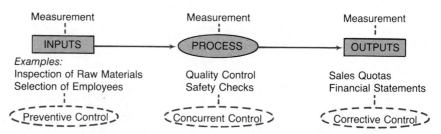

FIGURE 22–3   Stages of measurement and control

process stage is reached. A poor-quality product resulting from defective raw materials can be prevented through this form of control. Control based on measurement during the process stage is termed *concurrent control* because it occurs as the product or service is being produced. And measurement indicating problems at the output stage results in *corrective control,* or control after the fact.

Performance information is often channelled to the appropriate manager in the form of reports. If they are to be useful, reports should be specifically tailored to each manager's needs and must be timely and accurate. A computer-based management information system can be extremely useful in providing the up-to-date information necessary to effective control.

Not all information is formalized. Personal observation and informal discussions are used extensively in many organizations to keep managers in touch with units under their direction. In fact, informal systems are most appropriate for certain types of control situations. Most first-line supervisors, for example, must rely heavily upon such methods to keep in touch with their subordinates. At any level of any organization, some feedback is informal.

3 Taking Corrective Action

Corrective action is required when performance deviates significantly from the standard in an unfavorable direction. To prevent the deviation from recurring, however, such action must be preceded by an analysis of the cause of the deviation. If a student has established a standard of making a 90 on an exam and makes only a 60, he or she must determine the cause of the unfavorable deviation before taking the next test. To be effective, corrective action must locate and deal with the *real* cause.

Some deviation from the standard may be justified because of inaccuracies in the standard, changes in environmental conditions, or other reasons. The manager who states, "I don't want to hear excuses; I just want to see results!" fails to realize that standards may become unrealistic over time, and valid extenuating circumstances do occur. The data must be examined in the light of existing conditions. Such an examination may result in more realistic plans, goals, and control standards.

Finally, some processes are self-controlling. A common example is that of a heating system with a thermostat. Assume the thermostat is set at 65 degrees in the winter (the standard). The thermostat measures the temperature in the room and compares it to the standard. If the temperature is significantly less than 65 degrees, the thermostat activates the heating system (corrective action) to warm the room to 65 degrees. As long as the system works properly, no human is required to oversee it. In some industries—oil refining, for instance—computers are programmed to "control" intricate production processes in this way.

THE NEED FOR CONTROL IN THE SPACE AGE

"The president of one company grew increasingly suspicious when his competitor kept submitting bids a sliver below his own. One day he emptied his humidor, looking for a bug, but found nothing. Later, he learned that it was in a cigar on the bottom."

****

When the demand for integrated circuits (ICs) exceeded supply in 1980, a booming black market developed. The sellers were employees of the IC manufacturers who succumbed to temptation to "go into business" for themselves. Many found it easy to smuggle the small ICs out of the plant inside their clothing. The ICs could then be sold to industrial distributors for about $100 apiece.

Industry observers indicated that the electronic components industry was losing at least $20 million a year, with companies "experiencing losses they don't even know about."

SOURCES: "New 'Bugs' Make Spying Easier," *Business Week*, 12 July 1982, p. 74; and adapted from "In Silicon Valley, Goodbye, Mr. Chips," *Newsweek*, 12 May 1980, pp. 78, 81.

FINANCIAL CONTROL

Perhaps no area of control has received more emphasis in recent years than control over financial operations. Since cash and access to credit are integral to an organization's survival, this emphasis is understandable. Additionally, the lengthy economic recession, which has resulted in an unusual number of bankruptcies, has forced managers to pay close attention to their firms' financial status. This section reviews some of the important control tools and techniques in this area.

Sleepy Bedding Company
Balance Sheet
Year Ended December 31

Assets		_Liabilities & Net Worth_	
Current Assets		Current Liabilities	
Cash	$ 50,000	Accounts Payable	$ 90,000
Marketable Securities	170,000	Notes Payable	190,000
Accounts Receivable	250,000	Accrued Taxes	20,000
Inventories	350,000		
Total Current Assets	820,000	Total Current Liabilities	300,000
Fixed Assets		Long- term Debt	700,000
Plant & Equipment		Net Worth	
(less depreciation)	1,200,000	Common Stock	600,000
		(at par)	
		Retained Earnings	420,000
Total Assets	$2,020,000	Total Net Worth	1,020,000
		Total Liabilities and	
		Net Worth	$2,020,000

FIGURE 22–4   Balance sheet

Financial Statements

Balance Sheet. Perhaps the most visible accounting control tools are those reports detailing the organization's financial condition. The *balance sheet* (Figure 22–4) reports the organization's financial position as of the date of preparation. This requires a presentation of *assets* (what is owned), *liabilities* (what is owed), and the owners' *net worth* (the difference between assets and liabilities).

The Sleepy Bedding Company, which manufactures and sells mattresses and box springs, has current assets (those which are cash or will be converted into cash within a year) of $820,000. Besides cash, these assets consist of marketable securities (stocks and certificates of deposit), accounts receivable (the amount customers still owe the company), and inventories of mattresses and box springs (valued at cost). Fixed assets (those which will not be converted into cash within a year) consist of the organization's manufacturing facilities and tools, minus their depreciated value.

Current liabilities (those the company must pay within a year) amount to $300,000. The amounts owed include accounts payable (owed to suppliers), notes payable (short-term loans from banks), and accrued taxes (the tax liability already incurred). Long-term debt (which does not have to be paid within a year) amounts to $700,000. The difference be-

Sleepy Bedding Company		
Income Statement		
Year Ended December 31		
Net Sales		$3,500,000
Cost of Goods Sold		2,850,000
Gross Profit		650,000
Less: Selling Expenses	$35,000	
General and Administrative Expenses	50,000	
Depreciation	115,000	
Interest Expense	112,000	312,000
Net Income Before Taxes		338,000
Income Taxes		135,000
Net Income After Taxes		203,000
Cash Dividends to Stockholders		100,000
Increase in Retained Earnings		$103,000

FIGURE 22–5 Income statement

tween total assets ($2,020,000) and total liabilities ($1,000,000) represents the owners' equity or net worth ($1,020,000). This entry consists of the common stock purchased by investors and retained earnings (the firm's cumulative profits over the years after dividends).

Income Statement. The *income statement* (Figure 22–5) presents a more dynamic picture of the organization, showing over some period of time the amount of *revenue* which flowed into the organization less all *expenses* and *taxes* and the resultant *net profit* or *loss*. While the balance sheet indicates the net worth of the organization's owners, the income statement reveals how much money the organization made or lost over a given period of time.

The Sleepy Bedding Company sold $3,500,000 worth of mattresses and box springs during the calendar year. The production costs incurred during that time (raw materials, labor, and so on) amounted to $2,850,000, leaving a gross profit of $650,000. Other expenses, which are shown separately so that they might be compared to previous years' expense levels, amounted to $312,000, leaving net income before taxes of $338,000. Income taxes consumed $135,000 of that amount, resulting in net income after taxes of $203,000. After dividend payments of $100,000 to the stockholders, the retained earnings account increased by $103,000.

Ratio Analysis. Although financial statements reveal such figures as profit, net worth, and so on, these numbers alone provide us with limited information. Hence, *ratio analysis* is used to interpret the financial

LACK OF FINANCIAL CONTROL

Few major companies in recent years suffered more from financial woes than did AM International. Among other problems, the firm's operations were characterized by poor financial control. Consider the following appraisal of the financial operations of AM Jacquard, a division which produced word processors and small office computers:

Billing was haphazard. Some customers received invoices well before they received the product, while others were not billed until months after delivery. Jacquard was one of the divisions that contributed to the last-minute revenue shortfall [of AM International] in 1980. Insiders say that Jacquard did not distinguish properly between direct sales and dealer sales and thus did not take into account the lower price that independent dealers paid for the equipment.

SOURCE: "AM International: When Technology Was Not Enough," *Business Week*, 25 January 1982, p. 68.

statements by giving management more of the information it needs for control purposes.[2]

Examples of some of the more common—and meaningful—ratios are shown in Figure 22–6. Each ratio may be interpreted by comparing it to the firm's ratios from previous years (to discern trends) and/or to standard industry ratios. In Figure 22–6, the median ratios for small firms in the mattress/box springs industry are shown alongside the Sleepy Bedding Company's ratios. The median ratio, we should caution, is not necessarily a goal for which Sleepy Bedding Company should strive. Differences in accounting practices among firms may distort direct comparisons. Nevertheless, such evaluations are helpful in acquiring general impressions concerning the organization and its performance. Significant deviations from industry figures indicate that further analysis is required.

Some of the ratio comparisons in Figure 22–6 require further comment. The debt-to-net-worth ratio of Sleepy Bedding Company is below the industry's median. This comparison, combined with the current ratio which is above the median, indicates that the company, if it desired to borrow funds, would probably be looked upon with favor by its creditors. The company's average period for collecting payment from its customers, however, far exceeds the industry median. Since the normal sales terms in the industry are fifteen days, this deviation should alert management to take steps to expedite the collection of accounts receivable and, perhaps, to examine its credit policies.

Type of Ratio			Ratio for Sleepy Bedding Company	Median Ratio for Industry
Liquidity Ratio (ability to meet short-term financial obligations)				
Current Ratio $= \dfrac{\text{Current Assets}}{\text{Current Liabilities}} = \dfrac{\$820{,}000}{300{,}000} =$			2.73 times	1.95 times
Leverage Ratio (ability to meet long-term financial obligations)				
Debt-to-Net-Worth Ratio $= \dfrac{\text{Total Debt}}{\text{Net Worth}} = \dfrac{\$1{,}000{,}000}{1{,}020{,}000} =$			98.0%	114.9%
Activity Ratios (ability to employ resources effectively)				
Inventory Turnover $= \dfrac{\text{Sales}}{\text{Inventory}} = \dfrac{\$3{,}500{,}000}{350{,}000} =$			10 times	9.7 times
Average Collection Period $= \dfrac{\text{Accounts Receivable}}{\text{Sales/365 days}} = \dfrac{\$250{,}000}{3{,}500{,}000/365} =$			26 days	14 days
Profitability Ratios (ability to operate efficiently)				
Profit Margin on Sales $= \dfrac{\text{Net Income after Taxes}}{\text{Sales}} = \dfrac{\$203{,}000}{\$3{,}500{,}000} =$			5.80%	6.48%
Return on Net Worth $= \dfrac{\text{Net Income after Taxes}}{\text{Net Worth}} = \dfrac{\$203{,}000}{1{,}020{,}000} =$			19.90%	17.57%

FIGURE 22–6 Selected ratios for Sleepy Bedding Company
NOTE: Median ratios for the industry are from Dun & Bradstreet's 1980 *Key Business Ratios*, p. 48. The industry is Mattresses and Bedsprings (SIC 2515), and the ratios are for companies with less than $50,000,000 in net worth.

Finally, the profitability ratios indicate that Sleepy Bedding's return on net worth (often considered the final criterion of a firm's profitability) is higher than the industry median. Yet, the company receives less net income per dollar of sales than the industry median. This latter comparison requires management to analyze its expenses (cost of goods sold, selling expenses, administrative expenses, and so on) to determine if any of these areas are proportionately too high. This analysis can be accomplished by comparing current expense levels/sales with expense levels/sales of previous years. The company's prices for its products may also be lower than the industry median.

Limitations of Financial Statements. To use financial statements with any degree of sophistication, one must have some appreciation of their limitations. Only the naive manager accepts such statements as the simple truth. As a matter of fact, there are many limitations, only a few of which can be noted here.

As one example of these difficulties, the changing value of the dollar presents continuing problems. Assets are typically shown at cost or, in the case of inventory, at the lower of cost or market. But when general price levels change markedly, the worth of assets as shown on the books becomes unrealistic. Charging depreciation on the basis of cost, therefore, may be insufficient to make possible replacement of fully depreciated assets.

Another related difficulty is associated with the valuation of inventories. Some companies use a FIFO (first-in, first-out) method, while others use a LIFO (last-in, first-out) method. The FIFO method, for example, treats inventory costs as if items purchased first are sold or consumed first. When inventory is purchased at different prices over a period of time, asset values and profits differ according to the method of inventory valuation used. Someone's judgment regarding inventory valuation is involved, therefore, in "scientifically" determining profit results.

Many accounting figures must be approximations. Although a given obligation—a promissory note, for example—may be valued down to the exact penny, such precise calculations are not possible in all phases of the accounting process. As an example, the portion of equipment cost to be charged as an expense in a particular period must be estimated. The useful life cannot be predicted with complete accuracy. A particular machine may last well beyond its expected life or become obsolete earlier than anticipated. Either of these eventualities could cause depreciation estimates to prove inaccurate.

Accounting information, furthermore, supplies only part of the total relevant information for control purposes. Some aspects of business operations are difficult to reduce to a dollar basis for inclusion in financial statements. Suppose, for example, that two managers are being compared on the basis of the profit performance of their respective divisions. The fact that one division suffered the loss of several key executives during the year or that unexpectedly strong competition developed for one division may not be shown on the financial statements.

Budgets

Budgets were discussed in Chapter 7 as an aid to planning. As is the case with most planning tools, budgets are also useful control devices. Budgeted figures serve as standards to which actual performance can be compared. As a plan for expenditures, the budget provides preventive control, and as a means of pinpointing areas in which overspending is occurring, it serves as a corrective control tool. Budgeting, however, "should not be thought of as a device for limiting expenditures; the budgeting process is a tool for obtaining the most productive and profitable use of the company's resources."[3]

The overall budgeting process is illustrated in Figure 22–7. The organization's budgets are based on the firm's plans and forecasts. One set of budgets relates to manufacturing. Sales forecasts are translated into budgets for the actual production of goods or services, for materials, for labor, and for expenditures for new plant and equipment (capital expenditures). Budgets for advertising and selling what the firm produces are also needed. Budgets are likewise required for research on new products

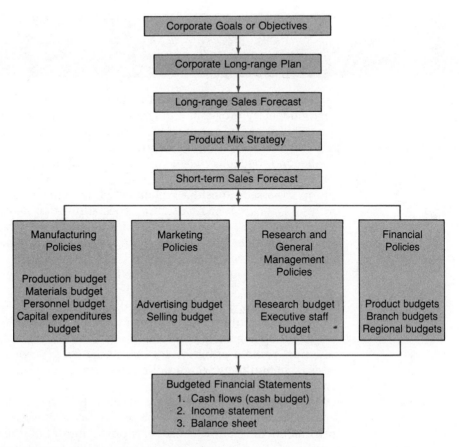

FIGURE 22–7 Overall view of the total budgeting process
SOURCE: From *Essentials of Managerial Finance*, 4th edition, by J.
Fred Weston and Eugene F. Brigham. Copyright © 1974, 1977 by the
Dryden Press, copyright © 1968, 1971 by Holt, Rinehart and Winston,
Inc. Reprinted by permission of Holt, Rinehart and Winston, CBS Col-
lege Publishing.

and the improvement of present products and for the organization's staff
of general managers. Finally, budgets for each product, each branch, and
each region are also formulated. The double arrow above these types of
budgets indicates that the budgets may also influence the organization's
forecasts. For instance, the size of the advertising budget will affect
sales.

The bottom of the diagram reveals that the various budgets may be
synthesized to yield predicted or *pro forma* financial statements. These
statements show the expected financial condition of the organization at
the end of the budgetary period.

Budgets can be used to control functional areas, product lines, and
subsystems such as branches or regions. They are, therefore, used to establish control standards for revenues, expenses, and profits.

PROBLEMS OF BUDGETING

Four major problems are encountered when using budget systems. First, budgetary programs can grow to be so complete and so detailed that they become cumbersome, meaningless, and unduly expensive. Overbudgeting is dangerous.

Second, budgetary goals may come to supersede enterprise goals. A budget is a tool, not an end in itself. Enterprise goals by definition supersede subsidiary plans of which budgets are a part. Moreover, budgets are based on future expectations that may not be realized. There is no acceptable reason for neglecting to alter budgets as circumstances change. This reasoning is the core of the argument in favor of more flexible budgets.

Third, budgets can tend to hide inefficiencies by continuing initial expenditures in succeeding periods without proper evaluation. Budgets growing from precedent usually contain undesirable expenditures. They sould not be used as umbrellas under which slovenly, inefficient management can hide. Consequently, the budgetary process must contain provision for reexamination of standards and other bases of planning by which policies are translated into numerical terms.

Finally, case study evidence suggests that the use of budgets as a pressure device defeats their basic objectives. Budgets, if used as instruments of tyranny, cause resentment and frustrations, which in turn lead to inefficiency. In order to counteract this effect, it has been recommended that top management increase the participation of subordinates during the preparatory stages of the budgets.

SOURCE: From *Essentials of Managerial Finance*, 4th edition, by J. Fred Weston and Eugene F. Brigham. Copyright © 1974, 1977 by the Dryden Press, copyright © 1968, 1971 by Holt, Rinehart and Winston, Inc. Reprinted by permission of Holt, Rinehart and Winston, CBS College Publishing.

Responsibility Centers

A *responsibility center* is an organizational subsystem which is charged with a well-defined mission and is headed by a manager accountable for the performance of the center. "Responsibility centers constitute the primary building blocks for management control."[4]

The logic behind the responsibility center concept is straightforward. Assume that an organization has no specific responsibility centers. Assume further that the company's year-end profits are significantly lower than expected. Where does the responsibility for the poor operat-

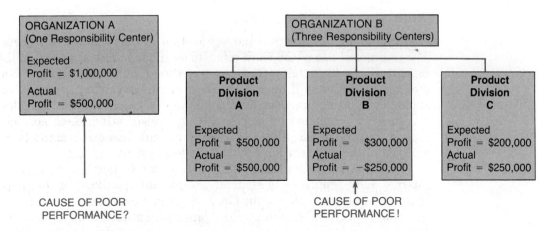

FIGURE 22-8   Pinpointing responsibility

ing performance lie? If the entire organization is the responsibility center, pinpointing the problem(s) would probably be quite difficult, meaning that appropriate corrective action will either not be taken or will be unnecessarily delayed.

If the organization, however, has three product divisions, each headed by a manager accountable for its performance, and an accounting system which measures the performance of each division, then control is considerably enhanced, as shown in Figure 22-8. In this case, management can analyze the operations of Product Division B while allowing Divisions A and C to continue operating normally. This process saves management time and facilitates corrective action.

The types of responsibility centers vary by organization and situation. A profit center, as illustrated in Figure 22-8, is responsible for both revenues and expenditures. The manager of a product division may be held accountable for the sales and expenses—and, hence, profits—associated with the operation of that division. This is a common arrangement in the retail industry (individual stores or even departments may be profit centers), in multiproduct (or service) organizations, and in organizations structured along geographic lines.

Many businesses with functional structures and most nonprofit organizations contain expense centers responsible for expenditures but not revenues. Business examples would include production departments, staff units, accounting and electronic data processing divisions, purchasing departments, public relations staffs, and so on.

Control focuses on measuring the profit or expenses of the responsibility center and comparing it with the figures of other responsibility centers as well as with historical trends. The object is to determine which centers are operating less effectively than others and, therefore, require corrective action.

Audits

Auditing is the examination and verification of the accuracy of records. The traditional use of the word refers to an independent appraisal of the organization's financial records by a certified public accounting firm seeking to determine if the records are accurate and reflect generally accepted accounting practices. In contrast to this *external audit,* an *internal* audit is conducted by members of the organization. Such an audit may go beyond verification of transactions and financial records to an analysis of the organization's overall control system.

The General Accounting Office (GAO), for instance, serves as the internal audit branch of the federal government. To illustrate the scope of its audit responsibilities, the GAO, in recent years, has criticized U.S. government contracts which allow Japanese coproduction of the McDonnell Douglas F-15 fighter as being a one-way flow of technological benefits to Japan; recommended that military training aircraft carry less equipment than combat-ready aircraft in order to reduce costs; and charged that the Reagan administration was using proceeds from the sale of excess materials from the national stockpile to reduce the budget deficit rather than to purchase strategic materials needed to maintain national security.[5]

DYSFUNCTIONAL CONSEQUENCES OF CONTROL

In the design of control systems and the application of controls to the organization, unanticipated and undesirable effects are often realized. Instead of, or in addition to, controlling organizational activity as intended, the controls produce side effects, a sort of by-product of the control system. Such dysfunctional side effects result from the human reactions of members of the organization.

The Narrow Viewpoint

One such undesirable effect is the tendency of some control systems to narrow one's viewpoint unduly. The controls act as a set of blinders to limit the individual's vision or concern to his or her own sphere, with possible disregard for broader organizational values. A pay incentive system in manufacturing, for example, may base the reward upon output to the extent that quality suffers. Such a system may give the individual little or no encouragement to think beyond the daily production record to the broader objectives of the organization and the contributions one might make to these. Absolutely no incentive for improvement in the operations and methods may exist. The incentive system has conditioned the employee to believe that only daily output is important.

Many college students—and faculty members, for that matter—complain that grades have similar undesirable effects. Studying for exams and writing term papers become ends in themselves rather than means to learning.

At a managerial level, an example may be found in the restricted viewpoints of managers of functional areas.

> A control system may be intended to contribute to profit and seek to control manufacturing efficiency by means of standard costing. Management may reward performance based upon variance measurement. However, unintended consequences of this control system may occur. It may lead persons responsible for standard costs to concentrate upon their measured performance, at the expense of other organizational goals, such as sales revenues, for which they are not responsible. Persons responsible for manufacturing cost centers may be reluctant or unwilling to modify production schedules to accommodate special customer requests, because of the effects of such changes upon manufacturing costs.[6]

UNREALISTIC PRODUCTION STANDARDS

Production standards, if unrealistic, can create considerable pressure for lower-level managers who must meet the standards. Plant supervisors at a Chevrolet truck plant in Michigan explained their problem as follows:

> At Chevrolet, we're given a production goal each week that's predicated on the assumption that everything will go perfectly. The problem is that on an assembly line, nothing ever does. There's always a conveyor breakdown or high absenteeism or something. As a result, we were constantly missing our targets, and the bosses were putting pressure on us to do something about it.
>
> We tried to explain our problems to higher-ups in the company, but we were told, "I don't care how you do it—just do it."

To cope with the problem, the managers installed a secret control box to speed up the assembly line and increase production. The assembly line workers, however, discovered and reported the secret control mechanism. The three supervisors were temporarily suspended and later transferred to other plants, and the United Auto Workers won $1,000,000 in back pay from General Motors.

SOURCE: Adapted from "Some Middle Managers Cut Corners to Achieve High Corporate Goals," *Wall Street Journal*, 8 November 1979, p. 26. Reprinted by permission of *The Wall Street Journal*, © Dow Jones & Company, Inc. 1979. All rights reserved.

The Short Run versus the Long Run

Another unfortunate consequence of some control systems is the premium they may unwittingly place upon the short run. The control system encourages a short-run course of action that may run counter to the long-run interests of the organization. Consider, for example, the profit control applied to the different divisions of a decentralized company. The profit goal of the division serves as a powerful incentive for the division manager who is under tremendous pressure to achieve that objective. Under certain conditions, this presents a strong motivation to win in the short run, even though the long-run effects may be disastrous.

The following decisions by division managers illustrate this type of undesirable short-run reaction to a control system.

> In order to increase his rate of return, a division manager reduced his research costs by eliminating all projects that did not have an expected payout within two years. He believed that if he did not improve his rate of return, he would be replaced.
>
> . . . .
>
> A division manager scrapped some machinery that he was not currently using in order to reduce his investment. Later, when the machinery was needed, he purchased new equipment.[7]

One study of managers in six major companies indicates that division managers who emphasize the attainment of short-run profits over long-term strategic goals often do so for two reasons.[8] The first is that the manager's performance evaluation (and financial incentives) often stress short-run criteria. The second is that short-term goals are more visible and easily comprehended than long-range objectives. Many lower-level managers are not fully aware of their organization's strategic goals.

Evasion of Controls through Falsification of Reporting

Pressure to achieve standards is an everyday fact of life for employees at all levels. Pressure, of course, can be useful in motivating individuals to high performance, but for some employees, the pressure becomes too intense and they find themselves faced with the choice of either being branded "incompetent" by their supervisors or resorting to falsifying reports.

This ethical issue is most often faced by middle- and lower-level managers, particularly in organizations in which these managers have little voice in setting their own performance goals. Such a situation evidently occurred in 1979 when middle managers chose to falsify reports in the "pressure-cooker" atmosphere of H. J. Heinz Company:

BOOMERANG THRIFT

"The manager of one of the major divisions of a large publishing company found himself with surplus budget funds at the end of the year. Thinking that he would become a 'fiscal hero,' he announced to his boss that he was giving back the dollars he had not spent. To his surprise he was told that he must be either a 'poor planner' (over-budgeted), 'incompetent organizer' (insufficient activity), or 'not growth oriented' (bigger and better budgets). In view of his unspent dollars, his request for funds for the following year was cut back. Thus, belatedly he learned that what he considered smart money management was regarded as unprogressive and almost un-American. Naturally, the next time he happened to be able to save the company money, he found other ways to spend the savings."

SOURCE: Charles L. Hughes, "Why Budgets Go Wrong," *Personnel* 42 (May–June 1965): 21.

"When we didn't meet our growth targets, the top brass really came down on us," recalls a former marketing official at the company's huge Heinz U.S.A. division. "And everybody knew that if you missed the targets enough, you were out on your ear."

In this environment, some harried managers apparently resorted to deceptive bookkeeping when they couldn't otherwise meet profit goals set by the company's top executives. Invoices were misdated and payments to suppliers were made in advance—sometimes to be returned later in cash—all with the aim, insiders say, of showing the sort of smooth profit growth that would please top management and impress securities analysts.[9]

Adverse Morale Effects

In view of the malfunctioning of control previously described, it is hardly surprising that morale may be impaired at times. The combination of pressure and seemingly necessary but illogical behavior would hardly make one wildly enthusiastic about the organization. In fact, management personnel may easily experience a strong reaction against such a control system.

Consider the attitude expressed by one department store salesperson concerning sales quotas:

Every day we are assigned a quota based on what was sold a year before. No account is taken of economic conditions, whether a holiday (such as Easter) comes early or late this year, or other such factors. In other words, only one criterion is used. When the quota is either too high or too low, my performance suffers. If it is too low, there is no challenge. If the quota is too high, which is worse, the quota is just out of reach. Management is plain being unrealistic. Why should I try to reach such an arbitrary quota? My attitude is negative.

If management appears unreasonable in the application of controls, the subordinate naturally becomes disturbed. A superior, for example, may refuse to accept reasonable explanations for delays. As a consequence, the subordinate must be content with an unfavorable evaluation by the superior or resort to one or more of the devious means available in combating the situation. A straightforward, honest effort may not secure the approbation of the superior. Those subject to such types of control are understandably critical.

Improving Effectiveness of Control

Managers, in installing and using controls, obviously do not desire the unfortunate effects previously described. Nor are these effects an inescapable consequence of all control systems. Establishing controls, however, does create pressures often leading to these undesirable effects. Managers should, therefore, be aware of this tendency and attempt to minimize the harmful effects.

Participative Management. To gain general acceptance, standards must be established so that they are perceived as fair by those whose performance is controlled. The use of participative management, for example, tends to induce acceptance of standards as reasonable. Standards which recognize some range of acceptable performance and which appear to be established objectively, as is the case with statistical quality controls, also encourage acceptance by those whose performance is controlled.

In addition, controls must be recognized as means and not as ends in themselves. Higher-level management can assure this, however, only by a reasonable interpretation of results being controlled. If all explanations, regardless of validity, are unacceptable, the control system will almost inevitably become an end in itself.

The Extent of Control. In any situation, the formality and nature of control can be varied. Control may be loose and general or close and detailed. The concepts of delegation and decentralization, for example, involve a philosophy of only general control. Higher management expects certain results but permits lower levels to proceed without detailed control in accomplishing those results. The extent to which a decentralized management approach is adopted, therefore, governs the closeness of control that may be used appropriately.

Improvement in managerial control may thus call for a paradoxical solution. By controlling less, the manager may control better. If a manager follows a natural bent toward overcontrol, on the other hand, the

MORE VERSUS LESS CONTROL

One writer stresses that an appropriate control process emphasizes strategic control with tactical flexibility. As a case in point, he relates the case of a company caught in a cost-cutting squeeze. To reduce its travel costs, management had two options. The first was to design a detailed travel authorization form, like most companies use, to be filled out by the employee who requests travel funds. This meant

- Every possible eventuality had to be included in the form which made it extremely complex.
- A great deal of the information required was hard for another person to evaluate—e.g., purpose of trip, reason for additional funds.
- The objective got lost in the means. People did not travel less—they became better advocates. They also lost their personal commitment as soon as the form was signed by their boss.

The second approach was to tell everybody to cut their travel costs: each person had to do so by a set percentage.
This had the following advantages:

- They found ingenious ways of cutting costs—e.g., different routes, cheaper flights, etc.
- There was no added cost from making up and chasing paperwork. The old system sufficed.
- There was a feedback on the total result which directly reflected the performance of the management.

SOURCE: David Mitchell, *Control without Bureaucracy* (London: McGraw-Hill Book Co. (UK), 1979), p. 29. Reprinted by permission.

results may be destructive rather than helpful. Within limits imposed by the situation, a manager may lighten control—delegating, avoiding close supervision, and eliminating burdensome control procedures—and still achieve greater success than otherwise.

Management by Objectives. The management-by-objectives (MBO) approach discussed in Chapter 7 tends to minimize undesirable behavioral effects. The principal feature of this type of management is the establishment of specific performance goals for each position, particularly for each managerial position. By stressing these objectives, overall control is achieved through self-control by individual participants. Rather than applying control from above, the emphasis is placed upon control from within.

Use of Strategic Control Points. The effectiveness of control partially depends upon the selection of the points at which control is applied. Consider a process or activity, for example, starting at point X and proceeding through stages a, b, and c to reach completion at point Y.

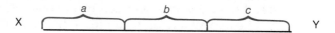

To control the process, checking may be employed at various points. The work may be checked at the end of the process, at the end of each stage, or at various points during each stage. The best combination of control points would keep the process in line with a minimum of cost and control effort.

Management by Exception. Economy of control effort uses the principle of *management by exception*. In using this approach, the manager devotes effort to unexpected or out-of-line performance. Some standard is established, and significant deviations from that standard are the exceptions. If performance conforms to anticipations, time spent in reviewing this fact is largely wasted. Managing by exception permits the manager to isolate nonstandard performance and to concentrate upon it.

Suppose that six sales territories are each expected to produce $50,000 in sales. If one produces $40,000, another $60,000, and four others between $49,000 and $51,000, the manager can focus upon two territories, thereby conserving time which can more profitably be devoted to planning and other managerial functions. Obviously, the existence of appropriate responsibility centers facilitates this process.

Expectations Approach. An interesting approach to control, developed in Great Britain by John Machin, is based on managerial "expectations."[10] All managers in the organization are asked to make an extensive list of the expectations they hold of the performance of other managers with whom they interact. Then the managers list the expectations they perceive other managers hold of them. The managers then meet to discuss the lists with each other.

As an example, the two managers illustrated below would discuss variations in their lists.

Manager A's List	*Manager B's List*
Expectations A holds of B ———————	Expectations B perceives A holds of B
Expectations A perceives B holds of A ———	Expectations B holds of A

Almost invariably, the expectations that A holds of B differ from B's perceptions of those expectations. Through interpersonal and, later, group discussions, managers reach a more accurate understanding of the inputs they expect from others and the outputs they are expected to supply to others. These expectations of performance are formalized and serve as standards to which actual performance may be compared.

SUMMARY

The purpose of control is to ensure the effective operation of an organization by focusing on all of its resources—human, material, and financial. The process of control is comprised of four steps: (1) establishing standards; (2) measuring performance; (3) comparing performance to standard; and (4) taking corrective action, if necessary.

An all-important area of control in contemporary organizations focuses upon the firm's financial operations. Financial control is attained through a number of means—*financial statements* interpreted through *ratio analysis*, *budgets*, the establishment of *responsibility centers*, and external and internal *audits*.

The control process has a tendency to produce certain unwanted *behavioral consequences* in the organization that is being controlled. Some of these undesirable reactions are narrowness of viewpoint, short-run expediencies with long-run disadvantages, evasion of controls through falsification of reporting, and reduced morale.

A number of possible variations or changes in control systems are available to managers who wish to improve their effectiveness. Harmful behavioral consequences may be minimized, for example, by careful development of the elements of the control system and its equitable administration. Improvement is also possible in many situations by reducing the extent of control through delegating authority and avoiding close supervision. *Management by objectives*, use of *strategic control points*, *management by exception*, and the *expectations approach* may also contribute to a workable control system.

DISCUSSION QUESTIONS

1. What is the relationship between *planning* and *control*?
2. Must all *standards* be quantified?
3. Distinguish between *preventive control*, *concurrent control*, and *corrective control*.
4. What is meant by the statement "*Financial statements* alone provide us with limited information"? How does the use of *ratio analysis* aid in financial control?

5. Explain how *budgets* serve as both planning and control tools.
6. Explain how the *responsibility center* concept aids in managerial control.
7. How can controls cause undesirably narrow viewpoints in individual members or departments of an organization?
8. "There is a direct correlation between increasing organizational control and improved organizational efficiency." True or false? Why?
9. Explain the principle of *management by exception*.
10. An office manager commented as follows: "It is my responsibility to keep up with all aspects of every activity and project that are assigned to this office." Evaluate this statement in the light of managerial control theory.

NOTES

1. Henri Fayol, *General and Industrial Management*, trans. Constance Storrs (London: Pitman Publishing, 1949), p. 107.
2. Excellent discussions of this area may be found in J. Fred Weston and Eugene F. Brigham, *Essentials of Managerial Finance*, 4th ed. (Hinsdale, Ill.: The Dryden Press, 1977), pp. 39–61; and James C. Van Horne, *Fundamentals of Financial Management*, 4th ed. (Englewood Cliffs, N.J.: Prentice-Hall, 1980), pp. 103–19.
3. Weston and Brigham, *Essentials of Managerial Finance*, p. 105.
4. Raymond M. Kinnunen and Robert H. Caplan III, "The Domain of Management Control," *University of Michigan Business Review* 30 (May 1978): 6.
5. "GAO Report Says Coproduction Pacts Aid Japan Industry," *Aviation Week & Space Technology*, 29 March 1982, p. 25; "GAO Raises Questions about F/A-18, AV-8B," *Aviation Week & Space Technology*, 22 March 1982, p. 28; and Jay C. Lowndes, "GAO Charges Stockpile Funds Misused," *Aviation Week & Space Technology*, 16 August 1982, pp. 20–21.
6. Eric Flamholtz, "Organizational Control Systems as a Managerial Tool," *California Management Review* 22 (Winter 1979): 50–59.
7. Bruce D. Henderson and John Dearden, "New System for Divisional Control," *Harvard Business Review* 44 (September–October 1966): 150.
8. Robert L. Banks and Steven C. Wheelwright, "Operations vs. Strategy: Trading Tomorrow for Today," *Harvard Business Review* 57 (May–June 1979): 112–20.
9. "Some Middle Managers Cut Corners to Achieve High Corporate Goals," *Wall Street Journal*, 8 November 1979, p. 1. Reprinted by permission of *The Wall Street Journal*, © Dow Jones & Company, 1979. All rights reserved.
10. John L. J. Machin, "A Contingent Methodology for Management Control," *Journal of Management Studies* 16 (February 1979): 1–29.

SUPPLEMENTARY READING

Banks, Robert L., and Wheelwright, Steven C. "Operations vs. Strategy: Trading Tomorrow for Today." *Harvard Business Review* 57 (May–June 1979): 112–20.

Buss, Martin D. J. "Penny-wise Approach to Data Processing." *Harvard Business Review* 59 (July–August 1981): 111–17.

Davies, Celia, and Francis, Arthur. "The Many Dimensions of Performance Measurement." *Organizational Dynamics* 3 (Winter 1975): 51–65.

Eiler, Robert G.; Goletz, Walter K.; and Keegan, Daniel P. "Is Your Cost Accounting Up to Date?" *Harvard Business Review* 60 (July–August 1982): 133–39.

Flamholtz, Eric. "Organizational Control Systems as a Managerial Tool." *California Management Review* 22 (Winter 1979): 50–59.

Hofstede, Geert. "The Poverty of Management Control Philosophy." *Academy of Management Review* 3 (July 1978): 450–61.

Machin, John L. J. "A Contingent Methodology for Management Control." *Journal of Management Studies* 16 (February 1979): 1–29.

Machin, John L. J., and Wilson, Lyn S. "Closing the Gap between Planning and Control." *Long Range Planning* 12 (April 1979): 16–32.

Merchant, Kenneth A. "The Control Function of Management." *Sloan Management Review* 23 (Summer 1982): 43–55.

Mitchell, David. *Control without Bureaucracy.* London: McGraw-Hill Book Co. (UK), 1979.

Naor, Jacob. "How to Motivate Corporate Executives to Implement Long-Range Plans." *MSU Business Topics* 25 (Summer 1977): 41–49.

Naylor, Thomas H. "Management Is Drowning in Numbers." *Business Week,* 6 April 1981, pp. 14–15.

Newman, William H. *Constructive Control: Design and Use of Control Systems.* Englewood Cliffs, N.J.: Prentice-Hall, 1975.

Ouchi, William G., and Maguire, Mary Ann. "Organizational Control: Two Functions." *Administrative Science Quarterly* 20 (December 1975): 559–69.

Pekar, Peter Paul, Jr., and Burack, Elmer H. "Management Control of Strategic Plans through Adaptive Techniques." *Academy of Management Journal* 19 (March 1976): 79–97.

Rhode, John Grant, and Lawler, Edward E., III. *Information and Control in Organizations.* Pacific Palisades, Calif.: Goodyear Publishing Co., 1976.

Smith, Howard L.; Fottler, Myron D.; and Saxberg, Borje O. "Cost Containment in Health Care: A Model for Management Research." *Academy of Management Review* 6 (July 1981): 397–407.

Tosi, Henry L., Jr. "The Human Effects of Budgeting Systems on Management." *MSU Business Topics* 22 (Autumn 1974): 53–63.

23

OPERATIONS MANAGEMENT

This chapter will enable you to

- *Understand the nature and importance of operations management.*
- *Describe the basic types of operations in organizations.*
- *Identify the various functions that managers must perform as they plan and organize operations.*
- *Discuss how managers control such operational areas as material requirements, inventory, and quality.*

The heart of every organization is its operational subsystem which is concerned with the conversion of inputs into final products and services. The efficiency with which these operations are managed is a key determinant of the organization's ability to compete and to operate effectively.

OVERVIEW OF OPERATIONS MANAGEMENT

Nature of Operations Management

Operations management focuses on the organizational subsystem that is responsible for transforming inputs into outputs. Its basic objective is to ensure that products or services are produced which have a value that exceeds the combined costs of the required inputs and the transformation process.

The first formal analysis of operations management began at the turn of the twentieth century with Frederick W. Taylor's work in scientific management (discussed in Chapter 2). In addition to Taylor's "scientific" study of work processes, the emphasis of this school of thought was exemplified by Frank B. and Lillian M. Gilbreth's time-and-motion studies, which helped workers reduce inefficiency and fatigue, and Henry L. Gantt's study of work scheduling. This focus on the technical aspects of organizational operations became known as production or manufacturing management.

In the 1930s, the Hawthorne Studies (see Chapter 2) expanded this view of operations to include human and social factors. It was not until the 1950s, however, that the technical and social perspectives of operations management were formally joined into a single school of thought known as the *sociotechnical approach* (Figure 23–1). Introduced by Eric Trist and his colleagues at the Tavistock Institute of Human Relations in London, this approach emphasizes that operations management is neither concerned with "adjusting" people to technology nor technology to people but with "organizing the interface so that the best match could be obtained between both."[1]

IGNORING THE SOCIAL SUBSYSTEM

Several years ago, Safeway Stores installed a computer-based system for determining an acceptable work pace for warehouse workers who manually loaded food cartons onto pallets. The computer combined time studies with analyses of workers' physical capabilities to arrive at a specific number of cartons that were to be loaded within a specified time period. The third time a worker failed to meet that standard, he or she could be fired.

The local union, affiliated with the International Brotherhood of Teamsters, objected to the system on two grounds: (1) the union members had not been consulted before installation of the new system; and (2) the system failed to consider the worker's age and sex (the system considered the average age of workers in a warehouse but not the age of each individual separately). As a result, 2,500 members walked off the job for fifteen weeks in the nine affected locals. As the sociotechnical approach emphasizes, it is not possible to "maximize" one subsystem while ignoring the other.

SOURCE: Based on "Productivity Goals Gall the Teamsters," *Business Week*, 6 November 1978, pp. 71-73.

FIGURE 23–1   The Sociotechnical Approach

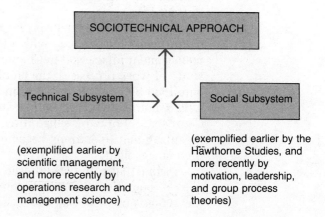

SOCIOTECHNICAL APPROACH

Technical Subsystem → ← Social Subsystem

(exemplified earlier by scientific management, and more recently by operations research and management science)

(exemplified earlier by the Hawthorne Studies, and more recently by motivation, leadership, and group process theories)

TABLE 23–1 Employment (in thousands) in selected industries

Industry	1920	1940	1960	1980	Growth Rate 1920–1980
Manufacturing	10,534	10,780	16,369	21,593	105%
Transportation, communication and public utilities	3,998	3,013	3,921	6,393	60%
Wholesale and retail trade	4,623	6,940	11,698	19,727	327%
Finance, insurance and real estate	1,110	1,436	2,494	5,860	428%
Services	2,142	3,477	6,673	27,983	1,206%

SOURCE: *Statistical Abstract of the United States,* 1981, p. 390; 1961, p. 207; 1951, p. 175.

Importance of Operations Management

Although the field of operations management has been associated most often with industrial manufacturing processes, it must be realized that managing operations is crucial to all types of organizations.

> Virtually everything one touches, uses, and consumes, and whatever one does is produced or affected by one or more manmade transformation processes: food, clothing, water, shelter, electricity, heat, refrigeration, transportation, money, communication, education, and so on. . . .
>
> The 1980s are times of challenge, opportunity, and threat. Society faces rampant inflation, imbalances of international payments, business cycles, increasingly scarce resources, declining morale and productivity, new technologies and automation, quality of working life issues, pollution, and the industrialization of services, to name but a few. *Every one of these major issues is related to the field of [operations management].*[2]

Additionally, focusing solely on manufacturing operations ignores the tremendous growth experienced by other sectors of the economy. Although manufacturing was by far the largest industry in the United States in 1920, it had become second to services and close to being overtaken by the wholesale and retail trade industry by 1980 (see Table 23–1). Because nonmanufacturing organizations are so important in our society, we must be aware that operations management concepts and skills apply to the operations of all types of organizations.

Productivity and Operations Management

Although a large number of factors influence organizational productivity (see Chapter 1), the greatest gains in productivity are often attained by increasing the efficiency of the operations subsystem. Efforts in this area, for example, may focus on improving job performance, updating technology, or improving coordination and scheduling processes.

Organizational emphasis on increasing productivity is directly related to the degree of competition the organization is experiencing. This fact explains why such significance has been placed on productivity improvements in manufacturing organizations over the past decade. During this period, the competition has expanded from what was primarily a domestic setting to encompass foreign manufacturers who often operate under very different rules and constraints. American manufacturing productivity, for instance, must keep pace with that of Japanese manufacturers if American products are to be competitive in price and quality.

Elsewhere, increasing competitive pressures in nonmanufacturing industries have caused managers who have only been peripherally concerned with operating efficiencies heretofore to place new emphasis on improving productivity. The retail industry, for instance, is attempting to increase its sales productivity.

> Although sales training is a common practice in other industries, retailers have dismissed it as a costly waste because employee turnover averages 60% annually. But with new store construction costs prohibitive, major markets saturated, and stores all carrying much the same goods, retailers are scrambling for ways to increase productivity at existing units. Now they are discovering that a trained sales force can set them apart from the competition, improve employee morale, and offer the greatest potential for lifting sales and profits.[3]

Even firms that sell services are developing productivity improvement programs. As a result of heavy competition from MasterCard and Visa, for example, American Express Company instituted a productivity program in 1978 to improve its customer service. Attempting to satisfy customers' desire for timeliness, accuracy, and company responsiveness, American Express broke down all service operations into the elements that fed into those three factors. After managerial task forces examined each discrete element, the managers set performance standards for each operation and devised ways to meet these new standards.[4]

Even though most of the publicity concerning productivity problems and improvements has centered on manufacturing operations, there are basic principles for increasing operational efficiency which can be applied to industrial and nonindustrial organizations alike.

Types of Operations

The specific type of operation an organization uses to transform its inputs into outputs depends on such factors as its industry, markets, competitors, strategies, image, available funds, and so on. In general, however, there are some general types of operations which may be used by both manufacturing and nonmanufacturing organizations alike. The following classification, for instance, is based upon the degree of process repetitiveness that characterizes an operation:[5]

1. *Continuous flow production*—characterized by a steady transformation of inputs into outputs. An oil refinery, for example, receives

from tankers a fairly continuous input of crude oil which is refined on a round-the-clock basis into products, such as gasoline, which are then pumped into tank trucks and railroad cars for shipment to customers.

2. *Mass production*—characterized by large production runs of a relatively standardized product requiring very specialized equipment and personnel. An automobile assembly plant is a common example.

3. *Large batch production*—characterized by the grouping of customer orders or products for large production runs. The production of different types of wine (rosé, burgundy, white, and so on) by a winery is an example.

4. *Job lot production*—characterized by production solely to customer order using short production runs and general-purpose equipment and personnel. A manufacturer of church pews, for example, produces no standard pews because each church requires different pew lengths, types of wood, and designs.

5. *Unique item production*—characterized by production of a "one-of-a-kind" product or service tailored to a specific customer so that, once the operation is completed, the same task never arises again. The work of a major repair yard for ships is an example.

Table 23–2 provides examples of all five types of operations in both the production and service sectors of the economy.

PLANNING AND ORGANIZING OPERATIONS

Management must perform a number of functions as it plans and organizes organizational operations. This section identifies these various functions, beginning with consideration of the physical facilities that are required to transform inputs into outputs.

Capacity Planning

The first function the operations manager performs involves planning the productive *capacity* required to meet the organization's sales forecast. To determine required capacity, the manager must convert forecasted dollar sales into physical units of output. In the automobile industry, for example, capacity is the number of cars that can be produced yearly, while an airline's capacity is measured by number of seats and a library's by number of volumes. The projected output requirements are then compared to the organization's current capacity to determine whether expansion, contraction, or maintenance of capacity at its present size is required.

Long-range planning may indicate that the organization needs to construct additional facilities or, conversely, sell some of its existing facilities or equipment. In the short run, capacity can be expanded through

TABLE 23–2 Examples of operations

Degree of Process Repetitiveness	Type of Operation					
	Production			Service		
	Manufacturing	Converting	Repairing	Protection	Logistics	Well-being
Continuous flow	Paper mill	Electrical power plant	Water-treatment plant	Prison	Gas pipeline	Hospital intensive-care ward
Mass	Automobile assembly plant	Open-pit coal mine	Large auto paint shop	U.S. secret service	Airline	Public school
Large batch	Winery	Scrap-metal reduction plant	Road-repair contractor	Traffic court	Grain elevator	Military basic-training camp
Job lot	Furniture maker	Custom slaughterhouse	Auto-body shop	Fire department	Trucking firm	Travel tour guide
Unique item	Office-building construction firm	Ship salvage company	Major ship-repair yard	Lloyds of London insurance	House mover	Management consulting firm

SOURCE: Stephen E. Barndt, Davis W. Carvey, Essentials of Operations Management, © 1982, p. 9. Reprinted by permission of Prentice-Hall, Inc., Englewood Cliffs, New Jersey.

such means as hiring temporary help, paying employees for overtime, renting space, or subcontracting excess orders. Likewise, capacity can be temporarily contracted through such actions as laying off employees, leasing idle space, or instituting shorter work weeks.

CAPACITY AS A CONSTRAINT

The inability to expand or update a firm's capacity due to financial limitations is the ultimate constraint on growth. Scott Paper Company illustrates this constraint. In 1981, one analyst estimated that 70 percent of Scott's capacity was "old technology" compared with 50 percent at competitor Kimberly-Clark Corporation and 20 percent at Procter & Gamble Company.

Although Scott's management recognized that much of its plant and equipment was too outdated to produce high-quality paper products, such as toilet tissue and paper towels, it lacked the cash or credit rating to conduct a major capital improvement program. As a temporary solution, Scott has modified the "marketing concept" of first identifying and then satisfying customer needs to a more pragmatic approach—that of producing and creating demand for the lower-cost products that its machinery can still make efficiently. Obviously, a longer-term solution must eventually be implemented.

SOURCE: Based on "Scott Paper Fights Back, at Last," *Business Week*, 16 February 1981, pp. 104, 108.

Site Location

New organizations and older ones which expand their operations must make decisions regarding the appropriate geographical *location* for physical facilities. Such decisions are complex because multiple factors must be considered (Figure 23–2) and because tradeoffs among these factors are inevitable. No site is optimal in every respect. A location with low land cost and taxes, for instance, may be far removed from a plentiful supply of skilled labor. The complexity of the decision, of course, is magnified when organizations locate branch offices or plants overseas and must deal with such additional complicating factors as different legal systems and cultures.

Although site decisions are important to all organizations, they are crucial for particular types of firms. For instance, organizations that supply other companies with parts or other goods often offer delivery time as an important part of their service. Firms that market directly consumed goods or services, such as restaurants, banks, movie theaters, and churches, can rarely succeed without convenient locations.

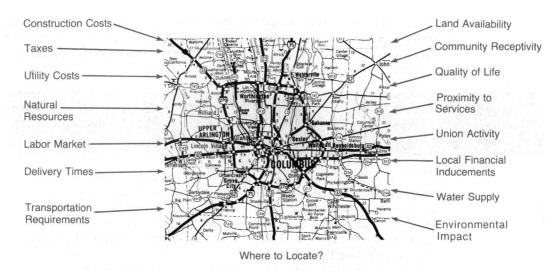

Construction Costs

Taxes

Utility Costs

Natural Resources

Labor Market

Delivery Times

Transportation Requirements

Land Availability

Community Receptivity

Quality of Life

Proximity to Services

Union Activity

Local Financial Inducements

Water Supply

Environmental Impact

Where to Locate?

FIGURE 23–2 Some factors in the site location decision

Process Planning

Once capacity and site decisions are made, management must determine the precise process that will be used to transform inputs into outputs. For any operations process, alternative means exist for converting inputs into final products or services. Automobiles, for instance, can be manufactured by mass production (General Motors), by autonomous work groups (Volvo), or by hand (Rolls Royce). The particular process chosen depends largely upon volume or capacity decisions, product design and quality, and the skill level of the organization's employees.

In general, any process design requires the following steps:[6]

1. Determining tasks and their sequence—this requires delineation of every operation, inspection, handling, and required wait (for drying or cooling, for example), and can be determined through assembly and flow process charting.

2. Determining type of process—this requires a decision on whether production should be continuous flow, mass production, large batch, job lot, or unique item.

3. Determining machines and work stations—this involves decisions about the kinds (general or special purpose) and number of machines, materials handling devices, and work stations.

These decisions in manufacturing organizations increasingly involve choices about automation. Although most often associated with continuous flow or mass production operations, automation has begun making inroads into large batch and job lot production in the form of computer-integrated manufacturing systems. In its most advanced state, known as a *flexible manufacturing system*, machine operations are controlled through a central computer which also provides for automated transfer of parts among the machines in the system.[7]

Layout Planning

More detailed than process planning, *layout planning* involves determining the precise configuration of the departments (and equipment within the departments) that constitute the transformation process. In-

---

ROBOTS

The use of robots in manufacturing—particularly in mass production operations—has increased rapidly in recent years, especially in Japan which employs more than half the world's robots. In a special *Business Week* advertising section, sponsored by Japanese industry, the following reasons for the Japanese adoption of robots are given:

1. Reduction of labor costs. "Take a company that purchases robots priced at $50,000 apiece. Each of these robots lasts six to seven years and replaces per shift one worker whose average annual wage-benefit package is about $21,000. When the robot operates two shifts daily, it pays for itself in just over a year. If there are three shifts, the payback is in less than a year."

2. Possibility for continuous operations. Although automation raises fixed costs and the firm's break-even point, robots can offset this increase by operating longer hours and providing a faster return on investment through higher productivity.

3. Greater efficiency in some operations than human workers. In painting, for instance, a robot uses 20 to 30 percent less paint than the human employee. "Robots do not require air conditioning, lighting or special protection. By taking humans out of hot, dirty or dangerous situations, a company can improve industrial safety without increasing expense."

4. Greater flexibility than other forms of automation. "Because they are easily reprogrammed, retooling and redesign are simpler. This makes it easier to do the short production runs that have become typical of many industries in the 1980s."

5. Insurance against a shortage of skilled labor. Japan expects its labor force to grow slowly in the 1980s, with most new entrants going into the service sector. The result will be a smaller, aging manufacturing work force, which will require robots for productivity improvements.

SOURCE: Based on Christopher S. Gray, "Japan: Corporate Strategies for the 80's," Special Advertising Section, *Business Week*, 19 July 1982, pp. 22, 26.

cluded in these plans are the specific locations of such peripheral areas as storage spaces, tool rooms, and rest rooms in factories, and customer service areas in such organizations as banks, offices, and supermarkets.

Although an infinite variety of layouts is possible, the following basic types of layouts are common:

1. The *product layout* arranges work centers in such a way as to assemble a product or serve a client through a standardized sequence of activities. This layout is used to produce a large volume of a particular product (an automobile assembly line, for instance) or to serve a large number of clients with similar needs (a cafeteria serving line, for example).

2. The *process layout* groups work centers together by similarity of function. The product being produced or the client being served is transported from one work center to another, depending upon the sequence of functions that is required. This layout is used when a number of different products are produced (a job lot production shop, for instance, has separate areas for lathes, drill presses, and so on) or when clients with different needs are served (an automobile repair shop has different areas for front-end alignments, tune-ups, and oil changes, for example).

3. The *fixed-position layout* brings the appropriate work centers to the location of a stationary product or client. This layout is used when the product or client cannot be moved (a farm, for example) or when it is not feasible to move the product or client (such as consulting on-site for a client).

The layout not only affects the organization's physical operations and financial requirements, but greatly influences the activities, interactions, and sentiments of the organization's employees.* Some of the technical and human consequences of the layouts described above are shown in Table 23–3.

Aggregate Planning

Once capacity requirements have been determined and the facility design completed, management must plan the firm's aggregate (total) production requirements (versus the requirements for a particular item). In its simplest form, aggregate planning involves consideration of the organization's beginning inventory, the forecasted demand for its products, and the desired target figure for ending inventory. From these figures, management can determine the amount of production that will be re-

---

*In planning for operations, management must consider the safety and health of its employees not only for the obvious ethical and moral reasons but also because such protection is required by law. The Occupational Safety and Health Act of 1970 (OSHA) requires that businesses establish and enforce strict health and safety standards. Failure to comply can result in fines and even jail sentences.

quired for some future period of time. Decisions can then be made concerning the number of workers to be employed for this period.

Since production requirements vary from one time period to another due to fluctuations in market demand, management must make choices regarding its work force policy. Some organizations may hire and lay off workers as production requirements change, while others maintain a steady work force size over time but vary the intensity with which it is used. During slack times, for instance, the length of the work week (or work day) might be reduced. During peak demand periods, employees might work overtime. Another common means of maintaining a constant work force size involves producing to inventory; that is, allowing stocks of finished goods to accumulate during slack demand periods and to be depleted during peak sales periods. Each of these alternatives has certain benefits and costs, both human and financial.

Scheduling

From the aggregate plan, the *master schedule* is derived to indicate which products will be produced, in what quantities, and by what dates. This schedule provides the following:[8]

1. A basis for estimating the workload of various work centers.
2. A yardstick by which to measure performance.
3. The basis for *detailed schedules*.

Detailed schedules, in turn, enable management to

1. Assign jobs to work centers.
2. Sequence operations.
3. Determine when each job is to start and finish at each work station, machine, or specialist.
4. Determine the need for special setups, tools, facilities, and equipment.
5. Forecast inventory.
6. Balance machines, work centers, and individuals' availability with jobs.

Such planning tools as Gantt Charts and PERT, discussed in Chapter 7, have obvious uses in scheduling.

Procurement

Procurement involves purchasing the materials and equipment required for planned organizational operations. After identifying the needs of operations managers, procurement personnel must evaluate alternative sources of supply to obtain items of the desired quality and quantity at

TABLE 23–3   Characteristics of layout designs

Aspect of the Conversion Process	Product-Oriented	Process-Oriented	Fixed-Position
Product characteristics	Layout geared to producing a standardized product, in large volume, at stable rates of output	Layout for diversified products requiring common fundamental operations, in varying volume, at varying rates of output	Low volume, each unit often unique
Product flow pattern	Straight line flow of product; same sequence of standard operations on each unit	Diversified flow pattern; each order (product) may require unique sequence of operations	Little or no product flow; equipment and human resources brought to site as needed
Human skills requirement	Tolerance for performing routine, repetitive tasks at imposed pace; highly specialized work content	Primarily skilled craftsmen; can perform without close supervision and with moderate degree of adaptability	High degree of task flexibility often required; specific work assignments and location vary
Supporting staff	Large administrative and indirect support staff for scheduling materials and people, work analysis and maintenance	Must possess skills for scheduling, materials handling, and production and inventory control	High degree of scheduling and co-ordinating skills required
Material handling	Material flows predictable, systematized and often automated	Type and volume of handling required are variable; duplication of	Type and volume of handling required are variable, often low; may

the lowest possible price. Purchasing also involves consideration of raw materials inventories so that the requirement for uninterrupted production is balanced with the need to minimize the size of the inventory. Purchasing personnel also serve as a primary source of information to operations managers concerning the availability of new materials and equipment from suppliers.

While American procurement managers often change suppliers for reasons involving cost, delivery, or quality, some Japanese companies enter into an "everlasting partnership" with their suppliers. Once a supplier has demonstrated its reliability by consistently delivering high-quality raw materials, the relationship between the supplier and the customer takes on a permanence rarely found in the United States.

One simply does not develop a relationship with an everlasting customer in the same way that one makes a one-time sale—the two require com-

TABLE 23–3 (Continued)

Aspect of the Conversion Process	Product-Oriented	Process-Oriented	Fixed-Position
Material handling (continued)		handling often occurs	require heavy-duty general purpose handling equipment
Inventory requirements	High turnover of raw material and work-in-process inventories	Low turnover of raw material and work-in-process inventories; high raw materials inventories	Variable inventories due to lengthy production cycle can result in inventory tie-ups for long periods
Space utilization	Efficient utilization of space, high rate of product output per unit of space	Relatively low rate of output per unit of facility space; large work-in-process requirements	For conversion within the facility, a low rate of space utilization per unit of output may occur
Capital requirements	High capital investment in equipment and processes that perform very specialized functions	Equipment and processes are general purpose and feature flexibility	General purpose equipment and processes that are mobile
Product cost components	Relatively high fixed costs; low unit direct labor and materials costs	Relatively low fixed costs; high unit costs for direct labor, materials (inventory) and materials handling	High labor and materials costs; relatively low fixed costs

SOURCE: Everett E. Adam, Jr., Ronald J. Ebert, *Production and Operations Management, Concepts, Models, and Behavior,* 2nd Edition, © 1982, p. 241. Reprinted by permission of Prentice-Hall, Inc., Englewood Cliffs, New Jersey.

pletely different expectations and approaches. Nor does one disappoint an everlasting customer by delivering defective products or by failing to meet delivery schedules. One does not disappoint a supplier-partner by not buying from him if his prices are somewhat out of line, although one certainly works with him to help him get prices back in line with those of competitors.[9]

CONTROLLING OPERATIONS

As we saw in the preceding chapter, control requires standards to which actual performance can be compared. Hence, the actual process of production is controlled through the master and detailed schedules. "Events presented in the schedules, such as 'start assembly of wheels' or 'end interview phase' or 'complete first lot of 500 fire extinguishers' are on the one hand objectives to guide action, and on the other hand standards against which progress is compared."[10] In addition to these time and quantity standards, management establishes standards for the quality of inputs and outputs and for the costs of various aspects of operations, such as direct labor and material, inventory, and maintenance of equipment. This section examines three areas that receive considerable management emphasis—the control of material requirements, inventory, and quality.

Controlling Material Requirements

As the previous section indicated, the number of products or services to be produced in a given period of time may be found on the master schedule. From this figure, the operations manager can derive the demand for the raw materials and component parts which are required to produce these outputs. Many organizations use computerized *Material Requirements Planning* (MRP) systems which determine material requirements and purchase schedules from such inputs as the master schedule, the bill of materials (which lists all of the materials and parts required to produce a single product or service), and current inventory levels of materials and parts. Although the MRP concept is useful for virtually any organization that requires materials or parts, its greatest contribution is in the manufacturing of complex products built from numerous components, such as diesel engines or radar equipment.[11]

Computerized systems are particularly useful because they react well to changing conditions. If significant increases or decreases in demand force modification of the master schedule, the MRP system can quickly refigure the organization's need for materials and parts. When these components number in the hundreds, the advantage of this control system becomes clear. Additionally, a good MRP system can help management reduce inventory and production lead time and make more realistic delivery commitments to customers.[12]

Controlling Inventory

In many organizations, inventory is the largest current asset. For this and other reasons, inventory control is essential for business success. From a cost standpoint, control of inventory quantity is necessary. If a substantial investment in inventory is required, the expense of maintaining it is considerable. These costs are of several types. The cost of capital invested in excessive or unnecessary inventory represents a waste. Interest costs on such capital may be avoided, or the money may be invested more profitably elsewhere by the use of effective inventory control. Other costs arise from increased warehouse space requirements, insurance, and taxes. In addition, inventory items may be subject to deterioration or obsolescence as well as to loss through price changes. Limitation of the inventory to the smallest practical size serves to minimize these losses.

JAPANESE INVENTORY CONTROL

Rather than subscribing to the economic order quantity concept, many Japanese manufacturers have patterned their inventory processes after Toyota's famous "just-in-time" system. Under this concept, inventory is almost nonexistent because the manufacturer requires suppliers of raw materials and parts to make multiple deliveries daily just as the components are needed in the production process. As one senior manager in a Japanese manufacturing plant put it:

> We feel that inventory is the root of all evil. You would be surprised how much you simplify problems and reduce costs when there are no inventories. For example, you don't need any inventory managers or sophisticated inventory control systems. Nor do you need expediters, because you can't expedite. And, finally, when something goes wrong, the system stops. Immediately the whole organization becomes aware of the problem and works quickly to resolve it. If you have buffer inventories, these potential problems stay hidden and may never get corrected.

The U.S. automobile industry is rapidly switching to the Japanese philosophy of inventory control. In only eight months under the new system, Pontiac managed to cut its inventories by 30 percent. Since General Motors' inventory was valued at $9 billion in 1982, the potential dollar savings are enormous.

Incidentally, the Japanese borrowed this "new" inventory system from a similar concept pioneered by Henry Ford in the 1920s.

SOURCE: Above quotation reprinted by permission of *Harvard Business Review*. Excerpt from "Why Japanese Factories Work" by Robert H. Hayes (July–August 1981). Copyright © 1981 by the President and Fellows of Harvard College; all rights reserved. Other background information based on "U.S. Auto Makers Reshape for World Competition," *Business Week*, 21 June 1982, pp. 83–84, 85, 88.

Effective inventory control also is essential for operating efficiency. If a production tie-up is caused by an out-of-stock part, the resulting costs may be staggering. In a retail store, customer dissatisfaction occurs if the shelf is bare when the customer wishes to buy. The objective of inventory control, then, is an adequate but not excessive inventory.

Effective control of regularly stocked inventory items requires an accurate determination of minimum and maximum inventory levels. In calculating the size of the minimum reserve stock, some judgment is necessary concerning the seriousness of stockouts. If stockouts are extremely dangerous—say a part whose shortage would shut down a production line—the minimum reserve stock must be higher than would otherwise be necessary. The pattern of withdrawals also has a bearing

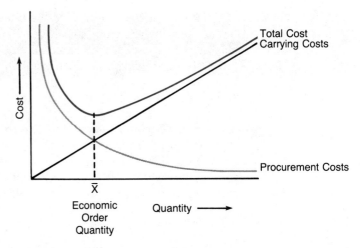

FIGURE 23–3 Inventory costs and economic order quantity
SOURCE: Adapted from Richard J. Hopeman, *Production and Operations Management: Planning, Analysis, Control,* 4th ed. (Columbus, Oh.: Charles E. Merrill Publishing Co., 1980), p. 368.

on the proper level. A relatively large stock is required in the case of items in which withdrawals occur irregularly and possibly in large quantities.

Given a specified minimum stock level, the maximum is determined by the amount procured at one time. Buying in large quantities increases both the maximum and average inventory size. To determine the most economical level, the manager must calculate an amount known as the *economic order quantity.* This is the purchase quantity that minimizes total costs by properly balancing costs associated with large orders (such as cost of money tied up in inventory and warehouse space) and costs associated with small orders (such as loss of quantity discounts, cost of stockouts, and overhead clerical cost in placing purchase orders).[13] In Figure 23–3, the optimal order quantity is the point where total cost is at a minimum.*

Controlling Quality

Purpose of Quality Control. Product quality is directly related to the basic objectives of the firm and rests, therefore, upon fundamental policy

---

*The economic order quantity may be determined mathematically by the following standard formula:

$$EOQ = \sqrt{\frac{2DC}{I}}$$

where D = expected annual product demand in units
C = procurement costs per order
I = inventory carrying cost in dollars per unit per year

For example, if the expected demand is 1,000 units, the cost of placing an order is $20, and the annual inventory carrying cost per unit is $.16, then

$$EOQ = \sqrt{\frac{2 \times 1000 \times \$20}{\$.16}} = 500 \text{ units.}$$

decisions of management. One manufacturer, for example, may elect to sell to a segment of the market desiring superior quality, while another may decide to sell to the mass market which accepts a lower-quality product. Such decisions entail evaluation of market potential at various levels as well as evaluation of production capacity to produce at these levels. Production cost is also pertinent. Higher quality typically entails higher production cost. Quality objectives emerge in this way from the general strategy and purposes of the enterprise.

The manufacturer's concept of quality may involve standards for a number of different characteristics such as physical dimensions, chemical composition, weight, color, strength, freedom from scratches, and so on. In the light of market and cost conditions, the manufacturer chooses a specific quality level, not necessarily the best. But, having chosen it, he or she attempts to meet that standard consistently.

Inspection. Although inspection is an integral part of quality control, it is not fully synonymous with control of quality. Inspection provides feedback to management by measuring the product to determine the extent to which it conforms to established standards. Control also includes those steps necessary to regulate and correct the manufacturing process to meet the stipulated standards.

Some type of inspection is required in the quality control process. This inspection may be limited to the finished product and occur at the end of the production process, or it may occur at different stages during the process. A key question, in fact, concerns the number of times the product should be inspected. The ideal is to minimize inspection costs without losing control of the product. Other questions relating to inspection concern the number of items to be inspected—100 percent or some fraction of the items—and the location of the inspection—floor versus central inspection.

Statistical Quality Control. Statistical quality control applies the theory of probability to the process of inspection and quality control. Even without statistical quality control, inspection is often conducted on the basis of systematic sampling. Rather than using 100 percent inspection, only a part of a lot is singled out for inspection. The assumption is that the quality of the entire lot will be indicated by the inspected items. Lacking statistical methodology, however, there is little knowledge of the degree of risk involved.

By the use of statistical quality control methods, management is able to make a choice as to the degree of risk that can be tolerated—that is, the proportion of below-standard items that can be accepted (such as 1 percent or 5 percent). The extent of risk can be specified by the statistician, and the risk (of accepting defective items) can be reduced with the expenditure of additional time and money. Statistical quality control tells the manager how likely it is that bad products will slip by with a given inspection plan. He or she can then weigh this problem against the increased cost required to reduce that risk.

THE LINK BETWEEN INVENTORY AND QUALITY CONTROL

Quality control is closely related to the control of inventory. As firms move in the direction of "just-in-time" inventories, what were acceptable quality levels of defective parts are no longer acceptable. L. Jerry Hudspeth, vice president for productivity and quality at Westinghouse Electric Corporation, links inventory and quality control in the following statement:

> If you can operate, like Toyota, with one or two hours' worth of inventory, you clearly have to have a smooth-operating division. . . . With minimal inventories, we can't accept a 1% AQL [acceptable quality level of 1 defective part per 100]. I'm not going to live with this anymore. There are new ground rules.

SOURCE: "Quality: The U.S. Drives to Catch Up," Special Report, *Business Week*, 1 November 1982, p. 67.

The same statistical principles can be applied to the production process itself. Machines and various processes can be checked periodically to ensure that they are operating within acceptable limits. If they are "out of control"—as shown on a statistical chart—corrective adjustments can be made immediately.

Figure 23–4 illustrates one type of statistical quality control chart—the mean chart. The vertical scale shows gradations for plotting the

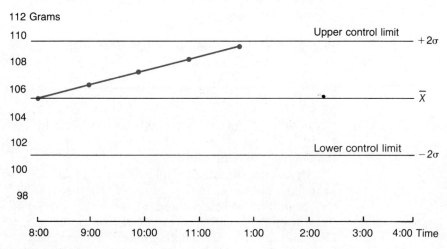

FIGURE 23–4 Sample mean chart

SOURCE: Richard J. Hopeman, *Production and Operations Management: Planning, Analysis, Control,* 4th ed. (Columbus, Oh.: Charles E. Merrill Publishing Co., 1980), p. 477.

arithmetic means of random items that are selected from the production process. In this situation, the items are packed by the case, with 16 items in each case. The mean weight of the cases should be 105.633 grams, with an allowable variation for deviations from the mean ranging from two standard deviations below (the lower control limit) to two standard deviations above (the upper control limit) the mean. The horizontal scale indicates hours of the day at which sample cases are randomly selected and weighed.

The samples taken at 8:00 through 1:00 indicate that the mean is shifting upward and the production process is out of control. If the trend line revealed only chance variations from the mean, the sample weights would fluctuate both above and below the mean. In this case, the trend is not due to chance but to some assignable cause such as tool slippage or tool wear, poor raw materials, inattention of the worker, or a gradual malfunctioning of the machine. A quality control manager would take corrective action before the 2:00 report.[14] The emphasis in this case is on correcting the manufacturing process to prevent the production of defective items rather than identifying the defective items after they have been produced.

SUMMARY

Operations management focuses on the organizational processes that transform inputs into outputs. An outgrowth of early scientific management and the later human relations movement, operations management integrates both technical and human considerations in its emphasis on improving operational efficiency. Although operations management has traditionally been associated with industrial manufacturing processes, its basic principles are today being applied to all types of organizations, including retail and service establishments. Even though specific activities will vary from one type of organization to another, the following general types of operations may be used by both manufacturing and non-manufacturing organizations: *continuous flow production, mass production, large batch production, job lot production,* and *unique item production.*

Management must perform a number of functions as it plans and organizes organizational operations. These include planning the productive *capacity* of the organization; selecting an appropriate geographical *location* for operations; determining the precise *process* that will be used to transform inputs into outputs; planning the *layout*—or precise configuration—of departments and equipment within those departments; forecasting the firm's *aggregate* (total) production requirements; *scheduling* which products will be produced, in what quantities, and by what dates; and *procuring* the materials and equipment required for organizational operations.

Once actual production begins, the process of controlling various aspects of operations becomes important. An increasing number of organizations are controlling their material requirements through computerized *Material Requirements Planning (MRP)* systems which can determine the organization's material needs for many different products under changing conditions. Much emphasis has recently been placed on minimizing *inventory*, with some manufacturing organizations adopting the just-in-time inventory control concept popularized in Japan. As inventory levels are lowered, the control of the *quality* of products and the processes used to manufacture them becomes increasingly important. Many organizations use statistical techniques to aid in this procedure.

DISCUSSION QUESTIONS

1. Briefly explain the *sociotechnical* view of operations management.
2. Are operations management concepts and principles transferable from manufacturing to nonmanufacturing organizations? Explain.
3. What types of organizations are more likely to emphasize *productivity* increases? Why?
4. Contrast *mass production* operations with *job lot production*.
5. Distinguish among *capacity planning*, *process planning*, and *aggregate planning*.
6. Is the *site* for a university important? Why or why not?
7. Is *scheduling* a planning or a control tool? Explain.
8. What are the two major competing types of costs involved in *inventory control*?
9. Can you think of any disadvantages associated with *just-in-time* inventory systems?
10. Explain the concept of *statistical quality control*.

NOTES

1. Eric Trist, "A Socio-Technical Critique of Scientific Management," in *Meaning and Control: Essays in Social Aspects of Science and Technology*, ed. D. O. Edge and J. N. Wolfe (London: Tavistock Publications, 1973), p. 103.
2. Charles G. Andrew and George A. Johnson, "The Crucial Importance of Production and Operations Management," *Academy of Management Review* 7 (January 1982): 146.

3. "Retailers Discover an Old Tool: Sales Training," *Business Week*, 22 December 1980, p. 51.

4. "Boosting Productivity at American Express," *Business Week*, 5 October 1981, p. 62.

5. This is a traditional classification of types of operations or technological processes based upon the work of Joan Woodward, *Industrial Organization: Theory and Practice* (London: Oxford University Press, 1965), Chapters 3 and 4.

6. Stephen E. Barndt and Davis W. Carvey, *Essentials of Operations Management* (Englewood Cliffs, N.J.: Prentice-Hall, 1982), p. 43.

7. See Melvin Blumberg and Antone Alber, "The Human Element: Its Impact on the Productivity of Advanced Batch Manufacturing Systems," *Journal of Manufacturing Systems* 1 (August 1982): 43–52; and Donald Gerwin, "Do's and Don't's of Computerized Manufacturing," *Harvard Business Review* 60 (March–April 1982): 107–16.

8. Barndt and Carvey, *Essentials of Operations Management*, pp. 64–67.

9. Reprinted by permission of *Harvard Business Review*. Excerpt from "Why Japanese Factories Work" by Robert H. Hayes (July–August 1981). Copyright © 1981 by the President and Fellows of Harvard College; all rights reserved.

10. Barndt and Carvey, *Essentials of Operations Management*, p. 101.

11. Ibid., p. 78.

12. Everett E. Adam, Jr., and Ronald J. Ebert, *Production and Operations Management: Concepts, Models, and Behavior*, 2d ed. (Englewood Cliffs, N.J.: Prentice-Hall, 1982), p. 522.

13. For a well-reasoned criticism of the economic order quantity concept, see John E. Bishop, "Integrating Critical Elements of Production Planning," *Harvard Business Review* 57 (September–October 1979): 154–60.

14. Example based on Richard J. Hopeman, *Production and Operations Management: Planning, Analysis, Control*, 4th ed. (Columbus, Oh.: Charles E. Merrill Publishing Co., 1980), pp. 476–77.

SUPPLEMENTARY READING

Adam, Everett E., Jr., and **Ebert, Ronald J.** *Production and Operations Management: Concepts, Models, and Behavior*, 2d ed. Englewood Cliffs, N.J.: Prentice-Hall, 1982.

Andrew, Charles G., and **Johnson, George A.** "The Crucial Importance of Production and Operations Management," *Academy of Management Review* 7 (January 1982): 143–47.

Barndt, Stephen E., and **Carvey, Davis W.** *Essentials of Operations Management.* Englewood Cliffs, N.J.: Prentice-Hall, 1982.

Benson, P. George; Hill, Arthur V.; and **Hoffmann, Thomas R.** "Manufacturing

Systems of the Future—A Delphi Study," *Production and Inventory Management* 23 (Third Quarter 1982): 87–105.

Blumberg, Melvin, and **Alber, Antone.** "The Human Element: Its Impact on the Productivity of Advanced Batch Manufacturing Systems." *Journal of Manufacturing Systems* 1 (August 1982): 43–52.

Davis, Louis E. "Optimizing Organization-Plant Design: A Complementary Structure for Technical and Social Systems." *Organizational Dynamics* 8 (Autumn 1979): 3–15.

Gerwin, Donald. "Do's and Don't's of Computerized Manufacturing." *Harvard Business Review* 60 (March–April 1982): 107–16.

Hancock, Walton M. "Quality, Productivity, and Workplace Design: An Engineering Perspective." *Journal of Contemporary Business* 11 (Second Quarter 1982): 107–14.

Hayes, Robert H. "Why Japanese Factories Work." *Harvard Business Review* 59 (July–August 1981): 57–66.

Judson, Arnold S. "The Awkward Truth about Productivity." *Harvard Business Review* 60 (September–October 1982): 93–97.

Leonard, Frank S., and **Sasser, W. Earl.** "The Incline of Quality." *Harvard Business Review* 60 (September–October 1982): 163–71.

Limprecht, Joseph A., and **Hayes, Robert H.** "Germany's World-Class Manufacturers." *Harvard Business Review* 60 (November–December 1982): 137–45.

Miller, Jeffrey G. "Fit Production Systems to the Task." *Harvard Business Review* 59 (January–February 1981): 145–54.

Miller, Stanley S. "Make Your Plant Manager's Job Manageable." *Harvard Business Review* 61 (January–February 1983): 69–74.

Nellemann, David O., and **Smith, Leighton F.** " 'Just-In-Time' Vs. Just-In-Case Production/Inventory Systems Concepts Borrowed Back from Japan." *Production and Inventory Management* 23 (Second Quarter 1982): 12–20.

Schonberger, Richard J. "The Transfer of Japanese Manufacturing Management Approaches to U.S. Industry." *Academy of Management Review* 7 (July 1982): 479–87.

Trist, Eric. "A Socio-Technical Critique of Scientific Management." In *Meaning and Control: Essays in Social Aspects of Science and Technology,* edited by D. O. Edge and J. N. Wolfe. London: Tavistock Publications, 1973, pp. 95–116.

Wheelwright, Steven C. "Japan—Where Operations Really Are Strategic." *Harvard Business Review* 59 (July–August 1981): 67–74.

24

SOCIAL RESPONSIBILITY AND ETHICAL BEHAVIOR

This chapter will enable you to

- *Provide a rationale for the social responsibilities of organizations and point out the limitations of business corporations in discharging these responsibilities*
- *Recognize the role of the social audit in evaluating social performance.*
- *Identify a variety of ethical problems in contemporary organizational life and explain the relationship of the managerial system to ethical performance.*
- *Point out the basis of ethical decisions.*
- *Explain the responsibility of the board of directors for social and moral leadership in the organization and show how the board's membership and committee structure affect its leadership.*

Managers now recognize a responsibility to society that extends beyond narrowly defined service objectives and strategies. The impact of business and other organizations on the physical environment, employees, local community, and other parts of society has led to public expectations of "responsible" performance. In this chapter, therefore, we shall examine the once peripheral but now vitally important areas of social responsibility and ethical behavior.

SOCIAL RESPONSIBILITY

Open Systems and Social Responsibility

All organizations, as explained in Chapters 2 and 3, are open systems which interact with their environments. Managers must be concerned, therefore, with public expectations and requirements affecting the functioning of their organizations.

Public expectations of responsible performance apply, moreover, to all types of organizations. Government agencies, labor unions, hospitals, universities, and business corporations are all institutions whose operation affects the public interest. Our society is increasingly demanding that these institutions take responsibility beyond their own specific mission, particularly in areas closely related to their primary fields of operation.

Large business corporations in particular are among the most powerful social institutions of our time. Their social performance has become, therefore, a matter of growing public concern, and much of the social responsibility debate has focused on the relationship of business to society.

The Changing Social Contract

Justification for a sense of social responsibility is grounded in the freedom accorded by society to business and other organizations. We may visualize the existence of a _social contract_. A business corporation, like other legitimate organizations, is given freedom to exist and to work toward some legitimate objective. The payment for that freedom is the firm's contribution to society. Terms of the contract, moreover, are not permanently fixed, but change over time as business firms are expected to assume increasingly broader responsibilities to society.

At one time, business responsibilities were defined narrowly as consisting of those pictured in the center circle of Figure 24–1. These responsibilities for providing jobs, goods, and services are still primary responsibilities, but many, if not most, observers now see business obligations extending to other issues related to business operations—the type listed in the intermediate circle. The outside circle contains social needs of a more general character—aid to education, urban development, and so on. Public opinion is mixed as to business responsibilities in these areas. There is no question, however, but that the social contract has been expanding to include more and more obligations outside the center circle.

Arguments Supporting Socially Responsible Management

Managers must respond to the changing demands of consumers, employees, and the general public. Such demands are forced upon them in many ways. The most obvious is public regulation that prescribes standards of behavior in many areas—environmental protection, equal opportunity employment, honesty in advertising, political contributions, product warranties, employee safety, and so on. Little in the way of a corporate "conscience" is involved in a minimal response to legal requirements.

A corporation's profit motive sometimes justifies concern for social obligations.[1] Honoring product warranties, for example, may build customer loyalty. The following statement shows the profitability of a chemical company's efforts to control pollution:

> In Dow's view, pollution is a wasted resource—valuable material dumped into the air and water or fed into costly treatment plants. The company is out to eliminate pollution at the source, by changing production processes and by recycling waste streams for further processing. So far, Dow has re-

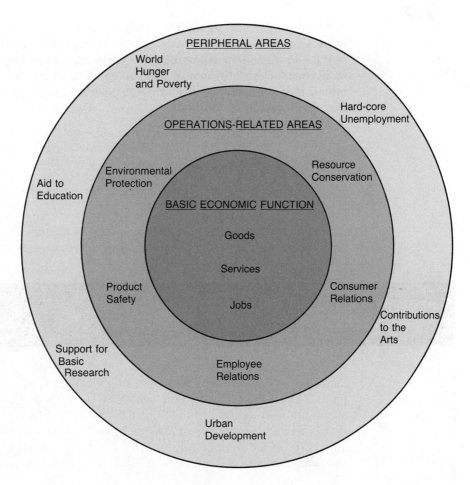

FIGURE 24–1 Areas of corporate social responsibility

covered enough valuable chemicals and boosted its process efficiencies so much that its abatement program is more than paying its own way.[2]

As another example, American Express devised a way in which to use charitable contributions as a marketing tool.[3] In cities where this program was used, American Express contributed small amounts to local arts programs each time its charge cards or travel services were used in those cities. They advertised the program in those cities and viewed it as a successful commercial venture.

There is also a price in ignoring social responsibilities. The threat of government control is always in the background. In a broader sense, the future of business is entwined with the future of society. Decay in society does not lead to health in business. In recognizing social responsibilities, then, management is not disregarding the best interests of business owners. The assumption of at least minimal social responsibilities represents an act of "enlightened self-interest" by corporate management.

It has also been argued that social responsibility should be accepted by business organizations as a matter of conscience. This view represents a change in perspective from traditional thinking which regards conscience as an attribute of the person. The actions of specific corporations are thought to reflect a kind of moral judgment comparable to that displayed by individuals.

> Hence, corporations that monitor their employment practices and the effects of their production processes and products on the environment and human health show the same kind of rationality and respect that morally responsible individuals do. Thus, attributing actions, strategies, decisions, and moral responsibilities to corporations as entities distinguishable from those who hold offices in them poses no problem.[4]

According to this view, corporations should consider obligations which extend beyond the making of profits and observance of the law.

PINTOS AND AUTO SAFETY

Rising public expectations of socially responsible performance is illustrated by customer insistence on safe products. Ford Motor Company became the target of more than fifty lawsuits during the 1970s as people were injured in fiery crashes of Pintos. Plaintiffs charged that Ford had installed faulty gas tanks in Pintos made between 1971 and 1976. Juries were openly sympathetic to their claims and awarded damages as high as $6 million in one case. One juror was quoted as saying:

> "The jury wanted a verdict that was high enough to hit them [Ford] hard and try to force them to make a safer car."

The many suits and the multimillion dollar awards are representative of the "new climate" in which business is expected to assume full responsibility for its actions.

Arguments against Social Responsibility

The concept of social responsibility is not without its critics. The most notable opponent of extensive business involvement in social endeavors is Milton Friedman who argues that the business system functions best when business firms stick to their primary mission—producing goods and services.[5] According to this view, corporations are obligated to operate in accordance with the law. However, they are not obligated to go beyond what the law requires.

According to the critics, business has no special expertise in solving social problems. It is improper, therefore, for corporate executives to spend the money of stockholders for public purposes. Stockholders should be permitted to spend their own money as they see fit. Furthermore, it is not the place of business to establish social priorities—to decide, for example, whether a new hospital or little league ball park is more important.

In reflecting upon these arguments, it is well to remember that business corporations enjoy the benefits of our social institutions. Is it unreasonable, therefore, that they should be expected to contribute to the general welfare? They may, for example, employ the graduates of educational institutions whose revenues must come from contributions as well as from tuition. Should they not contribute to the support of those universities? They also find it desirable to locate their plants and offices in communities offering cultural attractions and a clean environment. Does this impose obligations on them? The controversy reflects differing perceptions of the role of business, but an extremely narrow view of business responsibility is becoming increasingly less tenable.

Social Responsibility and Profits

In some instances, exemplary social performance results in profits. The experience of Dow Chemical Company cited above is a case in point. In other cases, good corporate citizenship may be unrelated to profits. Providing equal opportunity in employment, for example, might have little observable effect on profits. Nevertheless, many programs of social responsibility are costly, and it is conflict of this type that we examine in this section.

What, then, is the controlling objective? Must profit be regarded as the basic or primary goal and all conflict resolved in favor of the profit objective? "The governing rule in industry," according to one critic of the social responsibility doctrine, "should be that *something is good only if it pays*."[6] This seems to have a natural appeal, at least in theory, to managers who are accustomed to emphasizing the profit objective.

A realistic view of social responsibility must certainly recognize the economic constraints which limit managerial discretion. Corporate survival is a prerequisite for corporate responsibility, and corporate survival necessitates corporate profits.[7] Unless a firm attains a reasonable profit level, there is absolutely no way it can act as a good citizen by investing large amounts in programs for the public good. Profits are thus a necessary foundation for social expenditures. Even healthy corporations, moreover, operate in a competitive environment. As a result, they cannot disregard economic realities and function as philanthropic institutions. If one firm in an industry assumes heavy social costs that are not assumed by its competitors, it may bankrupt itself. These economic forces impose limits on the financial commitments which are possible.

Nevertheless, many corporations are financially healthy, and their managers are free, within limits, to support social action programs. Some programs may be costly in terms of short-run profits but logical in terms of long-run survival. Edward G. Harness, chairman of Procter and Gamble, expressed it this way:

> "Company management must consistently demonstrate a superior talent for keeping profit and growth objectives as first priorities. However, it must also have enough breadth to recognize that enlightened self-interest requires the company to fill any reasonable expectation placed upon it by the community and the various concerned publics."[8]

In summary, business firms must be profitable in order to be socially responsible. Even profitable firms, moreover, must take into account the financial costs of such programs, the extent of their resources, and the actions of competitors as they formulate their social objectives. These factors set limits on the social commitments which are possible. Within these limits, corporate managers may elect to act in a socially responsible manner. And, indeed, their long-run profitability and survival may require some attention to the broader social issues.

Corporate Responsiveness to Social Issues

How aggressive should corporations be in fulfilling their social responsibilities? Within the limits of their financial resources, they may choose to do little or much. Figure 24–2 shows a number of responsiveness strategies, ranging from "fight all the way" to "lead the industry."

When the Firestone 500 steel-belted radials were found (according to federal authorities) to be prone to blowouts, Firestone reacted defensively by contending there was nothing defective in the tire design and by resisting investigation of the tire. Procter and Gamble, on the other hand, showed a much more proactive response regarding Rely tampons. When these tampons were linked to the disease known as toxic shock syndrome, Procter and Gamble moved in a very short time to stop production and take the product off the shelves of stores where it was being sold.[9]

Assuming a willingness to accept some degree of social responsibility, where should a corporation begin? One corporation obviously cannot solve all of the world's social problems, and corporate managers must choose where to focus their efforts. Most firms elect to relate their

FIGURE 24–2   Levels of social responsiveness

SOURCE: These categories of responsiveness were suggested by Terry W. McAdam, "How to Put Corporate Responsibility into Practice," *Business and Society Review*, No. 6 (Summer 1973): 14.

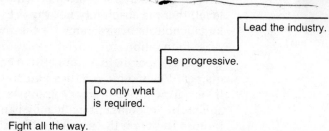

social involvement to areas related to their endeavor and expertise. An automobile manufacturer, for example, may devote special effort to automobile safety.

Such a posture is consistent with a conceptual model developed by Lee E. Preston and James E. Post.[10] They argue that a corporation's social responsibility encompasses both the "primary" and "secondary" involvement of the firm with its environment. An automobile manufacturer's involvement would include not only the primary areas of production and marketing, but also such secondary areas as environmental pollution, training opportunities for disadvantaged workers, product safety, and the impact of facilities on the physical environment. The Preston-Post model sets boundaries by suggesting that responsibilities extend only to *related issues.*

> To repeat, managerial responsibility, in our view, extends as far as the limits of secondary involvement, *but no further.* It is not the case, as some "social responsibility" enthusiasts apparently hold, that the private firm is charged with improving social conditions or resolving social problems regardless of their character or cause.[11]

The automobile manufacturer, for example, would find air pollution within, but water pollution without, its area of secondary involvement.

To obtain guidance in decision making within its area of primary and secondary involvement, managers should, according to Preston and Post, attune their actions to prevailing public policy. This means that they would attempt to discern public expectations not only from the letter of the law but also from the "spirit of the law"—the social traditions and values which underlie the law. The guidelines thus are broader than the statutes themselves but narrower than purely personal standards of corporate managers.

Assessment of Social Performance

As a result of the growing emphasis on social responsibility, some corporations now attempt to evaluate the quality of their social performance. Such an assessment procedure, often described as a *social audit,* identifies corporate activities believed to have a positive social impact.[12] Some social audits merely describe such corporate activities, while others attempt to assign a dollar value to them. Most social contributions are difficult to quantify, however, and even the most rigorous social audits lack the precision of financial audits.

Even though they lack the rigor of financial audits, social audits can serve as information systems for managers wishing to monitor social performance. As such, they can identify the important social issues facing a specific organization, develop performance measures, and evaluate corporate performance in terms of some standard. A corporation, for example, might compare its contributions to education with those of similar organizations.

ETHICS IN MANAGEMENT

Ethics and Organizational Activity

Organizational activity, as a part of life, poses ethical problems for management. Personal life and organizational life cannot be neatly compartmentalized with respect to moral judgments. The manager's standards of right and wrong must apply to both areas.

In the wake of the Watergate scandal, the ethical standards and behavior in many areas of society were questioned. Business organizations and business managers did not escape such observation and judgment. Unethical behavior of many business leaders has been exposed and widely reported in the news media. The significance of these flaws in contemporary business behavior is emphasized in these comments of Max Lerner:

> The predators used to be the swaggering piratical captains of industry; they have now become the managerial heads of impersonal corporations, conglomerates, multinationals. Doubtless, what they do is not so vicious as what the faceless bureaucrats of closed societies do. But the question still lingers, What shall it profit a civilization if it builds its industrial empires but loses its sense of moral direction?[13]

The Pervasive Problem of Business Ethics

Ethical problems exist in all types of organizations—educational, governmental, religious, business, and so on. In recent years, public attention has focused particularly on the ethical performance of business firms.

Problems of ethical behavior are widespread at all levels of our business institutions. The spotlight shifts over time from one sensitive area to another—from conflicts of interest to industrial espionage to tampering with the system of government regulation. From time to time, such issues erupt into national and even international scandals. In the aftermath of Watergate, executives of major corporations admitted illegal contributions of millions of corporate dollars to political campaigns. In July of 1973, for example, American Airlines publicly admitted that $55,000 of the $75,000 in cash that its officials contributed to the Committee to Re-elect the President was actually corporate money. American's chairman was quoted as saying that such *sub rosa* corporate financing of contributions supposedly originating from their employees is so common that it "creates a significant national problem."[14] Others that acknowledged illegal contributions included Ashland Oil, Gulf Oil, Phillips Petroleum, Braniff Airways, Goodyear Tire and Rubber Company, and Minnesota Mining and Manufacturing Company.

In 1975, a number of major corporations disclosed payoffs running into millions of dollars to foreign officials or political parties. United Brands allegedly paid $1.25 million to a high official in Honduras to get its taxes reduced. Gulf Oil, Northrop, and Exxon also made disclosures of overseas payoffs. The identity of these companies makes it clear that ethical issues plague even blue-chip corporations. In a survey of *Harvard Business Review* readers, two-thirds of the responding executives indicated there were industry practices which they considered unethical.[15]

Review of the tragedies in business morality should not be allowed to obscure the ethical behavior which does exist. Without doubt, much business behavior is commendable and representative of high ethical standards. The purpose of these examples is to develop an awareness of the serious and pervasive nature of ethical issues. There is obviously great opportunity for improvement in ethical performance generally.

Thorny Nature of Ethical Questions

People have a tendency to oversimplify the nature of ethical problems in business organizations. Frequently, we see decisions as involving simple choices between right and wrong, black and white. As a matter of fact, decisions with ethical overtones are often considerably more complex. The "right" decision from an ethical standpoint may indeed be hazy. Often there are conflicts in values, and the manager perceives different obligations which seem to conflict in their implications.

THE EQUITY FUNDING SCANDAL

One of the country's major business scandals involved a company known as the Equity Funding Corporation. The scandal surfaced in 1973, and the corporation filed for bankruptcy in that year. The corporation had grown rapidly since 1960 when Stanley Goldblum and three associates took control of a tiny company and began developing their mutual fund and insurance program. The spectacular growth of the company made it a stock market favorite, and its price soared from $6 a share in 1964 to $80 a share in 1969.

Equity Funding was accused of cheating thousands of small investors out of their savings as well as bilking dozens of insurance companies. At the time it filed for bankruptcy, Equity Funding owned four life insurance companies, three mutual funds, a savings and loan association, and a bank in the Bahamas. Among other things, the firm was charged with the creation of more than 50,000 policyholders out of thin air!

Multinational business firms, for example, must operate in countries whose cultures apparently condone the acceptance of personal and political payoffs as a part of commercial transactions. In some less-developed countries, payoffs are virtually a way of life. Even phone operators in Zaire must be paid privately to secure overseas lines, and hotel reservations in Nigeria must be "reconfirmed" to avoid losing one's lodging.[16] Foreign competitors, moreover, are seldom bound by bribery laws as strict as those which apply to U.S. firms. In the interest of protecting corporate interests, therefore, multinational managers face strong pressure to engage in questionable deals to obtain contracts of vital importance to their corporations and to the employees and stockholders of those corporations.

It has also been argued that investment decisions should consider issues of social responsibility. If a corporation acts in an antisocial manner, stockholders holding such stock should presumably bring pressure on its management. However, it is difficult to evaluate issues of this type. Should Xerox be commended for its job training of disadvantaged workers and aid to ghetto business or condemned for doing business in South Africa?[17] Another type of dilemma confronts the manager who must decide whether to lay off a less efficient employee who has given many years of service or a newer employee with greater skill and vigor.

In addition, it is difficult for managers to free themselves from bias and prejudice and to look at issues objectively. In spite of good intentions, the individual becomes involved in the situation and becomes identified with certain positions or points of view. It becomes difficult to step back and to take a detached point of view in examining the issue from an ethical standpoint.

The Managerial System and Ethical Behavior

Let us turn now to the relationship of the managerial system to the organization's ethical performance. We hold that a mangerial system is not neutral. A bad system can corrupt good people, and a good system can strengthen the moral intent of organizational members. Managers must supplement personal piety with appropriate organizational measures, therefore, in order to extend their ethical influence beyond their immediate personal associations.[18]

Organizational Priorities and Ethical Performance. Managers are concerned with many facets of organizational behavior—ethical matters and also technical and economic matters. Almost any organization, for example, is concerned with productivity and the extent to which it meets specific service goals. A basic question in each organization, therefore, is the extent to which its management emphasizes ethical behavior in comparison with these other factors. In many situations, the relative importance of ethical and technical considerations is ambiguous. It is difficult to tell how management values one vis-à-vis the other.

We might guess that the establishment of values and conveyance of feelings about priorities are a bit more subtle than making a simple announcement. If top management says, "Let's be ethical about this," subordinates may reason that management is simply making a public relations gesture. The manager's practice, behavior, and decisions undoubtedly provide more reliable information about organizational priorities.

In spite of difficulties in clarifying priorities, managers regularly attempt to do so. Speaking of a Koppers Company "ethics" letter to its managers, Board Chairman Fletcher L. Byrom commented as follows:

> The thing we as a corporation wanted to do was to remove what might be considered by some to be an ambiguity between economic performance and ethical conduct. . . . And we wanted to make it clear that we did not expect anybody to do something that was inconsistent with their ethical standards under the guise that it was for the benefit of the Company.[19]

In summary, a system characterized by unclear priorities or an extreme emphasis on purely technical and economic factors creates pressure for cutting corners.

Organizational Goals and Organizational Ethics. The manager must also be concerned with the dilution of ethical standards by emphasizing organizational goals. Most of us recommend goal setting and respect those organizations and people who are goal-directed. We view the establishment of goals as a step toward purposeful and productive activity.

Goal setting which has these desirable effects may simultaneously have dysfunctional effects on ethical standards, however.[20] Reflect for a moment on the context of goal setting and the reasonableness of goals. Suppose a goal is attainable only with extreme effort and a little luck. The practice of setting very difficult goals and then applying pressure to reach these goals creates conditions favorable to producing unethical behavior. Is it always clear to personnel that they are expected to attain goals only within the confines of ethical performance? Or, is the emphasis upon goals so intense that attention is directed to the goals and not to means of achieving those goals?

In a survey of ethical standards in American business, business managers were asked to respond to the following statement.[21]

> "Managers today feel under pressure to compromise personal standards to achieve company goals."

The managers responded as follows:

Disagree	24.6%
Somewhat disagree	11.0%
Somewhat agree	43.2%
Agree	21.2%

A remarkable 64 percent understood the pressures of organizational goals on personal standards—an interesting commentary on the ethical hazards of goals. Managers must establish goals with great care. If goals appear difficult to attain, managers must realize the strains that are created and make the ethical constraints clear. Otherwise, the ends may come to justify the means.

Control Systems and Ethical Performance. A control system is presumably conducive to ethical performance, and the quest for honesty is one reason for the development of control systems. Indeed, the basic concept of internal control is a system of checks and balances to eliminate intentional as well as unintentional errors. When Congress enacted the Foreign Corrupt Practices Act in 1977, it included in the act not only specific prohibitions against bribery and other corrupt practices but also requirements for accurate record keeping and internal control. Good internal control is no guarantee against bribery and corrupt practices, but it certainly makes such practices more difficult.

Although control systems may thus help to stimulate ethical performance, they also may undermine it. In other words, a control procedure may contain "bugs" that reduce its effectiveness. One problem is associated with the use of numbers. To find out how we are doing, we count something. This process of counting or numbering affects the very process that is being investigated. What we count becomes important. Numbers that go to managers are important numbers.

The process of quantification, therefore, directs attention to factors that can be easily measured. And what are these? We can count and measure most easily the technical and economic factors. How difficult it is, in contrast, to measure and tabulate the ethical levels of organizational performance. Measured standards and measured values may drive out those values and considerations that are not measureable. Careful design of control systems, therefore, is essential in creating a favorable environment for ethical behavior.

The Chain of Command and Ethical Performance. Another feature of the management system that may affect ethical performance is the chain of command itself. A time-honored principle of management holds that you "go through channels." One who understands organizational etiquette does not "go over the head" of the boss.

Excellent logic supports this principle. It is intended to establish lines of authority and responsibility and thereby to assure a productive organization. The relationship of this chain to ethical standards lies in the fact that total reliance on the chain of command cuts off any individual's "escape route." Suppose one is pressured by an unethical superior: what are that person's alternatives? The next higher level typically backs the immediate supervisor. The organization has constructed a system by which authority runs downward. If that authority becomes misused at some point, there is little provision for correction built into the system.

The obvious question is whether subordinates are ever badgered by their immediate superiors to engage in behavior that they regard as unethical. The following statement is based on a study of testimony before a congressional committee investigating price-fixing practices in the electrical equipment industry.

> Time and again, throughout the testimony, deeply ingrained respect for the line-of-command concept is evident. When asked directly why he did not report illegal activities to higher management, one witness simply replied: "I had no power to go higher. I do not report to anyone else except my superior."[22]

Another finding from the survey of managerial opinions touched on the inclination of junior managers to accept the standards of those higher in the chain of command. Executives were asked to respond to the following statement:

> "The junior members of Nixon's reelection committee who confessed that they went along with their bosses to show their loyalty is just what young managers would have done in business."[23]

The response of the executives was as follows:

Disagree	24.6%
Somewhat disagree	16.1%
Somewhat agree	35.6%
Agree	23.7%

Almost 60 percent acknowledged the tendency of those in the chain of command to "go along" with the boss.

The ethical dangers in rigid adherence to the chain of command provide a dilemma for managers. They must provide some type of appeal system without destroying the chain of command itself.

Codes of Ethics and Ethical Performance. Business leaders may attempt to extend their ethical standards throughout an organization by using formal ethical codes. A survey of large U.S. corporations (673 responses from 2,000 questionnaires) revealed that 77 percent of the corporate respondents had a code of conduct.[24] (The largest corporations were most likely to use codes—97 percent of those in the largest size category indicating their use of a code.) The adoption of codes has been strongly encouraged by the provisions of the Foreign Corrupt Practices Act which requires effective systems of internal control.

Even though most corporations now use codes, there is disagreement regarding their effectiveness. Some see codes as mere scraps of paper, unrelated to the real behavior which would fulfill or deny such codes. Some argue that statements of this kind may be dysfunctional in emphasizing the negative.[25] Clearly, little would be gained from merely preparing a statement of business ethics that is not taken seriously.

On the other hand, a code can provide an explicit definition of ethical standards. There is some advantage in being specific, rather than issuing statements so vague that they are virtually meaningless. Assuming clarity in ethical standards, the next question concerns the seriousness with which a code is taken and communicated. Some organizations, for example, require a signed statement from management employees that they understand and will adhere to the company's code and make an annual compliance review, the results of which go to the audit committee of the board of directors.

Enforcement of any code is essential if it is to be taken seriously. Fred T. Allen, chairman and chief executive officer of Pitney Bowes, has urged a rigorous application of ethical codes:

> How should the corporation respond to the individual who is guilty of violating its ethical code? From the pinnacle of the corporate pyramid to its base, immediate punitive action, commensurate with the degree of transgression, is the only choice. The corporation thus says in the clearest terms that it will not tolerate corporate wrongdoing of any kind by anyone.[26]

The majority of respondents to the 1976 *Harvard Business Review* survey expected that an ethical code would help executives to raise the ethical level of their industry, define the limits of acceptable conduct, and refuse unethical requests.[27] Although some members of an organization may look for every possible way to be unethical, others want to do the right thing. An ethical statement can strengthen their "backbone" when they find themselves in difficult situations. It is helpful for the individual who desires to observe good ethical standards to be able to say in times of stress, "I'm sorry but our policies do not permit such behavior." Some limited research evidence supports the view that a clear set of rules makes a difference in employee conduct.[28] To the extent that ethical codes can be used effectively, they can carry ethical standards to organizational levels and segments beyond the leaders' immediate personal control (Figure 24–3).

Corporate codes show considerable diversity in content. Table 24–1 shows topics which appeared in many of the codes sampled in the survey cited above.[29]

Foundations for Business Ethics

Ethical values in the business world reflect the ideals and standards of the society of which it is a part. Each culture has a distinctive system of moral values. It is unlikely that the general level of ethical standards in business conduct will differ in any substantial way from the ethical standards observed in nonbusiness areas of society. In considering business ethics, therefore, we are dealing with only one part of the broader issue of ethical standards in society.

The ethical concepts of any country are associated with its religious beliefs. In the United States, the strongest religious tradition is the Judeo-Christian heritage. Other religious viewpoints also have ethical content, of course, but the Judeo-Christian tradition has played the dominant role in shaping this country's ethical standards.

1. THE INCOMPLETE DISCLOSURE. Provide more information rather than less, even if it goes beyond what the Securities & Exchange Commission and other agencies require. Put yourself in the investor's place and ask, "What do I want to know?" The SEC keeps requiring fuller disclosure, and failure to disclose can bring a suit.
2. THE CORRUPT BOSS. Many middle managers have gotten into serious trouble— and a few have wound up in jail—by caving in to a boss who cared more about ends than means. Speak up as soon as you are faced with an ethical problem; you may set things straight. "If you can't, get out," says a Xerox director.
3. THE CORRUPT SUBORDINATE. As a senior man, don't worry about rocking the boat, just get rid of him. A tolerant, "nice guy" attitude can put both of you in trouble. And his misdeeds can infect his coworkers.
4. THE INADVERTENT REMARK. Think twice about what you tell anyone about your business—at lunch, in the locker room, over the bridge table. A chance remark might get you nailed for leaking company secrets. And the law about passing "inside information" is vague. You could wind up in a courtroom.
5. THE 'PURIFIED' IDEA. You can usually find a lawyer or a CPA who will endorse a questionable idea or plan—especially if you phrase it just the right way. Just remember, the plan is still questionable and it can get you in trouble.
6. THE PASSIVE DIRECTOR. Whether you are an inside or an outside director, don't just sit back silent and rubber-stamp management. You can be sued, and the courts take a hard line nowadays on director liability. "Speak up or drop out," says one man who has served on 11 boards.
7. THE EXPENSE-ACCOUNT VACATION. Go easy on tax deductions for combination business-pleasure trips. Deduct for your wife only if she is actually involved in your business. . . .
8. THE STOCK OPTION TRAP. Beware of "fast" option transactions—buying and selling your company's stock within the six-month trading rule period for insiders. More businessmen are getting tripped up on this one.

FIGURE 24–3 Guidelines for eight gray areas

TABLE 24–1 Typical topics included in corporate ethics codes

Corporate Code Topics	Percentage of Codes in Which Subject Is Addressed
Acceptance of gifts	77%
Conflict of interest (general)	73%
Compliance with applicable laws	67%
Political contributions	67%
Payments to government officials/political parties	63%
Inside information	63%
Giving gifts, favors, entertainment	57%
Undisclosed or unrecorded funds or assets	53%
False entries in books and records	50%
Confidential information	40%

To illustrate more specifically the connection between religious values and business practices, consider Harold L. Johnson's explanation of the linkages between historic Christian doctrines and business ethics.[30] Johnson holds, for example, that the concept of God as a personal transcendent Being places everything human under the rule of God and warns against the idolatry of putting the business firm or career at the center of life. The doctrine of creation, which holds that material things are gifts of God, furnishes a part of the religious foundation for the philosophy of the social responsibility. The Christian view of the nature of man reveals his weaknesses, serving as a warning to ambitious executives and against an inflated view of their own abilities. It warns managers at all levels that self-interest and pride may be woven into decisions believed to be objective. It also cautions against excessive optimism that human relations and social responsibility can bring the heavenly city here on earth by teaching that all, including ourselves, have the taint of sin.

Although there is no monolithic code of ethics in society, some of the general cultural values condition the viewpoint of most managers. In view of the diversity in this area of our culture, however, there is still a principle of individual responsibility and choice. A executive may follow ethical standards that are regarded as either more or less acceptable in terms of generally prevailing beliefs. Although the individual manager cannot be completely indifferent to generally accepted standards, managerial choices must also reflect his or her personal code. The individual's personal values and beliefs are thus of prime importance, and they deserve serious study and careful choice.*

BOARDS OF DIRECTORS AND SOCIAL RESPONSIBILITY

The post-Watergate disclosure of corporate wrongdoing focused attention on the country's leading corporations and their chief executives. An obvious question arose: "Where were their boards of directors?" This question points to the underlying issue of the board's responsibility for ethical performance and social responsibility.

Board Responsibility for Moral Leadership

Traditionally, directors have functioned as guardians of the financial interest of stockholders with a specific concern for earnings and dividends. Even this role has been performed in a largely passive manner. Now, in

---

*The fact that beliefs and values are matters of individual choice and commitment does not make all beliefs equally valid. However, the discussion of personal faith is beyond the scope of this book. For reasoned presentations of the Christian faith, involving a minimum of theological jargon, see the following: C. S. Lewis, *Mere Christianity* (New York: Macmillan, 1960) or Paul Little, *Know Why You Believe* (Downers Grove, Ill.: Inter-Varsity Press, 1968).

the aftermath of major business scandals, the system of corporate governance and the role of directors have become subjects of special interest.

To meet such demands, boards must extend their oversight beyond traditional matters of profits to areas of ethics and social responsibility. A concern for ethical performance is not necessarily inconsistent with stockholder interest, of course, but the connection between ethics and profits is often unclear.

We desire moral leadership from the board because as directors, they presumably have the power to require ethical performance by management. The overall organizational impact of a board which demands ethical performance is greater than that of a vice president who does the same.

Recognition of the growing responsibility of directors is not entirely voluntary. The courts and the Securities and Exchange Commission are actively involved in expanding areas of board responsibility. In a number of cases, the SEC has brought legal action against individual outside directors as well as against corporations. For example, the SEC named three outside directors of Penn Central for aiding and abetting frauds allegedly perpetrated by management.[31]

In holding board members responsible, the SEC has taken the position that anyone in a position to know what is going on and to do something about it will be held liable. Overt action or direct participation in a fraud is unnecessary. Directors presumably have access to the facts or should probe sufficiently to get the facts.

Problems in Achieving Strong Board Leadership

There are difficulties in correcting board performance to make it an effective agency for control. In practice, directors often lack the power they have in theory. To be sure, they are not powerless. From time to time, directors act decisively—for example, by dismissing a chief executive or even "blowing the whistle" on management. A director of Superscope called the New York Stock Exchange on one occasion to report apparent irregularities. As a result, trading of the company's stock was halted for more than a day.[32] (During that day, the company increased substantially the estimate of its second-quarter loss.) The director who blew the whistle controlled a substantial block of Superscope stock. Such an incident is exceptional, although it does show the potential power of a properly structured board.

Even though pressure on individual directors is increasing, the balance of power still favors the senior management group. In large corporations, this group continues to influence the selection of board members and to guide their deliberations. The unbalanced strength of a well-established management team vis-à-vis the relatively small individual stockholders still exists. A distinguished scholar on the role and functioning of boards of directors, Myles L. Mace, contends that little has changed.

"The CEO," he argues, "has de facto control of the proxy system, to determine who serves on the board, who gets invited to serve on the board, who stays on the board, how many meetings are held, what items are on the agenda, how much board members are paid, what management information is provided to board members, and basically what board members do or not do. . . ."[33]

Another limitation arises from the competing functions of boards of directors. Busy directors must devote attention to their traditional role of evaluating management's profit performance as well as their social responsibility role. This limits the time they can devote to guarding the company's morals.

Board Structure

Board effectiveness in providing moral guidance is related to its composition and organization. Independence is the basic requisite. A judge beholden to the accused is a weak judge. Independence of board members is jeopardized by their role as insiders, as suppliers of corporate services, or as management cronies. McDermott, Inc., which builds gigantic offshore oil platforms, provides a dramatic example of a company whose inside directors failed to exercise adequate surveillance.

Until five years ago, a board dominated by inside directors ran it like a private company. In the 1970s the government charged McDermott with all manner of corporate wrongdoing: phony accounting, kickbacks to a customer, illegal campaign contributions, and price-fixing. Managers who were put on probation for price-fixing kept their jobs.[34]

A first step in building a strong board, therefore, is the appointment of outside directors. This does not guarantee moral wisdom and courage, of course, but it does remove a potential handicap from board members. To realize the potential benefit from independent directors, corporations must seek out qualified individuals who are capable of asking tough questions and demanding responsible performance. Such directors may also represent the traditional interests of stockholders by monitoring the overall effectiveness of management, rather than giving routine approval to management programs.

The committee organization of the board constitutes another point of strength or weakness. The audit, nominating, compensation, and other key committees should be composed primarily, if not exclusively, of outside directors. For maximum effectiveness, the audit committee should work directly with the firm's internal and outside auditors.

In most corporations, the chief executive officer also serves as chairman of the board. Chairman Harold M. Williams of the SEC has argued for separation of chairman and chief executive functions as follows:

Control of the agenda process is a powerful tool, and the issues presented at board meetings should be determined by a chairman who is not a member of management. The substance and process of board deliberations, and the priority which the board assigns to the matters before it, should not be management's prerogatives. And this also means that hard decisions concerning what the board will take up when time is short and the issues are many should not be dictated by management. Finally, the intimidating power of the chair, when occupied by a chief executive in situations where the majority of the board are indebted to him for their directorship, is avoided.[35]

Prospects for Effective Control by Directors

The need for directors to perform the control function contemplated in the law is widely recognized. Structural changes, however, cannot guarantee a board that will act in the public interest. The cynic may feel that "the more things change, the more they stay the same." The limitations of board reform have been aptly stated by Professor Mace:

> You can talk all you want about mechanical contrivances or artifices or techniques, but if the CEO doesn't want nominating committees or committees of directors, he pays no attention to them.[36]

Boards of directors have been strengthened in recent years and show some signs of more effective control in the areas of ethics and social issues. We must be wary, however, of assuming that restructuring boards will in itself greatly improve corporate behavior.

SUMMARY

Society gives business corporations and other organizations the right to exist; it expects socially responsible performance in return. Such expectations are not fixed, however, and increasing demands are being made upon all organizations, particularly business corporations. Some socially desirable activities are profitable, but many are costly to the corporation. Profits are essential if a corporation is to invest substantial amounts in programs for the public good. Within the limits of their financial resources, however, corporations may choose to do little or much. The *Preston-Post* model of social responsiveness holds that corporate social action should extend as far as the corporation's primary and secondary involvement in society but no further. To evaluate their social performance, some firms now use a method of assessment known as a *social audit.*

Ethical decisions are involved in all aspects of organizational life. Even though much business behavior is highly ethical, evidence of malfeasance exists in many areas. Organizational ethics are affected by various features of the managerial system such as organizational priorities, organizational goals, control systems, the chain of command, and codes of ethics. The foundations for ethical behavior are found in our underlying values, particularly those associated with the *Judeo-Christian heritage*.

Boards of directors have major responsibilities for providing social and moral leadership in organizational life. The Securities and Exchange Commission has brought legal action against individual directors who allegedly failed to display such leadership. Board membership and committee structure are important factors in determining the effectiveness of the board's moral leadership.

DISCUSSION QUESTIONS

1. How does the concept of the *social contract* relate to corporate management?
2. Using Figure 24–1, explain the changing nature of the *social contract*.
3. What is the profit impact of socially responsible corporate action?
4. How does the factor of market competition affect corporate decision making on social issues?
5. How does a *social audit* differ from a financial audit?
6. Corporations have an obvious interest in politics and government regulation. What was wrong with their political contributions to the Committee to Re-elect the President?
7. Why do managers experience difficulty in deciding what is ethical or unethical in specific situations?
8. Why should an emphasis on organizational goals be a threat to ethical performance?
9. Of what value is a *code of ethics*?
10. What general viewpoint has been expressed by the Securities and Exchange Commission regarding the responsibilities of directors for ethical conduct of a corporation?
11. Explain the relative strength of an *inside* versus an *outside* board in overseeing company morality.
12. Identify the key committees of a board of directors and explain their significance in achieving ethical performance by corporations.

NOTES

1. Evidence on the overall relationship of social responsiveness and profitability is conflicting. See Peter Arlow and Martin J. Gannon, "Social Responsiveness, Corporate Structure, and Economic Performance," *Academy of Management Review* 7 (April 1982): 235–41.
2. "How Business Tackles Social Problems," *Business Week,* 20 May 1972, p. 97.

3. "AmEx Shows the Way to Benefit from Giving," *Business Week*, 18 October 1982, pp. 44–45.

4. Kenneth E. Goodpaster and John B. Matthews, Jr., "Can a Corporation Have a Conscience?" *Harvard Business Review* 60 (January–February 1981): 135.

5. Milton Friedman, "The Social Responsibility of Business Is to Increase Its Profits," *New York Times Magazine*, 13 September 1970, pp. 33, 122–25.

6. Theodore Levitt, "The Dangers of Social Responsibility," *Harvard Business Review* 36 (September–October 1958): 48.

7. The need for corporate profitability has been likened to human physiological needs in Maslow's need hierarchy. See Frank Tuzzolino and Barry R. Armandi, "A Need-Hierarchy Framework for Assessing Corporate Social Responsibility," *Academy of Management Review* 6 (January 1981): 21–28.

8. Elizabeth Gatewood and Archie B. Carroll, "The Anatomy of Corporate Social Response: "The Rely, Firestone 500, and Pinto Cases," *Business Horizons* 24 (September–October 1981): 9.

9. Ibid., pp. 9–16.

10. Lee E. Preston and James E. Post, *Private Management and Public Policy* (Englewood Cliffs, N.J.: Prentice-Hall, 1975). Also see Lee E. Preston and James E. Post, "Private Management and Public Policy," *California Management Review* 23 (Spring 1981): 56–62.

11. Preston and Post, *Private Management and Public Policy*, p. 97.

12. Archie B. Carroll and George W. Beiler, "Landmarks in the Evolution of the Social Audit," *Academy of Management Journal* 18 (September 1975): 589–99.

13. Max Lerner, "The Shame of the Professions," *Saturday Review*, 1 November 1975, p. 12.

14. "The Detectives Hunt for Illegal Givers," *Business Week*, 14 July 1973, pp. 27–28.

15. Steven N. Brenner and Earl A. Molander, "Is the Ethics of Business Changing?" *Harvard Business Review* 55 (January–February 1977): 60.

16. Sandra L. Caron, "Politics and International Business: The Impact of the Foreign Corrupt Practices Act," *Journal of Contemporary Business* 10 (3rd Quarter 1981): 17–28.

17. For a discussion of the complexity of moral choices in portfolio management, see Burton G. Malkiel and Richard E. Quandt, "Moral Issues in Investment Policy," *Harvard Business Review* 49 (March–April 1971): 37–47.

18. Kenneth R. Andres, "Can the Best Corporations Be Made Moral?" *Harvard Business Review* 51 (May–June 1973): 64; and Thomas J. Peters, "Management Systems: The Language of Organizational Character and Competence," *Organizational Dynamics* 9 (Summer 1980): 3–26.

19. "A Conversation with Fletcher L. Byrom," transcript of an interview by Dr. John F. Steiner, Center for the Study of Business and Society, California State University, Los Angeles, California, 1978.

20. For a review of the ethical issues involved in management by objectives, see Charles D. Pringle and Justin G. Longenecker, "The Ethics of MBO," *Academy of Management Review* 7 (April 1982): 305–12.

21. Archie B. Carroll, "Managerial Ethics: A Post-Watergate View," *Business Horizons* 18 (April 1975): 77.
22. James A. Waters, "Catch 20.5: Corporate Morality as an Organizational Phenomenon," *Organizational Dynamics* 6 (Spring 1978): 6.
23. Archie B. Carroll, "Managerial Ethics," p. 79.
24. Bernard J. White and B. Ruth Montgomery, "Corporate Codes of Conduct," *California Management Review* 23 (Winter 1980): 80–87.
25. See, for example, Robert W. Austin, "Code of Conduct for Executives," *Harvard Business Review* 39 (September–October 1961): 53.
26. Fred T. Allen, "Business Ethics," *The Management of International Corporate Citizenship*, Top Management Report (Washington, D.C.: International Management and Development Institute, n.d.), p. 23.
27. Brenner and Molander, "Is the Ethics of Business Changing?" p. 66.
28. Cited by Norman Bowie, *Business Ethics* (Englewood Cliffs, N.J.: Prentice-Hall, 1982), p. 92.
29. Bernard J. White and B. Ruth Montgomery, "Corporate Codes of Conduct," *California Management Review* 23 (Winter 1980): 84. Copyright © 1980 by the Regents of the University of California. Reprinted from *California Management Review*, Vol. XXIII, No. 2, pp. 84 by permission of the Regents.
30. Harold L. Johnson, "Can the Businessman Apply Christianity?" *Harvard Business Review* 35 (September–October 1957): 68–76.
31. "Questioning the Role of Outside Directors," *Business Week*, 11 May 1974, p. 34.
32. "A Funny Thing Happened on the Way to the Office," *Forbes*, 11 December 1978, pp. 33–34.
33. "The More Things Change . . .," *Forbes*, 11 June 1979, p. 112.
34. Shawn Tully, "The Mismatched Merger That Worked," *Fortune* 105 (April 19, 1982): 168.
35. Harold M. Williams, "Corporate Accountability," address to the Fifth Annual Securities Regulation Institute, San Diego, January 18, 1978.
36. "The More Things Change . . .," *Forbes*, 11 June 1979, p. 112.

SUPPLEMENTARY READING

Baruch, Hurd. "The Foreign Corrupt Practices Act." *Harvard Business Review* 57 (January–February 1979): 32–50.

Bowie, Norman. *Business Ethics.* Englewood Cliffs, N.J.: Prentice-Hall, 1982.

Bock, Robert H. "Modern Values and Corporate Social Responsibility," *MSU Business Topics* 28 (Spring 1980): 5–17.

Brenner, Steven, and **Molander, Earl A.** "Is the Ethics of Business Changing?" *Harvard Business Review* 55 (January–February 1977): 57–71.

Camenisch, Paul F. "Business Ethics: On Getting to the Heart of the Matter." *Business and Professional Ethics Journal* 1 (Fall 1981): 59–69.

Carroll, Archie B. "Managerial Ethics: A Post-Watergate View." *Business Horizons* 18 (April 1975): 75–80.

_____. "A Three-Dimensional Conceptual Model of Corporate Performance." *Academy of Management Review* 4 (October 1979): 497–505.

Cavanagh, Gerald F.; Moberg, Dennis J.; and **Velasquez, Manuel.** "The Ethics of Organizational Politics." *Academy of Management Review* 6 (July 1981): 363–74.

DeGeorge, Richard T. *Business Ethics.* New York: Macmillan Publishing Co., 1982.

Donaldson, Thomas. *Corporations and Morality.* Englewood Cliffs, N.J.: Prentice-Hall, 1982.

Donaldson, Thomas, and **Werhane, Patricia H.** *Ethical Issues in Business.* Englewood Cliffs, N.J.: Prentice-Hall, 1979.

Goodpaster, Kenneth E., and **Matthews, John B., Jr.** "Can a Corporation Have a Conscience?" *Harvard Business Review* 60 (January–February 1982): 132–41.

Johnson, Harold L. "Ethics and the Executive." *Business Horizons* 24 (May–June 1981): 53–59.

Lewis, Ralph F. "What Should Audit Committees Do?" *Harvard Business Review* 56 (May–June 1978): 22–26; 172–74.

Nash, Laura L. "Ethics without the Sermon." *Harvard Business Review* 59 (November–December 1981): 79–90.

Palmieri, Victor H. "Corporate Responsibility and the Competent Board." *Harvard Business Review* 57 (May–June 1979): 46–48.

Pringle, Charles D., and **Longenecker, Justin G.** "The Ethics of MBO." *Academy of Management Review* 7 (April 1982): 305–12.

Purcell, Theodore V. "Management and the 'Ethical' Investors." *Harvard Business Review* 57 (September–October 1979): 24–44.

Rudd, Andrew. "Social Responsibility and Portfolio Performance." *California Management Review* 23 (Summer 1981): 55–61.

Sethi, S. Prakash. "A Conceptual Framework for Environmental Analysis of Social Issues and Evaluation of Business Response Patterns." *Academy of Management Review* 4 (January 1979): 63–74.

Steckmest, Francis W. *Corporate Performance: The Key to Public Trust.* New York: McGraw-Hill Book Co., 1982.

Steiner, George A., and **Steiner, John F.** *Issues in Business and Society,* 2d ed. New York: Random House, 1977.

Waters, James A. "Catch 20.5: Corporate Morality as an Organizational Phenomenon." *Organizational Dynamics* 6 (Spring 1978): 3–19.

CASES

CASE 1: STEWART'S DEPARTMENT STORE*

Stewart's Department Store had been in existence 97 years when a firm of retail consultants was approached to solve the store's complex problems. Its founder, Jack Stewart, had come over from Scotland as a young man. After moving about the country, working and saving his money, he opened a small dry goods store in a village about one hundred miles from a large city. The village was surrounded by prosperous farmers and had good road and rail connections to the city. Because it was so easy to go to town, Stewart was able to make frequent trips to wholesalers in the city and soon learned he could buy goods as he required them. In this way he was able to finance the store, first from his savings and then from his profits. Thus, although he was not aware of the value of maintaining low inventories, he reaped its benefits through fast turnover, continuous fresh stock, and high markups.

When Stewart opened his business, there were two stores larger than his in the village. He soon surpassed these competitors because he was very personable and learned to buy only those goods his customers wanted. Moreover, he adopted a number of new retailing techniques that were being introduced by the more progressive stores in the city. Some of these retailing principles were prices clearly marked on all merchandise, money refunded if goods not satisfactory, and clearance of old stock. On the other hand, his competitors continued to do business as they always had done; that is, buying what they liked, haggling over every sale, and allowing no merchandise returns or cash refunds.

Stewart also threw himself into the life of the community and became known for miles around as a good man whose store was a pleasant place to visit and who sold good merchandise at fair prices. As he accumulated more wealth than his business required, Stewart invested it in real estate and in shares of certain industries that began to move into the area. He was as shrewd an investor as he was a merchant; when he died, he left his son James with the largest store in the area and a very comfortable income from his real estate and stock holdings.

James Stewart was not only as able a business man as his father but much more ambitious. He decided to increase his father's estate and also to be a social leader in the community; and, on the whole, he succeeded. Because he was so well known and thought of in the community and because he was a good merchant, the store grew until it covered half a city block and consisted of a complete basement and five selling floors. In James Stewart's lifetime, Stewart's became the only full-line department store in what had grown from a village to a town, and it actually dominated the entire retail area for miles around.

James had his faults. He was a complete autocrat and demanded unquestioned obedience from his employees and his family. He worked

*Case prepared by Professor Harold Shaffer of Sir George Williams University.

very hard because he never learned to delegate authority and so made all administrative decisions himself. But hard work seemed to agree with him, for he lived until he was 81 and actively ran the store and his other possessions until the day he died.

However, during the last eight years of his life, James was a wheelchair cripple. Nevertheless, he still came to the store every day and as he wheeled about the various departments, he greeted customers, gave orders, and made both major and minor decisions.

James had only one son, Bill Stewart, who wanted to be an engineer, but his father would have none of that nonsense. After the boy finished college, he went into the store as a receiver and slowly moved up the ladder until, at the time of his father's death, he had become an assistant buyer in the men's furnishings department. James, always impatient and critical, was even more so with his son. He criticized him continuously, usually within the hearing of customers or staff. The young man had no alternative but to cringe and become less and less certain of himself and his ability as a merchant.

Even though James was incapacitated during the last years of his life, he left the store in excellent condition. Moreover, his estate included a considerable fortune in real estate holdings, stocks, and bonds. He left the store and a small part of his investments to Bill and the balance of his estate to his wife.

Thus, Bill became president of Stewart's. He soon discovered, however, that he was incapable of making executive decisions and that there was no one in the store who could help him. Moreover, as the staff kept comparing him to his father and grandfather and found him wanting, they soon became openly hostile to his leadership. Soon Bill began to drink heavily, and although he put in as many hours in the store as any of his employees, he isolated himself in his office and so saw less and less of his staff or his customers. The organization rapidly fell apart, yet for one reason or another, the staff remained loyal to the store, with the employees trying to operate as they thought the old man would want them to.

As sales dropped, Bill not only drank harder, but began to stay away from the store for days on end. Under these circumstances, Miss Beach, the office manager, took it upon herself to move into the administrative vacuum. Miss Beach had idolized James Stewart and so had nothing but contempt for his son. Nevertheless, in her new role, Stewart's became her whole life. She had always worked hard, but now she spent even longer hours in the store trying to keep up with the office routine, listen to employee complaints, and make whatever administrative decisions she felt were required. But although she acted as chief administrator, she always felt uncertain of her decisions and resented the fact that she, rather than Bill, was making them. This attitude increased her loyalty to the store and her animosity towards its president.

In spite of Miss Beach's efforts, Stewart's continued to lose money and Bill was forced to sell more and more of his outside investments. Occasionally he would sober up and try to run the business himself but even when he set up good administrative policies, he could never obtain the desired results. For example, he hired a capable executive, Al Smith, to be his general merchandise manager. However, he never formally announced the appointment to his staff, the people in his area, or his vendors, nor would he support Smith against the open hostility of the buyers and Miss Beach.

At first Smith attempted to gain and exert control over the buyers by devious methods. For example, he persuaded Bill to install a retail inventory method. However, it was never used because the buyers simply ignored it; Smith, without Bill's authority behind him, could not force them to adhere to their open-to-buy positions or even to plan merchandise budgets. Moreover, they persisted in going to Miss Beach rather than to Smith for any major merchandise decisions.

Smith then installed a stock-age system, but the buyers ignored this too. Finally, he attempted to compare each department's cumulative daily sales against their former figures, in the hope that this tactic would increase the buyers' incentive to make more sales and so turn to Smith rather than Miss Beach for advice. But the store's sales tabulating system made it impossible to obtain department sales figures soon enough for this purpose.

Because both Jack and James Stewart felt that balancing the cash was more important than knowing what merchandise was sold, the store's daily cash was totalled first, and then, in their spare time, the office staff would break down the sales slips into departments and tabulate department figures. Thus, the buyers received their sales progress so late they could not use this as an active merchandise control.

Smith tried to reverse the process and use the sales slips to first report the merchandise sold by departments and then to balance the cash. Stewart agreed to the new procedure, but when it was actively opposed by Miss Beach he withdrew his support and left Smith to cope with the problem alone. The new system soon became inoperable; after this experience, Smith decided not to fight the system but to accept the situation as gracefully as he could.

As sales and profits continued to fall, Bill Stewart was faced with the possibility that he would have to liquidate the last portion of the estate his father had left him. In desperation he searched for a magic formula that would relieve him of his administrative duties and decisions, yet increase sales and turn losses into profits. In this way, he would prove to the staff and to himself that he was every bit as good a merchant as his father and grandfather had been. He decided that modernizing the store was the answer and sold this idea to his mother, who said she would help to finance it.

Bill threw himself into this project with unaccustomed zeal and enthusiasm. He obtained the services of a reputable fixture house, who researched the size and locations of the store's present departments and then made a number of recommendations for improving the Stewart operation. For example, they suggested that the ladies' hosiery, blouses, and skirts department should be moved from the third floor and placed on the street floor, immediately to the right of the entrance. Currently this area was taken up with ankle sox, umbrellas, and handbags. They also thought that the piece goods department should be moved from the main floor to the third floor, and so on.

Again, they suggested closing up nonprofitable departments such as notions, and using the area to enlarge more profitable departments, or to establish new departments or merchandise classifications.

They also pointed out that Stewart's millinery department carried the highest priced hats in town, while its dress department was unsuccessfully competing with the town's chain stores and implied that a uniform buying and price-lining policy would be much in order.

Stewart agreed with the fixture people, but those department heads who felt they would suffer or lose face if the plans went into effect, objected to the proposals. They were supported by Miss Beach, who took the position that what was good enough for Bill Stewart's father was good enough for his son. Thus, while Stewart's acquired modern floor coverings and light fixtures, colorful walls, and functional open shelving fixtures, little was done to improve the store's profit position, for the merchandising techniques remained almost as old-fashioned as when Jack Stewart first opened his store.

Actually, the interior alterations had been only phase one of Stewart's plan to renovate the store. Phase two was to modernize the store's exterior, but after the poor results of his interior project, his mother refused to throw good money after bad. Thus, the store remained with a late nineteenth-century exterior, including bust forms and other fixtures of the period, while its interior was modern.

About this time, Stewart was offered a handsome price for the store. He would have been happy to sell it, but he had a son who was studying business administration and who showed a marked desire to go into Stewart's when he graduated. Moreover, the boy seemed to have his grandfather's flair for store leadership. During the summer vacations when he worked in the store, Stewart's employees, including Miss Beach, were more content and happy than at any other time of the year.

Unfortunately, Stewart did not get along with his son and they quarrelled incessantly, with their bitterest fights over store policy. Aside from other considerations, then, Bill Stewart felt that if he sold the business, there might be less tension in the family. But Bill's mother put a lot of pressure on him not to sell. She wanted to keep the business in the family, if at all possible, and felt that her grandson would be capable of making the store an even greater success than her husband had done. Therefore, she said she was quite prepared to keep financing the business until the boy graduated.

Stewart, as usual, accepted his mother's decision but felt his position of president, with whatever status it entailed, was in jeopardy. He became so obsessed with this hazard that he turned to a firm of retail consultants and asked them to suggest what could be done to make the business profitable within the next three years. In this way, he felt he would build up his reputation as a merchant and secure his position as president of Stewart's.

The consultants made surveys of the community and found that Stewart's had enormous potential. Industry was moving into the area rapidly, yet there was no store within thirty miles of Stewart's that could compete with it, providing it were run properly. Moreover, a consumer survey produced a surprisingly strong loyalty to Stewart's. People wanted to shop there and were angry that the poor merchandise selections made this impossible. The consultants felt that with proper management Stewart's could rapidly increase its business and soon make a satisfactory profit.

After interviewing most of the personnel at Stewart's, however, some of the executives in the consulting firm were vehemently opposed to becoming involved with the store. They did not argue its business potential or that it could be made to run at a profit. What worried them was that Bill Stewart was the store's president and owner and that they would have to work through him. Yet it was obvious that he was unable to exert real power. Moreover, Smith, Stewart's assistant, seemed too weak to be able to carry out orders even if they were given by Stewart. In their interviews with Miss Beach, the consultants found her both negative and frightened. Apparently she was afraid of losing her job if any changes were made. To some extent, she was now enjoying the power she wielded in the store and would be most reluctant to give it up.

The personnel situation was further complicated by Stewart's peculiarly stubborn loyalty to his staff. He would not fire anyone. He admitted his fear of Miss Beach and his desire to get rid of her, but because she was loyal to him "in her way" he must be loyal to her. Nor would he change accountants, even though the present one, "a friend of his father's," was 82 and too old and sick to even see the books. Miss Beach, for years, had drawn up the annual statements, and the old man had merely signed them.

Questions

1. Name and discuss the major management considerations that are illustrated in this case.
2. What further arguments could the consultants give for accepting the case?

3. What further arguments could the consultants give for not accepting the case?
4. Assuming the consultants agreed to accept the assignment, what steps should they take to solve Stewart's problems?

CASE 2: A MANAGEMENT DILEMMA

Susan Williams, 53, had more departmental seniority than any other employee, including Carole Anderson, the department manager in a major insurance company. Susan was considered one of the more capable employees, although her efficiency had declined somewhat during the past five years. Even so, Carole realized that she was extremely conscientious and that she earned every penny of her paycheck. As a result of her ability and seniority, she customarily received the choice work assignments and was the highest paid employee in the department. Although there was no formal designation of various "special" projects as belonging to Susan, she handled them as a matter of course.

A problem developed when Carole employed Ann Bentley, 21, a personable, intelligent, and diligent employee. Ann's two years' prior experience in closely related work made it possible for her to catch on to work routines much more rapidly than was customary for a new employee. She was both hard working and aggressive. On several occasions, Carole became aware of tension or hostility developing between the two women. However, she did not wish to intrude into personal conflicts, and the work was being accomplished on schedule.

One afternoon, the controversy reached the boiling point when Susan Williams decided her personal duties were being taken over far too extensively by the new employee. She practically pulled Ann to the front of Carole's desk and demanded, "Will you please tell her once and for all which projects are mine and which are hers?" The office suddenly became quiet as everyone awaited Carole's reply. The abrupt confrontation made further procrastination impossible.

Questions

1. In what way has the manager's organizing function contributed to this problem? Could it have been avoided by better organization? How?
2. Evaluate the leadership or motivational approach evident in this department.
3. Evaluate Carole Anderson's performance as a "controller."
4. How should Carole Anderson respond to the demand of Susan Williams?

CASE 3: WORRY AT WERNETT'S*

Jeanne Jones felt confused and frustrated as she walked slowly toward the Receiving Department, pondering the impossible order her boss had issued only moments before. Not only the sheer impossibility of carrying out the order, but serious doubts as to the legitimacy of the directive had driven Jeanne into her current quandary.

Having been appointed assistant buyer in Women's Sportswear at Wernett's Department Store only three months earlier, she had established a smooth and rewarding working relationship with Helen Fabian, the department's buyer and one of the store's "rising stars." Since the Christmas selling season had begun, however, the air of compatibility had dissipated as Helen had grown increasingly tense and grouchy.

About one-fourth of the store's annual sales came during the weeks between Thanksgiving and Christmas. Since a buyer's income and opportunities for promotion depended upon being able to exceed last year's sales, the Christmas selling season was of paramount importance.

Under the leadership of Helen Fabian, sales in Women's Sportswear had consistently exceeded last year's sales by 20 percent since January. This increase had risen to about 23 percent the first two weeks of the Christmas season. But this record—easily one of the best among the store's 80 buyers—did not seem to satisfy Helen.

Only a few minutes ago, she had called Jeanne into her office. "Jeanne, our sales this week are up over last year's by about 23 percent. We should be able to do better than that, however. On the way back from lunch, I stopped at the loading docks and saw our overdue shipment of suede blazers arriving. If we could get those onto the selling floor by this evening, I think we could beat last year's figures for this week by close to 30 percent. I'd like you to go see Charlie Barnoski, the head of Receiving, and get him to move those blazers up to the front of the receiving line so we can get them on the floor before the evening rush."

As Jeanne walked reluctantly toward Receiving, she pondered her predicament. The store's policy on receiving was quite clear. All goods were checked against purchase orders for quantity, quality, size, and color; marked with price tags; and sent to the selling floor *in the order they arrived at the store*. Although temporary help was hired during the Christmas season to increase the size of the Receiving Department staff, the average time period between the arrival of the goods at the store and their actual display on the selling floor was three days. Obviously this period was too long for Helen!

Now, as she arrived at Receiving, Jeanne dreaded having to request an exception to store policy, especially since she had never even met Charlie Barnoski.

---

*Prepared with the assistance of Anne Marie Pringle.

Questions

1. Analyze this situation from a systems viewpoint:
   a. What is the rationale behind the store's receiving policy?
   b. What are the systems implications of Helen Fabian's order to Jeanne?
2. What should Jeanne do?

CASE 4: SELECTING A NEW SUPERINTENDENT*

Max Henson, president of the Canyon City School Board, sat at the head of the table and reflected on the tumultuous two-hour meeting that had just ended. Most of the meeting had been a discussion of the largest budget in school district history. Constituent groups were unhappy that several minor sports programs were being cut, teachers were irate that their planned 8 percent pay hike fell short of the projected rate of inflation, and several maintenance programs were deferred because the budget didn't stretch far enough.

But the bombshell was dropped near the end of the meeting when the school superintendent, William Anderson, tendered his resignation to be effective at the end of the school year—just six weeks away. Bill Anderson's decision was not anticipated. However, he said his decision, for reasons of health, was final. Because Max was an executive in a local firm, the other board members asked him to prepare a statement of qualifications to be used in advertising for, interviewing, and eventually selecting a replacement for Bill Anderson.

The Organization

Canyon City School District had grown dramatically in the nineteen years since Bill Anderson was named superintendent. When he took over as the first superintendent, the district had two elementary schools and a combined junior-senior high school. The total enrollment was slightly less than one thousand students and there were forty teachers. For ten years there had been very little growth. Then, just a decade ago, the student population began to increase.

In the early days, most of the children in Canyon City schools lived on a government installation that provided the only industrial base for the city. Federal-government support of the schools was generous, substituting per capita subsidies in lieu of property taxes that could have been raised had the homes not been on federal property. In fact, the

---

*Case prepared by Professor Robert L. Taylor of University of Wisconsin–Stevens Point. Used by permission of Houghton Mifflin Company, © 1982.

financial support was greater than any other adjacent school district enjoyed. As a result, the Canyon City School District funded many model programs. Real estate ads touted the district as the best place to build a home if the buyers wanted the best in schools for their children. Three new elementary schools and a junior high school were built and paid for out of accumulated surpluses.

The past five years were a different story. First, the district grew to where, last year, there were over 6,000 students and a teaching staff of 290. Second, the federal government significantly reduced its support. Third, several hundred homes had been built in the district but would not produce property tax revenue for another year or two. The new industries employing the home-owners were located outside the district, thus providing no financial support to the schools. Fourth, every school was overcrowded, yet parents and students were vehemently opposed to split sessions or year-round schools; they wanted new schools. Fifth, surrounding districts were losing students and the general trend was a decrease in the number of school-age children. Sixth, voters had just approved a bond issue to build two more elementary schools and a new high school, but they would not be completed for another two years.

The Environment

Canyon City is a community on the outskirts of a large metropolitan area of the Rocky Mountain West. It is a wooded area of zoned one-acre or larger home sites with an unsurpassed quality of life and a superb climate. Industrial growth in neighboring areas combines with excellent roads, making Canyon City the target of several real estate speculators and developers.

Unfortunately, shopping centers and plants are being built outside the district limits, depriving Canyon City of the needed tax base. Yet as more homes are being built, the number of students is increasing, putting more strain on existing and planned schools.

The Job

Bill Anderson is the last of his breed. He is a softspoken man who has risen "from the ranks." Starting as an English teacher, he became principal of the original rural high school. Then, when Canyon City organized as an independent school district, he was unanimously chosen by his colleagues as the first school superintendent.

His management style is paternalistic. Through the years he learned to know each of the district's teachers in a very personal way. In fact, until the last five years, Canyon City School District had been one big happy family. Bill selected his good friends to assist with other administrative tasks so that the main office was staffed with close, personal colleagues. There was no formal organization structure; teachers, administrators, and school board members related to each other in a casual, informal way—until last year.

The last year had been traumatic for Bill Anderson. Overcrowding and scheduling problems complicated every staff meeting. Most of the original cadre of teachers had retired, and the new young teachers seemed impatient in dealing with the administration. Financial problems had forced Bill to cancel the art and foreign language programs in the elementary schools. At the same time, federal mandates for educating the handicapped and children with learning disabilities put new strains on the budget. Most recently, reductions in athletic programs and inadequate pay raises for teachers had caused considerable furor. The latter led to the formation of a militant teachers' association.

One of the reasons Bill decided to retire now was that he recognized he was no longer able to fight the battles necessary to take the Canyon City schools through the next stage of growth. Not only was his health failing, he sincerely believed that he should turn the reins over to someone younger—someone who understood today's students, the needs of teachers, and the complexities of leadership in a changing world.

The Decision

Max was serving his first year on the school board. He had been elected because of his business experience and affable personality. Yet he quickly realized that there are significant differences between managing a business and setting policy for a public sector organization where there is no profit and loss statement.

He really appreciated Bill Anderson's caring and concern. In fact, Max felt that Bill was just the right person to have guided the district through its formative years. Canyon City still had a reputation for scholastic excellence, and it was clear that the teachers really cared about their students.

Max pondered the situation carefully. He believed that a different kind of leader was needed now—someone with creative vision. At the same time, Max knew that the new superintendent must address the critical issues now: teacher demands for economic equity, overcrowding and scheduling problems pending the completion of new schools, declining economic bases, and the evolving environment. He could not avoid it, and so he picked up his pencil and started to draft a set of criteria.

Questions

1. What are the most important changes that have occurred in the school district's specific environment?
2. Was Anderson's management style effective or ineffective for this changing environment?

3. Max Henson believes that a "different kind of leader" is needed now. Do you agree? Why or why not?

4. What are the most important actions the new superintendent should take?

CASE 5: THE ROAD TO HELL*

John Baker, Chief Engineer of the Caribbean Bauxite Company of Barracania in the West Indies, was making his final preparations to leave the island. His promotion to production manager of Keso Mining Corporation near Winnipeg—one of Continental Ore's fast-expanding Canadian enterprises—had been announced a month before and now everything had been tidied up except the last vital interview with his successor—the able young Barracanian, Matthew Rennalls. It was vital that this interview be a success and that Rennalls should leave his office uplifted and encouraged to face the challenge of his new job. A touch on the bell would have brought Rennalls walking into the room but Baker delayed the moment and gazed thoughtfully through the window considering just exactly what he was going to say and, more particularly, how he was going to say it.

John Baker, an English expatriate, was 45 years old and had served his 23 years with Continental Ore in many different places: in the Far East; several countries of Africa; Europe; and, for the last two years, in the West Indies. He hadn't cared much for his previous assignment in Hamburg and was delighted when the West Indian appointment came through. Climate was not the only attraction. Baker had always preferred working overseas (in what were termed the developing countries) because he felt he had an innate knack—better than most other expatriates working for Continental Ore—of knowing just how to get on with regional staff. Twenty-four hours in Barracania, however, soon made him realise that he would need all of this "innate knack" if he was to deal effectively with the problems in this field that now awaited him.

At his first interview with Hutchins, the production manager, the whole problem of Rennalls and his future was discussed. There and then it was made quite clear to Baker that one of his most important tasks would be the "grooming" of Rennalls as his successor. Hutchins had pointed out that, not only was Rennalls one of the brightest Barracanian prospects on the staff of Caribbean Bauxite—at London University he had taken first-class honours in the B.Sc. Engineering Degree—but, being the son of the Minister of Finance and Economic Planning, he also had no small political pull.

---

*Case prepared by Gareth Evans for Shell-British Petroleum Development Company of Nigeria. Used by permission of Professor John J. Gabarro of the Harvard Business School.

The company had been particularly pleased when Rennalls decided to work for them rather than for the Government in which his father had such a prominent post. They ascribed his action to the effect of their vigorous and liberal regionalisation programme which, since the Second World War, had produced eighteen Barracanians at mid-management level and given Caribbean Bauxite a good lead in this respect over all other international concerns operating in Barracania. The success of this timely regionalisation policy has led to excellent relations with the Government—a relationship which had been given an added importance when Barracania, three years later, became independent—an occasion which encouraged a critical and challenging attitude towards the role foreign interests would have to play in the new Barracania. Hutchins had therefore little difficulty in convincing Baker that the successful career development of Rennalls was of the first importance.

The interview with Hutchins was now two years old and Baker, leaning back in his office chair, reviewed just how successful he had been in the "grooming" of Rennalls. What aspects of the latter's character had helped and what had hindered? What about his own personality? How had that helped or hindered? The first item to go on the credit side would, without question, be the ability of Rennalls to master the technical aspects of his job. From the start he had shown keenness and enthusiasm and had often impressed Baker with his ability in tackling new assignments and the constructive comments he invariably made in departmental discussions. He was popular with all ranks of Barracanian staff and had an ease of manner which stood him in good stead when dealing with his expatriate seniors. These were all assets, but what about the debit side?

First and foremost, there was his racial consciousness. His four years at London University had accentuated this feeling and made him sensitive to any sign of condescension on the part of expatriates. It may have been to give expression to this sentiment that, as soon as he returned home from London, he threw himself into politics on behalf of the United Action Party who were later to win the preindependence elections and provide the country with its first Prime Minister.

The ambitions of Rennalls—and he certainly was ambitious—did not, however, lie in politics for, staunch nationalist as he was, he saw that he could serve himself and his country best—for was not bauxite responsible for nearly half the value of Barracania's export trade?—by putting his engineering talent to the best use possible. On this account, Hutchins found that he had an unexpectedly easy task in persuading Rennalls to give up his political work before entering the production department as an assistant engineer.

It was, Baker knew, Rennalls' well repressed sense of race consciousness which had prevented their relationship from being as close as it should have been. On the surface, nothing could have seemed more agreeable. Formality between the two men was at a minimum; Baker was delighted to find that his assistant shared his own peculiar "shaggy dog" sense of humour so that jokes were continually being exchanged; they entertained each other at their houses and often played tennis together—and yet the barrier remained invisible, indefinable, but ever present. The existence of this "screen" between them was a constant source of frustration to Baker since it indicated a weakness which he was loath to accept. If successful with all other nationalities, why not with Rennalls?

But at least he had managed to "break through" to Rennalls more successfully than any other expatriate. In fact, it was the young Barracanian's attitude—sometimes overbearing; sometimes cynical—towards other company expatriates that had been one of the subjects Baker had raised last year when he discussed Rennalls' staff report with him. He knew, too, that he would have to raise the same subject again in the forthcoming interview because Jackson, the senior draughtsman, had complained only yesterday about the rudeness of Rennalls. With this thought in mind, Baker leaned forward and spoke into the intercom. "Would you come in Matt, please? I'd like a word with you," and later, "Do sit down," proferring the box, "have a cigarette." He paused while he held out his lighter and then went on.

"As you know, Matt, I'll be off to Canada in a few days' time, and before I go, I thought it would be useful if we could have a final chat together. It is indeed with some deference that I suggest I can be of help. You will shortly be sitting in this chair doing the job I am now doing, but I, on the other hand, am ten years older, so perhaps you can accept the idea that I may be able to give you the benefit of my longer experience."

Baker saw Rennalls stiffen slightly in his chair as he made this point so added in explanation, "You and I have attended enough company courses to remember those repeated requests by the personnel manager to tell people how they are getting on as often as the convenient moment arises and not just the automatic 'once a year' when, by regulation, staff reports have to be discussed."

Rennalls nodded his agreement so Baker went on, "I shall always remember the last job performance discussion I had with my previous boss back in Germany. He used what he called the "plus and minus" technique. His firm belief was that when a senior, by discussion, seeks to improve the work performance of his staff, his prime objective should be to make sure that the latter leaves the interview encouraged and inspired to improve. Any criticism must, therefore, be constructive and helpful. He said that one very good way to encourage a person—and I fully agree with him—is to tell him about his good points—the plus factors—as well as his weak ones—the minus factors—so I thought, Matt, it would be a good idea to run our discussion along these lines."

Rennalls offered no comment, so Baker continued: "Let me say, therefore, right away, that, as far as your own work performance is concerned, the plus far outweighs the minus. I have, for instance, been most impressed with the way you have adapted your considerable theoretical knowledge to master the practical techniques of your job—that ingenious method you used to get air down to the fifth-shaft level is a sufficient case in point—and at departmental meetings I have invariably found your comments well taken and helpful. In fact, you will be interested to know that only last week I reported to Mr. Hutchins that, from the technical point of view, he could not wish for a more able man to succeed to the position of chief engineer."

"That's very good indeed of you, John," cut in Rennalls with a smile of thanks. "My only worry now is how to live up to such a high recommendation."

"Of that I am quite sure," returned Baker, "especially if you can overcome the minus factor which I would like now to discuss with you. It is one which I have talked about before so I'll come straight to the point. I have noticed that you are more friendly and get on better with your fellow Barracanians than you do with Europeans. In point of fact, I had a complaint only yesterday from Mr. Jackson, who said you had been rude to him—and not for the first time either.

"There is, Matt, I am sure, no need for me to tell you how necessary it will be for you to get on well with expatriates because until the company has trained up sufficient people of your calibre, Europeans are bound to occupy senior positions here in Barracania. All this is vital to your future interests, so can I help you in any way?"

While Baker was speaking on this theme, Rennalls had sat tensed in his chair, and it was some seconds before he replied. "It is quite extraordinary, isn't it, how one can convey an impression to others so at variance with what one intends? I can only assure you once again that my disputes with Jackson—and you may remember also Godson—have had nothing at all to do with the colour of their skins. I promise you that if a Barracanian had behaved in an equally preemptory manner I would have reacted in precisely the same way. And again, if I may say it within these four walls, I am sure I am not the only one who has found Jackson and Godson difficult. I could mention the names of several expatriates who have felt the same. However, I am really sorry to have created this impression of not being able to get on with Europeans—it is an entirely false one—and I quite realise that I must do all I can to correct it as quickly as possible. On your last point, regarding Europeans holding senior positions in the Company for some time to come, I quite accept the situation. I know that Caribbean Bauxite—as they have been doing for many years now—will promote Barracanians as soon as their experience warrants it. And, finally, I would like to assure you, John—and my father thinks the same too—that I am very happy in my work here and hope to stay with the company for many years to come."

Rennalls had spoken earnestly and, although not convinced by what he had heard, Baker did not think he could pursue the matter further except to say, "All right, Matt, my impression *may* be wrong, but I would like to remind you about the truth of that old saying, 'What is important is not what is true but what is believed.' Let it rest at that."

But suddenly Baker knew that he didn't want to "let it rest at that." He was disappointed once again at not being able to "break through" to Rennalls and having yet again to listen to his bland denial that there was any racial prejudice in his make-up. Baker, who had intended ending the interview at this point, decided to try another tack.

"To return for a moment to the 'plus and minus technique' I was telling you about just now, there is another plus factor I forgot to mention. I would like to congratulate you not only on the calibre of your work but also on the ability you have shown in overcoming a challenge which I, as a European, have never had to meet.

"Continental Ore is, as you know, a typical commercial enterprise—admittedly a big one—which is a product of the economic and social environment of the United States and Western Europe. My ancestors have all been brought up in this environment for the past two or three hundred years and I have, therefore, been able to live in a world in which commerce (as we know it today) has been part and parcel of my being. It has not been something revolutionary and new which has suddenly entered my life. In your case," went on Baker, "the situation is different because you and your forebears have only had some fifty or sixty years' experience of this commercial environment. You have had to face the challenge of bridging the gap between fifty and two or three hundred years. Again, Matt, let me congratulate you—and people like you—once again on having so successfully overcome this particular hurdle. It is for this very reason that I think the outlook for Barracania—and particularly Caribbean Bauxite—is so bright."

Rennalls had listened intently and when Baker finished, replied, "Well, once again, John, I have to thank you for what you have said, and, for my part, I can only say that it is gratifying to know that my own personal effort has been so much appreciated. I hope that more people will soon come to think as you do."

There was a pause and, for a moment, Baker thought hopefully that he was about to achieve his long awaited "breakthrough," but Rennalls merely smiled back. The barrier remained unbreached. There remained some five minutes' cheerful conversation about the contrast between the Caribbean and Canadian climate and whether the West Indies had any hope of beating England in the Fifth Test before Baker drew the interview to a close. Although he was as far as ever from knowing the real Rennalls, he was nevertheless glad that the interview had run along in this friendly manner and, particularly, that it had ended on such a cheerful note.

This feeling, however, lasted only until the following morning. Baker had some farewells to make, so he arrived at the office considerably later than usual. He had no sooner sat down at his desk than his secretary walked into the room with a worried frown on her face. Her words came fast. "When I arrived this morning I found Mr. Rennalls already waiting at my door. He seemed very angry and told me in quite a peremptory manner that he had a vital letter to dictate which must be sent off without any delay. He was so worked up that he couldn't keep still and kept pacing about the room, which is most unlike him. He wouldn't even wait to read what he had dictated. Just signed the page where he thought the letter would end. It has been distributed and your copy is in your 'in tray.' "

Puzzled and feeling vaguely uneasy, Baker opened the "Confidential" envelope and read the following letter:

From: Assistant Engineer

To: The Chief Engineer, Caribbean Bauxite Limited

14th August, 196_

ASSESSMENT OF INTERVIEW BETWEEN MESSRS. BAKER AND RENNALLS

It has always been my practice to respect the advice given me by seniors, so after our interview, I decided to give careful thought once again to its main points and so make sure that I had understood all that had been said. As I promised you at the time, I had every intention of putting your advice to the best effect.

It was not, therefore, until I had sat down quietly in my home yesterday evening to consider the interview objectively that its main purport became clear. Only then did the full enormity of what you said dawn on me. The more I thought about it, the more convinced I was that I had hit upon the real truth—and the more furious I became. With a facility in the English language which I—a poor Barracanian— cannot hope to match, you had the audacity to insult me (and through me every Barracanian worth his salt) by claiming that our knowledge of modern living is only a paltry fifty years old whilst yours goes back 200–300 years. As if your materialistic commercial environment could possibly be compared with the spiritual values of our culture. I'll have you know that if much of what I saw in London is representative of your most boasted culture, I hope fervently that it will never come to Barracania. By what right do you have the effrontery to condescend to us? At heart, all you Europeans think us barbarians, or, as you say amongst yourselves we are "just down from the trees."

Far into the night I discussed this matter with my father, and he is as disgusted as I. He agrees with me that any company whose senior staff think as you do is no place for any Barracanian proud of his culture and race—so much for all the company "clap-trap" and specious propaganda about regionalisation and Barracania for the Barracanians.

I feel ashamed and betrayed. Please accept this letter as my resignation which I wish to become effective immediately.

c.c. Production Manager
     Managing Director

Questions

1. What were John Baker's reasons for holding this final meeting with Matthew Rennalls?
2. What do you think of Rennalls' behavior during the meeting?
3. Analyze Rennalls' behavior following the meeting.
4. What role did "racial consciousness" play in this situation?
5. Can you foresee any short-term or long-term repercussions that are likely to grow out of this incident?

CASE 6: SAY IT ISN'T SO!*

For fifty years, the major business of the A. O. Smith Corporation has been manufacturing automobile frames—primarily for General Motors' cars. As far back as the 1930s, management recognized the risk associated with high dependency on one customer and one product line and, hence, diversified into products ranging from water heaters to computer programs for inventory control. In four decades, the proportion of A. O. Smith's sales accounted for by automobile frames declined from 90 percent to 40 percent. Unfortunately, management discovered that even 40 percent was far too large: GM notified Smith in 1981 that it would have no need for frames after 1983.

GM's decision was the result of decades of experimentation with unitized construction—the process of manufacturing a car by integrating its structural parts into the body itself, thereby eliminating the need for a separate frame. Unitized construction permits greater use of robots on the production line—and, hence, lower costs—and enhances the customer's perception of driving a more "solid" automobile. Both of these advantages are likely to help U.S. automakers compete more effectively with the Japanese in such areas as cost and quality.

A. O. Smith's management fought the trend toward unitized construction for years. When GM introduced its X cars with unitized bodies in 1979, Smith spent $300,000 to demonstrate how the Chevrolet Citation could weigh less and ride more smoothly if it were built with a separate frame. As Smith's president put it: "We became zealots for frames."

Automobile industry observers, however, believe that Smith's management failed to discern the trends foretelling the eventual demise of frame construction. One expert concluded that "A. O. Smith took its bread-and-butter product for granted too long and did not read the signals right that were coming from Detroit."

---

*Based on information contained in "A. O. Smith: 'Safe' Diversification That Is Endangering Profits," *Business Week*, 21 September 1981, pp. 82–83; and *Standard & Poor's Corporation Records* (New York: Standard & Poor's Corporation, Publishers).

The announcement from GM could hardly have come at a worse time for Smith. Among other factors, poor economic conditions and foreign currency devaluations caused Smith to incur a loss of $16.8 million on sales of $694 million in 1982, compared with a 1981 profit of $5.4 million on sales of $784 million.

Smith's management believes that its best strategy at this time is to accelerate its internal diversification program by continuing to build on the product lines with which management is already familiar. Negative past experiences with external acquisitions have made management averse to growth through the purchase of other firms.

In early 1983, Smith received some strategic breathing room. GM notified Smith's management that it would extend until mid-1986 its contract to purchase frames for use in intermediate- and full-size car models.

Questions

1. Analyze A. O. Smith's environmental scanning activities.
2. How might the use of *dialectical analysis* have helped prevent the present situation from occurring?
3. What should the A. O. Smith Corporation do now?

CASE 7: "UNBUNDLING" AT WORLD DATA PROCESSING*

World Data Processing Company is a giant of the computer field. One of the first to become involved with electronic digital computers, its sales are now in the billions per year. Although its products are not technically superior to its competitors, the company has bettered the others by virtue of its aggressive marketing and servicing. Whereas its largest competitor hired engineers and trained them as salesmen, WDP looked for sales types regardless of education and gave them strong technical support. Until four years ago, WDP marketed through salespeople and systems engineers located all over the country. A salesperson and a systems engineer worked together as a team with the salesperson assigned total customer responsibility while the systems engineer provided technical expertise. The entire marketing program of preproposal studies, proposals, sales, installation, and service was conducted as a sales and systems

*From Ross A. Webber, *Management Pragmatics: Cases and Readings on Basic Elements of Managing Organizations* (Homewood, Ill.: Richard D. Irwin, 1979), pp. 230–32.© Richard D. Irwin, Inc., 1979. All rights reserved.

team effort. In many cases the team worked so closely that roles overlapped.

The systems engineer, therefore, played a key role in WDP's marketing strategy. Continued technical support after sale was a central selling feature because computers require substantial debugging and training of user personnel after delivery. The owner just can't plug it in and expect it to work on Monday morning (although many of them thought so when they first signed the sales contract). In many large accounts, this support required permanent assignment of WDP systems engineers to a customer computer center. All of this service was provided free. When WDP sold or rented a computer, a person went along with it at no extra charge.

In January four years ago, the attorney general of the United States filed an antitrust suit against WDP designed to reduce its primacy in the computer field. The company immediately announced the formation of a special study committee composed of top executives "to investigate the changing data processing market." Data processing had expanded in size and complexity over the years. In addition to equipment manufacturers, the industry now included leasing companies, software houses selling programs, service bureaus, consulting firms, and data processing schools. The results of the study were to be published in six months.

Nothing more was heard about the government suit, the company's response, or the committee's deliberations until June when an announcement summoned all field personnel to their regional offices around the country for a mandatory two-day meeting. It was announced by an executive from the headquarters that marketing and service would be separated or "unbundled." The salesperson would handle all sales but was now to sell equipment and services separately. The systems engineer would report to a different superior and would charge for services at a rate that combined time and task complexity. All other services would also have a price tag including education, manuals, books, and programs.

The new policy would be in full effect immediately along with a 3 percent across-the-board reduction in rental prices. This reduction was described as being the cost of services formerly provided free. Prices to purchase equipment were unchanged. Finally at the end of the meeting, the executive stated that failure to strictly adhere to the policy would be grounds for dismissal.

The company's voluntary policy change was reputedly to appease the federal government and discourage further intervention and prosecution. Whatever it was, the announcement was a complete shock to employees, customers, and competitors. Anger and confusion were rampant for a long time. The systems engineers felt that their status was undetermined because they were no longer part of a professional sales team in this marketing-oriented organization. Indeed, they became a little uneasy because their activity was entirely dependent on the sales of a salesperson who might be more interested in selling hardware than services. Whereas sitting in the office rapping with fellow engineers might have been fun sometimes in the past, after the policy change it engendered fear that they had nothing to do and were expendable. In general, salespeople found it difficult to sell something that they formerly had given away free. The close relations between salespeople and engineers were severed. And field management was often confused about what specifically was included under the new sales and rental contracts.

The difficulties in the policy change were reflected in a series of modifications in the compensation plan for salespeople and systems engineers. In the first year after the announcement, salespeople were paid 50 percent salary and 50 percent commission based on sales of both equipment and services. The systems engineers were paid 80 percent salary and 20 percent commission based on exceeding an office services quota. Few salespeople made their goals that year, and fewer engineers received any bonus. Complaints among both groups increased.

The next year, WDP put systems engineers on straight salary. The salespeople's salary percentage was raised to 60 percent and commissions were based only on selling equipment. An extra bonus could still be made for selling services however.

In the third year after the change, salespeoples' salary percentage was further increased to 90 percent with 10 percent commission based solely on equipment sales. There was no bonus for service sales. As the years have passed, however, local management has become more and more lenient in its interpretation of company policy regarding free technical service to customers.

Since WDP was the dominant computer company, management assumed that their competitors would also separate sales and services. Some did so but others did not. Management also assumed that customers would spend on services approximately the amount by which rental charges were reduced. This prediction was in error. Small companies spent much more because they were so dependent on WDP, but the larger customers decided to develop their own service capability by hiring their own engineers and computer specialists. Their use of WDP systems engineers dropped greatly and total sales were less than predicted.

Questions

1. What was the WDP Company's strategic response to the government antitrust action? What was the objective in this response? Was it achieved?

2. Why was the company's former strategy superior to the separated sales of equipment and services?

3. Why did the company fail to achieve its sales goals in the two years after the change?

4. Should the field managers, salespeople, and engineers have been consulted by corporation executives in formulating the new policy? What might they have told the executives? How should the company have developed and announced the policy change?

CASE 8: THE VESSEL APPAREL SHOP*

The Vessel Apparel Shop is a sole-proprietorship owned and operated by Edwin and Susan Stockley. Located in the small rural farming community of Adairville, Kentucky, the Apparel Shop carries a line of sports clothes and accessories for men and women. Since taking over Vessel nine months ago, the Stockleys have more than doubled average weekly sales on their product line for men and women. The store currently stocks approximately $15,000 in inventory of 30 well-known brands and labels. The Stockleys, who are both in their mid-thirties and still attending college, employ one part-time sales clerk to help with customer service.

The Stockleys paid $16,000 for the store, which included $6,000 of merchandise inventory, and agreed to pay off the principal over ten years in annual lump sum payments of $1,600. They presently rent the building from the previous owner for $100 per month.

Ed Stockley has no prior experience in retailing but is experienced as a realtor and manufacturer's sales representative. Ed currently holds several part-time positions in Adairville, including emergency medical technician and police court justice of the peace. Both he and his wife are finishing up their undergraduate degrees in business administration at Western Kentucky University (located 55 miles to the northeast in Bowling Green). Sue Stockley has had prior retailing experience as a buyer for the Top Dollar General Store chain. She also worked for a county attorney's office. The Stockleys have no children.

Ed Stockley feels that the overall track record of the store over its 13 years of previous ownership was inconsistent. "I think the store had some good years and some bad years. Still, when I looked into the business before purchasing it, I felt strongly that it could be doing better than it was. From talking with the previous owner, there were some unprofitable years, but I have no idea when they were. One of the problems with the previous owners is that they would get into and out of different lines, such as children's clothes, and lose money."

Operational responsibilities at Vessel are divided up fairly equally between Ed and his wife. Sue takes care of the merchandising activities, including buying, inventory control, and displays. Ed concentrates more on the financial end of the business, such as credit and bill-paying. Both the Stockleys wait on customers and carry out maintenance duties on the physical facilities. Ed states that "The day-to-day management of the store is played by ear. We certainly don't fight over who's boss."

In discussing his goals for the Vessel Apparel Shop, Ed Stockley comments that "As far as the major goals my wife and I have discussed for the store, two broad alternatives are seen: expanding by setting up a

---

*This case was developed by Philip M. Van Auken (Baylor University), William W. McCartney (Central Florida University), and Harold D. Fletcher (Western Kentucky University). An expanded version of the case is available through the Intercollegiate Case Clearing House, Soldiers Field, Boston, Mass. 02163.

chain of clothing stores in the Western Kentucky area, or selling out, whenever the time is right. The real problem with either goal is finding someone either to help us expand or to buy us out. Finding motivated, capable people isn't easy."

Ed plans to continue with running Vessel Apparel upon his graduation from college, but he doesn't know what he wants to be doing over the long run. "I know I want to continue as the town's medical technician and that I want to buy a new house here in Adairville. However, I haven't really decided on a long-run goal, except that we know we won't stay with just one store for any period of time. We will either sell out or start a chain. We really haven't been in business long enough to finalize our long-range plans. I do know that once I get clear of school and my term as judge runs out in four months, I'll have a lot more time for planning."

The Stockleys have not tried to formulate an overall competitive strategy. Sue explains, "We don't have any competition—we're the only clothing store in town." Beyond their long-range plan to expand or sell out, they have not worked up any operational goals or policies. "Right now we pretty much try to make it from day to day. We really don't know where we stand after just eight months of operation. We are definitely open to suggestions from knowledgeable outsiders on where to go with the business."

Sue Stockley goes to trade shows in Louisville and Lexington, Kentucky, as well as Nashville, Tennessee, where she purchases the Vessel Shop's line of sportswear for men and women. She shops for ages 13 and up, maintaining a slightly larger inventory for women than for men. Even with its limited inventory, Vessel Apparel carries a fairly full line of sizes and age group styles. According to Sue, "We try to cater to mainstream fashions, but definitely not youth-oriented fads. Adairville is a rural farming community, and people are fairly conservative. We do carry quite a wide selection of inventory, even though carrying enough sizes is difficult. We take care of most customers with no problems, though."

Besides sportswear, Vessel handles a few jewelry and gift items, as well as belts, wallets, and a few linens. "We don't carry watches, because they are too expensive to handle, and besides, the mark-up on watches isn't very good."

Under its previous management, Vessel catered largely to the fashion needs of older women. The Stockleys decided to reverse this trend and instead to emphasize more youthful fashions. According to Ed, "We want to keep our older trade but at the same time pick up more younger people."

Ed Stockley feels his store has a marketing problem with older men. "One of the problems we have with older men is that they often don't realize that we carry what they're looking for. The younger trade know us better, and they're profitable. They'll come in and pay as much money for a pair of fancy jeans as they will for dress slacks."

In the area of generating a marketing information system, the Stockleys have found lack of time to be a real problem. "Sue and I have talked about doing some sort of a marketing survey, but we really haven't had the time." The Stockleys try to talk informally with customers in order to get a better idea of their needs, and a list of customers purchasing gift items in the past has been kept. "We try to make sure that we know the names of better customers, but there are plenty of $5 and $10 customers whose names we never have learned."

The Stockleys are not sure what group of customers constitutes their most profitable market, but they have observed quite an increase lately in the patronage of teenagers. Ed estimates that "50 to 60 percent of the people who come in usually buy something, but I'm not sure what our average sale per customer really is. We probably get from 15 to 20 people in a day."

In promoting Vessel Apparel, the Stockleys have relied primarily on word-of-mouth local advertising. The store has experimented with advertising in a Russellville, Kentucky, newspaper and over that town's youth-oriented radio station, but the Stockleys felt the results were lackluster. "Word of mouth is our best approach to advertising. The other, more costly, means just don't appear to be that effective in a small town like this."

Since taking over the store nine months ago, the Stockleys have seen sales increase at a fairly steady rate. The apparel shop's sales began at a level of $500 per week and since that time have reached as high as $1,200 weekly. The unfortunate lack of financial records for previous years of operation has made it all but impossible for the Stockleys to identify the store's sales trends and seasonal fluctuations. Despite sketchy information about Vessel's financial performance, however, Ed Stockley perceives the store to be in satisfactory financial shape. Humorously he explains, "I pretty well leave it to my accountant to tell me if we're about to have any financial troubles. I've done business with that lady for about 13 years and have come to trust her advice and thinking. As long as she accepts my check for her services, I figure the business must be okay. When she refuses to take my check, then I'll know the business is in trouble!"

Commenting further on sales performance, Stockley notes that sales peaked in December, dropped sharply in January, and then resumed growth in February. "We haven't had any week less than $500, however. This appears to be our break-even point as nearly as I can figure." Stockley feels confident that sales can continue to grow. "I think the growth is there if we can just find a way to tap into it." He projects that the store's weekly sales potential is at least $2,000 to $3,000.

Financial statements for Vessel Apparel have been drawn up only since the Stockleys assumed management. Ed Stockley explains that he has been too busy with running the business thus far to study his accountant's reports. "Once things settle down, I expect to review financial statements about every six months."

Vessel Apparel has no outstanding receivables and has been granted a credit line of $3,000 by the local bank. "Credit is no problem for us. We really can get all we want from our banker. The problem is knowing if we can pay it back. Right now, we're not sure enough of our cash flow situation to feel very confident about borrowing. This is the biggest financial matter worrying me now." Stockley feels occasional 60-day notes from the bank are sufficient for handling financial needs in the foreseeable future.

Stockley refers to inventory financing as his number one operational problem and managerial headache. He points to cash flow dilemmas caused by having to purchase large inventories of merchandise often far in advance of sales. Inventory ordered at trade shows is shipped by the 25th of the month specified by the Stockleys, with payment due by the 25th of the following month. If payment is made by the 10th of the following month, a discount of 8 percent accrues on all ladies' fashions. No such discounts are available on merchandise for men.

Stockley elaborates on his inventory purchasing problem: "Our inventory payment schedule and resulting cash flow are pretty much hit and miss. With as little sales as we have starting up the business, we haven't been able thus far to come up with a smooth inventory payment system. We try to keep track of when ordered merchandise is about to arrive and hope that there will be enough cash on hand to handle it."

Stockley is also troubled by the absence of a purchasing and inventory budget. "It worries me that we don't have a purchasing or inventory budget, but in just eight months we haven't been able to figure out things well enough to lay out a budget. As a result, cash flow is a real problem, particularly in financing the inventory. I would like to be able to know how much we're going to pay for and sell each month."

Ed estimates that inventory is purchased approximately four times a year for women and three times annually for men. Fashions for each group are purchased two seasons ahead, something Stockley describes as "a very difficult thing to do because of the long lead time involved."

"Getting back to the cash flow thing, I'd have to say that our number one problem is having to pay for merchandise before we have a chance to see it. Times arise when a lot of ordered merchandise comes in, but sales are slow. Coordinating the two has eluded us at times. You think that everything has come in but then find a large shipment arriving that you had forgotten about. We haven't been able to plan our purchases well. It's sort of like using a credit card; you don't realize all you spend until you get the bill at the end of the month."

The Stockleys have not yet prepared any financial plans or cash flow statements in their management of Vessel Apparel. They are in the process of gathering sales information for the past nine months, however, which they hope to use in plotting sales trends.

Ed Stockley offers these comments on his future financial plans for Vessel: "We have talked about opening up a second clothing store in Adairville by transferring our men's apparel to a separate retail establishment. The banker seems to be cooperative about this. We might even want to sell out, although I don't know that we could find someone to pay what we'd want for the store."

Questions

1. To what extent have the Stockleys actively planned for Vessel's operations over the past nine months? What planning deficiencies are evident?
2. In what specific areas is more planning warranted by the Stockleys? What aspects of their personal lives require additional planning?
3. What are the most important planning issues for Vessel in the short run? the long run?
4. What information would be most useful to the Stockleys in future planning?
5. What does the case illustrate about the realities of managerial planning?

CASE 9: ABUSE OF SAFETY RULES*

William Jones, an employee of a large hospital, was observed by a security guard smoking in a non-smoking area of the hospital while on his way to the exit. The guard asked him to refrain from smoking. Mr. Jones ignored the guard's request and continued walking toward the exit. When the guard confronted Mr. Jones, he responded with a contemptuous and very obscene remark against the guard, continued on his way, and left the hospital.

The guard reported this incident to the security chief who, in turn, reported it to the employee's supervisor. Mr. Jones was suspended without pay for one day for smoking in a restricted area, and for his obscene and abusive remarks to the guard.

Questions

1. Do you think the hospital administration acted properly in suspending Mr. Jones? Why? Why not?
2. What additional information would be useful to be quite sure your judgment is correct?
3. Under what conditions will the suspension be regarded as fair by other employees who know Mr. Jones?
4. To what extent should the supervisor be allowed to use his or her judgment in resolving a case of this type?

*Case prepared by Professor Kenneth A. Kovach of George Mason University.

CASE 10: DELTA CORPORATION*

Bill Joiner studied carefully the draft of performance objectives he had just received in the mail from one of his new sales representatives, Ralph Stone. He pondered what steps he should take next and wondered just what approach he should take in reviewing the objectives with Stone.

Bill Joiner was the Florida District Sales Manager for Delta Corporation, a national distributor of construction tools and equipment. Joiner's primary responsibility was the supervision of a seven man field sales force covering the state of Florida.

Stone had just joined Delta two months earlier. This would therefore be the first time that Joiner would go through the cycle of the MBO program with him. At Delta, subordinates drafted new objectives and reviewed them with their superiors every six months.

Bill remembered that the company had stressed the importance of mutual understanding and agreement between subordinate and superior as the keystone of the MBO program. He wondered what action he should take in response to Ralph Stone's first attempt at drafting objectives (see Exhibit 1).

Name: Ralph Stone	**Department:** Fla. District Sales
Title: Field Sales Rep.	**Supervisor:** Wm. Joiner

Objectives	Target Date for Completion
1. Significantly increase market share of the Delta product line in my territory	continuing
2. Develop additional contacts within my present customers' organizations as well as prospecting for new business with firms we do not now service	daily
3. Strengthen my knowledge of the Delta product line	(as soon as possible)
4. Achieve a total sales volume of $326,000 for all products this quarter	June 30
5. Improve customer relations	continuing
6. Develop my management potential by completing at least one evening course this year at Florida Atlantic University	December 31

EXHIBIT 1 Delta Corporation: Management by objectives worksheet

---

*Reprinted from *Contemporary Issues in Human Resources Management* by Fred E. Schuster, published by Reston Publishing Company, Inc., 1980.

Questions

1. How did Ralph Stone set his objectives?
2. Are there any problems with the approach he used?
3. Analyze each of the goals Ralph has set.

CASE 11: THE CONSULTING CLIENT'S COMPLAINT*

You are regional manager of an international management consulting company. You have a staff of six consultants reporting to you, each of whom enjoys a considerable amount of autonomy with clients in the field.

Yesterday you received a complaint from one of your major clients to the effect that the consultant whom you assigned to work on the contract with them was not doing his job effectively. They were not very explicit as to the nature of the problem, but it was clear that they were dissatisfied and that something would have to be done if you were to restore the client's faith in your company.

The consultant assigned to work on that contract has been with the company for six years. He is a systems analyst and is one of the best in that profession. For the first four or five years, his performance was superb, and he was a model for the other more junior consultants. However, recently he has seemed to have a "chip on his shoulder," and his previous identification with the company and its objectives has been replaced with indifference. His negative attitude has been noticed by other consultants, as well as by clients. This is not the first such complaint that you have had from a client this year about his performance. A previous client even reported to you that the consultant reported to work several times obviously suffering from a hangover and that he had been seen around town in the company of "fast" women.

It is important to get to the root of this problem quickly if that client is to be retained. The consultant obviously has the skill necessary to work with the clients effectively. If only he were willing to use it!

Questions

1. State the problem and outline at least three possible alternatives.
2. In what ways will "values" enter into the manager's decision in this situation?

---

*Taken from Victor H. Vroom and Arthur G. Jago, "Decision Making as a Social Process: Normative and Descriptive Models of Leader Behavior," *Decision Sciences* 5 (December 1974): 168.

3. To what extent should this manager bring his subordinate (or subordinates) into the decision-making process?
4. What are likely to be the major difficulties in reaching a totally rational decision in this case?

CASE 12: NEW BUSINESS APPLICATIONS*

James Lahiff was hired recently to head up the computer-based information systems area for a large consumer goods manufacturer. One of his first tasks was to examine the kinds of business applications for which the computer was currently being used. After five weeks of careful investigation, he concluded that most of the computer's use was for routine data processing applications. Computer users in the various departments seemed satisfied with the applications and felt Lahiff's department was doing a good job servicing them.

Lahiff was pleased at the perceptions of the computer area that he encountered, but he felt the company ought to be doing more in the area of decision-support-oriented applications. Top management supported his belief, but he knew that any initiative in this direction was going to have to come from him. The potential users in the firm did not seem to know much about this kind of business application.

Questions

1. How should Lahiff go about his task of increasing the decision-support applications in the firm?
2. What difficulties is he likely to encounter in this process? How should he deal with these difficulties?

CASE 13: LIQUID ASSETS COMPANY†

You are the manager of Liquid Assets. Your company produces two grades of solvent, regular and premium. When sold at retail, each barrel of premium-grade solvent will return a net profit of $12, while each barrel of regular-grade solvent will return a $4 profit. The two grades are produced by heating the basic chemical in a pressure tank and then heat-

---

*From Hugh J. Watson and Archie B. Carroll, *Computers for Business: A Managerial Emphasis*, rev. ed. (Plano, Tex.: Business Publications, 1980), p. 243. © Business Publications, Inc., 1976 and 1980. All rights reserved.

†Case prepared by Gerald Perselay of Winthrop College.

ing the fluid in an open tank. Each barrel of premium requires four hours under pressure and ten hours in the open tank, while each barrel of regular requires two hours in the pressure tank and two hours in the open tank. Because of budget constraints (and a cheap management), only forty hours of pressure-tank time and seventy hours of open-tank time are available during the coming week.

Question

1. As the person responsible for production, you must decide which combination of barrels of premium- and regular-grade solvent will return the maximum net profit to the Liquid Assets Company. Naturally, your decision about the best (or optimal) mix of barrels of premium and of regular must be made with the limitations imposed by the available number of hours in each of the tanks. Solve this problem using the graphic method of linear programming.

CASE 14: SOLAR-HEATING EXPANSION*

A company that builds home heating systems is trying to decide whether it should expand its old building or build a new plant which will produce home solar-heating systems. If the old building is expanded at a cost of $2 million, it is estimated that the present value of resulting operating profits (without allowing for increased costs) will be $4 million.

Management is somewhat uncertain about how successful the solar-heating system will be in terms of sales. A major promotion effort will be undertaken, and the marketing research department predicts there is a 0.3 chance of a significant demand for the solar systems and a 0.7 chance of no significant change in the demand for the systems. If a new plant is built for the manufacturing of solar systems, the cost will be $15 million. The estimated present value of resulting operating profits (without allowing for increased costs) is $20 million if there is a significant demand and $16 million if there is no significant change in the demand for the systems.

Questions

1. Draw a decision tree for this problem.
2. What decision should the company make, and what is the expected value?

---

*Case prepared by Professor Kris K. Moore of Baylor University.

CASE 15: HOUSTON WIRE ROPE COMPANY

As president and major stockholder of the Houston Wire Rope Company, a relatively young organization, Paul H. Rogers was attempting to develop an organizational arrangement and operating methods which would maintain and improve the efficiency and profitability of the business.

Background of the Company

In 1951, Mr. Rogers, then a sales representative for a major producer of wire rope, conceived the idea of a business which would specialize in the purchase and resale of used wire rope. Acting upon the idea, he established his business in Houston, Texas, purchasing used wire rope from the oil fields and selling it to mining, logging, and marine companies. In addition to purchasing and selling, some processing of the used rope was required. This involved rewinding on to new reels, inspection and grading of the rope, cutting out seriously defective pieces, and lubrication. The company quickly gained market acceptance and increased its sales volume each year.

The company later added new wire rope imported from Holland, Belgium, Germany, and Japan to supplement its lines of used rope. Sales were divided roughly equally between used and new rope. Approximately 50 percent of used rope sales were made to the marine industry (including substantial sales to large dredging companies), 30 percent to the logging industry, and 20 percent to the mining industry. Of the imported new rope sales, about 60 percent went to industrial customers, 25 percent to marine customers, and 15 percent to oil producers.

Sales were made to a nationwide market and even to a few accounts in Canada. Branch warehouses had also been established in Jeanerette, Louisiana; Odessa, Texas; and Norman, Oklahoma. Although the major purpose of the branches was to purchase used rope from the oil industry in their respective areas, they also made sales in the same areas.

Home Office Personnel and Organization

Both Mr. Rogers, the president, and the sales manager maintained offices at the Houston headquarters of the company. Their activities were devoted to the company as a whole. In addition, the following positions comprised what might be thought of as the Houston branch:

- 1 branch manager and inside salesperson
- 1 outside salesperson
- 1 bookkeeper and secretary
- 2 warehouse employees
- 1 truck driver

All employees had a close personal relationship with Mr. Rogers, who had hired each of them. The employee who had been with the company almost from its beginning was designated as manager of the Houston branch. His major responsibility was that of maintaining customer contacts and selling by telephone, although he did exercise some supervision over the warehouse employees and truck driver. The outside salesperson reported both to the sales manager and to Mr. Rogers. The bookkeeper-secretary, whose work also applied to the entire company, was personally responsible to Mr. Rogers, although the sales manager directed some of her activities.

Position of Sales Manager

Two years earlier, Mr. Rogers had employed as sales manager a person with extensive experience in the sale of wire rope. The sales manager had assumed a variety of sales and administrative activities. He had engaged in direct selling, worked out adjustments with dissatisfied customers, participated in the purchase of new imported wire rope, surveyed prospective locations for new branches, and exercised some supervision over branch managers.

There was some tendency for overlapping in the duties of Mr. Rogers and the sales manager. There had been no careful division of responsibilities between the positions. They both had contacts with the same customers and the same employees of the company. Their trips to branch offices were typically made at different times.

One effect of the somewhat nebulous division of responsibilities between these two top positions was a certain amount of confusion and uncertainty in the minds of other employees. All employees, including those in branch offices, had enjoyed a warm personal relationship and friendship with Mr. Rogers. His complete candor, personal interest, and generosity in the past had developed a strong sense of personal loyalty to him. It required time for them to accept and understand the new position of sales manager and its relationship to them. For example, branch managers would not hesitate to check back with Mr. Rogers concerning some policy or instruction they had received from the sales manager.

Branch Office Organization

Each of the three branch offices (Jeanerette, Odessa, and Norman) was expected to contain a total of three employees. The branch manager was directly responsible for overall supervision of the branch. In addition, he purchased used wire rope and made sales calls in his area. Purchasers of wire rope tended to be few in number and to purchase in large quantities. Considerable time was required, however, to cultivate customer goodwill and to seek out new customers. The firm was interested in developing new markets and discovering new uses for wire rope.

Backing up the office manager were a warehouse employee and a truck driver. As noted above, some processing of newly purchased used rope was required in addition to transporting and storing it. Of course, some stock of new rope was also maintained in branch warehouses as required by customer demand in each area.

Relationships between Home Office and Branch Offices

One of the policies Mr. Rogers attempted to follow closely in dealing with branch managers was that of decentralization and delegation of authority. As he visualized it, each branch manager should operate like an independent businessperson, making the decisions pertinent to the business in his or her own area. In fact, Mr. Rogers took considerable pride in the development of branch managers in his organization.

Each of the branch managers had started with inadequate experience but had proceeded to grow in his or her managerial position. For example, the manager of the Jeanerette branch had previously worked as a warehouse and office employee with a wire rope company but lacked selling experience prior to joining the Houston Wire Rope Company. He had assumed the responsibility placed upon him and developed an outstanding business record in his branch. The manager of the Odessa branch had nonselling experience as a refinery worker before joining the Houston Wire Rope Company. The Odessa branch had been successful, although it was conceded that the manager's selling abilities needed further development. The manager of the Norman branch had some previous experience as a salesperson of office equipment and insurance, although she had no prior contact with the wire rope business. The branch had not been established a sufficient length of time to permit a full evaluation of her efforts, but she seemed to be making good. Each of these managers had some training in selling and in company operations—from three to six months—before being placed in charge of a branch.

Each branch manager was made responsible for an account in a local bank and paid all bills locally. The sum of $1,000 was deposited in the account initially, and the amount fluctuated from time to time with the needs of the branch. When the cash balance was low and funds were needed, the branch manager requested additional funds from the home office, usually by telephone. Although a shortage of working capital in the business was partially responsible for this arrangement, it also provided a close control over most financial commitments by branch offices. The branch manager, for example, would often request funds to raise the bank balance sufficiently to permit a particular purchase of wire rope. Individual purchases were typically for amounts less than $300.

Personal visits were made to branch offices by either Mr. Rogers or the sales manager on the average of once a month. These visits were used to discuss branch problems, review sales contacts, and make sales calls with the branch manager.

Because of the diversity in their background and experience, the branch managers differed in the progress they had made in developing a strong branch organization. The Odessa manager had experienced some difficulty in fully delegating authority and responsibility to his subordinates. He tended to supervise those working for him closely and to be exacting in his demands upon them. At the same time, he had indicated a desire for greater guidance and help from the home office.

Formal Planning and Control

The company had never used a budget for overall operations or for activities of branch offices. As a result, there were no predetermined expense or sales standards that a branch manager was expected to achieve. The operating results of each branch were shown separately and thus provided a summary report of branch operations.

Similarly, the company had not yet grown to the point that written policies had been developed. For example, major personnel decisions were made through agreement between the branch manager and Mr. Rogers on the basis of the individual circumstances. One employee of a branch office who was ill for several weeks was continued on the payroll for an extended period. No decision had ever been made concerning overall company policy in such cases.

The Houston Wire Rope Company had expanded rapidly and gave every indication of continuing its expansion. Several possible expansion moves had been under consideration for some time. Enthusiasm for various of these possibilities had a tendency to rise and fall with changes in competition, fluctuation of sales to existing customers, progress of existing branches, and development of new information concerning proposed locations. It was possible that a decision might be made rather suddenly concerning establishment of a new branch. There was no plan which specified expectations concerning additional branches for the following six months, one year, or five years. As new branch offices were opened, some managers would no doubt be shifted into new locations. While this provided an opportunity for advancement, it also introduced some uncertainty and insecurity into their thinking.

Organization Planning

Mr. Rogers realized the importance of loyal, enthusiastic personnel and the value of present employees to the company. As the business continued to expand, however, it would be desirable and necessary to adapt the company's organization and operating methods to the changing needs of the business. The question was whether the most desirable organizational arrangements and procedures, considering the size and status of the business, had yet been developed.

Questions

1. Evaluate the position of the sales manager and his placement in the organization structure. Can Mr. Rogers make this position any more effective? If so, how?

2. What weaknesses are apparent in the home office organization?
3. What is Mr. Rogers' organizational philosophy in dealing with branch offices? Does he operate consistently with this philosophy?
4. What connection is there between planning and control on the one hand and organizational arrangements on the other hand?

CASE 16: THE PRICE OF AMBITION*

Ted Michod graduated from the Newark College of Engineering as an electrical engineer and went to work for a small but growing computer manufacturing firm in Philadelphia which employed about 10,000 people. His first position with the company was that of a junior engineer in the data processing systems division. He worked with twenty other junior engineers designing primary computer circuits and electro-mechanical linkages. Basically, Michod's job consisted of fitting various electrical and mechanical components into a package which would perform logical and arithmetic operations with the greatest reliability for the least cost. Most of the time he worked out designs on paper, although, on occasion, Ted actually tried his ideas out in the lab.

After two years, Ted received a promotion which, along with an increase in pay and status, provided him with an opportunity to expand greatly his knowledge of the industry. As an associate engineer in the programming systems division, he served as a liaison between his old design group and a systems engineering team which was responsible for the creation of new programming languages. Ted's duties were to make sure that the programming languages being developed were consistent with design capabilities which were being incorporated into new computer systems by his old work group. Thus, he was able to relate his previous experience with hardware (circuits) to the creation and design of software (program languages) and round out his technical education.

After a year in his new position, Ted began to realize that while he was mastering the technical end of the computer business, he was unprepared for the managerial responsibilities it entailed. Furthermore, it seemed to him that a graduate degree in business administration would improve greatly his chance for promotion in the future. After giving the problem much thought, Ted decided to take a two-year educational leave of absence to work on an MBA degree. His decision was based on the fact that in addition to his need for managerial development, his interests had gradually shifted from the technical to the administrative aspects of the industry.

Ted Michod graduated from the local university, finishing in the top twenty percent of his MBA class. Within two weeks of graduation he was married, and he decided to return to work with his old company.

*Case prepared by Professor Robert A. Ullrich of Vanderbilt University.

This time, at his request, he was assigned to the midwestern marketing regional office in Chicago as a customer engineer. Ted felt that experience in the field of customer relations together with his previous technical work would increase greatly his worth to the firm and thus his chances for success. For this reason, both Ted and his bride viewed their move to the Chicago office as a "step in the right direction."

Once settled in Chicago, Ted reported to the customer engineering manager, John Lucas. Mr. Lucas assigned Michod to the customer education section as an instructor. The section's purpose was to train customer employees in the installation and use of computer systems. Since this was not considered a full-time assignment, Ted was given additional duties as the supervisor of a program modification team. This second job consisted of giving technical assistance and direction to a group, consisting of four programmer trainees, which was modifying existing computer programs written by the manufacturers for the customers to keep them consistent with improved methodology and technology. Both positions required that he report directly to Mr. Lucas. On the average, Ted taught about thirty hours a week and devoted fifteen hours to his second job.

As a result of the group's work modifying a set of market forecasting programs, Ted hit upon the idea of using a form of the Markov Process to predict growth in sales of new industrial products. [The Markov Process is a statistical approach which basically views life as a series of probabilities that an event will (or will not) occur given that it has (or has not) taken place in the past.] Ted had learned about this technique in his MBA program. He studied the problem evenings at home and in mid-October submitted his idea to Lucas in the form of a well researched and documented proposal. Lucas seemed interested in the project but told Ted it would have to be shelved until the necessary manpower and finances became available.

About two months later, however, Ted's program modification team completed its assigned projects and the group was disbanded. When he reported to Lucas to be reassigned, Michod was instructed to see Wayne Smith, the head of the computer installation department. Smith, like Lucas, was the head of a staff department. Smith and Lucas enjoyed equal rank within the firm and reported to the same district manager.

Smith outlined Ted's next assignment as follows. Ted would supervise two junior systems engineers in the installation of small computers and would have complete responsibility for each installation project. The job, at first, would require about twenty hours a week of his time. In addition Ted would continue to serve in his present capacity of instructor until the middle of the year. At this time, an additional instructor would be transferred to the midwestern region and Ted would be relieved of his teaching responsibilities to devote his entire efforts to the installation department. Until then, however, he would report to Smith concerning installation problems and to Lucas for matters involving the education program.

The following day, Ted received a note from Lucas to see him as soon as possible. Upon entering Lucas' office, Ted found himself engaged in the following conversation.

Ted: You wanted to see me, Mr. Lucas?

Lucas: Yes, Ted. Sit down. You know, I liked the proposal you submitted for forecasting with Markov Processes. I'd like you to work up some programs and make it operational. Do you think you could wrap up the job in two months?

Ted: Well, I could if I had the time, but as you know I'm still working as an instructor and I've just taken over an installation team for Wayne Smith.

Lucas: Yes, I know about that. You'll have some free time on Wayne's project though. I don't see why you won't be able to fit my project around your other work. It won't take long, will it?

Ted: I just don't know. I can make a wild guess at 120 working hours. I don't think I'll have the time to tackle it.

Lucas: Sure you will, Ted. Smith's project won't take all your time. Besides, 120 hours isn't very much. Why, it's not even two weeks' work.

After leaving Mr. Lucas' office, Ted stopped in to see Wayne Smith.

Ted: Hi. I was just wondering when I should start working for you.

Smith: Today! Now! (Jokingly.)

Ted: Well, what I mean is will it be full time at first or will I have some time on my hands?

Smith: No. It should be a full twenty hours a week right from the start. Why did you ask? Any special reason?

Michod told Smith about his conversation with Lucas and explained that he didn't think he would be able to handle all three projects. Wayne Smith agreed but felt that there had been some misunderstanding. He told Ted that he would talk to Lucas that afternoon and that Ted should let the matter ride until it had been looked into further.

Ted: Good. I hope this gets cleared up soon.

Smith: Don't worry, Ted, we just have our wires crossed. Stop in and see me first thing in the morning.

The next day the following conversation took place between Ted and Mr. Smith.

Smith: Ted, I saw John Lucas yesterday and I'm not sure I've solved your problem. He said that the project he had in mind wasn't very big and that you should have plenty of time to get it done.

Ted: But I told him it would take 120 hours. Since then I've been worried that my estimate was way too low.

Smith: Well, you'd better talk with him again. I understood that I was to have you for twenty hours a week, and believe me, I need every bit of that time!

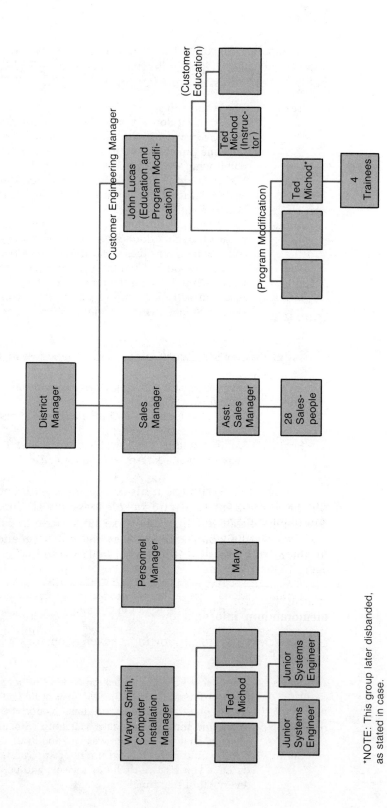

EXHIBIT 1 Midwestern marketing region partial organization chart

*NOTE: This group later disbanded, as stated in case.

Ted saw Lucas a few hours later and explained again his commitments and lack of available time. He went on to suggest that he could instruct a new person to carry out the project if that was acceptable to Lucas.

> Lucas: I don't know who else would be available to do this type of work. . . . Look, Ted, just fit it in around your other work. You'll have time to do it. . . . Oh, before I forget, see Mary in personnel on your way out. They need some information for your records. And tell my secretary to come in, will you? I have a stack of letters to get out.

Ted walked down to personnel wondering how he wound up in the middle of all this. Furthermore, he wondered what he should do next.

Questions

1. What are the nature and cause of the problem?
2. How is this situation explained by organization "principles"?
3. What damage, if any, is resulting from the problem?
4. What should Ted do next?

CASE 17: E. G. LOMAX COMPANY*

The purchasing agent, production manager, production control manager, and plant manager at the Scott branch plant of the E. G. Lomax Company were all astounded upon coming to work one morning to find waiting on their desks identical copies of a memorandum from the general manager, blistering them for acting without proper authority in jointly making the previous day what they had all regarded at the time as a purely routine decision to drop a vendor, the Castle Stamping Company. The memorandum informed them that the general manager was reversing their decision and that in the future no final actions on such "important policy matters" were to be taken without his specific approval.

The reprimanded executives immediately got together to talk the matter over. None of them had spoken to the general manager since the meeting at which the decision had been made. They concluded, therefore, that the only other man present the day before must have been the one to bring it to the general manager's attention. This man, chief tool

---

*From Austin Grimshaw and John W. Hennessey, Jr., *Organizational Behavior* (New York: McGraw-Hill Book Company, 1960).

engineer at the company's parent plant 200 miles distant, had formerly worked for the Castle Stamping Company. He had been instrumental in having Castle selected as the second source for a new stamping to be used in large quantities at the Scott branch.

Castle had been a source of supply, for some years previously, for other parts used in both Lomax plants. During the early part of this association, while business was generally slack, Castle had been reasonably satisfactory as to delivery and price, although never as reliable as one other stamping source used by Lomax. In the previous year, however, business had been brisk and stampings procurement had become difficult. The attitude of Castle executives remained on the surface as cordial as ever, but deliveries were consistently late, sometimes by as much as six months, and prices were high. Extra charges were billed for short runs made by Castle at Lomax's urgent request in order to keep its lines from shutting down, in spite of the fact that it was Castle's lateness in delivery which caused the emergencies.

Feeling that the amount of business currently being placed was not enough to make Lomax a preferred customer, the latter had offered Castle a share of the business on a new large volume part. This offer had been enthusiastically received; Castle had made dies at a cost to Lomax of $6,500 and accepted an initial order for 50,000 stampings.

The decision to drop Castle and to call all dies from its plant had been reached the previous day because, in spite of repeated promises, no stampings had been received in the six months since completion of the dies. Also, deliveries on other parts purchased from Castle were most unsatisfactory. The consensus of the meeting, with the exception of one dissenter, the chief tool engineer from the parent plant who happened to be in town and was consulted as a matter of courtesy, was that Castle would never be a trustworthy source of supply and would continue to get the Scott branch into trouble, as long as the supply situation remained tight. The dissenter's point of view was (1) that the difficulties could be straightened out, (2) that Castle made good parts and could be brought into line on prices, and (3) that the parent plant would be embarrassed by calling in of the dies, since it was currently getting some parts from Castle and might itself be dropped as a customer as a direct result of such hostile action.

The parent plant chief tool engineer requested that Scott's general manager be called in before the decision was made final. The others present at the meeting refused, saying that the general manager knew all about the troubles with the Castle Stamping Company and on several occasions had indicated that he favored dropping it as a vendor just as soon as this could be done without endangering shipment to Lomax customers.

The production manager said that it was a routine problem with which the general manager should not be bothered, that he customarily left such decisions to the men present at the meeting, that he spent very little time on plant matters, visited the shop only occasionally, and concentrated mostly on sales and product engineering problems.

The group also indicated a belief that each of the company's two plants should make its own independent decisions on purchasing. The parent company plant was free, they said, to keep or drop Castle, as it thought most advisable, regardless of the branch plant's action. Finally, the group argued, the general manager was out of town on a sales trip and the time of his return was indefinite.

The group then discussed what should be done about several dies that had been built for the branch plant's own presses at the parent plant, under the supervision of the parent plant chief tool engineer. These dies had been tried out at Scott and had not fitted its presses exactly, according to the production manager. Nor had they incorporated several features of design which the branch plant tool engineer had requested prior to their construction. The meeting broke up in order to permit all interested parties to visit the punch press department where the dies had been specially set up for retrial and for observation of the disputed points about their operation.

After rehashing the previous day's discussion with the others present, the plant manager, with a copy of the memo in his hand, went in to see the general manager. The general manager, without any preliminaries, immediately said: "I got home hot and tired after a long trip, late last night, and found Tom Norcross (the parent company chief tool engineer) waiting for me. What do you mean telling Tom that I never get into the shop any more and that I leave all production decisions to the plant executives? Maybe I don't get into the shop during working hours much now, but I often go in there evenings, when I come back to clear my desk, and on weekends. You know very well that I've had trouble more than once with the president because people at the main plant have distorted things we have said and done down here. Try to be more careful what you say to all of them in the future."

Three months later, following a series of completely unsatisfactory further dealings with the Castle Stamping Company, it was dropped as a vendor at the general manager's express instruction, and dies were called in.

Questions

1. Was the decision to drop Castle Stamping Company a routine decision or a basic policy matter? Was it a "good" decision?
2. How do you explain Norcross's disagreement? Did the committee exercise good judgment in dealing with him?
3. Evaluate the action taken by Norcross in calling on the general manager.
4. What will be the probable effect of this incident upon delegation of authority in the future?

CASE 18: ATLANTIC STORE FURNITURE*

Atlantic Store Furniture (A.S.F.) is a manufacturing operation in Moncton, New Brunswick. The company located in the Industrial Park employs about 20–25 people with annual sales of about two million dollars. Modern shelving systems are the main products and these units are distributed throughout the Maritimes. Metal library shelving, display cases, acoustical screens and work benches are a few of the products available at A.S.F. The products are classified by two distinct manufacturing procedures which form separate sections of the plant.

The Metal Working Operation

In the metal working part of the plant, sheet metal is cut and formed into shelving for assembly. The procedure is quite simple and organized in an assembly line method. Six or eight stations are used to cut the metal to the appropriate length, drill press, shape, spotweld, and paint the final ready-to-assemble product. The equipment used in the operation is both modern and costly, but the technology is quite simple.

The metal working operation employs on average about eight or ten workers located along the line of assembly. . . . The men range in age between 22 and 54 and are typically of French Canadian background. Most have high school education or have graduated from a technical program. The men as metal workers are united by their common identity in the plant and have formed two or three subgroups based on common interests. One group, for example, comprising the foreman and three other workers, has seasons tickets to the New Brunswick Hawks home games. Another group bowls together in the winter and attends horse races in the summer months.

The foreman's group is the most influential among the workers. The men in this group joined the company at the same time and James Savoie, the foreman, was once a worker with the three other men in the group. The group characteristically gets to the lunch counter first, sits together in the most comfortable chairs and punches the time clock first on the way out of work. Conrad LeBlanc, another group member, has a brother who plays professional hockey in the N.H.L. and he frequently describes the success of the team and the large home his brother lives in.

The metal workers as a group operate on one side of the plant and work at a very steady pace. The demand for their products in this section is high and the production is usually constant. The group adjusts well to changes in the order requests and the occasional overtime pressures. The salesmen on the road provide a constant flow of orders to the point where there is a small backlog of requisitions to be filled. The products

---

*Case prepared by Professor Peter B. McGrady of Lakehead University, Thunderbay, Ontario.

vary in size and style but for the most part they are standardized items. A small amount of work is performed on a customized basis.

Woodworking Operations

The woodworking operation differs considerably from the metal working operation. It is a new addition to the plant and has had some success. It is separated from the metal production unit by a sliding door.

The organization of the wood shop is haphazard. Some areas are organized to produce standard products like screening but the majority of the woodworking section is organized around a particular project. . . . Typically tools, equipment, and supplies are left in the area of the partially completed projects.

Custom cabinets and display cases are made for large department and retail stores. A small line of products is produced as a regular line while the rest of the products are custom designed. The flow of work is basically steady in the shop, but there are stages where the work orders become intermittent. Though the appearance of the woodworking shop is quite disorganized and messy, reflecting the nature of the work, the workers in this section of the plant see themselves as real craftsmen and take considerable pride in their work. Typically two or three projects are in progress simultaneously along with the normal run of standard products. The metal workers store some of their completed units in the woodworking area to the dislike of the woodworkers and to the disorganization of the section.

Unlike the metal workers there is a distinct hierarchy among the woodworkers based on seniority and ability. The apprenticeship program within the company has produced a number of good carpenters. This section of the company, though still relatively young, has produced good work and has a reputation for quality craftsmanship.

The morning coffee break for the woodworkers follows that of the metal workers. Lunch hour is staggered by twenty minutes as well. Only a minimal amount of interaction occurs between the wood and metal workers as there tends to be rivalry and competition between the two groups.

The supervisor that oversees the two sections of the plant (plant manager) is Ralph Jamieson, a production engineer from a local university. As plant manager he reports to the vice-president. He is responsible for the plant operation which includes the metal and woodworking shops. At the time of his hiring, A.S.F. had not developed the woodworking section of the plant. Jamieson's work at the University became integrated into the production line when he discovered a method of galvanizing the product in final stages of production. He spends a good deal of his time in the metal working operation planning and discussing problems in production with the foreman, James Savoie. Laboratory research is another occupation assigned to Jamieson who enjoys experimentation with new methods and techniques in design and fabrication of metal products. Jamieson and Savoie are good friends and they spend a good deal of time together both on and off the job. James Savoie is quite happy with the way his operation is running. He has a very good rapport with his men and absenteeism is minimal.

A recent personnel change that has occurred within A.S.F. is the addition of two new salesmen who are on the road in New Brunswick and Nova Scotia. Their contribution to the company is most notable in the metal work area. They have placed many orders for the company. The new sales incentive program has motivated these people to produce and their efforts are being recognized.

Sam Kirby, the woodworking supervisor blew up at the plant manager the other day after the metal workers had pushed open the sliding doors with an interest in storing more excess shelving units in the woodworking area. Sam is a hothead sometimes and has become quite annoyed recently with all the intergroup rivalry that has been going on between the metal workers and the woodworkers. Storage space has been a sore point between the groups for the last six months or so, ever since the metal workers became very busy. Jamieson and Howard Wylie, the vice-president, were asked to settle the problem between the two shops and decided that the metal workers were only to access the woodworking shop if absolutely necessary and with consent of the foreman or supervisor.

This latest incident really upset the boys in the woodworking shop. The woodworkers feel intimidated by the metal workers who are taking space and interrupting their work.

In a later conversation Kirby and Jamieson smoothed things over somewhat. It was explained to Kirby that it was the metal workers who were really turning out the work and that they need the space. The area that metal workers want to use is not really needed by the woodworkers, rather it is simply an area around the perimeter of the room by the walls.

Kirby did not like Jamieson's response, knowing full well his commitment to the metal working operations. With this decision, the metal workers proceeded to use the area in the woodworking shop and never missed an opportunity to insult or criticize the woodworkers. The effect of the situation on the respective groups became quite obvious. The metal workers became increasingly more jocular and irritating in their interactions with the woodworkers.

The fighting continued and became of more concern to the president and vice-president. For example, the large sliding doors separating the shops were hastily closed one afternoon on a metal worker who was retreating from a practical joke he was playing on a woodworker. The resulting injury was not serious but it did interrupt a long series of accident free days the company had been building up. This incident further divided the two groups. Meetings and threats by management were not enough to curtail the problems.

The woodworkers were now withdrawing all efforts to communicate. They ate lunch separately and took coffee breaks away from the regular room. Kirby became quite impatient to complete new products and to acquire new contracts. He urged management to hire personnel and to solicit new business. The climate changed considerably in the woodworking shop as the workers lost their satisfying work experience. Much of the friendly interaction that had gone on previously had ceased. Kirby's temper flared more frequently as small incidents seemed to upset him more than before. After work get-togethers at the tavern were no longer of much appeal to the men.

The metal workers were feeling quite good about their jobs as the weeks passed. Their orders remained strong as demand continued to grow for their products. The metal workers complained about the woodworkers and demanded more space for their inventory. The metal workers were becoming more cohesive and constantly ridiculed the woodworkers. Their concern for the job decreased somewhat as back orders filled up and talk of expansion developed for the metal work operation.

Just as the metal shop became more confident, there were more difficulties with the woodworking shop. The woodworkers were completing the final stages of an elaborate cabinet system when information came regarding a shipping delay. The new store for which the product was being built was experiencing problems, causing a two or three month delay before it could accept the new cabinet system. Kirby was very disturbed by this news as the woodworkers needed to see the completion of their project and the beginning of a new one.

The predicament was compounded somewhat by the attitude of the metal workers who heard of the frustration of the woodworkers and added only more jeers and smart remarks. Morale at this stage was at an all time low. The chief carpenter, an integral member of the woodworkers, was looking for a new job. One or two of the casual workers were drifting into new work or not showing up for work they had. Contracts and orders for new products were arriving but in fewer numbers and casual workers had to be laid off. Defective work was beginning to increase to the embarrassment of the company.

Management was upset with the conditions of the two operations and threatened the foreman and supervisors. Kirby was disturbed at the situation and was bitter about the deteriorating state of the woodworking plant. Despite many interviews, he was unable to replace the head carpenter who had left the company attracted by a new job prospect. Efforts to reduce the intergroup conflict were tried but without success.

The president of A.S.F., William MacDougal, was alarmed with the situation. He recognized some of the problems with the different operations. One operation was more active and busy while the other section worked primarily on project work, i.e., building a custom display cabinet for a retail company. The organization was designed, he thought, with the normal structure in mind. The men in the company, he thought to himself, were very much of the same background and what little diversity there was should not have accounted for this animosity. As president, he had not developed climate of competition or pressure in the company.

The disorganization and chaos in the woodworking plant was alarming and there was very little that could be done about it. Kirby had been discussing the problem with the president trying to identify some of the alternatives. This had been the third meeting in as many days and each time the conversation drifted into a discussion about current developments in Jamieson's metal working pursuits. James Savoie felt that there was too much worrying going on 'over there'!!!

Plans for expanding the building at A.S.F. were developing at a rapid pace. The president felt that more room might alleviate some of the problems particularly with respect to inventory, warehousing and storage.

Kirby became enthusiastic about the prospects of some relief for his side of the operation. He was very much aware of the fact that the performance of his operation was quite low. The president of the company felt satisfied that the woodworking concern was going to improve its performance. One or two new contracts with large department stores inspired the effort to improve the operation.

The men in the woodworking section became relaxed. A few positive interactions between the wood and metal workers became evident. One afternoon about two weeks after the disclosure by the president of the new plant development, Kirby observed blueprints for the new expansion. The plans had been left on Jamieson's desk inadvertently and to the surprise of Kirby revealed full details of the expansion for the new building.

Kirby sat down and examined the details more carefully and recognized that the woodworking area was not to be included in the expansion plans. Kirby left the office in a rage and stormed into the president's office and demanded an explanation.

EXHIBIT 1 Organizational chart

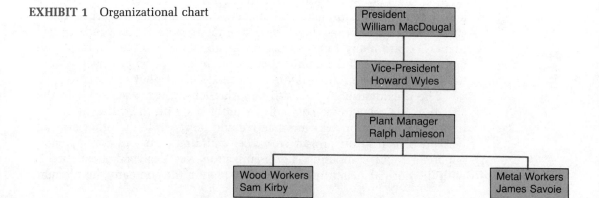

Kirby shouted that he had changed things around in the woodworking shop on the promise of more room and possibility of expansion. The president shook his head and apologized and explained he was going to be told, but nothing could be done. The demand was simply just not that great for wood products. Kirby left the office and went straight for his car and drove off.

Questions

1. What are the primary factors contributing to the self-image or esprit de corps of the two primary work groups?
2. What shows the relative status of the two groups?
3. Compare the manufacturing methods involved in the two work units. What is the apparent effect of these differences in terms of effective teamwork?
4. What are the primary points of conflict between the two groups?
5. What approach might be used to reduce the conflict that exists and to restore a spirit of teamwork?

CASE 19: THE TOKEN WOMAN*

The Mainstream Life Insurance Company, to forestall possible affirmative action pressure because of the lack of women in the insurance industry's managerial ranks, decided to actively recruit a woman to fill a recent opening in the Research Division of the company's Trust Department. The vacant Research Analyst position is one of several middle-management jobs at Mainstream that traditionally have been the stepping stone for promotion to the executive rank.

The required credentials for this particular opening in the Research Division of the Trust Department are an MBA degree (or a comparable graduate degree with a major emphasis in finance), at least two years of academic or business experience, and proven research capability in the investment field. An exhaustive search and meticulous screening resulted in the insurer's hiring Claire Meredith, an attractive 27-year-old single woman whose MS degree in finance was awarded "With Distinction" (i.e.; with high honors) and whose master's thesis was published by a prestigious university press. Ms. Meredith was previously employed as a broker in a highly respected Wall Street investment banking firm. In addition, she has authored numerous publications that were the result of extensive theoretical and applied research projects. Mainstream

*Case prepared by Professor Linda Pickthorne Fletcher of Louisiana State University and Professor Susan M. Phillips of the University of Iowa.

was able to hire Ms. Meredith only after John Forbes, her potential immediate "boss," assured her of equal opportunity on all possible levels.
Additional inducement to Ms. Meredith's accepting the Mainstream offer was supplied by the starting salary, which was $2,000 higher than
her other recent employment offers.

At the end of her third month on the job, Ms. Meredith privately
acknowledged a pervasive feeling of frustration in connection with her
new position. She began reviewing the activities of the past three
months in an attempt to determine the basis of her negative reaction.

During the first day on the job, each of Ms. Meredith's colleagues
had expressed enthusiastic delight at having her "on board." One colleague observed that "it's high time the company hired a woman for our
section—we've needed some beautification of the office for a long time
now." Another chimed in with the remark that "we better tell our wives
that Claire is married so they won't think we're researching monkey
business!" When Claire, in reply, suggested that they all have lunch together, Roy James, a division programmer, told her that "each of the guys
brings a brown bag for lunch and we eat and talk shop in one or the
other's office." Accordingly, Claire decided to emulate her colleagues
and announced that she was joining the brown bag league. She was surprised, therefore, when at noon the following day Roy James opened his
office door and urged, "Come on, you guys, let's research our brown
bags—Frank, you and Jim get the coffee while David and I get the ice
cream, and don't forget Don wants double cream in his coffee." Since
Claire's name was not mentioned specifically, she decided—after some
hesitation—to eat alone in her office. Claire did not feel she should join
the secretaries and clerks for lunch although she knew she would be
welcome. This routine, with minor variations, was then the established
pattern.

Breaks for coffee in the company cafeteria were no exception to the
seemingly established separation principle—only once in that three-
month interval had Claire been invited to join her colleagues for coffee.
At that particular coffee break, Claire remembered, she felt particularly
uncomfortable. Although she felt she had an excellent working relationship with her associates, she had little in common with them outside of
the work environment. In addition, it was quite obvious that the men in
the division seemed to plan social gatherings for both after work and the
week-ends. Although her colleagues were very friendly in the office,
they never seemed to think to include her in their plans.

Having reviewed the informal social structure of her employment,
Claire recognized similar frustrations with respect to various functional
aspects of her position. She recalled John Forbes, the head of the Research Division, explaining the operational features of the section: "We
meet once a week in committee to determine the status of current projects, discuss proposals for the future, and make individual assignments
of new research projects to be initiated. Any ideas you have—write them
up in memo form for distribution to everyone prior to the next meeting,

and we'll all go over your suggestion at the earliest possible meeting to determine the feasibility of your idea."

Because she was the most recent addition to the staff, Claire deliberately maintained a low profile during the first few weekly committee meetings of the Research Division. The other members of the committee appeared to endorse her strategy by seeking her opinions only infrequently and by failing to draw her into their policy deliberations. During the fourth weekly gathering, John Forbes, who acted as chairman, noted that his secretary was unable to be present as usual to record the minutes of the meeting. Frank Howard suggested sending for a replacement from the secretarial pool, but Mr. Forbes shook his head and casually replied that "a replacement is unnecessary since the logical substitute is Ms. Meredith—besides, brushing up on her shorthand will give her something to do during the meeting." Claire hastened to observe that "since I do not know shorthand, I must decline the honor of this additional responsibility." At this point, Claire recalled, she decided to abandon her sideline role at the next conclave of the committee by presenting a research proposal that she had been developing in the area of commission reduction through utilization of regional exchanges.

To date, Claire's specific assignments include responsibility for several ongoing projects which require only infrequent attention. The major portion of her time, however, is spent on the "Cost Allocation" project. Cost Allocation is a computer system which will, when completed, provide complete investment information for each of Mainstream's trust customers. All trust funds are pooled for investment purposes. The pooling is necessary since some of the trust accounts are so small that investment income would be difficult to generate for these accounts. Any income would virtually be "wiped out" by the commission expenses of such small transactions.

The current method of determining investment income for each trust account is to apply the average new investment rate to the pro rata portion of each account's share of the total investment funds. Consequently, several of Mainstream's larger trust accounts had complained that their investment income was "supporting" the smaller accounts. Threatened with the loss of these large trust accounts, the financial Vice-President of Mainstream, Bill Newbit, instructed John Forbes to develop some type of allocation system within his department so that each account could be properly charged with expenses while simultaneously enjoying the investment income of the pooled fund investment mechanism.

John Forbes developed the specifications for the Cost Allocation system and turned over the system design and programming to a Research Analyst who had resigned several months before Claire joined the division. She later found out through the grapevine that he quit because he felt he was getting nowhere with Cost Allocation. Claire recalled that when she was hired, she was told she would have full responsibility for the completion of the system, including supervising the programming by

Roy James, developing comprehensive test data, and ultimately getting the system on line. Since investment income for each account was currently calculated by hand under the supervision of Frank Howard, Claire anticipated the usual problems of employee resistance to a new computer system. She therefore had begun some system orientation classes for the personnel involved. Claire had determined that the existing personnel, with training, would be adequate to use and run the new system effectively. No personnel displacement would be necessary.

Claire was currently in the final stages of testing the system with Roy James, the programmer assigned to her. When she took the first run of the test data into John Forbes, he expressed complete surprise. He admitted, "I can't believe that Cost Allocation has ever gotten off the ground. This system has been knocking around for three years—we had just about counted the $800,000 developmental costs spent so far as sunk. In fact, we were going to write them off this year. I guess we'll have to start thinking about moving on this thing . . . manpower planning and so on."

When Claire left John Forbes' office, she was shocked and disappointed at his reaction. As she reviewed his comments, she really began to wonder just what she was supposed to be doing at Mainstream and how she could go about doing it.

Questions

1. Describe and evaluate the informal structure of the Research Division of the Trust Department and its effect on Ms. Meredith's relationships.
2. Why was Ms. Meredith hired?
3. Discuss Ms. Meredith's role in the weekly policy committee meetings. How might she change her established role in these meetings?
4. Why was Ms. Meredith disappointed at John Forbes' reaction to the first run of the test data for the cost allocation project?
5. What should Ms. Meredith do about her feelings of job frustration?

CASE 20: COOLAIRE CORPORATION*

Phil Waverly was just beginning to figure it all out. Somehow he had become caught in the middle of something he sensed as impending disaster. There was no way he could fulfill the biggest service contract his

---

*From Daniel Robey, *Designing Organizations* (Homewood, Ill.: Richard D. Irwin, 1982), pp. 246–49.

branch had ever seen with the personnel and resources allocated to the project. His service technicians were already working 12 hours of overtime each week, and the office staff had fallen three weeks behind in its paperwork. On top of this, three senior technicians, each with over 10 years of service, had just resigned because of job pressures. Two of the branch's most competent clerks had also quit recently. With profits rapidly eroding, Phil felt powerless to change anything. But at least he was beginning to see how it all began.

Phil Waverly is the manager of one of the Coolaire Corporation's largest regional branches. The Coolaire Corporation, one of the world's major manufacturers of air conditioning and refrigeration equipment, surpassed $2 billion in gross sales for the first time in 1978. In 1979, Coolaire was acquired by means of an unfriendly takeover by a large multinational conglomerate, Allied Industrials. Coolaire became the fourth major section of the Allied empire, the other three being the Allied Power Group, the Allied Electronics Group, and National Elevators.

Coolaire's Machinery and Systems Division comprises two departments with parallel structures: sales and service. The service department's role in the organization is to maintain large-capacity industrial refrigeration and air-conditioning equipment manufactured by Coolaire, and some of that manufactured by the organization's competitors as well. At the local branch level of the service department are the technicians, clerks, and secretaries. These people report to service supervisors. The service supervisors report to branch managers who are responsible for 10 to 40 employees and from $1 to $4 million of Coolaire's business. Anywhere from three to six branch managers report to each district manager, each of whom is, in turn, responsible to a zone manager, of which there are only four in the nation. Zone managers report to the national manager, who is a company vice president. This hierarchy is shown in Exhibit 1.

The Service Contract

Recently, Coolaire was one of a handful of companies invited to bid on a large service contract. A meeting was held of all Coolaire's branches in the Birmingham district (as this is where the contract would be executed), to come up with ideas on how to manage the contract in the event it was awarded to Coolaire. Three major possibilities were explored: (1) to treat the contract as an extension of ordinary business, with several branches participating on the basis of geographic location; (2) to create a new branch to manage this contract exclusively; and (3) to manage the whole contract from a single existing branch. This third proposal was adopted by the group, and Phil Waverly's branch was chosen to manage the contract if the bid was won.

Phil recalled his feelings after the meeting was over.

EXHIBIT 1   Coolaire service hierarchy.

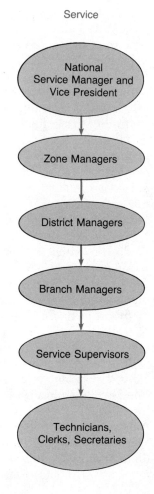

Service

This was the first time that the branch managers really provided input for a big decision, and I felt that we did it very well. Each alternative was evaluated systematically, taking into account the extra work and the extra personnel required to manage the contract. Everyone left the meeting with a feeling of contribution and accomplishment. I was really pumped up just imagining myself running such a big contract.

Coolaire's bid was more than 30 percent lower than its closest competitor's, and Coolaire was awarded the contract. The bid itself was prepared by the Southeast zone manager in consultation with the national service vice president with no input from the branch managers who had attended the meeting in Birmingham. At the time Phil thought little of this exclusion because he was accustomed to administering contracts rather than preparing bids. He never guessed the extent to which he had become a pawn in someone else's chess game.

Strategy behind the Bid

Coolaire's exceedingly low bid was part of an emerging struggle between Coolaire's service group and National Elevator's service group. Coolaire's takeover by Allied Industrials left many of Coolaire's top service managers uncertain about their future with the organization. A cold war of sorts was the result, with the service departments of Coolaire and National Elevator battling to become the core of Allied's planned consolidated service department, with the majority of the managers in the new centralized service organization coming from the ranks of the surviving department. As Coolaire had recently lost three large contracts, success on their latest bid was crucial.

Responsibility for fulfillment of this contract was delegated to Phillip Waverly's branch in hopes that giving one branch full responsibility for the contract would provide a tighter rein on expenditures and simplify managerial accounting and paperwork. Phil recalled, "Part of the deal was that additional office and field personnel would be an absolute necessity for any branch attempting to fulfill the contract on its own." But as he researched the problem further Phil uncovered a particularly dismaying bit of information. Three years earlier, Coolaire had bid on and lost the same contract. At that time, 4 branch managers, 9 supervisors, 52 service technicians, and 6 clerks had been allocated to the contract. Under Waverly there would be only 3 supervisors, 23 service technicians, and 2 clerks—a reduction in staff size of over 50 percent to fulfill a contract that had increased in size during the three-year period.

The air-conditioning equipment being maintained by the branch has rapidly deteriorated as the field personnel have become overtaxed just doing emergency repairs, with no time for routine preventive maintenance. Profit margins have become microscopic, and since the contract contained no allowances for inflation during its three-year term, profits will continue to erode and probably disappear altogether. Phil privately wondered if the next scene in the unfolding drama would be one called scapegoat. If so, he surmised that those pulling the strings would have no trouble identifying the actor to play that role.

Questions

1. How can the bid on the service contract be understood from a formal organization perspective?
2. Phil fears that he will become a scapegoat. Help him map out a strategy that would avoid this outcome.

CASE 21: THE COMPANY TRAINING PROGRAM*

Widget Manufacturing Company believed in providing every possible aid and encouragement to the development of its management personnel. Among the many extras that it provided was attendance for thirty or forty people each year at the Industrial Management Conference. These conferences were held in a college town and were widely attended, with as many as 1,200 people from various companies present at the annual three-day sessions. The sessions were divided into workshops and discussion groups, with a liberal sprinkling of speakers—experts in various phases of industrial management. The meetings concluded with a major speech and banquet, followed by entertainment.

When John Hamilton joined the staff of the Widget company, he was greatly impressed by the efforts of top management to provide such continuous development of its supervisory staff. He took advantage of the extension courses offered, was present at all foremen's classes, and generally considered himself lucky to be part of such an organization. When one of the supervisors approached him and asked if he would like to attend the conference, he was delighted. It seemed to him that it would be an excellent opportunity to sample some of the best thinking of men who were specialists in their fields.

Customarily the men were sent down in several cars to the conference. John Hamilton found himself in a car with three other men, one of which was Jim Warner, an old-line supervisor. He noted the holiday atmosphere from the beginning of the trip and felt that the men must indeed get a great deal out of the conferences because of the enthusiasm with which they greeted the prospect of attending. Several times on the ride to the conference John tried to draw out Jim on the subject matter of the conferences. All he got was remarks such as "You're sure to enjoy yourself, John; just relax."

Following the registration, John told Jim that he was going to his room and freshen up. He wanted to be sure and catch the first speaker. Before John could leave, Jim said, "Sure, John, just stop in room 325 before you go."

A little while later John knocked on the door of room 325 and was admitted to the smoke-filled room. Two of the desks had been pushed together and a blanket thrown over them. The supervisors he knew were sitting around in their shirt sleeves, playing poker and drinking. Before John could say anything, someone put a paper cup of lukewarm whisky and ginger ale into his hand. "There's plenty of time before the first speaker," said Jim. "Why don't you play a couple of hands."

---

*Case prepared by Professor Kenneth A. Kovach of George Mason University. Copyright © 1980 by Kenneth A. Kovach.

Hamilton didn't want to miss the speech; neither did he want to antagonize the other foremen by refusing a few friendly hands of poker with them. "Okay," he said. "But I'm only going to play one deal around; then I'm taking off." Five hands later Jim asked him, "How do you like the conference?"

"Look, Johnny boy," said Jim, "this is the conference. That speech making and all the other stuff is hogwash. The whole purpose of these conferences is to give the boys a three-day vacation for a little drinking and poker playing."

"That doesn't sound right to me," said John. "From the look of the program, a lot of people have worked hard to line up a very good conference. "It doesn't make sense to me," said John, "to drive all the way down here to hear these experts speak and stay in our rooms and play poker."

"This is the way the company wants it," said Jim. "The main idea is for the foremen to get together and get to know each other better. It makes a closer spirit among the foremen."

Hamilton was in a quandary. He wanted to attend the program, but he knew that if he spurned the poker session more than half of the foremen he knew would think him a "square."

Questions

1. Weigh the costs and benefits of (a) conforming to the foremen's behavior and (b) refusing to conform.

2. Should John somehow let his supervisor know what went on when he returns and take the chance of being "blackballed" by the rest of the foremen?

CASE 22: THE PROBLEM WITH PROBLEM SOLVING*

In mid-October, 29 year old Bill Meister, president of Artisan Industries, had to meet with his management group to consider increasing prices. A year before he had taken over the failing nine-million dollar a year wooden gift manufacturing company from his father. It had been a hectic year but he had arrested the slide to bankruptcy. Much work was still needed in almost every area of the company. In his office for the 11:00 meeting were:

---

*Case prepared by Professor Frank C. Barnes of University of North Carolina at Charlotte.

Bob: Thirty year old V.P. of Finance. He had three years with the company, coming from the staff of a big eight accounting firm. He headed accounting and the office staff in general.

Cal: Thirty-five years old, he had been with the company eight years. Though he had a B.A. in accounting, he had held many jobs in the company. Now he was installing a small computer system and reported to Bob.

Edith: Forty year old sister of Bill and manager of the routine sales activity as it interfaced with the home office. The sales force was comprised of independent sales reps. She had only clerical people reporting to her. She had no college training.

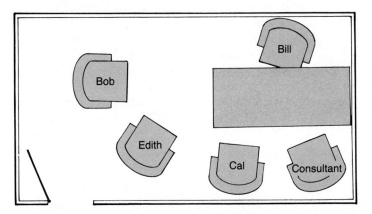

Bill called the meeting to order in the presence of a management consultant who happened to be visiting to discuss other plans for improvement.

Bill: O.K. we've been discussing the need for a price increase for some time now. Bob recommends increasing prices 16% right away. I'd like to get all of your thoughts on this. Bob.

Bob: My analysis of profit statements to date indicates that a 16% increase is necessary right now if we are to have any profit this year. My best estimate is that we're losing money on every order we take. We haven't raised prices in over a year and have no choice but to do so now.

Cal: I agree. What's the sense in taking orders on which we lose money?

Bob: Exactly. If we raise prices across the board immediately, we can have a profit of about $300,000 at year end.

Cal: It would've been better to have increased prices with our price-list last May or June rather than doing it on each order here in the middle of our sales season; but we really have no choice now.

Bob: There's just no way we can put it off.

Bill: *(pausing, looking around the room)* So, you all recommend a price increase at this time?

Cal & Bob: Yes.

Bob: We can't wait to increase prices as new orders are written in the field or through a new pricelist. Right now we already have enough of a backlog of orders accepted at the old prices and orders awaiting our acknowledgment to fill the plant until the season ends in 6 to 8 weeks. We must only accept orders at the new prices.

Cal: If we acknowledge all the orders we have now, like that 30-page one Edith has for $221,000, then the price change won't even be felt this year.

Bob: No, we should not acknowledge any orders at the old prices. I would hold the orders and send each customer a printed letter telling them of the price increase and asking them to reconfirm their orders with an enclosed mailer if they still wanted it.

Cal: Orders already acknowledged would keep the plant busy until they responded.

Bill: So, is this the best thing to do?

Bob: We're in business to make money; we'd be crazy not to raise prices!

Bill: Edith, you look unhappy. What do you think?

Edith: *(shrug)* I don't know.

Bob: *(visible impatience)* We're losing money on every order.

Edith: I'm just worried about trying to raise prices right in the middle of the season.

Cal: Well, if we wait we might as well forget it.

Bob: Just what would you suggest we do, Edith?

Edith: I don't know. *(pause)* This order *(picking up the 30-page order)* took the salesman a month to work-up with the customer. There are over 175 items on it and the items must be redistributed to the customer's 9 retail outlets in time for Christmas. I'm worried about it.

Bob: It's worthless to us as it is.

Cal: Look, in our letter we can mention the inflation and that this is our first increase in a long while. Most customers will understand this. We've got to try, it's worth the risk. Isn't it, Edith?

Edith: *(shrug)*

Bill: What do you suggest, Edith?

Edith: I don't know; we need the increase, but it bothers me.

Bob: Business is made of tough decisions; managers are paid to make 'em.

(All become quiet, look around the room, and finally look at Bill).

Questions

1. Explain what happened at this meeting. What was each person doing and trying to do? Was it a good meeting? Why?
2. What is going to happen now? What is the decision going to be?
3. What do you think of the decision? Can you think of ways to improve upon it?
4. What would you do if you were there?

Consultant: *(calmly)* I think Edith has raised a good point. We *are* considering making a big move right in the middle of our busy season. It will cause problems. If we can't avoid the increase, then what can we do to avoid or minimize the problems?

Bob: *(hostile and obviously disgusted)* It would be ridiculous to put off the price increase.

Consultant: *(calmly)* That may be true, but is it being done in the best way? There are always alternatives to consider. I don't think we are doing a good job of problem-solving here. *(pause)* Even with the basic idea of an increase, it can be done poorly or done well. There is room for more thought. How can it be done with the least penalty?

(All quiet, as consultant looks around the group, waiting for anyone to add comments. Hearing none. . . .)

For example, by the time we mail them a letter and they think about it and mail it back, 2 or 3 weeks may pass. The price increase wouldn't take effect until the season is almost over. How can we get the increase making us money right away? And though we are bound to lose some orders, what can we do to minimize these? *(pausing to allow comments)*

Edith: Yes, that's what I meant.

Consultant: On this order for example, (picking up the $221,000 order) we could call them right now and explain the situation and possibly be shipping at the higher prices *this afternoon.*

Bob: (with no hostility, with an apparent positive attitude) O.K. I will call them as soon as we leave here.

Cal: We have a pile of orders awaiting acknowledgement. . . .

Bob: Right, we can get some help and pick out the bigger orders and start calling them this afternoon.

Consultant: How about involving the salesmen?

Edith: Yes, the salesmen know the customers best. We should call them to contact the customer. They got the order and know the customer's needs. But we will have to convince the salesmen of the necessity of the increase. I can start getting in touch with them by phone right away.

Bob: O.K., we can handle the bigger orders personally by phone and use the letter on the small ones.

Consultant: What do you think about making them act *to keep* the order? Why not make it so *no action* keeps the order. Tell them that we are saving their place in our shipping schedule and will go ahead and ship if they don't contact us in 5 to 7 days. Is it best to put the control in their hands?

Edith: That bothered me. Increasing the price is serious and we need to handle it carefully if it's to work. I think most people will go ahead and accept the merchandise.

Bob: Edith and I can get together this afternoon on the letter.

(All become silent again.)

Bill: O.K., can you all get started after lunch and let's meet in the morning to see how it's going?

Questions

1. What do you think of the decision now? Is it improved? Why might you call the first decision "suboptimal"?
2. Would the group have made the new decision without help? Why?
3. It can be said initially the group was not involved in problem-solving. Why?
4. What did the consultant see had to be done with the group? How could he do it? Did the consultant want to make the decisions himself? Could Bill have taken this role?

5. What does this incident say about the management team and the work environment at Artisan? What should and could be done about it?

6. What does this case illustrate about group problem-solving? About communications?

CASE 23: CHALLENGE*

Delaware Community College is a small, state supported school situated in a quiet, rural area just south of the state capital. Chartered in 1911, it has become an integral part of the community with programs aimed primarily at preparing students to enter four year colleges and universities, although a few are two year para-professional programs. Like most schools, Delaware uses a traditional grading system. Karen Mayes, an instructor at Delaware, was soon to find herself seriously questioning this time-honored tradition.

Karen took her teaching seriously, working hard to balance the demands of her doctoral studies at the University with her teaching duties at the community college. In the classroom, Karen was "relationship oriented," trying to involve the students in active discussions of the material. The students seemed to respond well.

Today she had taught her Intro to Mangement class. The class became energetic and she too got caught up in their enthusiasm. The cause of the excitement was a case study about grading and the problems it caused at a particular university. The case itself was complicated because the class had been subjected to three different teachers during a term. Predictably, these teachers had different styles and different expectations.

The class discussion quickly became a discussion of grading at Delaware Community. Here, too, many teachers at the college had different styles. Some lectured exclusively; others, like Karen, lectured and led class debate; others relied almost entirely upon class participation. Professors used different testing methods—objective tests, essay tests, or both. Nevertheless, despite these varied inputs, practically all teachers used the traditional grading system, and in the opinion of the class members it left a lot to be desired.

"Grades, grades, grades, why do we need them anyway?" Leroy Mark asked.

"You don't like them because you can't get good ones—that's why you complain." Pamela Johnson said.

---

*This case was prepared by George E. Stevens and Penny Marquette when they were at Kent State University. All names are disguised. Copyright © 1977, George E. Stevens.

"It's not that at all; they just aren't fair. They don't measure what I've learned. You mean to tell me that when I can answer questions well in class, but not on some test, I should only get graded for my test answers? That's not fair!" Leroy retorted.

"That's true, Leroy's got a point. Plus we know teachers use the old A, B, C scale. Somebody's got to get the D's and F's. But what happens if the whole class is pretty smart?"

"Well, why don't they give all A's and B's, then nobody's hurt," Richard Green suggested.

Peggy Vandero chimed, "Now that idea I like!"

And so the discussion raged, back and forth, back and forth. Alternatives were suggested and rejected. Even when the bell rang the discussion went on; no one in the class moved! Finally, Karen stopped them. But now, reflecting on what she'd suggested, she was beginning to wonder if she'd let things go too far.

I hate to interrupt this lively discussion, but the bell's rung, and there's another class coming in. To summarize, I hear you saying that there are a number of grading systems being used including our traditional A, B, C, D, F system. Furthermore you believe the traditional system is not fair and does not always reflect the quality of your work. Here today you've discussed some alternatives including Pass/Fail and blanket grades, yet these appear to have faults as well. Let me make a proposition. I challenge you to put your money where your mouth is. We're only in the second week of class and if YOU can come up with a grading system that meets the dual criteria of being fair and reflecting the quality of work done, I'll implement it. You have from now until Friday to prepare your proposals either individually or in groups. During Friday's class, the proposals can be presented and voted on, and the one deemed most acceptable will be instituted.

Questions

1. Grading, of course, is a form of performance appraisal with which all students can readily identify. What are some of the more common types of grading systems?
2. What factors influence the grade a student may be assigned?
3. How might the grades and grading systems used affect people after graduation?
4. Does the problem go beyond just grading? What are the social implications of coping with varying grading systems? Dealing with the existence or non-existence of equity in the university environment?
5. If a university changed its grading system from an A, B, C, D, F scale to pass-fail, what might be some of the behavioral implications?

CASE 24: NORTON CONSOLIDATED*

Douglas Downing, purchasing manager for Norton Consolidated, a large defense contractor, was startled by the phone ringing at his elbow. He had been deep in thought as he tried to find an answer to the growing problem of supervisor turnover at Norton. Not that this was anything new, of course, but higher management was becoming more concerned because of the increasing realization that in many cases it was the better people who were leaving. "Hello. Yes, this is Doug Downing. Oh, hi, Frank; how are things in personnel these days? What can we do for you? Hmmm. Well, I guess you might as well send the authorization on through to corporate: Ray is a good man and I think he would benefit considerably from this type of graduate study. I do have the budget to cover it, and you of all people know that I encourage my employees to continue their education, particularly when an evening program is available."

Doug hung up the phone with mixed feelings. On the one hand, he knew that Ray would be better off in the long run by completing his MBA program; on the other hand, he also knew that from the company's standpoint it meant losing another promising young manager. He had seen the same pattern develop time after time, and he knew that graduate work was only one more step in the process that began with the promises made to these employees when they were recruited to work for the company. He knew all too well that the "stimulating environment" and "rapid advancement" would soon disappear into the drab workaday world of reality. Given the inevitable, somehow it seemed a shame to offer the encouragement of graduate school, knowing full well that the company had no real plan for either using or continuing their development. The really unfortunate part was that many managers in the company recognized the need to retain the talent available through such employees, but were unable to offer more than personal encouragement—which was not reflected tangibly by the company. Frequently this meant that opportunities did not meet even the minimum expectations of these individuals concerning their personal growth and growth opportunities. As a result, most of them would soon find it necessary to choose between a long-term "seasoning" process based primarily on chance, if they chose to stick it out, or leaving Norton for the immediate challenge of a new job with another firm. The ironical part is that the greater an individual's potential, the more likely he or she is to leave—and probably the sooner.

Doug was well aware of the pressures that would develop since he, too, had found it necessary to change companies to achieve what he considered to be reasonable growth in his work. He had even been idealistic (or naive) enough to think that his leaving might have some impact toward improving the system at his previous company. He had come a

---

*Case prepared by Professor Davis W. Carvey of Pacific Lutheran University.

long way since then, mostly in spite of the system. On the other hand, now he was the system—or at least part of it. Maybe this was the time to put some of those earlier thoughts into practice.

The next day Doug dictated the following memo to the vice-president of personnel and industrial relations. The memo outlined what he felt was a positive program to develop and encourage those individuals in his department who had management potential.

MEMORANDUM

TO: Richard Chapman, Vice-President
Personnel and Industrial Relations

FROM: Douglas Downing, Purchasing Manager

SUBJECT: Proposed Management Development Program

As you know, the company is currently encountering a two-faced dilemma. On the one hand, business is slack with resultant open capacity—both facilities and manpower. On the other hand, potential business opportunities necessitate that capacity, even though currently in excess of requirements, be kept available for future ventures.

Traditionally, this situation has been resolved primarily through management inaction, that is by attrition, which does, in fact, reduce manpower to acceptable levels based on a "head-count" philosophy. Along with attrition, some effort is usually made to use facilities through a change in the make-or-buy structure of our programs and a variety of make-work programs.

Unfortunately, this approach seriously hampers our ability to recover from periods of reduced activity as we, in effect, compound the problem. What is not considered is that individuals with education, foresight, drive, ability, and other desirable leadership attributes are those who often resign during these periods. This is the type of person who should be most encouraged to remain with Norton for planning, developing, and staffing future programs.

It appears that a limited attempt is being made at this time to solve the problem by offering lateral "experience transfers" to a few employees with potential. This, while a step in the right direction, is certainly inadequate to reduce significantly the loss of good personnel.

Based on the present situation, it would seem that an effective and appropriate course of action would include the following steps:

1. Designate a number of potential management employees to be included in an advancement/training program.
2. Discuss the program with these people on at least a department manager level and let them know that they are part of the program, possibly even in writing.
3. Pay the designated personnel increased salaries to the point of making it worth their while to become personally committed to their own development.
4. Lay off less productive employees in sufficient numbers to make up the budget money used for step 3.

5. Give these individuals as much experience as possible, including frequent job changes, management exposure, and formal training.

6. Establish "innovation sessions" as part of the training program with the purpose of acting as a group to establish new and/or better systems, organizations, or work methods. These sessions should be free flowing and include management participation on an as-required basis. Constructive ideas resulting from these sessions should be examined objectively and implemented whenever possible.

7. Each participant should be promoted as appropriate, with others added to the group as required and/or available.

All promotions should be based on merit; thus, the plan would involve no company commitment other than putting the individuals into the group and giving them sufficient encouragement, including money, to remain with Norton.

The approach suggested will decrease the number of employees, yet at the same time upgrade the quality of the manpower pool available for future expansion. Part of the training group assignment could also be to develop new business and facility usage ideas, thus helping solve the excess capacity problem as well.

I would appreciate your comments concerning this proposal since we are planning to implement it on an experimental basis in the purchasing department as soon as we work out the details.

Once the approach proves successful in our department, it could then be expanded to include other departments in the near future.

Questions

1. What is management development? How does it fit into an overall scheme of human resource planning?

2. What are some of the possible *negative* effects of proceeding with the plan suggested by Douglas Downing?

3. What are some of the possible *positive* effects of proceeding with the plan proposed by Downing?

4. How might this plan be most effectively implemented to maximize the positive results while minimizing its negative impact?

5. What are some practical alternatives to Downing's plan? How might these alternatives be integrated into a realistic overall personnel plan?

CASE 25: JOB ENLARGEMENT*

The manufacturing operations at Plant Y of the Crestline Corporation consist of fabricating and assembling a major consumer durable product. Traditionally, the manufacturing systems have been designed and built around the typical high-speed assembly-line operation.

As general production superintendent of Plant Y, Mr. Brown, who has developed through the management ranks largely by following traditional management principles, must give final approval to all systems changes that will affect his operations.

A new design of one of the major components for the ultimate product has been completed by product engineering. In turn, it has been released to manufacturing engineering for implementation into the assembly-line system.

The manufacturing engineering group recently studied the available research relative to the advantages of the job-enlargement principle versus the paced-conveyor system in terms of providing relief from monotony and boredom. Realizing that job dissatisfaction has been and continues to be an apparent problem, a system which includes job enlargement was developed to assemble the new component along with the traditional pace-conveyor system. Each system was then presented to Mr. Brown for his approval, with the recommendation from the manufacturing engineering group that he adopt the job-enlargement systems design.

Mr. Brown, being aware of the perceived monotony and boredom of the assembly line, decided to accept the recommendation and adopt the job-enlargement principle.

As the production date arrived, the facilities were completed and a number of operators moved from the assembly conveyor to a new job. They, in turn, were told to completely assemble the component and stamp their work with a personalized identification stamp which had been provided.

Output and quality during the first week was below that which was anticipated and showed very little improvement during the next several weeks. In fact, the output was significantly below that of similar work at an adjacent paced-conveyor operation.

Mr. Brown's boss is upset, to say the least, since efficiency is low and excessive overtime is necessary to meet schedules. Mr. Brown, realizing that he is responsible for production, is trying to determine what happened and what course of action to take now.

---

*From John V. Murray and Thomas J. Von der Embse, *Organizational Behavior: Critical Incidents and Analysis* (Columbus, Oh.: Charles E. Merrill Publishing Co., 1973), pp. 214–15.

Questions

1. What are the possible reasons that job enlargement has failed to increase or even to maintain productivity?
2. Evaulate Mr. Brown's approach in adopting and installing the new system.
3. What effect might the compensation system have on the job-enlargement plan?
4. In view of the present problem, what should Mr. Brown's next move be?

CASE 26: THE CASE OF THE RELUCTANT LOAN OFFICER*

Betty Hampton graduated from State College with a Bachelor's Degree in English. For three years, she had worked for a local bank during the day and attended classes at night. At this bank, Betty had held various jobs, such as teller, loan clerk, secretary, new accounts clerk, and loan processor. Although her major area was English, she had taken enough courses to have a second unofficial major in business administration. Upon graduation, Betty had difficulty finding a challenging job. Finally, in desperation, she accepted a secretarial position with Third National Bank of Brookfield, Betty's home town. A very personable and attractive woman, as well as intelligent, she was easily able to master the routine secretarial chores as well as handle some other areas of responsibility such as new accounts, loan documentation, statement analysis, and computer input.

Betty's work was soon noticed by Ralph Wheelen, the Senior Commercial Loan Officer, who remarked to others that since Betty seemed to be doing such a good job processing loan applications, she might make a good loan officer. There was some reluctance on the part of top management to have a female loan officer since it was "well known" that women are easily swayed by their emotions. There was some fear that Betty might be taken advantage of by some customers. It was feared by Mr. Louis, the bank president, that a young attractive woman might not project the stable and conservative image he felt was necessary in a good loan officer. At this point in time, only three women in the bank had supervisory responsibilities. Two women were in operations—one supervising the bookkeeping department and the other overseeing tellers. There was also one female branch manager (with whom Mr. Louis quite openly had more than a simple business relationship). Mr. Louis believed these women to be appropriately placed, since they primarily supervised other women and had nothing to do with what he considered to be the key profit area in the bank—commercial loans. Nevertheless, on the basis of Wheelen's recommendation and EEO (Equal Employment

---

*Case prepared by Professor J. David Hunger of Iowa State University.

Opportunity) considerations, Betty was given the chance to move up to loan officer.

Betty realized that the bank was using her as a test case and that the president was concerned she project a "proper" image. Consequently, Betty dressed in long sleeve blouses with high neck collars. She wore mainly dark colors and attempted to maintain a serious "Marian, the librarian" appearance and demeanor at all times both on the job and in the community. Of eight banks in the city, only Third National had a female lender.

The first few months on the job were very challenging ones for Betty. She enjoyed her job and seemed to be progressing well. She was having no real problems getting commercial customers to accept her as a lender or in conducting her "officer calls" during which she visited local business people to encourage them to do business with Third National.

One morning, Betty joined eleven other bank officers (loan officers and branch managers) in the conference room for the weekly business development meeting. The meeting was conducted, as usual, by the Senior Vice President, Bill Weber. After discussing the week's officer call reports, Bill Weber asked the group how the bank could increase its holdings of mortgage loans. John Sullivan, a loan officer of many years, suggested that someone talk with Amos McLaren, a successful realtor in the community. "If someone could just talk Amos into mentioning Third National to his customers," suggested John, "we could really pick up the business!" "That's an excellent idea," responded Weber. "But, we have to be careful in how we approach him." Turning to Betty, Weber said, "Betty, I think you ought to take Amos out tomorrow night and do whatever is necessary to get his business."

Betty was astounded at the implications of Weber's statement. "Who does he think I am?" she wondered to herself as she looked at the eleven other people in the conference room. Susan Spriggs, a branch manager and the only other female in the room, was looking at the floor and nervously adjusting her watch. No one else seemed to be reacting except for Joe Bibbins, a young but experienced loan officer, who seemed to have a slight smirk on his face. Betty had heard the rumors circulating around the bank of various people sleeping together, but she never realized how far things seemed to be going!

After a moment's hesitation, Betty looked the Senior Vice President in the face and said, "You have other women on the staff whom you've hired for that purpose. Let them do it."

Questions

1. Evaluate Betty Hampton's response to Bill Weber's suggestion.
2. Analyze the nature of the role conflict evident in this case.

3. Evaluate the ethical climate of Third National Bank.
4. How should Betty Hampton deal with the role conflict in the future?
5. What are the strengths and weaknesses of management in this bank?

CASE 27: NATIONAL INSURANCE COMPANY*

For nearly 30 years, the National Insurance Company had operated their Investment Division as shown in the organization chart (Exhibit 1):

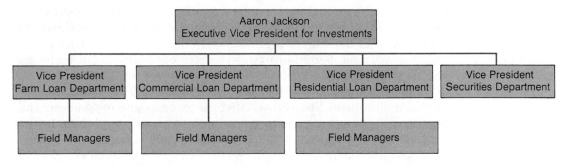

EXHIBIT 1

Aaron Jackson, Executive Vice President for Investments, was responsible for all company investments including mortgage loans, securities (stocks, bonds, etc.), and the small amount of company-owned real estate.

In the last ten years National had significantly increased its sales of large group insurance policies and was administering several large trust funds, such as state teachers retirement funds. These changes resulted in great sums of money which had to be invested, in accordance with various legal and fiduciary restrictions, in treasury bills, bonds, other securities, and real estate. Also, top management had decided to decrease its involvement with residential mortgages because of their relatively low yields in relation to the costs of processing and servicing these loans. It now appeared that the commercial loans and real estate were more promising investment alternatives.

Two major problems had developed with the existing organization given the changing needs of the Investment Division. Mr. Jackson, the Executive Vice President was concerned that he had too many people reporting directly to him. His day-to-day involvement with the Securities Department was rather extensive, as he had formerly headed up this Department and had maintained a close association with it in his current

---

*Case prepared by Professors Thomas R. Miller and James M. Todd, Memphis State University.

position. He felt that he could not "keep up" with the operations under him. Furthermore, with the de-emphasis on residential loans, there were now too many employees in the Residential Loan Department with not enough work to do, both at the headquarters level in Chicago and at the field-level offices in the smaller cities.

In an effort to deal with the changing demands on the Investment Division, Mr. Jackson appointed a committee to conduct a study of the current organization and submit its findings and recommendations to him for submission to the Board of Directors. Six months later the organization plan shown in Exhibit 2 was recommended to and then later approved by the Board for implementation early in the following year.

Under the reorganization plan, there was to be a change from three Vice Presidents reporting on mortgage loans to one Senior Vice President in charge of all mortgages. This made it necessary to consolidate the three mortgage departments into one. With the increased activity in real estate investment, a new real estate section was to be placed under the Senior Vice President.

Early in January the management team of the Investment Division including the Field Managers was called to a meeting in Chicago. This had been billed as the announcement of the reorganization of the Investment Division. In presenting the restructure, the Executive Vice President for Investments stated that there were two major reasons for the organizational change: (1) there had been too many people reporting directly to him, and (2) the investment market today made it necessary to have an organization that was fluid enough to shift its efforts to the most desirable investment opportunities. He explained that the reorganization would require retraining and recycling some employees in order for them to meet their new responsibilities effectively. However, in accordance with established company policy, no employees would lose their

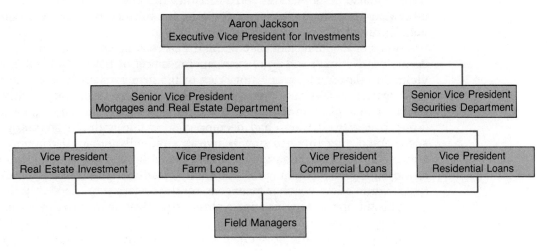

EXHIBIT 2

jobs nor would anyone receive a cut in pay. (In fact, many of the employees affected actually received increases in pay, partly due to inflation and partly because it was thought this would promote their acceptance of the new organization.) He announced the appointments of the two Senior Vice Presidents and the four Vice Presidents of Real Estate Investment, Farm Loans, Commercial Loans, and Residential Loans; charged them to commence implementation of the necessary changes in their units immediately; and wished them well in their new positions.

Although everything was worked out "on paper," soon problems began to emerge in the mortgage loan units. The three Vice Presidents who had formerly been department heads were now only Vice Presidents reporting to a department head. They did not relish their reduced status. At the level of the Field organization there were also subsequent changes. Where before, there had been a Field Manager for each of the Farm, Commercial, and Residential Loan units, there was now only one Field Manager for all mortgage loans. Thus, where there had been three Field offices in each major city, there was now one office per city for all mortgage loans. Some former Field Managers were now only Field Representatives reporting to a Field Manager. As the Field Offices were consolidated, there were also shifts among the administrative and clerical employees. With the change to one Field Office, there was a need for just one Office Manager—not three, and this was not well accepted by the women who were no longer managers. In several instances in the Company, employees who had worked together as peers for many years were now cast into the roles of superior and subordinates with restructured jobs and reporting relationships.

For some employees the restructure seemed to offer expanded opportunities, and they were eager to "get the show on the road." However, others felt that they were not getting their "share of the grapes" and were somewhat resistant and even uncooperative. Although earnest efforts were made to convince the personnel that the new organization would ultimately provide greater opportunities, for various reasons they were not all convinced.

Some of the managers affected by the reorganization had spent many years with National and were approaching retirement age. They felt that they had "paid their dues" in service to the firm over many years, and they knew that National would not terminate them after long faithful service. Some of them had spent 15 to 20 years doing the same job and doing it very well. They had become comfortable with the status quo and wanted everything to stay as it was. Gradually, some discontented workers adjusted and continued to make excellent employees with their new assignments. Others withstood their dissatisfaction until they could retire, while a few younger managers left the organization.

Specific forms of resistance to the reorganization were varied. One Senior Appraiser who had previously worked in a small Field Office did not like it because his new office didn't open into the reception area. Certain long-time residential appraisers felt it "beneath their dignity" when now called upon to appraise farm property. A farm appraiser left the company because he felt farm loans would eventually be cut out. Others resented the loss of status of their job functions under the new organizational pattern.

As certain key positions were filled with people from Commercial Loans, it was rumored "This is not a reorganization but a Commercial Loan Department take over." One of the reasons for the reorganization was to make better use of the large Residential Loan workforce by transferring them to work with Commercial Loan units which were now under staffed. The rumor then started that the same thing would happen to the Farm Loan employees unless they worked harder and produced a high volume of farm mortgages. This proved to be unsettling to the Farm group.

In retrospect, one thing that National apparently overemphasized was the belief that existing personnel could be retrained to assume all positions in the new structure. While some employees were successfully retrained, such as residential appraisers who became competent to do commercial appraisal work, it was found that outside specialists had to be brought in to fill certain key positions, particularly in the Commercial Loan and Real Estate Investment units.

Questions

1. What forces caused Aaron Jackson to perceive the need for organizational change?
2. Note the positive aspects of the firm's approach to the organizational change.
3. What actions did the firm take in planning and implementing change that you would disagree with?
4. Why was the change resisted by some individuals?
5. Would coercion have been more effective in reducing resistance in this case?
6. Could organization development (OD) have been useful in this situation? Why or why not?

CASE 28: DEVELOPING A CAREER PLAN*

The speaker is Lee Summers. He works as a collection correspondent in the credit department of a large retail sales organization. He is also completing his master's degree in business administration at a local univer-

---

*Case prepared by Richard L. Garman.

sity. At age 26, Summers considers himself lucky to have had a taste of several diverse careers but now seems desirous of settling into a stable, satisfying position.

"I remember when I was in high school I wasn't especially oriented toward any specific career. My parents had suggested several careers such as law or mechanical engineering. Several of my friends intended to go 'pre-med' at college and then go on to medical school. Probably half of my class, in fact, wanted to be pre-med, and it sounded like a pretty good idea to me too. It would be a prestigious, 'professional' career, and that looked very attractive. My high school guidance counselor, on the other hand, thought I should be a disc jockey or TV commentator. I had a good speaking voice and excelled in public speaking and debate, but there was just no way I would end up as a disc jockey. Talk about unglamorous, low-paying jobs! That didn't interest me at all.

"When the time came for me to leave for college, I had decided to go pre-med. And yet, I wasn't really interested in the required course work for that major. As my interest dropped, so did my grades. I quickly went from an A-student to just struggling for C's. After three semesters of mediocre performance, the most important thing I had learned was that I didn't really want to go into medicine. My stomach was so weak I'd never have made it past the cadavers at medical school. My career interests were uncertain, but I was sure I had gotten off the track with any career plans. Emotionally, I was at low ebb and felt like a lot of time had been wasted. Against the advice of parents and friends, I decided to quit school and look for a job.

"I went back to my home town and got a job as an apprentice machinist. Machine work was very enjoyable. I liked the technical nature of the job and the precision it required. And the money was great—of course, I had to join the union. All in all, it was a very educational experience and not just in a technical sense. I learned a lot about unions and labor relations. We even had a wildcat strike while I was there. More important still, I learned about the average factory worker in the average factory. I worked with them. I was one.

"After a year and a half, though, I decided to return to college and complete my degree. I liked being a machinist, but I guess I was ambitious. I wanted more. One of my close friends was a business professor at the university. I'd never taken any business courses or considered a career in business. My friend suggested I take a couple of business courses and see how well I liked them. Well, I took his advice and had never enjoyed school so much—or gotten such good grades! I quickly finished my bachelor's degree in business management and began to look for my next goal. Graduate school seemed like a good possibility, and an M.B.A. was highly coveted by every job seeker.

"I was sidetracked for a semester when I decided to help a friend start his own small business. He wanted to form a partnership, but I was reluctant. So I offered to act as a sort of independent consultant. I helped him do all of the planning and organizing right from day one. In only one month, we'd gone from only an idea to a well-documented, on-paper business plan. In two months, the business was fully operational. It's been four years now, and the business is really going strong. I was certainly very happy with that achievement. Anyway, after a few months of 'consulting,' I went on to graduate school to work on my M.B.A. It wasn't long before I was sidetracked again.

"My experience in working with the small business was so enjoyable that I thought I'd try to start my own. I wanted to start a small machine shop in the town where I was living, and so I borrowed the money to buy some of the necessary machinery and rent a building. Against my better judgment, I entered this venture with two financial partners. Unfortunately, they didn't know anything about machine shop operations, and we consequently had several hassles about various business decisions. I ran the operation for two years and then sold out. For a while I worked as a tool designer for another machine shop in town. Finally, I decided to go back to school and finish my M.B.A. I was very intent on finishing my degree without further interruptions, but I had to take a part-time job since most of my savings had gone into my own business venture. That's when I went to work for the retailer. They have been very flexible about working hours and so forth, so the job doesn't interfere with my school work. There's not really much to say about my job now. It's almost strictly clerical—certainly no decision making involved. I guess it's sort of a means to an end, and I'm just grateful to have a job that will allow me to finish school."

Questions

1. Evaluate Summers' career planning (or lack of it) in his educational and work experiences thus far.

2. In view of his interest and experience in machine work, should Summers be encouraged to seek a managerial position in manufacturing? What steps might he take to do so? What should he highlight in a résumé for a prospective employer?

3. Would Summers' experiences suggest a career in management consulting? If so, should he work independently or for a large consulting firm? What steps could he take to build a consulting practice of his own?

4. In view of Summers' enjoyment of academic pursuits, would a teaching career seem practical? How might he pursue an academic career?

CASE 29: VALUE OF RECOGNITION*

The Purity Chemical Corporation† was a large American manufacturing company. The plant involved in this case was one of the largest in the corporation and had been established to fill the needs of a growing market. The primary product of the plant sold well, as its quality was high, and the capacity of the plant, though large, was continually oversold. In the manufacturing process a by-product was produced and was "drawn off the stream" in such quantities that it was thought of as a co-product rather than a by-product; it also required a high degree of purification.

A large technical department was headed by a technical director who had several assistants, each in charge of a given phase of the department's activities. One of these assistants, Mr. Roberts, was in charge of a group of chemists and chemical engineers whose primary duties related to the important by-product. The men in this group reported directly to Mr. Roberts. He, in turn, reported to the technical director. Research problems, product development, quality, and the like were handled by the personnel in this group, reviewed by Mr. Roberts, and passed along to the technical director. Since the purification operations and quality control associated with the by-product were so technical, the group members also served as supervisors for the operating crews of the by-product plant.

Joe Brown, a chemical engineer, was a member of the technical group under Mr. Robert's supervision. He became completely absorbed in the research work in that area and set out to "learn everything there was to know about it."

At the start of the project, he was pleased with the potential it held and would half-jokingly say, "I'm going to make myself an expert in this field."

Elaborate research was conducted for about a year, and Joe thought the results he achieved were well worth the effort. However, about six months after he started, Joe sensed that his work was being taken for granted and that his superiors had not given the project the importance it deserved. Joe did not let this lack of recognition affect his work, however, and the quality and value of his work and research findings remained high. He expressed his feelings to some of his associates, but since they were not as close to the problem as he, their replies were more humorous than serious. This reaction did not help Joe's feelings one bit, but he increased his efforts and did an excellent research job.

He reported the results completely and thoroughly in a well-written, well-documented report. As was the practice in the group, all copies of the report were delivered to Mr. Roberts, who was to review the report,

---

*Case prepared by Professor Leon C. Megginson of University of South Alabama. Reprinted with permission from Megginson, *Personnel: A Behavioral Approach to Administration*, rev. ed. (Homewood, Ill.: Richard D. Irwin, Inc., © 1972), pp. 592–94.
    †All names have been disguised.

present it to the technical director, and arrange for necessary meetings to discuss practical applications of the findings.

Joe waited about a month for action on his work, but none came. He was given some other minor assignments, and he helped on routine work. He found it difficult to approach Mr. Roberts concerning the report and was put off time after time when he inquired about the project.

Mr. Roberts was called out of town on a business trip, and Joe was assigned the duty of "pinch-hitting" for him while he was gone. One day the technical director gave Joe the key to Mr. Roberts's desk and asked him to get a file which he knew was there. When Joe opened the desk, he saw all the copies of his report lying there, apparently unread. This discovery caused Joe considerable trauma, since he was confident that by this time some of the copies of the report had been delivered to the technical director and other company officials.

Joe's feeling of worth was reduced to nothing, and with it went his feeling of pride in his work. He was so shaken by this experience that he resigned from the company.

He was immediately hired by a competitive concern, where his success in his chosen field has been outstanding. He is now an outstanding authority in pollution control.

Questions

1. Evaluate Joe Brown's behavior by using expectancy theory. What was the significance of Joe's finding his reports in Roberts's desk?
2. Evaluate Joe's behavior by using behavior modification theory.
3. Does this case illustrate management's failure to motivate properly or an employee's failure to adopt reasonable attitudes concerning his projects?
4. If you were in Mr. Roberts's position, how would you attempt to motivate Joe Brown's replacement?

CASE 30: "THINGS ARE DIFFERENT AROUND HERE"*

"Things are different around here" were the first words that Jill was told by the new manager. Mr. Tyler was welcoming Jill back to another summer of working at Trams, a nationwide discount store. Jill was not at all thrilled with the prospect of another summer at Trams.

Reluctantly, Jill had returned to Trams where she worked in the ladies and childrens apparel department. Her job consisted of folding

---

*This case was prepared by Ann Marie Calacci, student at St. Mary's College in Notre Dame, Indiana, under the direction of Professor Frank Yeandel.

clothes, fixing the racks, and going to the registers for "price checks." In the summer after her sophomore year in college, Jill had hoped to find something a bit more stimulating or better paying. But jobs were hard to find, so Jill had returned to Trams to work the 6 p.m.–8 p.m. shift.

Her past memories of Trams were filled with strong disdain. She was originally hired since the management found that college students work hard, and work hard she did. Under the regime of Mrs. Williams, Jill began her employment at Trams. Mrs. Williams had strict rules that were to be adhered to or else you were fired.

Jill's stomach tied in knots as she remembered Mrs. Williams and her rules. There was to be no talking between employees, or to friends or family who entered the store. Since the department was located by the main doors and the store was only a block from Jill's house, it was a difficult rule to comply with. Each of the four girls who worked the night shift were assigned a section of the department and would be held responsible for it. With the clientele and the amount of price checks, it was nearly impossible to finish. Yet each night, Jill would do the impossible as she would race against the clock to finish her section. Exhausted at the end of the night, Jill would gaze at her completed job and think of the fruitlessness of it all. For the next day, the customers would ruin it all and she would again do it over.

It seemed from the minute she got there until the minute she left, there was not even time to breathe. She did have a fifteen minute break, but it could not be a second more than that. Mrs. Williams would look through a one way mirror, so everyone was alert at all times. The pressures of being silent in front of friends and relatives who did not know there was a silence rule, trying to beat the clock, and trying to keep her mind occupied as the taped music droned on repetitiously, made Trams an unpleasant place for Jill to work.

As she talked to Mr. Tyler, she sensed that things really were different. He seemed like such a nice man. One by one the new girls she would be working with were introduced to her. Surprisingly, they all seemed to know each other well. Jill was shocked to see them actually smiling as they came in to work. Jill was anxious to see how things were now run. Mr. Tyler then left at 6 p.m., leaving the night crew under no supervision. Jill asked Tara, one of the only remaining old employees, who was in charge. Tara explained that no one was in charge of assigning sections any more, they all worked together as a team.

Jill noticed how the talking ban was lifted. There was a constant chatter among the girls and they eagerly asked Jill about college and how Trams was under Mrs. Williams. Jill was hesitant in talking at first, but after a while she became comfortable talking and working, a thing she had never attempted in the past. The girls teased her for working so quickly as they reminded her they were a team and they would all pitch in to complete the section. At break time, Jill became very uncomfortable as the time was going on twenty minutes and no one attempted to move. Her past training was making her very uncomfortable in the new way of working. That night, amazingly to Jill, all the work was finished with time to spare. All the girls sat around or ate popcorn, while Jill nervously double checked to make sure everything was done.

At first Jill was appalled at the amount of goofing around the girls did, but as time passed Jill found herself enjoying it and participating too. She actually enjoyed coming in to work. It was so different for her to get to know the people she worked with, especially because they were so different from those she went to school with. The night crew was a team. They had so much fun, Jill felt guilty, as if she was getting paid to do nothing. She still was good naturedly teased about being a worrier, a clockwatcher and a workhorse. They reminded her that the kind Mr. Tyler was in charge and Mrs. Williams was long gone. Jill, a naturally lazy person by nature, began to act more and more like the others.

Then one day the district manager came to the store and said that things were to be done much neater since sales took a turn for the worse. Suddenly Jill was thrown back into the time watching method. As the new girls complained, Tara and Jill saw how little they had been doing before. Mr. Tyler enforced this new method for a week and then, slowly but surely, the old ways started to surface, and then came out with a bang.

Breaks turned into forty-five minute affairs. Eating was done after and during work. The girls became sloppier than ever in their work. They started calling in sick often. Jill liked the relaxed atmosphere but thought that this was ridiculous.

Jill felt responsible for the decline in sales, since the department was so untidy. She hated to see inefficiency and for the sake of the store wanted to do something about it. She began to suggest things to the girls, but they rejected her ideas. She knew she was in a bad position to suggest things since they were wary of her education. They resented her level of education, sometimes referring to her language as college talk and too difficult for them to understand. So that they would not call her a college snob, Jill made her suggestions to Mr. Tyler. He agreed that they were excellent suggestions, but he never mentioned them to the others. Jill was frustrated.

The behavior became even more lax, with no comments from Mr. Tyler. Jill enjoyed this freedom less and less. One day, Sue did not come in to work or call in sick. This meant that three had to do all the work that four were to do. After this kept up for a week, the girls were sure that Sue would be fired. But Mr. Tyler could not bring himself to fire Sue, so he gave her a warning. The girls were outraged.

In rebellion, the breaks became an hour long. They reasoned that if Sue could miss days and not be fired, certainly ten minutes here or there would not make a difference. They did not do their job completely, and what they did was done sloppily. Jill participated in the breaks and the quality of her work went down, but she still tried to do her job and the job of the others. Again Trams became a nightmare for her.

Then one day, Tara approached Jill and asked her to ring up a dress for $2. Jill replied that the tag said $25 and not $2. Tara said that Jill was right, that was what the tag said, but it made no difference. Tara explained how she worked hard for years, did her job and never received any reward. She reasoned the store owed her this "discount." Jill adamantly refused to ring it up. Tara went to the register and rang up $2. Jill knew now it was time for her to act.

Questions

1. Analyze the relationship between Jill's job satisfaction and job performance last summer under Mrs. Williams's supervision.
2. Analyze the relationship between the sales clerks' job satisfaction and performance at the beginning of this summer under Mr. Tyler.
3. What is the current relationship between job satisfaction and performance among the department's employees? Why has it changed since the beginning of the summer?
4. What style of leadership is Mr. Tyler using? Why is this style inappropriate in this situation?
5. What can be done to improve both job performance and satisfaction?

CASE 31: QUESTION OF BEHAVIOR MODIFICATION*

"Peg, order some flowers to be sent to Kathy—she'll be out of the hospital tomorrow, so have them sent home. Call Chuck Klein and Wayne Drake to see if the meeting can be switched to 3:30 p.m. I'll need a flight to Chicago on the fifteenth, return flight on the seventeenth—but that's tentative. You might as well have the pension report run. It looks like Kathy is going to be out for the rest of the week, so we can't delay it any longer. Also, hold all my calls for the next hour, I've got to trudge through this computer printout. Thanks, Peg, you're a dear."

Peg Moore's hand was still racing across her steno pad as Liz Reilley closed the door to her office. "That is some lady," Peg thought as she looked over the items on her list, hoping she remembered them all. Indeed, Liz Reilley is a woman to be admired; she has gotten quite far in the business world for a woman with a high school diploma. Liz, now the Personnel Systems Manager, started as a secretary with Austin Chemical Corporation ten years earlier.

Austin Chemical Corporation, a New York based company, is the third largest chemical company on the east coast. It is also very male-oriented. The internal structure of the company is a central corporate headquarters governed by a board of directors and a corporate president.

*This case was prepared by Virginia Kearney, student at St. Mary's College in Notre Dame, Indiana, under the direction of Professor Frank Yeandel.

The company's profits are generated by its six independent divisions, each of which is headed by a division president. The divisions are subordinate to the corporate office. The company is well established. However, in recent years it has been named in several million dollar lawsuits due to various chemical fires and explosions.

Liz, now age forty, came to Austin in 1968 as the secretary to an assistant manager in the corporate Personnel Department. After an unhappy marriage which ended in divorce, Liz wanted to get involved in the business world, and also support herself (she had had no children while she was married). A friend told her of the job opening in Austin, she applied and was hired immediately at her interview. Liz's secretarial skills were superb, and she was able to learn the company's operations within a few weeks. Physically, she was a striking looking woman (dark brown hair, crystal blue eyes, and delicately refined facial features), very poised for her five foot nine inch slender frame, and also well liked by her fellow employees. Liz was considered a definite asset to the Personnel Department, as well as the company.

Over her ten years with the company, Liz has proven to be extremely competent and efficient. She has worked her way up the scale from secretary to the managerial position she holds with the company today. She is a strong advocate of women's equal rights, and has had women appointed to the subordinate positions under her authority.

When Liz first stepped into the position of Personnel Systems Manager, she was faced with piles of paper work, and a fairly stable output. However, she literally turned the department around, creating a noticeable difference in its performance. Men had previously held this position, but their efforts took a back seat to her achievements.

She was looked upon as the "Golden Girl" in the company's eyes. Liz sounds like the perfect success story of a young woman and, indeed, she is successful. However, she is the cause of problems within the department.

Behind her friendly smile is an ambitious nature that is determined to execute the job faster than what is accepted as the company's normal rate. This improved output is not just minimal; it has increased 237.4%. Consequently, her staff has borne the brunt of this increase, and it has taken its toll both mentally and physically on them.

Personnel Systems is a service department responsible for maintaining current records on Austin's thirty-five thousand employees. Also, it generates weekly, monthly, and quarterly reports for associated departments. In order to ensure the latest records, Liz undertook a major project by changing the filing system from a manual to a computerized operation. The system was rather expensive, but the speed at which the information can be obtained is much faster than pulling files from the manual system.

With this system in use, Liz maintains a full-time employee staff of six. There is a fear of job stability among them if further modernization techniques occur. Liz also employs three to five temporary employees, depending on the time of the year. Because of the fast pace at which Liz demands her staff to work, she allows no time for the staff to check their work, and she has no checking system working in the department. If six boxes of keypunch cards are run through the central computer, and there is a mistake in the batch, any card after the mistake is rejected by the computer. This costs the department hundreds of dollars to find the error, correct it, and run the remaining batch through again, hoping no other mistakes will be found. Rejections occur weekly in Liz's department. In fact, they are almost expected. The emphasis is on how fast they can be corrected and rerun. As a result, the staff takes no pride in their work.

Liz's budget balances out because the department's minimal salary expense offsets the cost of computer rejections. Temporary employees are paid at a lesser salary than full-time employees; they are paid by the hour (which Liz regulates), and they do not receive employee benefits. The full-time employees did not adjust to the change of systems very well, and are finding it increasingly difficult to keep up with the pace demanded of them. Kathy Larkin is a prime example.

Kathy was moved from the College Relations Department to the position of assistant manager after Liz's appointment. Kathy was always a hard, dependable, and responsible worker, so her choice to fill the position was perfect under normal circumstances. However, Liz's demands were not normal, and the job had physical effects on Kathy: after one year she was hospitalized for hypertension.

There is no love lost between Liz and the staff. They resent her constant driving, feeling she is using them to better her position in the corporation. She realizes these feelings exist, but they are of no special consequence to her if the job is accomplished. There is also a noticeable increase in the amount of quarreling and bickering among the staff themselves. They continually place the blame on each other when a batch is rejected, and there is no time to assist each other since their only concern is completing the job on time. Unity does not exist in the office; to the staff it is a question of daily survival.

Liz not only makes hard demands on her department, but on other departments which work with Personnel Systems as well. These departments cannot supply her with the information she needs and handle their own work load in the normal five day work week. They have discussed this with Liz, but her demands cease to lighten.

Finally, one of these associate managers went to Liz's immediate supervisor, Dan Gulett, and informed him of Liz's unfair requirements. Mr. Gulett privately talked with Liz's staff and the grievances brought against Liz were confirmed. He also examined the department's financial statements and saw the great expense she was incurring due to careless errors. It was evident that the lack of concern for her staff, and her intense ambition were the cause of the low morale, the ill feelings, and the mental and physical fatigue of her staff. This was also starting to develop in associate departments.

Liz's outstanding record had made her the prime candidate for a directorship, an executive position immediately below vice president. A director position has never been held by a woman in Austin's history. However, with the new light shed on Liz's character, her supervisors have some doubts. They discussed the problems found in her department with her and told her she would have to slow down the pace to build office morale. She felt she should be allowed a larger budget with which to work; they did not favor this suggestion because of the recent expense of computerizing the filing system. Liz then agreed to slow down the work pace so as not to jeopardize her chance for the directorship. Some of her superiors were satisfied with this decision; others felt it was only a superficial change. Once Liz was given the authority of Director of Personnel, she may abuse it. This time the entire corporate personnel office would be at stake. It boils down to a question of whether such a deeply rooted character trait, such as ambition, can be greatly modified in Liz, or will it always be the driving factor in her life.

Dan Gulett was seriously perplexed. Since he is Liz's immediate superior, his opinion would greatly influence the board. There was no doubt in his mind that Liz was capable of handling the job but, in the long run, her appointment may prove detrimental to the company. In all fairness to Liz, he would have to present the facts objectively to the board, giving his opinion only when the board asked for it.

The board was scheduled to meet and vote on the matter at 11:00 a.m. Liz sat anxiously sipping coffee at her desk. It was 11:43 a.m.

> "Peg, when Dan Gulett calls, put it through immediately. Hold all others until then . . . please."

Questions

1. Should Liz Reilley be named Director of Personnel?
2. How would you describe Liz Reilley's leadership style? Is it likely that her leadership style can be substantially changed at this stage in her career?
3. Evaluate Liz Reilley's leadership in terms of path-goal theory and Fiedler's contingency theory.
4. Would you like to work for Liz Reilley? Why or why not?
5. What stress problems are created by Liz Reilley's leadership style? What can be done to correct these problems?

CASE 32: HAS THE WORM TURNED?*

The foreman watched as Alan Boswell, assistant to the factory manager, posted a memorandum on the bulletin board of the management lounge.

---

*Case prepared by John E. Schoen and Jerry L. Crowder.

It seemed as if there had been an endless stream of memoranda relating to policies, procedures, rules, and regulations since George Parker became factory manager five months ago. In addition, too many of the old department heads and management staff had been replaced by M.B.A.'s in vested suits, with Boswell being the worst.

For five months, Parker and his boys had harped on efficiency and had managed to drop the plant from second to fifth place in the division by stumbling over one another. However, Parker was a hard man to talk to—and not a man to cross, because of his temper and autocratic style. Poor old Jimmy Collins found out about that after he spoke up in the annual budget meetings last month.

When Boswell had gone, the foremen approached the bulletin board, shaking their heads wearily, to read the message.

CONFIDENTIAL

TO: All Department Managers   May 10
       All General Foremen

FRIDAY STAFF MEETING

"15 Minutes From the Jaw"

As mentioned in the last staff meeting, we will devote the last 15 minutes of each weekly staff meeting to a review and an answer period (a chance to get acquainted). Subjects may be presented verbally or in writing; the latter may be in a sealed envelope, unsigned, and directed confidentially to the writer.

The purpose of this discussion is to strengthen our managerial team by communication, affording all managers an opportunity to have their questions concerning plant administration thoroughly analyzed, clarified, and answered.

A well-informed management team is one of our key objectives. This team's knowledge and skill, ability to plan and organize effectively, to direct and control, and to evaluate and critique thoughtfully are requisites for effective and outstanding management.

We deal mostly with people, and we must be adequately prepared to:

1. Set goals and meet quotas
2. Work efficiently and effectively
3. Build sound, effective, and loyal teams
4. Stimulate and motivate
5. Develop others for promotion

Topics for discussion should not be limited, but must be meaningful and objective. They may relate to (1) improving individual performance, (2) clarifying procedures and policies, (3) improving leadership styles, or (4) any appropriate subject of your choice. Let's communicate and direct our efforts toward making the management team outstanding in each of its management responsibilities.

(signed)

George Parker
Factory Manager

Questions

1. Evaluate the probable effectiveness of the message in stimulating two-way communication in the staff meeting and/or generally.

2. Evaluate the content of the message with respect to management principles and/or a participative approach to management.

3. Who has responsibility for establishing communication after managerial succession?

4. Evaluate the method the factory manager has used to communicate instructions regarding the Friday staff meeting.

CASE 33: MONITORED PHONE CALLS*

On a Friday afternoon Gil Harris, National Insurance Regional Manager, called his accounts division manager, Earl Bennett, into his office and explained to him that he had, for some time, been considering a program which he felt could reveal any possible problems with customer service. Now he was prepared to implement it. Over the weekend the telephone company was to install new equipment allowing incoming and outgoing phone calls to be monitored. The program involved three managerial and nine clerical employees, all of whom had either agent or policy holder contacts. Mr. Harris was to maintain the tapping device in his office. Not only did he wish to supervise the program personally, but he felt that employees would be enthusiastic about an opportunity to prove themselves before higher management. As Bennett attempted to express his reservations, Harris ended the talk by saying that his decision was good and that Bennett should notify his people of it. Monday morning Bennett called the twelve employees together and told them of Mr. Harris's wishes.

The announcement was followed by a great deal of grumbling. One woman was overheard telling her coworkers, "I've always prided myself in doing a good job. We should go in there and complain, but he would probably fire the lot of us."

During the first month of monitoring, absenteeism nearly doubled, and two employees notified Bennett they wished to transfer to another section. When asked why, they replied they couldn't stand being "watched" all the time. Bennett knew he would be held responsible for this activity and didn't know what to tell Harris. His problem compounded when he received the following memo from Harris:

"Earl, it appears as though I have been successful in uncovering problem areas. Your people don't seem to spend enough time with agents or policy holders. They act as though they are in a hurry and on

---

*John V. Murray and Thomas J. Von der Embse, *Organizational Behavior: Critical Incidents and Analysis* (Columbus, Oh.; Charles E. Merrill Publishing Co., 1973), p. 190.

occasion are downright 'rude.' Be in my office at 10 a.m. tomorrow morning with your recommendations on how you are going to straighten this out."

Questions

1. Evaluate Gil Harris's statement that "employees would be enthusiastic about an opportunity to prove themselves before higher management."
2. Evaluate Mr. Harris as a leader and a communicator.
3. What should be done to correct the present situation?

CASE 34: AM I A TOUGH GUY?*

A friend of mine recently said that 1975 is going to be the year of the tough guys, and that's right. It's for guys and gals who care enough to put everything they've got into what they're doing, and do their best. It's not the year for sitting around and letting everyone else do it for them. It's a good year for challenge and productivity because there is still money there, and there are still people who are ready to spend it. It's up to the tough guys, to the ones who merit being the ones with whom that money is spent!†

Dorothy Barton, sitting at her desk in the small office just off the Style Shop sales floor, pondered this quotation which happened to catch her eye as she leafed through the latest edition of the *Dallas Fashion Retailer*.

In the women's ready-to-wear business, as in many other businesses, 1974 had been a rough year. It was particularly rough, however, for the attractive, energetic Style Shop owner. Wife, and the mother of four teenage daughters, Mrs. Barton saw her sales fall 12.5 percent from 1973 to 1974; but, more significantly, her net profit plunged 62.5 percent over the same time period. Untold hours she spent on the sales floor catering to her customers' eye for quality and fashion; in the office appealing to manufacturers to ship the next season's orders even though the current ones were yet to be paid; and at the Dallas Apparel Mart buying just the fashions she hoped would fit the needs and desires of her customers. At the same time, she was spending many hours each week in an effort to help her husband get his infant construction business off the ground.

She remembered hearing one "expert" say, "This is not a time for pessimism, nor a time for optimism. This is a time for realism." And an economic prognosticator had indicated that he saw a good future in the

---

*Case prepared by Professor Janelle C. Ashley of Stephen F. Austin State University.
†"Merchandisers Must Provide Leadership," *Dallas Fashion Retailer* (June 1975): 17.

industry, despite the economic slowdown. Buyers, he noted, are working a little more cautiously right now. They are still buying, just looking at things a little more carefully.

"But what is 'realism' for me?" she asked herself. "Am I one of the tough guys who can stick it out and 'merit being the one with whom the money is spent!'?"

Style Shop Location and Background

The Style Shop opened its doors on February 12, 1954, in Lufkin, TX, and in 1969 it moved to its present location in the Angelina Mall. The mall contains a major discount chain store, two full-line department stores, and a number of specialty shops. Located nearby are a twin cinema, motel, and junior college. The mall serves as the hub of a trade area extending over a radius of more than 100 miles. The only centers comparable to the Angelina Mall at the time were as distant as Houston, 120 miles to the southwest, and Dallas, 166 miles to the northwest.

Dorothy Barton, the present owner, began with the Style Shop as a part-time accountant in March, 1962. She became a 50-50 partner when the new shop opened in 1969 and purchased the 50 percent belonging to the other partner in January, 1974. She operates the business as a sole proprietorship.

The Style Shop up to 1974

Personnel.   The Style Shop employed four full-time clerks, one alteration lady, and a maid. A former employee and the teenage daughter of Mrs. Barton were frequently called in for part-time work during peak seasons.

Mrs. Flo Gates had been with the shop for 10 years. She worked as a clerk and floor manager and accompanied Mrs. Barton to market. The other three clerks had been with the Style Shop from one to three years each. Personnel turnover and apathy had been problems in the past, but Mrs. Barton was quite pleased with her present work force.

Policies.   The Style Shop operated with no formal, written policies. Personnel were paid wages and benefits comparable to other workers in similar capacities in the city. They enjoyed a great deal of freedom in their work, flexibility in hours of work, and a 20 percent discount on all merchandise purchased in the shop.

Competition.   Lufkin had an average number of retail outlets carrying ladies' ready-to-wear for cities of its size. Several department stores and other specialty shops carried some of the same lines as did the Style Shop, but they were all comparable in price. The Style Shop did handle several exclusive lines in Lufkin, however, and enjoyed the reputation of being the most prestigious women's shop in town. Its major competition was a similar, but larger, specialty shop complete with a fashion shoe department in neighboring Nacogdoches, 19 miles away.

Inventory Control. The Style Shop used the services of Santoro Management Consultants, Inc., of Dallas, TX, for inventory control. IBM inventory management reports were received each month broken down into 23 departmental groupings. These reports showed beginning inventory, sales and purchases for the month and year to date, markdowns, ending inventory, and various other information. Cost for the services was $110 per month.

Financial Position. It is often quite difficult and sometimes next to impossible to evaluate the "true" financial position of a single proprietorship or a partnership due to the peculiarities that are either allowed or tolerated in accounting practices for these forms of ownership. This is evident in looking at the Style Shop's five-year Comparative Statement of Income (Exhibit 1), the Comparative Statement of Financial Condition (Exhibit 2), plus the 1974 Statement of Income (Exhibit 3) and 1974 Statement of Financial Condition (Exhibit 4). Key business ratios (median) for women's ready-to-wear stores are also given for comparative purposes in Exhibit 5.

EXHIBIT 1 Comparative statement of income

Item	1970	1971	1972	1973	1974
Sales	$200,845.43	$213,368.15	$216,927.31	$217,969.59	$190,821.85
Cost of sales	132,838.30	$133,527.91	131,900.84	138,427.14	121,689.74
Gross profit	$ 68,007.13	$ 79,840.24	$ 85,026.47	$ 79,542.45	$ 69,132.11
Expenses	60,727.46	70,051.29	67,151.58	69,696.93	65,438.20
Net profit	$ 7,279.67	$ 9,788.95	$ 17,874.89	$ 9,845.52	$ 3,693.91

EXHIBIT 2 Comparative statement of financial condition

Item	1970	1971	1972	1973	1974
Current assets*	$38,524.93	$ 70,015.11	$ 66,749.78	$ 58,530.44	$ 68,458.34
Inventory	23,039.00	37,971.00	33,803.00	36,923.00	35,228.00
Fixed assets	7,314.58	86,504.94	83,924.45	80,534.06	63,943.67
Total assets	$45,839.51	$156,520.05	$150,674.23	$139,064.50	$132,402.01
Current liabilities	$35,892.81	$ 19,586.45	$ 20,161.93	$ 31,587.57	$ 55,552.70
Long-term liabilities	none	39,042.90	33,680.07	26,841.76	20,003.45
Total liabilities	$35,892.81	$ 58,629.35	$ 53,842.00	$ 58,429.33	$ 75,556.15
Net worth	9,946.70	97,890.70	96,832.23	80,635.17	56,845.86
Total	$45,839.51	$156,520.05	$150,674.23	$139,064.50	$132,402.01

*Current-asset values include the amounts shown for inventory.

EXHIBIT 3   Statement of income

Style Shop Statement of Income For Year Ended Dec. 31, 1974		
Sales		$190,821.85
Cost of sales:		
Beginning inventory	$ 36,923.00	
Purchases	119,994.74	
	$156,917.74	
Ending inventory	35,228.00	121,689.74
Gross profit		$ 69,132.11
Expenses:		
Advertising	$ 3,034.63	
Auto expense	1,509.63	
Bad debts	(439.83)	
Depreciation	1,580.49	
Freight, express, delivery	2,545.90	
Heat, light, power, and water	1,847.96	
Insurance	1,431.80	
Interest	4,064.25	
Legal and accounting	2,034.74	
Rent	11,220.40	
Repairs	528.98	
Salary	26,227.69	
Supplies	5,138.11	
Tax—Payroll	1,656.18	
Tax—Other	604.62	
Telephone	784.67	
Dues and subscriptions	601.89	
Market and travel	1,066.09	65,438.20
Net profit		$ 3,693.91

Two explanatory footnotes should be added to these statements. The jump in fixed assets between 1970 and 1971 (see Exhibit 2) and the subsequent changes were due in large part to the inclusion of personal real estate on the partnership books. The long-term liability initiated in 1971 was an SBA loan. Caught in a period of declining sales (due in part to the controversy over skirt length and women's pantsuits) and rapidly rising expenses in the new mall location, the Style Shop owners found themselves in that proverbial "financial bind" in late 1969 and 1970. They needed additional funds both for working capital and fixed investments. Since a big jump in sales was anticipated in the new location, additional working capital was necessary to purchase the required inventory. The new tenants also desired fixed-asset money to purchase display fixtures for their new store. They obtained this money through a local bank in the form of an SBA-insured loan.

EXHIBIT 4   Statement of financial condition

Style Shop Statement of Financial Condition Dec. 31, 1974		
ASSETS		
Current assets:		
Cash on hand and in banks		$ 4,923.92
Accounts receivable		21,306.42
Inventory		35,228.00
Cash value—Life insurance		7,000.00
Total current assets		$ 68,458.34
Fixed assets:		
Furniture and fixtures and leasehold improvements	$27,749.94	
Less: Allowance for depreciation	9,806.27	$ 17,943.67
Auto and truck		9,500.00
Real estate		20,000.00
Furniture		10,000.00
Boat and motor		2,000.00
Office equipment		2,500.00
Jewelry		2,000.00
Total fixed assets		$ 63,943.67
TOTAL ASSETS		$132,402.01
LIABILITIES AND CAPITAL		
Current liabilities:		
Accounts payable		$ 30,413.12
Accrued payroll tax		825.64
Accrued sales tax		1,193.94
Note payable—Due in one year		9,420.00
Note payable—Lot		10,700.00
Note payable—Auto		3,000.00
Total current liabilities		$ 55,552.70
Note payable—Due after one year		20,003.45
Total liabilities		$ 75,556.15
Net worth		56,845.86
TOTAL LIABILITIES AND CAPITAL		$132,402.01

The Style Shop, 1975. "Certainly there is no longer an arbiter of the length of a skirt or the acceptance of pantsuits," Mrs. Barton mused. "The economic picture is looking brighter. The experts tell us there will be more disposable personal income and a lower rate of inflation. Yet this is a time for 'realism.' Am I a 'tough guy'?"

EXHIBIT 5   Key business ratios for women's ready-to-wear stores

Ratio	1974	1973	1972	1971	1970
Current assets / Current liabilities	2.65	2.81	2.51	2.38	2.50
Net profit / Net sales	2.05	2.30	1.81	1.86	2.18
Net profit / Net worth	8.92	8.53	6.68	7.14	8.73
Net profit / Net working capital	11.43	10.96	8.64	9.98	10.92
Net sales / Net worth	3.82	3.96	3.95	3.76	3.78
Net sales / Net working capital	4.61	4.92	4.73	4.90	4.49
Net sales / Inventory	6.7	6.7	6.6	6.7	6.1
Fixed assets / Net worth	18.3	18.2	18.6	17.5	14.7
Current liabilities / Net worth	49.4	49.2	51.0	54.5	56.5
Total liabilities / Net worth	98.5	100.1	104.0	124.1	125.8
Inventory / Net working capital	73.0	72.3	76.7	71.1	78.3
Current liabilities / Inventory	84.6	87.2	87.0	93.9	86.6
Long-term liabilities / Net working capital	30.1	33.2	29.8	34.0	30.8

NOTE: Collection period not computed. Necessary information as to the division between cash sales and credit sales was available in too few cases to obtain an average collection period usable as a broad guide.
SOURCE: *Dun's Review* (September issues, 1970–1974).

Questions

1. Calculate and interpret the five-year trends for the Style Shop in the following areas:

   a. Current ratio
   b. Debt-to-net worth ratio
   c. Inventory turnover
   d. Profit margin on sales
   e. Return on net worth

2. Evaluate the overall performance of the Style Shop. What is the outlook for the store?

CASE 35: MADISON ELECTRONICS*

The Madison Electronics Company manufactures electrical components for a variety of major U.S. firms. The standards for the components vary with the customer but usually must conform to rather close tolerances. Despite receiving some large orders for components in recent years, MEC is currently being forced to lay-off employees.

Part of this lay-off can be attributed to an efficiency team brought into the organization one year ago to redesign jobs and workflow to increase productivity and reduce per unit costs. One of the recommendations of this group of consultants was the implementation of a bonus system. MTM [motion and time method] was used to establish rates for the various jobs throughout the facility. While there was initial resistance to using such a system, most employees have discovered that they can exceed the rate and so earn more than their base pay.

One of the jobs which has been unable to meet the rate is that of the employees which trim the various parts prior to their being assembled and sold to the customers. The parts are sent directly to the trimmer from the casting department. The trimmers insert the part into a shearing machine which trims away burrs and other irregular formations on the parts. After trimming, the parts are sent to milling where they are smoothed and prepared for assembly and shipped to the intended customer as shown in Exhibit 1. If the part does not fit into the shearing equipment, it is rejected and returned to the casting department for possible reworking.

The standard rate set for the trimmer is 500 units per hour or 4,000 units per day. When the casting machines are properly adjusted this rate can be attained by a diligent worker. However, if the trimmer rejects a part because it does not fit the shearing machine, it is not counted as a unit completed and does not count toward the rate set for the operator.

*Case prepared by Professor Joe Thomas of Northeast Missouri State University.

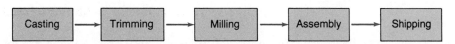

EXHIBIT 1   Workflow of cast components

Since the dies in the casting department are allowed to become quite worn before replacement, it becomes increasingly difficult for the trimmer to achieve the established rates of production. This creates special problems, since once the parts are trimmed, other workers in assembly and shipping are able to achieve their rates and earn their bonus. Trimmers are quite dissatisfied with the existing system, and turnover for the department is excessive.

The manager of the trimming department has asked the casting manager numerous times to replace the dies before they become so worn. The casting manager is reluctant to replace the dies sooner than is absolutely necessary because this increases the down time for his workers and keeps them from achieving their established rates. Doing maintenance also causes increased operating costs for the department.

The personnel manager has been very reluctant to change the established bonus system. The standard reply has been that the system was developed by specially trained time and motion experts and that they knew what they were doing.

Questions

1. What do you believe is the major problem in this case?
2. How might this problem be effectively resolved?

CASE 36: SOUTHERN CAMERA*

Rusty Veron, the owner of Southern Camera, had just received the results of the 1980 fiscal year's operations from his outside accountant. He was reviewing these statements with his general manager, Roger Nelson, and with the assistant manager, Cindy Jean Williams. During the course of this meeting, Rusty outlined several areas of concern. He asked Roger and Cindy Jean to investigate these areas and to formulate recommendations. These items are:

1. The decreasing profit margins and increasing inventory levels (see Exhibit 1).

*Case prepared by Professor John Chaney of California State College, San Bernardino.

2. The possibility and desirability of instituting a formal inventory system.

3. The feasibility of the institution of a computerized inventory control system.

4. The desirability of opening a new store in a neighboring community.

History of Southern Camera

Rusty Veron started this business in 1970 as Southern Photo and Instrument which operated as a camera repair service. After two years he moved to a larger location and began retail camera sales. Until 1978 his business activities included:

- retail sales of cameras and accessories
- photo finishing
- camera repair
- sale of surveying instruments

In 1978 the photo finishing lab was closed and now all photo finishing is sent out for processing. The sale of surveying instruments has been organized as a separate business, and the main retail camera sales and repair business is called Southern Camera.

Rusty has until recently managed the business by himself. In January of 1980 he hired Roger Nelson as general manager in order to leave

EXHIBIT 1 Summary of selected ratios—Southern Camera
(Fiscal year ending July 12, 1980)

		Figures as % of Sales			
Year	Sales	Inventory	Net Profit[1]	Cost of Sales	Wages
1980	$585,000	36	9	68	13
1979	$551,000	33	14	65	14
1978	$398,000	30	16	67	12
1977	$347,000	35	12	70	16
1976	$286,000	37	8	72	15
Industry averages[2] for 1979		20–25	10–15	60–70	12–17

[1]Before owners draw or salary.
[2]Estimated from data gathered from trade publications on similar types & size camera shops.

himself more time to set objectives and to plan the expansion of the business. Rusty is well liked by his employees and has built a reputation in the community and among his customers of being a fair and highly competent businessman. He feels that his business is sufficiently financially stable and successful to warrant expansion to a second location, but at this point has not conducted feasibility studies on this expansion.

Personnel

There is much competition in the retail camera and photo finishing market. Rusty views his business as serving that portion of the market which values personal attention and expert advice. Because of this, Southern Camera's sales personnel are hired for their prior knowledge of cameras and enthusiasm to provide a high level of personal service.

In the past year, Southern Camera has experienced a high employee turnover. Rusty feels that this turnover has had several negative consequences for his business:

1. The shipping and receiving department has been staffed by untrained, part-time personnel. This has contributed to the lack of adequate records on orders, items received, and inventory levels. No continuity in procedures has been maintained.
2. With rapid salesperson turnover it is difficult for the repeat customer to build rapport with the sales staff.
3. In several instances, an employee who had resigned had to be consulted for information that no one on the staff could furnish.

The high turnover resulted partly from the type of employees hired, often students working their way through college, and partly from the wages, which are low in comparison to many other sales jobs. Turnover has also been high in the managerial ranks. In the past year, Southern Camera has had two assistant managers, the administrative assistant and the manager of the repair department, resign.

Customer Profile

Rusty conducted an in-store survey of Southern Camera's customers. The majority (60%) of the customers interviewed had heard of Southern Camera by word of mouth. Thirty-nine percent of the customers were in the store to buy film and/or accessories; 34% were shopping for cameras; 14% were in for photo finishing and 11% were purchasing darkroom supplies. Sixty-seven percent of the customers owned 35mm cameras, 25% instant cameras, 5% pocket cameras and the rest owned other types of cameras. The vast majority of those surveyed considered themselves to be amateur photographers.

The age break-down of the customers was 31% in the 25–30 range;

25%, 31–40; 23%, 19–24; 19% over 41; and 2%, 18 and under. Seventy-three percent of the customers were male. Fifty-four percent of the customers identified themselves as white collar workers, 11% as students, 11% as blue collar and the remaining 6% were housewives or unemployed.

Internal Systems and Record-Keeping

Currently, ordering may be done by the repair technician (parts), the administrative assistant (office supplies), the general and assistant managers (merchandise inventory), and any salesperson (merchandise and special orders). In the past, many items were ordered without purchase orders. This contributed to lost special orders and a higher than necessary inventory level.

Accounts Payable are handled by a part-time bookkeeper. Accounts Receivable are handled by the Administrative Assistant. There is not sufficient allocation of employee time to keep these accounts current and late billing and paying of bills due has become a problem.

The inventory is divided into two parts for record-keeping purposes. Small items are replenished by the sales representatives of the supplier. No records are kept on these items. High value items are recorded by serial number at the time they are received on index cards which are maintained by the shipping and receiving department. A tag is placed on each item, listing the serial number. The items are then priced and placed into stock. When completely filled, the purchase order on which the items were ordered is removed from the current file. These purchase orders are not monitored or checked before they are completely filled.

As items are sold, the salespeople are to remove the inventory tag and attach it to the sales receipt copy. The administrative assistant then uses these receipts to fill in the portion of the inventory card which deals with sales price, date, and customer name. This removes the item from inventory.

Rusty does not know the number of separate items that are carried in inventory on a regular basis, but estimates the number at about 2,000 different items. This inventory ranges from one or two of each of the popular high-priced cameras and lens sets to an undetermined number of lower priced items such as film, accessories and cleaning supplies.

Rusty feels that his present inventory system has several drawbacks and problems:

1. Net cost of items received is not recorded on inventory cards. This makes it impossible to accurately determine cost-of-goods-sold for financial statements and tax forms.
2. The inventory card entry is not cross-referenced to the purchase order number.

3. There is no way to indicate on the current inventory cards when more items have been ordered and on the way.

4. Salespeople neglect to place the inventory tag on the sales receipt copy.

5. Current inventory cards are highly inaccurate. There is no system for auditing the inventory cards periodically and reconciling them with items physically on hand.

6. Items are not removed from inventory records on a current basis. This stems from an insufficient allocating of employee time for record-keeping purposes.

It is Rusty's belief that these problems could be solved by the institution of a computerized inventory system. He currently has an electronic cash register which has the capacity to generate data which could be sent out to a computer service for processing. He has received several quotes for this service ranging from $150 per month to $725 per month. The lower quotes would buy a listing of sales by item and a monthly updating of inventory records. The higher quotes would include detailed sales analysis organized to his specifications, inventory updates, and a listing of accounts receivable and accounts payable, all with a two-week turnaround.

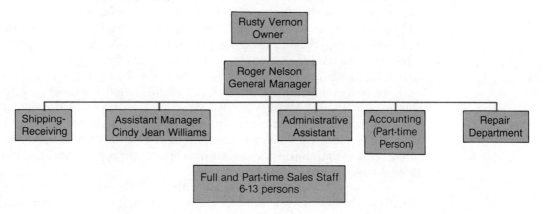

EXHIBIT 2 Organization chart of Southern Camera

Questions

1. What are the major personnel problems in Southern Camera and how would you solve them?

2. What specific steps would you advocate in improving the inventory control system of Southern Camera?

3. What other control problems—aside from personnel and inventory—do you see in the operations of Southern Camera and how would you alleviate them?

4. What are the advantages of a computerized inventory system for Southern Camera? The disadvantages? How would you recommend that such a system be implemented?

CASE 37: WALTER STANTON: EMPLOYEE RESPONSIBILITY AND THE USE OF TIME*

Walter Stanton, in discussing the responsibility of an employee to his or her employer with a group of MBA students at a southwestern business school, was surprised at the number of questions he received and the diversity of opinion he found among his students regarding the use of time on and off the job. In order to give some focus to the discussion, he asked each student to write up a short incident describing a specific situation in his own experience in which this question had arisen. The following are a few of the incidents reported by the students.

Jerry Donaldson

"Last summer I was employed in a serivce station in my home town in Idaho. Besides selling petroleum products, this station had a Big O Tire and Honda motorcycle franchise. My responsibilities included pumping gas, fixing tires, greasing cars, making minor motorcycle repairs and assembling new motorcycles which came in crates from Japan. I also assisted the mechanic and the manager whenever they needed me.

"Early in the summer, the manager decided that it would be profitable to stay open 24 hours a day. Many tourists traveled through our town during the summer months and they had no place to purchase gas after 10:00 p.m. The manager also thought that the night man could clean up the station, do the necessary motorcycle repairs and assemble at least two motorcycles each night shift.

"Although I was reluctant to work the 10:00 p.m. to 7:00 a.m. shift, I finally agreed to rotate every other week with another of the employees.

"During my first week of working night shifts, I went over the detailed list of duties for the night man to perform and planned out how much time I had to accomplish each assigned job. I tried to use all of the time allotted to each job even if it meant doing the job very slowly. This method allowed me to be busy the whole night and made the time go faster. I also found that if I wasn't busy all the time, I became very bored and drowsy. Therefore I always tried to stay busy.

"About the third week of working night shifts, however, I started to see how fast I could finish all of the assigned tasks. I worked out a whole series of short-cuts for cleaning the station and found that I could do it

---

*Case prepared by Professor Clinton L. Oaks of Brigham Young University.

in an hour less than it had taken me previously. I also found that I could up my efficiency in working motorcycle repairs and in assembling new Hondas. I made a game out of pushing myself and found that I could do all the jobs and still have at least two hours left after they were all completed. At first I did not know what to do during the two hours, and they went by very slowly. I have always enjoyed tinkering with my car, however, so I decided that during this spare time I would wash and wax it, work on the tune-up and make all of the little repairs that it needed. I always felt a little guilty working on my car while I was getting paid, but since I was doing a good job of finishing all the assigned tasks, I felt I was justified in using any spare time on my own projects.

"My boss evidently was pleased with my work because he frequently commended me on doing my job well. Several times I heard him 'chewing out' the other employee for not doing a good job. I never told him that I worked on my car, but since I had him get some parts for me I was pretty sure he knew what I was doing. He never said anything to me about it.

"Towards the end of the summer, by boss announced that the corporation that owned this station had decided that it would be beneficial to the company if every employee in the company received a polygraph test at least once a year. They had all of their employees sign a statement that they agreed to take the test.

"Early one Saturday morning when I arrived at work, I discovered that the test administrator was at our station and that I was to take the test that morning. I was not alarmed since I had been honest in putting all money that I had received in the till and making a proper receipt out after each sale.

"After putting all of the equipment on me and turning on his tape recorder, the man began asking me some general questions regarding my honesty. I felt very comfortable telling him I had never stolen any money from the till and that I always accomplished tasks that were assigned to me. Towards the end of the test he asked, 'Do you make good use of all of your time at work?' Suddenly, I felt very uncomfortable and could feel my heart start to beat a lot faster."

Questions

1. What should Jerry Donaldson tell the polygraph operator?
2. Is the company's use of the polygraph ethical?

Allen Knight

"After I finished my undergraduate work in mathematics and computer science, my wife persuaded me to take a job for a couple of years so that we could pay off some of our bills and get ahead a little before I started on my MBA. She was also concerned that I wasn't spending enough time with my two young sons. Between the demands of my course work and a part-time job, I usually left early in the morning and often was not home until after they had been put to bed.

"One of my undergraduate professors was instrumental in getting me a job with Nelson Data Processing. I understood before I started that they were a hard-driving firm with a reputation for high quality work. Once aboard, I found that the company had a large backlog and that management was encouraging everyone to put in overtime, for which they paid a generous hourly rate on top of the employee's salary.

"We needed the money and the work was interesting. Before long, I found myself working late almost every night. Barbara, my wife, didn't say much at first, but I could tell she wasn't happy with the way things were working out. Finally one day she said, 'Allen, you were spending more time at home when you were in school then you are now.' I mumbled something about 'trying to cut it down a little' and dropped the subject.

"The next day at noon when another employee and I were on our way out to grab a sandwich, I mentioned that my wife was unhappy about all the time I was spending away from home. He said, 'Look, Allen, you don't have to punch a time clock on those extra hours. A lot of the guys just take their work home with them. Keep track of your time and turn it in just like you do now. I'm not sure what the company policy is, but I have been doing this every so often for several months now, and nobody has ever said anything about it.'

"The more I thought about the idea of doing my overtime at home, the better I liked it. I could spend the early evening with the family and then, after the boys were to bed, I could really get some work done. As I had expected, Barbara was elated when I explained to her what I was going to do.

"The first few nights I found it hard to get up to speed again after letting down for dinner and roughhousing with the kids. As I got into the swing of it, however, I found that since there was no distractions, as there often were at the office, I could do a lot more at home in an hour than I was doing at work. Whenever I needed someone to help with the checking or sorting, Barbara was always available and seemed to enjoy working with me. I found that there were some things she could do faster and more accurately than I could. One night after we had finished a particularly long and involved task in about half the time it would ordinarily have taken me, I said, 'Barbara, there ought to be some way to put you on the payroll.' She laughed and said, 'Why don't you just increase the number of hours put in for yourself to cover it?'"

Questions

1. Should Allen Knight report his wife's working time as part of his own working time and thereby receive compensation for it?

2. Does the arrangement whereby work is performed at home present any particular ethical problems?

Weldon Gates

"I had been working for Patterson Engineering for nearly a year when I decided to come back and get my MBA. About three weeks before school was to start, I gave my supervisor, Jim, who was really a great boss, my two-week notice. Since he and I had talked a number of times about my going on to school as a preparation for a move into management, he was not at all surprised. He asked me to come in his office for a few minutes later that morning to make plans for my departure. I thought he might be concerned about several things I was working on that would be hard to turn over to anyone until I completed my present segment. I wasn't too concerned, however, because I had worked out a careful schedule and I figured I would just have time to do it all in those last two weeks.

"When I entered my supervisor's office, he said, 'Weldon, you have done a great job for us, and when you finish your education, we want you to keep us in mind. You said that school started right after the first of next month?' I nodded, and he went on to say, 'I imagine that you have a lot of work to do to get packed and moved, don't you?' I replied, 'Boy, I'll say! Moving is always such a hassle. We want to get out of our apartment by the fifteenth so that we can get our deposit back. I would like to have allowed myself a few more days, but when we figured out what we would need for school this year, we found that the money from these last two weeks was really crucial.'

"My supervisor smiled and leaned back in his chair. 'Yes,' he said, 'I remember how is was. I think, though, that I can help you out. According to my records, you have accumulated about 12 days sick leave. Is that right?' 'Yes,' I answered. 'Well, as you know, the firm doesn't pay any sick leave unless you are actually sick. In your case, though, you are going to be sick—sick of moving. I want you to spend this afternoon acquainting Tom with where you are on each one of your projects. Then each morning for the next two weeks I want you to call in sick. If there is any question about it, I'll cover for you.'

"That night I thought a lot about what Jim had said—but I just didn't feel good about it. Tom was a good man, but it would take someone else at least twice as long to finish the things I was working on as it would take me. One of the projects was the kind that someone new would almost have to start over. The executives at Patterson had really been good to me in terms of the kinds of assignments they had given me—and I had been given a pay raise every six months instead of every year as was typical with new employees.

"I went in early the next morning and was right in the middle of my most important project when Jim came by. He frowned when he saw me at my desk. 'I thought I told you to take these two weeks off. I don't want to see you in here after today!' "

Question

1. Should Weldon Gates accept his supervisor's offer and take sick leave during the time he is moving?

Lorraine Adams

"When I was an undergraduate, I worked summers on an electronic composer for Brown Publishing. This is a typewriter with a memory which enables it to type course material in columns and justified (flushed right) margins. Because it is difficult to determine how long it takes to type material into memory and play it back, I often went for four hours without taking the fifteen-minute break we were supposed to have both morning and afternoon. Some of the other girls, who had the same problem, kept track of the breaks they didn't take and then used them as justification for leaving a half hour early or arriving a half hour late, recording their time as if they had left or arrived at the normal time. One girl even saved hers for two weeks and then took an afternoon off to do some shopping. I am sure that this was contrary to company policy, but our supervisor was a very relaxed and friendly woman who never seemed to notice when someone was gone.

"Another problem I had with breaks is 'What can constitute a break?' If a friend, who wasn't an employee of the company, dropped in for a few minutes, I always thought of that as a break. But what if some other employee who is tired, bored, or worried comes by and spends a few minutes talking about her work, her plans for the weekend, her current boy friend or some personal problem? Should you count that as a break? One morning our supervisor talked to me for twenty minutes about job opportunities for women with MBAs. Was that a break?

"Accounting for my time has always been a problem for me. Last summer, I worked as a department manager in a branch of a large department store in Los Angeles. A number of the department managers would arrive at 8:00, as we were supposed to do, and then take off across the mall to a coffee shop 'to make plans for the day.' They usually got back just before the store opened at 9:30. I went with them a couple of times and found that if they discussed anything related to their work in the store, it was only an incidental part of their conversation. A couple of these guys would also regularly take up to an hour and a half for lunch and then check out right after five. Since we didn't have to check in and out for breaks or for lunch, their time card would show an eight-hour day. When I said something to one of them about it one day, he answered, 'Listen, Lorraine, summer is a slack time around here. You ought to be here during the Christmas rush. We work a lot of hours then that we don't get paid for. The store owes us a chance to relax a little when the heat is off.'"

Questions

1. What constitutes a legitimate break? Is it ethical to save up breaks and use them at other times?
2. Are the department managers acting ethically in taking extended coffee breaks and lunch hours?

Robert Jeffries

"Before I came back to school, I worked for two years for a branch of Jefferson Sporting Goods. Jefferson had five large stores located in different metropolitan areas in the state and did a large volume in men's and women's sports clothes. Our branch wasn't the largest in the chain but would have been second or third.

"The store manager, Rand Walker, had been manager since the store was opened. He had previously had soft goods experience with several other stores and really knew that part of the business.

"We got along really well. Not long after I came to work, Rand put me in charge of the shoe department. Later he made me manager of the men's clothing department, and, a year later, he made me assistant manager. He always saw that I got a substantial raise after each six month review. He seemed to have a lot of trust in me. I noticed, for example, that even before I had been there for a year, he shared a lot of confidential figures with me that he didn't show to any of the other managers.

"One day Rand called me into his office. He had me shut the door so that no one else would hear our conversation. 'Bob,' he said, 'I've got a chance to buy the Blue Hills Pant Depot and I want to know what you think about it.' Blue Hills was in a suburb about ten miles north of our store. Rand proceeded to tell me the details of the offer. 'It looks like a good deal as far as I can tell,' I said, 'but would it be as profitable for you as Jefferson's has been?' (I was assuming he would quit when he bought the store.) 'Oh,' he said, 'I'm not going to quit unless Elliot Jefferson, the owner, tells me to.' I was surprised because it looked to me like a clear case of conflict of interest. I knew that Rand had been looking at some outside investments since he had done very well at Jefferson's, but I hadn't thought he would consider buying another clothing store.

"I didn't say much after that, trying not to get too involved with what was happening. Many times Rand would come to me to ask my opinion on certain clothing lines. He asked me to give him a list of the top five pant vendors and their salesmen's names and addresses, which I did.

"Several weeks later, I asked Rand if he had made a decision on the store. He said he had gone ahead and bought it. He said he put it under his wife's name, and that she was going to run it; that way he felt he could justify continuing his work at Jefferson's.

"After that, I noticed that Rand spent a lot more time in his office and less time out on the floor. Occasionally, I would drop into his office to see him and find him paying invoices and doing book work for his pant store. I never asked anything about it and, in fact, tried to keep our conversations on problems that needed attention at Jefferson's.

"This situation remained unchanged for several months. I concentrated my attention on doing my job and kept my thoughts to myself. Many of the other employees kept asking me about the Pant Depot. They wanted to know, for example, who really owned it, Rand or his wife. I would just tell them I didn't know.

"In October, Rand came to me again and said that he was planning on acquiring a second pant store in another suburb about fifteen miles south of our store. A clothing store in that town was going out of business, and he had a chance to rent the building. This really surprised me. I kiddingly asked if he was planning to open a whole chain. He replied that he would like to open several stores similar to the one he had already and that all he needed was to find good locations where he could rent store space cheaply.

"On November 1, Rand opened his second store. It immediately became a success, almost equalling the volume of the first.

"After that, I seldom saw Rand on the floor. He was either in his office or gone. I found myself trying to cover for him when we would get calls from the home office. This situation made me very uncomfortable. When he did come in, he seemed a lot more absent-minded about things in our store.

"I wondered how much Elliot Jefferson knew (or suspected) about Rand's involvement in these other stores. I wondered, too, if I should tell the home office why our reports were slow and why our sales had stopped increasing as rapidly as they had when Rand spent full time managing the store."

Questions

1. Did Rand Walker experience a sufficient conflict of interest to constitute an ethical problem?
2. Does Robert Jeffries have an obligation to report Walker's outside business involvement to the top management of Jefferson Sporting Goods?

GLOSSARY

Acceptance theory of authority: A theory associated with Barnard which suggests that a subordinate's decision to accept a superior's order is the ultimate source of authority.

Adaptive management: Management that properly relates an organization to its environment by responding to and/or challenging conditions in the environment.

Administrative management: The early study of management from a top-level perspective. Associated with Henri Fayol, this field of thought identifies the functions of a manager, and a set of basic principles or guidelines for management to follow.

Aggregate planning: Determining the firm's total production requirements.

Assessment center: A technique of evaluating employees through simulation exercises, interviews, psychological tests, and group exercises to determine the degree to which they possess management potential.

Authority: The official (institutionalized) right and power to make decisions affecting the behavior of subordinates. It includes the right to give orders and exact obedience.

Autonomous work group: A small group that is given the responsibility for planning and carrying out a whole task. The group provides its own leadership and determines the roles each member will play. Compensation and feedback about performance are based on group—rather than individual—accomplishments.

Behaviorally anchored rating scales (BARS): A performance appraisal form designed by the raters themselves that uses critical behavioral incidents as points (anchors) on the rating scales.

Behavior modification: A motivational concept based on operant conditioning theory. It proposes that certain events which follow particular forms of behavior can affect the probability that those behaviors will be repeated in the future.

Board structure: General organization, including committees and board membership, of boards of directors.

Boundary: The area of contact between an organizational system and its environment.

Bounded rationality: Decision-making conditions under which the manager identifies and analyzes only a few possible alternatives and then selects, from these few, an alternative which he or she predicts will yield a satisfactory return to the organization.

Break-even analysis: A planning and decision-making tool which indicates the level of operations required for total revenue to equal total cost.

Budgeting: The process of planning and controlling financial expenditures to aid the organization in goal attainment.

Bureaucratic management: The early study of how managers should structure organizations. Associated with Max Weber, the term "bureaucracy" refers to a rational model of organization structure that is intended to be highly efficient for the operation of large organizations.

Burnout: A stressful condition so severe that the victim becomes virtually incapacitated.

Capacity planning: Ensuring that the organization has the capability to produce a desired number of units of output.

Career planning: Decisions involved in career choices—the planning of one's life work.

Chain of command: The communications and order-giving chain of superior-subordinate relationships in an organization.

Classical management thought: The earliest formal compilation of management concepts and principles. Stretching from about 1895 until approximately 1920, this school of thought was comprised of three related fields—scientific management, administrative management, and bureaucratic management.

Code of ethics: A basic statement specifying ethical and/or unethical practices for an organization or an industry.

Cohesiveness: The degree to which group members act as a single unit—rather than as individuals—in the pursuit of group objectives.

Command group: A formal group composed of a manager and his or her immediate subordinates.

Committee: A formal group of individuals who are officially drawn together to consider issues pertinent to the organization or to function in a certain capacity.

Communication: An interactive process in which a sender transmits a message—containing facts, feelings, and attitudes—to a receiver who sends a return message indicating his or her reception and degree of understanding.

Compressed work week: A work schedule which involves more hours per day and fewer days per week.

Compulsory staff consultation: An organizational policy requiring operating (line) managers to confer with appropriate staff personnel before taking action.

Concurrent staff authority: An organizational policy requiring line managers to obtain the agreement of appropriate staff personnel on specified types of issues before taking action.

Conformity: Individual adherence to group norms as a result of perceived group pressure. There are two types of conformity: (1) *compliance*—a change in behavior resulting in closer adherence to group norms; and

(2) *private acceptance*—a change in behavior *and* belief resulting in closer adherence to group norms.

Contingency management: A contemporary school of management thought that attempts to determine the circumstances under which certain managerial actions will yield a particular set of results.

Contingency model of leadership: A leadership theory, formulated by Fiedler, that proposes that the most effective style of leadership depends upon the particular situation.

Contingency planning: The process of developing a set of alternative plans to fit a variety of future conditions.

Control: The managerial function of assuring the effective performance of the organizational system through establishing standards of performance, comparing actual performance with the standards, and taking corrective action, when necessary.

Controllable factors: Factors under the direct control of the manager, such as selling price, product design, inventory, organizational structure, and so on.

Conventional rating scale: A performance appraisal form containing a list of qualities, characteristics, or traits upon which the employee is rated on a scale ranging from "poor" to "outstanding."

Core job characteristics: Features of jobs such as skill variety and autonomy which affect the attractiveness of jobs.

Data base: An interrelated collection of data stored together in a computer to serve one or more applications.

Decentralization: The systematic delegation of authority on an organization-wide basis, involving the creation of relatively autonomous divisions.

Decision-making style: The way in which a manager defines, analyzes, and solves unstructured problems.

Decision support systems: A computerized system containing decision models and a data base which provides managers with the capability of manipulating and analyzing data in order to answer "what if" types of questions.

Delegation: The act of a manager in granting a subordinate the right to act or make decisions.

Delphi technique: A group forecasting and decision-making technique in which the members, rather than interacting, independently respond to sequential questionnaires asking for their expert judgments on a particular topic.

Deterministic model: A mathematical model in which all variables are assigned exact values.

Dialectical analysis: A process that attempts to improve the quality of a strategic decision by questioning its basic assumptions and forming a set of opposing assumptions to develop a counterstrategy, in order to ensure that important aspects of the strategic situation are not overlooked.

Distinctive competence: The ability of an organization to do some things particularly well in comparison to its competitors.

Distributed data processing: The decentralization of computer hardware and access to that hardware from a central location into the offices of managers in various departments and functional areas.

Divisionalized organization: An organization structured at the top level in terms of products or geography.

Dual-career marriage: A marriage in which both husband and wife are pursuing professional careers.

Dynamic environment: An environment characterized by rapid change, creating problems for managers who must try to anticipate the direction and magnitude of change.

Economic order quantity (EOQ): The quantity of raw materials, parts, products, or supplies that should be purchased to minimize total inventory costs.

Environmental scanning: Gathering and analyzing information concerning relevant events and changes in the environment.

Executive committee: A group of persons who serve as an organization's top management team.

Expectancy theory: A motivation theory which proposes that people make conscious behavioral choices based on their expectations about the future.

Extinction: The withholding of positive reinforcement following a particular form of behavior in order to decrease the probability that the behavior will be repeated in the future.

Extreme job specialization: Subdivision of work to the point that it results in routine, monotonous jobs.

Flexitime: A system for scheduling work which permits individual variation in the hours of the day which are worked.

Focal person: The individual whose role is being considered.

Forecasting: Estimating the probability of the occurrence of future events.

Formal communication channels: The network designed and sanctioned by management through which messages move from senders to receivers. Such channels may be downward, upward, or horizontal.

Formal group: A collection of individuals formed by management and charged with the responsibility of contributing to the organization.

Formal organization: The management-specified structure of relationships and related procedures used to manage organizational activity.

Functional pattern: An organization pattern whereby jobs and activities are grouped on the basis of function—for example, sales, manufacturing, and finance.

Functional status: Status derived from one's profession or type of work.

Gantt chart: A simple network technique designed to aid management in scheduling and controlling activities.

General environment: External components and conditions that are of common concern to all organizations.

Geographic pattern: An organization pattern whereby jobs and activities are grouped on the basis of geographic location.

Grapevine: The organization's informal communication network which arises spontaneously without management's sanction.

Group: Two or more individuals who are psychologically aware of one another, perceive themselves to be a group, and interact to a significant degree in the pursuit of a common goal.

Hawthorne Studies: A series of experiments conducted in the Western Electric Company's Hawthorne Plant, beginning in 1924, which modified the rational/technical assumptions of the classical school by emphasizing the importance of the human element in management.

Individual differences: The variation among human beings in terms of needs, aptitudes, abilities, attitudes, interests, and so on.

Individual-role conflict: Conflict between individual capacity or interest and job requirements.

Informal group: A collection of individuals which arises spontaneously as a natural outgrowth of human interaction and develops without formal management sanction.

Informal organization: Interpersonal relationships arising spontaneously and supplementing the formal organization structure.

Information overload: A condition in which the volume of information being received by an organization or individual is greater than the capacity to handle it.

Inputs: The materials, information, and other items which a system imports from its environment. Raw materials are an input for a manufacturer.

Interdepartmental conflict: A form of conflict that arises between two or more departments because of conflicting interests, limited resources, communication problems and/or differing perceptions.

Interface: The boundary or area of contact between an organizational system and its environment.

Interrole conflict: A conflict between a person's roles—such as one's role as manager and one's role as parent.

Intersender role conflict: Conflicting expectations from two or more persons. Two managers, for example, may differ in the performance they expect from a particular employee.

Intrasender role conflict: Inconsistency between one person's various expectations regarding another's behavior. A manager, for example, may expect rapid work and a high quality level that is impossible at a rapid pace.

Inventory turnover: A comparison of sales to average inventory levels over a specified period of time as an indicator of the effectiveness of inventory control.

Jargon: The special language used by members of the same department, functional area, organization, or occupational group to facilitate communication among the members of that particular unit.

Job analysis: A systematic study of a job which includes the compilation of a job description—containing the specific duties and responsibilities of the position—and a job specification, which defines the education, experience, skills, and behaviors required of the position holder.

Job enlargement: An attempt to make jobs more interesting and satisfying by increasing the variety of duties.

Job enrichment: An attempt to make routine jobs more meaningful by providing more challenging tasks, responsibility, and autonomy.

Job evaluation: The systematic analysis of jobs within an organization to determine their relative financial value.

Job rotation: A personnel development technique designed to increase an employee's experience by shifting him or her periodically from one job to another.

Job satisfaction: A multidimensional concept composed of the attitudes a person has toward such work dimensions as the organization, immediate supervisor, financial rewards, fellow employees, and the task.

Judeo-Christian heritage: Fundamental ethical concepts and traditions associated with, and originating in, the nation's religious life.

Lateral relationships: Horizontal relationships among organizational components—that is, direct relationships among units at the same organizational level.

Layout planning: Determining the precise configuration of the departments (and equipment within the departments) that will be used to transform inputs into outputs.

Leadership: The managerial function of securing the cooperation of others in accomplishing an objective.

Leadership style: The way a manager behaves in his or her role as leader. The two most widely discussed leadership styles are task-oriented and relationship-oriented behavior.

Leadership substitutes: Variables that reduce the leader's power to improve or retard the performance or satisfaction of subordinates.

Liaison unit: An organizational unit having responsibility for coordinating the activities of two or more components of an organization.

Line and staff organization: A form of organization in which primary activities are performed by *line* units and supporting functions are performed by *staff* units.

Linear programming: A deterministic model which yields the optimal allocation of limited resources having alternative uses—if all of the relationships in the model are linear and all variables can be quantitatively measured.

Line function: A primary function which contributes directly to an organization's output, such as teaching in a university or production in a manufacturing firm.

Logical incrementalism: The concept that managers in rapidly changing environments, since they deal with events in an incremental (or bit-by-bit) fashion, may not know precisely their ultimate objective or their entire strategy at a particular point in time.

Management: The process of acquiring and combining human, financial, and physical resources to attain the organization's primary goal of producing a product or service desired by some segment of society.

Management by exception: Focusing managerial attention on organizational subsystems in which actual performance deviates significantly from the established standard.

Management by objectives (MBO): A planning technique in which a subordinate and immediate superior jointly establish goals for the subordinate. The goals are used to motivate, develop, control and evaluate the subordinate's performance.

Management functions: The basic activities required of managers in the performance of their jobs. The major management functions include planning and decision making, organizing for effective performance, leading and motivating, and controlling performance.

Management information system (MIS):   A system which collects data on internal operations and the external environment and transforms the data into information which is presented to managers in usable form.

Management process: The activities which take place in the managerial subsystem.

Management science: A mathematical application of the scientific method to the solution of organizational problems.

Managerial Grid: An organization development technique, developed by Blake and Mouton, which has as its underlying assumption that the best managers are those who are both highly task-centered and employee-centered.

Material Requirements Planning (MRP):   A computerized system that integrates the purchase and production of all materials and parts needed to produce the required quantity of a good or service.

Matrix structure: A type of organization involving multiple lines of command such as project organization in which both functional and project managers exercise authority over the same organizational activities.

Maximizing: Decision-making behavior in which the manager selects the *best* alternative (that is, the one that will yield maximum returns to the organization) from all possible alternatives.

Mentor: An older, more experienced individual who provides guidance and assistance to a newcomer in an organization.

Mission: A statement of purpose that distinguishes a business from other firms of its type and identifies the scope of its operations in product and market terms.

Model: A simplified representation of an actual system, containing only the most important and basic features of that system.

Motivation: A concept that refers to the direction, strength, and persistence of an individual's behavior.

Multinational corporation: A corporation having branches, divisions, and/or subsidiaries that straddle national boundaries. An example is an industrial organization with production facilities in many different countries and sales organizations in still other countries.

Multiple scenarios: A set of differing assumptions which are used in planning.

Need hierarchy: The theory, developed by Maslow, that human needs are arranged in a distinct hierarchy, ranging from physiological needs to self-fulfillment needs. An individual is motivated by the desire to fulfill the lowest-level needs which are not yet satisfied.

Negative reinforcement: The removal of an unpleasant event following a particular form of behavior in order to increase the probability that the behavior will be repeated in the future.

Nominal group technique: A group decision-making technique in which the members identify alternative solutions to a problem independently without interacting. The alternatives are then discussed, and the members vote on a solution by secret ballot.

Nonroutine decision: Decisions which deal with unstructured, nonrecurring problems which have no accepted method of resolution.

Norm: A generally agreed upon standard of behavior to which all members of the group are expected to adhere.

Objective probability: An estimate, based upon historical data, of the chances of the occurrence of a future event.

Objective rationality: Decision-making conditions under which the manager identifies all possible alternatives, accurately predicts the consequences of each, and selects the one which will maximize returns to the organization.

Official objectives: The publicly espoused goals of the organization. Less specific than operative objectives.

Open system: A system which interacts with its environment. Management concepts related to open systems emphasize openness, sharing, and adaptation.

Operating core: The central part of an organization—that part which produces an organization's goods and/or services.

Operational planning: A type of planning which is less basic than strategic planning and which involves preparation of plans for specific business functions.

Operations management: The managerial process that focuses on the organizational subsystem that is responsible for transforming inputs into outputs.

Operations research (OR): A mathematical application of the scientific method to the solution of organizational problems.

Operations research team: A group commissioned to analyze, using mathematical models, a complex organizational problem and to formulate recommendations for management.

Operative objectives: Goals that the organization actively pursues. More specific than official objectives.

Organizational culture: The values and patterns of belief and behavior that are accepted and practiced by the members of a particular organization.

Organizational effectiveness: The degree to which an organization attains its primary goals (those tied to satisfying the needs of the organization's primary client group) and secondary goals (those tied to the satisfaction of the needs of secondary beneficiary groups, such as employees, the public, suppliers, and so on).

Organizational environment: The external setting including physical elements, people, other organizations, and social systems surrounding any particular organization.

Organizational system: A system composed of human beings, money, materials, equipment, and so on, which are related in the accomplishment of some goal or goals.

Organization development (OD): A planned, organization-wide effort to increase the organization's effectiveness and health through behavioral science-based interventions.

Organizing function: Managerial activity involved in creating a formal structure of tasks and authority.

Orientation: The process through which newcomers to an organization are introduced to their jobs and new surroundings.

Outputs: The materials, information, and other items which a system exports to its environment. Finished products are an output of a manufacturer.

Parkinson's law: C. Northcote Parkinson's contention that work expands to fill available time, resulting in organizations that grow regardless of work load.

Participative leadership: A leadership style in which the leader consults with subordinates and involves them in the decision-making process.

Path-goal theory of leadership: A leadership theory which views the leader's function as clarifying the subordinates' paths to work-goal attainment and increasing their opportunities for personal satisfaction.

Performance appraisal: A form of control designed to measure how effectively the organization's human resources are used. Performance appraisal provides feedback to each person concerning his or her job performance and how performance might be improved.

Personal status: Status derived from one's personal characteristics and accomplishments.

Planning: Managerial activities involved in defining goals and determining the means to achieve those goals.

Planning premise: A planner's assumption about some aspect of the future such as the health of the economy.

Policy: A basic statement serving as a guide for administrative action. Policies are more general in nature than rules and procedures.

Political power: Power derived from informal relationships and contrasting with that conferred by official grants of authority.

Positive reinforcement: An event that follows a particular form of behavior and increases the probability that the behavior will be repeated in the future.

Power: The ability to influence the behavior of others.

Power structure: The positions of influence within an organization. Positions in the power structure exist because of formal authority, informal power, or some combination of the two.

Probabilistic model: A mathematical model in which the values of some variables are uncertain.

Procedure: A statement prescribing the chronological sequence of steps or tasks in a given activity.

Process planning: Determining the precise means that will be used to transform inputs into outputs.

Procurement: Purchasing the materials and equipment required for planned organizational operations.

Product pattern: An organization pattern whereby jobs and activities are grouped on the basis of types of products (or services).

Productivity: A measure of economic output per person.

Professional management: Management based on qualifications derived from knowledge and experience in various functional areas rather than from ownership.

Program evaluation review technique (PERT):   A sophisticated network technique designed to aid management in scheduling, coordinating, and controlling the sequence and timing of activities in large, complex projects.

Quality circle: A group of employees who meet regularly on a formal basis to devise means of improving productivity and product or service quality.

Ranking: A type of performance appraisal in which the rater ranks his or her subordinates from highest to lowest, based on some criterion.

Ratio analysis: Analysis of financial statements through a comparison of one figure (such as net profit) to another (such as sales or total investment).

Reciprocal causation: The process in which the leader influences the behavior and attitudes of subordinates while, simultaneously, the subordinates influence the leader's behavior and attitudes.

Responsibility center: An organizational unit charged with a well-defined mission and headed by a manager who is accountable for the unit's performance. Types include profit centers (in which the manager is responsible for both revenues and expenditures) and expense centers (where the manager is responsible for expenditures, but not revenues).

Role: Behavior or set of activities expected of a particular individual (position).

Role ambiguity: Uncertainty regarding role expectations.

Role conflict: Conflicting role requirements arising from the multiplicity of roles or from differences between individual characteristics and role expectations.

Role set: The various individuals and/or groups having expectations regarding a focal person's behavior.

Routine decision: Decisions which deal with well-structured, recurring problems to which standard decision procedures apply.

Rule: A statement prescribing specific action to be taken and permitting little or no discretion on the part of a manager.

Satisficing: Decision-making behavior in which the manager selects an alternative which is "good enough" (that is, one which will yield a satisfactory return to the organization).

Scalar status: Status derived from one's hierarchical level in an organization.

Scheduling: Determining the time sequencing of events in the operations process.

Scientific management: A turn-of-the-century management movement, founded by Taylor, which aimed to increase employee productivity through systematic analysis of work, culminating in "one best way" to perform a task.

Sensitivity training: A form of training intended to develop a greater understanding of self, others, and interpersonal relationships.

Serial transmission effect: The distortion in communication that occurs when a message is transmitted through a series of individuals.

Simulation: A mathematical model which represents the operation of a real system by describing the behavior of individual components of the system and the effects of their interaction. Decisions—and their possible outcomes—may be "simulated" without affecting the real system.

Social audit: An identification and evaluation of organizational activities believed to have a positive social impact.

Social contract: A model conceptualizing the relationship between an organization and society as a whole, whereby the organization is granted freedom to exist and is obligated to function in the public interest.

Social responsibility: The expectation that organizations, particularly business firms, should act in the public interest and contribute to the solution of social and ecological problems.

Social system: The system of interpersonal relationships among members of an organization. It includes both formal and informal relationships.

Socialization: The process through which a newcomer to an organization adjusts to the job requirements and the organization's culture sufficiently to become a full-fledged member of the organization.

Sociotechnical approach: An approach to designing work organizations that gives explicit consideration to the workers' needs for social and psychological satisfactions, and the technical requirements of the organization.

Span of control: The number of subordinates reporting directly to a given manager.

Specific environment: The external components and conditions that directly affect a particular organization's operations. Although all organizations share a common general environment, each organization has a unique specific environment.

Staff function: Service, advisory, or otherwise supportive activities performed by staff units in line and staff organizations.

Standing plans: Objectives, policies, and other plans which are continuing in nature.

Static environment: An environment which changes relatively slowly and permits managers to predict the direction and magnitude of change.

Statistical quality control: Monitoring the quality of products (or services) by inspecting a random sample of the total batch.

Status: The relative standing or prestige of a person or group compared with other persons or groups.

Status symbols: External indicators of status, such as private offices and special privileges.

Strategic apex: The top-management group which makes strategic decisions for an organization.

Strategic business unit (SBU): An organizational subsystem which has a market, set of competitors, and mission distinct from the other subsystems in the firm.

Strategic contingencies theory of power: A theory which holds that any unit's power is contingent upon that unit's relationship to the problems and uncertainties facing the organization as a whole.

Strategic planning: A basic type of planning by which an organization formulates its long-range goals and selects activities for achieving those goals.

Strategic posture: The orientation of an organization to its environment that is reflected in the way its resources are deployed at a given time.

Strategy: Basic long-range objectives and the approaches or "routes" taken by an organization to achieve those objectives.

Stress: The emotional and physiological condition which results from tension and pressure of work as well as from other causes.

Stressor: An external agent which disturbs a person's equilibrium and produces stress.

Subjective probability: An estimate, based upon the manager's intuition or "feel" for the situation, of the chances of the occurrence of a future event.

Suboptimization: Operating at a less-than-optimal level in one segment of an organization in order to optimize the functioning of the organization as a whole.

Subsystem: An interdependent part of a larger system.

Survey feedback: An organization development method characterized by the gathering of attitudinal data (via questionnaires) from organization members, followed by a presentation of the results to the members to aid them in diagnosing where change is needed.

System: A set of components that are related in the accomplishment of some purpose.

Task force: A team of individuals, often representing various departments or interests, which has responsibility for coordinating a study or other efforts involving a number of organizational units.

Team building: An organization development method designed to improve the functioning of groups or work teams through the intensive interaction of group members.

Technological forecasting: The prediction of scientific and technological developments.

Technology: Machinery, methods, and techniques (both physical and mental) used in performing work.

Technostructure: Analysts and departments which provide technical assistance and support to line managers.

Theory Z: Refers to the style of management characteristic of large Japanese firms and exhibited by a few U.S. corporations. Some of its essential elements include long-term employment for organizational members, consensual decision making, moderately specialized career paths, and slow evaluation and promotion.

Trigger points: Events which are designated to set in action a contingency plan.

Two-factor theory: A motivation theory, developed by Herzberg, which proposes that factors associated with the job context (hygiene factors) keep employees from becoming dissatisfied while factors associated with the job content (motivators) make individuals satisfied with their jobs and help to motivate them.

Uncontrollable factors: Factors beyond the direct control of the manager, such as competitors' activities, international developments, economic conditions, and so on.

Unity of command: A precept which holds that any employee should receive orders from only one superior.

Vroom-Yetton model of leadership: Theory of leadership that clarifies the conditions under which subordinates should participate in decision making and to what extent.

Zero-base budgeting: A financial planning tool which requires an assessment and justification of the cost and benefits of all current and proposed organizational activities.

Zone of indifference: A category of subordinate attitudes toward authority in which certain orders are accepted without question.

NAME INDEX

Abouzeid, Kamal M., 109
Ackerman, Robert W., 110
Ackoff, Russell L., 119, 193, 194
Adam, Everett E., Jr., 523, 531
Adizes, Ichak, 22
Aetna Life & Casualty, 301
Agarwala-Rogers, Rekha, 480
Alber, Antone, 531
Alderfer, Clayton P., 416
Allan, Peter, 22
Allen, Fred T., 548, 556
Allen, Louis A., 263
Allen, Richard K., 480
Allen, Robert L., 361
Allied Corporation, 137
Alluto, Joseph A., 219
Alpander, Guvenc, 339
American Airlines, 542
American Express Company, 514, 537
American Motors, 73
American Telephone & Telegraph
    Company, 349, 372, 393
AM International, 494
AM Jacquard, 494
Andres, Kenneth R., 555
Andrew, Charles G., 530
Andrews, Kenneth R., 110
Ang, James S., 129
Anthony, William P., 384
A. O. Smith Corporation, 576–77
Aplin, John C., Jr., 149
Apple Computer, 368
Argyris, Chris, 35, 66
Arlow, Peter, 554
Armandi, Barry R., 555
Arnett, P., 473
Arthur Andersen and Company, 57
Arvey, Richard D., 324, 339, 422, 432
Ashkenas, Ronald N., 407
Ashland Oil, 542
Ashley, Janelle C., 418
Aston Group, 205
Atkinson, John W., 416
Austin, Robert W., 556
Avery, Sewell, 121

Babb, Harold W., 431
Badawy, M. K., 87
Baird, John E., Jr., 480

Baird, Lloyd, 432
Baker, Douglas, 423
Ball, George W., 86
Banks, Robert L., 508
Bannister, Brendan D., 455
Barker, Larry L., 481
Barnard, Chester I., 36, 37, 45, 162, 225,
    241, 272, 284
Barndt, Stephen E., 516, 531
Barnes, Frank C., 613
Bartlett, Christopher A., 76
Bartolomé, Fernando, 397, 398, 506
Basadur, Min, 170
Basek, John, 87
Bass, Alan R., 340
Bass, Bernard M., 449, 454
Baty, Gordon B., 406
Baumback, Clifford M., 406
Beach, Lee Roy, 156, 169
Bechtel Group, 6
Beckhard, Richard, 383
Beer, Michael, 368, 383
Behling, Orlando C., 455
Beiler, George W., 555
Bell, Cecil H., Jr., 379, 383, 384
Bell, Gerald D., 242
Bell Laboratories, 438
Bell System, 372
Bendix Corporation, 236
Bennett, George F., 354
Benson, Herbert, 361
Berg, Per Olaf, 384
Bethlehem Steel Company, 26, 28, 29
Billingsley, Edmond, 390, 391
Bishop, John E., 531
Bittel, Lester R., 19
Blake, Robert, 378, 384
Blanchard, Kenneth H., 445
Blank, Stephen, 87
Blumberg, Melvin, 307, 432, 531
Blumethal, W. Michael, 236
Bock, Robert H., 142
Boeing Company, 155
Bohlander, George W., 361
Bolles, Richard Nelson, 390, 391
Boone, Louis E., 7
Booz, Allen, and Hamilton, 142
Borden, Donald, 455
Boston Consulting Group, 103–4

Bowie, Norman, 556
Bowman, Edward H., 66
Braniff International, 98–99, 542
Bray, Douglas W., 406
Breaugh, James A., 339
Brenner, Steven N., 555, 556
Bridwell, Lawrence G., 431
Briggs, Jean A., 114, 449
Brigham, Eugene F., 497, 498, 508
British Steel Corporation, 237, 348
Brown, Charles L., 372
Brown, Rex V., 194
Bruce-Briggs, B., 88
Bruning, Nealia S., 454
Bucy, J. Fred, 126
Burger, Warren, 255
Burnham, David H., 416
Burnham, James, 21
Burroughs Corporation, 236
Business Roundtable, 57
Butler, Richard J., 220
Byrom, Fletcher L., 545

Calabro, P. J., 480
Calacci, Ann Marie, 633
Cameron, Kim, 384
Camillus, John C., 118
Campagna, Anthony F., 361
Campbell, John P., 333, 340, 430, 431
Campbell, Richard J., 406
Campbell Soup Company, 78
Campion, James E., 324, 339
Campion, Michael A., 339
Cao, A. D., 87
Caplan, Robert H., III, 508
Capon, Noel, 110
Career Blazers, 323
Carey, Alex, 44, 45
Carlson, John G., 432
Caron, Sandra L., 75, 555
Carrell, Michael R., 316, 321, 339
Carroll, Archie B., 39, 555, 556, 587
Carter, Jimmy, 140
Cartwright, Dorwin, 284, 294, 307
Carvey, Davis W., 516, 531, 620
Casey, Samuel B., Jr., 120
Catalyst, 399
Cavanagh, Gerald F., 285
CBS, 336

SUBJECT INDEX

681